S0-CAZ-160

# MAGILL'S SURVEY OF CINEMA

# MAGILL'S SURVEY OF CINEMA

## Foreign Language Films

VOLUME 7
TAL-Z

*Edited by*

FRANK N. MAGILL

*Associate Editors*

PATRICIA KING HANSON

KAREN JAEHNE

SALEM PRESS
Englewood Cliffs, N.J.

**Library of Congress Cataloging-in-Publication Data**

Magill's survey of cinema, foreign language films.

Includes index.

1. Moving-pictures—Plots, themes, etc.—Dictionaries.

I. Magill, Frank Northen, 1907-

PN1993.45.M34 1986 791.43'75 85-18241

ISBN 0-89356-243-2 (set)

ISBN 0-89356-256-4 (volume 7)

FIRST PRINTING

PRINTED IN THE UNITED STATES OF AMERICA

# LIST OF TITLES IN VOLUME SEVEN

## LIST OF TITLES IN VOLUME SEVEN

# MAGILL'S SURVEY OF CINEMA

# THE TALL BLOND MAN WITH ONE BLACK SHOE (LE GRAND BLOND AVEC UNE CHAUSSURE NOIRE)

*Origin:* France
*Released:* 1972
*Released in U.S.:* 1973
*Production:* Alain Poire and Yves Robert for Les Productions de la Gueville, Gaumont International, and Madeleine Films
*Direction:* Yves Robert
*Screenplay:* Francis Veber and Yves Robert
*Cinematography:* René Mathelin
*Editing:* Ghislaine Desjonquères
*Art direction:* no listing
*Music:* Vladimir Cosma
*MPAA rating:* PG
*Running time:* 88 minutes

*Principal characters:*
François .......................... Pierre Richard
Toulouse .......................... Jean Rochefort
Perrache .......................... Paul Le Person
Milan .......................... Bernard Blier
Christine .......................... Mireille Darc
Maurice .......................... Jean Carmet
Paulette .......................... Colette Castel
Orchestra conductor .......................... Yves Robert

Most films dealing with government invasion of privacy, such as *The Conversation* (1974) and *All the President's Men* (1976), address their subject from a sober and moralistic perspective. *The Tall Blond Man with One Black Shoe*, however, examines the issue with a wry smile. Under the direction of Yves Robert, this proves to be a remarkably incisive and assured approach.

It was with this modest but confident film that Robert established his reputation as a solidly commercial director and Francis Veber as France's foremost comedy screenwriter. Two of the film's principals, Pierre Richard and Jean Rochefort, vaulted from its box-office success to become among the most sought-after actors in France. The film even spawned a sequel and rights were acquired in 1983 for an English-language remake.

Several universal themes frame the film's topical right-to-privacy message and probably account for the enduring appeal of its story. One of these is about the impact of innocence on a cynical, amoral environment. Another contrasts two worldviews, the aesthetic and the pragmatic and suggests their basic incompatibility. Also relevant is the interplay of illusion and reality: Significantly, the film's credits roll against a background of card tricks.

Notwithstanding these weighty issues, the film floats along on a tone of sheer merriment, owing largely to its sardonic characterizations and swiftly paced rhythms. The story is divided into three parts. The first introduces the population of the Paris Bureau of the French Secret Service: Louis Toulouse (Jean Rochefort), the urbane, aloof, humorless bureau chief; Perrache (Paul Le Person), his wry but benevolent assistant; Bernard Milan (Bernard Blier), Toulouse's jowly, shrewd first lieutenant, who has designs on his boss's job; and Christine (Mireille Darc), Milan's svelte blonde assistant, the Mata Hari of the group.

As the skullduggery begins, it is revealed that Milan's plot to disgrace and supplant Toulouse has provoked retaliation. Toulouse, aware that Milan has bugged his apartment, turns this to his own advantage by allowing Milan to eavesdrop on a conversation with Perrache in which Toulouse confides a plan to import a secret superagent to "clear up this mess" in the bureau. This is a ruse to trap Milan and divest him of power and support. Actually, Toulouse has instructed Perrache to select someone at random (from the passengers arriving at Orly) to serve as bait for the trap. For Toulouse, people are merely pawns in a game. This emotional detachment is reflected in the stark aridity of his living quarters. Throughout the film, there are also subtle allusions to his homosexuality—Classical Greek male statuary, his uncharacteristic interest in a passing male athlete, his apartment's proximity to the phallic Eiffel Tower, and the fact that he still lives with his mother—all of which suggest detachment from emotional, procreative relationships as well.

The second part of the film introduces the remainder of the cast, all members of the local symphony: the title character, François Perrin (Pierre Richard), a gangling, guileless romantic with endearing charm; Maurice (Jean Carmet), his rascally friend, a tympanist much given to percussive teasing and exploding cigars; and Paulette (Colette Castel), Maurice's wife and François' soon-to-be ex-mistress, a harpy of a harpist. The story continues at Orly the next morning, with François descending the escalator from the heights, replete with halo of blond hair and mismatched shoes (one black, one brown—their mates having been nailed to the floor the night before by mischievous colleagues). Pierre Richard's bumbling naïveté is clearly reminiscent of Cary Grant in *Bringing Up Baby* (1938), of Peter Sellers in *The Pink Panther* (1964), and of almost all the great silent comedians. Comical and vulnerable, he is selected as victim by Perrache, who betrays him to Milan's forces with a kiss on the cheek. (The Christ-like imagery connotes innocence and heavenly protection; he is, indeed, the "divine fool" of literature.)

Oblivious to the portentousness of the gesture and to the subsequent pandemonium storming around him, François goes about his daily activities (attending to a toothache, practicing violin, disengaging from his awkward affair with Paulette, sporting about town with Maurice, performing under the watchful eye of his conductor, played by Robert himself) unaware that his every move is being scrutinized, photographed, and recorded by agents of both factions, who attribute cryptic significance to the banalities that they breathlessly report up the chain of command. Within moments, Milan has compiled an intimate dossier on him, complete with photo montage. His home is ransacked and bugged. (Notably, his somewhat stark apartment is warmed by flowers, musical instruments, and pictures of famous composers, contrasting it sharply to the total sterility of Toulouse's residence.) To François' obsessed eavesdroppers, immersed as they are in deception, double entendre, and illusion, his ingenuous behavior is inscrutable. They are incapable of recognizing that his behavior is what it is, that it springs from a sense of delight and simplicity, and that he is the reverse of a spy: He wears no cloak to conceal a dagger, no illusions to mask his reality, so they conclude that he must be the most dangerously subtle of secret agents. In an effort to ferret out François' "game," then, Milan dispatches Christine to seduce him. She presents herself at his door on the pretext of seeking violin lessons for her (nonexistent) son and, justifiably confident of François' attraction to her, invites him over to view her collection of eccentric musical instruments (including a giraffe piano and bagpipes with a life of their own).

Part three of the story opens on a seduction scene lifted from the pages of *Playboy* magazine: fur rugs, a trick bed, and audiovisual surveillance equipment. As François fumbles, stumbles, and finally succumbs to Christine's allure, Milan and the others look on in the dark, as though from a box at the opera, their entrainment obvious as they unconsciously mime each of his actions. The message is clear: Vicarious experience is as close to life and reality as these people get; they are symbiotically bound to François by what would seem to be an electronic umbilical cord. Following this scene, the pace accelerates as Milan is driven by desperation to order François' "liquidation" (the words "death" or "murder" are never used). In response, Perrache doubles security around François. This independent display of concern is consistent with Perrache's character. He functions as an intermediary between François (life-affirming energy) and Toulouse (life-denying energy), and thus his personality is an amalgam of both. Christine, similarly, serves as a bridge between Milan (the primitive) and François (the aesthetic); she epitomizes the fusion of woman-as-seductress and woman-as-romantic-ideal. (Woman-as-mother is represented by Toulouse's mother, and Paulette is woman-as-shrew.)

As the story continues, François is aflutter with love for Christine, and she, having been transformed by his gentle but potent charms, is no longer of use to Milan. She has crossed the bridge from deceptive illusion to the reality of guileless love. Love, however, is not without its complications. Milan's agents are hot on her trail as well as on François', and when he leaves his apartment to rescue her, two agents break in only to be confronted by two of Perrache's agents. There follows a strangely underplayed scene in which the four face off, briefly attempting to reason with one another before coolly shooting it out with silenced guns. One of Perrache's agents survives and hides behind a door, awaiting further developments. This encounter introduces an element of irrational destructiveness into François' creative environment, thereby not only fortifying the idea that such mentalities have little reverence for humanity, but also suggesting that they destroy mindlessly. Their methods are not loud and blatant; they are quiet, efficient, and frighteningly passionless.

Across town, Maurice has discovered François' and Paulette's faithlessness and has set out for François' home, gun in hand. The ensuing scenes are punctuated with appearing and disappearing bodies, as Maurice is driven to distraction by his inability to convince François (who has since returned, without Christine) that there are bodies in the apartment. In one scene, Maurice has discovered a corpse in the refrigerator. Through one of the film's wonderfully clever visual moments, the camera's point of view stays with Maurice as François is seen disappearing into the kitchen and heard fumbling about, creating the expectation that he will shriek, but, instead, he returns unruffled. The audience's curiosity is piqued along with Maurice's: The next sequence follows him to find a now normally stocked refrigerator. Maurice thinks that he is crazy. A more chilling thought is raised in the mind of the viewer: These spies are so frightfully efficient that they can silently and antiseptically whisk away a dead body in a matter of seconds.

In the final scenes, François leaves the apartment just before Milan's arrival; Milan quietly kills and is killed by the remaining agent. This final desecration of François' living space actually has a positive side. The dark elements have repeatedly launched assaults on his privacy and his person but have succeeded only in destroying themselves. François' innocence is inviolable; his genuineness remains intact.

The film concludes at Orly airport, with Maurice and Paulette together again, a little the worse for wear, and with François and Christine affirming their love as they depart for Rio, she, in a steamer trunk, implying that nascent innocence requires insulation and protection from a harsh world. Finally, in voice-overs, Toulouse and Perrache speculate that François will return again, for "he has promise."

*The Tall Blond Man with One Black Shoe* is a technically superior film. Its direction is lighthanded, its writing is understated, and its editing is exceptionally fluent. The camera work tends to be rather static, theatrical, and favors close-ups in shallow focus, but, overall, it captures the dexterous physical quality of the comedy. Much of the lighting is symbolic: François and Christine are usually lit in high key, Toulouse and Milan are usually in low key, often emerging from total shadow, sometimes lit eerily from below.

The major theme of the film is philosophically and chronologically relevant. Released in the United States amid the distrust and paranoia of the Watergate era, its pointed commentary was especially pertinent, and it remains so. This is a dramatization of the plight of contemporary man in a time of eclipsed gods and their sorry substitutes, Science and Technology, a time of counter-Renaissance, of man-abasing rather than man-ennobling influences. On deeper levels, these characters are engaged in ancient conflicts. For example, Toulouse symbolizes the loss of innocence, detachment from life, the world of appearances, and Thanatos. He stands in an objective relationship to beauty, unable to enter into it. François, on the other hand, is the embodiment of innocence. He is engaged in life and symbolizes the world of reality and of Eros. As a creative artist (musician, composer), he partakes of beauty and contributes to it. Though his actions, especially with Paulette, are not always angelic (he does, after all, have one *black* shoe), innocence and beauty augment each other in his relationship with Christine, strengthening him and softening her. Milan represents primal, regressive forces (symbolized by his placement in darkness). In his pragmatic cynicism, he is opposite to François' aesthetic romanticism, which he finds incomprehensible; in his baseness, he is opposed to Toulouse's urbanity.

The narrative and dramatic richness underlying the film's entertaining veneer attests its thoughtful construction and refined composition. It effectively mobilizes the cinematic medium to explore the tantalizing imperfection of human life from a fresh, deceptively light perspective.

*Marc Mancini*
*Nancy Clark*

# TALL SHADOWS OF THE WIND (SAIEHAIEN BOLAN DE BAD)

*Origin:* Iran
*Released:* 1978
*Released in U.S.:* 1980
*Production:* Bahman Farmanara for Telfilm and Iran Biograph Film Center
*Direction:* Bahman Farmanara
*Screenplay:* Hushang Golshiri and Bahman Farmanara; based on the short story "Ma'sum-e Avval," by Golshiri
*Cinematography:* Alireza Zarindast
*Editing:* Abbas Ganjavi
*Art direction:* Malekjahan Khazai; set decoration, Mehdi Bahmanpur
*Special effects:* Mehdi Bahmanpur
*Makeup:* Abdollah Eskandari
*Costume design:* Malekjahan Khazai
*Sound:* Lauri Clarkson and John Stevenson
*Music:* Ahmad Pejman
*MPAA rating:* no listing
*Running time:* 110 minutes

*Principal characters:*
Abdollah ..................... Faramarz Gharibian
Mohammad ....................... Saiid Nikpour
Narges .......................... Nadia Khalilpur

Iranian cinema since its inception has benefited from the rich heritage of Persian literature and from the collaboration of contemporary fiction writers. Many Iranian films have been inspired by or adapted from foreign films and literature, but the collaboration of engagé Iranian writers with the new generation of filmmakers in the late 1960's and the 1970's was pivotal in creating a short-lived but significant surge of high-quality films. Named the New Wave movement, this burst of creativity produced films which won popular and critical acclaim both at home and abroad.

Another salient factor in dealing with Iranian cinema is the effect of the political climate on films. Authoritarian regimes have often pressured artists and filmmakers into seeking indirect methods for expressing their ideas, and symbolism has been one such method favored by Iranian writers and filmmakers.

*Tall Shadows of the Wind* should be viewed in the context of these two factors. It is an offspring both of the collaboration of a writer with a filmmaker and of the authoritarian political climate which forced its creators to use a variety of symbols and iconography to express their more subversive ideas. Hushang Golshiri, one of the most promising young engagé writers of Iran, collaborated with the New Wave director Bahman Farmanara on both of his major feature films, *Shazdeh Ehtejab* (1974; *Prince Ehtejab*) and *Tall Shadows of the Wind*. Golshiri helped Farmanara to adapt Golshiri's stories into screenplays.

With a budget of some $200,000, *Tall Shadows of the Wind* is a story of fear, superstition, and authoritarian rule. It deals with the way in which human beings create deities in the first place and subsequently themselves fall captive to them. This visually engrossing film begins with a slow trucking shot of a large group of villagers seated on the ground in some unknown locale in Iran. As the shots truck, pan, and cut from the somber face of one villager to another, a choral chant from a Zoroastrian text is heard imploring God for assistance: "May he come to help us, may he come to care for us, may he come to comfort us, may he come to untie our knots, may he come for our victory, may he come for our happiness, may he come for our justice." Throughout, the wind whistles by and blows the colorful shawls of the villagers.

This mysterious and mystical beginning sets the tone for the entire film. The villagers construct a scarecrow and install it in a field outside the village. The scarecrow has one leg, wears a long, black robe, and his head and face are wrapped with a white cloth. When a bus fails in its attempt to ascend the steep, sandy grade into the village, the driver, Abdollah (Faramarz Gharibian), sends the passengers and his assistant to the village for help. Meanwhile, he himself ambles along toward a brook irrigating the fields. While drinking vodka from his pocket flask, he senses a kind of premonition and soon notices first one pebble, then another, then another falling into the brook. A cut to the scarecrow in the distance creates the impression that it is throwing the pebbles. After a few pebbles land in the water and splash him, Abdollah reaches out and retrieves one. This tiny monolith becomes a charisma, a symbol of power.

Abdollah walks toward the scarecrow and faces its mysteriously wrapped face, which is highly reminiscent of René Magritte's painting of a wrapped face. He draws a face on the scarecrow and puts his own hat on its head. The power is now transferred to the scarecrow.

Back in the village café, the villagers congratulate him for the lifelike quality of his work on the scarecrow. That night, while Abdollah and his mother are sleeping, in a parallel editing sequence, the villagers are seen in bed talking about what Abdollah has done to the scarecrow. This device is used again later. Outside, the empty alleys are alive with mystery and premonition. A lush musical score, which combines effectively Persian motifs with Western instrumentation, accompanies the images and gives them dimension and force.

Soon the ill effects of the power become visible. An old woman on her way from the fields into the village is found unconscious. When she awakes, she is delirious and seems possessed. Among the villagers gathered, some speculate loudly that this event is caused by Abdollah's making up the scarecrow. The next night a farmer working in the fields cannot light his pipe because of wind, sees mysterious flashes of light, and finally discovers a dead chicken swinging in the wind from one of the scarecrow's arms. In his fright he rushes into a stranger's house and severely frightens the pregnant woman of the house, causing her to miscarry. When the villagers ask the village chief for assistance, he responds by saying, "I am not the master of people's fears." Their fear is shown effectively through the same parallel cutting device. Again villagers are seen in bed unable to sleep, discussing their fears and premonitions. Outside, in the alleys, the sound of the wind and the footsteps of a one-legged person are heard.

One night Abdollah calls upon his old drinking buddy, Mohammad (Saiid Nikpour), the school headmaster, to go for a walk. Here, in a sequence reminiscent of Kenji Mizogouchi's style, the headmaster complains that the situation is getting out of hand. Abdollah admonishes him for becoming a believer in superstition and says: "For me he is only a scarecrow made of wood. The others must discover this for themselves." Mohammad responds: "No, he is no longer made of wood and I am afraid that people will begin to revere it." This is a key discussion by the two protagonists of the film, who symbolically stand for Iranian social classes.

More mysterious things happen: Mohammad's dog is found dead one night, and the village chief's daughter Narges (Nadia Khalilpur), who was to be Abdollah's future wife, disappears. When a score of villagers arrive, they find her dazed and possessed near the scarecrow. Apparently she has buried something there (the villagers speculate that it is her child conceived by the Devil). A series of quick cuts establishes the mounting fear. Villagers board their windows, lock their doors, and menfolk walk their womenfolk to the public bathhouse. Long-shots of the village again emphasize that it is located within a high-walled, imposing fortress.

One night Abdollah's drinking buddies challenge him to do away with the scarecrow and to check the grave of Narges' child. They make a bet and Abdollah, with a shovel in his hand, sets out for the scarecrow. In the dim light of his lantern, he mockingly gazes into the scarecrow's face and proceeds to dig for the grave. Suddenly in the darkness Abdollah's frightening cry is heard. A close-up reveals his severed toes.

Days later, it turns out that Abdollah has developed gangrene, but he refuses to allow his leg to be amputated, because he does not want to have only one leg like the scarecrow. The power has worked its way full circle. It has consumed its creator. Before he dies in front of his friends, however, Abdollah's wishful thinking finds its expression in a visually stunning dream. A group of sixteen scarecrows are lined up across a hilly field. Suddenly, a large group of villagers, including Abdollah and Mohammad, all wearing shocking red outfits and carrying red banners, are seen running across the fields toward the black-robed scarecrows. High-angle shots establish the battle lines. Close-ups express the intensity of the villagers' emotions. Suddenly, Abdollah gives out the call for battle and the villagers attack the scarecrows and burn them to the ground, leaving only their charred skeletons. Here a long dissolve between one such skeleton and the dying driver in his bed completes the identification of the scarecrow and the driver. When he awakens, Abdollah reaches in his pocket and, with his last gasps, hands Mohammad the little monolith.

Late that night, one sees Mohammad at his desk. The wind blows his papers around. He rises, puts the monolith on the papers, and resolutely walks toward the window and gazes outside. He has made up his mind to carry on the mission left to him by the driver. The last shot shows the monolith on a sheet of paper bearing the following words: The sea is jealous of the depth of the well from which you have drunk.

The main theme of this film is the manner in which power is created and sustained. According to the film, traditional societies are susceptible to suggestion and superstition and they turn toward mystical and supernatural forces for answers to their dilemmas. Thus, religious and political leaders are created. Once the leaders and gods are created, however, they can no longer be controlled by their creators. Abdollah the driver, a symbol of Everyman, is inadvertently instrumental in creating a powerfully perceived god, but he, too, fails to control its actions. On the whole the film seems ambivalent about the effectiveness of the intellectuals as represented by Mohammad the headmaster. On the one hand, he seems a rational and progressive force, but on the other, he is politically ineffective because he stands apart from the average people. Mohammad himself testifies to this point when he tells Abdollah during their night walk that they have fallen away from the people. The driver is uneducated but enlightened. The headmaster is educated but is given to speculation, and there is no evidence in the film that he will be capable of carrying the torch passed on to him by the driver.

An ancillary notion to this populist point of view is the idea, proved by the failure of Abdollah to defeat the scarecrow, that single-handed actions are insufficient. Only group and communal actions can succeed, as attested by the final dream sequence.

Another theme of the film, which is alluded to in the film's title, is the way that irrational fear eats at a community, dissolving existing structures and preventing rational solutions. It is in this atmosphere that authoritarianism finds fertile ground for growth. The film skillfully correlates the rising level of fear with the increasing powerlessness of the community. Music and color intensify the message. As fear mounts, the music becomes more haunting and infuses the scenes with mystery and suspense. At the beginning of the film, the colors are bright and intense. With the increasing fear, however, the colors gradually become subdued. That is why the dream sequence at the end appears so shockingly vivid.

The solution that the film offers for combating irrational fears is knowledge; as Abdollah says to the headmaster, each villager must discover for himself or herself what the scarecrow is. Farmanara himself indicates that the message of the film is that once one has discovered the source of the wind, one will no longer be afraid of the tall shadows of the wind.

The symbolic iconography of the film provides important clues. The most obvious symbol is the scarecrow. Dressed in a long, black robe and imbued with mystical powers, the scarecrow is seen by the director as a symbol for retrogressive religions. On the other hand, the villagers, dressed in red and carrying red banners in Abdollah's last dream, are seen as symbols of progressive revolutionary movements. The showdown between these two forces in the dream may also be considered the inevitable battle between these forces. It is an ironic testimony to Farmanara's astuteness as a socially conscious filmmaker that the film has been viewed with disfavor by both the Pahlavi regime, under which it was produced, and the Islamic government, under which it was first publicly exhibited. The government of the Shah Mohammad Reza Pahlavi considered the scarecrow a symbol of the Shah and his repressive apparatus, and the Islamic government interpreted the same symbol as standing for the Ayatollah Ruhollah Khomaini and his doctrinaire Islamic regime. After only three days of public exhibition in Tehran, during which the film was applauded by audiences, the Islamic authorities banned the film.

The charisma retrieved from the stream by Abdollah is clearly a symbol of religious inspiration and supernatural power. In a way, the fortress inside whose high, thick walls the villagers live represents the Iran of the 1970's. Yet the film does not identify the location or the people, and the village and the fortress could also represent any community on earth in the grip of its own fears. It is this which elevates the film from its concern with only local issues to the level of a universal statement on the creation and evolution of power.

*Hamid Naficy*

# THE TASTE OF WATER (DE SMAAK VAN WATER)

*Origin:* The Netherlands
*Released:* 1982
*Released in U.S.:* 1982
*Production:* Jan Musch, Orlow Seunke, and Tijs Tinbergen for Maya Film
*Direction:* Orlow Seunke
*Screenplay:* Dirk Ayelt Kooiman and Orlow Seunke; based on the novel by György Konrad
*Cinematography:* Albert van der Wildt
*Editing:* Tom Erisman and Orlow Seunke
*Art direction:* Dorus van der Linden
*Costume design:* An Verhoeven
*Music:* Jan Musch
*MPAA rating:* no listing
*Running time:* 100 minutes

*Principal characters:*

Hes.............................Gerard Thoolen
Anna............................Dorijn Curvers
Schram..........................Joop Admiraal
Student.........................Hans Van Tongeren
Wife............................Olga Zuiderhoek
Prostitute......................Moniek Toebosch
Landlord........................Standa Bareš
Porter..........................Ab Abspoel
Man in bar......................René Groothoff
New colleague...................Jean Pierre Plooij
Barsch..........................Bram van der Vlugt
Doctor..........................Roelant Radier
Nurse...........................Elsje Scherjon
Italian man.....................Omar El Jout

Taking narrative cues from François Truffaut's *L'Enfant sauvage* (1970; *The Wild Child*)—and, to a lesser degree, Werner Herzog's *Jeder für sich und Gott gegen alle* (1974; *The Mystery of Kaspar Hauser*) and George Bernard Shaw's *Pygmalion* (1913), an original shaping of that legend—Orlow Seunke's *The Taste of Water* has as its subject the rehabilitation of a young savage.

In the Truffaut film, young Victor (Jean-Pierre Cargol) is plucked, wild and naked, from the Aveyron forest and taught to speak by Dr. Itard (Truffaut). Herzog employed his bizarre yet poignant acting find Bruno S.

as the deaf and dumb foundling discovered one day in the main square of Nürnberg, a prayer book in one hand and a letter addressed to a local dignitary in the other. Shaw took the legend of Pygmalion and fashioned it into a quintessential battle of the sexes, laced with social satire. Set in Victorian France and filmed in a black-and-white style that deliberately evoked the early, self-conscious American cinema, *The Wild Child* is a mythic exploration of personal freedom and dependency. *The Mystery of Kaspar Hauser* is steeped in German Romanticism, paying its awestruck respects to the mysteries of life and affirming the virtue of a natural order of things. Shaw's play, which has been the springboard for all sorts of adaptations and interpretations, is at heart an entertainment, albeit an intellectual one. As such, there is a happy ending.

*The Taste of Water* updates the scenario to a modern-day Dutch bureaucracy (that remains nameless throughout the film) and jettisons myth and romance for uncompromising practicality. Hes (Gerard Thoolen) is a "social regulator" in his late thirties. He is also a dedicated civil servant, who shares a large, shabby office with other branches of social service: judges, firemen, nurses, and even nuns.

Hes's job encompasses all areas of social welfare, from unemployment benefits to public housing. This overwhelming work load has caused Hes to develop a rock-hard professional cynicism. With it has come a cagey understanding and intuitive sense for the absurd logic of bureaucratic channels. In response to the unrelenting misery that surrounds him each and every day, Hes has become a survivor.

The film opens with a shot through the bars of a cage, as Hes watches the day's cases. This device foreshadows the trapped feeling he will have later in the film, as the maze that he has learned to navigate so well begins to change direction on him.

A young probationary student (Hans Van Tongeren) is astonished and angered at what he interprets to be a cavalier approach to dealing with human suffering. When he confronts Hes and challenges him to reconsider the methods and effects of their work, the student—and the audience—is given a crash course in survival. After years of daily exposure to this crushing poverty, Hes patiently explains, indifference is not only necessary, but it is also inevitable. Besides, he says, efficiency is essential if everyone is to be given the same chance at state aid—and efficiency means speed.

The moral validity of this point is the film's first hurdle. As short-staffed as the office obviously is (at least in comparison to the tidal wave of humanity that swirls through its corridors), the best regulators are the ones who can "help" the most people in the least amount of time. Hes, for all of his distance, is the best. Not consciously mean to any of his cases, his usefulness stops just short of personal involvement. In short, Hes is the perfect bureaucrat. Hes is only human, however, and no one is completely immune to destitution. A tragedy in the office involving one of his clients serves to remind him that they, too, are human and that they are subject to the same frustrations as anyone else.

If this event opened his eyes, the discovery of Anna (Dorijn Curvers) turns his head around. The fourteen-year-old daughter of an elderly, impoverished couple whom Hes has known for years, Anna, for reasons destined to remain forever unknown, has been neglected for her entire life. Apparently raised in the cupboard in which Hes discovers her, she is now an orphan: The elderly couple has died. The surviving family members do not want her, the neighbors have no interest, and Hes is only too aware of what his system will do to her: They will, no doubt, lock her in a state-funded cupboard. Another hurdle thus develops, this one for Hes. To care for Anna properly requires time, and with a wife and child to care for, in addition to official duties, the prospect of educating this rather large infant looks remote. Yet there is an aspect to this case that fascinates Hes. Anna's behavior is riveting: all greasy hair and rags, she dashes out of the cupboard only when offered the bread-and-milk mush she needs to survive. She rarely talks, and when she does, it comes out as guttural gibberish. Hes softens at once to the child and is soon coaxing her out of hiding. Without consciously deciding to do so, Hes violates the cardinal rule of his profession and becomes emotionally involved with Anna and her strange case, dedicating himself to her care and education.

The process is gradual and at times excruciatingly slow for Hes. At first he waits hours simply for a glimpse of her, and on more than one occasion he ends up wearing what was intended as her meal. He takes much satisfaction in his work with Anna, however, and his personality develops a relaxed, more spontaneous side. Like a new, frightened pet, Anna is at first wary of Hes, but she slowly comes to feel comfortable with his presence outside the cupboard. Like Jean-Pierre Cargol and Bruno S., the young Dorijn Curvers is the focal point around which the whole film revolves. If her Anna becomes an evil or threatening figure to the audience, the film loses its idealistic power, a power based on sympathy. To her credit, it never does. Her performance is brilliant and brilliantly directed, and it never once strays from the narrow path that the story provides.

As Hes begins to make progress with Anna, the question of his effectiveness looms larger and larger in his mind. What difference has he made to Anna or any of his clients? Has he ever really helped anybody? Why is he rejecting a job that he is so good at for a dirty, illiterate waif? He is fired from the social service office, primarily for never being there. His colleagues are also becoming concerned about what they see as sloppy tendencies in a man once known for exactness and predictability. Committing himself totally, he leaves his family and moves into the dilapidated, deserted flat with Anna. She still has not permanently left the cupboard, but her progress is both steady and sure.

Here, again, Seunke displays the depth of his craft. Showing remarkable restraint for a first feature, he consistently refuses to rush Anna's development or glamorize Hes's achievements. Like the identity of the office in which he works, the time span of Hes's relationship with Anna is left purposefully vague, a device mentioned in the very first sentence of the official synopsis provided in the press kit: "[*The Taste of Water*] is set in an imaginary world not tied spatially or temporally to our present reality." This could happen anywhere, at any time, to anybody. So, too, the psychological repercussions of Hes's decision are logical and unforced. He commits to Anna on a whim born of resolve and guilt, but even he cannot foresee the inevitable: When he decides that adoption is the only way to keep Anna, he is forced to apply at his own office for aid.

Naturally, only the student on probation is sympathetic when the disheveled Hes appears, and, naturally, the adoption is rejected. They offer him his old job back one last time if he will abandon this folly. Hes refuses, and he withdraws even more. The final heartbreak is a climactic, quite moving trip to the beach with a now decidedly childlike Anna. While at the sea, he realizes that Anna is only a taste of water, and that the relentless lapping of the bureaucratic waves will wash her away from him, leaving him completely alone. Defeated by the faceless muscle of the system, he gives up the child. In the final shot, he is leaning against a wall filled with her nonsensical paintings, alone for the first time in the filthy apartment in which she was discovered. He is drained.

As it so often happens in intimate film communities such as the Dutch enjoy, Seunke had worked previously with nearly everyone involved in the creation of *The Taste of Water*. Developed over a period of four years, the film benefited from input by both Thoolen and Curvers, who had already been confirmed for their respective roles early in the film's development. Seunke's self-confessed aim in making *The Taste of Water* was to explore a protagonist who felt powerless. "In my films," he has said, "I try to release people's emotions, I want to move them with emotion deeper than just an identification with the main character." Shot through with an honest, no-nonsense style and much sincerity, *The Taste of Water* is a vivid and satisfying emotional experience.

*Edward W. Cockrell, Jr.*

# TEN THOUSAND SUNS (TÍZEZER NAP)

*Origin:* Hungary
*Released:* 1967
*Released in U.S.:* no listing
*Production:* Mafilm Studio
*Direction:* Ferenc Kośa
*Screenplay:* Ferenc Kósa, Imre Gyöngyössy, and Sándor Csoóri
*Cinematography:* Sándor Sára
*Editing:* Maria Szecsenyi
*Art direction:* József Romváry
*Sound:* György Pinter
*Music:* András Szöllősy
*Running time:* 109 minutes

*Principal characters:*

| | |
|---|---|
| István Széles | Tibor Molnár |
| Juli | Gyöngyi Bürös |
| István's son | András Kozák |
| Fülöp Bánó | János Koltai |
| Széles' mother | Ida Siménfalvy |
| Balogh | János Rajz |
| Uncle Sándor | Sándor Siménfalvy |
| József Bócza | János Görbe |
| Policeman | Péter Hauman |
| Mihály Csere | László Nyers |

Although *Ten Thousand Suns* was completed in 1965, problems over its controversial treatment of the forced collectivization of land in the early 1950's delayed its release for almost two years. Finally, it was officially approved for showing at the 1967 Cannes International Film Festival, where it won for its thirty-year-old director the prize for best direction. Released in Hungary after that, it became recognized as one of the key films of that nation's cinematic revival in the mid-1960's, both for the honesty and boldness of its political content and for a sense of visual style and composition that constantly recalls the work of Sergei Eisenstein.

The film began as Ferenc Kósa's diploma work at the end of his training at the National Film School, and, in its origins at least, was largely a cooperative work between several students in their final year. Kósa finally emerged as sole director; like his coscriptwriters Imre Gyöngyössy (also a director) and the poet Sándor Csoóri, he came from peasant stock, and the trio spent several months traveling across Hungary and interviewing peasants who had gone through the kinds of experiences presented in the film.

The result has an authenticity that contrasts sharply with the blandly optimistic official versions of the preceding decade, in which opposition to social change was presented as exclusively the work of evil, unregenerate "kulaks," while the peasants were alleged to be enthusiastically in support. Like his cinematographer Sándor Sára, who directed the fine *Feldobott kö* (1968; *The Upthrown Stone*) on a similar theme, Kósa expresses outspoken anger and outrage at the brutality and insensitivity with which land reforms (which, like most Hungarians, he accepts as being, in their essence, necessary and long overdue) were forced upon a bewildered and helpless population. A just and decent society will place human needs ahead of mere ideology: Changes must come with the consent, cooperation, and full understanding of those affected by them and not be imposed upon them against their will. Specifically, the authorities should recognize the peasant's age-old hunger for security, expressed as a piece of land of his own, and attempt to work in harmony with this desire rather than ignore it.

The film covers a time span of thirty years, from the mid-1930's to the mid-1960's (roughly the scope of "ten thousand suns," though the main character's son, in his monologue that closes the film, speaks also of his vision of "ten thousand suns" illuminating the sea). The central character, István Széles (Tibor Molnár), begins as a landless farm laborer and, throughout the film, sees himself as the victim of social changes that he cannot understand, despite constant reassurance from those in power that they are all taking place for his benefit and that of those like him. He is "given" land, for example, and yet told that he must hand over most of what "his" land produces to the government. Contrasted with him is his friend Fülöp Bánó (János Koltai), a convinced but undogmatic Communist who is aware of and regrets the suffering caused by the social upheavals but persists in believing that a genuinely free and humane society will emerge as a result. Several scenes of the film involve debates between the two and also between Bánó and Széles' adolescent son (András Kozák), who represents a new generation impatient with the lies and deceptions of the past and eager to see the incessantly repeated promises of a better future actually fulfilled.

The opening scenes of the film, set in the mid-1960's, immediately establish the contrasts between old and new that are central to the film as a whole. Széles' son is seen packing to leave home, watched by his aged grandmother; inside the traditionally furnished farmhouse with a huge stove dominating the room, a television screen shows pictures of modern jet-fighter planes. In the village street outside, Széles and Bánó discuss whether Communism has brought the benefits it promised: not yet, Bánó admits, but it will. Yes, but at what cost? inquires his friend.

A flashback to the mid-1930's follows. Juli (Gyöngyi Bürös) is hired as a laborer by the local landlord Balogh (János Rajz), who examines her as if she were a horse or some other beast of burden. Meanwhile, the peasants are entertained by the spectacle of a dancing bear. Juli is then seen sorting a huge pile of potatoes while Széles declares his intention of marrying her (after which he asks her what her name is). Moving forward in time, one sees Juli and other women at work in the fields; their children (including Juli's young son) are kept safe by being buried up to their waists in holes dug in the ground.

Winter: Széles is being interrogated by some gendarmes about straw that has been stolen: Three of the landlord's pigs have died from cold because there was no straw to keep them warm. Balogh insists that Széles "apologize" to the dead animals and orders him to kneel in front of them. The indignant Bánó attempts to intervene but is taken away by the gendarmes. Széles makes the apology and is accused of cowardice by Bánó; resenting his humiliation, he fights with his friend and then strikes Juli when she attempts to remonstrate with him. Their subsequent quarrel ends in a visually exotic scene that shows her massaging her exhausted husband by trampling over his back as he lies on their bed, performing an authentic and age-old peasant remedy.

Széles further displays his lack of political awareness by refusing to take part in a strike and continuing to work for the reduced wages offered by his boss. He and a few fellow strikebreakers are treated as traitors: Tied up against wheelbarrows, they have dirt thrown in their faces. More humiliation follows at a local fair: He offers to sell his cow in part exchange for a horse but is contemptuously told to keep his money and buy a present for his child.

Newsreel scenes of World War II follow, after which Bánó is seen talking to a group of hymn-singing peasants about Karl Marx and the need for redistribution of the land. They remain skeptical and unconvinced but show interest when he tells them that the grain harvested from land previously belonging to Balogh is now communal property. Each insists on claiming "his" share immediately; ignoring Bánó's protests that they have missed the point, they scramble to stuff the grain into sacks and run off with it as Bánó attempts in vain to stop them. One by one they collapse under the weight of their burdens until, in a magnificently composed extreme long-shot, they are seen lying in an immense zigzag of fallen bodies that stretches across the whole width of the CinemaScope screen.

After this, things seem to improve: At a joyous picnic, the peasants celebrate and watch a dumpling-eating contest between Bánó and Mihály Csere (László Nyers). Széles, however, is still discontented; he wonders why some of "his" grain has to be handed over to the government, though it is Juli who actually articulates his protest for him. His aged mother curses Bánó for "stealing" their grain; Bánó tells her that, under Communism, sharing is necessary.

That night, Széles tries to take back his "own" sacks of grain and is arrested. Cseres, who has helped him, starts a fight with the local policeman; Széles watches apathetically as the massive Csere almost strangles his opponent and is then shot by him in self-defense, staggering out to collapse in the courtyard as the other peasants crowd around him. The terrified policeman flees, while Bánó rebukes Széles for his passivity.

Széles is sentenced to a period of forced labor and is seen working in a barren quarry as Juli comes to visit him, pretending to be the wife of an ordinary worker in the quarry, as visits to prisoners are forbidden. By the time Széles is released, his son has reached the age of eighteen, and the political situation takes another turn with the 1956 uprising.

The handling of this event is the least satisfactory element of the film, though the reasons are understandable if one remembers that the film was made barely a decade after the uprising, when the wounds created by it were still very raw. Nevertheless, whereas elsewhere in the film conflicting viewpoints are given a fair and sympathetic hearing, in these scenes the revolutionaries are presented simply as murderous thugs who kill their opponents in cold blood and spare Bánó's life only because they respect his courage and his defiance of them. Meanwhile, Széles plays a typically passive and neutral role, associating himself with the revolutionaries but rejecting their invitation to shoot Bánó and other Party members with a gun thrust into his hands. His son, however, the viewer learns, actually joined the revolutionaries for a time.

Once again things settle down: Bánó and Széles' son argue over the political situation, while life gradually improves for the peasants as a whole. Széles remains discontented, however; for him, Communism remains only a fine dream that will never actually be realized. Reconciled with Bánó, he still questions him about his political faith: *When* will Communism be achieved; who will benefit from it? His sense of dissatisfaction with his whole life comes to a head as he broods on his unworthy conduct during the war, when he lied about the size of his family in order to avoid conscription. Unable to face up to himself or his situation any longer, he tries to hang himself, but Juli rescues him in time and revives him.

The final scene of the film takes the form of a monologue spoken by Széles' son as he paces along the seashore, asking the questions of a younger generation that had not experienced the hardships undergone by their parents and are now impatient to reap the long-promised rewards. He has come into a strange inheritance, he muses, and faces a strange responsibility; like others he will have to learn to cope with the world as it actually is, without utterly losing the sense of vision that will inspire him to build a better future.

The film as a whole is more concerned with posing questions (many of them previously ignored and long overdue) than with offering solutions.

Bánó, Széles, and the latter's son are all presented sympathetically, despite their sometimes incompatible viewpoints. The crucial questions that Kósa poses, and which have proved to be central to the development of his country's cinema over the next two decades are: How was it possible for people with good intentions to cause such suffering to others? Could that suffering have been avoided? Will it be possible to learn from the experience of the past and go on to build a genuinely just and humane society that puts the human being at the center of its concerns?

At the same time, *Ten Thousand Suns* is more than a mere series of debates, regardless of the importance of the political issues the film raises. From beginning to end, it is the work of a born filmmaker, full of dazzling and unforgettable images. On the basis of the later films on which they worked together, both Kósa and his cinematographer Sára can be credited for these: a superb use of pictorial space in which diagonal, vertical, and horizontal patterns are constantly recombined and reworked to maximum thematic and visual effect; striking contrasts of black and white (assisted by the black clothing worn by the peasants and the whitewashed exteriors and interiors of their houses); the creation of bizarre and memorable images such as Juli's massaging of her husband, or the Party members in 1956 made to stand immersed to their waists in the waters of a lake while the revolutionaries decide what to do with them, or the peasants later enjoying a swim in the lake, with most of the men still wearing their hats.

Kósa was hailed as "a new Dovzhenko" with the appearance of this film, but, though his later films are never without either visual or thematic interest, he has not produced anything to match the combination of commitment, passion, and visual skill that makes *Ten Thousand Suns* an enduring landmark of his country's cinema.

*Graham Petrie*

# DAS TESTAMENT DES DR. MABUSE

*Origin:* Germany
*Released:* 1933
*Released in U.S.:* 1943
*Production:* Seymour Nebenzal for Nero-Film
*Direction:* Fritz Lang
*Screenplay:* Thea von Harbou (German) and A. René-Stil (French)
*Cinematography:* Fritz Arno Wagner and Karl Vash
*Editing:* no listing
*Art direction:* Karl Vollbrecht and Emil Hasler
*Music:* Hans Erdmann
*Running time:* 122 minutes
*Also known as: The Last Will of Dr. Mabuse* and *The Testament of Dr. Mabuse*

*Principal characters:*

Dr. Mabuse .................... Rudolf Klein-Rogge
Dr. Baum ........................... Oskar Beregi
Karl Lohmann ..... Otto Wernicke (German version)
Jim Gerald (French version)
Müller ................................ Klaus Pohl
Dr. Kramm ........................ Theodor Loos
Landlord ........................... Karl Meixner
Lilli .................................. Wera Liessen
Kent ................................. Gustav Diesel
Juewlen-Anna ...................... Camilla Spira
Hardy ......................... Rudolf Schundler
Lithographer ...................... Paul Henckels

Undertaken by the firm of Tri-Ergon, research in sound technology provided Germany with a head start among European film capitals. As early as 1929, Marlene Dietrich was featured in a musical, *Ich küsse ihre Hand, Madame* (*I Kiss Your Hand Madame*), and productions in the early 1930's included Leni Riefenstahl's first directing assignment, *Die blaue Licht* (1932; *The Blue Light*) and Slatan Dudow's *Kühle Wampe* (1932; *Whither Germany?*), made the Communist resources that included the skills of author Bertolt Brecht and composer Hanns Eisler. Two period films still cited for imaginative employment of sound are Josef von Sternberg's *Der blaue Engel* (1930; *The Blue Angel*) and Fritz Lang's *M* (1931).

Viennese by birth, Lang (1890-1976) studied art in Paris before World War I, fought in the German Imperial Army, and started to write stories and film scripts while convalescing from military injuries. His first film, a detective thriller directed by Joe May, *Die Hochzeit in Ekzentrik Klub*

(1917) drew on the pulp fiction that Lang had enjoyed since his youth. This idiom soon proved to be a characteristic mode for Lang. From 1919 to 1929, Lang directed a succession of internationally popular and artistically successful German silent films, whose subject matter ranged from crass heroics in *Die Spinnen* (1919, 1920; *The Spiders*) to legend in *Die Nibelungen* (1924); from moody mysticism in *Der müde Tod* (1921; *Destiny*) to science fiction in *Metropolis* (1927). Commencing with *Das wandernde Bild* (1920; *The Wandering Image*), Lang usually cowrote his films with Thea von Harbou, whom he married in 1922. Von Harbou's work emphasized popular nationalist fervor couched in heavily plotted melodrama. She provided scripts to directors such as F. W. Murnau, Carl Theodor Dreyer, and E. A. Dupont as well as working with Lang and Joe May.

An especially successful von Harbou-Lang collaboration proved to be a two-part film centering on the schemes of a super criminal whom they named Dr. Mabuse. In part 1, *Ein Bild der Zeit* (1922), variously titled *A Picture of the Times* and *The Great Gambler*, Dr. Mabuse is introduced as an evil force dominating a city's underworld, controlling his victims through drugs, crooked gambling, hypnotism, and murder. Pitted against Mabuse is Chief Inspector von Wenck, who finally penetrates the disguises that Mabuse assumes to maintain anonymity and freedom of movement. During part 2, *Inferno, ein Spiel von Menschen unserer Zeit* (1922; *Inferno, a Play About People of Our Time*), Mabuse kidnaps Countess Told. In a ferocious gun battle, the police lay siege to Mabuse's headquarters. He escapes through sewers to a counterfeiters' den, where he is captured, an insane man, crouched in the forged currency.

*Das Testament des Dr. Mabuse* finds the doctor, again played by Rudolf Klein-Rogge, committed to a lunatic asylum whose administrator is Dr. Baum (Oskar Beregi). Mabuse dominates Baum through hypnotism, and through Baum, he continues his criminal strategies. He plans to take over Berlin through acts of terrorism, debasing the currency, and attacking chemical plants and transportation centers. His own identify shrouded, Baum transmits Mabuse's orders to the criminal gang, now occupied with amassing stolen wealth in preparation for the political coup.

Mabuse's adversary is now Chief Inspector Lohmann, played by Otto Wernicke, who had been Superintendent Lohmann in Lang and von Harbou's *M*. Balking at an order to commit murder, a gang member, Kent (Gustav Diesel), tries to break away but is captured with his girlfriend, Lilli (Wera Liessen). Following threads of evidence, Lohmann locates Mabuse, now dead, in the asylum and captures the gang. Kent and Lilli escape and identify Baum for Lohmann. Now completely possessed by the dead Mabuse, Baum initiates the reign of terror but is spotted at the site of a fire and is pursued by Lohmann and Kent to the asylum. There, Baum is discovered in a cell, raving mad, convinced that he is Mabuse.

So garish a plot reconstruction fails to recognize what have become distinguishable Langian themes and effects. Many of these occur when sound and picture unexpectedly conjoin. Graphic sophistication is retained from Lang's silent films. An opening sequence is exemplary. Darting and probing around the crates and machinery of an industrial warehouse where counterfeit printing presses operate, Lang deploys the camera of Fritz Arno Wagner into the building's recesses, there to spot a police informant desperately hiding from Mabuse's gang, who know that he is somewhere about. The mood is intensified by the steady drone of printing machinery, whose ambient sound, first unrecognizable to the audience, then identifiable, finally seems to echo the mounting anxiety of the fugitive. Filmed without dialogue, the episode is reminiscent of Peter Lorre's efforts to hide in *M*, and Lang also turns to similar visual cues (as in the chalked M on Lorre's overcoat) in this film. In *Das Testament des Dr. Mabuse*, the criminal doctor is first identified by Lohmann by means of a name scratched backward on a piece of window glass by a police agent. As cinematographer Wagner panned the faces of Lorre's kangaroo criminal court in *M*, here he traces rows of medical students in an amphitheater where Dr. Baum is describing the case history of his most illustrious inmate. In fact, Wagner's contributions to the full repertory of classic German film deserve broad recognition. As a major staff cameraman for the Ufa studios, his close work with set designers helps to account for the look of such Lang films as *Destiny* and *Spione* (1928; *Spies*), as well as major works by G. W. Pabst, F. W. Murnau, and Arthur Robinson. Wagner continued to work in Germany until the late 1940's. Among others, the French director Claude Chabrol was deeply impressed by one *mise en scène* in the Mabuse film, in which Dr. Baum sits in his study, which is dimly lit, emphasizing walls dressed with African masks. Here, Baum reads the papers scrawled by Mabuse in his cell, purportedly the scribbles of a madman, actually plans to conquer Berlin.

Where Expressionism figured heavily in the silent Dr. Mabuse film, in the third film it is confined to hallucinatory effects, most noticeably during the climatic chase in which Baum is pursued to the asylum. As images of trees and foliage (projected in negative so that the black-and-white polarities appear ghostly) fly past the speeding car, a transparent Mabuse appears in the car windshield. Murnau and Wagner had used the device of negative imagery in *Nosferatu* (1922), and Jean Cocteau repeated it in *Orphée* (1949; *Orpheus*).

Another motif equates Mabuse's evil purpose with machinery. He writes, "The individual has no existence except as part of the machine—the individual is nothing, the machine everything." Some devices facilitate Lang's unexpected use of sound-infected dialogue. Baum, for example, covers his absences from the sanatorium by rigging a phonograph to the door of his study so that when the door is opened, a recording of his voice announces,

"Go away. I do not wish to be disturbed." Similarly, Baum speaks to the criminal gang by way of a microphone and loudspeaker system linked to a wooden silhouette situated behind a translucent curtain.

Lang also used sound to bridge his cuts: A character's dialogue anticipates a forthcoming visual but in an unexpected fashion. For example, viewing a former police officer rendered insane by terror, Lohmann mutters, "I'd like to get my hands on the man responsible for driving this fellow insane." Overlapping his last words, one sees Mabuse in his cell, crazily scrawling orders to be passed to Baum.

In the film's spectacular conclusion, depicting a gasworks torched by the gang, Lang blends the sounds of sirens, falling chimneys, a locomotive, motorcycles, and the fire itself to orchestrate a counterpoint to the imagery of flames and falling debris, much of which was filmed in miniature.

Where Dr. Mabuse preserves something of past generations' romantic villains, defeated finally by madness, Inspector Lohmann plays a kind of English detective implant, courageous enough, yet unfortunately disposed toward pondering, slow burns, and double takes. In final estimation, *Das Testament des Dr. Mabuse* proves less successful than *M* not because of diminished skills in execution but by reason of its mundane plotting and characterizations, which overexaggerate qualities that characterize Fritz Lang at his best.

German censors refused to certify the film, and it was never released in that country. Joseph Goebbels appears to have disliked it because it seemed to glorify criminals. Enthusiastic toward *Metropolis*, he offered Lang a leading position in the new German film industry. Instead, the director, whose mother was Jewish, fled to Paris with a print of the French version of his new film. An English-dubbed version of the film (using the German rather than the French version) was first circulated in New York City in 1943. At that time, Lang emphasized Goebbels' ban and said that his own intentions had been to "denounce the terrorist methods of Adolf Hitler. Slogans and doctrines of the Third Reich have been put into the mouths of criminals in the film."

Such a proposal seems questionable at best. The story too closely resembles a succession of previous Lang-von Harbou collaborations, and by the time it was produced, Lang's wife had embraced National Socialism. The couple separated before Lang's departure; she remained in Germany, writing and directing films until her death in 1945. In 1960, Lang undertook a last Dr. Mabuse film, his second postwar German production, after spending years in Hollywood. *Die tausend Augen des Dr. Mabuse* (*The Thousand Eyes of Dr. Mabuse*) proved to be Lang's last film. It disappointed both critics and the director, who finally admitted, "I would rather not have made it."

*John L. Fell*

# THAT MAN FROM RIO (L'HOMME DE RIO)

*Origin:* France and Italy
*Released:* 1964
*Released in U.S.:* 1964
*Production:* Alexandre Mnouchkine and Georges Dancigers for Les Productions Artistes Associés/Dear Film
*Direction:* Philippe de Broca
*Screenplay:* Jean-Paul Rappeneau, Ariane Mnouchkine, Daniel Boulanger, and Philippe de Broca
*Cinematography:* Edmond Séchan
*Editing:* Laurence Méry and Françoise Javet
*Art direction:* no listing
*Music:* Georges Delerue
*Running time:* 120 minutes
*Running time in U.S.:* 114 minutes

*Principal characters:*

Adrian Dufourquet ............ Jean-Paul Belmondo
Agnès .......................... Françoise Dorléac
Professor Catalan ..................... Jean Servais
Lola ............................. Simone Renant
Tupac ............................ Milton Ribeiro
Sir Winston .................. Ubiracy de Oliveira
Señor De Castro ..................... Adolfo Celi

Brash screen heroes—from Harold Lloyd, in his various cinematic disguises, to James Bond and Indiana Jones—have thrilled film audiences for decades. A superior film in that mold, internationally popular when released, is Philippe de Broca's *That Man from Rio*. It was rightly labeled a James Bond spoof—long before the Bond films came to parody their own genre.

In *That Man from Rio*, Jean-Paul Belmondo stars as Adrian Dufourquet, a provincial French airman who is first seen boarding a train for Paris, where he plans to spend his eighty-day furlough with Agnès (Françoise Dorléac), his fiancée. While he innocently commences his journey, two South American Indians pilfer a priceless Amazon statuette, a sort of religious effigy, from the Musée de l'Homme in Paris and order Professor Catalan (Jean Servais) into their car. The professor had found the statuette while accompanying Agnès' archeologist father on an expedition to the Amazon four years earlier, during which the archaeologist died under mysterious circumstances. Catalan is convinced that the statuette is one of a trio, all identical in appearance, which holds the key to a secret "Maltec" treasure.

As Adrian arrives at his fiancée's home, he observes the Indians abducting Agnès, who is the sole person who knows the whereabouts of the other two statuettes. Adrian follows them on a motorcycle to Orly Airport and is horrified as he watches Agnès dragged through customs and hurried into an airplane. He sneaks aboard, just before the plane takes off for Rio de Janeiro. Adrian is soon discovered and identified as a stowaway and tells the pilot the truth, but Agnès has been drugged and cannot identify him. The soldier is sure to be arrested when the plane lands, but he eludes the police and wanders around Rio.

The hero then strikes up a friendship with Sir Winston (Ubiracy de Oliveira), a young bootblack. Their initial meeting offers a fine demonstration of the film's sense of fun and is one of its comic highlights: Adrian's shoes are white, but Sir Winston begins to shine them black. Adrian cannot pay for the work, and he does not complain that his shoes are ruined; he merely changes places with the bootblack and begins to polish *his* shoes.

The character of Sir Winston is not simply a humorous diversion; he helps Adrian pick up the trail of Agnès and her kidnapers. They find and rescue her—she has been hidden in a room in a luxury hotel—but Adrian must dangle from a tenth-story window before she can breathlessly explain the significance of the statuette. It seems obvious that the thieves are in Rio to retrieve its mates. Adrian, Agnès, and Sir Winston decide to prevent any further thefts.

Agnès takes them to the spot where her father had buried one of the statuettes, but as they dig it up, they are attacked by two Indians, who make off with it. Adrian and Agnès then drive to Brasília to meet with Señor De Castro (Adolfo Celi), a rich industrialist who owns the third statuette. While en route, they find the Indians' car and Professor Catalan, whom they rescue before continuing on to Brasília.

De Castro is at first reluctant to show Catalan the statuette, but he finally agrees in order to assure the professor of its safety. He takes Catalan to his strong room, but the professor quickly turns on him, murders him, stealing the statuette. Catalan is the real villain—it is he who planned the museum robbery, staging his own abduction as an alibi. He is now in possession of all three statuettes.

Catalan and the Indians kidnap Agnès again, then escape in a seaplane—before Adrian even discovers De Castro's body. The hero then steals a plane of his own and pursues his girlfriend and her captors to the jungle. There, he parachutes out, landing on an alligator, and soon finds himself in a floating waterfront café operated by Lola (Simone Renant), who had originally financed Catalan. Adrian is informed that the professor killed Agnès' father, and that his fiancée is being held on a boat. The soldier hangs from its side as it sails upstream and docks. Catalan treks off to the underground location of the treasure, an ancient temple, where, with the three statuettes, he operates the complex mechanism that opens the temple's gigantic portals. Before him are shimmering jewels, remnants of the Maltec civilization, but he has little time to enjoy his riches: An explosion, set off by a nearby demolition crew constructing a highway, results in the destruction of the site, as well as the demise of the professor. Adrian has already rescued Agnès once again, and the couple leave the jungle and fly back to Paris, just in time for Adrian to arrive at the train depot to catch his ride back to camp.

Despite the murders, kidnapings, thievery, and constant danger—which could easily make up the elements of a straightforward thriller—all of the action is played tongue-in-cheek. As each unlikely event leads to an even more unlikely one, the film takes on elements of the "caper" genre, including an extended and nonsensical chase. There is virtually no character development in the film; the "bad guys" are thoroughly evil and equally incredible; the single resourceful "good guy" aggressively and optimistically pursues them while constantly and unthinkingly punching at foes whom he obviously will be unable to knock out. The action offers several amusing vignettes: At Orly airport, for example, Adrian steals a passport from an octogenarian general in a wheelchair after the vehicle is sent spinning into the men's room; Lola's waterfront dive, with its seedy patrons and easily broken furniture, is the epitome of the saloon of the untamed Western town or the sleazy bar of the big-city slum. There are many close calls: At one point, Adrian is nearly run over by a speedboat; he rescues himself by grabbing on to a pretty waterskier who happens to zip past him in the water. Agnès is kidnaped on what seems to be a daily basis, always followed by Adrian running across rooftops or swinging from vines to rescue her. The hero is barely harmed in these exploits. The final, ironic joke occurs when Adrian, supposedly on leave from his military duties, must return to his post having lived through stress that rivals that of war and without the anticipated romantic weekend with his fiancée.

All of these adventures are cleverly directed by de Broca, whose other credits include *L'Amant de cinq jours* (1961; *The Five-Day Lover*), the cult favorite *Le Roi de cœur* (1966; *King of Hearts*), and *Tendre Poulet* (1977; *Dear Inspector*). Two years before *That Man from Rio*, de Broca and Belmondo made *Cartouche* (1962), a lampoon of the swashbuckler genre; they also worked together in *Les Tribulations d'un Chinois en Chine* (1965) and in the intriguingly titled *Comment detruire la reputation du plus célèbre agent secret du monde* (1973; *How to Destroy the Reputation of the Greatest Secret Agent*). During the 1960's, French filmmakers delighted in paying homage to American directors and film genres. In Jean-Luc Godard's *À bout de souffle* (1960; *Breathless*), for example, Belmondo pays his respects to Humphrey Bogart. In *That Man from Rio*, de Broca and his coscreenwriters emulate Alfred Hitchcock, Tarzan, the Hollywood Western, *The*

*Perils of Pauline*, Harold Lloyd, Humphrey Bogart in his straight adventure-intrigue films, and Bogart again in the wryly comic *Beat the Devil*.

The cast is excellent. Belmondo, coming into his own as a star in the early 1960's, shines as Adrian in a physical tour de force worthy of Sean Connery and Roger Moore. Pretty, red-headed Françoise Dorléac, sister of Cathérine Deneuve, is a fitting Agnès. (Sadly, her career was cut short when, in 1967, she died in a car crash at age twenty-six.) Offering excellent support is Jean Servais, a veteran of French films since 1931, whose international reputation was made when he starred as the gang boss in Jules Dassin's *Rififi* (1955), one of the best caper films ever made.

*That Man from Rio* was shot on location in Paris, Rio de Janeiro, Brasília, and elsewhere in Brazil; the film is almost a travelogue of exotic places, with generous, vividly photographed footage of each locale. The film opened in Paris in February, 1964 (as *L'homme de Rio*) and later that year played in Rome (as *L'uomo di Rio*) and the United States. In France, where it received fine reviews—*Le Figaro* called Jean-Paul Belmondo "the 1964 Musketeer of the Impossible"—it did brisk business, outgrossing all other films in release there; in the United States, it attracted large crowds of filmgoers at New York's Paris Theater. Prints were dubbed in English, with the expectation of mass audience response outside the art-house market.

Reviews were mixed but generally favorable. Some critics believed that the film was simply an illogical, incredible parody of bad action films, but others recognized its worth in its deft, self-conscious, and often hilarious fulfillment of the expectations of such a genre.

*Rob Edelman*

# THAT OBSCURE OBJECT OF DESIRE (CET OBSCUR OBJET DU DÉSIR)

*Origin:* France
*Released:* 1977
*Released in U.S.:* 1977
*Production:* Serge Silberman for Greenwich/Galaxy/Incine
*Direction:* Luis Buñuel
*Screenplay:* Luis Buñuel and Jean-Claude Carrière; based on the novel *La Femme et le pantin*, by Pierre Loüys
*Cinematography:* Edmond Richard
*Editing:* Hélène Plemiannikov
*Art direction:* Pierre Guffroy
*Music:* Richard Wagner
*MPAA rating:* R
*Running time:* 103 minutes

*Principal characters:*
Mathieu .......................... Fernando Rey
Conchita............ Carole Bouquet/Angela Molina
Judge ........................... Julien Bertheau
Valet............................ André Weber
Psychologist ............................ Pieral

Luis Buñuel's *That Obscure Object of Desire* was a great success with the critics both in Europe and in the United States. It was praised by reviewers of popular television as well as by historians of serious film. More than a dozen critics in the United States called it one of the best ten films of the year, and it was nominated for the Academy Award in the Best Foreign-Language Film category. What the critics did not always agree about, however, was their interpretation of the film and the reasons that they thought it was good. This confusion is not surprising, for the films of Buñuel often have a Surrealistic element that makes them difficult or impossible to explain by ordinary logic.

Buñuel's first film was *Un chien andalou* (1928; *An Andalusian Dog*). Artist Salvador Dalí collaborated with him on the script, and the two have said that they tried to avoid meaning in the film, discarding any ideas that were rational or could be explained. This was done because one intention of Surrealism is to reach the subconscious rather than the conscious mind. The film opens with a famous shot of a razor slicing open the eye of a woman and continues for some fifteen minutes to immerse the viewer in the irrational, the irreverent, and the unexpected. Buñuel made a number of important films in the decades following *An Andalusian Dog*, but he never completely turned away from the Surrealistic element of the 1928 film. In 1972 he made *Le Charme discret de la bourgeoisie* (*The Discreet Charm of the Bourgeoisie*), which began as a seemingly straightforward film but became increasingly absurd as it continued, taking the surprised viewer once again into the realm of the irrational and the incongruous. Five years later, in *That Obscure Object of Desire*, Buñuel combined aspects of the method of *The Discreet Charm of the Bourgeoisie* with an examination of the extremes of desire, love, and manipulation.

The film begins with Mathieu (Fernando Rey), a well-dressed man in his late fifties or early sixties, booking a railroad passage from Seville to Paris. As he is being driven to the train, a car in front of him is blown up by terrorists, but the only effect it seems to have on Mathieu is to make him concerned about reaching the railroad station on time. He does reach the train in time and takes his seat in a compartment.

Before the train leaves the station, however, a young woman with a black eye and bandaged head comes to the door of his car saying, "You don't understand. Please don't go." Mathieu responds by pouring a pail of water on her. Because this act intrigues his fellow passengers in the compartment, particularly a dwarf professor of psychology (Pieral), Mathieu begins telling them the story that led to that act. His story then takes up virtually all of the remainder of the film. The viewer usually sees the events that he describes, but the narrative occasionally withdraws again to the train, drawing attention to the storyteller and the listeners.

Mathieu first meets the young woman, Conchita (played by Carole Bouquet in some scenes and Angela Molina in others), when she is hired as a maid in his house in Paris. He is attracted to her and tries to kiss her, but she refuses his advances and quits the job. Three months later, in Switzerland, he meets her accidentally and discovers where she lives with her mother. Mathieu gives money to the mother, but Conchita continues to resist him. Mathieu then meets the mother alone and tells her that he will support both of them handsomely if Conchita will come to live with him. The mother accepts the proposition, but Conchita refuses, and she and her mother move without telling Mathieu where they have gone. Mathieu then becomes unresponsive and distant. He often confides in his cousin (Julien Bertheau), who is a judge. He cannot, he tells his cousin, merely find another woman. Then, apparently quite by accident, he meets Conchita again. This time she agrees to go with him to his country house and be his mistress.

Once they reach the house (which has no electricity that night because terrorists have damaged the power station), Conchita refuses to stay in one bedroom because Mathieu's wife, who has been dead for seven years, slept there. In another bedroom she delays entering the bed as long as she can, and when she finally does so, she has put on an undergarment that has so many ties that Mathieu cannot get it off. Thus begins a long series of encounters in which Conchita professes love but refuses to consummate their relationship. Neither Mathieu nor the audience knows whether she is telling the truth. He continues to become frustrated, but he cannot give up his obsession with Conchita. She says that he would no longer love her if she gave him everything he wanted.

Finally, Conchita disappears again and the still-obsessed Mathieu goes to Seville in hopes of finding her. Again, by chance he meets her, this time in a café where she dances the flamenco. The sequence at the café is revealing for the depth of Mathieu's obsession and for his gullibility. After Conchita dances downstairs in the café, she tells Mathieu that it is a policy of the management that the dancers rest between numbers, and that she must go upstairs. Later, however, another dancer tells Mathieu to go upstairs and he finds Conchita dancing naked before a primarily male audience. He is enraged, but again he accepts her very transparent explanation, and she (too easily) persuades him to buy her a house.

After she moves in, she tells him to come and see her the next night at exactly midnight. Instead of letting him in the gates, however, she leaves him outside beyond the iron bars, tells him that she detests him, then makes love with a young man right before his eyes.

The next day, she goes to see him to see "how he died," because, she tells him, she thought he loved her enough to commit suicide. She asserts that his buying her a house gives him no rights to her, and when he begins slapping her savagely, she claims that the whole scene was only staged and that she is still a virgin. By now her nose is bleeding, but she gives him the key to the house and asks him to come to her there. This time he refuses and leaves.

The film returns to the train compartment where Mathieu is telling the story, and Conchita comes to the door of the compartment and pours a bucket of water on him just as the train reaches Paris.

The ending of the film is deliberately bizarre and ambiguous. Mathieu and Conchita leave the railway station together and stroll down a street of shops. A burlap sack, which may or may not be one that the viewer has occasionally seen throughout the film carried either by a workman or by the impeccably dressed Mathieu himself, is opened in a shop window and white lace nightgowns are taken out. One is stained with blood, but a streamstress begins working on it nevertheless. As Mathieu and Conchita continue walking, there is a huge explosion between them and the camera that engulfs the screen and ends the film.

The film contains many Surrealistic touches, such as a woman carrying a young pig in a blanket as if it were a human baby. There are also less obscure devices such as a mouse being caught in a trap at the moment Conchita's mother mentions marriage to Mathieu.

The series of what must be seen as sadomasochistic exchanges between Conchita and Mathieu may reveal psychological truths about obsession, desire, and the willingness to accept humiliation, but the visual depiction of many incidents is provocative and disturbing. Both in the direction of his actors and in the visual conception, Buñuel shows his masterful command of the medium of cinema. In a painterly manner, each shot is well composed and well integrated into the whole. The acting of Fernando Rey as Mathieu is superbly smooth and lends credence to a series of incredible acts of passion. The supporting characters—particularly André Weber as Mathieu's imperturbable valet—are also excellent. The device of using two actresses to play Conchita was decided upon when the star of Bernardo Bertolucci's *Last Tango in Paris* (1972), Maria Schneider, who was originally signed to play the role by herself, quit the film shortly before filming began. Some critics have said that the two actresses show the duality of the character, while others have said that they show that the subject of the film is Mathieu's obsession rather than the "object" that supposedly inspires it.

*Timothy W. Johnson*

# THEOREM (TEOREMA)

*Origin:* Italy
*Released:* 1968
*Released in U.S.:* 1969
*Production:* Franco Rossellini and Manolo Bolgnini for Aetos Film
*Direction:* Pier Paolo Pasolini
*Screenplay:* Pier Paolo Pasolini
*Cinematography:* Giuseppe Ruzzolini
*Editing:* Nino Baragli
*Art direction:* Luciano Puccini
*Music:* Ennio Morricone and Wolfgang Amadeus Mozart
*MPAA rating:* no listing
*Running time:* 98 minutes
*Running time in U.S.:* 93 minutes

*Principal characters:*

Lucia .......................... Silvana Mangano
Visitor .......................... Terence Stamp
Odetta.......................... Anne Wiazemsky
Paolo .......................... Massimo Girotti
Pietro .......................... Andrès José Cruz
Emilia .......................... Laura Betti
Angiolino.......................... Ninetto Davoli
Old peasant .......................... Susanna Pasolini

*Theorem* detonated one of the most violent controversies in the turbulent career of Pier Paolo Pasolini. At Venice in 1968, it was awarded the prize of the Catholic International Film Office, while many Catholics, including the Pope himself, vigorously denounced it as "a Black Mass with Freud and Marx as assistant celebrants." The Italian authorities prosecuted Pasolini for blasphemy and immorality, and, although he was exculpated, the Catholic prize was eventually withdrawn as an error of judgment.

Paolo (Massimo Girotti), a Milanese industrialist, has transferred ownership of his factory to his work force. After television-interview-style shots of reporters and workers, equally bemused, the film becomes a flashback of the "inside story." First, black-and-white, almost silent, sequences introduce Paolo's family. Returning from school, his son, Pietro (Andrès José Cruz), clowns about, while his daughter, Odetta (Anne Wiazemsky), skips away from an admirer after showing him a photograph of her father. Paolo's wife, Lucia (Silvana Mangano), is as beautiful as a statuesque doll, and their house is as immaculate as it is luxurious. In the shiny modern kitchen, the maid, Emilia (Laura Betti), a stocky peasant woman, seems quite out of place. From a cheerful, clownlike messenger, Angiolino (Ninetto Davoli), she takes a telegram which she brings to Paolo at the table. It reads, "Arriving tomorrow."

With the arrival of the Visitor (Terence Stamp), color returns. A handsome youth, the Visitor never acquires a name. As he responds to the friendship and interest of each member of the family, each confesses or indicates his or her love for him and is gently fulfilled. First, Emilia, after clearing cigarette ashes from his trousers, runs into the kitchen to gas herself. As if sensing her distress, the Visitor follows her, and after rescuing her, he makes love to her, despite their differences in class, beauty, and age. Although Pietro's low self-esteem renders him awkward and shy, the sympathetic Visitor takes the initiative in a gently fraternal way. The proud Lucia is arrested by the sight of the Visitor's heap of abandoned clothes. From the summerhouse, she watches him hunting in a nearby wood. She removes her clothes, and, to make the gesture irreversible, throws them onto the lawn before calling him. Paolo, ailing and suffering from insomnia, sees the Visitor in bed with his Pietro. He falls ill, but the Visitor makes him more comfortable by lifting both his legs up from the bed. Odetta shares with the Visitor her photographic interests, showing her family album and photographing him with her father in the garden. He understands her signs of desire. Intending to remonstrate with the Visitor, Paolo invites him for a country drive. The Visitor playfully spars with Paolo, finally making it easy for Paolo literally to come down on him.

In a second round of scenes, each member of the family in turn gratefully confesses to the Visitor the new insights into themselves that he has revealed. A second telegram, however, triggers his abrupt departure.

Still the members of the family scarcely communicate with one another. Emilia takes the train to her home village. She sits immobile on a farmyard bench, eating only stewed nettles, as the villagers venerate her saintliness. The sores on a boy's face are miraculously healed, and in a miracle of levitation, Emilia rises above the rooftops. Odetta retires to her room and sinks into a catatonic trance, one hand obstinately closed. No one can revive her. Pietro quits home to become a painter. Eventually he resorts to postmodernist experimentation, blindfolding himself and urinating on a canvas depicting an azure sky. Lucia refuses her husband, but takes to cruising the city by day, picking up youths who physically resemble the Visitor and offering herself to them—at one point, in a ditch. In the Milan railway station, Paolo is suddenly fascinated by the bulging jeans of a male prostitute and divests himself of his clothes amid the rush-hour crowd. Leaving her village, Emilia has a peasant woman bury her in the soil of a building site up to her eyes, which seem to weep "tears of renewal." The film ends, however, with one of its intermittent scenes of deserts and dust clouds. This time, Paolo wanders nude across the slopes of a volcano, uttering a cry of spiritual anguish.

Pasolini wrote *Theorem* as a verse play but then decided that its theme called for a kind of silence. He adapted it, virtually simultaneously, both as a film and as a novel (which intermittently breaks into verse), regarding the film as a "correction" of the novel, which therefore is not the "key" to it. He describes the film's first part as the theorem: A bourgeois family encounters an incarnation of the divine. Their fates are the corollaries. Hence, *Theorem* is often bracketed with Pasolini's *Edipo Re* (1967; *Oedipus Rex*) for contrasting, in its very different way, the mythic, sacred, preindustrial world with the uncertainties of a modern, rational, alienated man.

Where *Oedipus Rex* is a myth, *Theorem* is a parable. Like poetry, myths complicate and enrich a plot's meanings, whereas parable, like allegory, is the simpler form. Yet *Theorem* avoids the patness of the message film, thanks to its visual style and the ambiguity of the Visitor. His aloof yet magically understanding character, his kindness and absence of need, swiftly link him to the long tradition of stories in which Christ moves unrecognized among men. Nevertheless, that reference seems difficult to connect with the political themes of the opening interviews and with the Visitor's extreme sexual promiscuity.

In its relation to Christianity, the film is open to various interpretations. It can be construed as a purely negative, destructive, blasphemous parody, although Pasolini's style is oddly reverential and gentle. It can seem a thoughtful repudiation of Christianity along 1960's lines, suggesting that Marxism and eroticism, though superseding religion, were themselves expression of the religious urge, and, as such, the antithesis of materialism and hedonism; hence the emphasis on seeking, suffering, and disorientation. Pasolini, however, was already criticizing Marxism for having assimilated excessive bourgeois materialism and rationality into itself. A certain Father Marc Gervais defended *Theorem* for vindicating the painful search for some profound spiritual link between man, men, and nature, so that sexuality is merely the point of entry of an essentially religious yearning.

Pasolini first intended the Visitor to personify "a fertility God, the typical God of non-industrial religion, the Sun-God, the Biblical God, God the Father" (as distinct from God the Son—presumably because he summons the family into the wilderness rather than exemplifying a new form of love). Responding to the personality of Terence Stamp, however, Pasolini reconceived the Visitor as "a generically ultraterrestrial and metaphysical apparition; he could be the Devil, or a mixture of God and the Devil." For Pasolini, the Visitor's essential trait is his power of authenticity, despite his touch of "bourgeois vulgarity." Since the Visitor is merely a catalyst for the characters' reactions, he could be construed as a hallucination, a phantasm, like the Lee Marvin character in John Boorman's *Point Blank* (1967).

The film's simple story line deftly combines many contemporary preoccupations. Sexual liberation was in full swing. *Theorem* was among the first films to present homosexuality without guilt, shame, or foreboding, as equal to heterosexuality. Affluence was rendering the working classes more bourgeois, while bourgeois youth was discovering many kinds of radicalism. (Hence, this bourgeois Visitor can resemble Pasolini's lumpenproletarian youths in his self-sovereignty.) Workers' ownership and control were live issues, and although bourgeois and Marxist thinkers held differing attitudes toward affluence, all saw it as a "crisis of opportunity" entailing identity crises, alienation, and profound moral problems.

Indeed, *Theorem* converges on Michelangelo Antonioni's style, with its blank, ominous landscapes and its glossy, civilized people discovering emotional emptiness as a schizoid condition. Several critics bracketed *Theorem* with Jean-Luc Godard's *La Chinoise* (1967), which also depicts members of the bourgeoisie trying to think through arduous mutations of their very souls (with only books, in Godard's case, and only memories, in Pasolini's). Pasolini's viewpoint, however, was unique, thanks to his peasant roots and nostalgia, personified in the maid.

Plot and dialogue are exceptionally terse and elliptical; the story is exposed, never explained. France Farago suggests that the characters share one, understandable, error: All cling to one particular individual (the Visitor) as an incarnation of the Absolute, whereas his nature is to be nonlocalizable, an ongoing flow, an adventurous welcome to each new "other." This moral-psychological interpretation agrees with the following approach to the plot imagery, though neither can, nor should, exclude many different avenues of approach.

Disclaiming easy criticism of bourgeois patriarchy, Pasolini presents a father (Paolo) who is lucid, generous, and gentle. Perhaps his "tragic flaw" is the reasonableness that allows him to postpone discussion of his son's seduction. Hence, a certain passivity, which renders him vulnerable to the male prostitute's bulging virility (whereas the Visitor carefully allows him the superior position in their embrace). Perhaps his self-expropriation contains a hint of masochism, like his public self-stripping—although that humility also proclaims, calmly, a human truth. His gift of the factory is a decisive act, and, if it risks rendering the workers as bourgeois as he is, that cannot be considered his fault, but theirs—or that of the situation. Pasolini chose for him a strong, smooth actor, reminding one that Paolo is potentially a king. His very openness to social possibility enables him to "see" modern life as a sulphurous desert, perhaps even as Hell.

Initially, Lucia is interested only in her immaculate person and her home. Yet she responds to the Visitor's roughly disordered clothes and his energy as a huntsman in a wood—the contrast to her sheltered inactivity. She throws down her clothes, like his, as if to leave a trail, a scent, for him. After his departure, she quits her home to "go hunting." She is still side-tracked by physical appearance, however, and may only have replaced self-grooming by self-soiling. The nearby church could indicate another "false trail" but allows one to hope that her fixation is not permanent. Perhaps she is in Purgatory.

If Lucia's progress is away from home, centrifugal, Odetta's is a retreat. Her initially swift movements become ever more lost, forlorn, slow, until she subsides into immobility. Perhaps her clenched fist "matches" her mother's obsessive self-opening. Catatonic, she has become as still and abstract as the photographs that preoccupied her—whether taking or showing them. Her cruel fate is to become a photograph, a moment's pose prolonged for an eternity. Perhaps she is merely willing herself into a too well-protected Limbo.

Image-making preoccupies Pietro. To the Visitor he explains his admiration for Francis Bacon. After failing to achieve the Visitor's portrait from memory, however, he settles for "experiments" intended not to portray but to mask his own self-hatred. At least he admits his dissatisfaction to himself, and perhaps there is hope in that—and in his inability to achieve Bacon's perfect, but all the more self-enfolding, self-expression.

Emilia can return to her peasant origins, which give her such strong, naïve, unanalyzed impulses. At first they drive her to suicide; later they lead her, through acceptance of nature's wildness (eating stewed nettles) to the wildness of supernature (Pasolini presents her miracles of simple faith with brutal literalism, as if to defy our rationalist skepticism). Eventually, her spiritual force becomes more equivocal. Burial, as rebirth, evokes some fertility-myth concept of the seed reborn but cannot link with the machinery around her. Whereas the children relate with images, the maid hides herself, except for her eyes, which weep. Perhaps she and Paolo, the father, are the real forces for renewal.

In telling this story, space, posture, and gesture are beautifully deployed and merit detailed analysis. Stylistically, Pasolini achieves a remarkable combination of opposites. On one hand, he generates an oppressive sense of lonely schizo-alienation; on the other, his characters' carnal-animal presence is emotionally rich, warm, and explosive.

Critic Stephen Snyder has splendidly begun the analysis of Pasolini's armory of devices for suggesting the coldness of the modern world: bright, flat surfaces, linear perspectives, geometric layouts, pictures-within-the-picture. Often these elements imply the semiological vision of human beings as no more than mindless signs existing primarily for others. If this side of Pasolini's style matches Godard's blank faces in blank spaces, other elements are as forceful and passionate as in the "mythic" films. Pasolini stressed his affinities with Tommaso Masaccio, Giotto, and the fourteenth century primitive painters, "who placed man in the centre of every perspective." He likewise commented that his camera style "isolates and idolizes" people, objects, landscapes, for its inspiration is his "fetishistic love" for creation (even at the expense of impeding a proper flow and continuity between them). To contrast with this cold, thin world, Pasolini's attentive camera rivets on faces and bodies; often a single, sustained shot transmits a landscape's mood, whether that landscape is of suburban sunlight or forest pools. The secret is Pasolini's painterly eye for light. The narrative is enigmatic, elliptical, discontinuous—whence emanates the strange sense of suspended time. The sparsity of words and sounds enhances the effects.

These niceties are "humanized" by the contained strength of the actors. Though gently seductive as the Visitor, Terence Stamp is a sphinx in human form—a modern counterpart, in a rationalizing culture, of the Monster-Sphinx in *Oedipus Rex*. Silvana Mangano plays another majestic maternal figure, this time more nervous and fragile. Ninetto Davoli plays another "herald"—the bringer of telegrams. Flapping his arms like wings while prancing free-spiritedly around the front garden, he suggests, like several other Pasolini characters entrusted to this actor, an open-minded joy which is not quite effective, or undoes itself. Emilia is played by Laura Betti, a redoubtable influence in Roman artistic circles and a formidable defender of Pasolini; her interpretation won for her Venice's Best Actress Award. The woman who buries her is played by Pasolini's mother.

*Raymond Durgnat*

# THERE WAS A FATHER (CHICHI ARIKI)

*Origin:* Japan
*Released:* 1942
*Released in U.S.:* no listing
*Production:* Shochiku
*Direction:* Yasujiro Ozu
*Screenplay:* Tadao Ikeda, Takao Yanai, and Yasujiro Ozu
*Cinematography:* Yuharu Atsuta
*Editing:* no listing
*Art direction:* Toshishichiro Isono
*Costume design:* Taizo Saito
*Sound:* Kozaburo Matsuo
*Music:* Gyoichi Saiki
*Running time:* 94 minutes

*Principal characters:*

Shuhei Horikawa.................... Chishu Ryu
Ryohei Horikawa .................... Shuji Sano
Ryohei as a young man .......... Haruhiko Tsuda
Makoto Hirata ................ Takeshi Sakamoto
Fumiko Hirata .................... Mitsuko Mito
Yasutaro Kurokawa.................. Shin Saburi
Minoru Uchida.................. Shinichi Himori
Seiichi Hirata ................ Otsuka Masayoshi

Yasujiro Ozu occupies a special place in the Japanese psyche. Long considered the most "Japanese" of Japanese directors, Ozu remains a beloved figure long after his death. Ozu's grave occupies a prized place in the prestigious Engaku-ji Temple in Kamakura; his gravestone receives constant care. In the West, Ozu's reputation is less emotionally grounded, but equally prestigious. This status is based on Ozu's film style, which, grounded in traditional Japanese culture, diverges significantly from the Hollywood mainstream model. Unfortunately, the appraisal of Ozu's film style has a significant drawback for a complete understanding of his cinema. The focus on technique, whether as a manifestation of traditional Japanese cultural practices or as a style at variance with that of Hollywood, tends to dehistoricize his films, removing them from their specific context in Japanese history. To compare his films produced during the 1930's, for example, to his efforts in the 1950's from the point of view of his stylistic evolution is certainly of some value, but it would neither account for their importance to Japanese culture, nor would it reveal the kinds of historical tensions to which film, more than any other art, seems to be subject.

An examination of Ozu's *There Was a Father* is as good a place as any to bring historical analysis into the criticism of Ozu's canon. Produced at the height of World War II, *There Was a Father* was subject to certain restrictions and guidelines. The way the film diverges from the typical Ozu work may be ascribed to this historical circumstance; the way the film manifests Ozu's special insights and concerns may reveal the manner in which a genuine auteur can continue to make personal statements even within a restrictive context. *There Was a Father* is by all means the kind of contemplative, episodic family drama that one has come to expect from Ozu. The story spans approximately fifteen years in the lives of a widowed father, Shuhei Horikawa (Chishu Ryu, Ozu's favorite actor), and his son, Ryohei (Haruhiko Tsuda as the young Ryohei, Shuji Sano as the older Ryohei). At the film's start, Shuhei Horikawa is a junior high school mathematics teacher living in Kanazawa with his young son Ryohei. Horikawa and a group of other teachers, with Horikawa in charge, lead a class trip to Tokyo and its famous suburbs. Horikawa, nicknamed "the badger," is a kind, well-liked teacher, very much concerned for his students. The group travels to a large lake, where one of the students is killed in a boating accident. Though completely blameless (Horikawa told the students not to take out the boats), Horikawa feels responsible for the young boy's death. He talks to his best friend, Makoto Hirata (Takeshi Sakamoto), telling him that he feels compelled to resign from his teaching position because of the accident.

Horikawa and Ryohei move to Horikawa's boyhood hometown in Ueda. Horikawa takes a job in the village registry office and lives in a temple with his son. When it is time for Ryohei to enter junior high school, Ryohei must move full-time into the dormitory as Ueda is too far away from school to commute. Horikawa soon comes to realize that he must leave Ueda if he is to be able to pay for Ryohei's advanced schooling, as he wants the boy to continue on to high school and then university. Ryohei, however, will continue to live apart from his father.

Many years pass, and Horikawa is now a middle-level executive in a Tokyo factory. Ryohei attends the national university in Sendai, thus continuing to live apart from his father. When Ryohei is graduated from college, he takes a job in an industrial school in Akita, far to the north of Tokyo.

At a *go* parlor (*go* is a traditional Japanese board game, similar to checkers and chess), Horikawa sees Hirata, who is now retired, a widower living in Tokyo with his daughter, Fumiko (Mitsuko Mito), and his small son, Seiichi (Otsuka Masayoshi).

Horikawa and his now-grown son are able to spend only a few days together at any one time. One such vacation together finds them at a hot springs resort. Horikawa brings up the subject of Hirata and his daughter Fumiko, who, at age twenty-one, is ready to be married. Ryohei says that he will think about marrying. He also says that he wants to quit his job in Akita and live with Horikawa in Tokyo. Horikawa, however, does not think it is a good idea. As they part, Ryohei offers his father some money, which he gladly accepts.

Yasutaro Kurokawa (Shin Saburi) and Minoru Uchida (Shinichi Himori), two former students of Horikawa, invite him and Hirata to a reunion party in their honor. At the party, attended by a dozen or so former students, Horikawa and Hirata realize how much time has passed—all the boys are now successful businessmen, husbands and fathers. After the party, Horikawa asks his son Ryohei, who is in Tokyo for a visit, if Ryohei will marry Fumiko Hirata. Ryohei agrees to the wedding. Ryohei tells his father that he has passed the conscription test for the military, but it is not mentioned whether he will be called to serve. At the end of the evening, Horikawa suddenly falls ill. He is taken to a hospital where, with his son, Hirata, Fumiko, and Seiichi present, he dies peacefully.

Fumiko and Ryohei take the train to Akita, where they will live together as husband and wife. Ryohei tells Fumiko how much he will always treasure his last week together with his father. Fumiko begins to cry as the train rides off into the night.

Ozu wrote a draft of the script for *There Was a Father* in 1937, but was called up for military service in July of that year, following the outbreak of the Sino-Japanese War. He returned to Japan, and to the Shochiku studios, after serving two years. Ozu found himself in a Japan whose film studios were subject to fairly strict censorship codes wherein all scripts were required to meet with the approval of the Censorship Office of the Home Ministry. There were a number of "do nots" imposed upon filmmakers and their scripts: Do not make light of the military or military matters; do not do anything to lower the morale of the conscripted men and their families; do not show scenes of corruption and/or merriment; do not portray individualism in a positive light; do not fail to glorify traditional Japanese art and culture.

An awareness of the conditions during the production of *There Was a Father* is quite necessary to a full appreciation of the finished film. One can see many little moments in the film that at least pay lip service to the national policy ideology. While none of these scenes can be construed as offensive, or even as overtly propagandistic in any pejorative sense, they should be acknowledged in order to situate the film properly within its sociohistorical context.

The first hint of the wartime production of the film comes when one of Ryohei's students in Akita asks to return home for a few days because his mother has just given birth to a new son and his older brother has been drafted. Ryohei gives the boy permission to go home, with the proviso that he not be a burden to his mother. Later in the film, when Ryohei is visiting his father in Tokyo, Horikawa calls Ryohei's attention to a museum exhibition of traditional Japanese art which he regards as particularly moving. (Without doubt, Horikawa's sentiments on traditional Japanese art are quite true, now harmless but clearly meant to fulfill an ideological position in 1942.) The most major, indeed, inescapably ideologically motivated moment occurs when Ryohei tells his father that he wants to quit his school job in Akita in order to live with Horikawa in Tokyo. Horikawa forbids the boy to do so and goes on to make what amounts to a speech about work and duty. (Long speeches are quite rare in Ozu's cinema, and the mere presence of one here should stand as a significantly overt intrusion of the wartime censoring ideology.) Horikawa says, "We each have our own jobs. Once we have them we must consider them our missions whatever they may be. Every man has his duty which he has to carry out by all means." He goes on to say that teaching is an important job and that people must not think only of their individual happiness. Obviously, the speech was written with the censorship code in hand.

Nevertheless, while such a speech is clearly intended for a wartime audience, to inspire citizens to put aside individual wants and buckle down to the needs of the nation, it is a tribute to Ozu that the speech works in a more timeless, universally emotional context: Horikawa is also saying that events and circumstances have a way of interfering with one's wishes, that there is little one can do about that, except to persevere. This transcendental attitude is very much in keeping with the mainstream of Ozu's cinema and helps one to understand how this film, produced during the war, so easily overcomes its origins.

The propagandistic aspects aside, *There Was a Father* manifests many of the essential Ozu traits for which he is justly famous and praised. The basic parent-child relationship is central to Ozu's cinema, and it has never been handled with more emotional appeal and sensitivity. Ordinary people in every way, the Horikawas speak to the very essence of the parent-child bond. The ordinariness of the characters is reflected in the episodic, offhand way the plot unfolds. The film is extremely simple, but as in many of Ozu's films, one must pay careful attention to the narrative, for time passes quite deceptively, and it is not until some time into the new scene that one becomes aware of just how the plot has progressed. (This is the principle of "retrospectivity" which is fundamental to Ozu's conception of cinematic storytelling.) For example, in one scene Horikawa tells Ryohei that he must move to Tokyo to get a better job in order to afford Ryohei's schooling. The next scene shows Horikawa working in a factory, at a middle-management level, where one may assume he has recently become employed. Nevertheless, a conversation soon reveals that Ryohei has, in the meantime, been graduated from high school (in the previous scene he has just started junior high) and now attends a university. Similarly, when, shortly after this scene,

Horikawa meets his friend Hirata at a *go* parlor in Tokyo, one suddenly learns that Ryohei is now twenty-five years old, a graduate of the university and now teaching in Akita.

The typically Ozu-like narrative structure is also accompanied by Ozu's use of the "coda"—a still-life shot used as punctuation between scenes. The most common coda in *There Was a Father* is a straight-on shot of a traditional Japanese stone lantern. The obvious temptation in dealing with an Ozu film is to try to put forth symbolic interpretations of the coda-image as a transitional device, but, as the formalists have correctly concluded, such devices have no narrative weight. Shots of the stone lantern serve as the site across which narrative events may transpire but in and of themselves have no more weight than other Ozu still-life devices, such as shots of clotheslines, bird cages, alleyways, and office buildings. The codas do have a certain emotional weight, as Ozu, here as usual, is careful to utilize an image that relies on the Zen concept of presence-in-absence. The stone lantern speaks of the human presence (as do clotheslines and bird cages), but such presence is felt by its absence. Thus, Ozu may quickly evoke an emotional response from his Japanese audience. It may also be the case that the stone lanterns are there to evoke the traditional Japanese aesthetic concept of *sabi*—the valuation and honor of the old, which would be in keeping with wartime ideology. Yet, this may be reading too much into a strictly formal component.

One is also in familiar Ozu territory in the many scenes that rely on the concept of the "dailiness of daily living." Although *There Was a Father* begins with a traumatic scene involving the death of the junior high school student (a death alluded to, but not shown, in a shot of an overturned boat) and climaxes with the death of the father, in between the film is nothing other than strictly ordinary events, some humorous, some touching, some sad, but nothing overwhelming. On the humorous side (and humor is an often overlooked quantity in Ozu's films), Ozu works hard to build a small gag which, in typical Ozu fashion, is merely tossed away. When young Ryohei learns from his father that they must move to Ueda from Kanazawa, he finds some small solace in the fact that his new friends will not know that his father is nicknamed "the badger" and he will, consequently, no longer be called "son of badger." A number of scenes later in the film, Horikawa comes to visit Ryohei at his junior high school dormitory. When Ryohei and Horikawa leave, his new friends decide that Horikawa needs a nickname—one wit quickly decides upon "badger." (The nickname never comes up again in the film.) On the more ordinary side, Ozu delivers two scenes, one with the young Ryohei, the other with the grown-up one, in which father and son quietly enjoy fishing together in a small stream. One of the longer scenes with Horikawa and Ryohei together merely finds them bathing together in a hot spring, then sitting down to a leisurely meal. "The dailiness of daily living" also helps explain why Ozu finds it necessary to show a scene at the film's beginning of Horikawa teaching a mathematics class, and one much later of Ryohei teaching a chemistry class. In neither sequence does anything of any narrative or dramatic significance occur, but Ozu believes that it is important to show what people do, for, after all, this is how people actually spend their time. Besides, it is precisely in the ordinary, in the dailiness of daily living, that people, at least in Ozu's films, must come to terms with the ultimate meaning of life.

Coming to terms with life also means, for Ozu, coming to terms with the inevitable changes that life has in store. This is shown most clearly in the party sequence in which Horikawa and Hirata are honored by their former students. Much is made in this scene of how the young boys have now grown up, how they are parents themselves, an indication of life's inevitable cycle. This is further impacted into the film's structure by Horikawa's death, which occurs in the next scene, almost immediately after Ryohei agrees to marry Fumiko. Seeing his students in adulthood and knowing his son is on that path almost inspires Horikawa's death, as it were, so that he may participate in the never-ending mythic cycle.

No discussion of an Ozu film would be complete, would completely convey the special properties of his cinema, without acknowledging the ultimate "Ozu scene." It is almost a signature for Ozu to have one or more of his characters make some seemingly harmless comment, usually about the weather, at a particularly emotional moment. Such moments, interestingly, usually occur about two-thirds of the way into the film. Here that moment occurs in the sequence in which Horikawa and his son are at the hot springs. Following Horikawa's speech about each man's duty, Ryohei offers his father some money, which the older man accepts. Horikawa Shuhei then goes to the balcony of their room, quietly looks out, and says, "The nightingales are singing." An understanding of this moment is an understanding of why Ozu will live forever in the psyche of traditional Japan.

*David Desser*

# THÉRÈSE DESQUEYROUX

*Origin:* France
*Released:* 1962
*Released in U.S.:* 1963
*Production:* Eugène Lépicier for Filmel
*Direction:* Georges Franju
*Assistant direction:* Georges Casati
*Screenplay:* François Mauriac, Claude Mauriac, and Georges Franju; based on the novel by Mauriac
*Cinematography:* Christian Matras and Raymond Heil
*Editing:* Gilbert Natot
*Art direction:* Jacques Chalvet
*Makeup:* Maguy Vernardet
*Sound:* Jean Labussière
*Music:* Maurice Jarre
*Running time:* 109 minutes

*Principal characters:*

Thérèse Desqueyroux ............ Emmanuelle Riva
Bernard Desqueyroux .............. Philippe Noiret
Anne de la Trave ....................... Edith Scob
Balionte ............................ Jeanne Perez
Jean Avézédo .......................... Sami Frey
Mme de la Trave .................. Renée Devillers
Aunt Clara..................... Hélène Dieudonné
Hector de la Trave .............. Richard Saint Bris
Jérôme Larroque ...................... Lucien Nat

Georges Franju is well-known for the influence of his work on the New Wave filmmakers. At the beginning of his career in the 1940's, Franju showed deep concern for social themes which positioned him as a politically "engaged" filmmaker. It was his critical view of French institutions which attracted such New Wave filmmakers as Jean-Luc Godard and Claude Chabrol. Franju's denunciations of French society and his ambiguous narratives were very radical for their time: His work as a filmmaker was at the center of the debate on cinema as a means of political and personal expression. Franju's criticism of French society and its shortcomings ranged from the slaughtering of animals, in *Le Sang des bêtes* (1949), to government asylums, in *La Tête contre les murs* (1958; *The Keepers*).

*Thérèse Desqueyroux* itself is a statement on the need for individual freedom. As in his other films, Franju concentrates on an individual who does not fit into his own world. In a deliberately slow pace, the suffocating life of heroine Thérèse Desqueyroux (Emmanuelle Riva) is captured in all of its harshness. As Franju presents Thérèse's claustrophobic world and her problems with her husband, Bernard Desqueyroux (Philippe Noiret), he offers a detailed portrayal of rural life. Like the Italian neorealists, Franju relies on a faithful rendition of daily life to convey Thérèse's loneliness. Yet *Thérèse Desqueyroux* goes further than the use of realistic techniques: Georges Franju's reality is always surrounded by a poetic ambiguity.

The film opens at the courthouse of Bordeaux. As Thérèse's father, Jérôme Larroque (Lucien Nat), talks to her, the viewer learns that Thérèse has been found innocent of a murder attempt on her husband, and it is Bernard's false testimony that has saved Thérèse. Thérèse is driven back to her house, where Bernard waits for her. Traveling throughout the night, she reviews the major moments in her life which led to her tragic and futile gesture. This series of flashbacks form the first part of the film. The second part begins as she meets Bernard, who refuses to hear Thérèse's explanation. For the sake of appearances, he will not seek a divorce, but he will keep her prisoner in their own home. Under these conditions, Thérèse soon becomes very ill. Eventually taking pity on her, Bernard allows her to leave for Paris. The film closes on an image of Thérèse walking through the crowds of Paris.

While being very complex, the structure of the narrative is so well organized that the viewer is transported gracefully from one moment to another. The first part of the film is built on flashbacks appearing in a chronological sequence. The transitions from present to past are very innovative: In an early scene when Thérèse remembers her friendship with the husband (Richard Saint Bris) of her sister, Anne de la Trave (Edith Scob), Thérèse, whose face is surrounded by the darkness of the night, bends over the car window to look outside. Suddenly, Anne's image appears on the car window. The next shot brings the viewer back to the past as Anne and Thérèse are riding their bicycles in the country. The movement from dark to light gives these transitions the seductive appearance of a dream. The unreal quality of the transitions imposes an impressive subjectivity on the narrative.

To resolve the difficulties usually posed by time, Franju uses voice-overs in a remarkable manner. The voice-over of Thérèse meditating on her life establishes a link with the numerous flashbacks. The device of the voice-over also serves to reveal the heroine's inner thoughts, as in the scene in which she meets Anne's lover, Jean Avézédo (Sami Frey). She does not say anything to Jean as he reads his letter to Anne. Her voice-over, however, expresses her reaction: She thinks that this letter (of separation) is cruel. The voice-over becomes a key to an understanding of Thérèse's soul.

The chronological order of the flashback permits the establishment of an evolution in Thérèse's behavior. From the first flashback, in which she appears as a carefree adolescent, to a later one in which she begins poisoning Bernard, the viewer notices a dramatic change. While in the early stages of her life she wears white clothes; she later dresses in darker colors. As the film progresses, her faces takes on a look of anxiety. The most noticeable change in the character, however, is in her use of gestures. In the scenes from her earlier years, she moves in an abrupt and decisive manner; later, her movements become slower, contrasting with the other characters who seem to be moving much more rapidly than she. Thérèse's progressive alienation from her family is presented through a pathetic lapse into silence. During her honeymoon, she has repeated arguments with her husband. She criticizes Bernard's values and his patronizing attitude. As the story unfolds, however, she takes refuge in silence, and she allows people to talk without even taking notice of them. By the time Thérèse decides to poison Bernard, she seems more like a phantom than a person.

If the first part creates a subjective atmosphere, the second part is objective and yet more dramatic, through the use of cinematic technique. In the reunion scene between Bernard and his wife, Bernard is shot from a low angle while a high angle is used for Thérèse's close-up. This composition increases the position of superiority of the husband, deaf to his wife's explanations. The dramatic tone that Franju gives to this second part is based on his obvious desire to maintain the film's momentum. Franju has an uncanny ability to build in intense emotion through the use of image, as in the scene in which Thérèse is sequestered, under the surveillance of the family domestic. Lying in bed and ill, she sees her cigarettes taken away from her. In a mechanical gesture, she flicks the ashes of an imaginary cigarette. Franju's close-up of her hand captures all the despair of her situation.

In *Thérèse Desqueyroux*, many such scenes carry a narrative meaning without the support of words. Franju allows the image to speak for itself. In the wedding scene, for example, conceived with great attention to depth of field, the camera is held on Bernard and Thérèse in the foreground. As they exchange their vows, the guests and the church alley are seen in the background. Thérèse's face grows anxious as she begins to panic. Suddenly, in the background, the viewer sees the church door closing. At the same time, the viewer can observe the expression of dreadful apprehension on Thérèse's face as she realizes that there is no escape. Franju uses depth of field to enhance the narrative in another scene, in which the family comes to see Thérèse during her time of "imprisonment" by her husband. The characters stand at different spatial levels in the room, staring anxiously at the door while they wait for Thérèse to enter. When the door opens, the characters' reactions become slowly inscribed on their faces. The effect is stunning as the viewer contemplates the various reactions, from bemused to horrified.

Franju's use of camera movement and of long-shot composition is similar to that of Jean Renoir. The director of *Thérèse Desqueyroux* captures the characters' movements within their environment in a way that displays a realistic picture of their inner states. In a family dinner scene after Thérèse's honeymoon, the gestures of the family members seem to grate on Thérèse, who appears to find them unbearable. The camera movement is fluid as it follows the characters around. As Thérèse's sense of entrapment increases, the camera moves closer to her, as space gradually closes in on her. The restriction of her movement effectively reproduces a claustrophobic world.

Shot on location, *Thérèse Desqueyroux* takes place in the Region of Girondes, near Bordeaux. As in all of his other films, Franju successfully exploits the surroundings. Following the tradition of the Swedish naturalistic movement of the 1920's, Franju relies on nature to represent Thérèse's feelings. Nature becomes associated with the drama taking place. In an early scene Anne is seen sleeping on Thérèse's knees, the sun reflecting on the sand dunes. The natural scene expresses her sense of calm and happiness. When Thérèse meets Jean and they talk about life and passion, the viewer can see the herbs on fire behind them. Lying in bed in her prison, she stares outside the windows at the trees bending over in the wind and rain. Franju creates a poetic atmosphere with his association of images to narrative. The lighting in the film, too, corresponds to Thérèse's story; as the heroine's destiny becomes more dramatic, the scenes are shot under a darker sky. The sunlight present in the early flashback of Thérèse's youth reappears only at the end, when she is finally set free in Paris. It is in this metaphoric function of the image that one finds the ambiguity always present in Franju's films. Franju often relied on the sole power of the image, giving life to a startling level of meaning. Such is the case in the scene in which Bernard shows a captive bird to his wife. Thérèse's fearful look and the bird's violent attempt to escape establish a link between their mutual loss of freedom.

While entering Thérèse's consciousness, the viewer discovers and experiences her relationship to the world. The slow camera movement and the composition re-create her perceptions. Concentrating on Thérèse as narrator, Franju develops an accurate portrayal of French provincial life. Like Thérèse, the viewer judges the hypocrisy of Bernard, who goes to church for the sake of appearances only. The fact that Bernard never notices Thérèse's strange behavior reveals his inability to question himself.

*Thérèse Desqueyroux* is the story of an individual's rebellion against her empty life. While Franju shows Thérèse's passions for life being crushed by her community, he seems to plead for the right to individualism. As in all of his other films, Franju concentrates on an individual whose attempts to challenge conventional behavior reveals the need for such a right. Franju's love and respect for a worthy life can be retraced through this story.

*Françine Blais*

# THÉRÈSE RAQUIN

*Origin:* France and Italy
*Released:* 1953
*Released in U.S.:* 1958
*Production:* Paris Film Production/Lux Film
*Direction:* Marcel Carné
*Screenplay:* Charles Spaak and Marcel Carné; based on the novel by Émile Zola
*Cinematography:* Roger Hubert
*Editing:* Henri Rust
*Art direction:* Paul Bertrand
*Costume design:* Mayo
*Music:* Maurice Thiriet
*Running time:* 110 minutes
*Also known as: The Adulterers*

*Principal characters:*

| | |
|---|---|
| Thérèse Raquin | Simone Signoret |
| Laurent | Raf Vallone |
| Witness | Roland Lesaffre |
| Camille | Jacques Duby |
| Mme Raquin | Sylvie |

Carné's *Thérèse Raquin* was "inspired," in the words of the credits, by Émile Zola's nineteenth century novel of the same title, but changed the setting to Lyons in 1950. The story is otherwise essentially the same as Zola's, relating an ill-fated love affair which results in destruction for all the main characters. In the film, the sickly Camille Raquin (Jacques Duby) lives in a passionless marriage with Thérèse (Simone Signoret), which was arranged by his domineering mother (Sylvie). When Camille introduces the Italian truck driver Laurent (Raf Vallone) into his home, Laurent and Thérèse fall in love. Laurent argues that they should run away together without thinking of the consequences, but Thérèse is unable to take this step. Laurent tells Thérèse that he cannot stand the lying and hiding and then confesses to Camille, who determines to reconcile with his wife on a holiday in Paris. Laurent also is aboard the train to Paris, and when Camille finds the lovers on the platform, he starts a fight. Laurent throws him from the moving train in a fit of passion. Upon hearing the news of her son's death, Mme Raquin has a stroke which leaves her paralyzed. Thérèse then has to nurse the old woman, who is unable to speak and follows her every move with her eyes.

The police suspect either murder or suicide in Camille's death but cannot prove anything, so the railroad pays Thérèse a small sum in compensation.

Meanwhile, a sailor (Roland Lesaffre), who was asleep in the compartment and testified that he saw nothing, blackmails Thérèse, saying that he saw her leave the compartment before Camille did. Thérèse and Laurent pay off the sailor with the settlement money, but he is killed in the street by a runaway truck, and the letter that he has left at his hotel as a safeguard is sent to the police.

There were two previous versions of *Thérèse Raquin*: a 1915 Italian film directed, by Nino Martoglio, and a 1928 German film by Jacques Feyder. Both renditions have disappeared, and the only records of their existence survive in archival data.

Besides updating the Zola original, Carné and his scenarist, Charles Spaak, changed Camille's death from a murder by drowning in a river to an unpremeditated shove from the train. The film also omits the novel's end—the marriage of Thérèse and Laurent, whose relationship is altered from a crazy shared desire to a situation in which their life together is a prison. In the original ending, Thérèse and Laurent develop a mutual loathing and plan to kill each other, but at the last moment, they experience a surge of their former love, and together they commit suicide.

Carné and Spaak, in modernizing the story, lost the social pressures of provincial, middle-class life that were brought to bear on the Thérèse and Laurent of the previous century. They sacrificed Zola's emphasis on the determinism of character by heredity and environment and substituted chance as the deciding factor in the lovers' alliance. In the film, the first meeting, their affair, Camille's demise, and the death of the blackmailer, which ends in their destruction, all result from accidents. Carné carries forward some of Zola's intentions, but they are at odds with the social realities of Carné's period. The Thérèse of 1950 presumably has options not open to the Thérèse of 1867, and a modern Camille would certainly be abnormal if he thought that he could confine his wife in order to make her forget her lover.

Carné's *Thérèse Raquin* is a film of contrasts. Impulse fights with reason, passion with reserve; the vitality of an earthy Italian truck driver is set in opposition to the impotence of a sickly, mother-dominated weakling. Romance wars with bourgeois pretense. The outdoors is presented as the antithesis of the Raquins' stuffy shop and apartment.

Laurent is carried away by his romantic notions. He urges Thérèse to run away with him without hesitation but realizes that she is tied to the security provided by her middle-class existence, her "little life" as he refers to it. Even in love, Thérèse's fervor does not approach that of Laurent. He will risk everything for her, but her face remains closed, rarely betraying any depth in her passion. In Carné's conception and in Simone Signoret's performance, Thérèse is an enigma. One wonders if she thinks that she can have both her affair with Laurent and her secure life with Camille. She is cool, reasonable, and implacable. Although the audience believes in the force of her love and the respite that it provides her from the confines of the Raquins' dry goods store and the apartment above, her ardor is rarely visible.

Laurent is open and strong. He accepts Thérèse straightforwardly and warmly. In the person of Raf Vallone, Laurent is virile and life-embracing, as opposed to the spindly Camille portrayed by Jacques Duby, with his weak chin and pointed nose. Laurent takes Thérèse in his arms and kisses her passionately. Camille's strongest emotions are reserved for a board game that he plays every Thursday with his mother's friends, fighting heatedly over points. Camille and Thérèse never embrace; instead, she puts him to bed with a hot water bottle when Mme Raquin suspects that he may have caught a chill.

In the first scene between Laurent and Camille, Camille vents his prejudices against foreigners to Laurent, the Italian, repeating them more vehemently to Thérèse after Laurent has told him of the affair. Indeed, he is particularly ashamed of being cuckolded by a foreigner, and he whimpers about what people will think of him. He complains that he will die without Thérèse and promises her a holiday at his aunt's apartment in Paris as a means of making her forget Laurent. He then tells his mother that he will lock Thérèse in that apartment with no money and no telephone to punish her for her infidelity.

The film is as savage about petit-bourgeois respectability and ideas of propriety as Zola was. The status quo, whether it is the maintenance of a loveless marriage or the care of an infirm mother-in-law, no matter how unhappy she has made one's life or how much she is hated, must be preserved. Mme Raquin's disapproval of Thérèse, who seems to be spiritually absent throughout much of the film, is noted in the old woman's insistence on tending her son, claiming that Thérèse ignores his well-being.

All life is squashed in this setting. The only activity which animates the Raquins is the weekly game, which explodes in passionate accusations about cheating and about who is ahead, but from which Thérèse remains conspicuously aloof. In this milieu, Laurent, with his smoldering glances and attentiveness, is a breath of fresh air.

The atmosphere at the Raquins' is as stuffy as the conservative values by which they live. Downstairs, Thérèse works in the drab dry goods store, with its rows of fabric in dark cases; upstairs, the apartment is full of draperies, fringes, fussy pictures, and imposing furniture, the stultifying minutiae of cluttered but empty lives.

Carné contrasts the oppressive interiors with a few shots of the outdoors. In the opening scene, when the three Raquins walk beside the Rhône, Camille animatedly watches the townsmen playing boules on the quay while Thérèse stares at the water, lost in her thoughts. As Thérèse walks down a lane toward a rendezvous with Laurent at a country inn, the open air is seen as a relief, a means of escaping into the light from the dark, going from emotional deprivation toward sensuality. These moments are brief; Carné keeps the emphasis on the smothering aspects of the indoor scenes.

*Thérèse Raquin* is practically a *film noir*, but the principals do not voluptuously embrace their fates, as in the classic *noir* films, or throw their lives away almost capriciously after some enormous emotional or romantic reversal. Stylistically, however, *Thérèse Raquin* is dark enough to stand beside Carné's best work in the genre, *Le Jour se lève* (1939; *Daybreak*) and *Quai des brunes* (1938; *Port of Shadows*).

*Judith M. Kass*

# THEY DON'T WEAR BLACK TIE (ELES NÃO USAM BLACK TIE)

*Origin:* Brazil
*Released:* 1981
*Released in U.S.:* 1982
*Production:* Leon Hirszman for Embrafilme
*Direction:* Leon Hirszman
*Screenplay:* Gianfrancesco Guarnieri and Leon Hirszman; based on the play by Guarnieri
*Cinematography:* Lauro Escorel
*Editing:* Eduardo Escorel
*Art direction:* Marcos Weinstock and Jefferson de Albuquerque
*Costume design:* Yurika Yamasaki
*Sound:* Juares Dagoberto
*Music:* Radamés Gnatelli and Adoniram Barbosa
*MPAA rating:* no listing
*Running time:* 120 minutes

*Principal characters:*

| | |
|---|---|
| Romana | Fernanda Montenegro |
| Otávio | Gianfrancesco Guarnieri |
| Tião | Carlos Alberto Ricelli |
| Maria | Bete Mendes |
| Braulio | Milton Gonçalves |
| Sartini | Francisco Milani |

Although he has directed relatively few feature fiction films, Leon Hirszman has been one of the prime movers of Brazilian cinema since the early 1960's, when, together with Glauber Rocha, Carlos Diegues, Nelson Pereira dos Santos, and Ruy Guerra, he helped found that decade's *Cinema Novo*. Hirszman began by directing a short episode, "Pedreira de São Diogo" ("São Diogo Quarry"), which was incorporated into the feature-length *Cinco Vezes Favela* (1961; *Favela Five Times*), a collaborative film produced by the leftist Popular Center of Culture. In the episode, Hirszman deploys Eisensteinian montage strategies in the service of his progressive vision of worker solidarity. His first feature film, *A Falecida* (1965; *The Deceased Woman*), was based on a story by Brazilian playwright Nelson Rodrigues, and chronicles the tragic alienation of a lower-middle-class woman obsessed by religion and death. The film marked the screen debut of Fernanda Montenegro, a celebrated stage actress who also plays the role of Romana in *They Don't Wear Black Tie*.

*Garota de Ipanema* (1967; *The Girl from Ipanema*), Hirszman's next film, was *Cinema Novo*'s first color feature and offers music by Vinícius de Moraes and other bossa nova composers. This sensuous film not only explores the myth of the suntanned "girl from Ipanema" but also questions that very myth. Hirszman's next film, *São Bernardo*—made in 1971 but released only in 1972 because of censorship—reflected a moment of severe political repression in Brazil. Based on Graciliano Ramos' classic 1934 novel, the film recounts the metamorphosis of an exploited peasant into a powerful plantation owner. In a distanced, Brechtian style, the film exposes the social alienation of a protagonist who has become deformed through his lust for power and property. The film also typifies the allegorical strategies adopted by Brazilian directors in the face of official censorship. The protagonist, for example, is authoritarian and rabidly anti-Communist, not unlike Brazil's military leaders, and, like them, he comes to power through force and intimidation.

*They Don't Wear Black Tie* continues Hirszman's ongoing search to combine intense political and social concern with a certain popular appeal. The film won numerous international awards, including the Special Golden Lion at the Venice International Film Festival. Adapted from the play of the same title by Gianfrancesco Guarnieri, which marked the emergence of a Brazilian political theater in the mid-1950's, *They Don't Wear Black Tie* focuses on a São Paulo working-class family that becomes deeply divided over a strike at the factory in which both father and son, along with the son's fiancée, work. The father, Otávio (Gianfrancesco Guarnieri), is an old union activist who has spent three years in prison for his activism. Against the impatient radical Sartini (Francisco Milani), both Otávio and his fellow activist Braulio (Milton Gonçalves) argue that the strike is premature, although they finally support it in a spirit of solidarity. The son, Tião (Carlos Alberto Ricelli), meanwhile, is planning to marry his pregnant fiancée, Maria (Bete Mendes), and is more concerned with providing for his family-to-be than with the political issues involved in the strike. When the strike breaks out, Tião crosses the picket line. Police repression sends Otávio to jail and Maria to the hospital. Otávio's wife, Romana (Fernanda Montenegro), gets Otávio out of jail, but both Otávio and Maria reject Tião as a strikebreaker. Later, a police agent kills Braulio, whose death is commemorated by a huge funeral procession winding through the streets of São Paulo, intimating the promise of democracy and justice for the workers of Brazil.

Rather than treat the source play as a museum piece to be respected at all costs, Guarnieri and Hirszman transpose it into the Brazil of the 1980's. In this sense, the film reflects two interrelated historical phenomena: the political liberalization called *abertura* (opening) and the emergence of a strong workers' movement, especially in the São Paulo area. While *Cinema Novo* rarely focused on working-class characters, preferring instead marginal figures from *favela* (slum) and *sertão* (backlands), *They Don't Wear Black Tie* puts a diverse gallery of such characters at the center of its tale. The working class is not seen as an idealized monolith, but rather as a diversified and conflicted group, ranging from the passionately committed Otávio to the hotheaded radical Sartini, through the vacillating, but never despicable Tião, to the "apolitical" Romana. Hirszman treats all the characters as humanly complex figures, each with understandable motives for their participation or nonparticipation in the strike. Tião chooses to pursue personal and family advancement rather than participate in oppositional politics, and although the film clearly represents his decision as politically misguided, his actions are depicted as humanly comprehensible. Maria's rejection of Tião, meanwhile, has as much to do with his machismo as with his refusal to support the strike. All the major characters of *They Don't Wear Black Tie* are treated as complex human beings with desires, hesitations, and contradictions; they are not one-dimensional ideological projections of the filmmaker.

Hirszman has been known for his fine work with actors—for example, with Fernanda Montenegro in *The Deceased Woman*, and Othon Bastos and Isabel Ribeiro in *São Bernardo*—and *They Don't Wear Black Tie* is no exception to this rule. The excellent ensemble acting, achieved through repeated group readings and discussion, melds brilliant individual performances into a powerful whole. Guarnieri, who at age twenty-four played the role of the strikebreaker Tião, here plays Tião's father with great power and resourcefulness. Fernanda Montenegro's Romana is quietly charismatic, an example of a nonacademic actress who combines deeply rooted Brazilian cultural values with universal appeal.

Stylistically, *They Don't Wear Black Tie* eschews the Brechtian distance that marks *São Bernardo* in favor of what Hirszman calls "popular emotion." *They Don't Wear Black Tie* emphasizes familiar warmth and affectivity, clearly departing from the ironic strategies typical of many *Cinema Novo* films of the late 1960's and 1970's. Those films typically used music, for example, only for social portraiture (for example, the songs of the Brazilian Northeast in Glauber Rocha's films) or for ironic effect (opera counterpointing samba, for example) while *They Don't Wear Black Tie* uses the clearly commentative, emotionally affecting "mood" music of Adoniram Barbosa. The cinematography, too, despite the relatively poor working-class environment depicted, is lush, far from the calculated "ugliness" of the early films of *Cinema Novo*. In another sense, however, *They Don't Wear Black Tie* continues the didactic tradition of *Cinema Novo*, offering a kind of filmic "pedagogy of the oppressed." Hirszman's cinema aims at raising the spectator's consciousness, like early *Cinema Novo*; only the means have changed by becoming more accessible. Although somewhat "nostalgic" in aesthetic terms, *They Don't Wear Black Tie* is burningly contemporary in its subject matter. The film transmits a strong sense of sincerity within a style that Hirszman calls "democratic realism." It largely succeeds in fulfilling the director's goal of fusing political consciousness and popular emotion, of using the force of feeling in the service of enlightenment.

*Robert Stam*

# THE THISTLES OF THE BARAGAN (CIULINII BĂRĂGANULUI)

*Origin:* Romania
*Released:* 1958
*Released in U.S.:* no listing
*Production:* Bucureşti Studios; released by Romaniafilm
*Direction:* Louis Daquin
*Screenplay:* Louis Daquin, Antoine Tudal, and Alexandru Struţeanu; based on the novel by Panait Istrati
*Cinematography:* André Dumaître
*Editing:* Eugenia Gorovei
*Art direction:* Liviu Popa
*Costume design:* Maria Bortnovski
*Sound:* Ionel Iliescu
*Music:* Radu Palade
*Running time:* 140 minutes
*Also known as: Baragan Thistles*

*Principal characters:*

Matache ............................ Nuţă Chirlea
Tudoriţa ............................ Ana Vlădescu
Tănase ............................ Florin Piersic
Stana ............................ Ruxandra Ionescu
Marin ............................ Nicolae Tomazoglu
Duduca ............................ Clody Berthola
Ursu ............................ Marcel Anghelescu
Boyar ............................ Mihai Berechet

*The Thistles of the Baragan* belongs to the beginning of the state cinema in Romania (established in 1948), a period which was to end in 1965, with the first major achievement of a Romanian film at an international level—the prize for Best Direction at the Cannes International Film Festival for *Pădurea spînzuraţilor* (1965; *The Forest of the Hanged*) by Liviu Ciulei. Typical of infant film industries, this period was dominated by adaptations from the national literature. Preference was given to works extolling love for the motherland and the struggle of the common people to achieve social justice and equality.

Following the pattern in postwar Eastern European cinema, a national film institute was established, and from time to time, experienced foreign directors were invited to make films in Romania. In this context, on the occasion of the fiftieth-year commemoration of the great peasants' uprisings to make the screen version of the novel *Les Chardons du Baragan* (1928;

*The Thistles of the Baragan*). The literary work not only corresponded perfectly to the above-mentioned criteria of cultural policy, but it also offered other advantages. Its author, Panait Istrati, was a proletarian writer like Jack London or Maxim Gorky: a self-taught man, a lover of freedom, and at the same time an incurable wanderer.

As a young man, Istrati had traveled widely, generally working at menial jobs but demonstrating his literary gifts as a journalist. In 1921, in Nice, worn down by poverty and lack of recognition, he cut his throat. He was saved, and, a letter was found in his suitcase addressed to the great French writer Romain Rolland, who encouraged him to write. Thus, between 1921 and 1929, Istrati made a name for himself as a French writer of a great force and special originality. His case is perhaps comparable to that of Polish-born writer Joseph Conrad, who became a great English-language writer (the difference residing in the fact that, after becoming well-known in France, Istrati returned to Romania). His popularity the world over was instantaneous. Ernest Hemingway, among others, held him in great esteem.

The novel *The Thistles of the Baragan*, regarded as one of Istrati's finest works, was dedicated to the eleven thousand peasants who were victims of the bloody repression of the uprising of 1907. Although the plot does not incorporate the actual event and ends on the eve of its outburst, the analysis of the conditions leading to the uprising, considered to be very penetrating while the violent and cruel realism moderating the romanticism of the characters has been compared to that of novelist William Faulkner.

Louis Daquin, one of the most venerable craftsmen of the French cinema to emerge after World War I, had been in love with Istrati's works ever since his youth, and he had cherished the hope of a film adaptation, but he realized that this could only be done in Romania. The Baragan, the endless flat plain in the south of the country, is different from the Russian or Hungarian steppes. It cannot be reconstituted in any other part of the world. This inferno teeming with mirages could only be comparable to the Brazilian *sertão*, the hunger reigning there contributing to people's obsession with escaping from it. The autumn wind which, on its endless stretches, chases away the thistles—thorny vegetation having the hardness of steel—strengthens the wish to escape. On such days, there was a custom for bold people, and particularly for children, to run in search of their luck after the thistles as they were rolled ahead by the wind.

It is with such an unusual scene that the film *The Thistles of the Baragan* begins, followed by an introduction of the family of little Matache (Nuţă Chirlea), who did not dare to run away with his friends. Upon pricking her hand with a fish bone and developing an infection, the child's mother dies after having invested her money in a poor cart for trading fish. In spite of this, Marin, the father (Nicolae Tomazoglu), goes together with Matache to sell fish, but business turns out to be poor. The fish rots, the horse dies, and the father and the son get work with Duduca (Clody Berthola), a strange gentlewoman. On being sent to steal from the land of another boyar, Marin is torn to pieces by the watchdogs.

Tudoriţa (Ana Vlădescu), the young peasant girl, who becomes a kind of protector of the child, takes him to her native village. There, the village boyar (Mihai Berechet) forces Tănase (Florin Piersic), Tudoriţa's lover, to marry Stana (Ruxandra Ionescu), a peasant woman who was the boyar's mistress and is now pregnant. For fear that Tănase will be killed if he opposes the master's will, Tudoriţa rejects her lover's proposal that they run away together. The wedding takes place but the peasants fail to turn up at the feast, preferring to enjoy themselves on their own. Having become the village miller, Tăsnase cannot bear to see his friends starving (the peasants who existed more as serfs were obligated to finish work on the big land of the boyar first, and the bad weather had ruined the ungathered crop on their small plots), and he facilitates the theft of several sacks of maize. The theft is discovered, but the investigation made by the gendarmes fails to find the maize, and the blame is laid on a poor peasant who, in despair, commits suicide.

A very hard winter sets in, and the wolves threaten the village. The boyar agrees to give guns to the peasants for a great hunt, during which someone wounds the boyar, who then demands that the culprit show up. If he does not, all forty men who have received guns will be arrested. As this would mean death or forced labor for them, Tănase surrenders. His being killed without a trial angers the peasants, who all go to the manor, but the boyar has run away. While the peasants are looking for their contracts in order to destroy them, Stana—crazy because of Tănase's murder—sets fire to the manor. The peasants leave the village, and the soldiers brought by the boyar bomb the grove where they have taken refuge. Matache is the only survivor of this slaughter.

This world of poverty and violence, a world which preserved a semi-feudal organization, meant deprivation for the Baragan peasant, to whom bread was a dream. Matache's mother dies absurdly, pricked by a fish bone. A cart with fish represents the only solution for acquiring even minimal wealth—or even being able to eat something else. The loss of this investment means the loss of any hope for Matache and Marin. Violence is the means with which this state of things is maintained; the attack of property or of the owner's life is punished on the spot as demonstrated by the deaths of Marin and Tănase. The system works irreproachably: When necessary, violence is turned upon people belonging to the ruling classes. Duduca, though a boyar's daughter, is an outcast, punished for having eloped with a coachman. Violence exists in peasants, too, but in a smoldering state and is only manifested in indirect ways, such as in the scene of the feast taking place at the very time of the wedding, in which the *hora* is the expression of the collective rage. A special accumulation of unfair acts is necessary for the peasants to react, as happens at the end of the film. Yet when they attack the manor, their object of destruction is neither the boyar nor his house, but the contracts. Convinced that the army, also made up of peasants, will not shoot, they are surprised and killed by organized violence.

The film's characters are types rather than fully realized individuals. The peasants are obedient, patient, hating their lot, yet passive. They always cherish some hope: that God will grant good weather, that the boyar will be kinder, that something to their advantage will occur. The boyar is conceited, wicked, and cruel. His men are servile and also cruel (to others) in order not to lose their positions; the village authorities—the mayor, the gendarmes—are afraid of the boyar and carry out his orders blindly. Practically, there is no evolution except for the schoolmaster who, in the end, joins the peasants, and for Stana—the owner's former mistress—who, from an obedient servant, becomes a rebel. Yet what is surprising in the screenplay of the film is the inconsistency in the narrative, initially conceived only to be seen through Matache's eyes. All sorts of events take place which the child does not witness, and, in the end, Matache ceases to be the main character as he is in the book.

Even if he had had at his disposal a flawless script, Louis Daquin's task would have been no easier. Yet he managed to make a film (and not a transcription of the literary text) which is also Romanian. His main contribution lies in the pictorial quality of the black-and-white photography, beginning with the way in which he was able to "capture" the Baragan: the steam of the plain, dotted by wells, a stone cross, a flock of sheep, and the only moving elements—the dust and the thistles. A cloud or a sunbeam suddenly changes the landscape, while the mist brings about an image apparently from another world. The skill of cinematographer André Dumaître, the lack of ostentation of the interiors and of the costumes, the solid documentation and ethnographic research, provide a vivid and historically accurate image of the Romanian peasant. It would be unfair, however, to mention only the plastic function of the camera work without considering the importance of the sound track: the long traveling shots through the cornfields accompanied by bits of dialogue in the scene of crop gathering and particularly the overlapping of barks and shouts with the image of the reeds in movement, which suggests the savage way in which Marin is killed.

The other noteworthy element of the film is Radu Palade's music. The haunting theme present in the sequences showing father and son wandering about the Baragan, then the wailing of Tănase's mother beside her murdered son, and finally the theme of the *hora*, a prelude to the uprising—all of these are taken over and amplified in the swelling chorus in the last segment of the film. Pain, sorrow, rage, terror are conveyed by the music more powerfully than by the dialogue. Indeed, the moment of maximum emotion of the film, that of the fierce peasants' *hora*, derives much of its force from the music.

The film was not completely successful; the peasants' performance, for example, was disappointing. Nevertheless, it is a tribute to cross-cultural exchange: a Frenchman's film adaptation in Romanian of a novel written in French by a Romanian.

*Aura Puran*

# THOMAS L'IMPOSTEUR

*Origin:* France
*Released:* 1965
*Released in U.S.:* 1972
*Production:* Eugène Lépicier for Filmel
*Direction:* Georges Franju
*Assistant direction:* Christian de Chalonges and Michel Worms
*Screenplay:* Jean Cocteau, Georges Franju, Michel Worms, and Raphaël Cluzel; based on the novel by Cocteau
*Cinematography:* Marcel Fradetal
*Editing:* Gilbert Natot
*Narration:* Jean Marais
*Art direction:* Claude Pignot
*Special effects:* Angelo Rizzi
*Makeup:* Pierre Néant
*Costume design:* Pierre Nourry and Simone Henry
*Music:* Georges Auric
*MPAA rating:* PG
*Running time:* 94 minutes

*Principal characters:*

Princess Clémence de Bormes ..... Emmanuelle Riva
Guillaume Thomas de Fontenoy .... Fabrice Rouleau
Pesquel-Duport ........................ Jean Servais
Henriette de Bormes................ Sophie Darès
Dr. Verne ......................... Michel Vitold
Mme Valiche........................... Rosy Varte
Captain Roy ..................... Édouard Dermit
Dr. Gentil ...................... Bernard Lavalette
Thomas' aunt .................. Hélène Dieudonné
Bishop .................... Jean-Roger Caussimon
Nurse ................................ Édith Scob
Elderly man at the ball.............. André Méliès
Fortune-teller.................... Gabrielle Dorziat

*Thomas l'Imposteur* is the product of a collaboration between two very distinctive talents: director Georges Franju and writer Jean Cocteau, the poet, novelist, dramatist, artist, filmmaker, and intellectual celebrity upon whose 1923 novel the film was based. Cocteau was also a coauthor of the screenplay, although he died in 1963, before *Thomas l'Imposteur* went into production.

Franju is one of the most individualistic yet elusive of modern French directors. The pattern of his career—documentary shorts in the early and mid-1950's, first feature film in 1958-1959, peak in the early 1960's—is homologous with that of the most famous French New Wave directors, and he is often identified with that movement. Franju, however, is considerably older than his New Wave contemporaries, and his films have strong affinities with earlier, more archaic and classical styles. These include the French pioneer filmmakers Georges Méliès and Ferdinand Zecca, and various directors with especially strong mixtures of realism and expressionism/poeticism/fantasy—notably, Louis Feuillade, F. W. Murnau, Fritz Lang, and, in a more anarchic, surrealist vein, Jean Vigo and Luis Buñuel. This strong sense of film history is not surprising in the man who, with Henri Langlois, founded the Cinémathèque Française in 1936.

Franju first gained attention for a series of remarkable, original documentaries ranging from the eccentric *Le Grand Méliès* (1952) to the iconoclastic *Hôtel des Invalides* (1951) to the shocking *Le Sang des bêtes* (1949). Since his graduation to features, several of Franju's films have been adaptations of prestigious literary properties—including, besides *Thomas l'Imposteur*, François Mauriac's 1927 novel *Thérèse Desqueyroux* (filmed in 1962), Émile Zola's 1875 *La Faute de l'abbé Mouret* (*Albine: Or, The Abbe's Temptation*; filmed in 1970 as *The Demise of Father Mouret*), and Joseph Conrad's 1917 *The Shadow-Line*, filmed in 1971 as *La Ligne d'ombre* (*The Shadow-Line*). In this respect, Franju is related to yet another cinematic tradition—the so-called Tradition of Quality which dominated French cinema in the 1940's and early 1950's. This tradition, specializing in reverent, polished adaptations of classic French novels, was the special anathema of the New Wave generation and the subject of a famous attack by François Truffaut in the magazine *Cahiers du cinéma*. Owing to the elegant and classical elements of his style, Franju can easily be misidentified with Tradition-of-Quality-type cinema, and, in fact, he is not wholly unrelated to it.

In effect, Franju has had two careers, the first as a maker of idiosyncratic documentaries, the second as a maker of feature and television films which are largely text-oriented—whether that text be a novel, a previous film (*Judex*, 1964), or a script by a prestigious screenwriter. These two sides of Franju's career have a fundamental element in common: the use, as the basis of the film, of "found material" (a segment of the nonfictional world in the documentaries, a preexisting text in the features), to which the film stands in a certain position of externality and commentary. A paradigm for this position is the relationship of the voice-over narration to the images in a documentary. Indeed, one of the most important elements in the film *Thomas l'Imposteur* is a voice-over narration, composed of quotations from and expansions upon Cocteau's novel. This narration serves to evaluate characters and interpret their motivations in a very authorly way, and also to provide a running commentary for documentarylike passages depicting the strange mutations of ordinary reality spawned by the war. Franju, however, goes even further than this in the film: The relationship of the narration to the images is often overdetermined to the point where it becomes part of a general strategy of expressing certain aspects of Cocteau's novel while also commenting on them. Franju's relationship to his source material here is a tricky one, half-in and half-out—almost as if the film were at the same time a faithful rendering of Cocteau's novel and a documentary about it—a fact and a commentary upon that fact.

Like Cocteau's, Franju's style has strong surrealist qualities, but it is quite different in several respects. Cocteau's literary style is light, mercurial, ornamental, and somewhat precious. Franju's style is heavier, more solid (even, at times, more stolid), more concrete and integral. Closely linked to Franju's poetic side is a visceral, even brutal side—amply demonstrated in the *abbatoirs* of *La Sang des bêtes*, the mutilated war veterans of *Hôtel des Invalides*, and the gory crescendos of the horror film *Les Yeux sans visage* (1960; *Eyes Without a Face*). Franju's style complements Cocteau's without duplicating it, investing Cocteau's brittle arabesques with a substantiality and impact often lacking in the poet's solo works.

Despite the wide range of influences and modes which constitute Franju's style, it rarely seems like a pastiche. It is precisely his ability to comprehend extreme paradoxical contrasts in an integral and almost serene manner that is perhaps the most striking feature of his style, which is both documentary and expressionistic, materialist and metaphysical, shocking and poetic. These dualities are ideally suited to many of the central concerns of Cocteau's tale of Thomas the Impostor.

The story opens in 1914, a time when, the opening title notes, "vivacious disorder triumphed over stolid order." Princess Clémence de Bormes (Emmanuelle Riva) is giving her last ball. The Germans are at the gates of Paris; trenches are being dug in the Bois de Boulogne. For the princess, an eccentric, still-beautiful widow adored by her teenage daughter Henriette (Sophie Darès) and persistently wooed by the newspaper editor Pesquel-Duport (Jean Servais), the curtain is going up on the greatest theater of them all. In the same spirit with which she might embark on a garden party, she decides to lead an automobile convoy to evacuate wounded soldiers from the front. Her cohorts in the venture include the bemused Dr. Verne (Michel Vitold) and the half-mad Mme Valiche (Rosy Varte). Denied an official permit, the princess thinks her game is lost until out of nowhere appears a mysterious young man in uniform who calls himself Guillaume Thomas de Fontenoy (Fabrice Rouleau), nephew of the celebrated General de Fontenoy. Using his name as an Open Sesame, Thomas takes the princess and her convoy to the front lines, "behind the scenes of the drama," where they are swept up into a chaotic maelstrom of blood and destruction. Chastened, the princess returns to her mansion.

The gentle, enigmatic Thomas is, one learns, not the general's nephew at all, but a sixteen-year-old orphan in an actor's uniform living a half-life of lies and dreams. Henriette falls desperately in love with him, but he is too absorbed in his masquerade to reciprocate. Thomas gets himself adopted by a group of Marines on the Belgian front, a desolate region of bombed-out summer resorts and windswept marshes. While running through the flare-illuminated fairyland between the lines, Thomas is shot by a German patrol. His last thought is, "I'm lost if I don't play dead."

Straightforward realism has generally proven a limited (though often popular) vehicle for dealing with the enormity of modern warfare. In literature as well as film, the most effective styles for dealing with the subject have usually been some form of modified, dreamlike surrealism. *Thomas l'Imposteur* sets out to capture the reality of war precisely by capturing its unreality. War is rendered via a battery of distancing effects, as if viewed through a series of filters.

The film's opening scenes, set in Paris, establish an extremely solid visual context, with crisply focused deep space and high-contrast black-and-white photography accentuated by the literally white-and-black costumes worn by the actors in the ball scene. This initial tone serves two important functions. First, it evokes the high-contrast orthochromatic look of pre-1925 cinema and thus introduces a note of deliberate archaism and pastness into the film. Second, it sets up a visual contrast with the war scenes that alternate with the Paris scenes in the remainder of the film. The battlefield always seems less substantial, immediate, and "real" than the glittery artifice of Parisian society, epitomized by the chandelier that opens the film. Shots are generally roomier and more distanced in the war scenes. The brown of military uniforms breaks up the pure blacks and whites of the first part of the film. Photography in the war scenes is more gray-toned, and the images are softened by a variety of atmospheric effects, including haze, smoke, dusk, mist, rain, snow, and flickering firelight.

This visual context imparts a ghostly, hallucinatory quality to the graphic horrors of war, producing some of Franju's most powerful and haunting images. Nighttime explosions burst in dreamlike reflection on automobile windows. Treetops shoot out fire like Roman candles. A lone painting hangs crooked on an otherwise bare wall exposed by shelling. In the film's most terrifying apparition, a white horse suddenly gallops by with its mane on fire. Debris rains down from a smoke-enshrouded cathedral as if tossed by a hidden, capricious deity. In the final battle scene, drifting flares and silent explosions transform the trenches into a shimmering arena where Thomas plays his final scene.

The dominant metaphor of Cocteau's novel is theatricality, realized in a multitude of conceits and comparisons linking the battlefield and the stage, with Thomas as the star role-player in both theaters. The theatrical metaphor relates to the characters' (and, more self-consciously, the novelist's) inability to grasp the full reality of modern warfare, to conceive it as anything more than a make-believe pageant from which they can remain detached, either as "spectators" (Henriette, Pesquel-Duport, Dr. Verne) or as "performers" (Thomas, the princess, Mme Valiche). For example, in a line lifted almost verbatim from the novel, the narrator relates, "The princess was a born actress and her daughter a born spectator, whose favorite actress was her mother." These categories are not necessarily hard and fast: the princess starts out as a full-fledged performer and then becomes more of a spectator; Thomas is an elusive mixture of actor and spectator, both distanced from and involved in the war through which he glides.

The film expands Cocteau's theatrical conceit in several ways, so that it becomes a more concrete distancing device—unlike the novelist, Franju can show actual performances and stagelike spaces against the backdrop of war. There is much attention given to characters' entrances and exits, often handled at ostentatious length. Several sequences are built on characters histrionically taking the foreground before speaking, as if they were stepping up to the footlights. The spectator/performer pattern is reinforced in the film by point-of-view configurations, and by the structuring of many scenes around an "audience" character, who watches and reacts to the action more than participates in it. Characters functioning as spectators tend to be associated with windows and balconies, while characters functioning as performers tend to be associated with mirrors. In a short but striking passage, Thomas wanders off behind a farmhouse and fires a pistol at a mirror image of himself. As if in reply, artillery fire bursts in the distance. Thomas looks back and forth from his shattered reflection to the explosions breaking up the horizon, then walks off contentedly. Besides establishing Thomas' illusory position as stage manager of the events, this scene underscores the fundamental narcissism behind his masquerade—that he sees no distinction between the war (the explosions) and himself (the mirror), the one being merely an extension of the other.

The framings of the shots are generally quite spacious, especially in the war scenes, giving a distanced, proscenium quality to much of the action. This effect is intensified by the frequent use of window shots to display the action, occasionally with actual curtains to frame the "stage" outside. The most striking example of this occurs when, through a window, Thomas and the princess are seen getting into a car in Paris; the shot slowly dissolves to a flaming battlefield, momentarily framed between the curtains of the window.

The style of Cocteau's novel is attenuated and oblique, with a pared-down narrative adorned with delicate metaphors whose effect derives from their very inappropriateness to their wartime context. The sound of cannons is compared to that of a distant orchestra; guns pop like bottles of dry champagne; bullets hum like bees in flowers; flares illuminate the battlefield like flickering candlelight; mud clutches at crawling soldiers with the embrace of an affectionate nurse. The filth and carnage of the battlefront are continually being converted into gossamer conceits about fairies and phantoms.

The film creates similar distancing effects through expressive incongruity, a disjunction between means and subject matter. The film's style, based on elegance and precision, stands at the opposite pole from the illogic and disorder associated with war in the narrative and thus serves to frame its subject rather than mirror it. The film is built largely on leisurely, sweeping camera movements, which impart a gliding, waltzlike flow to even the most violent settings. Compositions often have a very formal and overarranged quality, most blatantly in a bizarrely comic effect involving the receding figure of an angry bishop exactly centered (via a process shot) through the rear window of the princess' car as it drives off.

The self-questioning artifice and precision of the film's style extends to the relationship between the voice-over narration and the images which accompany it, often *too* precisely. Near the end of the ball scene, the narration relates that "a deadly night fell over Paris"; at that exact moment, the camera tracks over to a night-blackened window. Under the narrational phrase "shielded once more by the spreading fan of his lies," the shot zooms back from the fanlike pattern of a skylight in a train station. At an overcrowded battlefront hospital, the narration observes, "They let gangrene grow over him as ivy grows over a statue," and the camera trundles over to an open window to disclose, right on cue, an ivy-covered statue outside; a shell bursts behind it, providing a neat exclamation point to round off the shot.

Other examples of this hyperchoreographed correspondence between word and image abound in the film. Their frequent association with windows which frame the conceits underscores the excessive contrivance of their design. Franju's visuals often serve Cocteau's text too deferentially, in the manner of a suspiciously overunctuous servant, so that they begin to bracket it and call it into question. The film works to objectify some of the attitudes represented by the novel—most notably, the aestheticization of war fashionable among certain intellectuals and artists of the 1910's and 1920's, the type of impulse that, at its most perverse, inspired Italian Futurists to rhapsodize over the flowerlike patterns of bomb explosions and the musical screams of the wounded.

The film opens with the Princess de Bormes' "last ball"—a scene which has no equivalent in the novel. A last ball at the opening of the film; the final blaze of the prewar aristocracy; cutaway shots to scandalized gossipers; a nostalgic sense of a bygone age; the extensive use of deep-focus photography and gliding camera movements; periodic narration and bridging passages; a plot centered on a much-indulged, narcissistic young man who finally gets his "comeuppance"—these elements evoke one film above all:

Orson Welles's great, fragmented masterpiece, *The Magnificent Ambersons* (1942).

Why should Franju want to bring up *The Magnificent Ambersons* and place it, like a ghostly superimposition, over Cocteau's story? Primarily for one reason: to invoke that film's powerful sense of nostalgia, of passing history, of bygone and somewhat foolish innocence. This strong dimension of pastness differentiates the film from Cocteau's novel and also includes the novel within that sense of the past, as an ambivalent relic of an era when war could still be considered a great adventure for imaginative souls, and a source of provocative and scintillating imagery for aesthetes, rather than a massive depersonalized killing machine.

In effect, the concept of "vivacious disorder"—the aestheticization (or theatricalization) of war—is framed three times by the film. The attitudes of Cocteau's characters are called into question by Cocteau's novel, which, in turn, calls itself into question; the attitudes of Cocteau's novel are called into question by the film, which, in turn, calls *itself* into question. The subject of war is grasped only indirectly, as a reflection of a reflection of a reflection. Franju's film is more substantial and self-aware than Cocteau's novel (just as Cocteau's novel is more substantial and self-aware than its characters), but it does not presume to place itself outside the inadequacy of representation that it represents.

*Martin Rubin*

# THE THREEPENNY OPERA (DIE DREIGROSCHENOPER)

*Origin:* Germany
*Released:* 1931
*Released in U.S.:* 1931 and 1960 (first complete version of German original)
*Production:* Seymour Nebenzal for Nero-Film
*Direction:* G. W. Pabst
*Screenplay:* Leo Lania, Béla Baláz, Ladislaus Vajda, Solange Bussi (French version), and Ninon Steinhoff (French version); based on the play by Bertolt Brecht
*Cinematography:* Fritz Arno Wagner
*Editing:* Hans Oser; French version, Henri Rust
*Art direction:* Andrei Andreiev
*Music direction:* Theo Mackeben
*Music:* Kurt Weill
*Running time:* 111 minutes; French version: 104 minutes

*Principal characters:*

| | |
|---|---|
| Macheath | Rudolf Forster |
| Polly | Carola Neher |
| Tiger Brown | Reinhold Schünzel |
| J. J. Peachum | Fritz Rasp |
| Mrs. Peachum | Valeska Gert |
| Jenny | Lotte Lenya |
| Vicar | Hermann Thimig |
| Street singer | Ernst Busch |

Along with Fritz Lang's *M* (1931), Leontine Sagan's *Mädchen in Uniform* (1931; *Girls in Uniform*), and Josef von Sternberg's *Der blaue Engel* (1930; *The Blue Angel*), G. W. Pabst's *The Threepenny Opera* represents the best of German film production after the addition of sound to filmmaking in the late 1920's and before the Nazis' rise to power in 1933. All four films contain strong elements of social criticism. While the other three films scrutinize German society particularly, however, *The Threepenny Opera* tackles capitalism and human nature in general.

*The Threepenny Opera*'s pedigree dates back to 1728, when John Gay scored a popular success with *The Beggar's Opera*, a ballad opera peopled with unscrupulous prostitutes, highwaymen, police, and businessmen. After a successful London revival of *The Beggar's Opera* in 1920, Bertolt Brecht modified and adapted Gay's work to achieve a similar stage success with his *Der Dreigroschenoper* (*The Threepenny Opera*) in Berlin in 1928. It is on this latter work, if somewhat indirectly, that Pabst based his film.

From both a political and aesthetic perspective, *The Threepenny Opera* marks a turning point for Pabst in a curiously uneven career. Having begun in the theater, he had already directed such films as *Die freudlose Gasse* (1925; *The Joyless Street*) and *Westfront 1918* (1930), which realistically presented contemporary social problems resulting from World War I. Because Pabst was also involved with various leftist production and distribution organizations, he must have seemed a sympathetic choice to transfer Brecht's Communist analysis of the deterioration of human relations under capitalism from stage to screen.

Pabst, however, was also the director of *Geheimnisse einer Seele* (1926; *Secrets of a Soul*) and *Die Büchse der Pandora* (1928; *Pandora's Box*), works which forsake social realism to explore the psychology of male and female sexuality. A superb editor, Pabst was fascinated with the Soviet theories of montage developed by Sergei Eisenstein and Vsevolod Pudovkin. His fascination, though, was with the aesthetic rather than political implications of what was once known as "Soviet editing." In fact, Pabst's politics were so nebulous that he eventually drifted into making films for the Nazis.

Pabst's lack of political commitment makes it no surprise, therefore, that Brecht felt betrayed by the film of his play. He sued the German production company, Nero-Film, and thus, indirectly, Warner Bros. First National, the Hollywood production company which stood behind Nero-Film. When Brecht lost, it was a blow to authors as a group, since the court's ruling effectively curtailed an author's rights to control the ideological content of work associated with his name. This court case was all the more fitting in the light of *The Threepenny Opera*'s story.

Set in an imaginary, late Victorian London instead of Gay's eighteenth century venue, *The Threepenny Opera* tells a story of love, betrayal, and avarice among thieves. The biggest criminal of all, Macheath—known also as Mackie Messer, or Mack the Knife, and stylishly played by Rudolf Forster—falls in love with Polly (Carola Neher) at first sight. That night they marry, in a ceremony attended by many respected members of London society, including Police Commissioner Tiger Brown (Reinhold Schünzel), who turns a blind eye to the plunder brought by Macheath's gang as tribute to the bride. Polly, however, is the daughter of J. J. Peachum (Fritz Rasp), king of the beggars. Incensed by the marriage and loss of his daughter, Peachum seeks revenge. He engages Jenny (Lotte Lenya), Macheath's jealous mistress, to betray her lover when next Macheath appears at her brothel. Tiger Brown, loyal to his friend, can only be persuaded to bring Macheath to justice when Peachum threatens to disrupt the queen's coronation by flooding the streets with his beggars.

In a twist peculiar to the film, Polly opens a bank, and with it proves that legal exploitation can be more profitable than criminal activities. When Jenny's love overcomes her jealousy, she helps Macheath escape from jail. He rejoins his successful wife and even offers to share this success with Peachum and Tiger Brown, both of whom were undone when they lost control of the beggars during the coronation parade.

Certainly a major component of Gay's original work was the satire of contemporary politics, but equally important was his satire of English society's acceptance of the new Italian form of opera at the expense of an indigenous musical tradition. The greatest change Brecht and his musical collaborator, Kurt Weill, made in transforming *The Beggar's Opera* into *The Threepenny Opera* was to write a new score incorporating contemporary jazz and cabaret idioms for a brash, sometimes abrasive sound which complemented the acerbity of Brecht's dialogue. The troupe of actors trained by Brecht to accentuate the play's harshness in its Berlin performances largely reappeared in the German filmed version.

Because the German company, Tobis Klang-Film, owned various necessary patents, the German national cinema could continue to compete with Hollywood productions after the coming of sound. The German language alone, though, presented technical difficulties unique to itself, which Brecht's pointed diction and Weill's disturbing music highlighted. For a German cinema which favored the softer Southern dialect and Viennese waltzes, this abrasiveness represented something of a departure. Even the French version, which Pabst filmed simultaneously (using the same sets and costumes), retained some of Brecht's influence on the actors, for Margo Lion, the French actress who played Jenny, had close ties with Berlin's cabaret theaters.

Generally, though, Pabst's interpretation of the work softened rough edges. Where the songs had served to counterpoint Brecht's dialogue, Pabst used them more for decorative purposes. More obviously, the film score eliminated several of the play's raciest songs, such as the "Ballad of Sexual Submissiveness." With his cinematographer, Fritz Arno Wagner, Pabst again achieved the strikingly beautiful images which characterized their work together in *Die Liebe der Jeanne Ney* (1927; *The Love of Jeanne Ney*). Whenever possible, Pabst has the camera flow through streets, down stairways, and around characters. On other occasions, he creates the same effect of fluidity through the smoothness of his editing.

Not averse to teamwork, Pabst again collaborated with Andrei Andreiev, a Russian architect, whose sets for the London scenes with Jack the Ripper in the earlier *Pandora's Box* look like a run-through for *The Threepenny Opera*. The combination of heavy sets and costumes with the thick fog and chiaroscuro lighting create a dreamlike effect of reality and fantasy intermingled. The wedding scene between Macheath and Polly, for example, takes place in a warehouse which is almost but not quite transformed into an elegant hall through the presence of an overabundance of stolen decorations.

Pabst's emphasis on atmosphere and mood leads the audience into an emotional involvement which runs counter to Brecht's famous call for an "alienation effect." The latter evokes a critical distance enabling an intellectual rather than emotional response. Although Pabst had often used his editing skills in earlier films to curtail scenes just short of their full emotional flowering, he did not follow Brecht's theatrical precepts.

Instead, Pabst's film seems more firmly embedded within the Expressionist aesthetic which dominated German filmmaking in its golden age. Macheath, for example, at one point wears a pair of light-colored gloves whose black ribbing echoes the costumes for Robert Wiene's *Das Kabinett des Dr. Caligari* (1919; *The Cabinet of Dr. Caligari*). Pabst's use of mirrors and glass to create dynamic relations among characters also harks back to the Expressionist tradition; for example, when Jenny broods over Macheath's perfidy, the backdrop of the brothel windows seems to entrap her in her violent passion. When Polly longs for the wedding gown behind the shop window, Macheath creeps up on her, much as the murderer creeps up on his small victim in *The Threepenny Opera*'s contemporary, *M*. *The Threepenny Opera* borrows some of the cabaret seaminess from another of its contemporaries, *The Blue Angel*, for the brothel scenes with Macheath and Jenny.

There is, in fact, an odd jangling of styles in *The Threepenny Opera*. The beggars, for example, are consistently filmed in a style the realism of which highlights the contrasting dependence on atmosphere and mood that characterizes the remainder of the film. This often creates a startling effect, as when, at day's end, their "work" done, the "crippled" beggars suddenly rise to walk while the blind open their eyes to see. Pabst's appreciation of the beggar's imagistic power caused a change in his personal style as well. His previous, largely decorative use of shadows, derived from the Expressionist tradition, shifted to something more purposeful, as when Peachum's shadow over the beggar mob indicates his control over it.

From a critical tradition which, since the 1940's, has viewed the early German films as a reflection of the political strains within pre-Nazi Germany, it is difficult not to see a prophetic note in Pabst's version of *The Threepenny Opera*. Peachum's demagogic exploitation and control of his beggars suggests the role that Adolf Hitler had already begun to play in German society. The film's association with various leftist artists makes it no surprise that the Nazis suppressed it once they were in power. Whatever Pabst's "true" political sympathies may have been, read this way, his version of *The Threepenny Opera* remains an aesthetic betrayal of Brecht's artistic vision only if one maintains that the director is merely an interpreter and that cinematic presentations of successful stage plays must be slavishly faithful re-creations.

Pabst, after all, was known for his films with Louise Brooks, Greta Garbo, Brigitte Helm, and Asta Nielsen. He was a cult figure, a director hailed internationally as an artist. He was known for a special ability with actresses, but this aspect of his directorial abilities was unnecessary for *The Threepenny Opera*. Full of character parts, the film was brilliantly cast with a group of actors hardly in need of Pabst's direction. As Pabst's attention was in fact focused elsewhere, the film preserves a record of acting styles which no longer exist. Carola Neher and Lotte Lenya, as already noted, were products largely of the Brechtian stage. Rudolf Forster and Fritz Rasp, on the other hand, were stars of the cinema carrying on the tradition of a heavier, more physical acting style. The French version as well brought together an odd ensemble. Along with Margo Lion, there were Albert Préjean, who often worked for the French filmmaker René Clair; Gaston Modot, who appeared in Jean Renoir's most classic films; and even the renegade Surrealist, Antonin Artaud, who had a minor role.

Admittedly, *The Threepenny Opera* may be difficult and confusing for the uninitiated viewer. The style is heavy and disconcerting, while the plot has been telescoped beyond terseness. It is a film very much of its own time, yet somehow ahead of its time. The Germans were leaders in devising successful solutions to technical and aesthetic problems created by mechanical limitations, which were increased with the addition of sound. Pabst and the various experts he gathered around him had already proven themselves more than competent at challenging the Hollywood monopoly, especially in the areas of aesthetic and technical innovation. After the successes of Ernst Lubitsch, Rouben Mamoulian, and René Clair with their groundbreaking musicals—a genre newly available to filmmakers with the coming of sound—curiosity and expectations were always high when a master director put his hand to the genre.

As a cult director, Pabst was a center of attention. People noticed not only his creative talent but also his social consciousness. He was, in other words, a director with a tremendous influence on the other directors of his time, as well as of another generation.

*Harriet Margolis*

# THRONE OF BLOOD (KUMONOSU-JO)

*Origin:* Japan
*Released:* 1957
*Released in U.S.:* 1961
*Production:* Sojiro Motoki and Akira Kurosawa for Toho
*Direction:* Akira Kurosawa
*Screenplay:* Hideo Oguni, Shinobu Hashimoto, Ryuzo Kikushima, and Akira Kurosawa; based on the play *Macbeth*, by William Shakespeare
*Cinematography:* Asaichi Nakai
*Editing:* Akira Kurosawa
*Art direction:* Yoshiro Muraki and Kohei Ezaki
*Music:* Masaru Sato
*Running time:* 105 minutes
*Also known as: The Castle of the Spider's Web* and *Cobweb Castle*

*Principal characters:*

Taketoki Washizu .................. Toshiro Mifune
Asaji ............................. Isuzu Yamada
Yoshiaki Miki ..................... Minoru Chiaki
Kuniharu Tsuzuki .................. Takamaru Sasaki
Weird woman ....................... Chieko Naniwa

*Throne of Blood* is the title given by distributors in the West to Akira Kurosawa's Japanese version of William Shakespeare's *Macbeth* (1606); Kurosawa's more subtle title is *Kumonosu-jo*, meaning "Castle of the Spider's Web." Shakespeare's plays are much appreciated and frequently performed in Japan, and *Macbeth* is the Shakespearean tragedy that comes closest in spirit to the Japanese concept of tragedy, which differs markedly from that obtaining in traditional Western culture. For the Japanese, an individual should fatalistically accept deeply adverse circumstances; traditional nobility of behavior lies in fulfilling this ideal. In Western culture, great men or women with a "tragic flaw" which leads them to do wrong nevertheless become elevated in stature through suffering; the universality of Shakespearean tragedy suggests that intense suffering to the point of death can ennoble the protagonists, transforming them from erring individuals into exemplars of human greatness. This is seen in *King Lear* (c. 1605-1606) and *Hamlet* (c. 1600-1601), even in *Othello* (1604), but barely in *Macbeth*, whose hero dies unrepentant with savage ferocity, the victim of human betrayal through the evil forces of the supernatural. The only positive human value in *Macbeth* lies in the close affection between this ill-fated couple; though their relentless ambition destroys them, they never lose their devoted loyalty to each other. This loyalty is stressed in Roman Polanski's 1971 film version of the play.

In response to certain specific questions put to him on behalf of the writer by the noted Japanese film historian, Tadao Sato, and published in *Shakespeare and the Film* (1971), Kurosawa said that he chose to film *Macbeth* because of its closeness of spirit and action to the period of the civil wars undertaken by rival regional warlords in Japan during the fifteenth and sixteenth centuries, when the weak became prey to the strong. Kurosawa responded to the savage intensity of Shakespeare's violent characters, so like that of the Japanese themselves. These qualities, he believed, had much in common with his own work, especially his masterpiece made three years previously, *Seven Samurai* (1954).

Kurosawa had no intention, however, of trying to emulate the essentially Anglo-Scottish character and setting of Shakespeare's tragedy; he transposed the action entirely to fifteenth or sixteenth century Japan, while retaining the grimly poetic atmosphere of the play. There was also no question of using a translation of Shakespeare's text. Kurosawa described the speech used in his original script, in which actual dialogue is reduced to a minimum, as contemporary Japanese slightly stylized to suggest period, but presenting none of the difficulties that Shakespeare's dialogue presents to English-speaking audiences. On the other hand, some verse style in the manner of Nō songs is introduced in a chant that stresses at the outset the traditional nature of the story. The makeup used by the principals is closely modeled on Nō masks. The highly volatile face of Washizu (Toshiro Mifune), is perhaps least like that of a Nō warrior mask, but Asaji (Isuzu Yamada) has Nō-like mask makeup, that of a woman in middle age, beautiful but about to go mad. Nō acting involves the static alternating with very violent movement, and this is the manner in which Mifune performs. The rapidity of the editing tempo during scenes of intense action is very marked—for example, the scene succeeding the murder of the overlord, or that at the banquet when Washizu encounters the ghost of Miki (Minoru Chiaki). These scenes are highly choreographed and visually stylized.

There is also the important matter of the differences in the treatment of the supernatural between East and West. In the West, it is important for audiences to perceive the witches as fearful and all-powerful influences on the superstitious nature of Macbeth; they should not be presented as merely grotesque background figures, as twentieth century audiences tend to regard them. Polanski solved this problem by making them members of a sinister coven, at once weirdly loathsome and threatening. For Kurosawa, the problem lay in the fact that there is no tradition of witchcraft as such in Japan. He used therefore an evil hag (Chieko Naniwa), or demon of the woods, a nearly sexless creature with a spinning wheel, a kind of "fate" weaving men's destinies, a figure not unknown in Nō drama. This female demon, with her mocking laugh, chants her prophecies, appearing and disappearing in the misty maze of the haunted forest to which Washizu is constantly drawn, as if by hypnosis. Mist and fog for the Japanese are symbolic of the hidden and mysterious. The forest, once entered, seems to offer no means of escape; Kurosawa terms it a labyrinth. Even the horse that Washizu rides is terrified.

Asaji presented another problem in her relationship to Washizu. Given the period, no woman in traditional Japan could have influenced her husband in the way that Lady Macbeth controls Macbeth. For this reason, Asaji is represented as much older than her husband, since age gives women a certain precedence in the traditional Japanese family. She is sinister and static, whereas he is dynamic. She adopts Nō-like postures and speaks in a mocking tone when Washizu resists the idea of murdering Tsuzuki (Takamaru Sasaki), the overlord; in the crucial, virtually wordless scene of the murder itself, she guides her husband, who seems terrified and seemingly transfixed in all of his actions. Her heavy silk kimono swishes along the floors, a sound that is often the only sound to be heard in the scene, which is also punctuated by the sudden, terrifying screech of the night bird. Although more like an elder sister than a wife, she is pregnant (a fact that the viewer learns not by appearance, but by reference in the dialogue). Whereas the stress in Shakespeare's play is upon the psychology of the characters (Shakespeare reached far beyond the humors psychophysiology of his time in his profound intuition of the subconscious), the motivation of Kurosawa's characters (as Tadao Sato has pointed out) turns upon their basic behavior as they fulfill the destiny that has been apportioned them. The stress is on immediate, harsh emotion and consequent violent action. Kurosawa reinforces the horror of the murder situation by making the chambers used for the overlord's lodging rooms associated with past bloody deeds, the bloodstains on floor and walls being incapable of removal.

J. Blumenthal, in *Sight and Sound*, autumn issue, 1965, pointed out how Kurosawa has produced one of the most artistically satisfying of all the adaptations of Shakespeare to the screen, a point upon which both Sir Peter Hall and Peter Brook, both Shakespearean filmmakers themselves, have agreed. *Throne of Blood* is less an adaptation than a total transmutation, with the result that its powerful visual imagery dominates throughout. Words are always secondary; Kurosawa takes the dark spirit of Shakespeare's blood-soaked poetry (the root word "blood" recurs more than thirty times in this comparatively short play), and transmutes it into visual imagery—the stark countryside, the mysterious mists, the mazelike woodlands, the demon with her spinning wheel, the elaborately threatening armor and helmets, the pennants of warfare snapping in the fierce wind. The characters barely speak: They only use speech for essential communication, as in the initial scene between Washizu and Asaji (when she, in fact, does most of the talking). Shakespeare becomes the scenarist for *Throne of Blood*, not the dialogue writer. Not a line of his poetry occurs in the film.

The action follows closely and with marked economy the story line of the play, with certain notable deviations to increase verisimilitude for modern audiences. The film begins with a background chant (Nō style) on the theme, "ambition destroys," heard as mists are seen enfolding a barren landscape. A monolith emerges, marking the spot where the legendary Cobweb Castle had once stood. When the castle itself appears, headquarters of the overlord, the viewer sees a messenger on horseback with fluttering pennants, galloping to announce new victories. While the lord debates strategy with his generals, Washizu and Miki, journeying home on horseback, enter the rain-swept forest of the Spider's Web, where the demon-witch's eerie chant greets them with prophecies that Washizu will himself become overlord, but that Miki's sons will eventually succeed him. The demon vanishes, leaving behind a mound of skulls.

After Washizu has been rewarded by his overlord, there follows an almost lyric scene of Washizu and Asaji in their home-fort, peacefully surrounded by peasants cultivating the land. Asaji, static and expressionless, is urging Washizu to murder the overlord and take possession of Cobweb Castle; Washizu resists. When the overlord arrives on a visit, he is given one of the "forbidden" rooms in the fort, rooms associated with murder in the past. Asaji finally taunts Washizu into committing the murder. The sinister atmosphere intensifies as night comes; Asaji makes Washizu drug the guards and presses a spear into his wavering grasp. He groans and shudders but stalks out in silence as the owl shrieks. Asaji waits, anxiously pacing, the moment accompanied by Nō-like beats of timpani and the shrill of whistles. Washizu returns; he squats down, breathing heavily, exhausted. Asaji prizes the bloody spear that Washizu should have left out of his grasp and leaves him, putting the spear in the hands of one of the drugged guards. She fetches water and washes her hands feverishly. It is she who rouses the household, and her cries wake Washizu from his trance. He leaps to his feet, kills the guards, and the whole sequence explodes into a crescendo of shots of rushing men, galloping horses, and flying pennants snapping in the wind.

Miki, left in charge of the defense of the overlord's Cobweb Castle, is forced to open its gates to Washizu and Asaji when they approach in procession with the body of the overlord. The former allies, Washizu and Miki, are now tense rivals for absolute power. Without more ado, the scene cuts to Washizu and Asaji as lord and lady of Cobweb Castle; Asaji chooses this moment to announce that she is pregnant. In contrast, Miki's wife has committed suicide because of her husband's loss of power. Washizu has Miki assassinated, but Miki's ghost appears to fill his empty place at Washizu's celebratory banquet—Washizu, terrified, is restrained by Asaji when he tries to transfix the ghost with his sword. A messenger brings Miki's head wrapped in cloth, but when the messenger confesses that Miki's son has escaped, Washizu kills him. Then he is told of his wife's dire illness following the birth of a stillborn child.

Adversity now sets in. Thunder and rain accompany news that the forts under Washizu's command are to be attacked. Immediately, Washizu gallops away to consult the demon-oracle and is told that he can never lose a battle until Cobweb Forest is seen to move; the trees echo with the demon's fiendish laughter.

Washizu is preparing his defense when a dark flock of ravens invades the inner compound with a menacing swirl of wings. Weeping women come to lead Washizu to the room where his wife is feverishly rubbing her hands, washing them in dumb show and muttering continuously, "the smell of blood, the smell of blood." Outside there is panic among Washizu's warriors when the trees of Cobweb Forest are observed to be moving toward the fort. Magnificent shots show a wide panorama of trees in motion, their branches nodding. Washizu is finally killed, not by his advancing enemies but by his own men; flights of arrows are launched at him, a solitary, staggering figure on an upper gallery of the fort. Wounded many times, he appears to be impervious to death, until finally an arrow transfixes his throat in close-shot. He stumbles down the steps to oppose his retreating soldiers and collapses at last onto the mist-covered ground. The film comes to a close with a return of the chanting voices with which it began, and the mist-enfolded monolith replaces the fort in the barren landscape.

This richly designed and magnificently photographed film is directed and edited with absolute economy, and Washizu and Asaji are both played, largely in mime, with a stylized bravura and an intensity of emotional expression which seem unique to Japanese acting. *Throne of Blood* remains one of Kurosawa's masterpieces and a unique rendering of Shakespeare, both in its total deviation from the text of the play and in its remarkable transmutation of the grim poetic atmosphere of the tragedy in terms of visual atmosphere, sound effects, and music closely related to the Nō tradition.

*Roger Manvell*

# THROUGH A GLASS DARKLY (SÅSOM I EN SPEGEL)

*Origin:* Sweden
*Released:* 1961
*Released in U.S.:* 1962
*Production:* Svensk Filmindustri (AA)
*Direction:* Ingmar Bergman
*Screenplay:* Ingmar Bergman
*Cinematography:* Sven Nykvist
*Editing:* Ulla Ryghe
*Art direction:* P. A. Lundgren
*Music:* Johann Sebastian Bach
*Running time:* 93 minutes
*Running time in U.S.:* 91 minutes

*Principal characters:*
Karin.......................... Harriet Andersson
Martin.......................... Max von Sydow
David.......................... Gunnar Björnstrand
Minus.......................... Lars Passgård

*Through a Glass Darkly* marked an important turning point in the film career of Swedish director Ingmar Bergman. In this film, he adopted a more introspective, personalized, and thematically integrated style of filmmaking. This "chamber film," as he called it, shows a simplification of form in contrast to his earlier work. Using an isolated island setting, only four characters, and the classical time frame of twenty-four hours, *Through a Glass Darkly* dramatically expresses Bergman's familiar concerns: the meaning of life without God and the difficult necessity of establishing human contact. These issues would be of central importance in the trilogy of films begun with *Through a Glass Darkly*, followed by *Nattvardsgästerna* (1962; *Winter Light*), and completed by *Tystnaden* (1963; *The Silence*). Bergman characterized the first film as illustrating the concept of "certainty achieved," the second film as "certainty lost," and *The Silence* as "the silence of God." This thematic progression occurs on both a theological and psychological/emotional level in the three films.

*Through a Glass Darkly* is also important in that it demonstrates Bergman's continuing experiments with film space as an expressive means of revealing the inner turmoil of his characters. Bergman's treatment of space is crucial in shaping the audience's emotional reaction to the film. Space becomes an extension of the personal anguish of human isolation, both physical isolation and the isolation imposed by conflicting emotions and alienating behavior. *Through a Glass Darkly* shows the subtle ways in which Bergman uses lighting, composition, camera movement, and similar techniques for emotionally expressive purposes.

As in many of Bergman's later films, *Vargotimmen* (1968; *Hour of the Wolf*) and *Ansikte mot ansikte* (1976; *Face to Face*), *Through a Glass Darkly* traces the disintegration of a human mind, and, paradoxically, the suffering and the enlightenment that result. Unlike later Bergman films, however, the illusory states of mind within the film are not presented in a dreamlike distortion of space that confuses the audience's perception of what is real and what is not. Instead, Bergman relies on an objective view of the main character, Karin, and of her plummet into madness. He limits the role of the audience to that of the distanced observer rather than permitting it to become an active participant in dream/madness, as he does in *Persona* (1966) and *Hour of the Wolf*.

*Through a Glass Darkly*, filmed from Bergman's own screenplay, moves swiftly in establishing its characters and the dramatic course toward emotional crisis. Karin (Harriet Andersson), her doctor husband, Martin (Max von Sydow), her father, David (Gunnar Björnstrand), and her teenaged brother Minus (Lars Passgård) vacation together on a remote island. The opening shots of the film might appear to be casually constructed, but in actuality they carefully guide the audience's introduction to the characters. Against an unbroken horizon of placid ocean, the four family members briskly walk back from a swim. Their laughter and friendly chatter match the visual background of calm sea and sky. This is the deceptive starting point from which Bergman progressively strips away the characters' tenuously maintained façade of happiness and health. Ostensibly, this image, dominated as it is by horizontal lines, confirms the sense of peace and contentment evident in the family's good spirits, but the extreme long-shot, with the resulting diminution of the four figures, limits the viewer's capacity for involvement in their feelings of joy and unity. The extreme camera distance also evokes the family's isolation against an unlimited, empty, and somewhat ominous space reminiscent of the disquieting shot that ends *Det sjunde inseglet* (1956; *The Seventh Seal*). This spatial configuration not only lulls the audience into accepting the emotions superficially conveyed by the characters but also undercuts that acceptance with the disturbing qualities imbued by the subtle manipulation of film space.

The family returns to its summer home to prepare for supper. Minus and Karin discuss Minus' adolescent sexual confusion and Karin's recent mental illness. Karin sympathizes with her brother but also teases him cruelly. As Martin and David gather up their fishing nets, they discuss David's return from Switzerland and the progress of his new novel. At dinner, the family's relationships are further revealed. David is an absentee father whose career as a writer has taken precedence over his family. He loves his children but is incapable of showing that love adequately. He emerges as one in a long line of "cold" parents in Bergman films, whose actions inevitably leave their children neurotic, if not emotionally crippled. Like Professor Borg in Bergman's *Smultronstället* (1957; *Wild Strawberries*), however, David is not yet cut off from all feeling and is still capable of realizing his emotional failings. At one point in the dinner, he leaves the table, retreats to his room, and begins to sob uncontrollably. He is overcome by his own guilt as a negligent father and by the role which his emotional coldness has played in Karin's mental disintegration. Karin's schizophrenia is a repetition of his wife's mental illness. The hereditary cause of Karin's disease is thus established, but, as often occurs in Bergman's films, *Through a Glass Darkly* implies that emotional neglect in Karin's upbringing is also a factor in her illness. Karin has taken refuge from the real world in an alternate world of illusion. Her brother Minus takes similar refuge in the illusion of art. In direct emulation of Bergman's own childhood, Minus uses playwriting as an escape from his loneliness and anguish.

As an after-dinner entertainment, Minus and Karin present one of Minus' numerous plays. The play tells the story of an artist who falls in love with a dead princess but does not have the courage to fulfill his promise to follow her in death. The theme of the artist's failure to commit himself to love strikes a nerve in David. Minus has not consciously meant to hurt David, but he knows that his play has done so. In turn, David's "art" delivers a cruel blow to Karin. She discovers David's diary. In it, he has commented on the irreversibility of her illness and his misgivings about his own desire to watch her descent into madness so as to use these observations as material for his writing. This scene creates one of the most haunting moments in the entire film. With the sound track filled by the solemn music of Johann Sebastian Bach's Suite no. 2 in D Minor for violoncello, the camera closes in on Karin's face as she is confronted with the true nature of her father's feelings about her. Bergman's own discovery of his mother's diary after her death impressed him with the absolutely unknowable side of every person. Often, Bergman's films use the device of a letter or a diary to remind the audience of the ambiguity of human love and the secrets held by each individual. David's love for Karin is mixed with calculating self-interest and an almost unfeeling scientific curiosity. Karin tells Martin of her discovery, and when Martin and David leave the island on an errand, Martin confronts David with the cold, exploitative nature that the diary has revealed. David has no defense against Martin's accusations and begins to realize his own emotional hollowness.

Minus and Karin are left alone on the island. Minus begins to study, but Karin insists on taking him to the attic of their house. She believes that the walls of the attic are inhabited by "The Others," creatures who want her to join them in waiting for the imminent arrival of God. Minus, terrified by this sign of Karin's madness, leaves her writhing on the floor. His fears are allayed when Karin reappears downstairs. She seems to be lucid, but warns him against telling Martin and David about the attic. She then disappears. Minus searches for her and finds her in the dark, rotting hull of an abandoned boat. In this dreamlike setting, Karin's retreat into madness "explodes" Minus' reality. He goes to comfort her, but Karin draws him into incest. When Martin and David return, they help Minus take her back to the house. Karin realizes what has happened and tells David that she knows that she must return to the hospital, but she makes him promise that the hospital will discontinue her treatments. She is tired of being torn between the reality of others and her own hallucinatory world.

This short period of calm is broken by another hallucination. Karin sees God as a spider who attempts to rape her. Through the control of film space, Bergman makes it clear that Karin's image of the spider-rapist-god is linked to her relationship with her father. In her insanity, she achieves the awful certainty afforded by glimpsing her own version of God. If, as Corinthians 13:12 maintains, God only reveals himself "through a glass darkly," then Karin's experience confirms man's freedom to see a god who conforms to each person's lack of or attainment of faith.

In contrast with Karin, David chooses to affirm the positive presence of God in life. It is somewhat ironic, but not inappropriate, that David, the negative father-figure who was a catalyst in his daughter's madness, should be the one to offer an alternative to Karin's spider god. David has been a failure as a human being, but he talks to Minus about the way God is expressed in all types of love. Minus gains comfort, not so much by what David says, but from the very fact that his father has cared enough to speak to him. Many critics (as well as Bergman himself) have criticized this ending as being too simplistic and even false, but the ending is typical of the director. In spite of the pessimism in his work, Bergman's films usually affirm the value of human communication and love in giving meaning to life. As Bergman once remarked, "what matters most of all in life is being able to make contact with other human beings."

Although *Through a Glass Darkly* received an Academy Award for Best Foreign Language Film, the critical reaction to the film was by no means overwhelmingly positive. It is curious that Bergman's films usually receive very mixed reviews, in spite of the universal acknowledgment of Bergman's place as a master of the cinema. His films are often cited as being "interesting," but the lack of deep enthusiasm for his work may be related to the difficult nature of his emotional and theological concerns, and to the austerity of his style. *Through a Glass Darkly* was praised for its intensity and for the excellent acting displayed, yet it left some critics disturbed by the "abnormality" of its characters and its seemingly ambiguous conclusion.

*Through a Glass Darkly* remains a pivotal Bergman film in its step toward dissolving the boundaries between dream and reality in Bergman's film world. In Bergman's universe, reality can explode for anyone. *Through a Glass Darkly* confirms Bergman's belief that reality is not an unquestionable empirical truth but only a subjective experience. Faith in love may offer the only hope, for only in madness or death will certainty be achieved.

*Gaylyn Studlar*

# TIEFLAND

*Origin:* West Germany
*Released:* 1954
*Released in U.S.:* 1981
*Production:* Riefenstahl-Film
*Direction:* Leni Riefenstahl
*Screenplay:* Leni Riefenstahl and Harold Reinl; based on the opera by Eugen d'Albert
*Cinematography:* Albert Benitz
*Editing:* Erich Crane
*Art direction:* no listing
*Music:* Herbert Windt; with original selections by Eugen d'Albert
*MPAA rating:* no listing
*Running time:* 98 minutes

*Principal characters:*

Marta .......................... Leni Riefenstahl
Pedro .......................... Franz Eichberger
Don Sebastian .................. Bernhard Minetti
Doña Amelia .................... Maria Köppenhöfer
Nando .......................... Luis Rainer
Josefa ......................... Frieda Richard
Burgermeister .................. Karl Skraup
Natario ........................ Max Holzboer

*Triumph des Willens* (1935; *Triumph of the Will*), the notorious chronicle of the 1934 Nazi Party rally in Nuremberg, and the two-part *Olympiad* (1938; *Olympia*), a record of the 1936 Berlin Olympic Games, are both legendary, powerful documentary masterpieces. Their director, Leni Riefenstahl, is one of the most able women ever to work behind a camera. Riefenstahl did not, however, only make nonnarrative films—or propaganda exercises extolling the virtues of National Socialism. *Das blaue Licht* (1932; *The Blue Light*) is based on a legend of the Italian Dolomites; in story line and atmosphere, it is the predecessor of *Tiefland*, which took twenty years to produce from inspiration to completion.

*Tiefland* (lowlands) is based on the opera of the same title by Eugen d'Albert, which had its premiere in Prague in 1903 and became especially popular in Berlin during the 1920's. Riefenstahl, who also produced and coscripted, stars as Marta, a sensual gypsy dancer who is still "pure of heart." The setting is the Pyrenees, in both the lowlands and mountains of Catalonia, and the time is the eighteenth century. The film opens with a breathtaking shot of clouds and mountain peaks, and the first character introduced is Pedro (Franz Eichberger), a shy, strikingly handsome shepherd who has always been content to live in nature. A wolf peers over a ledge, and Pedro's sheep become uneasy. When he investigates, he is attacked, and he struggles furiously with the wolf. Pedro is bitten but finally is able to strangle his attacker.

After the sun rises, Pedro directs his flock to the "tiefland." Peasants are now seen laboring at an irrigation ditch on the dry plain. They desperately need water and beg their landlord, Don Sebastian (Bernhard Minetti), to allow them access to it from the highlands, but the don refuses, as he needs the water for his cattle. Later, at a banquet, he proposes to Doña Amelia (Maria Köppenhöfer), the daughter of the mayor, admitting that he needs the financial support of her wealthy father. Despite his castle and his power, Sebastian has little money.

Meanwhile, Pedro eats supper in Sebastian's kitchen, among the servants. The young women there flirt with him, but he is unresponsive. Soon, he strolls through the village and observes Marta, surrounded by a crowd, dancing to flamenco music. He immediately falls in love, but Sebastian soon arrives and takes Marta and the guitar player back to his castle. There, she dances for Sebastian, who, aroused, kisses her and carries her away.

Pedro returns to the highlands, but he is changed. He now decides that he wants a wife, a companion. Meanwhile, the drought becomes worse, and the peasants are clearly suffering. Sebastian, who still has ample water for his cattle, has set up Marta as his mistress. She wears an expensive dress and rides with him as he inspects his herd. As they do so, the peasants curse them. Marta is sympathetic to their plight and feels guilty that she benefits from Sebastian's generosity while everyone else suffers because of his selfishness. She therefore sets up a meeting between the villagers and her lover, who at first refuses to see them, but later relents at Marta's request. At the meeting, though, he only informs them that he will evict them from their land if they are unable to pay their rent.

The peasants are on the verge of revolt, when Marta gives the miller's wife a necklace, a present from Sebastian. She explains that it is to be sold and used to help pay the don. The miller, however, will not accept this "charity." While the plight of the villagers is disastrous, Sebastian suffers his own financial woes—a fact that Amelia learns from his scheming butler. She wants to marry Sebastian, but she first must discredit Marta. The miller's wife returns the necklace to the butler, who promptly delivers the evidence to Sebastian. In turn, he angrily beats Marta, and she runs away to the mountains. After collapsing, she is rescued by Pedro, but two of Sebastian's men have followed her. When she awakens, she thinks that she is in the don's presence, and the shepherd must restrain her. Sebastian's servants then arrive and take Marta back to the castle; Pedro follows them.

Sebastian cannot pay a bill he owes the mayor, who demands that he marry Amelia. The butler suggests to Sebastian that he indeed should wed her—but keep Marta as a mistress. He further suggests that the gypsy could wed someone in the village, but that that union need never be consummated. Sebastian enthusiastically agrees, but Marta now hates her benefactor, who tells her he would kill her first before losing her. Pedro, who has returned to the highlands, is informed that he is to marry Marta. Excitedly, he journeys to the village, where he is jeered by the peasants. Sebastian, meanwhile, is planning to come to Marta on his wedding night.

Marta reluctantly meets with Pedro and then refuses to look at him. They enter the church, just as Amelia and Sebastian's wedding feast begins. Marta and Pedro arrive at the mill, where they will live now that the miller's family has been evicted, but she believes that Pedro is in collusion with Sebastian and refuses his advances. The villagers gather outside the mill and continue to taunt the uncomprehending Pedro. When Marta tells him that she is involved with someone else, he leaves. A furious storm commences, disrupting Sebastian's wedding celebration. He excuses himself and walks through the storm to Marta, who by now realizes Pedro's innocence. She beckons him to return to her, and they kiss, but Sebastian arrives and pulls a knife. He and Pedro fight—in a scene reminiscent of the fight between the shepherd and the wolf—and the don, like the wolf, is strangled. At the end, Pedro and Marta return to his home in the highlands.

*Tiefland* is a simplistic, predictable melodrama of selfishness versus generosity, the lowlands versus the highlands, the corrupt Sebastian versus the innocent Pedro—with the love of a desirable woman in between. The acting is serviceable, although Riefenstahl and Eichberger are not unattractive performers. Originally Riefenstahl did not want both to act in and to direct the film, as she had in *The Blue Light*, her first feature, but she could find no one suitable to replace her in either capacity, so she decided to take on both roles.

Riefenstahl's direction easily outshines her performance. The opening and closing sequences, with Pedro battling the wolf and, then, Sebastian, are the film's highlights. The cinematography is above average: Using a special emulsion developed by Agfa and constantly experimenting with filters and aperture settings, Riefenstahl is able to create striking, painterly images of mountains, clouds, and waterfalls. The music, scored by Herbert Windt and performed by the Vienna Philharmonic Orchestra, is striking. Some is taken directly from the d'Albert opera, other parts are original, and still more is based on Spanish folk music.

*Tiefland* was Riefenstahl's last complete feature film. Originally, the director came upon a book containing photographs of Spain—specifically, Castille and its population—and became interested in shooting a film using its locales. She was familiar with the *Tiefland* opera, and saw in it the basis for the project. After writing the script, she planned a trip to scout locations. The year was 1934. Heinrich George was hired to play Sebastian, with Sepp Rist set for Pedro. Riefenstahl had hoped that G. W. Pabst would be hired as director, but the filmmaker had another commitment. The project quickly fell apart for a variety of reasons. George was available for only three weeks, and there was inadequate funding and insufficient time for all the preproduction details. Finally, while in Madrid, Riefenstahl suffered a nervous breakdown.

When she recovered, she was pressured by Adolf Hitler to begin preparation for *Triumph of the Will*. In 1933, she had made a seventeen-hundred-meter documentary, *Sieg des Glaubens* (*Victory of Faith*), on an earlier Nazi rally, and had no interest in making any further documentaries. She suggested that Walter Ruttmann work on the project, but Ruttmann, whose most famous work is *Berlin—Die Symphonie einer Grosstadt* (1927; *Berlin—Symphony of a Great City*), wanted to shoot *Triumph of the Will* as a historical record of the Nazis' rise to power—not as propaganda. He even shot some footage, none of which survives. Hitler, who had been extremely pleased with *Victory of Faith*, wanted Riefenstahl for *Triumph of the Will*, so *Tiefland* was delayed.

At the outset of World War II, Riefenstahl was seeking a film project that, as she has often claimed, would not involve her in the war or Nazi activities: thus, the resumption of her work on *Tiefland*. Because the film was not propaganda, Joseph Goebbels, the Minister for People's Enlightenment and Propaganda and controller of the German film industry during the Third Reich, attempted to sabotage the project. Riefenstahl asserts that she was constantly bumped from studio to studio, editing table to editing table, with her production company constantly near bankruptcy. She also could no longer shoot in Spain because of currency restrictions, so the production was moved to Bavaria, where a model Spanish village was constructed. Interiors were eventually filmed in a Prague studio. By the end of 1944, most of the film had been shot, with both G. W. Pabst and Veit Harlan (maker of the odiously anti-Semitic *Jud Süss*, 1940) allegedly directing some of the secondary scenes. The bulk of the postproduction, however, was not completed until years after the war's end. The French occupying forces confiscated the film, and much footage was lost before Riefenstahl successfully repossessed it in 1953.

The director was not pleased with her final cut: Although the story line remained coherent, many visuals contrasting the highlands and lowlands were lost forever. When the film was released in 1954, it was not a success, and after a short run, Riefenstahl took it out of circulation for some years. In October, 1981, it was screened in its American theatrical premiere for three weeks at New York's Film Forum.

*Rob Edelman*

# TIME FOR REVENGE (TIEMPO DE REVANCHA)

*Origin:* Argentina
*Released:* 1982
*Released in U.S.:* 1982
*Production:* Héctor Olivera and L. O. Repetto for ARIES Cinematografica Argentina
*Direction:* Adolfo Aristarain
*Screenplay:* Adolfo Aristarain
*Cinematography:* Horacio Maira
*Editing:* Eduardo Lopez
*Art direction:* no listing
*Sound:* Daniel Castronuovo
*Music:* Enrique Kauderer
*MPAA rating:* no listing
*Running time:* 112 minutes

*Principal characters:*
Pedro Bengoa .................... Federico Luppi
Amanda Bengoa .................. Haydée Padilla
Larsen ........................... Julio de Grazia
Torrens .......................... Rodolfo Ranni
Bruno Di Toro .................... Ulises Dumont
Rossi ............................ Aldo Barbero
Basile ........................... Enrique Liporace
Aitor ............................ José Joffre Soares
García-Brown ..................... Arturo Maly
Guido Ventura .................... Jorge Hacker
Don Bautista ..................... Cavetano Biondo
Lea .............................. Ingrid Pellicori
Jorge ............................ Jorge Chernov
Golo ............................. Alberto Benegas
Polaco ........................... Marcos Woinsky
Juez ............................. Jorge Velurtas

In view of Argentina's record of repression, any film that boldly depicts individuals battling against entrenched institutions and corruption is noteworthy; when such a film, as is true in the case of *Time for Revenge*, succeeds on both artistic and entertainment levels, there is added reason for the international film community to pay special attention.

*Time for Revenge*, written and directed by Adolfo Aristarain, is a compelling thriller with a powerful political undercurrent. Federico Luppi, a leading Argentine actor, is brilliant in his portrayal of Pedro Bengoa, an industrial demolitions expert. (Luppi won the Best Actor Award at the 1982 Chicago Film Festival for his work in *Time for Revenge*.) Married for twenty-five years and now in his mid-forties, Bengoa has been an outcast because of his record in the labor movement. Long blacklisted, he decides that he must put his radical past behind him. With forged papers, he is able to get an interview for a post with a major multinational corporation called Tulsaco. An excellent early scene in which he is interviewed for the job conveys the tension that he feels at concealing his past and suppressing his political convictions.

Despite his inner conflict, Bengoa survives the interview and is hired as foreman of a demolition crew at a remote mining camp, where working conditions are dangerous and repressive. Much to his surprise, he finds at the camp a man whom he knew in his days as a labor activist, and his old friend recognizes him as well, although they make no public sign of recognition. As this chance meeting indicates, it is impossible for Bengoa to forget his past and the values by which he has lived. The dangerous policies of the company—using much larger charges of dynamite than safety permits—pose a threat to the men. Bengoa's former acquaintance, Bruno Di Toro (Ulises Dumont), has been nursing his own scheme to avenge certain social injustices, and he soon apprises Bengoa of the plan and enlists his help.

Di Toro's plan entails faking an accident. He wants Bengoa to help him set up an explosion that will trap him amid the rocks, but he has figured out a way to be safe until Bengoa can rush to his rescue. Di Toro will then pretend that he has lost his power of speech as a result of the traumatic experience. He has already lined up a crooked lawyer who will take his case and, playing upon the company's corrupt activities, compel the company to make a compensation deal that will leave Di Toro in comfortable financial shape for the remainder of his life.

Although Bengoa at first does not want to become involved, a series of events leads him to change his mind. Two of his fellow workers die in an explosion that occurs because of the company's callous policies. There is also a personal tragedy. His father dies, and because he was very close to his father, who stubbornly adhered to his ideals throughout his life and castigated his son for moving away from his own militancy, his entire sense of values is called into question. Bengoa sees Di Toro's swindle as a means to strike back against corporate greed, and despite his reservations, he agrees to go along with it.

The plan backfires. Immediately before the explosion, Di Toro loses his nerve and panics. Despite Bengoa's heroic efforts to rescue him, Di Toro is killed, and it is Bengoa who is trapped. A unique opportunity presents itself as workers come to his rescue. Bengoa can trade places with Di Toro in the bizarre scheme. Now it is he who is unable to speak. His wife, Amanda

(Haydée Padilla), at first goes along with her husband's ruse and makes contact with Di Toro's lawyer, Larsen (Julio de Grazia), who sets up a chilling confrontation between Bengoa and the company chairman. A Mafia-like type who would normally not even see the supposed victim, the chairman is forced to make a deal because of the potential scandal. He is willing to buy off Bengo with $300,000, the amount that Larsen has demanded. To his own lawyer's surprise, Bengoa, sensing the powerful cards that he holds, refuses to make a deal, even when the amount is raised to half a million dollars. Acting on principle, he is determined to take the firm to court and expose its shady record.

Now the contest begins in earnest. The company sets out to break Bengoa, to prove that his muteness is a fraud. His phone is tapped, and listening devices are planted in his apartment. He lives under the shadow of threats every minute of the day and night, and when his wife can no longer withstand the intense pressure, she leaves him. Bengoa is a man alone, determined to fight back and win against this array of power and corruption. It takes a year for the case to be resolved, and he is indeed the victor. The firm is found guilty, its operation at the mine is halted, and an investigation is ordered. Nevertheless, his very victory condemns him; Bengoa is legally dumb and must remain so. Although he is awarded $200,000, which he must split with the lawyer, and although he and his wife, who has returned to him, can live comfortably if they can follow their plan and leave the country, the pressures on them continue. The company is determined to wreak revenge, and Bengoa is equally determined to fight back, no matter what the cost. He faces the challenge in the final scene and cuts out his tongue, rendering himself truly mute, but also incapable of betraying what he has done, no matter what the pressure.

If *Time for Revenge* were merely a film about an insurance fraud, it would still be a taut, exciting film in the *film noir* tradition, but Aristarain makes it far more than that at every turn. He has concocted a metaphor for present-day Argentina, pitting his protagonist, who represents ideals, militant action, and determination to be free, against industrial evil, a corrupt system in which such evil flourishes, and the people who thrive and rule in such an environment. By making the inability to speak the central device, Aristarain sharply dramatizes the concept of speech as a litmus test of freedom and shows that even silence can be turned against an oppressor.

By weaving this theme into a suspense pattern, the writer-director expresses his ideas in an extremely popular form, somewhat in the manner of Constantin Costa-Gavras in *Z* (1969). The film can be thoroughly enjoyed on any of its levels. It moves at a rapid clip, is rich in character study, has several crisp, incisive confrontations in which the dialogue is fascinating, and also contains vivid action sequences.

Aristarain has been active in film production for many years. In 1965, he worked as a second assistant director, and his subsequent experience included a six-year period in Spain, during which he was involved in various coproductions. He has worked with such diverse directors as the spaghetti-Western king Sergio Leone, British action director Lewis Gilbert, and American comedy director Melvin Frank. His major break occurred after he returned to Argentina and directed an eighteen-day-wonder of a detective story production, *La parte de León* (1978; *The Lion's Share*), which became something of a cult film in his country. He has since directed musicals as well as dramas, and he represents a vital strain of talent in contemporary Argentine cinema, as well as exemplifying the conscience of those who believe that the arts in Argentina must confront the issues facing that troubled land.

Aristarain was astute in his choice of actors. As Bengoa, Luppi is lean, determined, and stoic. He conveys the impression of being deeply introspective and has the gift of being able to project much more than is actually spoken. He acts as convincingly when he simply listens as when he must take charge. He moves with agile decisiveness in the action scenes, and in private, he suggests a sensitivity and tenderness underlying his strangely tested convictions.

Ulises Dumont, as Di Toro, creates a completely believable character. He appears to be a man with a dubious and difficult past and fits convincingly into the group of demolition men. Indeed, he at first seems to be a nonprofessional actor enlisted from an authentic mining crew, but his skill soon becomes evident. Julio de Grazia, as Larsen, the lawyer, is equally convincing. He is a model of sliminess, the shyster who has graduated to bigger prey. De Grazia makes him thoroughly mercenary yet capable of grudging admiration for Bengoa.

Haydée Padilla creates an interesting character in her role as Bengoa's wife. She is no simpering coward who is dragging down a man of principle; rather, she is a warm, devoted woman who simply has trouble surviving under the pressure. In effect, she is denied freedom of choice: Her husband's masquerade is a *fait accompli*, and she is put in the position of having to cooperate or betray him. Padilla conveys these nuances admirably and adds significantly to the film's believability.

In some respects, *Time for Revenge* suffers from the contrivances of its plot, however clever. Bengoa's sudden assumption of Di Toro's role is too neat, but after that, the scenario is played out with originality, and the cat-and-mouse game itself becomes compelling. The director's pacing is good, and he manages to keep the film within the confines of the material at hand, without succumbing to any temptation to try to inflate the story to a grander scale, to bring in extraneous ideas, events, or characters, or to preach. Whatever he has to say is said through action, characterizations, and conflicts intrinsic to the plot, not through forced dialogue.

Cinematographer Horacio Maira deserves credit for the realistic look of the film, in the effective outdoor settings, in the indoor confrontations, and in the action through the Argentine streets. He does this not through resorting to fancy cinematic footwork, but through intelligent angles and targeting of his subjects. In analyzing the "look" of a film, it is always difficult to distinguish the input of the cinematographer from that of the director. *Time for Revenge* appears to be the result of a harmonious collaboration between a director and a cinematographer who shared a clear vision of how to make a thriller with political overtones. In consequence, they produced a work that stands as a major achievement of Latin American cinema.

*William Wolf*

# TIME STANDS STILL (MEGÁLL AZ IDŐ)

*Origin:* Hungary
*Released:* 1982
*Released in U.S.:* 1982
*Production:* Mafilm-Budapest Studio Production
*Direction:* Péter Gothár
*Screenplay:* Géza Bereményi and Péter Gothár
*Cinematography:* Lajos Koltai
*Editing:* Mária Nagy
*Art direction:* no listing
*Music:* György Selmeczi
*MPAA rating:* no listing
*Running time:* 99 minutes

*Principal characters:*

Denes .......................... István Znamenák
Gabor .............................. Henrik Pauer
Pierre .............................. Sándor Sőth
Vilmon ............................. Péter Galfy
Magda .............................. Anikó Iván
Mother.............................. Agi Kakassy
Father .............................. Pál Hetényi
Bodor.................................. Lajos Őze
Form master ........................ Jozef Kroner

The title of this film is evocative of the state of Central Europe in the early 1980's. Time stands still in the sense that each generation gets caught in the same dilemma: How does one express individuality in the midst of tremendous pressures to conform to the political strictures of the State? Since the end of World War II, several Central European countries—Poland, Czechoslovakia, and Hungary in particular—have gone through cycles of change, through periods when political repression has been relaxed and when hopes have risen for a more flexible form of government. Always, such hopes have been dashed, and the drive for reform has been severely restrained or crushed.

*Time Stands Still* belongs, then, to a very rich body of work in cinema and literature that has increasingly commanded the respect and admiration of Western audiences. A truly Central European statement, it blends the styles and themes of East and West—of rock music, Hollywood films, and political dialectics—in a manner that it not usually found in Soviet, Western European, or American art.

The film begins in black and white, with newsreel footage dated November 5, 1956, the day after the Soviet army invaded Budapest and put down the Hungarian uprising. An era is thus quickly documented and objectified; the results of one rebellion are revealed before the next generation of 1963 arrives in the color photography and rock-and-roll sound track of the rest of the film.

In 1956, a family is breaking up in the midst of a society that is in ruins. A frightened wife (Agi Kakassy) stays behind with her two sons and seems paralyzed while her husband (Pál Hetényi) desperately prepares for his escape only steps ahead of the Russians. In 1963, the two sons, Denes (István Znamenák) and Gabor (Henrik Pauer), reflect the tensions inherent in their parents' generation, for the latter worries about getting ahead in his native land while the former opens himself up to the anarchic spirit of rock music and a culture of high individualism.

Much of *Time Stands Still* takes place in a high school, where Denes, the younger brother, takes up with a wild, older student, Pierre (Sándor Sőth), and a forward girl, Magda (Anikó Iván), who propositions him. Gabor, on the other hand, is concerned that his father's past will prevent his going to medical school.

Comparisons could be made between *Time Stands Still* and American youth films, but they would be misleading, since these Hungarian teenagers are not in anguish over their identities and do not contend with either affluence or poverty in the terms that Hollywood is accustomed to purveying. They are schooled, rather, in the assumption of false identities and drilled to perform in roles that they shuck off by acquiring what might be called the ethos of rock music.

That ethos is apparent in the line the teenagers sing from a Paul Anka record: "You . . . are . . . my . . . des-ti-ny." To romanticize a person in this way counteracts the fate that the State has in store for its young citizens. They seek to establish faith in one another with a longing intensity that is captured in Anka's aching sophomoric lyrics. Rock music for these youths dwells on the gaps in the self and the mysteries of human love and loyalty that the State would like to replace with a political allegiance to itself.

Denes is the focus of attention because he is neither as docile as his conventional brother nor as outlandish as the school tough, Pierre, who eventually leads his schoolmates on a destructive rampage. If Denes is not yet ready for sex with Magda, he is willing to take off with her and Pierre for the border in a stolen car. Like them, he sheds the inhibitions that his schooling would impose, playing close to the edge of what is permissible and, on occasion, going beyond it.

These students are not exactly dissidents, but they do manage to create considerable dissonance within a one-party state. Their own parties are uproarious and deliberately disorganized. They delight in the randomness that is not supposed to be part of a well-governed society. They rely on impulse, on an inimitable sense of style that prevents them from becoming the predictable partisans that the system tries to produce.

Yet the enormous spirit of these adolescents is doomed to dissipate, since they cannot go beyond the very same border that Denes' father crossed. Because they are not free to come and go as they please, they are dislocated. They do their best to make the rock songs their own, but—like so much of the shooting style of the film—their feelings for the songs are fragmented. They jump from one lyric to another—from "Don't Be Cruel" to "Jailhouse Rock" to "Tutti Frutti"—but cannot connect the sentiments of the songs into creative acts that will sustain them. They have the energy but not the resources to maintain a counterculture.

Time stands still in these musical phrases plucked out of context. Time is warped, truncated, and finally subdued in a miasmic, ambiguous atmosphere. Almost nothing in this film is shot in clear, bright light. Much of the color is dull green or gray—institutional color that subdues natural, vivid highlights. Occasionally the lighting is warmer and mellower—during one of the teenagers' parties, for example—but even that episode is more of a dream than a reality, a kind of digression from the coercive staleness and subterranean ambience of the school. At best, the students find a way to ventilate their environment, not to change it.

The camera seems on the side of these errant individualists, however, for it careens along hallways and streets, following them everywhere, looking over their shoulders, so to speak, in the classroom as it also tracks the outraged schoolmaster who tries to catch the student who laughed during an official speech. Seldom has camera work been this effectively employed to show how individuals can give a special tilt to a political structure imposed upon them.

The camera also reveals, however, that ultimately this world of youth will be skewed in the direction already established by the State. If Pierre is glimpsed headed for the United States in his stolen car, Denes is pictured on New Year's Eve, 1967, in a soldier's uniform, drunkenly urinating against the wall. Is he still his irreverent self? Maybe, but the uniform indicates exactly how solidly the boundaries have formed around his person. Is he free to do much more than have too much to drink on New Year's Eve? The film leaves the question open for this vulnerable, wobbling individual, the frail vessel of liberty so exuberantly himself in the earlier scenes.

What truly distinguishes *Time Stands Still* is its sense of style, of showing things that can be revealed only by a playful grasp of cinematic technique. The editing emphasizes the discontinuities of existence in contemporary Hungary. A more conventional narrative, with carefully managed transitions, would have imposed a false order on the chaotic emotions of adolescence, a false order inculcated by the authority figures in the film.

The deliberate awkwardness of the editing is somewhat mitigated by the passionately thorough performances not only of the students but also of their parents and teachers. Denes' form master (Jozef Kroner) is striking as a traditionalist who tries to teach his pupil about the spirituality of sex. He is replaced because "he doesn't fit in," and his successor is a lapsed but surprisingly calm hard-line Communist attempting to come to terms with a system in which she and her husband are now suspect. Bodor (Lajos Őze), an old friend of Denes' father, appears after serving several years in prison and becomes the lover of Denes' mother. As a surrogate father to Denes, Bodor expresses the paranoia acquired in his confinement. Each of these older generational representatives defines the perils ahead for students of the State. Resistance, accommodation, and compromise—each of these alternatives exacts a heavy tax on individuality—as is demonstrated at the end of the film when Magda has apparently chosen Gabor, the obedient older brother, and Denes' father returns on New Year's Eve, 1967, during a period of political liberalization that will be summarily destroyed seven months later in the Soviet invasion of Czechoslovakia.

*Carl E. Rollyson, Jr.*

# THE TIN DRUM (DIE BLECHTROMMEL)

*Origin:* West Germany
*Released:* 1979
*Released in U.S.:* 1980
*Production:* Franz Seitz and Anatole Dauman for Bioskop-Film, Artemis Film, and Argos Films (AA)
*Direction:* Volker Schlöndorff
*Screenplay:* Jean-Claude Carrière, Franz Seitz, Volker Schlöndorff, and Günter Grass; based on the novel by Grass
*Cinematography:* Igor Luther
*Editing:* Suzanne Baron
*Art direction:* Nicos Perakis; set decoration, Bernd Lepel
*Music:* Maurice Jarre and Friedrich Meyer
*MPAA rating:* R
*Running time:* 144 minutes

*Principal characters:*

Alfred Matzerath . . . . . . . . . . . . . . . . . . . . . Mario Adorf
Agnes Matzerath . . . . . . . . . . . . . . . . . . Angela Winkler
Oskar Matzerath . . . . . . . . . . . . . . . . . . . David Bennent
Jan Bronski . . . . . . . . . . . . . . . . . . . . . Daniel Olbrychski
Maria . . . . . . . . . . . . . . . . . . . . . . . . Katharina Thalbach
Sigismund Markus . . . . . . . . . . . . . . . Charles Aznavour
Anna Koljaiczek . . . . . . . . . . . . . . . . . . . . . . Tina Engel
Joseph Koljaiczek . . . . . . . . . . . . . . . . . Roland Beubner
Anna Koljaiczek, as an old woman . . . . . Berta Drews
Bebra . . . . . . . . . . . . . . . . . . . . . . . . . . . . . . . Fritz Hakl
Roswitha Raguna . . . . . . . . . . . . . . . . . Mariella Oliveri

Volker Schlöndorff, director of *The Tin Drum*, which was awarded the Gold Palm in Cannes in 1979 and in 1980, and an Academy Award for the Best Foreign Film, has admitted that he has always wanted to bring literature to the marketplace. Indeed, before directing *The Tin Drum*, Schlöndorff had already established a reputation for bringing literature to the screen, primarily with his films based on works by Heinrich Böll, Heinrich von Kleist, and Robert Musil, as well as his 1984 film *Un Amour de Swann* (*Swann in Love*), based on Marcel Proust's novel.

*The Tin Drum* is based on the Günter Grass novel of the same title. Grass's work, which first appeared in 1959, is presented as the autobiography of Oskar Matzerath, who at the age of three, after surveying the adult world, decides to grow no more. The novel, aside from being a record of

Oskar's life, ranges from the political background of the pre-World War II Nazi era in Danzig to Germany's economic recovery in the 1950's. The novel, translated into numerous languages, was a cultural as well as a literary phenomenon; more than three million copies of the book were sold.

A film based on this highly successful novel could hardly fail to be a success on its own. The concern of producer Franz Seitz, however, was not only that the film make a profit but also that the film have artistic merit, which could be ensured by choosing the right director. His choice was Volker Schlöndorff.

Volker Schlöndorff was born in Wiesbaden, Germany in 1939. His father, a physician, was too old to serve in the military. His mother was killed in a bombing raid during the war. He has very few memories of that era. At the age of fifteen, he continued his education in France. In the mid-1950's, he lived in Paris and worked at the *cinémathèque* in order to see films without paying. At this point, he was already determined to be a film director. Eventually, he worked as an assistant for several French directors, including Louis Malle, Alain Resnais, and Jean-Pierre Melville. In 1965, he returned to Munich with a script based on Musil's *Die Verwirrungen des Zöglings Törless* (1906; *Young Törless*, 1964). Taking advice from Werner Herzog, he filmed his first full-length work, which was a great success and established his name in German cinema.

Most of Schlöndorff's films are based on literary works. Schlöndorff has always been an avid reader and admits that for many years his life comprised literature rather than personal experience; his life experiences were reading experiences. He sees it as only natural that literature became the point of departure for his films. When he chooses a novel or short story for the screen, Schlöndorff says he is not so much concerned with the literary quality of the work but rather with the *Lebensqualität und Aussage über Leben*, the statement about life that the work reflects. In evaluating Grass's novel for the screen, his first reaction was that *The Tin Drum* was impossible to translate into film. The big question was how to portray history through the eyes of a child who has a mature mind.

The film opens in the year 1899 with Oskar's grandmother Anna (Tina Engel) sitting in a potato field and watching a fugitive pursued by the police. The voice of Oskar (David Bennent) informs the viewer that the young and inexperienced woman gives refuge to the pursued under her four long skirts, and it is at this time that his mother, Agnes (Angela Winkler) is conceived. Joseph Koljaiczek (Roland Beubner) spends a year with Anna and then again is pursued by the authorities. He escapes by jumping into the river, never to be seen again.

The time is now World War I, and the child conceived in the first scene has matured into a young woman. Agnes is concerned for her handsome cousin Jan Bronski (Daniel Olbrychski), who is about to be drafted. While working in a military hospital, Agnes meets the other man in her life, Alfred Matzerath (Mario Adorf), a German originally from the Rhine region. Although the two men are very different, they become friends, and, together with Agnes, form a close trio which Oskar in his narration refers to as the "trinity" that brought him into the world. Even though Agnes marries Alfred, one cannot assume that he is the father of her child. Oskar seems to be already aware of the world into which he is about to be born, and is reluctant to emerge from his mother's womb. The audience witnesses the birthing and even gets a glimpse of the hesitant fetus floating in the embryonic fluid. It is the delighted mother who shortly after the birth promises her newborn a tin drum when he is three.

The next scene is Oskar's third birthday party, September 12, 1927, in which several friends have gathered for the celebration. Sitting under the table, Oskar takes a critical view of the adult world and decides at this point that he does not want to become part of it. He resolves to grow no more. To achieve this, he deliberately throws himself down the cellar stairs. Alfred Matzerath had left the trapdoor open after fetching beer, and Agnes blames him for the accident. According to Oskar, however, the plan was a complete success; his growth is stunted. At this point the red and white tin drum also becomes more and more important. Oskar is never without it. It is his security blanket and his means of expression. His other extraordinary means of self-expression and protest is his high-pitched, screechy voice, which can shatter glass. His uniquely developed larynx is even entered in a medical journal, which makes Agnes very proud of her son.

For the first time, the historical background comes to the forefront. Nazi soldiers can be seen marching through the street. The film, at this point, still concentrates on Oskar's childhood. When, on the first day of school, Oskar brings his drum and refuses to surrender it to the teacher, the confrontation ends with his high-pitched screech, which shatters the teacher's glasses. In another scene the neighborhood children are concocting soup, which includes frogs and urine, which they force Oskar to taste. Oskar also makes Thursday trips into town with his mother, who has important business to conduct. While his mother meets Jan in a hotel room, Oskar usually stays with Sigismund Markus (Charles Aznavour), the toy store proprietor, who is obviously the supplier of his tin drums. His parents also take Oskar to the circus, where he is befriended by one of the midgets, who addresses him as one of his own kind. The fifty-three-year-old Bebra (Fritz Hakl) strikes a prophetic note when he tells Oskar that they will undoubtedly meet again.

Scenes of Oskar's childhood are now interspersed with scenes from the political world. Radios broadcast Adolf Hitler's speeches; Ludwig van Beethoven's picture above the piano is replaced with one of Hitler's; Alfred Matzerath, dressed in the Nazi khaki uniform, attends a Nazi demonstration. Oskar is there also, observing from underneath the bleachers. As the band plays a march, Oskar, who is never without his drum, drums along. He plays a three-quarter beat, however, and soon throws the entire band off rhythm. The spirited march becomes a Viennese waltz and swastika banners sway as people begin to waltz on the field. The scene is broken off by a rainstorm and the leaders are left alone, exasperated, on the muddy field.

The next family outing is to the coast. Jan Bronski is still part of the core family. Although Agnes is revolted by eels being caught in a horse's head and at first refuses to eat them, after Alfred prepares them in a dill sauce, she soon develops an uncontrollable passion for fish of all kind. Her Thursday trips to town, where she meets Jan, continue. In the church scene, Agnes confesses her sin of unfaithfulness and is simply told to pray. Meanwhile, Oskar offers his drum to the statue of the Christ Child at the altar. He is totally disappointed when the statue does not take the drum and questions Jesus whether he cannot or does not want to play.

Agnes' passion for fish grows. She devours entire cans of sardines as well as whole herring. There is no longer any doubt about her pregnancy. Alfred tries to comfort her and tells her that it does not really matter whose child it is. He even calls her mother, whose attempts to deal with her daughter's unhappiness are futile. Without any preparation to the viewer, Agnes dies in the toilet. Oskar plays his drum over his mother's grave, as the various ethnic and political groups are represented at the cemetery. Her German husband and her Polish lover mourn. The Nazi musician is prevented from playing his horn. As the Poles sing, the Jewish Sigismund Markus, who has been baptized, is first harassed by the Nazis but returns later to say a Hebrew prayer. At this point, the village idiot is also introduced. He was a former seminary student who has become mentally ill and is present in all the cemetery scenes. The funeral is climaxed by Oskar's narration that there once was a gullible people who believed in Santa Claus but that Santa Claus was the gasman in reality.

That gasman rears his ugliness on *Reichskristallnacht*. A synagogue is burning and Markus' store has "Jew" scribbled on its showcase window. Oskar enters the ransacked toy store and finds Markus slumped over his desk in the back. He has poisoned himself. Oskar's childhood and the political world merge in that scene. It is a sad but prophetic Oskar who states that there once was a toy dealer who took all the toys of this world away with him.

It is September 1, 1939, and the political confrontation becomes a military one at the Polish post office. Oskar and Jan Bronski arrive there just before the battle. Oskar is released unharmed but all the insurgents are eventually shot, including his "Uncle" Jan. Again, there is a cemetery scene, and it is the town idiot who knows the truth regarding the death of the men who had surrendered at the post office.

Hitler comes to Danzig and sixteen-year-old Maria comes to the

Matzerath household. Oskar at this point is also sixteen. Although he has not grown outwardly since his third birthday, he has obviously matured sexually. Maria, who smells of vanilla, becomes his first love. Alfred Matzerath, however, makes love to Maria also and she becomes pregnant. Another trinity is formed, and another child is born. Oskar considers the baby named Kurt to be his son and promises him a drum when he is three.

The midget Bebra, now wearing a uniform, is entertaining the troops. Oskar falls in love with the mind reader, Roswitha Raguna (Mariella Oliveri), also a midget, and joins the troupe. Oskar, too, wears a uniform and is presented as "Drummer and Glass Killer." The entertainers spend a night in a French castle as the Americans invade. Roswitha is killed as the Germans flee.

Oskar returns to Danzig just in time for Kurt's third birthday celebration. He presents him with the promised tin drum. The war is now coming to a close, and Danzig is under attack. Hitler's picture is removed and the picture of Beethoven, the genius, is back above the piano. The Matzeraths, along with several neighbors, seek shelter in their basement as the Russians enter the city. Alfred Matzerath desperately tries to hide his Nazi pin, which Oskar presses into his hand. In panic, Matzerath swallows it, only to choke and eventually be shot by one of the soldiers.

The war has ended, and Matzerath is buried in a coffin made of margarine crates. Standing over the open grave Oskar makes a decision. He throws his drum with the sticks into the grave and decides to grow. He is now twenty-one. Kurt, playing nearby, strikes Oskar on the head with a stone and causes him to fall into the grave. The town idiot suddenly appears, examines Oskar, and declares that Oskar, indeed, is growing.

The move to the West begins. Maria has packed up the baby buggy, which includes Oskar with bandages around his head. His grandmother confirms that Oskar, who had fallen down the basement stairs and stopped growing years ago, had recently fallen into a grave and started to grow again. Oskar's grandmother accompanies Maria and the two children to the railroad station and helps them onto the crowded train, but the old Kasubian woman, who describes herself as not Polish enough and not German enough, remains behind. The train moves slowly westward, leaving behind a potato field where an old woman is roasting potatoes.

The film ends with the westward migration. The action of the final third of Grass's novel, in which Oskar lives and works in West Germany and finally becomes an inmate of an insane asylum, is left out. As Schlöndorff says, this omitted section may provide the material for a sequel.

Schlöndorff found the ideal actor to portray Oskar. David Bennent, who was twelve years old at the time of the filming, had a medical condition that kept him at a height of 1.17 meters. His size, however, was only one of his assets. Bennent's large and probing eyes give Oskar that dimension of mischief and prophecy necessary for the role. Both his physical size and his expressive eyes were perfect to portray the stunted individual with a mature intellect and critical observation. He successfully portrays the unborn fetus as well as a twenty-one-year-old who could be mistaken for a three-year-old.

Schlöndorff, with the collaboration of Jean-Claude Carrière as well as Günter Grass, produced a film script based on a novel that he had at first considered impossible for film adaptation. The major part of the screenplay was written by Carrière, who could not read German, and who relied on Schlöndorff's instructions. The French was then translated back into German by Schlöndorff. Grass, who had retained final right of approval of the screenplay, also contributed to the dialogue in the film. After viewing the finished product, he said that he had forgotten all about his novel and saw only the film. Schlöndorff translated Grass's "mountain of words" into pictures, action, and emotion.

*Brigitte Pampel*

# TO FORGET VENICE (DIMENTICARE VENEZIA)

*Origin:* Italy
*Released:* 1979
*Released in U.S.:* 1979
*Production:* Ermanno Donati for Rizzoli Film-Action Film
*Direction:* Franco Brusati
*Screenplay:* Franco Brusati and Jaja Fiastri
*Cinematography:* Romano Albani
*Editing:* Ruggero Mastroianni
*Art direction:* Luigi Scaccianoce
*Music:* Benedetto Ghiglia
*MPAA rating:* no listing
*Running time:* 108 minutes

*Principal characters:*
Nicky/Nicky's father .............. Erland Josephson
Anna/Anna's mother ............ Mariangela Melato
Claudia .......................... Eleonora Giorgi
Picchio ......................... David Pontremoli
Marta .............................. Hella Petri
Rossino ......................... Fred Personne
Caterina ............................ Siria Betti

Franco Brusati's *To Forget Venice* won the coveted David Di Donatello Award for Best Italian Film of 1979, as well as a cluster of other Italian film prizes and a nomination for an Academy Award for Best Foreign-Language Film, but was subsequently dismissed by most Western critics. The reverse phenomenon had attended his only other film of the decade, *Pane e cioccolata* (1974; *Bread and Chocolate*), which first earned widespread popularity outside Italy before native audiences appreciated it. Ironically, there are several similarities in the films: Each has scenes of raucous comedy as well as intense drama; they share certain common themes (alienation and disconnection); and their characters are struggling against tremendous odds for survival. Their most radical differences are in style and structure. The earlier film is more conventional, a satire developed through essentially cinematic scenes and sequences, where *To Forget Venice* uses flashbacks and a more somber *mise en scène* investigating interior human landscapes. This film, with its somewhat Bergmanian sensibility and a Chekhovian plot, reveals Brusati's sensitivity to human suffering, expressed in a manner both poetic and theatrical, and in a tone that is always sympathetic.

The narrative of *To Forget Venice* weaves around the events of a brief summer reunion between Nicky (Erland Josephson), a middle-aged dealer in antique automobiles from Milan, and his elder sister, Marta (Hella Petri), a retired *prima donna*, at her country estate near Venice. Marta's ill health generates the film's central tensions as her imminent heart attack and death become the catalysts for radical change in the lives of those closest to her, and for whom she has served as surrogate mother, as an umbilical link to their childhood. Besides Nicky, who has arrived with his partner, chief mechanic, and lover, Picchio (David Pontremoli), it is Anna (Mariangela Melato), the niece of Marta's first husband, who runs the farm and resides in the villa with her childhood friend, now lover, Claudia (Eleonora Giorgi), who will be most profoundly affected by Marta's death.

Structurally, there are three major units, analogous to acts, through which the plot develops: Part 1 expositorily develops events of the afternoon and evening of Nicky's arrival, delineates relationships, establishes Marta's delicate health, and builds anticipation for the group's planned jaunt to Venice; part 2 details Marta's heart attack and its repercussions and climaxes with her death; part 3, an extended resolution, posits the characters facing new directions, new lives, uncertainty, and changed relationships with one another.

Brusati begins with a delicate, poetic, title sequence in which a group of children frolic with Claudia, their teacher, who is blindfolded and spinning, chasing them through the woods. As they return home, Claudia accidently sees a couple making love on the ground, partly hidden by bushes. She responds with a mixture of fear and curiosity. The brief, elegant sequence introduces at least three pivotal themes of the film: isolation, childhood, and sexual development. Brusati elaborates these in the next complicated sequence in which Anna is introduced. She is behaving petulantly and crudely responds to a flirtatious neighbor in the storage loft of the barn by hiking her skirts over her head and revealing her nakedness underneath, forcing him to retreat. His hurried exit marks a radical shift in the film's style; Brusati moves into a more novelistic, theatrical mode by staging the simultaneous entrance into the same space by Claudia, now seen as a little girl dressed in the gown and veil of First Communion. As she enters the loft, the camera dollies to reveal Anna present in the space in two incarnations, as both child and adult. This intricate filming and blocking bridges past with present, externalizes Anna's memories, and allows Brusati to dramatize the girls' early bonding, to accentuate their differences in personality—Claudia proudly demonstrates the dance steps she has learned in classes which her poor family can ill-afford to give her, while Anna is self-absorbed in hating her mother. Anna's hatred of both parents is externalized by her coaxing Claudia to join in pelting a photograph of her father and mother with darts and eggs. Brusati uses the end of this scene to underscore Anna's deep-seated rage as well as the imbalance in the relationship by having Claudia hug her desperately while Anna refuses to respond, sternly holding back and looking impatiently away.

Common themes and identical stylistic strategies characterize the next portion of the narrative, which introduces Nicky and Picchio. What begins conventionally as a scene involving Nicky and Picchio en route to Marta's house—they have stopped while Picchio joins briefly in a soccer game and Nicky polishes his vintage convertible—gradually develops into a merging of past and present, a manifestation of Nicky's memories as he first sees his childhood playmate Rossino, a young boy with red hair, dressed in a red cassock, then turns to recognize himself as a child running off the now empty game field. Nicky follows the boys into an old mill, watching and listening as Rossino makes explicit, vulgar comments on the pictures of nudes in paintings by Francisco de Goya and Giorgione, and then ridicules Nicky for having mistaken a Michelangelo figure for a woman (it possesses a penis). Brusati punctuates the moment with the metaphorical image of a broken tree branch moving outside the window. Sexual development in the two boys is further contrasted when Rossino sees a group of washerwomen bathing, rips off his cassock, and marches proudly from the building exhibiting his erection to the amused and annoyed women. Alone in the mill, Nicky undresses, covers himself with Rossino's torn cassock, and stands contemplating his image, reflected darkly in a mirror on the floor. Brusati shifts the narrative to the present by editing alternating close-shots of the adult Nicky with a long-shot of the room with Nicky's pictures scattered on the floor, to one of a dirty, abandoned floor into which a soccer ball suddenly rolls from outside. Nicky goes to find Picchio bloodied from the game; he washes his face with care and pride, then sits far removed from him and lights a cigarette. Here again, Brusati's thematic concerns are vividly portrayed.

Chief among the riches deriving from Brusati's application of these self-conscious flashbacks is the vivid character contrasts that surface as characters respond to themselves. Anna evidences little tolerance for her young self, appears to be disgusted by the child she was and has remained. Nicky, however, reacts affectionately to the narcissistic adolescent self whom he perceives. Historically, there are several earlier points of reference for this particular flashback strategy—notably in Federico Fellini's *Otto e mezzo* (1963; *8½*) and Woody Allen's *Annie Hall* (1977).

Throughout the ensuing scenes and sequences of part 2, Brusati adheres to conventional treatment of time and space. Nicky's arrival is sequenced in brief shots of ducks scurrying and squawking from under the fender of the automobile that is nudging them along the driveway; of Claudia calling for Anna; of the old dog barking and tugging at its rope; and of a woman's hands on the window ledge, in high-angle, as Nicky is seen leaping about with Anna and Claudia in the yard below. The woman's face remains outside the frame, her voice muttering that "magic" is about to happen as she sets to discarding medicine bottles and to applying makeup to her unseen face, items lifting and disappearing until her powder puff fills the shot with dust. The camera travels with her past a standing clock, its pendulum swinging, symbolically marking life's inescapable passing. Marta's face finally emerges in the next shot when she sweeps from the villa, greets Nicky, and causes Anna and Claudia anxiety because they mistake her coughing and choking sounds for a flare-up of her heart condition (she and Nicky have slipped and fallen to the floor while celebrating), although she is simply laughing hysterically with joy over Nicky's return. The last member of Marta's household to appear is Caterina (Siria Betti), the children's now senile nanny. While the others shower and dress for their evening of dining out (a sequence filmed with many visual symbols of "doubling" and edited to stress parallels between the two couples), Caterina sets the table with crystal and china for the supper that she will fail to prepare and which the others realize she soon will have forgotten.

Brusati brings part 2 to a climax in the next scenes at an outdoor café. A wedding party is under way as Marta's entourage arrives, filled with their own excitement, anticipating their trip to Venice the next morning. Flattered by an elderly waiter, Marta is inspired to entertain the crowd. Armed with a red carnation, she sings a few lines from Georges Bizet's opera *Carmen* (1875), then spoofs the tango in a delightful romp with Nicky. Her talents as an actress assist (just as the wig and makeup have camouflaged her age) in disguising the exhaustion caused by the impromptu performances. As night falls, the café's colored lights sparkle, and Nicky is confronted suddenly by what at first appears to be a ghost: The red-haired child, Rossino, is standing by a tree. Trailing him through the café, Nicky arrives at the wedding table where, rising to greet him, is the child's father—the adult Rossino (Fred Personne).

The rich texture of the scene further elaborates Brusati's earlier themes of sex (Rossino is still the sex-obsessed person whom Nicky remembers; Nicky later sees him forcing his wife to have sex standing against a bathroom sink at the restaurant); isolation (Nicky has nothing substantial to say to Rossino; he can only smile and nod at his remarks or correct him when he mistakes Marta for his mother); maturity and change (Rossino manifests outward signs of maturity—a wife and five children—but he is also ineffectual, mumbling platitudes to his pregnant daughter and to Nicky, whom he advises to forget Venice, to forget the past and live only in the present). The close of part 1 focuses on a simple action, a gesture which is resonant symbolically for Nicky's character in particular; it is a stylistic technique that Brusati employs again at the climactic piercing of Marta's heart in part 2, and again in part 3 with the smashing of the crystal ball. Here Rossino sends his son, who is possibly retarded, to deliver a gift, a flower from the bridal bouquet, to Nicky's table. After searching all the faces, the boy finally hands it to Picchio.

Marta's heart attack, precipitated by the excitement of leaving for Venice, provides the impetus to three additional flashbacks in the film's second major part. The first, showing Nicky as a boy, praying that his mother will live, is filmed and edited in a traditional filmic style. It is marked by an abstract *mise en scène*, a space that clearly represents Nicky's imagination, and unlike the film's other flashbacks, there is no evidence of the adult Nicky watching. Anna's "memory" is staged like the earlier flashbacks, with a character from the past entering into a space in the present, which in turn becomes the setting for a past experience. Additionally, Brusati repeats the theatrical casting of an actor in multiple roles (as with the boy Rossino) by having Melato portray Anna's mother as well as the adult Anna. This strategy is repeated in Nicky's next flashback when Josephson appears as Nicky's father.

Thematically, these two flashbacks contrast in striking ways. Anna's reaction to Marta's dying triggers a memory (which has a cold, searingly bitter edge to it) of her mother's faked suicide attempt. After hysterically locking herself in the bathroom and threatening to swallow pills, she eats soap instead and staggers to Anna, filling the air with bubbles. A shot of Anna's birthday cake is succeeded by a shot of a tea tray held by Claudia as she offers it to the adult Anna. Birthdays, parties, and Caterina's mention of Marta's crystal ball as she carries a rose to Marta's room are all elements that animate Nicky's memories of Marta's birthday party (probably her sixteenth) which Brusati stages using elaborate costumes of sparkling animal figures and photographs in the soft-focus of a magical fairyland. The adult Nicky enters the space, sits on the stairs, and watches his father, dressed in the robes and beard of a wizard, calling forth symbolic prophecies for Marta's future from his crystal ball. Her gifts are "beauty, wealth, and love." Then it is Nicky's turn to bestow a present. Emerging from his frog costume, little prince Nicky announces that he is giving her "everything" and hands her the crystal ball. After intercutting shots of her father with ones of Marta watching him adoringly from the stairs (the adult Nicky sits behind her), Brusati holds on her happy, youthful face, then dramatically cuts to a close-shot of her lifeless face on her deathbed. The second part ends as Nicky stands watching through the slightly opened doorway as the doctor punctures Marta's heart. Nicky gasps, and slams the door shut.

A door in the barn slams open, and Anna gasps. This doubling technique initiates the somewhat protracted resolution of the narrative in part 3, which dispenses with temporal and spatial disjunctions and allows characters to remain in their present situations, squarely facing the future, their ties with the past shredded if not entirely broken, their choices declared, and their first uncertain steps taken. Anna's two-day solitude, during which she is locked away in the barn, grieving, amid relics of her youth (a doll, her communion veil), is violated by Picchio's breaking in the door. Their scene together elaborates numerous themes already operating in the film, particularly that of sex. Anna again exposes herself (this time her breasts) and Picchio calls her childish. He counters her fears of him with gentle gestures, removing his clothes and encouraging her to trust him. She even puts her veil on his head and paints his cheeks and lips with wine. Significantly, Anna calls Picchio an "illusion" in Nicky's life, one easily provided by any attractive young man. In filming their final embrace, Brusati trains the camera below the table on the floor, framing them so that Anna falls down into the frame. This lowering, grounding of Anna marks a new vulnerability for her as expressed by her repeatedly sobbing to Picchio, "help me." Outside, the rain washes pebbles into a drain, pours off Nicky's car, and covers the estate with metaphorical tears.

The morning sunshine brings new direction, new beginnings to each of Brusati's characters. Caterina packs to go and live with her nephews, pausing to release her caged bird, which, unable to fly, falls to its death after she flings it from the upstairs window. Anna and Claudia will move into Nicky's flat in Milan, and Nicky tells Picchio to accompany them on the bus while he remains at the villa to put his own life in order; he is "tired of being young." The theme of change (maturity and growth) is dominant during the concluding sequence of the film, in which Brusati parallel-cuts shots of each character departing with shots of Nicky carrying a tray with his lunch and a book, Ludovico Ariosto's *Orlando furioso* into the garden. While Nicky eats, Claudia bids farewell to Caterina; Picchio and the local soccer players board the bus; and Anna and Claudia settle anxiously into their seats for the ride to Milan. The film's title and many of its themes are embedded in the symbol of the crystal ball which Nicky discovers accidently hidden in the undergrowth of the garden. He studies it, holds it forward, then drops it. Brusati films the ball rolling in slow motion; it traverses the downward slope of the yard and smashes into pieces against a tree. The Christoph Gluck aria accompanying this on the sound track abruptly stops and airplanes are heard (their sound occurred once before when Nicky and Picchio prayed together while Marta was dying). Two jets slice across the sky; Nicky watches two men ride by on bicycles; the old dog settles under a nearby tree; and Nicky picks up the book. As he turns, Brusati freezes the image of him in the garden, the villa behind him in the distance. This sustained, unchanging image synthesizes many of Brusati's central themes. Time is stopped; the past continues without development, without change, without life. Symbolic "doubling"—a motif apparent in Brusati's use of mirrors, of objects (a veil, twin beds, the crystal ball) in the *mise en scène*, of actors in multiple roles, and of the homosexuality of the two couples—reverberates in this closing moment. Interestingly, throughout Brusati treats sexuality in disturbing, even negative, imagery, both heterosexuality (the couple fornicating in hiding on the ground; the boy, Rossino, obsessed and exhibitionistic, even in adulthood; the possessive wife forcibly aroused and taken against the bathroom sink; the childish, pregnant bride; Nicky's childhood memories of a father alone, his mother absent, dying; Anna's despised, whorish mother and womanizing father, also in absentia) and homosexuality (Anna is miserable with the suffocating Claudia, and Nicky mainly appreciates Picchio's youth and athletic prowess). Brusati even presents Claudia as terrified and repulsed by her womanhood, symbolized by her monthly menstruation, as if to suggest that all sexuality is troublesome, unsatisfactory.

Produced when Brusati was in his mid-fifties, the film represents only his fifth directorial effort in commercial filmmaking, and as such it suggests aspirations in scope and dimension which far exceed his grasp. As both writer and director, Brusati overloaded his arsenal. This seems ironic in view of his considerable experience as a playwright and screenwriter (for Alberto Lattuada, Mario Monicelli, and Franco Zeffirelli) as well as his work assisting other directors (Renato Castellani, Mario Camerini, and Roberto Rossellini) since starting his career in theater and film in 1950, having earned his M.A. in political science. *To Forget Venice* is an intensely ambitious enterprise. It fascinates throughout, even achieves startling effects in numerous ways, yet it is ultimately both unconvincing and unsatisfying: Like a banquet whose tables are so overladen with delights, it leaves one bewildered and hungry. Its central weakness is its diffused focus between two major characters, Nicky and Anna, obscuring each where clarity is essential. If Brusati intended them to be perceived finally as a single entity, a kind of male/female duality, he does not substantially develop this intention. Additionally, the sheer weight and number of themes disturbs the film's balance. Nevertheless, it is an engaging exercise, noteworthy for Brusati's sensitive attention to visual detail, for his ability to elicit affecting performances (although casting Josephson, an actor primarily known for his films with Ingmar Bergman, may subvert rather than enhance the film's intentions), and for its blending of both comic and dramatic elements.

*Paul Trent*

# TOKYO STORY (TOKYO MONOGATARI)

*Origin:* Japan
*Released:* 1953
*Released in U.S.:* 1967
*Production:* Shochiku/Ofuna
*Direction:* Yasujiro Ozu
*Screenplay:* Yasujiro Ozu and Kogo Noda
*Cinematography:* Yuharu Atsuta
*Editing:* Yasujiro Ozu
*Art direction:* no listing
*Music:* Takanobu Saito
*Running time:* 139 minutes

*Principal characters:*
Shukichi Hirayama .................... Chishu Ryu
Tomi Hirayama ............... Chieko Higashiyama
Koichi ............................ So Yamamura
Shige.......................... Haruko Sugimura
Noriko ............................ Setsuko Hara
Kyoko ........................... Kyoko Kagawa

Nothing is more characteristic of Yasujiro Ozu's work than the understatement and obliquity of the scenes in *Tokyo Story*. Restraint becomes a virtue in itself. The plot of the film is easily told: An elderly, provincial couple, Tomi Hirayama (Chieko Higashiyama) and her husband, Shukichi Hirayama (Chishu Ryu), from the small town of Onomichi, make a pilgrimage to Tokyo to visit their grown children and their young grandchildren. The grandparents are simple, unworldly folk, with little experience traveling and the trip to the big city is a rare and potentially bewildering one for them. When they arrive in Tokyo, what they discover, not surprisingly, is that however important the trip may be for them, their children and grandchildren really do not have much interest in them or much time for them. They are too busy leading their own lives, with their own interests and their own circle of friends, and making ends meet financially. Ironically, the one young person who seems to care about them most affectionately, and who takes time to show them the sights of Tokyo, is not a blood relative at all, but the lonely, widowed wife of a son who died several years before. After spending a few days in Tokyo and another day at the resort town of Atami (where the children send them to be temporarily rid of them), Tomi and Shukichi head back to Onomichi, where the grandmother suddenly falls sick and dies. Thus, in the final scenes of the film, the busy, inconsiderate children from Tokyo gather together in Onomichi for the funeral rites and then depart, one by one, leaving the father alone at the end.

It is the simplest possible parable of human isolation, loneliness, and self-centeredness. The sheer simplicity of this story of children too busy with life to make time to love their parents before it is too late is what makes it one of the saddest and most touching of all Ozu's films. Yet what is most interesting about it is how sentiments such as these, about the essential isolation, solitude, and loneliness of the human condition, are, with one notable exception, never given direct utterance in the film. The grandparents go through the saddest and most pathetic recognition of their irrelevance to their children's lives, and yet at no point in *Tokyo Story* do they even articulate that recognition, much less bemoan the ingratitude or failure to love of their children.

Yet the reason such sentiments are studiously kept out of the mouths of the deeply wounded grandmother or grandfather in *Tokyo Story* is not merely Ozu's dislike for the platitudinous or sentimental remark. William Butler Yeats wrote: "Hamlet and Lear are gay. . . . They do not break up their lines to weep," and as much as one may disagree with the first clause of that formulation, the second contains a profound truth, without which the works of both William Shakespeare and Ozu are incomprehensible. Both men were infinitely more interested in trying to make something out of the inevitable sadnesses, confusions, and failures of life than in merely expressing the existence of those sadnesses, confusions, and failures. To paraphrase a phrase by Robert Frost, the genius of Ozu's work is not at all embodied in some recognition of the poverty or difficulty or diminishment of life, but in the effort that both Ozu and his characters exert of "what to make (artistically, socially, and personally) of a diminished thing."

For Ozu, as for Frost, Yeats, and Shakespeare, style (both personal and artistic) is what one makes of one's diminishments, one's sadnesses and impoverishments, and to "break up one's lines to weep," would be to abandon the faith that something, somehow, can be made of all that suffering, something that may even make it all worthwhile, or at least bearable. Where Ozu profoundly differs from these Western artists, who worked within a common Renaissance tradition in which stylistic bravado is the response to loss, is in offering the opposite of Lear's or Hamlet's (or Frost's or Yeats's) stylistic swagger as an adequate response. While Yeats, Frost, and Shakespeare (and the entire Western tradition) offer the "gaiety of language" and the delightful, playful complexities of expression as a response to their plight, Ozu holds up an opposite ideal of restraint, self-control, and resignation tantamount to stoicism. While the entire Western artistic tradition is, in some sense, devoted to the cultivation of an enriched personal consciousness (which is given dramatic outlet in an enriched personal expression), Ozu's work is dedicated to the opposite ideal of a stilled consciousness and a silenced expression.

Characters undergoing the greatest personal tragedy and the deepest disappointment express their feelings only at the rarest moments, and even these infrequent expressions of their feelings can only be understood, from Ozu's point of view, as moments of failure. One must find a style of inexpressiveness, a style of absolute restraint and self-composure with which to perform one's sadness or frustration. Not to do so is to be inadequate and immature. Confronted with their grandparents' imminent arrival, one of their grandchildren, whose desk has been moved to make space for them in the house, throws a temper tantrum. A little later in the film, the same child goes into another fit of petulance when a Sunday outing with the grandparents is frustrated. Such direct expressiveness of one's emotions is the property of children.

It is with this in mind that one must approach the scene near the end of the film in which the good, widowed daughter-in-law, Noriko (Setsuko Hara), talks with the daughter, Kyoto (Kyoko Kagawa), who lives at home with the grandfather. While all the other children only tried to get rid of the grandparents on their visit to Tokyo, Noriko has been the one to make time for them, to take them around the city, and she has been generous enough to share with them her cakes and wine. She is also the one most profoundly affected by the grandmother's death, and the one most hurt and disappointed by the apparent indifference of the other children. Alone with Kyoko after the funeral rites are over, she agrees when Kyoko says: "Isn't life disappointing?" by adding, "Yes, it is." If one is looking for a summary statement to take away from *Tokyo Story* (and almost all the essays written about the film have been looking), then this is, undeniably, the closest any conversation comes to summarizing the theme of the film. The grandmother and the grandfather make no remarks of this sort at all. What needs emphasizing, however, is that the response of these two young women, expressing their deepest feelings this way—this direct expression of feeling and consciousness (one almost every viewer wants to take away from the film as its point or moral)—is, from Ozu's point of view, inadequate and immature. That is to say, with this remark in the world of this film, the two girls inadvertently show themselves to be closer to the petulant children of the beginning than to the silent, serene grandfather of the end.

To agree with the girls, or even to take their statements as representing Ozu's reading of his own film, would be to prefer those who break up their lines to weep over those who do not, and Ozu's absolutely placid cinematic style, even at the moments of greatest agitation in this film tells the viewer where he stands on this. Yet he does, in the position of the crucial figure of Noriko in the film, acknowledge how very difficult it is to get beyond tears, pathos, and sadness to the calmness of acceptance that the grandfather or he, as a director, shows. The final minutes of *Tokyo Story* alternate uneasily between shots of the infinitely serene grandfather and shots of the agitated women who are unable to get beyond their emotions of grief and resentment (Noriko on the train headed back to Tokyo and Kyoko listening to the sound of the train whistle in the distance outside the schoolroom in which she teaches). Ozu's extraordinary cinematic achievement in these final moments is his demonstration that, even while honoring and respecting the women's sadness, he has stylistically moved beyond tears and moans and sadness himself, to the grandfather's infinite resignation and gentle serenity about life's essential and unavoidable tragedy. For that, audiences can be grateful, since, if Ozu himself had broken up his lines or shots to weep, they would have been denied this clear, placid masterpiece of infinite resignation and utter tragic acceptance.

*Raymond Carney*

# EL TOPO

*Origin:* Mexico
*Released:* 1971
*Released in U.S.:* 1971
*Production:* Roberto Viskin for ABKCO Films and Producciones Panic
*Direction:* Alexandro Jodorowsky
*Screenplay:* Alexandro Jodorowsky
*Cinematography:* Rafael Corkidi
*Editing:* Federico Landeros
*Art direction:* Alexandro Jodorowsky
*Music direction:* Nacho Mendez
*Music:* Alexandro Jodorowsky
*MPAA rating:* no listing
*Running time:* 123 minutes

*Principal characters:*

El Topo .................... Alexandro Jodorowsky
Brontis as a child .............. Brontis Jodorowsky
Woman in black ...................... Paula Romo
Mara ............................ Mara Lorenzio
Colonel ............................ David Silva
Brontis as an adult .................. Robert John
First master ......... Hector "El Barrado" Martínez
Second master .................. Juan José Gurrola
Third master ...................... Victor Fosada
Fourth master...................... Agustín Isunza
Dwarf ........................... Jacqueline Luis
Woman ..................... Graciela Covarrubias

A cult favorite at art-house midnight shows long before its official American debut, *El Topo* is a surreal, complex, and often perplexing pantheistic allegory in the guise of a phantasmagoric "spaghetti" Western. Director Alexandro Jodorowsky, of Chilean and Russian descent, borrows a number of images, epigrams, symbols, mythic characters, and dramatic themes from cosmology, Christianity, Judaism, Egyptology, medieval alchemy, Taoism, and Hinduism, among others, to create this violent, Felliniesque tale of religious rites of passage, barbarism, and spiritual rebirth.

With a story divided into sections titled, "Genesis," "Prophets," "Psalms," and "Apocalypse," *El Topo* opens with the black-bearded and black-clad title character riding horseback across the desert with his naked, seven-year-old son, Brontis (Brontis Jodorowsky). After a narrator's voice describes how the mole ("el topo") tunnels up through the ground in quest of the sun (and is always blinded by the sight of it), El Topo (Alexandro Jodorowsky) instructs his son to bury his first toy and a picture of his dead mother in the sand. Continuing their journey, the two enter a village that has been recently pillaged. Disemboweled animals, mutilated bodies, and pools of streaming blood form the basis of the tableau. The arrival of El Topo is noticed by four bandits who are counting their loot upon a nearby mountaintop. When they ride down to greet the dark stranger, El Topo demands the whereabouts of the warlord responsible for the massacre, and kills each of the bandits while getting the information.

At a nearby Franciscan mission, El Topo observes more bandits. They desecrate religious items, torture monks, and murder captive townsfolk. The festivities cease, however, upon the appearance of the colonel (David Silva)—a fat, vain bandit warlord who bears more than a passing resemblance to General Francisco Franco. The colonel offers his beautiful mistress, Mara (Mara Lorenzio), to the sex-starved bandits, which prompts El Topo to announce himself and gun down the outlaws. He spares the colonel's life, however, merely castrating him. El Topo takes Mara for his own and turns Brontis over to the monks—a turn of events which the boy accepts quite passively. Once again in the desert, El Topo performs miracles: digging turtle eggs from the sand and drawing water from a rock split with a pistol shot, to provide Mara with food and drink. When he professes his love for her, she spurns him, saying that he must prove himself as a master gunfighter by eliminating the four master gunfighters who rule the circular desert.

The first master (Hector "El Barrado" Martínez) they encounter on their inwardly spiraling journey is a bullet-scarred man living within an octagonal tower. He is protected by a double man, a legless man astride the shoulders of a man with no arms. A duel is arranged for the following day, and Mara talks the reluctant El Topo into using trickery to succeed. At the appointed time, a mysterious lesbian (Paula Romo) dressed in black appears. She watches as the first master drops into a hole secretly dug during the previous night; El Topo dispatches the first master with a single shot to the head. Ashamed of himself, El Topo drops his gun and Mara has to finish off the double man. The woman in black asks to join the travelers and offers to lead them to the second master. She gives a mirror to Mara, and El Topo becomes so irritated with Mara's constant preening that he shoots it and puts some of the shards in his pocket.

They find the second master (Juan José Gurrola) camped in a ravine with his elderly mother. Before agreeing to a duel, the master challenges El Topo to tests of Zen awareness and marksmanship. El Topo finally concedes defeat but uses the mirror shards to cut the feet of the mother, distracting the master's attention and allowing El Topo to kill him. Prior to his departure, El Topo puts a copper ashtray in his pocket.

The third master (Victor Fosada) is a dark Mexican Indian who is tending hundreds of rabbits. Immediately upon El Topo's approach, the rabbits start to die. The master tells El Topo that their death is caused by the evil harbored by the inferior gunfighter. The two face off for their duel, and the third master's draw is quicker; he sends a bullet aimed directly for El Topo's heart. El Topo is saved by the copper ashtray, and he shoots his opponent in the heart himself, killing him.

The fourth master (Agustín Isunza) is a thin old man clad in a loincloth and armed with a butterfly net that he uses to catch and return El Topo's bullets. Admitting defeat, El Topo surrenders his gun. To prove the futility of El Topo's despair over failing to kill him, the fourth master turns the pistol on himself and commits suicide. This final irony is too much for El Topo, and he retraces his journey, all the while cursing God for his fate and his pointless existence. Deciding that flinging himself from a suspension bridge is his only logical recourse, El Topo is stopped by the challenge of a final gunfight with the woman in black. He refuses, and she fires upon him, piercing his hands, feet, and lower abdomen in a pattern of Christ-like stigmata. Mara and the woman depart, leaving El Topo for dead. A band of cripples, pinheads, and other freaks happen upon his body and carry him away on a stretcher.

When El Topo regains "consciousness," he is twenty years older, and his hair and beard have turned totally white. His new home is a huge mountain grotto, inhabited by cripples and mutants, the imprisoned offspring of the incestuous townsfolk living near the mountain. El Topo's final act of penance is to shave his beard and head and don a monk's robe. With a female dwarf (Jacqueline Luis) as his companion, he escapes from the mountain cave and sets out to earn enough money to finance a tunnel in order to free the prisoners. Riding into the infamous mountainside town, El Topo and the dwarf woman are greeted by scenes of absolute decadence: public sex, parading transvestites, slavery, murder, and violence. Their arrival is treated as a joyous event, and El Topo acts the part of the imbecilic buffoon. After performing a dumb-show routine in which the dwarf woman climbs a stepladder to exchange affections, El Topo passes his hat among the crowd for a collection.

Their income assured, El Topo and his companion begin to dig the tunnel, using their earnings to buy dynamite. The appetites of audiences can be very fickle, and soon the dwarf woman and El Topo are forced to have sex in public view. Ashamed, El Topo escorts the dwarf woman to the church to marry her. To his surprise, he finds that the monk at the altar is his own son, Brontis. Brontis' first impulse is to draw his gun to kill his father, but the dwarf woman intercedes, explaining that El Topo has an important job to complete. Brontis reluctantly agrees to stay the execution until the tunnel is completed, even helping them to dig and blast.

As the work progresses, the dwarf shows evidence of being with child; her labor pains commence at the moment that they break through to the mountain's grotto prison. Brontis draws his gun and prepares to kill his father, however, he finds himself incapable of pulling the trigger. A torrent of freakish humanity streams from the tunnel and down into the town. The people in the community are waiting, and they gun down every one of the liberated inhabitants escaping from the mountain. Furious, El Topo takes up guns and dynamite and retaliates, killing or driving off the entire population of the town. His revenge complete, El Topo pours the contents of a kerosene lamp over his head and sets himself on fire. Brontis sees to the burial of El Topo's remains, and, with the dwarf woman and her newborn son, rides away on horseback.

Immediate critical reaction to *El Topo* drew comparisons between Jodorowsky's vision of evil and barbarism and the villainy within Luis Buñuel's *L'Âge d'or* (1930; *The Age of Gold*). When stylistic, cinematic, or narrative comparisons are made, the work of Federico Fellini, Sam Peckinpah, or Sergio Leone are often mentioned. Stripped of its gore, violence, religious imagery, freak-show casting, and agoraphobic landscapes, *El Topo* is a routinely religious allegory in which a man succumbs to his barbarity in order to discover Christian humanism. The muddle of religious and mythic imagery camouflaging this simple premise is the basis for much of the complaint that *El Topo* is a pretentious, philosophically confused bouillabaisse served hot and steamy for the indiscriminate palates of the same filmgoers who turned *Easy Rider* (1969) into a popular phenomenon. Jodorowsky, a onetime student of French mime Marcel Marceau, had one directorial credit prior to *El Topo*, the equally avant-garde *Fando y Lis* (1967). While editing *The Last Movie* (1971), director Dennis Hopper reportedly watched *El Topo* and drew upon it for inspiration. A subsequent film, *La montaña sacra* (1973; *The Sacred Mountain*), repeats Jodorowsky's nightmarish vision as a monk makes a pilgrimage to the sacred mountain where he will find eternal life. It is an even more extreme exercise in the pathos of irrationality.

*Tim Kennedy*

# TORMENT (HETS)

*Origin:* Sweden
*Released:* 1944
*Released in U.S.:* 1947
*Production:* Svensk Filmindustri
*Direction:* Alf Sjöberg
*Assistant direction:* Ingmar Bergman
*Screenplay:* Ingmar Bergman
*Cinematography:* Martin Bodin
*Editing:* Oscar Rosander
*Art direction:* Arne Akermark
*Music:* Hilding Rosenberg
*Running time:* 95 minutes
*Also known as: Frenzy*

*Principal characters:*

Caligula .............................. Stig Järrel
Jan-Erik Widgren ...................... Alf Kjellin
Bertha Olsson ........................ Mai Zetterling
Pippi ............................ Gösta Cederlund
Headmaster ..................... Olof Winnerstrand
Sandman ............................. Stig Olin
Pettersson ......................... Jan Molander
Teacher ...................... Gunnar Björnstrand
Jan-Erik's classmates .......... Curt Edgard, Anders Nyström, Birger Malmsten

One measure of the importance of *Torment* is its prominence in a pivotal chapter of Sweden's cinematic history. Far out of proportion to the country's small population, Sweden has been a major force in the world of film during the twentieth century's first decades, but a series of complex artistic and financial crises in the 1920's led to an exodus of its most creative artists. When the advent of sound undermined the foreign market for its silent films, this export of its talent accelerated, and the glories of the Mauritz Stiller-Victor Sjöström period faded quickly; Swedish film in the 1930's became formulaic in its brittle imitation of Hollywood and in its reliance on subjects with provincial appeal. Two factors led to a reversal of this decline: World War II, which stimulated the entertainment business generally while sheltering domestic films from foreign competition, and the reinvigoration of Svensk Filmindustri by a new executive head, Carl Anders Dymling, who welcomed the repatriated members of the older generation and sought out promising newcomers to learn from their experience. Although no renaissance was immediately evident in the early 1940's, the superior quality of a few films raised hopes of such an event. Whether, in retrospect, *Torment* was artistically the most distinguished among this small group is open to dispute, but it clearly had the greatest impact.

In a poll of Swedish critics, it received five awards—for Best Film, Best Director, Best Screenplay, Best Cinematography, and Best Actor (Stig Järrel); more valuable to an industry sensitive to foreign esteem, it also enjoyed an encouraging, modest success abroad. The most consequential judgment, however, was the reaction of a Swedish public which not only filled the theaters but also found a cause in the film's indictment of an authoritarian school system. Given the nation's political current during the following generation, the eventual reform in the schools was inevitable; even so, the emotion generated by *Torment* and the furor it stirred in the press helped prepare the way. This demonstration of the screen's potency as a weapon for protest also foretold the course that Swedish film would pursue through the present day. Although a reflection of reformist allegiances was already discernible in the silent era, in the postwar decades, the use of the medium to promote the social attitudes of the Left has become a preoccupation.

*Torment* acquires a quite different aspect if one addresses it as an auteurist. Cinematically Sweden's most gifted director between the heyday of Stiller and Sjöström and the international breakthrough of Ingmar Bergman, Alf Sjöberg made his debut in 1929 with *Den starkaste* (*The Strongest*), an extraordinary depiction of man's struggle within and against nature that had been a hallmark of early Swedish film. Unfortunately, however, this last product of the silent era slipped from attention in the excitement over the arrival of sound, and Sjöberg, remanded to the theater for the next decade, did not return to the film studio until 1939. His second film, *Med livet som insats* (1940; *They Staked Their Lives*), confirmed the promise of the first, and although he faltered in his next two films, his screen translation in 1942 of the celebrated folk drama *Himlaspelet* (*The Road to Heaven*) was a masterpiece. Even so, it was *Torment* that established his preeminence among the nation's film directors in the 1940's.

Stylistically, Sjöberg was no innovator, but if his eclecticism separates him from the truly great, his virtuosity in applying the techniques of others qualifies him for the next rank. More than any of his Swedish contemporaries, he opened himself to international influences, and *Torment* displays the full array of lessons he learned from his masters. The film's first "act"—in which Sjöberg exploits the magisterial interior architecture to imply oppression in the initial sequences and then, during the following scene, brilliantly orchestrates a relentless heightening of the tyranny in the classroom—bears the Russian stamp of Sergei Eisenstein and Vsevolod Pudovkin; the subsequent romantic complication reveals an indebtedness to the French cinema of Marcel Carné; the infusions of psychological terror suggest the German sources of F. W. Murnau and Fritz Lang. Remarkably, Sjöberg joins these diverse styles without having the seams show.

Yet it is not only through his strategy with the camera that Sjöberg makes *Torment* his film; as director, he also reoriented the screenplay by shifting its center from the young lovers to Caligula (Stig Järrel), the villainous Latin teacher, and by supplying the character with a political reference that had no basis in the original story. Because of German pressure on the Swedish motion-picture industry to avoid subjects relating to the war or reflecting unfavorably on the Third Reich, filmmakers disguised their anti-Nazism only enough to keep within the bounds of tolerance. Thus, in *They Staked Their Lives*, Sjöberg used a fictitious Baltic state to portray the ugliness of totalitarianism, and in *Kungajakt* (1943; *The Royal Hunt*), he selected an episode from eighteenth century Swedish history to serve as a parable about the current threat posed by Germany. In *Torment*, however, almost all pretense falls away. In appearance and manner, Caligula is a copy of Heinrich Himmler. Even the newspaper he reads (*Dagsposten*, the country's sole Nazi daily) points toward the identification. Although this superimposition on the script results in a muddling of the story's statement, the association of the teacher's psychopathic personality with Nazi sadism not only heightened the emotional impact on wartime audiences but also imbued the character with an evil energy that continues to affect viewers too young to recognize the allusion.

Curiously, despite the dominance of Sjöberg's fashioning hand, the film now tends to be credited almost entirely to its young screenwriter. Ingmar Bergman had been hired for the script department at Svensk Filmindustri two years earlier, after Dymling read admiring reviews of a student production of his first play. (At the time, Bergman's commitment to a career in writing and directing for the theater made him reluctant to take Svensk Filmindustri's offer, but as a newly married man suddenly faced with the additional expenses of parenthood, he found the money too tempting to refuse.) Had *Torment*, the first of his scripts to be accepted, been assigned to any director other than Sjöberg, the film almost certainly would have stirred little excitement; as it was, its financial and artistic success forced the industry to take note of Bergman as the voice of a new generation—a recognition he quickly used to lever himself into the corps of directors at Svensk Filmindustri.

Bergmanophiles searching his 1940's work for hints of his future prominence would find his plays for the stage far more productive than his filmscripts: Although his theatrical writing is often derivative and flawed by sententiousness, it clearly represents a higher magnitude of ambition. Nevertheless, films of this period furnish some telling clues to Bergman's perennial preoccupations before he was able fully to transform them into the stuff of art. None of these early efforts is more revealing than *Torment*, which expressed the formula that he would repeat for the rest of the decade.

To Bergman, the film revolved around neither the exposé of the schools which roused the audience's anger nor the devices of the thriller skewed by Sjöberg to make an anti-Nazi statement, but around the rebellion of a patently autobiographical middle-class youth against an unsympathetic, unjust society. Jan-Erik (Alf Kjellin) appears in the opening segment as a good student who seems certain to pass his university matriculation examination despite the petty tyranny of the Latin teacher. Yet one night he encounters Bertha (Mai Zetterling), the girl from the cigarette shop near the school, who has been drinking heavily to escape her fear of a shadowy tormentor; after he conducts her to her flat, they become lovers. The strain of preparing for the examinations while carrying on an affair with Bertha soon causes him to receive an academic demerit from Caligula, which in turn subjects him to upbraiding by his parents. Nightmarishly, the assumptions on which Jan-Erik had based his expectations of a comfortable future are quickly evaporating; as though he were falling through reality, the student lapses into a fever.

Shortly thereafter, Jan-Erik goes to Bertha's room, where he finds her dead and Caligula, babbling incoherently, hiding in the hall closet. Suddenly realizing that it was the Latin teacher who had been terrorizing her, the student reports the "murderer" to the police, but when an autopsy finds that she died of heart failure precipitated by alcohol abuse, Caligula is released. Subsequently, in a confrontation before the school's headmaster (Olof Winnerstrand), the teacher twists the facts to make it seem that he was at the girl's flat only to investigate the reasons for his student's bad behavior. The lie is so outrageous that Jan-Erik, unable to muster an effective defense, assaults Caligula—and thus ensures his own expulsion from school. On graduation day, the tormentor stands in his honored place among the faculty, but when he meets Jan-Erik in Bertha's flat, it is the young man who enjoys the final triumph: While Caligula, like a trapped, cringing child, pathetically beseeches his victim to turn on the light in the dark building, Jan-Erik strides manfully into the bright sunshine of the summer day.

In its plot and characters, Bergman's story reflects the clichés of pulp fiction. That Caligula should turn out to be Bertha's nemesis does not, in itself, exceed credibility, but that Bertha should not divulge his identity lacks motivation and seems designed for melodramatic effect; similarly, the figure of the cowering teacher pleading for the light to be turned on at the conclusion does not accord with his previous image as a specter skulking in the shadows. Even more strongly indicative of Bergman's callowness at this point in his career is the failure to expand a psychological complexity of his characters and to discover the drama within their relationships. Bertha is a stereotypical fallen woman of pure heart, and Jan-Erik is a conventional middle-class youth undergoing an initiatory experience; their mutual attraction lies at the heart of the story Bergman is trying to tell, and yet the bond that presumably unites them is never felt by the audience—not even at the level of animal eroticism. Given the film's focus on adolescent rebellion, one would expect the inability of Jan-Erik's parents to understand their son's turmoil to be a central dramatic element, but the cardboard cutouts Bergman presents are incapable of generating a tension between opposing values. Most flawed of all is the portrait of Caligula as, by turns, an incarnation of evil and a pitiable psychotic; the vacillation bespeaks an author unsteady in his purpose, not an ambiguity that drives the story's argument.

Yet if the *Sturm und Drang* lathering the script's surface is far removed from the hellish interiors in which the later Bergman films are set, *Torment* nevertheless introduces several of the motifs that persist in his more sophisticated works. Bergman has often expressed his belief that society and all its institutions (including religion) are built upon humiliation. That tenet, evident in such diverse works as *Det sjunde inseglet* (1956; *The Seventh Seal*), *Ansiktet* (1958; *The Magician*), *Vargtimmen* (1968; *Hour of the Wolf*), *Skammen* (1968; *Shame*), *Riten* (1969; *The Rite*), *Ormens ägg* (1977; *The Serpent's Egg*), and *Aus dem leben der marionetten* (*From the Life of the Marionettes*), operates here in two crucial respects: Jan-Erik's oppression by a social authority that cannot overcome the malignity within it, and the curious bondage in which Caligula holds Bertha. Closely related to Bergman's notions about humiliation is his lifelong enmity toward his father, expressed in terms of either a quarrel with God, as in *Nattvardsgästerna* (1962; *Winter Light*), or, as in *Torment*, of a contest between a son and a father figure for the affections of a mother or mother surrogate. (A shot, unfortunately missing from some prints circulated in the United States, graphically illustrates the Oedipal struggle that underlies the story: During Jan-Erik's febrile hallucinations, his father and mother appear to him as Caligula and Bertha.) Another aspect of the same conflict, which also recurs as a theme throughout Bergman's later films, surfaces in the misogyny of Sandman, Jan-Erik's Nietzschean friend who only functions in the story as the protagonist's alter ego.

Least apparent of these foreshadowings, yet no less central to Bergman's creative imagination, is the presentation of Bertha's flat as a refuge from a hostile world. Critics, in noting that island settings begin to dominate his films in the 1960's, have assumed that they symbolize an intellectual and emotional withdrawal from society which occurred at that stage of his life; in fact, however, the trope is already well rooted in his earliest screenplays. Like the "secret" rooms in director Gustaf Molander's *Kvinna utan ansikte* (1947; *Woman Without a Face*), like Bergman's *Fängelse* (1948; *The Devil's Wanton*), *Sommarlek* (1951; *Summer Interlude*), and *Sommarnattens leende* (1955; *Smiles of a Summer Night*)—and like the nursery to which Karin retreats in *Såsom i en spegel* (1961; *Through a Glass Darkly*)—the lovers' sanctuary is figuratively an island on which the illusions of childhood enjoy a short reprieve before being engulfed by life's cruel realities. In that respect, *Torment* is the paradigm from which all the rest of Bergman's writings develop.

*Frank Gado*

# A TOUCH OF ZEN
# (HSIA NU)

*Origin:* Taiwan
*Released:* 1969
*Released in U.S.:* 1976
*Production:* Sha Jung-Feng for International Film
*Direction:* King Hu
*Screenplay:* King Hu; based on the story "The Magnanimous Girl," by P'u Sung-Ling
*Cinematography:* Hua Hui-Ying and Chou Yeh-Hsing
*Editing:* King Hu
*Art direction:* King Hu
*Choreography:* Han Ying-Chien
*Music:* Wu Ta-Chiang
*MPAA rating:* no listing
*Running time:* 178 minutes

*Principal characters:*
Yang Hui-Chen ........................ Hsu Feng
Ku Sheng-Chai ........................ Shih Chun
Shih ................................. Pai Ying
Lu ................................... Hseuh Han
Hui Yuan ............................. Roy Chiao
Ku's mother .......................... Chang Ping-Yu
Ou-Yang Nin .......................... Tien Peng
Hsu Hsien-Chun ....................... Han Ying-Chien

While Bruce Lee popularized the martial arts in exploitation films in the West, King Hu established the genre as a major art form with films such as *Lung-men k'o chan* (1966; *Dragon Gate Inn*) and *Ying-ch'un ko chih feng-po* (1973; *The Fate of Lee Khan*). *A Touch of Zen*, Hu's three-hour classic, took two years to make and a further six to establish itself. Begun in 1966, it was completed in 1968 and first shown in a mutilated shortened version in Southeast Asia a year later. It was a failure. Then, in 1975, Hu released the original version of the film, which attracted public attention at the Cannes International Film Festival, winning the Grand Prix.

*A Touch of Zen* is a lyric mixture of personal, political, and religious philosophies, placed firmly within a martial arts context. Moving from a love story to a traditional ghost tale, through the corrupt politics of the court to a triumph of Zen Buddhism coupled with the overthrow of tyranny, the film operates on several levels, deepening its conception of the world as it passes along its various narrative phases.

The striking beauty of many of the compositions in the film may arise from Hu's own training as a painter and designer. He entered the film industry in 1950 as a set designer but soon moved on, acting, scriptwriting, and producing radio programs before directing his first film for the prolific Shaw Brothers in 1962. A few years later, he joined the newly formed Union Film Company in Taiwan, attracting new talent and ideas to join the studio. *A Touch of Zen*, starring Hsu Feng and Pai Ying, two of the actors trained at that studio, was made there, but the producers' subsequent mercenary manipulation of the film and use of Hu's name to sell others caused a rift, and Hu left to form his own independent production company.

*A Touch of Zen* intertwines three main themes. The first, based on a short story, "The Magnanimous Girl," in the collection *Strange Stories from a Chinese Studio*, by the Ming Dynasty writer P'u Sung-Ling, is essentially a love story, centering on the poor artist Ku and the more sophisticated stranger Yang.

Hu has a considerable knowledge of Chinese history and literature and chose to set this story during the Ming Dynasty in the seventeenth century. "It is a particularly controversial period, both in China and among overseas Sinologists. It was on the one hand the period when Western influences first reached China; on the other, it was one of the most corrupt periods in Chinese politics," he explained in an interview with Tony Rayns for *Sight and Sound*.

The second theme of the film is a more political one, bringing in the dictatorial power of the Eastern group, a secret service organized and maintained by the court eunuchs. The group had the sort of rule more usually associated in modern times with the reign of the Gestapo or the KGB. In the above-quoted interview, Hu elaborates his reasons for incorporating this subject into *A Touch of Zen*. "At the time, the James Bond movies were very popular and I thought it very wrong to make a hero of a secret service man. My films were a kind of comment on this."

From politics to spiritualism, the film moves on to its third and final phase, when the high priest Hui Yuan enters the intricate plot. Hu has stated that he is not a Buddhist and that the final victory of Hui's side is more an affirmation of traditional Chinese culture than a religious statement. Hu is not making a film that expounds Zen philosophy, but rather giving his audience a "touch" of one of the East's most pervasive philosophies.

The narrative of *A Touch of Zen* mirrors its intellectual development and falls into three main sections. The first part is set in a small village in the region of Shanhsi in northern China. Ku Sheng-Chai (Shih Chun), a young scholar, earns a meager living painting portraits. His mother (Chang Ping-Yu) continually nags him to concentrate on furthering his career and finding a girl to marry. When Yang Hui-Chen (Hsu Feng) arrives in town, camping out in a supposedly haunted fort, Ku is interested and woos her. She rejects his proposal of marriage, but one night, after a violent attack by another stranger, Ou-Yang Nin (Tien Peng), she offers herself to Ku.

Hu has consciously built into this section of the film a gradually increasing sense of unease. The unexplained arrival of Yang at the same time as that of two other shadowy figures—Shih (Pai Ying), a blind beggar, and the herbalist Lu (Hseuh Han)—adds to the sense of mystery, and glimpses of covert meetings in narrow alleyways hint at a hidden conspiracy of which Ku is unaware. It is as if Ku has tangentially contacted another, more ephemeral world, echoed by the rumors of ghosts in Yang's ruined retreat.

The forlorn beauty of the fort was carefully created by Hu, taking both time and money to achieve the desired effect. It took some nine months to erect the edifice of crumbling stone and establish its abandoned look with deliberately planted overgrown grass. Hu's attention to detail differentiates him from many of the other directors of Hong Kong and was one of the causes of his disagreements with the studio. The location, however, paid for itself amply by becoming the setting for more than two hundred other films.

The second narrative section, the part that moves the personal story on to the political plane, opens when Yang explains her history to Ku. With the use of flashbacks it becomes clear that Yang is the daughter of an official who has been victimized by the Eastern group under the leadership of the eunuch Wei. Shih and Lu are two of her father's generals who are protecting Yang from Wei's forces—although Yang, with her mastery of martial arts, seems to need little protection. Wei's army is approaching, and Yang enlists Ku's help in preparing a defense.

Ku's mother spreads the rumor that the fort is haunted (Hu here uses a multiscreen technique to effect), and when the army arrives, they are attacked by a series of clever devices carefully arranged by Ku to give the appearance of a ghostly advance. In the pale moonlight overhanging the fort, dummies, multiple catapults, bells activated by trip wires, and spears fired by springs are all used to reinforce this impression and frighten the oncoming army.

When Ku wakes in the morning, he laughs as he remembers the rout of the previous night, but he is first puzzled, then disturbed, to find that Yang and her generals have disappeared. If the first sequence represents the introduction of romance, the second part denies its possibility. Yang's one night with Ku can now more easily be reconciled as a maneuver in the plot than as an act of love. He is continually playing with his audience as well as his characters, constantly changing their perception of what is actually happening.

As Yang leaves Ku behind her to join her master, the priest Hui Yuan (Roy Chiao), in a Buddhist monastery, she is also leaving the material world (represented by the village) to join the spiritual one. The narrative once again paves the way for the third and final phase of the film, in which Hui's powers are brought into battle with the master of the Eastern group, Hsu Hsien-Chun (Han Ying-Chien).

After several months, Ku has finally traced Yang and Hui. On the rocks below the monastery, he finds a child with a note from Yang explaining that the child is his and that she can never see him again. On his way back to the village with the child, Ku is pursued by Hsu, but Yang, Shih, and Hui arrive in time to protect him, and in a breathtaking fight in a bamboo forest, they defeat the Eastern group. Hsu plays a final trick on Hui and, at the last moment, stabs him. As Hui dies, he bleeds gold, and the universe changes color as silver vultures inhabit golden skies. Whether this transformation is a hallucination of those living or a symbol of Hui's attainment of Nirvana is left unresolved, but the triumph of the philosophy is not in doubt.

It is the spectacular fight scenes that set *A Touch of Zen* apart from other martial arts films. Their formal beauty, their exciting pace, and the increase in tension and technique as the film progresses are the film's high points. In the first sequence, it is Ku who masterminds the battle plan; by the end, even Yang (who can throw four javelins at once with her left hand) is left on the sidelines watching the expertise of Hui. With scarlet cloaks flying, unimaginable leaps, whirling limbs, and incredible swordplay, the action often borders on the edge of what, in another culture, might be termed "magic."

Hu has brought the craft of the Peking Opera into his fight scenes, creating a pulsating rhythm out of dance and movement. His choreographer, Han Ying-Chien (who also plays the villain Hsu), trained at the Peking Opera, in which the combination of authentic swordplay, daring acrobatics, and stylized violence originated. Each fight is sketched out in advance and filmed to a precise tempo that makes these balletic compositions strikingly original. Mixed with a camera style that is rarely static and which makes full use of zooms, pans, and tracks, the excitement of the fight is played to its height.

The climactic battle in the bamboo forest is the ultimate exposition of Hu's art. Lasting only ten minutes on film, it took twenty-five days to shoot in order to capture the eerie effect of sunlight streaming through the forest and rising condensation.

When Hui first appears in the forest, he arrives in his saffron robes with the sun lined up behind him. His entrance is blinding—it is as though he has momentarily become the source of the sunlight—a remarkable visual anticipation of the transformation to come upon his death.

In *A Touch of Zen*, Hu has reached the zenith of the martial arts film, a genre which has been on the wane, even in Southeast Asia, since the late 1970's. His skill at organizing fights, elevating them from mere battles to a complex and engaging art form, combined with the intricacy of the plot as it moves from phase to phase, stripping off layers of consciousness as it progresses toward its finale, results in a unique martial arts film, aimed at the West as much as the more traditional market in Asia. Hu has stated (again in *Sight and Sound*) that his intention was to show something that could not be explained by the logical processes of Western philosophy: "It's like trying to explain to someone what 'sweet' is and finding it hard, but then giving them a lump of sugar to taste," he elaborated. With his rich cinematic art, Hu has succeeded. *A Touch of Zen*, widely distributed in the West, tantalizingly gives the flavor of what Buddhist philosophy must mean in a Chinese culture.

*Sally Hibbin*

# TRAGEDY OF A RIDICULOUS MAN (LA TRAGEDIA DI UN UOMO RIDICULO)

*Origin:* Italy
*Released:* 1981
*Released in U.S.:* 1982
*Production:* Giovanni Bertolucci for Fiction Cinematografica
*Direction:* Bernardo Bertolucci
*Screenplay:* Bernardo Bertolucci
*Cinematography:* Carlo Di Palma
*Editing:* Gabriella Cristiani
*Art direction:* Gianni Silvestri
*Music:* Ennio Morricone
*MPAA rating:* PG
*Running time:* 110 minutes

*Principal characters:*

| | |
|---|---|
| Primo Spaggiari | Ugo Tognazzi |
| Barbara | Anouk Aimée |
| Laura | Laura Morante |
| Adelfo | Victor Cavallo |
| Romola | Olimpia Carlisi |
| Maresciallo Angrisani | Vittorio Caprioli |
| Colonello Macchi | Renato Salvatori |
| Giovanni | Ricardo Tognazzi |

One sign of a major filmmaker is his ability to keep searching for differing means of expression while remaining consistent in point of view, that is, examining almost obsessively the subjects that are at the core of each of their works, yet managing those subjects so that in each successive film they receive a different treatment, a different way of seeing the problem.

Such is the case with Bernardo Bertolucci, who, after the overwhelming success (or scandal) of *Last Tango in Paris* (1972), dropped the erotic, lush style, the rich investigation of sex and politics of that film to seek after other, related problems and alternative modes of expression. *Last Tango in Paris* was followed by *Novecento* (1976; *1900*), a five-and-one-half-hour reverie on the peasant Communist movement in the north of Italy, spanning the period from the turn of the century to the end of World War II, concentrating on the relationship of two families: one of owners, the other, workers. The dreamlike, sometimes surreal style of Bertolucci's earlier works was here changed to a kind of realism, an almost romantic celebration of peasant life and struggle.

The film suffered commercially, particularly in the United States, partly because of its politics, but especially because its American distributor, Paramount, could not deal with its enormous length. They forced Bertolucci to cut it to four hours, then cut it further themselves, and finally gave it limited publicity and distribution. It reached a relatively small audience. Bertolucci followed *1900* with *La luna* (1979), in which he experimented with a highly melodramatic style, approaching, at times, the form of grand opera (the film is, after all, concerned with the torments of an opera singer with an incestuous desire for her son). *La luna* continued the obsessions of most of Bertolucci's films: the relationships and dynamics of the family, the psychological ramifications of emotional deprivation, the search, on the part of all the members of the domestic unit, for a consolidation of their needs and desires. Stylistically, *La luna*, like the family it portrays, could not find a satisfactory center. Its form seems to pull out odds and ends from Bertolucci's earlier work, unable to knit them together with complete success.

Obviously, the time had come for a reconsideration, a rethinking on Bertolucci's part of what he wanted to address in his next film and, most especially, the way in which he wished to address it. Part of that reconsideration may have been forced upon him. *Tragedy of a Ridiculous Man* is the first of his films since *La strategia del ragno* (1970; *The Spider's Stratagem*) not to have been photographed by Vittorio Storaro. Storaro's work for Bertolucci had become so admired by American filmmakers that he was called upon to photograph *Apocalypse Now* (1979) and *One From the Heart* (1982) for Francis Ford Coppola and *Reds* (1981) for Warren Beatty. Whether he was simply unavailable when Bertolucci shot *Tragedy of a Ridiculous Man*, or whether it was Bertolucci's conscious choice to make a film without him (the two events probably coincided), the result is a film that looks like none other that Bertolucci had made.

Gone are the rich pastels and lush coloration of the earlier works, the sweeping tracking shots and intricate manipulations of space that marked the collaborations of director and cinematographer. In their place, cinematographer Carlo di Palma creates a much cooler color scheme, not washed out, certainly, but with something of the look of a Kodachrome slide, rich but restrained. So, too, with the camera movements; they are present, but strongly controlled, with none of the bravura that one finds in the tracking shots of *The Conformist* (1970) or *Last Tango in Paris*. Thus, working with someone new, Bertolucci had the opportunity to try out a somewhat different stylistic approach, to make a film that in form and in content is more restrained and delimited than the work he had done heretofore. Form and content elaborate each other in the work of a good filmmaker, and in *Tragedy of a Ridiculous Man*, Bertolucci seeks what is for him a greater restraint than he had demonstrated in his earlier work, an eschewing of melodrama and operatic gesture. Instead, he creates another kind of intensity, one of silence and withholding.

*Tragedy of a Ridiculous Man* attempts to deal with one of the most difficult, controversial political subjects: terrorism. Other talented filmmakers, Claude Chabrol and Rainer Werner Fassbinder, for example, had attempted—without much success—to deal with the subject in, respectively, *Nada* (1974; *The Nada Gang*) and *Die 3. Generation* (1979; *The Third Generation*). One reason that these films do not totally succeed is that they attempt to deal directly with the personalities of terrorists as well as the reactions of the state against them, and they cannot overcome the ambiguities inherent in the conflicts. As a result, these films do not really enlighten the viewer about the phenomenon.

Bertolucci avoids these problems by not focusing on terrorism or terrorists as such. Rather, he assumes that his audience will have knowledge of the political situation in Italy in the late 1970's and early 1980's—when the Red Brigade and other groups were kidnaping and sometimes maiming or killing businessmen and political figures—and instead focuses upon a family that is affected by terrorist activity, their responses, and through those responses, suggests possibilities as to why terrorist activity exists. He makes no explicit value judgments, but does draw conclusions. Over all, he continues to work out one of his obsessive themes, the relationship of father and son.

For the first time in his films, Bertolucci adopts a first-person point of view in *Tragedy of a Ridiculous Man*. The narrative is told through the perceptions of the title character, the self-proclaimed "ridiculous man," Primo Spaggiari (Ugo Tognazzi), owner of a cheese and sausage factory near Parma (incidentally the city of Bertolucci's birth and the location of his 1964 film *Before the Revolution*). Yet like all good fiction-makers who use the first person, Bertolucci allows the viewer to see and know more than the central character, to pass beyond his perceptions and interpretations of events into a clearer knowledge of what actually transpires and why.

On his birthday, standing on the roof of his factory, ridiculously decked out in a captain's hat and binoculars which his son, Giovanni (Ricardo Tognazzi), had given him as presents, Primo Spaggiari, a thick featured, oafish-looking man, observes a terrible event. His son's car is pursued by another, overturns, and Giovanni is apparently taken prisoner. It seems to be the conventional terrorist act: A wealthy businessman is attacked, this time through his son, who is kidnaped, presumably to gain a large ransom from this captain of industry. Naturally, the immediate response of the parents, after their fear and grief, is to find a means to meet the ransom demand. Primo's wife, Barbara (Anouk Aimée), is especially obsessed with gathering the necessary funds, and both turn to the assets of their factory. The factory, however, is more than a means for this couple; it is a fetish. For Primo, it is his life; for Barbara, the inventory of their wealth. The first night after the kidnaping, after the police have made their initial investigation, searching the cornfield that was the kidnaping site (a place in which Primo seems to express genuine emotion, weeping among the cornstalks), the couple sleep in the factory among the cheeses.

Rather than return to their modern, luxurious villa, overlooking the countryside, they seek refuge and comfort among the things that produce their wealth. Primo refers to the cheese warehouse as his Fort Knox, and Bertolucci ironically infuses the room with a golden light. Nevertheless, Primo's Fort Knox is not as rich in its holdings as he would wish. Business has been bad. It will be difficult for him to raise money from the assets of his factory. What is more, his workers are not overly impressed by his calls for solidarity in the face of his troubles. In her growing anxiety, Barbara turns to other sources for comfort and financial assistance—her numerologist, who insists that Giovanni will be returned unharmed, and the town's rich usurers, a motley collection of local upper-middle-class businessmen whom she entertains. Sitting at a piano, looking for all the world like Joan Crawford in *Humoresque* (1946), she attempts to auction off her wealth in a desperate attempt to gain the ransom money.

These elements are enough in themselves to constitute Bertolucci's notion of the ridiculousness of a family whose members reduce themselves to barter and trade to redeem their son. A legitimate question is raised: What else are they to do in the face of such a trauma? If the kidnapers want money, and that money is difficult to find, a loving family will go to any ends to obtain it. Yet there is something wrong with the cool ferocity with which they make the attempt; it is somehow devoid of passion and care, too full of self-righteousness. Most important, they have no insight into who they are and why this is all happening to them. Primo, so full of himself, cannot see how he can be the target of the wrath of the Left. He evokes his peasant origins, speaks of how he felt like a Socialist hero standing among the milk cans in his youth, reminds the viewer of his work as a resistance fighter during the war.

He is blind to the fact that his past is severed from his present. As a failing captain of industry, he stands for the acquisitiveness, the fetishism of goods and wealth that are anathema to the Left. He is indeed their target, and he proves the accuracy of their aim. This fact becomes clear as two other figures move into prominence during the course of events that transpire during the wait for the release of Giovanni.

One figure is Giovanni's girlfriend, Laura (Laura Morante). The other, Adelfo (Victor Cavallo), a friend of Giovanni who tells Primo that he is a worker-priest (though an odd priest who has on his bookshelf a copy of an autobiography of Maria Callas and Kenneth Anger's book of scandals, *Hollywood Babylon*). Both work at Primo's factory, and both are profoundly involved with the kidnaping. They toy with Primo, bringing him alleged letters from Giovanni that tell about his condition and the demands of his captors. Laura plays seductress, proving further how ridiculous Primo is, easily enticing him sexually in the midst of his apparent misery. (Laura remains an intriguing and enigmatic character throughout the film, for the viewer often does not know quite how much she knows and at what crucial points she has the knowledge that is controlling the events.)

They toy with Primo because the entire event becomes a game, an elaborate plot to part a fool from his money, to aid the cause of the Left, and prove the ridiculousness of a man who, while proclaiming his love for his son, in fact loves mainly his factory and his position as boss. Adelfo and Laura convince Primo that Giovanni has been killed by his captors. Ever the pragmatic businessman, Primo sees now a chance if not to save his son, at least to save his business. He hides the news of the death from his wife, arranges with his business cronies to come up with the ransom money, and, he believes, with the help of Laura and Adelfo, to use this money to refinance his failing business.

The plan is hatched in the pig barns of Primo's factory, and as Primo elaborates the plot, Bertolucci intercuts shots of the slaughtering and skinning of pigs in the machines of Primo's factory. It is an apt montage, for Primo slaughters his conscience as easily as he does the pigs which are killed for his greater profit. There is an extra irony, however, for it is Primo himself who, figuratively, is a pig being led to slaughter. Giovanni is not dead. Giovanni is, in fact, a leftist himself (a fact that the viewer learns when the police search his room and find left-wing posters and books—and one wonders why his parents never referred to or even seemed aware of their son's politics). His kidnaping, it seems, was set up by him and his colleagues, including Laura and Adelfo, with, perhaps, the full knowledge of how his father would react.

React Primo does, still not telling his wife the truth, carrying through an elaborate plan to leave a suitcase full of money in the woods (money which he expects will be returned to him). Barbara takes it all very seriously, even threatening to shoot Primo as he bumbles and hesitates his way through the beautiful autumnal landscape where the money is to be left. When they return home, Primo reveals the plot to Barbara, but it is too late. Outside the people of the region gather under a tent for a dance. Primo goes with Laura and Adelfo because he thinks that they will be returning to him the money he left for Giovanni's ransom. Punk-rock music is played (the "worker-priest" Adelfo does a frantic dance by himself), followed by traditional Italian country melodies. Old and new meet in a cacophonous confusion. Giovanni appears, returned from his "kidnaping." Primo walks away as the film ends, and his voice comments upon the enigma of sons who die and are reborn again. He says that he will leave this mystery to the viewer, and Bertolucci irises in on him, isolating his distant figure on the screen, indicating that if any enigma exists, if there is any mystery, it is in the tragic foolishness of this ridiculous man.

The story line of *Tragedy of a Ridiculous Man* is as complex as any that Bertolucci has created—complex because, paradoxically, the visual form and narrative structure are among the simplest and sparest of all of his films. This is a quiet and withdrawn work, and in it Bertolucci is as interested in observing the dead times, the periods of waiting and uncertainty that the family endures while their son is missing. It is a deeply contemplative film, in which those quiet and empty times and spaces are openings for the viewer to muse about the relationships between the characters, and to work out the profound psychological and political subtexts that the film suggests without exploring. This is a film as much about husbands and wives, fathers and sons, friends and lovers as it is about political terrorism. The political terrorism it explicitly deals with does not so much concern the violent acts of political rebels, as the psychological-political terrorism that occurs when the love of money comes into conflict with the love that family members are supposed to feel toward one another.

*Tragedy of a Ridiculous Man* is very different from the visual and emotional bravura of Bertolucci's earlier films, indicative perhaps of a new stage in his development, a stage of greater subtlety, of a holding back, of a desire to confront his audience with a demand to reach into the work to deal with its complexities. If this is true, it is the sign of a filmmaker being very brave, and an encouraging sign that he believes his audience willing to do the work demanded of them.

*Robert Phillip Kolker*

# TRAGIC HUNT
# (CACCIA TRAGICA)

*Origin:* Italy
*Released:* 1947
*Released in U.S.:* 1948
*Production:* G. Giorgio Agliani for Associazione Nazionale di Partigiani Italiani
*Direction:* Giuseppe De Santis
*Screenplay:* Michelangelo Antonioni, Umberto Barbaro, Giuseppe De Santis, Carlo Lizzani, Cesare Zavattini, and Carrado Alvaro; based on an original story by De Santis and Lizzani
*Cinematography:* Otello Martelli
*Editing:* Mario Serandrei and Giuseppe Rosati
*Art direction:* no listing
*Music:* no listing
*Running time:* 80 minutes
*Also known as: Pursuit* and *The Tragic Pursuit*

*Principal characters:*
Daniela ("Lili Marlene") . . . . . . . . . . . . . . . . . Vivi Gioi
Alberto . . . . . . . . . . . . . . . . . . . . . . . . . . Andrea Checchi
Giovanna . . . . . . . . . . . . . . . . . . . . . . . . Carla Del Poggio
Michele . . . . . . . . . . . . . . . . . . . . . . . . . . Massimo Girotti

Italian director Giuseppe De Santis' *Tragic Hunt* was made during the heyday of neorealism. Preceded by the success in the United States of Roberto Rossellini's *Roma, città aperta* (1945; *Rome, Open City*) and *Paisà* (1946; *Paisan*) and by Vittorio De Sica's *Sciuscià* (1946; *Shoeshine*), *Tragic Hunt* played to American audiences familiar with the look and themes of neorealist films: a documentarylike representation of people struggling for survival and social justice in the aftermath of the fall of Fascism and the Liberation.

In *Tragic Hunt*, Italian peasants seize uncultivated lands in the Romagna region of the Po River Valley to form cooperatives with the help of the new, postwar, liberal government. The wealthy local landowners retaliate by hiring bandits who, operating from an ambulance, steal the money destined for the development of the farm collectives and kidnap a young peasant bride, Giovanna (Carla Del Poggio), as hostage. The sinister ringleaders of the gang, Daniela (Vivi Gioi), nicknamed "Lili Marlene," and her lover Alberto (Andrea Checchi), a former peasant, are unsuccessful in their terrorist act: The money is returned, the hostage escapes, and Alberto himself returns to his class, accepted and forgiven.

De Santis, in a choice that he was to repeat, based the story of *Tragic Hunt* on a real event reported in the newspapers: A small truck carrying money for a peasant cooperative had been assaulted and robbed by bandits in the province of Ravenna, which became the setting of his film. In the anarchy of the postwar years, this episode of banditry was not an isolated event; in the year that *Tragic Hunt* was made, a state of virtual civil war existed in the South over the question of landownership. As a neorealist, De Santis transformed the local event of peasants demanding a share of the land into a question of national justice.

As a former Partisan and a current member of the Communist Party at the time he made the film, De Santis affirmed in *Tragic Hunt* his faith in the people's ability to win their economic rights. Other neorealist directors foregrounded social problems such as unemployment (De Sica especially), but few gave the problem a national political perspective, as De Santis did. *Tragic Hunt* suggests that justice can be achieved through the collective efforts of the peasants, while De Sica's *Ladri di biciclette* (1948; *The Bicycle Thief*), in contrast, implies that justice is unattainable because society is too fragmented and selfish to observe the needs of individuals. In its social optimism, *Tragic Hunt* represents a tangent of neorealism that disappeared along with the militancy of the Communist Party in 1948, when the Demochristian reaction set in with censorship and close ties with the Vatican.

*Tragic Hunt* divorces itself from classic neorealist films in other than political ways. Its plot, a virtual tribute to the Hollywood movie, is packed with action unlike any neorealist film except for *Rome, Open City*. The model is the classic gangster film, complete with robbery, chases, shootouts, murders, and sex. In addition to the Hollywood tribute, De Santis includes an explicit allusion to Fritz Lang's *M* (1931) in the final trial scene of Alberto, when he is tried and forgiven by the collectivity of peasants, who cover him in soil in a gesture of ritual solemnity. Thus, *Tragic Hunt* is exuberant with references to film lore. Works by other neorealist directors strive to be more self-contained and less allusive, so that the Italian neorealist product may bear a national signature.

De Santis chose means to convey his national political intent different from those advocated by the neorealists. He turned to the methods of the Soviet cinema, and his frequent use of crane shots in *Tragic Hunt*, very unusual for the time in Italy, is indebted to Soviet directors, as is De Santis' ideology. *Tragic Hunt*, financed by the Associazione Nazionale di Partigiani Italiani (ANPI, the National Association of Italian Partisans), is unique among neorealist films because it highlights a frank and euphoric celebration of the class struggle. In this sense, *Tragic Hunt* is inspired by Sergei Eisenstein, Vsevolod Pudovkin, and Alexander Dovzhenko. Like them, De Santis conceived of the cinema as an instrument for social revolution, and, in their tradition, he gave epic dimensions to the conflict in *Tragic Hunt* between peasants and exploiters at the same time that he glorified the ordinary individual caught in the sweep of history (Giovanna, Alberto, and so on). The combination in the Soviet cinema of the ordinary person involved in extraordinary events is what De Santis called *coralita*—an untranslatable word that signifies the unification of the individual with his group.

The element that De Santis' *Tragic Hunt* conspicuously shares with other neorealist films is the use of the landscape. In the years of the early 1940's, when De Santis was a leading critic for the film journal *Cinema*, he was helping to lay the foundations of neorealism with his writings. He was particularly in favor of the use of natural landscapes, saying that without man the landscape is nothing but that the reverse is equally true. Much of this poetic attachment to the landscape was encouraged by the films of Jean Renoir, whom all neorealists acknowledged as a guiding spirit.

The choice of the Po River Valley as landscape for *Tragic Hunt* had a long evolution which began in 1942. Perhaps nothing in De Santis' early cinematic career was more instrumental in pushing him toward neorealist goals than his collaboration with Luchino Visconti on the screenplay of *Ossessione* (1942). Based loosely on James M. Cain's novel *The Postman Always Rings Twice*, *Ossessione* was not theatrically released in the United States because of a copyright war with Hollywood. With only a pirated copy of the novel in French (as legend has it, handed to Visconti by Renoir), De Santis and Visconti finished the script and went on location in the Po River Valley in 1942.

The location was chosen as the one best able to represent the spirit of the setting in Cain's novel: a place where the archaism of nature and the conflict imposed by human corruption could best be shown to coexist. The setting, furthermore, was a makeshift but apt reflection of Italian society at the time, struggling to rise from the soil into the industrial twentieth century—a historical movement that would be shown again in *Tragic Hunt*. The Po River Valley, thus conceived and captured in *Ossessione*, would become an iconic neorealist landscape embodying the essence of Italian moral, social, and economic reality. De Santis used it in *Tragic Hunt*, but it appears with obsessive frequency in other neorealist films: in Michelangelo Antonioni's documentary *Gente del Po* (1947) and in his feature films *Cronaca di un amore* (1950; *Story of a Love Affair*) and *Il grido* (1957; *The Cry*); in Rossellini's *Paisan*; in Federico Fellini's *I vitelloni* (1953); and, later, in Bernardo Bertolucci's *Prima della rivoluzione* (1964; *Before the Revolution*) and *Novecento* (1976; *1900*).

The influence of Brueghel the Elder in *Ossessione* is admitted by De Santis and is not surprising when one considers his enduring interest in the communal actions of the peasantry in *Tragic Hunt*. Perhaps the greatest stimulation De Santis derived from his work with Visconti, however, was the characterization of obsessive passion. If, with the use of the landscape, De Santis promoted the most essential basis of neorealism, his sally into eroticism was a highly personal departure from the constitutionally puritanical content of the best-known neorealist works. For De Santis, two elements marked the life of the peasantry: work and eros. With the exploration of the second element, he pioneered a political Freudianism that would not be picked up again in Italian cinema until Bertolucci's *1900*, a quarter of a century later, although Visconti would sustain the effort from *Ossessione* to his last films in a less pronounced Marxist vein than that worked by De Santis and Bertolucci.

The ethic of eros, as is obvious in *Tragic Hunt*, is not ruled, according to De Santis, by the family and the Catholic Church. For De Santis, the only sin is to go against one's nature and one's class. Thus, in *Tragic Hunt*, the evil Daniela, "Lili Marlene"—physically reminiscent of Rossellini's Gestapo lesbian in *Rome, Open City*—is sexually ambiguous, portrayed against a background of feral cruelty and charged with intimations of sexual perversion. With Daniela's character-type, De Santis seems to be suggesting an equation between ethical and sexual deviations. Her relationship with the kidnaped bride, Giovanna, is full of latent homosexuality, while with her lover, Alberto, the relationship is practically sadomasochistic. Not coincidentally, "Lili Marlene" is discovered to have been a Nazi collaborator.

*Tragic Hunt* is an essential film for the study of neorealism, as it both represents and deviates from this crucial movement in the history of the cinema. Though De Santis does not belong, by universal standards, to the pantheon of neorealist directors, his *Tragic Hunt* was widely acclaimed. It received special mention at the Festival of Karlovy Vary in 1948 and the Silver Ribbon for Best Direction at the Venice International Film Festival in 1947.

*Luciana Bohne*

# THE TRAITORS (LOS TRAIDORES)

*Origin:* Argentina
*Released:* 1973
*Released in U.S.:* 1974
*Production:* William Sussman
*Direction:* Raymundo Gleyzer (uncredited) and Grupo Cine de la Base
*Screenplay:* no listing
*Cinematography:* no listing
*Editing:* no listing
*Art direction:* no listing
*Music:* no listing
*MPAA rating:* no listing
*Running time:* 114 minutes

*Principal characters:*
Roberto Barrera, a corrupt labor leader
Paloma, Barrera's girlfriend, later his mistress
Señor Benitez, a company manager
Miguel Barrera, Roberto's father
Peralta, an uncorrupted labor leader
Chela, Barrera's wife

At the time of its release, *The Traitors* coincided with a spate of political features then being produced in Europe and the United States. Certain formulaic elements of hard-hitting action, along with the film's focus on corruption and betrayal, strategy and counterstrategy, suggest a superficial kinship with films such as Constantin Costa-Gavras' *State of Siege* (1972). Rather than focusing on historical personalities, however, *The Traitors* places fictional characters—paradoxically more "real" than any documentary figures, since their fictional nature is a composite of many actual people and events—in the complex world of Argentine labor politics over the nearly two decades between Juan Perón's ouster in 1955 and his return from exile in 1973.

The particular circumstances of the film's production and the role it played on the Argentine political scene—indeed, the very way its makers chose to define that scene—distinguish it from commercial thrillers. *The Traitors* is the most ambitious of a number of Latin American films which, because of their political sensitivity, have been shot, processed, and circulated clandestinely. More circumspect even than the prototype of this clandestine "genre," the epic documentary *La hora de los hornos* (1968; *The Hour of the Furnaces*), *The Traitors* maintains a rigorous anonymity, all the more remarkable in a full-length fictional film which uses a number of professional actors and aspires to high production values. The credits acknowledge only a single participant: the Grupo Cine de la Base (literally, "cinema group of the base"; more colloquially, "grass-roots cinema group").

*The Traitors* cannot be fully understood apart from the particular historical time and place in which it had its genesis. Argentina, along with Mexico and Brazil, lays claim to one of Latin America's three most important film industries. It has also had a significant if intermittent tradition of experimental and socially committed independents. Political instability has exerted an adverse effect on commercial and independent filmmakers alike.

General Juan Perón, a prolabor Populist, was elected president in 1946. A decade later, representatives of the middle sectors united to overthrow him and force him into exile, despite widespread opposition from the urban labor force, which Perón had enfranchised and defended. A series of *de facto* military governments struggled to maintain power for the next decade and a half until, in 1972, the indisputable evidence of their own failure to govern effectively compelled the military to revive political parties and arrange elections. Argentines who had been deprived of their rights to political participation were euphoric at their readmission into that arena. During the period which became known as the Argentine Spring, that euphoria sought cultural as well as political channels for expression. The Peronist candidate won the elections and, after only three months in office, stepped aside to allow Perón himself to return from exile and reclaim power. Both left- and right-wing Peronists applauded this long-awaited homecoming, but the gun battle at the airport welcoming ceremony left no doubt that expeditious pluralism had given way to deadly sectarianism. During the nine months of his presidency, Perón aligned himself increasingly with his more conservative supporters. Upon his death, he bequeathed the presidency to his third wife and vice-president, Isabelita, who would in turn be relieved of it in March of 1976, in yet another military coup, which brought the country full circle. There ensued a prolonged and ruthless war against "terrorists" and "subversives" in which thousands were killed or driven into exile.

*The Traitors* examines the tensions between different Peronist factions within the labor movement. Roberto Barrera is a Peronist union boss facing the first serious challenge to his power. A group of militant young workers, also loyal to Perón, stage a series of wildcat factory takeovers and propose an opposition slate in the imminent union elections. Barrera, seeking both to perpetuate his power and to punish the insurgents, engineers his own disappearance. While he enjoys a four-day interlude at a remote vacation house in the company of his lover, his presumed kidnaping is attributed to the rival faction, whose leaders are abducted and tortured. As he toasts his landslide election victory on the day following his "release," he is gunned down as a traitor to his class by militants of his own union. In the act of that assassination, these workers become guerrillas, deserting the electoral arena for that of armed struggle.

This final step in their political evolution has a kind of ironic circularity in the light of what the film reveals of Barrera's early political activity. In response to Perón's overthrow and the subsequent curtailment of workers' power and representation, the young Barrera engaged in indiscriminate terrorist attacks against the military, until his father, Miguel, eventually convinced him that organizing the workers was a more constructive political strategy. Suspecting the deception behind Barrera's disappearance and conveniently timed return, his own father joins the militant cell as it decides to adopt the strategy of organized violence. Barrera's progressive corruption and betrayal have driven those who justly oppose his hegemony to a course which is a more refined version of his own strategy in his days of genuine commitment to the workers' cause.

*The Traitors* interweaves three levels of action: the planning, execution, and outcome of the kidnaping scheme; a series of flashbacks detailing the personal life and career of the "victim"; and a set of documentary sequences which recapitulate the major events in Argentina over the same seventeen-year period. Barrera's progressive corruption is depicted in detail—from the cases of managerial liquor bestowed upon him in honor of his first election victory to his decision to make the union a profitmaking venture by running a numbers game among its members, as well as his elaborate scheme for sharing a portion of the workers' layoff compensation with management in exchange for deciding who should be laid off. More concerned with the historical and social causes and consequences of individual action than with inner motivation, the film never attempts—like Bernardo Bertolucci's *Il conformista* (1970; *The Conformist*), for example—to plumb the depths of the psyche—never, that is, with the exception of a single dream sequence whose surrealistic tone and absurdist humor are strikingly out of key with the only occasionally expressionistic realism which characterizes the remainder of the film.

Though the practical takes precedence over the psychological, the structure and content of the film make a continual connection between the public and the private, between Barrera's political stance and the events in his personal life. When Barrera, who has courageously served the interests and needs of the workers as a union delegate and has consistently refused the bribes of the management, is finally won over by the prospect of real power as the elected head of the union, he begins to "pay" immediately. His first concession—a small and strategic one—is to put a stop to the production slowdown on the grounds that any opposition to management's speed-up policies might reduce the chances for relegalization of the union. This decision distresses his girlfriend, Paloma, who intuits his compromise and realizes its implications. Her silent censure angers Barrera. Paloma is promptly replaced by Chela, whom Barrera officially designates as his fiancée.

Paloma is visually associated with Barrera's humble origins: a drab room much like one in his parents' home, a sad grassy spot under a railroad trestle. The flashier Chela stands as an emblem of Barrera's new status. In the house she has so pretentiously decorated (she measures books by the meter and displays them for their ornamental appeal), Chela bears and rears Barrera's children. Paloma, on the other hand, is escorted down grimy streets into the ramshackle patio of the abortionist. Barrera tries to retain both women, symbols of what he was and what he has become, but Paloma deserts him before their final tryst is over. The film wisely refrains from giving her decision a political motivation. Still unaware of his kidnaping stratagem, she deserts him on purely personal grounds. The opportunism and self-centeredness which drive her away clearly parallel Barrera's opportunistic manipulation of his political constituency.

In contrast to a number of Latin American films which have abandoned conventional fictional forms for a variety of documentary techniques—the "film essay," historical reconstruction, and interpretive documentary—*The Traitors* stands out for the traditionality of its narrative and visual style. Two assumptions motivate this choice of form: that conventional narrative cinema is most accessible to the working-class audience to which the film is directed, and that fictional film offers a greater potential for a synthesized, personalized, penetrating view than the external perspective of public or documentary sources.

Focusing as it does on the life of a single individual over many years, *The Traitors* raises problems of identification and continuity. The abruptness of Barrera's assassination is not mitigated by the surrealistic foreshadowing of the dream sequence, in which he attends his own funeral, or by any emotional association between the audience and the executioners, since the militants are numerous and are much more sketchily delineated than their enemy. The filmmakers' political commitment and their sense of the obviousness and urgency of the contemporary Argentine situation motivate their emphasis on the corrupt bureaucrat and their comparative failure to portray the human dimension of the opposition. The sheer size of the latter clouds certain transitions. The tie between the workers whom Barrera conspires to have laid off and the formation of the militant opposition cell, for example, is not immediately apparent. To see these militants subjected to beatings and torture, to see one of them brutally murdered, does not make them any more "real." Barrera's unctuousness and increasingly bombastic public rhetoric are criticized through the very mode by which they are conveyed in the film, yet the absence of this critical perspective in portraying the excessively rhetorical and oversimplified discussions among the militants reduces the credibility of the film and dilutes its impact. The workers—with the exception of one woman whose humiliation at the hands of a company physician generates a high degree of empathy—remain cardboard characters despite the filmmakers' obvious sympathies with the justice of their cause. Barrera, for all of his despicableness, is overwhelmingly and convincingly "real" precisely because of the efficacy of traditional identification mechanisms which are a function of the conventions of this "classical" narrative style.

Thus, in the last analysis, *The Traitors* ensnares itself in its own contradictions. Roberto Barrera is not inherently corrupt; he is not by nature bent to betrayal. On the contrary, he is depicted as an exemplary worker and comrade in his early years. The hook on which his corruptibility hangs is not money but power, though the latter most often brings wealth in its wake. What is there to guarantee that those who militate at the film's end for a "class tendency" which will both conserve and reach beyond the best of Peronist doctrine will not also eventually succumb to the seductions of power? A film which presents itself as a call to action and commitment can thus also be read as a rationale for inaction and cynicism.

*The Traitors* was an experiment which was not to be repeated—because the evolution of historical events forbade it, but perhaps also because its makers wished to avoid entrapment in a similar set of contradictions. For whatever reasons, the group subsequently narrowed its focus, its ambitions, and the resources needed to achieve them. The black-and-white documentary short *Me matan si no trabajo, y si trabajo, me matan* (1975; literally, "they kill me if I do not work, and if I work, they kill me"), made with and for a group of striking factory workers, was much more typical of the group's subsequent activity.

Given the historical circumstances, such a step was not surprising. Rather than a change in direction, it represented, for many members of the group, a return to well-traveled ground. Raymundo Gleyzer, a key member of the collective, had been making documentaries for more than a decade before beginning work on *The Traitors* and was the recipient of seven international awards. Of his ethnographic films, *La tierra quema* (1964), shot in Brazil, and *Ocurrido en Hualfin* (1966), codirected by Jorge Prelorán, are his most famous. His feature-length study *Mexico: La revolución congelada* (1971) has also received wide circulation.

During the short-lived Argentine Spring before Perón's return, many artists and intellectuals on the Left became more overt in their activities. The members of Cine de la Base, in contrast, went to great lengths to preserve their anonymity, but the very nature of *The Traitors* project seemed to undermine their precautions. The fact that many of the film's professional actors were known to audiences through previous screen or television roles facilitated their eventual persecution at the hands of military and paramilitary groups, who reportedly arranged "special screenings" in which the captive actors, under torture, were enjoined to identify fellow participants. Though his directorial responsibility for the film was not made public for years, Raymundo Gleyzer also fell victim to punitive political violence. On May 27, 1976, he was kidnaped by a heavily armed contingent of military police. Individuals and agencies within and outside Argentina, including officials from the United Nations, demanded information of his whereabouts to no avail. Intermittent, unofficial reports of his imprisonment and torture eventually ceased, and after a period of years of fruitless effort on his behalf, Gleyzer was presumed dead.

Their physical well-being so severely jeopardized, several members of the Cine de la Base group went into exile after Gleyzer's disappearance. Working anonymously in other Latin American countries, they released, in 1978, a seventeen-minute documentary entitled *Los Triple A*, about the reign of terror which the military regime was then imposing upon all sectors of the Argentine populace.

*Julianne Burton*

# TRANSES

*Origin:* Morocco and France
*Released:* 1981
*Released in U.S.:* 1983
*Production:* Izza Genini and Souhel Ben Barka for SOGEAV and Interfilms
*Direction:* Ahmed El Maanouni
*Screenplay:* Ahmed El Maanouni
*Cinematography:* Ahmed El Maanouni
*Editing:* Jean-Claude Bonfanti and Atika Tahiri
*Art direction:* Ahmed El Maanouni
*Sound:* Ricardo Castro and Michel Sonnier
*Music:* Nass El Ghiwane
*MPAA rating:* no listing
*Running time:* 87 minutes

*Principal characters:*
Boujema Hgour .......................... Himself
Omar Sayed ............................. Himself
Allal Yaala.............................. Himself
Aberrahman Paco ....................... Himself
Larbi Batma ............................. Himself

Ahmed El Maanouni's *Transes* both showcases a charismatic, unusual group of performers and illuminates a moment of cultural transition. The musicians that are the subject of the musical documentary want, as 1960's rockers did in the United States, to make revolutionary art with electric amplifiers, but they also want to rescue and preserve ancient traditions of Moroccan folk music. As a result, *Transes* does more than record a quixotic international show-business phenomenon. It is also an essay on the living transmission of folk culture in an age of mass culture.

Nass El Ghiwane (People of Song), an immensely popular five-man singing group, has performed throughout northern Africa and in France, where the group has attracted eager crowds of immigrant laborers, or "guest-workers." The musicians, who came out of the Moroccan slums, have become symbols of youthful idealism in the Maghreb cultures. Plugged into high technology and international fame, they also see themselves as carriers of the ecstatic and mystical folk tradition in which music is central. Their historical links are as important to them as the message of social justice that they preach in their lyrics.

*Transes* quickly makes the band members' appeal as performers understandable, even for cultural tourists. The film opens with dramatic concert footage. Nass El Ghiwane's routines are hypnotically entrancing and have a commanding rhythm; members of the group share an intensity untouched by histrionics. In contrast to the sound, the scene around them looks cheaply familiar: flashy neon and incandescent light displays, roadies scurrying about, and grim, uniformed security guards fighting off delirious crowds that break out of wild dancing to rush the stage. What initially looks like some Third World version of Beatlemania, however, soon takes on a different meaning. Going behind and beside the showbiz scene, *Transes* explains Nass El Ghiwane's popularity in its own terms. The film uses a syncretic style as unpredictable as the pop success of Nass El Ghiwane and as intriguing.

El Maanouni takes several approaches to his material, which he then interweaves. In one approach, he takes the viewer on an unsentimental journey through Third World urban life, where poverty and affluence, ancient parochial customs and space-age instant internationalism jostle one another. A beat-up horse and carriage racket through streets clogged with fancy cars; men in robes sit cross-legged sipping mint tea not far from a bar whose awning is bedecked with a "things go better with Coke" logo in Arabic. In the slums, artisans labor over inlaid tables and a street musician plays a folk tune on a flute not far from where street urchins mimic the singing group with makeshift wooden microphones.

In several self-conscious interviews, which portray a charming awkwardness in the interviewees, the members of the group describe their musical project. They see themselves as artists first, businessmen a very poor second. Their artistic ancestors were troubadours, who used to travel from *souk* (market) to *souk*, inventing songs out of the issues and news of the day. They want to perform the same function in the modern world, the band leader explains. At a time when young people were strongly attracted to the exoticism of an Eastern sound, the group's original leader, Boujema (now dead), instructed the group to identify as Moroccans, to use that tradition, to build on it, and only then to begin to create something new.

There was certainly enough mysticism to draw on in the Moroccan tradition to satisfy even the dreamiest in the group, a performer who has a George Harrison-like affect and talks soulfully of visions. The function of traditional music in ecstatic rituals is brought home in some scenes that could be straight out of an anthropological documentary. At a *zowiah*, or public meeting hall, a twenty-four-hour-long ceremony is held that involves the slaughtering of a goat and dancing the fervor of which puts the participants into trances. The scene of insistent, pervasive music—band members join the musicians—accompanying the trance dancers compares dramatically with the opening scene of young concert revelers dancing to Nass El Ghiwane's own compositions. In fact, the similarities are brought home by a moment in which the concert sound is superimposed on the folk ritual.

Finally, the film makes use of rare historical footage that, sometimes cryptically, draws parallels with the present. The importance of ecstatic expression in public life is emphasized with newsreel footage from the funeral cortege of a Moroccan king, during which men and women fall into fits and are carted away by officials. The presence of the military and of foreign influence in Moroccan life is starkly asserted with atrocity footage from the World War I occupation of Morocco by European troops. The musical tradition of the *souks* finds visual testimony in the sight of street musicians, who perform eagerly for the cameras of tourists and soldiers on leave in that era.

The technical sophistication of *Transes* is impressive, especially in contrast to the paralyzingly static and unfocused *Alyam, Alyam!* (1978; *Oh the Days!*), El Maanouni's first feature, which painstakingly described the physical universe of a peasant who has aspirations to become a guest-worker. (Originally an economics student, El Maanouni studied filmmaking in Belgium and then began work as both a director and a cinematographer.) The vivid camera work in the concert footage is full of movement; difficult interiors such as rehearsal rooms and slum alleyways are unobtrusively well lit. Editing gives the film its energy; El Maanouni crosscuts concert scenes, atmospherics, interviews, and ethnographic documentary in an abrupt and even provocative way. The rapid crosscutting sometimes puzzles, but it does not irritate or frustrate the viewer. There is an emerging logic to the juxtapositions, and the forced interplay in the editing makes the social milieu of the music and the immediate pulse of the sound parts of the same urgent story.

More puzzling and less effective is the use of historical material, where much of the meaning is lost on a foreigner. The death of a king and the sight of foreign uniforms on Moroccan streets are more than fortuitous bits of newsreel footage and more even than visual memory. They are clues to current issues—clues which remain elusive for the non-Moroccan viewer.

In fact, the political issues on which the group's songs comment, unlike their social context, are never made clear for the viewers who might never have heard of Nass El Ghiwane before. Although the lyrics apparently give voice to a general discontent, to an outsider they sound vague and sentimental. The authoritarianism of the Moroccan government of the early 1980's, the tensions in the international labor force at a time when European countries are expelling guest-workers, and the cruelties of industrialization in a Third World country make up the unseen background for the group's musical mission.

In general, the group's social message does not rise to the vitality of its sound. While eloquently making a case for the music's cultural roots, the film celebrates only the most banally international qualities of its lyrics. The occasional scenes of birds in flight, sunsets, and picturesque harbors match with unfortunate perfection the trite sound of lyrics that, to the uninformed ear, reduce peace, love, and justice to June-moon-spoon.

These puzzling and unsatisfying moments may be more than a filmic lapse of taste. They may be evidence of the uneasy quality of the meeting of Western and industrial influences on a tradition in which mysticism infuses social life. That uneasy ground is also where the film finds some of its more pointed ironies, as brought out in one of the group's rehearsal scenes. The singers grapple with their contract obligations and questions of cassette piracy, trying to make their legal arrangements jibe with their desire to share their music freely and to bring a message of social justice to the masses.

In the end, the music carries the film's message. The singing group's power to attract an audience with one foot in the sixteenth century and another in the twenty-first testifies to the power of cultural tradition to endure—and even to provide a vehicle in which to ride into an uncertain future with hope. As the lyrics of the finale put it, "Justice will lead us."

*Pat Aufderheide*

# THE TREE OF WOODEN CLOGS (L'ALBERO DEGLI ZOCCOLI)

*Origin:* Italy
*Released:* 1978
*Released in U.S.:* 1979
*Production:* Gruppo Produzione Cinema for Radiotelevisione Italiana
*Direction:* Ermanno Olmi
*Screenplay:* Ermanno Olmi
*Cinematography:* Ermanno Olmi
*Editing:* Ermanno Olmi
*Art direction:* Enrico Tovaglieri; set decoration, Franco Gambarana
*Costume design:* Francesca Zucchelli
*Sound:* Amendeo Casati
*Music:* Johann Sebastian Bach; performed by Fernando Germani
*MPAA rating:* no listing
*Running time:* 185 minutes

*Principal characters:*
Batisti .............................. Luigi Ornaghi
Batistina ........................ Francesca Moriggi
Minek ............................. Omar Brignoli
Widow Runk ................... Teresa Brescianini
Peppino ........................... Carlo Rota
Grandfather Anselmo ............ Giuseppe Brignoli
Bettina ....................... Maria Grazia Caroli
Maddalena ........................ Lucia Pezzoli
Stefano ......................... Franco Pilenga
Don Carlo ........................ Carmelo Silva
Sister Maria ................ Francesca Bassurini

Set in the Italian region of Lombardy at the turn of the century, *The Tree of Wooden Clogs* is Italian director Ermanno Olmi's tribute to the peasants and to the land that he remembers from his childhood. In the film, Olmi interweaves the stories of several peasant families living in a communal farmhouse, carefully selecting ordinary incidents related to the land, to the change of seasons, and to peasant life. His deliberate avoidance of the melodramatic gives the film a documentary quality that is reflected in its natural and almost inevitable rhythm as the film moves from one season to another and from one everyday event to another. Gradually the viewer is caught up in this seemingly effortless, unforced rhythm of the film as it depicts the day-to-day existence of the peasant families.

The peasants are sharecroppers, owning almost nothing: The land, the farmhouse, most of the farm tools and implements, much of the livestock, and two-thirds of the harvest belong to the landlord.

The film opens with Don Carlo (Carmelo Silva), the parish priest, telling Batisti (Luigi Ornaghi) and his wife, Batistina (Francesca Moriggi), that because their little boy, Minek (Omar Brignoli), is intelligent, he should be sent to school, almost unheard of for a peasant's son. Batisti grumbles but obeys. With another child on the way, this is an additional burden for the family.

The Widow Runk (Teresa Brescianini), another inhabitant of the communal farmhouse, does laundry to support her father and six children. Her eldest son, Peppino (Carlo Rota), gets a job at the local flour mill, and Grandfather Anselmo (Giuseppe Brignoli) helps watch the children, prepare meals, and tend the garden and their one cow. His youngest granddaughter, Bettina (Maria Grazia Caroli), constantly follows him about, asking questions and listening to his stories. Grandfather Anselmo's great ambition each year is to produce the season's first tomatoes, thus astonishing his neighbors.

Maddalena (Lucia Pezzoli), the beautiful daughter of the Brena family, is being decorously courted by Stefano (Franco Pilenga), a young peasant from a neighboring farm. As she walks home alone in the evening after leaving the spinning mill where she works, Maddalena is joined by Stefano. They scarcely speak to each other, but it is accepted by Maddalena's family that they will be married. Once, Stefano asks Maddalena to let him kiss her, but she replies that all that can wait until they are married.

When the Widow Runk's cow falls sick, it is a potential catastrophe for the family. After the veterinarian pronounces the cow's sickness incurable, the widow goes to church to pray for help. Returning with some holy water, she forces it down the animal's throat, and in a few days, the cow recovers. Meanwhile, the daily activities of the peasants' lives continue. The fields are planted and tilled, the harvest gathered, the grain sacked and weighed, and a hog slaughtered. In the fall, when the nights begin to turn cold, the peasant families gather in the stables for warmth and entertainment, the women mending and sewing, the men smoking and telling stories.

Maddalena and Stefano's courtship continues. At a fair in a neighboring town, one of the peasants listens uncomprehendingly to a political speech. While the speaker calls for solidarity among the oppressed, the peasant—whose family is dishonest and slovenly, in marked contrast to most of the dwellers in their commune—spots a gold coin which someone has dropped. He slides his foot over it, picks it up, and takes it home, but becomes so obsessed with hiding it for himself that he eventually loses it. When Batistina is about to give birth, she decides not to have a midwife assist at the birth, because she does not think she and Batisti can afford the expense. The delivery is successful, for which her husband is grateful, but now he must worry about another mouth to feed.

As the year turns toward spring, Grandfather Anselmo and Bettina plant the delicate tomato plants against a sunny stone wall and carefully cover them with chicken droppings saved for just this purpose. Such are the small moments of which the film is made.

For the most part, Olmi concentrates exclusively on the lives of the peasants, but in one telling sequence he implicitly contrasts their world with that of the landlord. It is night, and a piano recital is in progress at the landlord's richly appointed villa, but the landlord himself is outside in the dark, peering through his own windows. His face is contorted, his muscles clenched. Inside the brightly lit room, a small crowd of wealthy guests listens to a Mozart sonata. The pianist is young and attractive; nearby, occasionally turning a page for him, stands the landlord's pretty wife. With her eyes alone, she is making a cuckold of her husband, seemingly oblivious to the crowd. There is no dialogue in this expressive sequence, which conveys without a trace of didacticism the restless dissatisfaction of the rich: They have everything, and it is not enough.

Olmi's approach is similarly understated throughout. In the most important scene of the film, Batisti cuts down a young poplar tree to make his little son Minek a wooden clog sandal. Batisti has been unable to repair Minek's broken sandal, and it is still too cold for the little boy to go barefoot. In the middle of the night, so he will not be seen, Batisti slips out, chops down the tree, and conceals the deed as carefully as possible. Since the tree belongs to the landlord, it is a crime to cut it down without permission. Although the scene provides the central image for the film, Olmi does not linger on the incident. It is only in retrospect, after the viewer learns the consequences of Batisti's action, that the scene acquires vital importance.

As the film continues to unfold in a natural, unforced manner, one learns the outcome of earlier incidents. Maddalena and Stefano, the prescribed period of courtship over, marry and take a boat to Milan for a one-day honeymoon. They spend their wedding night in a convent where Maddalena's aunt is a nun.

The nun, Sister Maria (Francesca Bassurini), persuades them to take an orphan baby, because the convent will provide a small dowry of money and clothes for anyone who will adopt him; he can already help to pay his way. On their way to the convent, the young couple had seen political demonstrators violently repressed by soldiers, but they do not seem to understand what is happening.

Upon the couple's return to the communal farmhouse, everyone crowds around to see the baby and speculate about his parentage, someone saying that he might be the son of an aristocrat. Don Carlo, the parish priest, cuts short the discussion by telling them all that the boy is now a peasant's son, and that love is the most important thing he needs to be happy.

Meanwhile, the landlord has discovered the stump of the tree that Batisti cut down. When the bailiff traces the "theft" to Batisti, he and his family are immediately evicted. As Batisti loads the family's meager possessions into a cart, the other peasants stay inside, watching silently through their windows. Their faces express fear and a stoic, resigned sorrow. No one sympathizes with Batisti or offers to help him. Their fear of the omnipotent landlord keeps them within the protective walls of the farmhouse. After the family has driven off into the twilight, the other peasants come out and stand silently looking after them until they disappear in the deepening darkness. Again, without the aid of dialogue, Olmi eloquently depicts the tyranny of the landlord over the peasants' lives.

Thus, this quiet, seemingly apolitical film has deeper, subtler overtones, both social and political. Olmi's sympathies obviously lie with the peasants, and to some degree he has romanticized their lives. Olmi's peasants have, above all, a quiet dignity, emphasized by meditative cinematography and the music of Johann Sebastian Bach, which swells and soars in the background. Yet if he has glorified some of their virtues—the close-knit family life, the sense of community, the faith, the sacrifices, and the toil—he has also suggested some of the peasants' limitations: the narrowness and provinciality of their lives, their superstitions and fears, and their unquestioning obedience to authority.

Olmi shot the film in eleven weeks, characteristically using no professional actors. Instead, he went to Bergamo, where he was to shoot the film, and reportedly spent months interviewing more than two thousand people before selecting the performers. After completing the shooting, he then spent a year editing the film.

In an interview, Olmi said that *The Tree of Wooden Clogs* "is really a story of my childhood, stories that have long lived in my memory crying to be told." *The Tree of Wooden Clogs* represents, Olmi says, "a return to my origins, a look inside myself." *The Tree of Wooden Clogs* won the Gold Palm at the Cannes International Film Festival in 1978 and was acclaimed by reviewers, some calling it a masterpiece.

*Julia Johnson*

# THE TRIAL OF JOAN OF ARC (LE PROCÈS DE JEANNE D'ARC)

*Origin:* France
*Released:* 1962
*Released in U.S.:* 1965
*Production:* Agnès Delahaie
*Direction:* Robert Bresson
*Screenplay:* Robert Bresson
*Cinematography:* Léonce-Henry Burel
*Editing:* Germaine Artus
*Art direction:* Pierre Charbonnier
*Costume design:* Lucilla Mussini
*Music:* Françis Seyrig
*Running time:* 63 minutes

*Principal characters:*

Joan.......................Florence (Delay) Carrez
Bishop Cauchon.............Jean-Claude Fourneau
Jean Lemaître......................Marc Jacquier
Jean Beaupère.....................Roger Honorat
D'Estivet..........................André Régnier
Brother Isambart.................Michel Hérubel
Nicholas de Houppeville...........Marcel Darbaud
Duke of Warwick....................Richard Pratt
Jean de Chatillon....................Jean Gillibert
Guards...................Jean Payen/Nicolas Bang

The story of Joan of Arc, the Maid of Orleans, is one that every schoolchild knows, but the fascination with the warrior-heroine, the farm girl turned saint, extends beyond childhood, as the enthusiasm of many filmmakers for the subject proves. Obviously, the story of a teenager who takes up the cause of France in battle at the prompting of heavenly voices contains almost everything for which a director might hope: spectacle and mystery, patriotism and martyrdom. The only thing missing is romance, and some filmmakers have obligingly provided at least a hint of that as well, for the five-hundred-year gap in time conveniently affords the assurance of artistic "freedom." Cinematic interpretations have ranged from Georges Hart's earliest known film version to Roberto Rossellini's adaptation of Arthur Honegger's *Jeanne au bucher*. The most famous is Carl Theodor Dreyer's masterful silent classic *La Passion de Jeanne d' Arc* (1928; *The Passion of Joan of Arc*). The formal experimentation and artistic integrity of Dreyer's version stands in contrast with the uncomfortable results of Hollywood's several attempts to mix the spectacle and the spiritual in retelling the story. In 1917, Cecil B. De Mille offered audiences opera singer Geraldine Farrar in his silent film spectacular, *Joan the Woman*. With a robustly attractive Ingrid Bergman as Joan, Victor Fleming filmed his *Joan of Arc* in 1948. The film was visually appealing but demonstrated the limitations of Hollywood's sense of historical accuracy. Otto Preminger's *Saint Joan* (1957) was an ill-fated attempt to bring George Bernard Shaw's play to the screen.

Director Robert Bresson's use of the subject of Joan of Arc as the basis of a film marks a radical departure from the previous incarnations of Joan on film. Bresson's *The Trial of Joan of Arc* is neither spectacle nor historical reconstruction, nationalistic remythologization nor vaguely respectful romanticization. Bresson is not interested in Joan as the armored defender of Armagnac Gaul and the bitter foe of the Anglo-Burgundian alliance that sought to deny the Dauphin Charles's claim to the throne. In her own time, Joan was as much a center of political as of religious controversy. Opinion regarding her was divided strictly along party lines. To the Burgundians and the English, she was a witch, the Devil's child, a mannish madwoman or charlatan who supported a bastard for king. To the Armagnacs, she was the emblem of God's favor. She has remained, in spite of the countless books, plays, and films, a mysterious figure whose very existence might be doubted as romantic legend were it not for the records of her 1431 trial and those of the rehabilitation process which was begun twenty-five years later, at the prompting of her family (and, it is said, the French monarchy).

Basing his screenplay on these trial and rehabilitation records, Bresson ignores the nationalistic spectacle and the political controversy. Like Dreyer, Bresson offers only Joan's final days as she is interrogated by a court of French clerics who have been assembled by their English allies to convict Joan for heresy. Yet Bresson takes an approach that is very different, both aesthetically and thematically, from Dreyer's. Bresson has remarked that the goal of the film was to make Joan "as possible and true to life—or as impossible and untrue to life—as she was then." Joan is endlessly fascinating because she was a real person whose very practical influence on events was based on something that appeared impossible: her visions. The mystery extends to her ability to influence those in power, but Bresson centralizes the ambiguity of spiritual mystery—her implicit trust in the ineffable.

For Bresson, it is the question of the meaning of faith that is illuminated by Joan's trial and death. Many of the same issues revolving around the relationship of faith, God's grace, physical suffering, and spiritual being were also addressed in his earlier film, *Le Journal d'un curé de campagne* (1951; *Diary of a Country Priest*). *The Trial of Joan of Arc* uses the metaphor of imprisonment that was also used in *Un Condamné à mort s'est échappé* (1956; *A Man Escaped*).

The film begins with a simple scene. Joan's mother and brothers enter the cathedral of Notre Dame to ask the Church to reconsider Joan's condemnation at the hands of the Rouen ecclesiastical court. The faces of Joan's family are never seen. The credits appear and a drumroll announces the flashback to Joan's trial. Her hands appear on the Bible as she swears to tell the truth. The inquisitors, led by the august Bishop Cauchon (Jean-Claude Fourneau), begin to question her. They are curious about her origins as a farm girl and her claim of having heard angels and saints who, she has publicly declared, were sent to her by God. The judges' aim is clear: They wish to trick their prisoner into a contradiction in testimony or an ill-considered, theologically suspect answer that will prove her a liar, a fraud, and a heretic. The interrogation is presented by Bresson through alternation of medium shots of Joan with similar ones of her judges. Although criticized by one reviewer as amounting to nothing more than television camera technique, Bresson's visual style is an important part of his attempt to achieve a "pared image." The calmness of the proceedings, matched by the camera technique, also points up Bresson's interest in Joan, not as a figure who should elicit our emotional response, but as an embodiment of the strangeness found in the meeting of the supernatural and the physical.

Bresson's Joan, Florence (Delay) Carrez, reveals herself through her answers as intellectually audacious, confident in her faith, and sufficiently convinced of her deliverance that she questions Cauchon's authority. In spite of this, as with so many other Bressonian characters, she never reveals herself completely in a manner that conforms to the viewer's expectations of what film characters should do. She is, perhaps, as much a mystery at the end of the film as at the beginning. Bresson does not permit the audience to know Joan beyond her answers and her reticent demeanor. Carrez was a nonprofessional actor coached in the inexpressive style of presentation that Bresson used to try to avoid the false psychology and learned theatrical emotions of actors. Like the dying priest of Ambricourt (Claude Laydu) in Bresson's *Diary of a Country Priest*, Joan seems impassive, distant, unknowable, but her words (analogous to the curé's diary) and fleeting moments of reaction bring the audience closer to her in a way that Bresson hopes will reveal her soul, not her psychology. Such a moment occurs when women are sent to her prison cell to examine her to verify her claim of virginity. Joan covers her face with a sheet as if trying to retain her dignity and her privacy. In contrast, particularly to Dreyer's film, Bresson's very unemotional presentation of Joan places new demands upon the audience. While Dreyer's film matches Renée Falconetti's tearful, victimized Joan with an emotional camera style complete with canted frames, swinging camera movement, and the rhetoric of intimate close-ups, Bresson offers only a distanced view. All camera and editing flourishes are eliminated and the single shot itself seems incomplete, not as in Dreyer's film, where the close-ups of Joan tell all that the viewer needs to know about her. Just as Bresson has characterized Joan as a young girl who withdraws from the world little by little, so Bresson makes his audience withdraw from the crutches of conventionalized film technique and acting. Viewers must experience the film without the assumption that they will be easily and smoothly guided to a specific reaction.

As the questioning continues, Joan discovers that she does have sympathizers. De Houppeville (Marcel Darbaud) protests that the trial is really only a persecution. The English leader, Warwick (Richard Pratt), warns him that any attempt to counsel Joan will lead to his death as well as hers. Joan's predictions of an Armagnac victory are called into question, as is her belief that God will deliver her from prison. On her return to her cell, Joan's cell window is shattered by a stone. This becomes one of the few on-screen indicators of the presence of a hostile mob clamoring for Joan's execution. Joan does not appear surprised or perturbed. She quietly examines the rock, but as Bresson has stated, her calm response illustrates the depth of her belief that God will deliver her from prison.

On the resumption of the court interrogation, Joan is accused of knowingly and therefore blasphemously contributing to her own deification by the peasantry. Her vow of chastity is also called into question, but the physical examination confirms the truth of her claims. Warwick cynically declares that if her virginity is what gives her strength, they will take away her virginity. He voyeuristically watches her by means of a hole in the cell wall, but finally agrees with a colleague who says that it would be impossible to hurt her after having observed her. They acknowledge that the judges may strip her through other means. Her clothes have become a symbol of her spiritual otherness as well as the symbol of her political value (as a war leader) and a symbol of her confidence in her communion with the supernatural. Her voices have told her to wear men's clothing. The trial records confirm that Joan's masculine attire was used as a major point against her at the trial. To the judges, her clothing was the constant signifier of her blasphemy, her rebellion against nature.

In one of the several secret (and illegal) interrogations in Joan's cell, Bishop Cauchon offers Joan Holy Communion in exchange for her abandoning of male attire. Joan refuses. She is denied communion although it is Easter. Tearfully, Joan asks Brother Isambart (Michel Hérubel) what has happened to those (the king and his supporters) who believed in her cause. Isambart, who provided counsel at the trial, has no answer. Joan is left alone.

The trial questioning resumes, but Joan takes ill. She believes that she is dying, but Bishop Cauchon still denies her the Sacraments. When she is well enough to return to the courtroom, she declares her willingness to be judged by the pope and the Bâle assembly. Cauchon, however, refuses to allow these remarks to be noted in the trial proceedings. Put on the rack and told that she will be tortured and then promptly burned if she does not renounce her claims of divine inspiration, Joan relents and signs an abjuration. She is sentenced to life in prison. Later, Joan renounces the abjuration. She is told she will die.

After putting on a simple gown and receiving communion, Joan calmly tells Brother Isambart that she hopes to be in paradise that night. She accepts that her deliverance from prison can be only a transcendental one found in death. With her legs free of iron chains for the first time since the beginning of the trial, Joan virtually runs to the stake. She is bound, the pyre lit. In a strangely affecting detail characteristic of Bresson, Joan's shoes and clothes are heaved onto the fire kindling; the English want to ensure there will be no religious relics for the Maid's followers. Joan boldly declares a last time that her voices were from God and that she has not been deceived by them. Joan's body is obscured by the flames and smoke; the chains holding her are melted by the heat. Her last word is "Jesus."

Dreyer finalized this same moment in *The Passion of Joan of Arc* with an emotionally wrenching silhouette shot of Joan's burning body slumping down amid the flames. He then shifted attention to a riot among the spectators of the execution. Bresson chooses a different strategy that is less affecting on a superficially emotional level but equally valid. While Dreyer's final shot of Joan forces the audience to confront the physical horror of Joan's death, Bresson chooses to focus on something ambiguous, something that can be explained rationally or that can be viewed as miraculous. Joan's body is gone. The chains that bound her hang from the smoking stake. Like the shadow of the Cross at the end of *Diary of a Country Priest*, the empty stake shifts attention from Joan's physical death to the miraculous promise of her faith. She had told her judges that she knew her voices were those of angels because she had the will to believe they were. As Bresson has explained, Joan's will extended to accepting God's grace even if it meant the end of her earthly life and the beginning of a purely spiritual one. All the desperate machinations of the court have merely fulfilled the promise of Joan's faith.

*The Trial of Joan of Arc*, like many of Bresson's other films, was greeted by critical controversy but public indifference. Bresson's emphasis on the question/answer dialogue, the monotony of his detached camera style, and the inexpressive Bressonian nonacting style irritated many reviewers. Numerous critics, however, praised the film's realism, its purity, and its sincerity. Jean-Pierre Oudart proclaimed the film's formal experimentation in avoiding conventional cinematic rhetoric a stylistic breakthrough. Although it was named the French entry at the Cannes International Film Festival and took the Special Jury Award, *The Trial of Joan of Arc* was not a box-office success. Bresson's reputation as a stylistic iconoclast whose austerity of approach and narrowness of interest condemned him to be an unpopular master filmmaker remained sadly intact.

*Gaylyn Studlar*

# TRISTANA

*Origin:* Spain, Italy, and France
*Released:* 1970
*Released in U.S.:* 1970
*Production:* Robert Dorfmann, Epoca Films-Talía Films, Selenia Cinematografica, and Les Films Corona
*Direction:* Luis Buñuel
*Assistant direction:* Pierre Lary and José Puyel
*Screenplay:* Luis Buñuel and Julio Alejandro; based on the novel by Benito Pérez Galdós
*Cinematography:* José F. Aguayo
*Editing:* Pedro del Rey
*Art direction:* Enrique Alarcón
*Sound:* José Nogueira and Dino Fronzetti
*Music:* Frédéric Chopin
*MPAA rating:* PG
*Running time:* 105 minutes
*Running time in U.S.:* 95 minutes

*Principal characters:*
Tristana .......................... Catherine Deneuve
Don Lope............................ Fernando Rey
Horacio .............................. Franco Nero
Saturna ................................ Lola Gaos
Saturno ........................... Jesús Fernández
Don Cosme.......................... Antonio Casas
Bell ringer .............................. José Calvo

Luis Buñuel's *Tristana* is one of the most subtle and complex expressions of themes that are central to the Spanish filmmaker's creative canon: sexual politics, bourgeois hypocrisy, the futile pursuit of freedom in a repressive society. With Catherine Deneuve in the title role and Fernando Rey as her tutor and lover Don Lope, *Tristana* is also one of the rare Buñuelian works which is remembered for its outstanding dramatic performances as much as for its rich fabric of ideas and images.

When the opportunity arose for Buñuel to return to Spain in the 1960's under one of the by-then routine efforts by the Franco regime to court its most famous exiles, he proposed a project to Serge Silberman, his French producer, which he had been considering for some time: a film version of a novel by the nineteenth century Spanish writer Benito Pérez Galdós. Buñuel had earlier filmed one of Pérez Galdós' minor novels, *Nazarín* (1895), in Mexico in 1958, with a screenplay by fellow Spanish exile Julio

Alejandro. *Viridiana* (1961), another Buñuel-Alejandro script collaboration, was inspired by Pérez Galdós' *Ángel Guerra* (1890-1891). Silberman agreed to the new project, giving Buñuel complete artistic freedom in exchange for the director's accepting Catherine Deneuve, who had previously starred in the title role *Belle de jour* (1967). Buñuel had conceived of *Tristana* as a very Spanish film with an all-Spanish cast but acceded to his producer's conditions, eventually agreeing to the addition of the Italian actor Franco Nero in the role of Tristana's young lover to round out Silberman's proposed international cast. Despite such modifications in its conception, *Tristana* retains a profoundly Spanish flavor, strikingly foregrounded by the choice of the provincial city of Toledo as the sole location for the action.

The film is organized according to a tight symmetry of plotting, theme, and characters. Divided into two major narrative stages, separated by a two-year hiatus in Tristana's relationship with Don Lope, the plot centers on the character and motivation of an aging aristocrat, Don Lope (Fernando Rey), and his innocent ward, Tristana (Catherine Deneuve). Tracing the young woman's education in a world dominated by men, Buñuel deftly portrays his heroine's vulnerability in the first half of the story and, in the second, her revenge against those whom she feels have deformed her body and spirit. Within this two-part division, the story is structured so as to represent the unfolding of Tristana's tragic destiny, which neither she nor the spectator can fully discern until the very final frames of the film.

In the first phase of the narrative, Tristana, a recently orphaned young girl of about eighteen, is taken as a ward of the impoverished aristocrat, Don Lope. While teaching her to cherish personal freedom, he seduces the young girl and makes her his mistress. Some time later, she meets and falls in love with a young artist, Horacio (Franco Nero). With the assistance of her maid Saturna (Lola Gaos), Tristana is able to maintain a clandestine affair with Horacio. Lope eventually discovers her infidelity, thus precipitating an open conflict, the result of which is Tristana's departure from Lope's house and from Toledo with her new lover.

About two years later, Lope, now wealthy with a sizable inheritance from his sister, learns that Horacio has brought Tristana back to Toledo. She is suffering from a malignant tumor on her leg, and Lope willingly takes her in. To save her life, the doctors are forced to amputate Tristana's leg, which only cools even further Horacio's apparently fading passion for the woman to whom he once swore undying devotion. Lope, on the other hand, is perversely delighted by the turn of events, thinking that it will now be impossible for Tristana ever to run away from him again.

Abandoned by one lover and trapped by the other, Tristana's entire demeanor changes after the operation. She remains with Lope but does not disguise her animosity toward him. After much prompting by the local priest, she reluctantly agrees to marry Lope and thus end what the Church considers her sinful relationship with him. Now more than ever obsessed with revenge, Tristana awakens one night from a recurrent nightmare of Lope's decapitation, only to hear him gasping for breath in his bedroom. She feigns calling a physician and allows Lope to die without making any effort to help him.

The film's narrative scheme emphasizes the bitter irony of Tristana's double entrapment, first as the ingenuous victim of predatory men, then as the entrapped victim of her own uncontrollable desire for revenge. To underscore this thematic cluster, Buñuel constructs a dense web of symbolic relationships among characters in nearly every scene, weaving into these a number of visual figures in the first part of the film which are reinvoked at crucial points in the latter part of the plot. Action viewed in a linear, sequential progression in the early stages of the film is thus transformed into illuminating retrospection for both Tristana and the audience. The first major narrative sequence sets the stylistic and thematic model for this strategy and, to suggest a circular structure to the action, is repeated at the end of the film as a brief flashback.

Tristana, still in mourning for her recently deceased mother, accompanied by her maid, Saturna, approaches a playing field where a group of schoolboys are involved in a soccer match under the watchful eye of their teacher. Saturna has come to retrieve her deaf-mute son, Saturno (Jesús Fernández), from the school. The scene begins with a full-shot of the women approaching the playing field and then a close-up of the boys' legs. The loud kicking sounds heard on the sound track draw the audience's attention to the image of the youthful players' powerful legs, ironically relating to the later motif of Tristana's loss of sexual energy occasioned by her amputation. The match is halted when the two women arrive; Saturna speaks to her son's teacher while Tristana offers Saturno an apple. The latter image, in suggestive silhouette, underscores the iconography of the biblical Fall, which is a thematic key to the film as a whole.

The camera cuts to Saturna's conversation with the teacher. The feisty maid explains that as a widowed mother with a lazy, undisciplined son, she is dependent upon the kindness of her employer, Don Lope. The teacher knows Don Lope and praises his rectitude as a perfect Spanish gentleman. These final words of praise are spoken as the scene now cuts to a view of Lope walking down a street, eyeing a young woman and making a pass at her. This ironic linking of dialogue from the end of one scene to the introductory image of another subverts the false image of Lope held within the community.

This same editing strategy is used later to insinuate a dream structure into the narrative. A striking example is the scene in which Tristana, accompanied by Saturno and one of his deaf-mute friends, goes to the top of the church tower to view the city. The sequence begins when Tristana, visiting the tower with Saturno, stops at the dwelling of the church bell ringer (José Calvo), whose deaf-mute son is Saturno's friend. Tristana and the bell ringer chat about his profession, and she remarks that he must feel important working in such an elevated position over the city and announcing the hours for the community. The conversation is interrupted by the boys, who are impatient to ascend the tower.

When Tristana arrives at the top, she eyes the massive church bells, but, in a close-up of her face, one sees an expression of bewilderment as she utters a gasp. The image cuts to the other church bell with Lope's head in place of the clapper. A third shot in this series of images is a surprising juxtaposition of Tristana with the same expression of fright on her face, but now sitting up in her bed. Saturna enters to comfort her from what has obviously been a nightmare. Tristana's dream is imperceptibly triggered by her waking experiences, but one is not sure where those waking experiences end and the dream experience begins.

The image of Lope's head is repeated in another ironic twist of the dream motif. When Tristana finally establishes her relationship with Horacio, they come to his studio, where they prepare for their departure from Toledo. As Tristana is about to leave the studio, Horacio kisses her. At the instant of the kiss, a gasp is heard, and the image cuts to Lope in nightshirt and cap, awakening in his bed, the obvious implication being that he has had a precognitive dream of Tristana's infidelity.

At the start of the film, Tristana is viewed as the innocent, expressing her own simple aspirations: to be financially self-supporting and to make a career as a piano teacher. To these Lope quickly adds another: to be free. He teaches her to despise the institution of marriage as a form of social entrapment, and she gladly accepts his advice, integrating it into her own personal philosophy of action. Tristana sees the world as made up of differences, and she believes that between two obviously similar objects, one is always different. She attempts to live this simple philosophy of freedom and choice. It is all the more ironic that the sense of freedom that Lope cultivates in her leads her to encounter Horacio and to choose the younger, more attractive man as her preferred lover.

With Tristana's return to Toledo and the radical alteration in her appearance and spirit, Buñuel brings the audience not only to consider Tristana's new, embittered emotional state but also to appreciate how her predicament has flowed out of her earlier, ingenuous beliefs. Although Tristana's perverse motivational logic is never explicitly stated, hints of her diabolic plot against her two former lovers are posed in key dramatic scenes. Through dialogue, one learns that it was at Tristana's instigation that Horacio brought her back to Lope's house when she discovered the tumor. When Horacio visits her at Lope's house, she chides him for having brought her there, saying that Lope never would have brought her to another man's house. She has, it appears, forced him into this situation only to humiliate him, or worse, have him humiliate himself in the eyes of his rival, Lope.

Tristana is no kinder with the aging Lope. Living with him but refusing all his offers of marriage, she mocks Lope's amorous advances and tyrannizes him, making him feel somehow responsible for her physical condition. Her attitude is described as satantic by the priest who comes to convince her to accept the marriage offer. The viewer achieves a better sense of the motivation beneath her impenetrable grimace when she responds to Saturno's sexual advances by ordering him to the garden and exposing her naked body for him to view only as a voyeur. Strikingly, Tristana constructs her encounter with Saturno so as to place him in an inferior position and to make herself the untouchable object of desire. The scene is a further embellishment on the motif of the fall from the innocence of the garden with which the film began.

The logic of the second part of the film thus gradually becomes clear through the reiteration of a single underlying paradigm: In exchange for her lost sexual force, Tristana bitterly assumes the role of power and domination over the men around her; Horacio, Saturno, and, finally, Lope. If in the first part of the film she lived the belief in freedom and choice among men and destinies, she has now become bitterly disillusioned and acts on the certain knowledge that all men are the same and that somehow they are all responsible for having mutilated her.

In the final scene, after Tristana pretends to call a doctor for assistance, thereby letting Lope die, she hobbles on crutches to the bedroom window and opens it to look out at the snowy night. The window is barred, and a gust of wind is heard as images from her earlier life flash on the screen in reverse chronological order: the nightmare image of Lope's head in place of the bell clapper; her rejection of Saturno's advances; her marriage ceremony with Lope; her embrace with Horacio; Lope's seduction of her, finally, the image of Tristana and Saturna approaching the soccer field, thus closing the circle of the heroine's dream.

That closed circle is crucial to the understanding of Tristana's plight and the destiny that she has carved out of it for herself. Tristana's dream of self-fulfillment and liberation has been transformed into a nightmare of revenge upon the men who have mutilated her. The image of the barred window suggests the heroine's recognition of her own fall from innocence as enigmatically posed in the first scene. Freedom and choice, as Buñuel again demonstrates, are only illusions which entrap and victimize the ingenuous.

*Marvin D'Lugo*

# TUDO BEM

*Origin:* Brazil
*Released:* 1978
*Released in U.S.:* no listing
*Production:* Sagittarius Cinematic Productions
*Direction:* Arnaldo Jabor
*Screenplay:* Arnaldo Jabor and Leopoldo Serran
*Cinematography:* Dib Lufti
*Editing:* Gilberto Santeiro
*Art direction:* Hélio Eichbauer
*Sound:* Vítor Raposeira
*Music:* no listing
*MPAA rating:* no listing
*Running time:* 110 minutes

*Principal characters:*
Juarez Carioca .................... Paulo Gracindo
Elvira ...................... Fernanda Montenegro
Zezé................................ Zezé Motta
Aparecida de Fátima ................. Maria Silvia
Right-wing dentist ................... Jorge Loredo
Bankrupt industrialist.............. Fernando Torres
Tubercular poet ...................... Luiz Linhares
Bill Thompson ................. Paulo César Pereio

One of the founding members of Brazil's *Cinema Novo*, Arnaldo Jabor began his career as a theater critic and playwright, and his films are deeply marked by the theatrical tradition. After work as a sound technician in some early *Cinema Novo* films, Jabor made a documentary, *A opinião pública* (1967; *Public Opinion*), which won a prize in the Pesaro Film Festival. His second feature was an ambitious allegorical film entitled *Pindorama* (1971), which was a critical and box-office failure. Jabor reached his stride, however, with two filmic adaptations of the plays of Brazilian playwright Nelson Rodrigues: *Toda nudez será castigada* (1973; *All Nudity Shall Be Punished*) and *O casamento* (1975; *The Marriage*). Both were satiric melodramas which posit sexual decadence and repression as symptomatic of the political corruption and moral decay of the Brazilian upper class. Jabor made *Tudo bem* in 1978, followed by *Ey te amo* (1981; *I Love You*). The latter film featured Sonia Braga and was distributed in the United States, Latin America, and elsewhere.

*Tudo bem* shows Jabor at the height of his powers in an ironic film which is both critical and comic. The title mocks Brazilian optimism by alluding to the fairly standard Brazilian response to the question "How are You?"—"Everything's Fine." The film shows that in fact everything is not fine, by painting a satiric portrait of the social contradictions of Brazil. Jabor concentrates all of Brazil into the middle-class apartment of a Carioca family. The retired father, Juarez (Paulo Gracindo), naïvely reactionary and romantically patriotic, lives at home in his pajamas, surrounded by a private museum of nationalist relics. Counseled by the boisterous phantoms of his former friends—a drunken Fascist (Jorge Loredo), a failed spaghetti manufacturer (Fernando Torres), and a tubercular romantic poet (Luiz Linhares)—Juarez spends his time sending irate letters to newspapers, lamenting the decadence of contemporary mores, and proposing absurd solutions for the country's problems. He favors capitalism, for example, but he deplores profit. His wife Elvira (Fernanda Montenegro), meanwhile, has her own phantoms. Unable to accept the fact of her husband's impotence, she fantasizes an imaginary lover for him, describing her with obsessive fascination, to the point that Juarez actually falls in love with his wife's chimerical invention. Two children complete the family portrait—a bland public relations consultant working for a multinational corporation, and a daughter defined largely in terms of her search for a husband. Of two maids, initially the family's only contact with other social classes—one, Zezé (Zezé Motta), moonlights as a prostitute, while the other, Aparecida de Fátima (Maria Silvia), is a virgin and a mystic.

It is Elvira's decision to refurbish the apartment that sets the dramatic action in motion. The entry of the working class, come to "reform" the apartment into the comfortable home explodes all of its complacencies. In surreal conversation, Elvira complains about inflation, while the workers say that they worry about having something, anything, to eat. She says naïvely that they are "almost neighbors," forgetting that she lives in luxurious Copacabana while they live in a slum. In a politicized version of the Marx Brothers *A Night at the Opera* (1935), Jabor has all the dispossessed of Brazil symbolically "invade" the bourgeois apartment. The workers, seeing Elvira's generous intentions, invite their homeless friends, while the sick in search of healing come to visit Aparecida, who has become known as a miracle worker. The apartment becomes a microcosm of Brazil itself, a social synthesis which is both horizontal, in that it includes representatives of the diverse regions of the country, and vertical, in that it comprises all social classes. How many social contradictions, the film asks, can a nation accommodate before it explodes from the pressure?

Recontextualized within this bourgeois space, the Brazilian popular culture of samba, carnival, and Afro-Brazilian mysticism begins to seem subversive and incendiary. "The slave quarters," in Glauber Rocha's felicitous expression, "invade the Big House." The Utopian energy of carnival, led by the prostitute Zezé, threatens the order and progress of the respectable apartment. The harsh gutteral songs of the Northeast seem painful, disturbing, unbearable. The social and cultural contradictions of Brazilian life are made by Jabor to seem strange and therefore unacceptable, as Jabor gives a precise political meaning to the venerable Surrealist strategy of the absurd juxtaposition.

*Tudo bem* typifies the approach of much of *Cinema Novo* by employing Brechtian distancing strategies in the service of social demystification. The credits show eight millimeter footage of the director as a child. Elvira projects her jealous fantasies onto a movie screen. More important, however, the story structure of the film is Brechtian, consisting in autonomous sequences, each with its own style. Brecht argued for a "theatre for latecomers," in which it would matter little if the spectators arrived late, since the play would be composed of autonomous and independent segments. Jabor mimics this technique by a series of unattached scenes, which might have been edited in any number of distinct manners.

Anticipating his own later film *I Love You*—the title mockingly alludes to the prejudice, once widespread in Brazil, that Portuguese was not a "cinematic" language, since "I Love You" was so much more beautiful than "eu te amo"—*Tudo bem* also exploits the language of television. The film begins as a kind of television soap opera (telenovela) concerned with the emotional problems of a middle-class nuclear family, but soon transforms itself into the reverse of a soap opera by reminding the viewer of everything that soap operas usually leave out. The film ends with an amusing sequence in which the American Bill Thompson (Paulo César Pereio) sings the praises of the "global village." Thanks to communications satellites, he says, in an allusion both to the soccer of Pelé and to the "creative geography of (Lev) Kuleshov," a ball can be "kicked in New York, but received in Copacabana." He then leads the party crowd in a festive version of "Around the World I Searched for You." The mass media of the industrialized nations, Jabor seems to be suggesting, no longer need "eighty days" to circle the globe; their transmissions are instantaneous. Yet the masters of the media should not become overly complacent, the film implies, for Brazil, like the apartment of Juarez and Elvira, is still "under construction," and the reforms proposed might prove to be insufficient. Like Ruy Guerra and Nelso Xavier's *A oueda* (1978; *The Fall*), *Tudo bem* combines a thematic of construction with an aesthetic of deconstruction, combining humor and political purpose, energy and consciousness.

*Robert Stam*

# TURKISH DELIGHT
# (TURKS FRUIT)

*Origin:* The Netherlands
*Released:* 1972
*Released in U.S.:* 1973
*Production:* Rob Houwer for Rob Houwer Film Holland
*Direction:* Paul Verhoeven
*Screenplay:* Gerard Soeteman; based on the novel *Turks Fruit*, by Jan Wolkers
*Cinematography:* Jan de Bont
*Editing:* Jan Bosdriesz
*Art direction:* Ralf van der Elst
*Costume design:* Mia Houweling
*Music:* Rogier van Otterloo
*MPAA rating:* X
*Running time:* 102 minutes

*Principal characters:*
Olga........................Monique van de Ven
Eric..............................Rutger Hauer
Olga's mother..................Tonny Huurdeman
Olga's father..................Wim van den Brink

Dutch postwar cinema up to the 1960's consisted almost exclusively of documentary films. In the 1960's, the emphasis switched to feature films and a new wave surged forward. Paul Verhoeven boldly claimed to have opted for a more commercial, no-nonsense approach to filmmaking, wishing to be considered a straightforward storyteller. In the early 1970's, he attacked his colleagues by calling them pretentious and arty, or "whipped cream." Although he has frequently been damned with faint praise by the critics, the general public has responded with enthusiasm to his films.

Verhoeven started his career by making short films, among others a film on the Dutch marines, *Het korps Mariniers* (1966). Some years of television work followed, including a series of adventures under the title *Floris*, the name of a medieval warrior. In that period, he was lucky to find a good producer, Rob Houwer, and together with scriptwriter Gerard Soeteman, they formed a successful working team, which, during the 1970's, made a number of feature-length films, such as *Wat zien ik?* (1971), *Turkish Delight*, and *Keetje Tippel* (1975). All of these films have a somewhat fragmentary structure. They do not seem to form a continuous story, but rather a chain of rounded-off events: *Wat zien ik?*, a burlesque on prostitution in Amsterdam, presents a succession of independent short stories about visits by customers; taken as a whole, these stories form a "kind of doll's house," as

Paul Verhoeven himself once put it. *Turkish Delight* professes to be a love story with a beginning and an end, but in between there is only the arbitrary order of more or less noteworthy events. In *Keetje Tippel*, the lack of dramatic composition again was a serious problem for Verhoeven to solve, because the material on which the film was based consisted of selected chapters from different novels by Neel Doff. This film is about the (mis)-adventures of a poor working-class girl in nineteenth century Amsterdam, who succeeds in working her way up to romance and wealth.

Not only *Keetje Tippel* but also *Turkish Delight* was based on a novel. The best-seller of the same name by Jan Wolkers, one of the most popular of contemporary Dutch writers, was published in 1969 and, although it caused great consternation among the older generation, was received warmly by the young because of its daring personal and emotional tone, larded with plain, rather aggressive sexual descriptions. Verhoeven's intention to stick closely to the very personal, confessional character of the novel required a conscientious "literal" translation into film. The novelist cooperated in making the film; more than once, Wolkers was asked for his opinion, and he helped to set up the script as well.

*Turkish Delight* opens in a sudden and unexpectedly aggressive way. The audience is confronted with some rude charges made by a furious young man (Rutger Hauer) against two other people, a man and a woman. It seems a nightmare: The assault and the killing that follow are repeated several times. In the next shot, the same young man lies half-naked on his bed in a desolate studio, and the viewer learns that the foregoing events were indeed a nightmare, having occurred only in the young man's imagination. He picks up a pinup photograph of the girl he strangled, hit, and shot in his dream of a moment before, and while looking at it, he masturbates, cursing and swearing. This pitiable man apparently has been abandoned by his girlfriend, but the viewer has no time to sit back and ponder. The whirling tempo and drive of events have not yet slackened. In abrupt and quick rushes, the camera continues to follow the man's movements. He tries desperately to forget his love by seducing all the women he is able to lure into his bed, but all the same, he cannot be cured of his longing for Olga (Monique van de Ven). One day, he mistakes one of his sculptures for the real Olga, and the shock it gives him makes him realize that he cannot go on like this. Only at this point is the story of the love affair presented, as the action moves back two years in time.

Information is given about the person and character of the artist, Eric, a lusty "angry young man" who ridicules and lashes out at every kind of smug and bourgeois behavior he encounters. Olga, a seductive young woman with red curly hair, with whom he is falling in love, happens to come from such a bourgeois family. Olga's mother (Tonny Huurdeman), who is extremely vulgar and calculating, never ceases to provoke and disgust Eric. Despite her objections, but with the approval of Olga's father (Wim van den Brink)—a sympathetic, meek old man who always tells the same joke—Eric and Olga wed. At first, they are completely happy together: The couple is shown biking downtown, making love in the studio, rejoicing in their honeymoon on the beach. On the other hand, there are the family visits, the problems of making a living, and contact with the everyday "normal" world. In short, Verhoeven sets the lovers' isolated world of romance against the pressures of day-to-day living.

Eric and Olga's love eventually is not strong enough to withstand these pressures, and Olga goes off with another man. This brings the story up to the fictive present of the film. Eric tries to see Olga, but he does not succeed in making her change her mind and return to him. Time goes by, and then, by chance, they meet again in a warehouse. She invites him to have coffee, for she is by that time alone again. Just as they are planning to go for a ride to the beach together, Olga collapses on the spot. In the hospital, Eric discovers that she is dying from a brain tumor. He visits her faithfully and keeps her company to the very end.

The final scene is of a rare and moving beauty. Eric has brought Olga presents, a box with Turkish delight and a wig, since the hospital attendants have shaved off her hair. Olga duly swallows the entire contents of the box, having dressed herself in the wig. She naughtily tells Eric that she is secretly reading a dime novel, but as she tries to show him and read aloud, her state does not permit her to continue, and she stumbles over simple phrases. Eric takes over the reading, and by means of the clichés he is uttering, he conveys his most sincere feelings in an unsentimental way. The following night, Olga dies. Eric leaves the hospital carrying the wig, then throwing it away in a garbage can. The last scenes of the film show the red curls of the wig disappearing in the grinder of a garbage truck.

The use of small but constantly recurring motifs, such as the red hair, is significant. When Eric and Olga first meet (Olga has picked up the hitchhiking Eric), the radio is playing a well-known Dutch song about kissing girls with red hair. This song is repeated at various points during the film. Furthermore, the red hair thus not only refers to their love affair, but also becomes a link to Olga's future disease. Perhaps the red wig can even be considered an indication of "vulgarity." The Turkish delight functions as a similar metaphor: "Delight" conceals decay.

At first sight, Verhoeven is describing a tragic but ordinary love story in his controversial style. The shameless and comical presentation of sexual adventures in itself was, at the time the film was made, taboo-breaking and embarrassing. This approach, however, allowed Verhoeven to hold up a mirror to society by defying prevailing moral values and mocking them, not only by means of Eric's rebellious character but also by means of his reflections and critical remarks on bourgeois conformity. It is not so much the disease, Verhoeven seems to suggest, or even Olga's surroundings, that doom the innocent and spontaneous girl. Olga leaves Eric after a quarrel during a family party. They are having dinner at a Chinese restaurant (which in Holland is considered cheap and commonplace), and the company is behaving in such a banal and sick way that Eric cannot restrain his disgust. He is obliged to vomit, after which he slaps Olga in the face for having flirted with another man. When Eric meets Olga again in the warehouse, she has been metamorphosed into a rather vulgar woman, who shows a striking resemblance to her mother.

Verhoeven himself compared his style with the music of Igor Stravinsky. He wishes to keep an emotional distance and to avoid cheap sentimentality. The relationships of the characters may be as violent as possible, but emotions must be screened so that the viewer is left uncertain whether to laugh or to cry.

Sound and lighting are used to advantage to emphasize the film's structure and atmosphere. Noise suddenly replaces silence, and vice versa; dark suddenly switches over to light or the reverse, which causes a dazzling effect. Romantic scenes are often shot against the light: the resultant *clair-obscur* fits into the Dutch tradition of painting and its lyric manipulation of light. An interesting example of this is the morning after the first night Olga and Eric spend together. In the studio it is still dark, but outside, day is breaking. The picture is similar to a Dutch seventeenth century painting. Another romantic scene, in which the couple are on the beach watching the sunset, is too stereotypical and therefore less successful. The choice of setting on the beach, however, is not without importance. After Olga's departure, Eric takes care of a wounded seagull; later on, he sets it free on the beach, at dawn. The parallel with the story of Eric and Olga is obvious—the more so as their first encounter also ends in a car crash, the helpless Eric standing at the side of the road with an unconscious Olga in his arms. The camera is placed at a low angle, once more against the light, but this time creating an impressive silhouette.

The musical arrangement, by Rogier van Otterloo, contributes to the juxtaposition of the romance against the triviality of everyday life. The main theme harmoniously accompanies the sweet or tragic moments. At the unveiling of Eric's sculpture by the queen, Olga is so provocatively dressed that the municipal officials are shocked. This is conveyed in the film by the marching brass band. Olga's father is caricatured by his favorite Radetzky march, as well as by the trite joke he keeps repeating. At his funeral, the Bach Requiem sharply contrasts with the more suitable march, as Eric sees it in a visionary instant, and underlines once again the hypocritical conformity of society.

The principal characters of *Turkish Delight*, Eric and Olga, were brilliantly interpreted by Rutger Hauer and Monique van de Ven in their debut performances. (In the 1970's, they were cast in many parts in subsequent films. They became internationally famous and went on to work primarily in the United States.) Verhoeven himself realized the danger of unrealistic dialogue. He tried to cut down long conversations and, in fact, particularly between Eric and Olga there is little dialogue. They thereby manage to achieve an acceptable and credible interpretation. The other characters are not as convincing, their acting tending toward the stereotypical, but Verhoeven partly compensated for this by the quick tempo and shifts of action.

Before the production of *Turkish Delight* was complete, many skeptical voices asserted that it would be an irresponsible and risky production. In retrospect, it was called a commercial film, because of the enormous international success it achieved. Today *Turkish Delight* has partly lost its original significance: The public has become used to sexual display in cinema. On the other hand, the reflections on social and moral behavior remain. The film received an Academy Award nomination for Best Foreign-Language Film in 1973.

*Arjen Uijterlinde*

# 25 FIREMAN'S STREET (TŰZOLTÓ UTCA 25)

*Origin:* Hungary
*Released:* 1973
*Released in U.S.:* 1975
*Production:* Budapest Studio
*Direction:* István Szabó
*Screenplay:* István Szabó
*Cinematography:* Sándor Sára
*Editing:* József Romváry
*Art direction:* János Rózsa
*Music:* Zdenkó Tamássy
*MPAA rating:* no listing
*Running time:* 97 minutes

*Principal characters:*

Mrs. Gaskóy .......................... Rita Békés
Mária .......................... Lucyna Winniczka
János, Mária's husband ............... Péter Müller
Andris ............................ András Bálint
Julika ............................ Mari Szemes
Aranka ........................... Ági Mészáros
Mária's mother ...................... Margit Makai
Mária's father ...................... Károly Kovács

István Szabó began his filmmaking career as a member of the young generation of graduates from the National Film School who brought Hungarian cinema worldwide recognition in the mid- and late 1960's. Among his contemporaries were István Gaál, Pál Gábor, Judit Elek, Zsolt Kézdi-Kovács, and Ferenc Kósa, though all were for a time overshadowed by the influential and controversial figure of the slightly older Miklós Jancsó. Szabó's early films, such as *Álmodozások kora* (1964; *Age of Illusions*), *Apa* (1966; *Father*), and *Szerelmes film* (1970; *A Film About Love*), contain clearly autobiographical elements: The films deal with the central events of Hungarian history since the time of Szabó's own birth in 1938 and, in particular, the German occupation of Budapest at the end of World War II, and the 1956 uprising, seen from the perspective of a member of Szabó's own generation, in a role invariably played by András Bálint. The films are set in the present day, but are constructed in an intricate mosaic of often fragmentary flashbacks, sparked by a chance word or image, rather in the manner of the films made by Alain Resnais in the 1960's, though the tone and impact of Szabó's films are very different from those elements of Resnais' work.

These films brought Szabó attention and respect abroad, particularly in Western Europe, but it was the Academy Award-winning *Mephisto* (1981), a Hungarian-West German coproduction, that first received widespread acclaim in the United States and established Szabó as one of the most significant figures on the international film scene.

*25 Fireman's Street* shares the thematic preoccupations of these earlier films, but its structure is much more clearly that of the "portrait of a generation" that Szabó has said he intends his films to represent. Although András Bálint appears in the film, he is no longer the center of consciousness, and the action of the film revolves around the dreams and memories of at least a half dozen characters, the inhabitants of an old house on the eve of its demolition: Szabó himself has suggested that the film can be best understood as a dream experienced by the house itself, rather than as reflecting the mind of any character in particular.

The constant shifting from the memory of one character to that of another; the deliberate blurring of the distinctions between factual event, dream, and fantasy; the physical linking within the same shot of characters and incidents from two or more different time levels; and the matter-of-fact way in which living characters will converse with their dead friends and neighbors, who are seen in the same shot and sharing the same apparent physical reality, make it as difficult to construct an accurate narrative of what occurs in the film as it is with films such as Ingmar Bergman's *Persona* (1966) or Federico Fellini's *Otto e mezzo* (1963; *8½*). This is especially true of the first half of the film; the second half presents a slightly more chronological framework and centers on the experiences of the characters Mária and Mrs. Gaskóy in particular.

After an initial montage sequence of houses crumbling under the impact of demolition, accompanied by snatches of music that suggest the 1930's, viewers are quickly introduced to the inhabitants of the house, drifting in and out of their dreams and memories as they vainly try to sleep on a hot summer night. Some of them are thinking about food: an old woman goes over the recipe for a rich chocolate cake, while her daughter eats spoonful after spoonful of cream; and, in a scene which gives fact and fantasy the same apparent reality for the audience as for the characters themselves, a man dreams that a former girlfriend talks to him about his favorite soup, and the viewer sees her settle herself on the bed beside him, while his wife sleeps soundly at his side. Others think about romance, whether it is the young man who enters the bathroom to find a beautiful young girl standing naked in the bath and smiling an encouraging welcome, or his mother, Mária (Lucyna Winniczka), who remembers her own early love affairs and the competition of several suitors for her hand. One shot here conflates events from several years of Mária's life into a single continuous and elegant camera movement and ends with her talking to a friend who had committed suicide many years before.

Other characters are introduced: an old man who remembers (or imagines) singing to a group of small children in a carpenter's workshop, and two postmen, their coats covered with snow, who stand silently at the bed of a dying colleague. Gradually, however, with the introduction of a cluster of memories dealing with World War II, the focus narrows to a concentration on the experiences of Mária and the baker's wife, Mrs. Gaskóy (Rita Békés). The townspeople prepare to defend themselves against attack, trying on gas masks and digging trenches, then saying farewell to a group of young conscripts about to set off for the front; a sense of the communal solidarity of the period is suggested as a man buys a truckload of bread and gives it away to these youths. As conditions worsen, however, dissension and conflicts arise: some choose to collaborate openly with the Fascists, while others resist as far as is practicable. Still others remain neutral, taking neither side openly, but quick to profit from any misfortunes that may befall their neighbors. Mária is one of many people who are about to be deported, and she goes through the house from apartment to apartment, giving her clothes and furniture to friends, asking them to take care of them until she returns. The women are forced to strip and are subjected to a humiliating body search, conducted, in some cases, by their own neighbors; then, in a scene of complete and ominous silence, they walk through a pool of disinfectant, still clutching the remnants of their pitiful possessions; steam rises and swirls around them, shrouding them from view. Huddled in a basement cellar, they share what food they have brought with them, taking care to feed the children first. Mária is fortunate enough to be released and leaves her winter clothing for the others when she parts from them.

These scenes are not presented as a continuous narrative: They are fragmentary, interspersed with shots of Mrs. Gaskóy attempting to shelter fugitives from the Nazis and hide them in her attic. An atmosphere of constant fear, suspicion, and mistrust is created as the Fascists raid and search the house and there is always the possibility that one of her neighbors will betray her. Then, as a young German soldier walks down a flight of stairs, a shot rings out, signaling the liberation of the city, and a Hungarian flag is raised on the house.

Collaborators are now hunted down and punished, often by those whose own conduct had been most ambiguous. People come to Mrs. Gaskóy begging for character references that might save them, and even Mária, whose bedridden husband (Péter Müller) has finally died, cannot prevent herself from slapping one of her neighbors, who had gleefully taken part in supervising the deportations and who now tries to brazen out her conduct during the war. The film then moves to the late 1940's and the socialization of the country: Mrs. Gaskóy's bakery is brusquely taken over, and she is told that her admirable conduct during the war is no longer relevant; in 1956, however, the woman who had told her this comes to her begging for her protection. The uprising is defeated, and now it is the turn of the upper class to be dispossessed and sent away: An aged count asks Mária to look after his furniture for him until he is allowed to return. Gradually things sort themselves out and some kind of stability is achieved: The viewer sees the house being vacated, its past literally thrown out as the furniture tumbles in slow motion from the windows into the courtyard and the camera wanders through the deserted rooms. In a powerfully surreal image, an old clockmaker is seen among the jumble of broken and discarded clocks in his room; he takes a handful of flowers from a vase and starts to chew them; then he picks up a handful of broken glass and starts to eat that too. Other characters gather together in a room where a cheerful rag-and-bone man bids for their possessions; carried away with enthusiasm, he starts to take even the shoes from their feet and the coats from their backs. Mária's son, Andris (András Bálint), leaves the house and turns to take a final look at it: Lined up before it, as if for a photograph, are all its previous inhabitants from the film, whether alive or dead; the camera pans from face to face, then settles on the empty house for the film's final shot.

Like all Szabó's work, *25 Fireman's Street*, while fully conveying the horror and despair of the history of the last forty years, remains optimistic and quietly confident about the human potential for good as well as evil. There are people who are defeated, corrupted, or destroyed by their experiences, but there are also those who struggle to retain their sense of human worth and dignity and who succeed in doing so against all the odds. The mood of the film is quiet, reflective, and unsensationalized, but, aided by the effective use of both sound and silence and the brilliantly atmospheric color photography of Sándor Sára, *25 Fireman's Street* remains one of the most haunting and memorable of all Szabó's films.

*Graham Petrie*

# THE TWO OF US
# (LE VIEIL HOMME ET L'ENFANT)

*Origin:* France
*Released:* 1967
*Released in U.S.:* 1968
*Production:* Paul Cadeac for Production Artistique Cinématographique, Renn Productions, and Valoria Films
*Direction:* Claude Berri
*Screenplay:* Claude Berri, with Gérard Brach and Michel Rivelin
*Cinematography:* Jean Penzer
*Editing:* Sophie Coussein and Denis Charvein
*Art direction:* Maurice Petri and Georges Lévy
*Music:* Georges Delerue
*MPAA rating:* no listing
*Running time:* 86 minutes

*Principal characters:*

| | |
|---|---|
| Gramps | Michel Simon |
| Claude Langmann | Alain Cohen |
| Granny | Luce Fabiole |
| Claude's father | Charles Denner |
| Victor | Roger Carel |
| Maxime | Paul Préboist |
| Dinou | Élisabeth Rey |
| Schoolteacher | Jacqueline Rouillard |

Like many nations, France has long suffered widespread intolerance within its society, an embarrassment hidden well below the official surface of liberty, equality, and fraternity. Those illiberal tendencies, however, erupted during World War II, when the German-supported Vichy government under Marshal Philippe Pétain gave nearly official status to anti-Semitism.

In the postwar era, France pretended that certain ugly actions had been nothing but the mad vendettas of a disturbed few. It was not until 1969 that Marcel Ophüls galvanized the French with his television special *Le Chagrin et la pitié* (1969; *The Sorrow and the Pity*). Eventually released in theatrical form, the documentary accused the French public of tacit but widespread complicity with Vichy anti-Semitic policies. The documentary likewise spurred a cycle of dramas with similar themes, including such masterworks as *Les Violons du bal* (1974), *Lacombe, Lucien* (1974), and *Le Dernier Métro* (1980; *The Last Métro*).

Long before any of these films, however, Claude Berri made *The Two of*

*Us*. Intended as a first feature vehicle for the director (who had won an Academy Award for his 1966 short *Le Poulet*) and for veteran character actor Michel Simon, *The Two of Us* is one of the first motion pictures to treat the sensitive question of France's behavior toward Jews during World War II.

The film opens with a title card attesting the veracity of the story to follow. A voice-over narrator indicates that it is 1943 and that the boy trying to steal a toy tank is the narrator himself, Claude Langmann (Alain Cohen), a young Jew who is at this time eight years old. Claude is chased around the store in an amusing scene, but the frivolity ends as a German soldier stops the diminutive thief.

Back home, Claude does not understand the perils facing both him and his family. His father (Charles Denner) chastizes him for constantly endangering the family, but all is forgiven as Claude later jumps into bed with his parents. It is this tension, generated by Claude's innocent playfulness clashing with his family's apprehensions, which marks the rest of the film's first section. Claude is caught smoking in an outhouse. Claude engages in a mock sword fight, brought abruptly to a halt when a boy calls him a dirty Jew. Ominous radio broadcasts and air raids heighten the family's already substantial anxiety.

Finally, it is decided that, to protect everyone, Claude should be sent to the country to stay with a friend's elderly parents. There is one problem: The friend's father is a narrow-minded, cantankerous old man, so in order to avoid problems, Claude must pretend that he is Catholic and that his last name is Longuet. He is likewise warned to bathe privately, lest his circumcision betray him.

In the film's second section, the tension arises from Claude's efforts to keep his heritage secret, while the interest sustains itself through Michel Simon's magnificent portrayal of the old "Gramps." Gramps is a gruff curmudgeon who criticizes almost anyone who is not stolidly French. Yet both the script and the seventy-one-year-old actor consistently apply loving touches to the character to prevent him from sliding from antagonist to villain. He loves his dog Kinou, allowing the animal to eat at the dinner table and even take breakfast in bed. Gramps soothes Claude's psychological and physical wounds after the boy is roughed up at school. He pretends brandy is "medicine." He throws caught fish back into the water. Some of his actions (like the flaunting of his tatoos) allude to sympathetic characters which Simon had played three decades before (especially in *L'Atalante*, 1934).

Gramps, however, is also a bigot, weighed down by stereotypes turned to stone. He explains to Claude that Jews smell bad, have noses like fishhooks, have flat feet, and are obsessed with money. In his otherwise happy exile, then, Claude must be especially guarded. He mumbles the Lord's Prayer beside his bed but stops as soon as no one is listening. He pretends shame for his private parts so that Gramps's wife (Luce Fabiole) will not help him bathe. He avoids a "peeing" contest to which Gramps challenges him. Eventually, Claude, in innocent confusion, concocts an intuitively brilliant defense: He points out that Gramps has most of the characteristics that he has ascribed to Jews. Gramps's stereotyping is deflected back upon him, and Claude, who does not fully understand all of this, is left unharassed.

A quite different matter, however, does set off complications. Claude had earlier conducted a juvenile flirtation with Dinou (Elisabeth Rey), the young daughter of a neighboring farmer. Claude purchases a postcard to send to his sweetheart. He inscribes it with "I love you" and, at the mischievous suggestion of Gramps's son, Victor (Roger Carel), draws a cherry as his signature.

Dinou's father (Paul Préboist) is upset. He brings the postcard to school. The schoolteacher (Jacqueline Rouillard) tricks Claude into admitting to having sent it. In punishment, she shaves off his hair, a procedure which the school normally uses to delouse students' heads. The image of the tiny, bald Claude returning home to a compassionate Gramps is one of the film's most powerful and moving scenes. One cannot help but sense the irony in the old man's empathy for a child whose appearance reminds the audience of six million Jews whose fate has been sealed by the same kind of xenophobia which Gramps so glibly espouses.

The film's final movement marks the erosion of Gramps's safe but unreasonable world. Dinou dies. The Allies invade Normandy. The Vichy government collapses. Victor condemns Gramps's support of Marshal Pétain and moves out of the house. Even Claude must abandon Gramps, for with the end of the war, the child can now safely return to Paris and his parents.

Gramps never discovers Claude's ancestry, nor does he ever overcome his own prejudices. During the course of the film, his jocularity, compassion, and sensitivity are countered by an unforgivable tragic flaw: He prefers ignorance to knowledge, stubbornness to flexibility, stereotypes to what he perceives as exceptions to the rule. He may voice a comment toward the end of the film which, for him, seems enlightened ("Jews can't be much worse than the others"), but one suspects that he deeply regrets the loss of his comforting, petrified generalizations.

If *The Two of Us* seems heartfelt, it is because its story is rooted in personal experience. In the wake of the numerous autobiographical New Wave films which preceded it, the writer/director Berri has formed *The Two of Us* into the shape of his own childhood. Berri's actual name is Claude Langmann, the same as that of his protagonist. He, too, as a child was protectively sent away to live with an elderly couple during the war. Out of these experiences, Berri has gathered a bouquet of poignant moments, some praising the warmth of love, others condemning the intransigence of bigotry. That these contradictory elements are ironically fused in one character contributes to the film's splendid strength. Furthermore, there is little doubt that Berri intends Gramps to be a proxy for the French people themselves, whom Berri perceives as bemusedly intolerant, no matter what side they are on (a telling shot emphasizes the shaved head of a woman in the Allies' victory parade; she has consorted with a German soldier).

Not only does Berri embrace the New Wave's penchant for fastening onto personal experience; he likewise observes certain cinematographic rules set down by its aesthetic doyen, film critic and historian André Bazin. Bazin argued that in order to preserve the integrity of reality, one must present things visually as they are perceived in real life. Long takes must be favored over rapid editing, deep focus over limited planes of sharpness.

*The Two of Us* follows these precepts in an almost slavish manner. Most shots play for extensive blocks of time, with subtle, strategic camera movements deployed to reveal new information. There are, in fact, four shots that last for more than a minute, an unusually extended period for a length of film to go without a cut. Yet all of these shots occur at key dramatic moments in which Michel Simon's acting deflects any boredom that might arise. Only in the victory-parade scene does Berri employ rapid cutting.

Jean Penzer's deep-focus photography likewise pays homage to Bazin's theories, though at times at the cost of undermining the story, allowing the viewer to notice the often slipshod lighting setups. Georges Delerue, who scored many important New Wave works, composed the film's gentle, lyrical music. His score is thoroughly appropriate to a film which could have been angrily didactic but instead chose to reminisce through a child's eyes in a warm, innocent, and accessible manner.

*Marc Mancini*

# TWO OR THREE THINGS I KNOW ABOUT HER (DEUX OU TROIS CHOSES QUE JE SAIS D'ELLE)

*Origin:* France
*Released:* 1967
*Released in U.S.:* 1968
*Production:* Anouchka Films/Argos Films/Les Films du Carrosse/Parc Film
*Direction:* Jean-Luc Godard
*Assistant direction:* Charles Bitsch and Isabelle Pons
*Screenplay:* Jean-Luc Godard; based on articles by Catherine Vimenet
*Cinematography:* Raoul Coutard
*Editing:* Françoise Collin and Chantal Delattre
*Art direction:* no listing
*Music:* Ludwig van Beethoven
*MPAA rating:* no listing
*Running time:* 95 minutes

*Principal characters:*
Juliette Janson ........................ Marina Vlady
Marianne ........................... Anny Duperey
Robert Janson ................... Roger Montsoret
Roger .............................. Jean Narboni
Christophe.................. Christophe Bourseiller
Solange ......................... Marie Bourseiller
John Bogus............................ Raoul Lévy

The films of Jean-Luc Godard have had a profound effect on world cinema. A founding member of the French New Wave, Godard, the former critic for *Cahiers du cinéma*, brought to the commercial film industry a new kind of film: a film, both entertaining and serious, which functioned as a critical event. To make works of art that are self-critical, Godard employs a variety of antinarrative devices in order to force the spectator into an active dialogue with the screen images. In the process, Godard's films and videos have challenged virtually all accepted ideas about narrative conventions. He has broken down the barriers between documentary and fiction, and he has brought ideas associated with the European avant-garde into mainstream filmmaking.

*Two or Three Things I Know About Her* is one of Godard's most challenging works. Filmed simultaneously with Godard's *Made in USA* (1966), it was based on a series of newspaper articles, "Les Étoiles filantes" (prostitution in the high-rises), which appeared in *Le Nouvel Observateur* in 1966. Its idea is deceptively simple: to make a film that shows one typical day in the life of a Parisian woman who, as a married mother of two children, works for pin money as a prostitute. To present Godard's unique ideas, however, the film is made up of a series of disjointed scenes and sequences in which the words of one character are never corroborated by another. Godard himself offers commentary over images which appear contradictory. Intertitles announce a variety of political observations. The characters frequently appear to be bored, disengaged, and lacking narrative motivation. Nevertheless, the film is in many ways a profound and moving statement about modern consumerism and urban disaffection.

The film opens with several shots of modern Paris, a city being overrun by urban development. Construction cranes hover above the once beautiful and romantic city. Next the heroine is seen standing at her window, and Godard's voice introduces her as the actress Marina Vlady, who she is in real life. The next shot is identical to the first except for a change of angle, and Godard introduces the woman again. This time, however, he uses her fictional name, Juliette Janson. Later, she is seen looking into the camera and introducing herself a third time as both actress and heroine. The remainder of the action follows Juliette/Marina as she sleeps with a customer, buys clothes, goes with a girlfriend to have her car washed at the garage where her husband works. He, in turn, sits in a café and talks and later listens on his ham radio as President Lyndon Johnson orders the increased bombing of North Vietnam. Juliette's son relates a dream, and throughout the film, Godard intercuts shots of Paris, advertising slogans, and close-ups of consumer goods.

Godard has called *Two or Three Things I Know About Her* an essay, and it is clearly closer to that form than to the more novelistic narrative films of the dominant cinema; the title points to this fact. "Two or three things" refers to the rather self-consciously arbitrary nature of the ideas which Godard is sharing; it could as well have been two dozen. The point is that the film is part of an ongoing dialogue between Godard, the "I," and the spectator, whom he addresses each time a character looks into the camera. The essay form also allows Godard to use an episodic structure in which meaning comes from the individual ideas and actions themselves rather than from the accumulated effect of the film at its end. Unlike more traditional films, *Two or Three Things I Know About Her* is a collage of ideas and emotions.

The "her" of the title refers as much to the city of Paris as to the character of Juliette. For Godard, modern society is like a woman who is forced into prostitution against her will. In the film, Juliette sells her body so that she can buy the consumer products that advertisers tell her she must have regardless of her own needs. Likewise, Godard shows a Paris that is undergoing a drastic physical change not because people want it, but merely because politicians see it as a way of making themselves famous. This analogy between the heroine and the city allows Godard to devote as much screen time to objects and places as he does to the characters. Some criticize Godard for this, accusing him of coldness in not allowing his characters full emotional development. Others, however, see this technique as a way of illustrating how the world itself tends to fragment people, separating them from one another and depriving them of stability.

In Godard's search for a new narrative form, he has used this concept of fragmentation to great effect. Most of his films are made up of many dissimilar scenes arranged much like a mosaic with its own internal rules of order. The new arrangement of the narrative parts is Godard's way of showing new modes of perceiving modern life.

One of Godard's most consistent themes is the difficulty of modern communication. Not only do people have difficulty communicating with one another, but objects and things also communicate contradictory messages. For Godard, advertising and the government are responsible for this predicament, and he takes great pains to illustrate this in *Two or Three Things I Know About Her*. He concentrates his camera on a host of new apartment complexes, all designed according to the government, in order to offer people the best in new, reasonably priced housing. What the government does not say, however, is that to feel comfortable in these large concrete buildings, one must furnish them with all the latest consumer products. To afford these extras, the people who live there, especially the women, Godard maintains, must resort to prostitution. The sight of these buildings, therefore, communicates two contradictory messages: affluence along with debt, the good life and the inability to afford it.

For Godard, a third aspect of this theme is how artworks themselves communicate, and his experiments with narrative are designed to question the whole process of how a film communicates to an audience. This is the motivating force behind his use of a variety of stylistic elements which are self-reflexive. When the heroine of *Two or Three Things I Know About Her* looks into the camera, one is made aware that one is watching a film. The same effect is achieved when Godard's voice on the sound track addresses the viewer directly. The purpose of this procedure is to break down the imaginary relationship between the screen and the spectator. In this way, Godard believes, the filmmaker gives back to the spectator his freedom to make judgments about what he is seeing. This breaks one of the central rules of the commercial cinema: that the events are to be portrayed as if they could not have happened otherwise. When a character acknowledges the presence of the camera, the spectator is compelled to acknowledge the arbitrary nature of what he is watching. In theory at least, this allows him to propose alternatives to the action on the screen. The viewer thereby extracts himself from the tyranny of the image. His regained freedom, Godard believes, makes him less a prostitute, less someone who is forced to do and feel that which is not of his own choosing.

Many of Godard's ideas are derived from the writings of Bertolt Brecht. The reflexive techniques in Godard's films, for example, are similar to the alienation effect Brecht proposed in the theater. The purpose of these procedures is to make the viewer more aware of himself as an informed consumer. For Godard, films are products, like toasters and new apartments, subject to the laws of the marketplace that govern the production and distribution of all kinds of consumer goods. Thus, it is important for the viewer/consumer to know what he is being sold. He must be able to discriminate between valuable and unneeded merchandise. Since political and economic forces rule the film market, and since they determine what kinds of films are available to the public, going to films is a political act, whether the audience realizes it or not. Much of Godard's career has been spent in attempting to put this idea into practice by creating a new kind of political film. *Two or Three Things I Know About Her* is one of these attempts.

The radical nature of Godard's film experiments evolved. In the 1960's, he began each film in a style with which the audience was familiar. *Two or Three Things I Know About Her* opens like a documentary on modern urban development. It is soon obvious, however, that this is no documentary as theatrical conventions challenge the viewer's expectations. Similarly, in Godard's first feature, *À bout de souffle* (1960; *Breathless*), the action starts as a gangster film but quickly develops into a serious parody of itself with political overtones. *Bande à part* (1964; *Band of Outsiders*) is a gangster film that becomes a musical. In each case, Godard mixes genres so that film conventions thought to be understood become something quite different. Godard hopes that such juxtaposition of attitudes and styles will allow the viewer himself more creativity to think about his own life both inside and out of the cinema.

Godard's search for a political cinema was never totally successful, because the more overtly political his statements became, the less commercial the films were. Still, his influence on the United States was quite extensive because of his style of mixing genres. Films such as *Alice's Restaurant* (1969) and *Bonnie and Clyde* (1967) owe their appearances to this influence. Nevertheless, Godard's films underwent a change during the 1970's, and he turned to video, for which he believed a larger audience was available.

*Two or Three Things I Know About Her* is a complex film which stems from a simple idea. This is a defining characteristic of Godard's genius: to be able to pursue the most profound ideas within the most mundane activities. In the film, this proposition is illustrated in a unique scene: The camera frames Godard placing sugar into a cup of coffee. Next, the camera zeroes in on the cup, getting closer until the swirling dark liquid fills the screen. Over this static image, Godard speaks about the impossibility of language and the limitations of action. With poetic grace he voices his fears of the future and his regrets over the past. Because of the film's tone and its persuasive logic, this image is not boring or trite. Instead, it touches a deep cord in the viewer and conveys a sense of extreme emotional tension.

If Godard can find the world in a coffee cup, he also manages to create the opposite effect. Nothing is sacred to Godard, least of all notions of serious art. Continually, he turns high-minded ideas and conventions into comedy and farce. He is fond of using authentic French intellectuals in his films, but he has them recite riddles or philosophical jibberish. More important, Godard takes popular genre forms and treats them with the seriousness of high art. In *Alphaville* (1965), the hero, Lemmy Caution (Eddie Constantin), is a hard-boiled detective out of a *film noir* thriller who speaks like a French Existentialist philosopher. Thus, Godard blurs the distinction between serious and popular art, seeking a film form that speaks with emotional honesty. He is humorous and often brilliantly witty as he plants references throughout his work to comic books and literary masterpieces alike. Visual compositions in a neighborhood bar will be arranged like Impressionist paintings.

Godard shares an often whimsical quality with other members of the New Wave, notably François Truffaut, yet he alone went about challenging the very foundations of the film medium. Like the other members of the New Wave, he was greatly influenced by American films, yet his relationship with the United States has been an ambiguous affair. He has been popular with film students and radicals, while the general public has found him baffling and obscure. Still, Godard's uncompromising stance against the over-commercialization of world cinema and his creative brilliance have made him one of the most important filmmakers of his time.

*Robert N. Cohen*

# TWO STAGE SISTERS (WUTAI JIEMEI)

*Origin:* People's Republic of China
*Released:* 1964
*Released in U.S.:* 1981
*Production:* Tianma Film Studio
*Direction:* Xie Jin
*Screenplay:* Lin Gu, Xu Jin, and Xie Jin
*Cinematography:* Zhou Daming
*Editing:* Zhang Liqin
*Art direction:* Ge Shicheng
*Music:* Huang Zhun
*MPAA rating:* no listing
*Running time:* 114 minutes

*Principal characters:*

Chunhua .............................. Xie Fang
Yuehong ............................ Cao Yindi
A'xin ................................ Deng Nan
Teacher Xing ........................... Feng Ji
Landlord Ni .......................... Dong Lin
Manager Tang............................ Li Wei
Shang Shuihua ................ Shangguan Yunzhu
Mrs. Shen ........................... Shen Hao
Jiang Bo ....................... Gao Yuansheng
Commissioner Pan ..................... Ding Ran

Set against a backdrop of China in revolution, *Two Stage Sisters* is the saga of two women whose lives reflect the choices at stake in such a situation. Spanning a fifteen-year period, from 1935 to 1950, the film offers a vivid picture of life before and after the Revolution. The two central characters, Chunhua (Xie Fang) and Yuehong (Cao Yindi), begin as friends and sworn sisters but eventually choose separate paths that place them on opposite sides of the Revolution. *Two Stage Sisters* is the story of how they become the deepest of friends and the conflicting values that cause them to part ways.

The film begins in a town in South China in the year 1935. The Yangshun theater troupe is giving an outdoor performance of the Shaoxing Opera. While they are onstage, young Chunhua sneaks into the dressing room and hides herself in a trunk. After the opera, Yuehong, the troupe's lead performer, discovers the runaway and hides her from her parents, who are searching backstage. Once her parents leave, Chunhua pleads to work with the troupe, but its owner, A'xin (Deng Nan), believes that she will only be a problem. Yuehong speaks with her father, Xing (Feng Ji), the troupe's teacher, who intercedes on Chunhua's behalf. Xing senses that the young runaway has a certain quality that will work well on the stage and lets her join the company.

A'xin, however, will not allow Chunhua to enter the company without some profit for himself. He has her sign a contract stipulating that she will work three years as an apprentice and four years without pay, and that as owner he assumes no responsibility for her health. Thus, Chunhua learns her first lesson about the theater world: Onstage, things seem beautiful and attractive, but backstage, actors are exploited for their labor. As a runaway with neither family nor money, she signs the contract out of necessity.

While they are on a tour of the provinces, a local landlord sees the troupe perform and commissions a private show in his home. After the private performance, Landlord Ni (Dong Lin) attempts to seduce Yuehong. Ni is rebuffed, but the next day, at his prompting, Kuomintaing police raid the troupe during a performance. A brawl ensues, and Yuehong is arrested and charged with starting a riot. Her sentence is to be tied to a stake in public for three days.

Chunhua brings aid and comfort to Yuehong while she serves her sentence; the two are quickly developing a bond that seems unbreakable. After Yuehong is freed, the two women begin performing leading roles opposite each other. As a result of Xing's careful instruction, Chunhua's singing and dancing have become very popular with audiences.

During the winter of 1940, Xing becomes ill and eventually dies. Before his death, he instructs Yuehong and Chunhua to lead blameless lives. The troupe is grieved by the teacher's death, except for A'xin, who thinks in terms of money rather than people. He makes plans to disband the company and, in order to cut his losses, to sell Chunhua and Yuehong to another owner. By now, the two actresses are very skilled in their craft, and A'xin sees them as valuable commodities. They are sold to a prestigious Shaoxing Opera house in Shanghai, one of the theatrical and monetary centers of China.

After a tearful goodbye, the two actresses bid farewell to their now unemployed comrades. In Shanghai, Chunhua and Yuehong seek out their new employer, Manager Tang (Li Wei), whose treatment of actors and actresses differs from A'xin's only in terms of the money and prestige he possesses. Upon arrival in their new dressing rooms, the two sisters see the famous Shang Shuihua (Shangguan Yunzhu), renowned throughout the country for her stagework. Shang offers no greeting to the newcomers. An aging star, she senses that Tang has brought the two women to replace her. Her fears soon prove to be true. One night Tang has Chunhua and Yuehong stand in for Shang to test the audience's reaction. The two actresses are an instant success, and Tang is quite pleased with his new acquisitions. Later, Shang confronts Tang and asks what the two women's popularity will mean for her role in the opera. As if she were a mark on a ledger, Tang coldly informs Shang that he no longer needs her. He has made her the queen of Shaoxing Opera and that is enough; he brusquely states that he owes her nothing. Later, as Chunhua and Yuehong are accepting congratulations after their opening, they see Shang silently packing her things.

After several years of stardom, problems develop in Chunhua and Yuehong's friendship. Tang introduces the two women to Mrs. Shen (Shen Hao), a wealthy society woman who offers to be their patroness. Chunhua distrusts the woman and refuses, but Yuehong gladly accepts the offer, as she has become accustomed to her new life of stardom and a generous salary. She sees Mrs. Shen as a way to become firmly entrenched in a world of riches. Meanwhile, Chunhua has been giving some of her salary to Shang, who now has to struggle to get a minor part. An argument ensues after the meeting with Mrs. Shen. Chunhua believes that Yuehong is too flamboyant in her dress and behavior. Yuehong, who revels in her new status, claims that Chunhua is jealous of the attention Tang is giving her. Yuehong even brags that she plans to marry Tang. By now, the two sisters share few values. Yuehong retires from the stage, while Chunhua continues acting.

One day, Chunhua arrives at the theater to find that Shang Shuihua has hanged herself. A suicide note has been left accusing Tang of exploiting Shang for money and abandoning her. When Chunhua confronts Tang with the note, he tries to feign remorse, but she knows the truth and is not swayed. Mrs. Shen, who is cunningly polite, tries to curb Chunhua's anger as well as a scandal by suggesting that one must first bury the dead, and she offers to sponsor a regal funeral.

Chunhua's anger over the injustice done to Shang, however, does not subside. Jiang Bo (Gao Yuansheng), a Communist reporter, also senses wrongdoing and approaches Chunhua to learn the truth. The two quickly become friends as Jiang introduces her to leftist ideology. Jiang suggests that she could use theater as a tool to educate people against oppression. The idea is a turning point for Chunhua. Prior to this, her work as an actress has been separate from her compassion for the victims of oppression. Chunhua envisions immense possibilities in integrating the two interests and busily prepares herself to become involved in political theater.

The theater's next production is an adaptation of Lu Xun's *New Year Sacrifice*. The ruling Kuomintaing is not at all pleased with the progressive nature of the play, as Tang quickly learns. Tang makes plans to cancel the play and to put Yuehong back onstage in its place. Using A'xin, who has reappeared as Tang's henchman, he tries to bully the performers into stopping the production. Chunhua and the cast members, however, are undaunted and refuse to stop the play. As a last resort, the Kuomintaing bans the play, angering much of the Shanghai populace.

Chunhua remains committed to the play and to progressive theater. Along with other Shaoxing performers, she plans a benefit for a new theater. Commissioner Pan (Ding Ran) of the Kuomintaing gets word of the plans and orders Tang to stop Chunhua. A'xin, at Tang's orders, attacks Chunhua one night and throws lime in her face. She is temporarily blinded and the benefit is halted. The citizens of Shanghai are outraged at the crime, and A'xin is caught and brought to trial. Pan is nervous that the public might learn the truth from the trial, thus discrediting the Kuomintaing. He orders Tang to make Yuehong testify that she planned the attack out of jealousy over Chunhua's popularity.

At the subsequent trial, A'xin is the first witness. He feebly tries to read from prepared notes to support Pan's lie. Yuehong is next on the stand. She has been beaten by Tang to make her testify. Once on the stand, where she sees Chunhua in the courtroom, the memory of their long friendship is rekindled and she cannot tell the lies that have been prepared for her. Chunhua rises from the audience and speaks in her friend's defense, saying that the guilt lies with those who forced Yuehong to come to testify.

In the next scene, Shanghai has been liberated, the Communists have defeated the Kuomintaing, and Chunhua is leading a theater group. They travel to Hangxhou, where, Chunhua learns, Yuehong now lives in seclusion, having been left by Tang. After her performance, Chunhua searches for her long-lost friend and finally finds her. Yuehong is ashamed of her association with those who harmed her sister, but Chunhua understands the influences upon Yuehong and forgives her. The two women vow to act together for the rest of their lives.

Xie Jin's direction pays scrupulous attention to the details of the period. Peasant markets, theater interiors, and provincial countrysides are presented in such a way that they give the film epic dimension. Zhou Daming's cinematography creates a visual style that is precise and often stunning, beginning with the opening shot of the film, in which the camera cranes down to a crowded village marketplace, revealing various events before finally arriving at the opera troupe onstage. Considered one of the most talented of Chinese directors, Xie Jin has been involved in film since the early 1950's. His credits as director include *A Wave of Unrest* (1954), *Rendezvous at Orchid Bridge* (1954), and *Woman Basketball Player Number 5* (1957). In 1961, he gained prominence when his production of *The Red Detachment of Women* (not the ballet version known to the West) won the first 100 Flowers Award (China's Oscar) for Best Picture.

*Two Stage Sisters* features an original screenplay—an exception in an industry that traditionally relies on adaptations. Xie Jin's collaboration with writers Lin Gu and Xu Jin is exemplary: The course of Chunhua and Yuehong's relationship is drawn in such a way that the film never lags, and this even development from scene to scene contributes to the film's balance and scope.

Nevertheless, *Two Stage Sisters* was not well received upon its release. Completed at the beginning of the Cultural Revolution, the film was criticized both for its Western style and for its sympathetic treatment of the "bad" sister, Yuehong. Though she goes astray in Shanghai, Yuehong is, in the end, a sympathetic character. The film's critics would rather have had her condemned outright than have her shown as she is: a woman seduced by money who, ultimately, sees the error in her ways. After its condemnation, the film was not shown in China until 1979, when it proved to be the most popular film of the year.

*Douglas Wallick*

# TWO WOMEN
# (LA CIOCIARA)

*Origin:* Italy and France
*Released:* 1960
*Released in U.S.:* 1961
*Production:* Carlo Ponti for Champion-Film and SGC
*Direction:* Vittorio De Sica
*Screenplay:* Cesare Zavattini and Vittorio De Sica; based on the novel by Alberto Moravia
*Cinematography:* Gabor Pogany
*Editing:* Adriana Novelli
*Art direction:* Gastone Medin
*Music:* Armando Trovajoli
*Running time:* 105 minutes

*Principal characters:*

| | |
|---|---|
| Cesira | Sophia Loren (AA) |
| Rosetta | Eleonora Brown |
| Giovanni | Raf Vallone |
| Michele | Jean-Paul Belmondo |
| Floundo | Renato Salvatori |
| Michele's father | Carlo Ninchi |
| Fascist | Andrea Checchi |

*Two Women* was the sixth film upon which two of the great figures of Italian cinema, Vittorio De Sica and Cesare Zavattini, collaborated. Zavattini wrote his first screenplay in 1935, De Sica began his career as director in 1940, and they worked together for the first time in 1943, on the production of De Sica's *I bambini ci guardano* (1943; *The Children Are Watching Us*). Zavattini was also one of the most important voices of the theory of neorealism, and together De Sica and Zavattini were responsible for several of the monuments of this very important film style—*Sciuscià* (1946; *Shoeshine*), *Ladri di biciclette* (1948; *The Bicycle Thief*), and *Umberto D* (1952). The films of De Sica, Roberto Rossellini, and Luchino Visconti, to name only the principal neorealist directors, generally featured, in the 1940's and early 1950's, common people caught up in the trials of everyday life, a certain documentary look to the *mise en scène* and cinematography, shooting on location (as opposed to extensive studio work), and the use of nonprofessional actors. Film critics and historians, however, widely agree that *Umberto D* was the last neorealist masterpiece. Improving economic conditions in Italy, the popularity of American films, and an apparent desire among Italian filmgoers for lighter film fare contributed to the decline in popularity of the neorealist style, which had never enjoyed great commercial success in any event. Giuseppe De Santis' *Riso amaro* (1949; *Bitter Rice*) seems to constitute an example of what one might call the corruption of neorealism in its emphasis on sensuality and also the commercial appeal of a woman who was to become one of Italian cinema's most popular post-World War II stars, Silvana Mangano.

From at least one perspective, *Two Women* bears a similarity to *Bitter Rice*. De Sica, instead of relying upon nonprofessional players, as he had in his great films of previous years, chose to head his cast with actors who were already established and commercially "bankable" stars in the late 1950's or who would soon achieve international recognition. Sophia Loren, whose sensual appeal has become legendary, had starred in Italian, British, and American productions and was much in demand. She did, in fact, receive numerous awards, including a 1961 Oscar for Best Actress, for her role in *Two Women.* Raf Vallone, whose first film was *Bitter Rice,* was also a very popular leading man, and Jean-Paul Belmondo starred in one of the first classics of the French New Wave, *À bout de souffle* (1960; *Breathless*), and went on to become, like Loren and Vallone, an actor of renown around the globe. *Two Women* itself won no awards, and as one might expect from the recognition which Loren received, her powerful presence dominates the film. The English title of the film is an unfortunate choice, for *La ciociara*, which refers to a peasant woman of a region near Rome, emphasizes the importance of Loren's role as Cesira. Loren is on camera virtually all the time, Vallone has a very small part, and Belmondo's strength is inhibited by the nature of the character that he plays. Loren competes for the viewer's attention only with young Eleonora Brown, who plays Rosetta, Cesira's daughter.

If De Sica exploits the commercial magnetism of important professional actors, he and Zavattini remain faithful to the basic neorealist traditions which brought them so much success. The film does deal with the hardships of petite bourgeoisie and peasants who are trapped in the crossfire of warfare after the Allied landing in 1943: A fundamental theme of the film is survival, the will of ordinary people to hang onto life when all around them is chaos, anarchy, and death—the absurdity of war. Much of the film is shot on location in the Italian hills, although *Two Women* has a more polished, contrived, "studio" look than *The Bicycle Thief* or Rossellini's *Roma, città aperta* (1945; *Rome, Open City*). De Sica adds a certain documentary touch through the use of a series of still shots at the beginning of the film, shots of groups of war-ravaged civilians. Actual documentary footage is almost nonexistent in the film. Whether *Two Women* bears a positive message about human solidarity and moral values is debatable, but then, other neorealist films, *The Bicycle Thief* and *Umberto D*, for example, cannot be characterized as wildly optimistic works.

Cesira (Sophia Loren) is a strong, proud, resourceful, dignified, and earthy woman, whose abiding interest in life is her daughter. She married a man much older than she, not out of love, but because he represented for her a means to attain a better life in Rome, away from the rural poverty of her native village. She has outlived her husband, survived a loveless marriage, and been able to earn a comfortable living as proprietress of a small grocery in the city. Early in the film, Cesira decides that she must close her shop and get Rosetta (Eleonora Brown) to safety, out of the city, to the hills from which she has come. She asks her friend Giovanni (Raf Vallone), to mind her store while she is away. What follows is a rather cheerful, gentle seduction by Giovanni of Cesira, who protests, but not too vigorously. De Sica's concessions to the interest which Loren's potent sensuality provokes thus appear within the first five minutes of the film. Cesira's attitude toward her own obvious physical appeal is ambivalent. She draws lascivious stares from seemingly respectable men at every turn, and their looks and remarks often annoy her, yet it can be argued that she does not dress in an unprovocative manner. Throughout the film, Cesira will project the image of a woman who enjoys sex but can easily do without it; as she says, Rosetta comes first in her life.

Cesira and Rosetta make their way, first by train and then on foot, to her native country north of Rome. Eventually, mother and daughter are welcomed by friends and fellow refugees, who share their food and lodging and show Cesira the deference which they accord someone who has made a success in life in the city. Cesira meets young Michele (Jean-Paul Belmondo), a former student who is the most complex character in the film. For reasons that are not revealed, Michele has not participated in the war in a country where the Fascists and Nazis have surely inducted every able-bodied man who was available. Michele falls in love almost immediately with Cesira, who, while she resists his advances, accepts him as a friend. Rosetta too becomes quite fond of the kind and generous young man.

Despite Cesira's efforts to escape the war, its terror is present in the country too. She and Rosetta see an old man killed in completely gratuitous fashion when a German airplane strafes an isolated road. In one of the film's most moving scenes, Cesira and Michele meet a crazed young woman whose baby has been murdered by the Nazis; she offers them the milk from her breasts since she no longer has her child to suckle. Finally, Michele himself is killed after he is taken hostage by a group of German stragglers who are trying to get back to their unit.

As the Allies make their way north, the peasants pack their belongings in order to return to Rome on foot. They stop to rest in the church of an abandoned village, and this is the scene of the film's horrible climax. A band of marauding Moroccan soldiers gang rape Cesira and Rosetta, and the young girl is brutally traumatized. She is immediately transformed from

Cesira's innocent, kindhearted child into a young woman who has been forced to see the truly dark side of life. Rosetta no longer seems to care for herself or for the values which her mother has taught her: Cesira and Rosetta are conveyed to safety by a young truck driver, but to Cesira's dismay, Rosetta skips out of her bed in the middle of the night to go dancing with the boy. When her daughter returns home the following morning with a pair of nylon stockings which the young man gave her, Cesira flies into a rage. It is only when Cesira tells Rosetta that she has just learned of Michele's death that the hardness of the new Rosetta dissipates, and the audience and Cesira see once again in the weeping twelve-year-old the tenderness and compassion that had apparently disappeared. Mother and daughter embrace, reunited in their love, and Rosetta is once again Cesira's "sweet little angel." The last shot of the film is extraordinary. Cesira and Rosetta sit on the bed in a peasant cottage, locked in each other's arms. The camera begins to track slowly backward until something of a cameo is produced—ultimately the shot becomes a moving long-shot still of Madonna and child.

Cesira and Rosetta, Italy, and the free world have survived, but a terrible price has been paid by all. Life is very difficult, the film tells the viewer, but the bond among people who love one another can pull them through. What lies outside the individual, even though friends and chance acquaintances may often be kind and helpful, is contingent at best. War is senseless futility and tests the will to endure and the moral fiber of everyone; this message is not new, but its truth cannot be argued. The picture of wartime Italy which De Sica presents is not flattering. Almost all the people whom Cesira and Rosetta meet are interested only in surviving the war: Even though some of them still wear their Fascist lapel pins, it matters little to them who wins the war so long as their misery ceases. Benito Mussolini is roundly described by several characters as a hated, foolish figure, and the two Fascist soldiers who appear are corrupt and ineffectual. The country is crisscrossed by the frantic comings and goings of the soldiers of several armies—Englishmen, Fascists, Nazis, Russians, Americans, and Moroccans, but, for the most part, the people of the hills look on the troop movements in confusion and terror. After Cesira and Rosetta leave the church where they have been cruelly violated, a jeep full of American soldiers happens by. Cesira begins frantically to berate them for what has just happened: To her, soldiers are soldiers, bearers of pain, be they American, Germans, or Moroccans. The only German soldiers who appear for any length of time in the film are children in uniform who sing that the war will end by Christmas and an embittered officer who shouts at Michele that Italians are stupid idealists and that war is a glorious experience without which a man cannot be a man.

Michele is, as the Nazi officer accuses, an idealist, a bespectacled, disillusioned student of literature and the Bible who is apparently disgusted with his own failure to take an active stand against evil. It seems that he has chosen to hide in the hills and take refuge in his books and ideas rather than fight. Now, as the Fascists and Nazis are being routed, he announces to Cesira his intention to join the Resistance. Yet it is too late, and his death really has no meaning: It is not a heroic gesture—it is simply something over which he could exercise no control. If Michele is meant to represent the conscience of Italy, he is not an admirable figure.

There is no point in looking beyond the forces of this world for comfort and assistance. In *The Bicycle Thief*, De Sica's representation of organized religion is not a positive one, and in *Two Women*, God Himself seems to have taken leave of the world. When Cesira and Rosetta enter the church, they are clearly hoping to find sanctuary. Even though the building has been gutted by shelling, bombing, and looting, the altar is more or less intact, and Rosetta genuflects and makes the sign of the Cross before the Crucifix. After she lies down on a bench, however, she looks up to see a gaping hole in the church roof, and this sight gives her pause. The shot of the hole in the church roof, were it not repeated when Cesira regains consciousness, might seem insignificant. De Sica obviously means for the viewer to consider this shot as a depiction of the void, an image of the heavens from which no help comes. Rosetta's awful fragility and solitude are emphasized in the same sequence when her mother sees her stretched out on the floor in front of the very altar to which she had made her devotions only a short time before. The rape has caused Rosetta to see the nothingness around her and the emptiness above; after her terrible ordeal, she lies on the floor of the church staring at nothing, disillusioned in the true sense of the word. She will find salvation only in her mother's love. The conclusion of *Two Women* will remind the viewer of the final sequences of *The Bicycle Thief* and *Umberto D*, in which there is also a narrowing of focus. The protagonists of these films have been obliged to withdraw, to retreat from a cruel world to a single source of love and fidelity in which they can find solace.

*Two Women* is not a great film of the order of *The Bicycle Thief*, *Shoeshine*, and *Umberto D*, and it is perhaps vulnerable to attacks made by critics who charge that in the late 1950's and the 1960's, De Sica fell victim to the temptations of commercialism and the star system. The film nevertheless has many admirable qualities, not the least of which is the sensitive screenplay, the touching performance of Brown, and the vigorous, if perhaps somewhat overpraised, work of Loren.

*Gordon Walters*

# UGETSU
# (UGETSU MONOGATARI)

*Origin:* Japan
*Released:* 1953
*Released in U.S.:* 1955
*Production:* Masaichi Nagata for Daiei
*Direction:* Kenji Mizoguchi
*Screenplay:* Yoshikata Yoda and Matsutaro Kawaguchi; based on the stories "The House Amid the Thickets" and "The Lust of the White Serpent" from *Ugetsu Monogatari*, by Akinari Ueda, and "How He Got the Legion of Honor," by Guy de Maupassant
*Cinematography:* Kazuo Miyagawa
*Editing:* no listing
*Art direction:* Kisaku Ito
*Sound:* Iwao Otani
*Music:* Fumio Hayasaka
*Running time:* 96 minutes
*Also known as: Tales of the Pale Moon After the Rain*

*Principal characters:*

| | |
|---|---|
| Lady Wasaka | Machiko Kyo |
| Miyagi | Kinuyo Tanaka |
| Ohama | Mitsuko Mito |
| Genjuro | Masayuki Mori |
| Tobei | Sakae Ozawa |

For many years, *Ugetsu* was the only film by Japanese master director Kenji Mizoguchi to be widely known in the West. Encompassing both a compelling theme—moral disintegration and regeneration in periods of destructive social conflict—and a haunting ghost story, the work has long been regarded as one of the supreme masterpieces of cinema. As Mizoguchi's other films have come to be known, however, it has come to seem somewhat atypical in several respects. The dramatic emphasis is at least as much on the male characters as on the female ones—in contrast to most of his great films, from *Naniwa ereji* (1936; *Osaka Elegy*) and *Gion no shimai* (1936; *Sisters of the Gion*) to the magnificent *Saikaku ichidai onna* (1952; *The Life of Oharu*) and his last film, *Akasen chitai* (1956; *Street of Shame*). The pace and style of *Ugetsu*—while they could not be confused with those of any other director—are more subservient to a taut narrative line than in other Mizoguchi film. The long takes and distanced perspective characteristic of the director are present, but editing and dramatic camera angles play a larger role than usual. Mizoguchi and his loyal scenarist Yoshikata Yoda constructed many a fine film on the slow emotional evolution of a female protagonist; quietly absorbing scenes—punctuated by graceful camera movements as they unfold without a cut—characterize Mizoguchi's mature style to a greater extent than is true of any other major director.

Because it is such a singular film in the Mizoguchi oeuvre, it would be easy, though callous, to downgrade *Ugetsu* as a false classic. Many great directors who have been rediscovered and reconsidered have seen, in a new critical consensus, their official masterpieces displaced by other, initially overlooked, works. Thus, John Ford's *The Informer* (1935) and *The Grapes of Wrath* (1940) are now regarded by only a few eccentric Fordian scholars as equal or superior to his later Westerns *The Searchers* (1956) and *The Man Who Shot Liberty Valance* (1962). This kind of revisionism can be too radical—in the case of Ford, for example, the two earlier works, while they are less resonant than the two later ones, deserve something more than the scorn with which they are often treated; in the context of cinema as a whole, they are unsually rich and accomplished, and it is insensitive to ignore the centrally Fordian qualities that they do manifest. On the whole, however, revisions of received critical knowledge are usually fruitful and tend to lead to a fuller understanding of both individual artists and specific films. In the case of *Ugetsu*, appreciation of Mizoguchi's special qualities as an artist contributes to a deeper perception of the film, but at the same time, its distinctive mood—difficult to compare with that of any other film—should be appreciated for its appropriateness and for the imagination that it reflects. *Ugetsu* is in truth one of a very few films that has always deserved its high reputation. The broadest acquaintance with other Mizoguchi films does nothing to dispel the sense that *Ugetsu* is indeed one of his greatest works, and it is easy to understand why anyone might name it as his favorite.

Something of the film's special aura is evoked by the usual translation of the title: *Tales of the Pale Moon After the Rain*. An appropriately moody title for a collection of ghost stories (Akinari Ueda's 1776 collection provided two of the three stories interwoven in the ingenious screenplay), it also suggests poetic atmosphere. In the film, poetic atmosphere is indeed vital; despite the sixteenth century setting, the story has a timeless quality, and its otherworldly aspects impose themselves with a sense of reality equal to that of the more literal narrative events. Mizoguchi was not a specialist in supernatural subjects, but, through purely aesthetic means, he makes the supernatural palpable and believable—as well as an inevitable force in the larger flow of the story—in a way that few other artists in any medium have managed.

Initially, however, the story appears to be purely a forceful social drama, animated by the all-too-human flaws of greed and ambition. Genjuro (Masayuki Mori) is a potter who lives with his devoted wife, Miyagi (Kinuyo Tanaka), and their young son in a small village. His friend Tobei (Sakae

Ozawa), married to Ohama (Mitsuko Mito), is a farmer. During a period of civil war, Genjuro finds that he can make a lot of money by turning out quantities of pottery quickly. At the same time, Tobei—enlisted by Genjuro to help sell the pottery in town—dreams of becoming a great and honored samurai. Both wives are disturbed by their husbands' sudden, war-induced mania, though Miyagi stoically supports and helps Genjuro, while Ohama nags and belittles Tobei. After a destructive raid on their village by one of the warring clans, the four adult characters and the small child set off for town together. It is at this point that the character traits already manifested push the story in several different but complementary directions.

In order to avoid the ongoing violence, the group journeys by boat across Lake Biwa, but signs of possible danger prompt Genjuro to put Miyagi and their son ashore before the journey is completed, with the intention of assuring their safety. While Miyagi makes her way home, carrying the boy on her back, the others continue on to town.

Pottery sales are brisk, but Genjuro, Tobei, and Ohama are separated before they can return home. Tobei is pursuing his samurai career, and his neglect of Ohama causes her to be attacked by soldiers when she looks for him. She is raped in a deserted temple; then, anguished, she screams out her reproaches at the absent Tobei after she has been left alone. Meanwhile, Tobei is initially rejected by the warriors whom he approaches, but after he witnesses the suicide of a great samurai and brings back the samurai's head, claiming that he defeated the other in battle, he is skeptically accepted and made a leader. While these events are occurring, Genjuro is led into a strange supernatural adventure. The mysterious Lady Wasaka (Machiko Kyo) asks Genjuro to bring some pottery that she has purchased to the nearly deserted mansion where she lives alone with her nurse. When Genjuro arrives, the dilapidated mansion is eerily transformed into a place of elegance and refinement. Wasaka sings and dances for Genjuro, and finally seduces him.

Though it has been suggested only by stylistic means, Wasaka is a ghost. Forgetting everything but his passion for her, a transfixed Genjuro remains in residence at the mansion, seemingly under a spell that cannot be broken. The narrative focuses on the unearthly love affair during this section of the film, but its other threads are interlaced. Ohama becomes a prostitute, and an astonished Tobei happens upon her when he and his men enter the brothel where she is working; after she chastises him for the ambition that inadvertently led to her low estate, he sees the error of his ways and an uneasy reconciliation is effected. Meanwhile, Miyagi is attacked by robbers for the food that she carries as she makes her way homeward with her child. Mortally wounded by one of them, she staggers on. Genjuro is unaware of all these events, but when he goes into town to shop for Lady Wasaka, a Buddhist priest recognizes that he is under a spell. The priest inscribes a

Sanskrit incantation on his back, and when Wasaka sees it, she realizes that she will lose her power over him unless he rubs it off. The nurse explains why Wasaka (and the nurse herself) have lived on as ghosts—Wasaka died without ever knowing a man's love—but Genjuro, now repentant and intent on going home to Miyagi, does not respond to Wasaka's pathetic appeals to him. The ghosts disappear from the story's reality as quickly and unostentatiously as they were introduced into it, and Genjuro, ineffectually fighting shadows with a sword, finds himself alone in the once-again dilapidated mansion.

The second supernatural episode occurs during the film's final scenes. In a now peaceful land, Genjuro returns home. His house is dark and empty, but after he goes outside and reenters, he finds that a fire is lit and Miyagi is there waiting for him. A tender reunion occurs, and Miyagi continues to tend the household after Genjuro retires. Genjuro awakens to find that the house is once again deserted; Miyagi is indeed dead, as the narrative has earlier indicated, and friends have been taking care of the boy. Life in the village returns to normal, with Tobei and Ohama—sobered by their experiences—picking up the threads of their simple lives, but Genjuro is desolate at the loss of his wife. He finds the will to continue living by returning to his pottery wheel. There, his wife's voice guides him in his daily life. Not tangibly present, she assures him in a strong, serene voice that she is still with him and that he has become the man she wants him to be. As the story ends, the eternity in which Miyagi's spirit and Genjuro's earthly existence mingle is acknowledged when the son places a bowl of rice on her grave.

That graveside image underscores the transcendent vision that ultimately lifts a compelling tale above the tragic events which compose it. An aesthetic curve has graced the film since its beginning and is completed in the final shot. In the opening shot, a sweeping camera movement from right to left takes the viewer from a long-shot of the countryside to an image of the central characters in the village. In the final shot, the camera movement is reversed; after the boy places the bowl of rice on the grave, the camera continues to move from left to right, rising so that the final composition is one of the landscape meeting the sky. The visual reversal of the opening shot is not only gracefully symmetrical but also metaphysical: The camera movement links the village to the heavens in which Miyagi watches over her husband; the specific properties of "left" and "right" have philosophical and spiritual implications. In interpreting art, theories based on psychological understanding of the nature of created images have demonstrated that the left represents the past and the right represents the future. In *Ugetsu*, this would mean that the opening shot to the left—which introduces the self-destructive, negative drives of Genjuro, who is seen ignoring Miyagi's anxieties—is already, for the filmmaker, a past event, while the closing shot—defined both by the inner serenity that Genjuro has gained at tragic expense and by the sense of a higher self, represented by Miyagi, that gives positive direction to his life—represents the liberated philosophical perspective that has always lain ahead to give meaning to the characters' unhappy experiences and the cruel forces in life (the recent war) that played a part in defining those experiences. Even if the meaning of these shots could not be articulated by the viewer, that meaning is felt because of Mizoguchi's highly developed aesthetic sense and the differing moods that suffuse each of the shots described.

The director's stylistic assurance commands specific kinds of responses in the body of the film as well. The extreme delicacy with which the supernatural elements are introduced and elaborated attests not only Mizoguchi's subtlety but also that of master cinematographer Kazuo Miyagawa—an artist in his own right—and the director's other collaborators. Lighting, composition, sound, music, makeup, and acting are all vital to the absolute credibility of the story's supernatural threads. Three beautiful moments demonstrate how this conviction is achieved. The first occurs in a nonsupernatural sequence—the trip across Lake Biwa. Here, the boat and the characters who are traveling on it slowly emerge from the mist in a quiet, eerie long-shot. The shot is expressive because it suggests that the film is entering a magical realm even though there has been no hint of the ghost stories to come. Even more impressive is the first appearance of Lady Wasaka—in a fully realistic long-shot of the marketplace, she simply walks through a crowd with her companion and approaches Genjuro as he hawks his pottery. The next shot of her, however, is taken over her shoulder and registers Genjuro's startled response to her, so when a closer view of her follows, the sense of something strange about her is already taking shape in visual terms. Finally, before he goes to the Wasaka mansion, Genjuro looks at some beautiful, expensive kimonos that are being sold in the marketplace and imagines Miyagi wearing them—the fantasy image of a happy Miyagi radiant in the kimonos is interpolated with the same understated directness as Wasaka's entrance.

By the time the action reaches the Wasaka mansion, Mizoguchi has prepared his audience for visual and aural subtleties that will break down all sense of literal reality. Textured black-and-white cinematography breaks the mansion into areas of light, but as the mansion is transformed by the transfiguration of Wasaka from pale if beautiful presence to alluring, approachable woman, the lighting gradually, almost imperceptibly, changes, and the entire interior takes on a different look. Sourceless sound deepens the unsettling mood—as manifested in Wasaka's dead father joining his voice with hers when she sings and dances, an effect enhanced visually by a silhouetted view of Wasaka and a complementary shadow in the frame that could be that of the father (Wasaka's song is also heard after she has disappeared from the film, when Genjuro awakens in the abandoned mansion). Perhaps the most ineffable effect is the linking of two successive scenes that describe the love affair of Genjuro and Wasaka. The camera first travels to an image of the two characters bathing in a hot spring, at night, then travels on and—with an almost imperceptible dissolve as the light brightens on furrows of earth—reintroduces them in a long-shot that positions them on the grass beside a shimmering lake in a daytime exterior. The conception and lighting of this revered moment of cinematic poetry attest gifts possessed by Mizoguchi and Miyagawa that a painter might envy; the achieved visual beauty is not confined to a static image.

The most beautiful of the film's supernatural moments, however, is marked by a graceful simplicity. This occurs during the most moving scene, Genjuro's return home. Mizoguchi shows the viewer the house twice without a cut as Genjuro walks through, goes out, and reappears after the camera has tracked back to fix itself on the transformed image of Miyagi situated in an interior that is now clean, warm, and lit by the glow of the hearth. The materialization of the dead Miyagi has again been effected without any showy flourishes, and the ease with which the real and supernatural worlds meet gives an extra dimension to a scene that, as written and played, is already wrenchingly moving in the most direct manner possible.

Mizoguchi's long-take aesthetic philosophy—the guiding force of this scene and of many others—is demonstrably related to his scorn for conventionally elaborate effects in all the supernatural sequences. Mizoguchi is an artist who seeks images of harmony in which the dramatic action is sustained within a realistic sense of space. The principle of the long-shot is felt even in close shots: There are close-ups of a kind in *Ugetsu*—notably of Lady Wasaka—but they are enhanced in several ways; either the close-up is a foreground compositional element and other characters are in sharp focus in the background, or the characters are in movement as they pass in and out of close-up. A supreme example of the director's long-take/long-shot style is the attack on Miyagi; the scene is in fact filmed in a single shot, in the midst of which Miyagi is speared by one of the robbers. Setting his camera at a distance and moving the camera functionally, Mizoguchi refuses to manipulate the content of the scene by separating the sympathetic Miyagi from the context (the chaos of historical and social conflict) that has made her anonymous attackers so desperate. Paradoxically, the serene perspective to which he remains loyal makes the moment of the spearing much more piercing to the viewer than a cut to the attacker or the spear or Miyagi would be, yet it is impossible to imagine another director staging and shooting a sequence like this one in such a manner. One might note, as a parallel, less pure in the details of its execution but equally refined, that the rape of Ohama is constructed with comparable stylistic poise. Ohama is dragged into the temple in long-shot; the rape is not shown; an overhead shot of a prostrate Ohama surrounded by shadows is punctuated only by the sight and sound of a few coins tossed down at her; and, finally, as she emerges from the doorway of the temple, another long-shot integrates her with the now deserted exterior setting as she futilely voices her anguish to the absent Tobei.

Much of the action in *Ugetsu* is harsh and violent, so Mizoguchi's characteristic style must bend to the demands of a fairly vigorous pace. This necessitates a more elaborate editing, which the director provides without betraying his sensibility. It might be expected that moments of tension would rush by without imposing themselves in haunting, detailed images, but the opposite is true. When Genjuro is at his most manic, a highly dramatic deep-focus composition places him in left foreground, where he intently turns out pot after pot, while Miyagi, at the center of the image, is far back in the frame, operating the pump that drives the wheel. The image recurs immediately before the end, this time with Miyagi absent (except for her voice) and the wheel turning as if prompted by her spiritual encouragement. A good example of a scene broken down into shots that retains a completely Mizoguchian flavor is that of Miyagi and Genjuro shouting their goodbyes in the foggy night after Genjuro and his companions have let her off on the shore and are continuing their boat journey; here, parallel tracking shots, each with its characters absorbed into long views of their respective places in the scene, underscore the sense of impending doom and of a last earthly farewell.

It cannot be asserted strongly enough that Mizoguchi's grasp of the aesthetic potential of cinema—which led him to create some of the medium's sublime moments in this film—cannot be separated from that aspect of his sensibility that seeks to illuminate human truths. The progression in *Ugetsu*—in which characters lose and then regain their sense of life's most meaningful values, though at tragic cost—is a timeless, spiritual one derived from a profound understanding of human struggle. Mizoguchi is as good with actors as he is with a camera, and Tanaka (his favorite actress and ideal interpreter), Mori, Kyo, Mito, and Ozawa are all at the peak of their considerable talents—especially Kyo, whose remarkable incarnation of the ghost princess is so multidimensional that it arouses as much compassion as dread. Exquisitely beautiful in its details, *Ugetsu* is finally most memorable for its powerful and heartrending synthesis of drama and meditation.

*Blake Lucas*

# UMBERTO D

*Origin:* Italy
*Released:* 1952
*Released in U.S.:* 1955
*Production:* Giuseppe Amato for Rizzoli-De Sica-Amato
*Direction:* Vittorio De Sica
*Screenplay:* Cesare Zavattini
*Cinematography:* G. R. Aldo
*Editing:* Eraldo Da Roma
*Art direction:* Virgilio Marchi
*Sound:* Ennio Sensi
*Music:* Alessandro Cicognini
*Running time:* 89 minutes

*Principal characters:*
Umberto Domenico Ferrari........... Carlo Battisti
Maria............................ Maria Pia Casilio
Elena............................. Lina Gennari
Elena's fiancé.................... Alberto Barbieri

Vittorio De Sica's *Umberto D* is one of the half dozen or so films that are generally regarded as masterpieces of Italian neorealism; indeed, *Umberto D* may well constitute the last great film of what should probably be called a cinematic "movement" (for the purposes of historical and critical convenience). After World War II, several gifted Italian screenwriters and directors—most notably, Roberto Rossellini, Luchino Visconti, Cesare Zavattini, and Vittorio De Sica—took advantage of the freedom of the post-Fascist era to express their personal perspectives on life. Although it is clear that many of the works of these men have much in common, there is no strong evidence that would indicate that they in any way saw themselves as a school of filmmakers. Film historians have come to group much of the work of Rossellini, Visconti, and De Sica under the rubric of neorealism because of what appears to be the desire of these directors to react against years of filmmaking convention in Italy and to represent instead contemporary reality. A concern with social and political problems, the use of nonprofessional actors, shooting on location (as opposed to working in the studio), and, often, a relatively crude pseudodocumentary photographic style (especially in those films that were produced near the end of World War II and shortly thereafter) are traditionally accepted as among the most important characteristics of Italian neorealism. Such acknowledged classics as Rossellini's *Roma, città aperta* (1945; *Rome, Open City*), De Sica's *Sciuscià* (1946; *Shoeshine*), *Ladri di biciclette* (1948; *The Bicycle Thief*), and *Umberto D* feature ordinary people caught up in the desperate attempt to survive in a hostile environment inhabited, for the most part, by unsympathetic beings. The plots, settings, and characterizations of these and other neorealist films do suggest certain analogies between them and "realism" as it is expressed in Italian literature of the period, in French film of the 1930's, and in the European novel of the late nineteenth century.

*Umberto D* is the story of a retired civil servant whose meager government pension reduces him to a life of poverty. On the one hand, the film is about one man and his problems (De Sica dedicated the film to his father, thus signaling a certain subjectivity in the director's point of view). In a larger context, *Umberto D* depicts the cruel alienation inflicted upon the aged by a ruthlessly materialistic and morally bankrupt bourgeois society. The essential dilemma of Umberto Domenico Ferrari (Carlo Battisti) is readily presented in the film's opening sequences. As the credits come up on the screen, behind them one sees, in a high-angle extreme long shot, a Roman thoroughfare busy with automobiles, buses, and pedestrians. Into this long-shot comes a procession of old men—pensioners, including Umberto, who have tried to stage a protest against the economic conditions to which lack of government support condemns them. No one pays any attention to these unwanted, no longer useful, faceless men (even in medium shot, they appear remarkably similar); the buses do not stop to allow the procession to continue, pedestrians pass on their way, and eventually the police arrive to disperse the demonstrators. The pensioners scatter, in extreme long-shot, like ants. Much has thus been said within the first few minutes of the film. One observes the status of a disinherited, powerless caste, of which the protagonist is a member. Umberto always uses his full name when he introduces himself to others; the title of the film, however, expresses in Kafkaesque fashion the impersonality with which society views him. In this world of individual and collective callousness and brutality, "Umberto D" and his colleagues have no real identity.

Umberto's immediate practical problem is that his landlady, Elena (Lina Gennari), intends to evict him from his room unless he pays in full the rent that he owes her. Elena's lack of sympathy is in itself a betrayal, because Umberto had kept her from starving during the war by sharing his bread with her (she had called him "Grandpa" in those days). The narrative of the film relates Umberto's growing desperation—his attempts to raise money by selling his few possessions, a serious illness (he suffers from angina), his eventual despair in realizing that no one can or is willing to help him, and his ultimate decision to throw himself beneath the wheels of a passing train. As frantic as Umberto becomes in his situation, he nevertheless is conscious of his dignity. He never fails to maintain his appearance carefully, and he cannot bring himself to ask anyone directly for money. In a particularly touching sequence, the old man considers the possibility of begging on the street. He even practices the alien gesture of extending his open hand, but just as a passerby is ready to give him some spare change, Umberto withdraws his hand, palm down now, in order to give the man the impression that he had simply felt a drop of rain.

The only things in Umberto's life that retain any meaning, aside from his own sense of pride, are his furnished room, his dog Flag, and a young maidservant named Maria (Maria Pia Casilio), who works for Elena. Umberto clearly sees in Maria the daughter and family devotion that he has never had. Maria cares for Umberto when he is ill with tonsillitis, visits him during his brief stay in the hospital, looks after Flag, and shows a genuine affection for a man who is much kinder to her than her own father. Early in the film, Maria confides to Umberto that she is three months pregnant and that she is unsure of the identity of the father. On the one hand, Umberto's expressions of shock and dismay when Maria tells him of her condition reveals the extent to which the values of his generation differ from those of the young. Not only is Umberto a social outcast but he is also no longer in step with changing mores. The old man cannot comprehend Maria's frank acceptance of her pregnancy, which he regards as an attitude of shamelessness, anymore than he can tolerate the immorality of Elena, who rents rooms in her apartment by the hour to trysting couples. Nevertheless, Umberto's paternal feelings for Maria are so strong that he offers to intercede for her with the two young soldiers whom she has been seeing.

It is the relationship of Umberto and Flag that constitutes the heart of the narrative. From the beginning, the man and his dog are virtually inseparable. Unfortunately, while he is in the hospital, Umberto entrusts Flag to the care of Maria, and, unbeknown to her, Elena allows the dog to wander outside the building. When Umberto is released from the hospital, Maria tells him that Flag has disappeared. The viewer may find the old man's anger distasteful (he literally threatens to kill Maria if harm has come to Flag), but his sense of helplessness and compounded frustration are easily understood in the context of his devotion to the dog. Eventually, Umberto finds Flag at a city pound, but saving Flag from impending doom does not resolve his problem with Elena and the rent money. Umberto returns home only to find that Elena has had his room gutted as part of her renovation of the apartment. The old man's despondency inevitably encourages thoughts of giving up entirely, but before he can take suicide seriously, he must make an effort to see that his pet will be cared for properly. Umberto considers boarding Flag with an elderly couple, but he is put off by their lack of compassion for the dogs that they have taken in; he tries to give Flag to a little girl in a neighborhood park, but her governess refuses to allow the child to keep the dog; finally, he simply leaves Flag behind in the park, but the dog finds Umberto as he hides in the bushes near the entrance. At this point, there is no recourse: Umberto carries Flag off to a railroad siding with the intention of hurling himself and his faithful friend beneath a train. Flag jumps from Umberto's arms just as the train flies past them. The dog cannot accept what his master has just tried to do, and the film's last sequences portray the reconciliation of Umberto and the only source of love that remains to him. The film's finale is frankly sentimental but, nevertheless, profoundly moving. As touched as one might be by the love between a man and his dog, the viewer can hardly consider the end of the story a positive one. Umberto's problems are unresolved: Where will he go now? What will he do? He is, in reality, even more estranged from the people around him than he was at the beginning of the film.

One may argue that *Umberto D* is a realistic portrayal of certain events in particular lives at a certain time. If *Umberto D* is a realistic film, it is also true that De Sica's realism includes the unmistakable presence of poetic license and indirect commentary. Much has been made of a few scenes in the film wherein film time is real time; that is, the time consumed by what is taking place on-screen is in fact the amount of time consumed by these actions when they are performed by living beings in the real world. Even so, it is quite obvious that the scene of Maria's early-morning rising, for example, is an exception to the general practice of Zavattini and De Sica. The narrative of the film is by no means a moment-by-moment account, and the use of temporal ellipsis is really much more evident than any effort to reproduce chronological reality.

The alienation from others that is Umberto D's lot in life and that is the fundamental theme of the film is expressed cinematically in a number of scenes. The masterful *mise en scène* of *Umberto D*, particularly the use of deep-focus photography, is justifiably famous. Deep-focus photography may give the viewer a greater sense of the elements of everyday life and an opportunity to discover the richness of the world of *Umberto D*, but this technical strategy is exploited to reinforce thematic content and to interpret reality. Umberto takes his meals in a soup kitchen frequented by numerous men who are as aimless and downtrodden as he is. His loss of dignity in an indifferent society is as well represented by depth-of-field shots of the endless rows of beds in the hospital as it is by the compassionless doctors who are interested only in dismissing patients as soon as possible. In the bed next to Umberto, an old man lies dying. Two younger men, apparently his sons, ask the nun about their father's condition, clearly only mimicking concern. As soon as the nurse leaves, they return to their conversation about their real interests: money and women. This vignette relates pertinently to Umberto's own situation. When Umberto goes to the dog pound in search of Flag, he encounters similar signs of depersonalization and degradation. He finds long lines of people who are looking for their lost animals; they must take a number and wait to be interviewed by an official. Dogs are routinely put to death if their owners cannot pay the necessary fees or if they remain unclaimed. Once more the viewer is reminded that all too often money can spell the difference between life and death: one observes the painful quandary of an elderly man who must pay 450 liras, a sum that he obviously cannot afford, or allow his dog to be killed. Finally, the camera lingers in several shots upon the ovens in which unclaimed dogs are destroyed.

It is evident that the long-shot is used most effectively by De Sica to emphasize Umberto's sense of alienation and insignificance. The film's first shots have already been cited in this context. Sequences in Elena's apartment are often prefaced by low-level deep-focus shots that serve to express Umberto's physical fragility and the dominance of Elena. Such shots show Elena's rooms at the end of the corridor; lights behind the French doors that lead to her sitting room cast her grotesquely menacing shadow on the glass. Later, when Umberto takes Flag and leaves the apartment for good, he says goodbye to Maria and boards a bus. As the bus pulls away, Umberto looks up to see Maria, his only real human friend, watching his departure from an upstairs window. The bus continues on its way, and Umberto gazes up at a series of apartment-building façades: His sense of loss is deepened by the sight of nothing but empty windows and closed shutters. The final shot of the film is technically similar to the shots of the corridor in Elena's apartment. The last images of Umberto and Flag are a long take in low-angle deep-focus: The old man and his dog gradually recede into the distance beneath the canopy of trees in the park. Ironically, a group of shouting children run into the foreground of the shot, completely hiding the figures of Umberto and Flag.

Sound and music, music which comes from outside the story space as well as from within, are among the most admirable features of *Umberto D*. Several scenes contain sounds of various sorts that are skillfully employed as means of creating or heightening dramatic tension. Near the end of the film, when Umberto's depression seems darkest, Maria tries to cheer him up and draw him into conversation. Umberto, however, is beyond chitchat, and the long pauses between Maria's words and his unenthusiastic responses are punctuated by the insistent amplified ticking of Umberto's bedside alarm clock. The audience is thus made even more conscious of the silence—of the distance that now exists between Umberto and Maria and of the very real void in Umberto's life. This is the hour of decision for the old man: Time is running out, Elena continues to press him for her money, and his home is being torn down around him. Maria leaves, and Umberto is alone with Flag. The viewer suddenly hears again the grating sound of the electrical sparks that come from the tram lines outside the window. This sound, which is accompanied by flashes of light thrown into the room, has been heard before, when Umberto sullenly takes stock of the wreckage of his room, and even earlier, when he is ill and is trying to fall asleep. The sound is unpleasant in itself, but it ultimately signals Umberto's decision to end his life. He goes to his window and looks down at the trolley tracks (a zoom of the tracks is very effective here). It is a short distance in Umberto's mind from tram tracks to railroad tracks, even though his thoughts of self-destruction are, for the time being, interrupted by the consoling presence of Flag. Umberto sits up all night on his bed, thinking. When morning comes, Umberto is presented in close-up, but all he hears—and the only thing the viewer hears—is emptiness, once again emphasized by the inordinately loud ticking of his clock. Later, when Umberto leaves the couple who take in stray and unwanted dogs, one hears a series of strong blows: A woman is hanging a rug out of an upstairs window and is beating it. The source of this noise is seen only after Umberto passes out of frame. Even though one realizes that the source of the noise has in reality nothing to do with Umberto, the loud blows seem to mock the futility of his very existence—the ominous sound might well be that of the hammer of a coffin maker. Ultimately, Umberto makes his way with Flag to the railroad tracks. The sound-track music comes up and then suddenly stops. The only sounds are those of the rapidly tolling electric signal which announces the approach of the train, then voices of bystanders talking loudly (the volume of the sound is already increasing), and, finally, the dramatic climax of this tense scene is accompanied by the deafening passage of the train and its piercing whistle.

In addition to the use of a traditional kind of background score, De Sica also employs a musical device borrowed from operatic tradition in order to aid in characterization and to enhance the emotional impact of important scenes. Each of the major characters, Umberto, Maria, and Elena, is connected with certain leitmotifs. The lilting, rather somber music that is heard at the beginning of the film is actually what one might call Umberto's theme; it is repeated many times during the film, especially when life weighs heaviest on the protagonist. Elena's great joy in life is her singing, and the opera phrases which almost constantly come from her apartment are an inescapable irritation for Umberto. The presence of Maria's soldier-lovers and of her dilemma is always signaled by bugle calls. As fond as she is of Umberto, the sound of the bugle easily distracts Maria and clearly indicates where her real loyalties lie.

The acting of the principals merits admiration, especially in view of the fact that the film features nonprofessionals. Carlo Battisti was, in fact, a university professor from Florence, but he brings a very effective understatement to the title role. Maria Pia Casilio could not have been better in her interpretation of the vulnerable, naïve, yet childishly sensuous Maria. While the acting of Battisti and Casilio is moving in its subtlety, the role of the villainous Elena, a large women of domineering and selfish nature, is rather broadly rendered by Lina Gennari. In addition, there are numerous small parts that are memorable: Umberto's former colleague, the Commendatore, who makes a perfunctory effort to be kind to his old friend only to find that they no longer have anything to say to each other; the grotesque couple who try to eke out a living by taking in abandoned dogs; the adulterous friend of Elena who refuses to talk to Umberto because he knows the truth about her hypocrisy; the governess and her young admirer who briefly but effectively articulate the myopic attitudes of a more comfortable and complacent generation.

Although Cesare Zavattini and Vittorio De Sica collaborated on films into the 1970's, they never again, with the possible exception of *Il giardino dei Finzi-Contini* (1970; *The Garden of the Finzi-Continis*), produced a film of the stature of *Umberto D*. As prosperity slowly returned to Italy in the late 1940's and early 1950's, the relevance of neorealism seemed to wane. Italians turned to more entertaining, escapist films, and commercialization bastardized the neorealist aesthetic, its theories and ideals. *Umberto D* stands, however, as a film of magnificent universal appeal. Its narrative and cinematic rendering of the themes of fundamental human isolation, of the loneliness of modern city life, and, especially, of the heartless treatment of the elderly is truly timeless—as viewers who see the film for the first time decades after its initial release will quickly attest.

*Gordon Walters*

# THE UMBRELLAS OF CHERBOURG (LES PARAPLUIES DE CHERBOURG)

*Origin:* France and West Germany
*Released:* 1964
*Released in U.S.:* 1964
*Production:* Mag Bodard for Parc Film/Madeleine Films/Beta Film
*Direction:* Jacques Demy
*Screenplay:* Jacques Demy
*Cinematography:* Jean Rabier
*Editing:* Anne-Marie Cotret
*Art direction:* Bernard Evein
*Music:* Michel Legrand
*Running time:* 95 minutes
*Running time in U.S.:* 90 minutes

*Principal characters:*
Guy Foucher .................... Nino Castelnuovo
Geneviève Emery............... Catherine Deneuve
Roland Cassard ...................... Marc Michel
Madeleine ............................ Ellen Farner
Madame Emery .................... Anne Vernon
Aunt Elise ........................ Mireille Perrey

*The Umbrellas of Cherbourg* is distinguished on several counts, beginning with its rigorous use of music and its expressive use of color. These unrealistic elements lend distinctiveness to what *The Umbrellas of Cherbourg* shares with other French New Wave films of the late 1950's and early 1960's: the realism of being shot entirely on location. In one sense, Jacques Demy surpasses most of his contemporaries in realism, since the action of his film hinges on events in the wider world—the drafting of the protagonist into military service in Algeria.

The film has another, more difficult distinction. While other New Wave filmmakers acknowledged their love of Hollywood with reflections of its tougher genres—the *film noir*, the action film, or the screwball comedy—Demy showed an affinity not only for the American musical but also for the sentimental drama whose paradigm begins, Boy Meets Girl, Boy Loses Girl. Yet *The Umbrellas of Cherbourg*'s continual appeal to the emotions, which repels some critics, forms an inseparable part of the film's achievement.

The setting is Cherbourg, a major seaport on the Normandy coast. The action of the film takes place between November, 1957, and December, 1963, and is divided into three parts. Part 1, "Departure," introduces Guy

(Nino Castelnuovo), who lives with his Aunt Elise (Mireille Perrey) and works at a service station, and Geneviève (Catherine Deneuve), who helps her widowed mother, Mme Emery (Anne Vernon), run an umbrella store (called "the Umbrellas of Cherbourg"). Guy and Geneviève are in love. After they have sex for the first time, Guy receives draft papers. The two part, promising to love each other forever. Meanwhile, a young businessman, Roland (Marc Michel), has visited the umbrella shop and fallen for Geneviève. In part 2, "Absence," Geneviève discovers that she is pregnant. There is no word from Guy. Roland, who has befriended the Emerys, offers to marry Geneviève and treat her child as his own, and finally Geneviève agrees. Only then does a letter arrive from Guy saying that he has been wounded, in the leg. Roland and Geneviève marry and leave for Paris. In part 3, "The Return," Guy arrives back in Cherbourg. He falls into a depression over the loss of Geneviève, and his loneliness intensifies when his aunt dies. A young woman named Madeleine (Ellen Farner), who had been taking care of Aunt Elise, is secretly in love with Guy. He asks her to stay on for companionship. Later, he proposes marriage, and Madeleine, weeping for joy, accepts. In an epilogue, Guy is now running his own service station, and he and Madeleine have a son named François. Geneviève happens to drive in. In a brief and apparently unemotional scene between her and Guy, she mentions that they have a daughter named Françoise. Then Geneviève drives off and Guy returns to his wife and son.

When Demy first started working on the script of *The Umbrellas of Cherbourg* he did not think of it as a musical. He got the idea from talking with Michel Legrand, who had composed the incidental music for Demy's first feature film, *Lola* (1961). Demy and Legrand worked together for six months, preparing and integrating the script and score. Meanwhile, producer Mag Bodard was trying to raise the necessary money, which was more than usual for a New Wave feature because of the use of color and the exigencies of filming with music. The entire score was recorded in advance, with professional singers in the "speaking" roles, even before all of the money had been raised. One week before filming was due to begin, Bodard arranged a coproduction with a West German company for the outstanding funds, and Demy had to replace two of his cast with German players, including Ellen Farner, who took the key role of Madeleine. The filming lasted eight weeks.

In casting the role of Roland, Demy deliberately forged a link with *Lola*. In the earlier film, Marc Michel played a young man who was hopelessly in love with the elusive Lola (Anouk Aimée); in *The Umbrellas of Cherbourg* he has a solo, based on a theme from *Lola*, which accompanies a key setting from that film, a shopping arcade in the city of Nantes. In Demy's later film, *The Model Shop* (1969), which takes up Lola's adventures in Los Angeles, there is a much briefer reference to *The Umbrellas of Cherbourg*, in the form of a photograph of Catherine Deneuve. His *Les Demoiselles de Rochefort* (1967; *The Young Girls of Rochefort*), which has no plot connection with the other films but stars Catherine Deneuve, includes references to Cherbourg. Thus Roland's experiences from *Lola* to *The Umbrellas of Cherbourg* echo those of Guy in the latter: Each loses his first, all-absorbing love, and each attains a less romantic love with another woman.

That echo is only one of many devices by which Demy enlarges and transfigures what may seem at first to be a banal sentimental drama. A more pervasive strategy consists in shifting between different levels of realism. Such shifts occur in most Hollywood musicals, but there they nearly always coincide with the beginning and end of each musical number. In *The Umbrellas of Cherbourg*, the combination of real settings with totally sung dialogue establishes a home base midway between realism and stylization, and from it Demy can (and does) swing easily in either direction. On the one hand, Demy uses straightforward shots of simple, everyday objects in normal-looking settings, as when Guy returns from the army and is reminded of his lost love by the sight of two empty chairs at the café where he and Geneviève sat before going to his room, or of the cold fireplace that had blazed for their lovemaking. On the other hand, Demy qualifies the realism by various means, perhaps most obviously when Guy and Geneviève "float" from the café to Guy's home. More often, Demy relies on the transformative power of music and color: He may let the music shape either the action (as in the opening scene with its high-angle view of an "umbrella ballet" of passersby) or the flow of scenes (as when each shot of Geneviève's return home after making love with Guy is cut on a main beat); or he may suffuse the real settings with paint or colored lighting, so that the floating journey to Guy's home passes through streets bathed in blue.

The roles of both color and music go beyond such isolated effects. The broad color scheme of the film is summarized in the opening shot, as bright-colored umbrellas begin the "ballet" and black ones end it. The first part of the film glows with saturated colors. The earlier scenes with Guy and Geneviève are keyed to warm hues, such as the crimson light that bathes them at a dance hall. After the arrival of Guy's draft notice, and especially after he and Geneviève make love, the hues become wilder, first with the blues mentioned above and then, for Geneviève's return home from Guy's room, with an irruption of greens, yellows, and blacks amid the blues and reds. The scenes with Roland, by contrast, are pale and bright, and these tones predominate in part 2. When Guy proposes to Madeleine, there is a sudden return of warm saturated hues as an orange-red partition forms a backdrop to Madeleine's emotional acceptance. The epilogue, which takes place at night in snow, is keyed to black and white but also has touches of warm color: This enigmatic sequence is discussed separately below.

Legrand's score to a large extent follows the tradition of haunting, bittersweet melodies with which composers such as Maurice Yvain, Jean Wiener, Paul Misraki and Georges Delerue have embroidered countless French films. It differs largely in the length and structure of its melodies, which include many phrase patterns that are repeated in shift after shift of key. These patterns make it possible for a set "number" to emerge from and merge back into the background music or sung dialogue without any forced break. Although the score has frequent changes of rhythm and tempo, it is easy to understand why an unsympathetic critic referred to it as "sewing machine music." Except at crucial moments—as when Guy and Geneviève sing "I Will Wait for You" at the café, or when this main theme is reprised orchestrally at the end—the purpose of the music is not to assert itself but, precisely, to establish an underlying pulse. For this aural continuity, Legrand's score is ideal.

Continuity, in the sense of the flowing and linking of events, is the essence of *The Umbrellas of Cherbourg*. In addition to the *moto perpetuo* of the music and the overarching color scheme, the camera movement often serves to bind one action to another. After Roland visits the umbrella store in hopes of seeing Geneviève, for example, the camera follows his car past the service station where she is meeting Guy; when Roland and Geneviève drive off toward Paris, their car "leads" the camera to Madeleine. Other links arise from the choice of content, like the café chairs and the fireplace that mark the passage of time and the changes it brings. Characters, too, may serve a similar purpose: Aunt Elise and Mme Emery both die, offscreen and undramatically, while François and Françoise are born, in one revolution of an endless natural cycle. Demy projects this kind of continuity outside the confines of *The Umbrellas of Cherbourg*, reaching back to *Lola*, and forward (potentially) to *The Young Girls of Rochefort*.

Since the sequence of scenes in even a routine film can establish a continuum—a fictional world that viewers can accept temporarily as real—the impact of Demy's multiple continuities is powerful indeed. As the events of six fictional years pass by in a dense stream of colorful images and musical sounds, the viewer undergoes a double experience: Each moment is vividly *there*, its presence metrically required by the score, and yet it is immediately gone; to put it another way, the continual sense of loss (for not only Guy but also the viewer loses Geneviève, Mme Emery, and Aunt Elise) is compensated by the emergence of new images and sounds from those that have vanished. Some critics have been tempted to suggest that *The Umbrellas of Cherbourg* reflects the thought of Henri-Louis Bergson and Marcel Proust, but this burdens the film with a portentousness it never claims. A more apt comparison is with Thornton Wilder's *Our Town* (1938): Demy and Legrand likewise celebrate the passing moments of life, though without recourse to a stage manager or the knowing dead.

The epilogue goes further. While the previous sequences were spread fairly evenly across a span of eighteen months, the epilogue comes after a four-and-a-half-year gap. The stream of sentiment has been interrupted: The viewer does not know what Guy is supposed to have experienced during that time and must find fresh clues to what he (and Geneviève) may be feeling. Such clues are ambiguous throughout. In color, for example, the black of night and the white of snow cover the largest areas of the screen, yet they are dominated by the red of the Esso sign on Guy's service station. This suggests that passion still survives—but in and for whom?

The music raises similar questions: By the end of the epilogue, as Geneviève drives away and Madeleine and young François return, the sound track has built up to a full orchestral reprise of the main "love" theme. This could mean either that Guy's and Geneviève's love still survives or that it has migrated to Guy and Madeleine, or the music could be a comment, elegiac and ironic, on the exchange of that love for domestic comfort, or even a romantic assertion that all past events continue to exist in some dimension of time. As for the noncommittal words and gestures between Guy and Geneviève, they might equally well betray the lack as the suppression of emotion; it could be either reluctance to play an outdated role or fear of reawakening the past that makes Guy decline Geneviève's invitation to see their daughter Françoise.

There is no contrived mystification in this ambiguity. Since the images and sounds could fit either the survival or the death of Guy's and Geneviève's love, Demy need not have decided which was "true." (It is also reasonable to assume that Guy and Geneviève themselves might be uncertain about their feelings.) Colors and music flow by in the epilogue as smoothly as in the rest of the film, but they no longer evoke simple emotions. Instead, they resonate with the many possible outcomes of Guy's and Geneviève's love, ending the film on a complex chord of passion, regret, and contentment.

In France, *The Umbrellas of Cherbourg* was both a critical and a popular success. In other countries it enjoyed popular favor but was treated harshly by many critics, who tended to see it as a vacuous story tricked out with pretty colors and repetitive music. Undoubtedly, it suffered from following on the more obviously serious films of such French New Wave directors as Jean-Luc Godard, Alain Resnais, and François Truffaut. In any event, *The Umbrellas of Cherbourg* was awarded the Golden Palm at the Cannes Festival in 1964. In France, the film also received the Louis Delluc Prize and the Méliès Prize; in the United States, it was nominated as Best Foreign-Language Film in the 1964 Academy Awards and nominated again for Best Score, Best Song, and Best Original Screenplay in 1965. A stage version, directed by Andrei Serban, was produced in New York City in 1979.

With one exception, the popularity of *The Umbrellas of Cherbourg* had little effect on the careers of the people involved in its making: Catherine Deneuve, though only nineteen when the film was released, had already made several screen appearances without attracting much attention; suddenly she became a star. Legrand was already well established as a composer of film music, but the box-office success of *The Umbrellas of Cherbourg* undoubtedly helped him extend his career to Hollywood. Demy's subsequent films have never approached the popularity of *The Umbrellas of Cherbourg*, partly because he has never tried to repeat its formula. The second musical that he made with Legrand, *The Young Girls of Rochefort*, differed from *The Umbrellas of Cherbourg* in several basic ways: It featured not one but three couples of different ages; it involved much ensemble singing and dancing; it had a complex plot that ranged from humor to mystery; and it included spoken dialogue. Whereas in *The Umbrellas of Cherbourg* Demy and Legrand had stayed within strict stylistic limits—and perhaps within their own limitations until they broke out magnificently in the epilogue, in *The Young Girls of Rochefort* they tried to break out from start to finish. Too many divergent parts—some of them outstanding—undermine the whole, which is an honorable (and enjoyable) failure. In retrospect, it throws an even brighter light on the achievement of *The Umbrellas of Cherbourg*.

*William Johnson*

# UNDER THE ROOFS OF PARIS (SOUS LES TOITS DE PARIS)

*Origin:* France
*Released:* 1930
*Released in U.S.:* 1930
*Production:* Films Sonores Tobis
*Direction:* René Clair
*Assistant direction:* Marcel Carné and Georges Lacombe
*Screenplay:* René Clair
*Cinematography:* Georges Périnal and Georges Raulet
*Editing:* René Le Hénaff
*Art direction:* Lazare Meerson
*Music:* Armand Bernard
*Songs:* Raoul Moretti and René Nazelles
*Running time:* 96 minutes

*Principal characters:*

Albert .............................. Albert Préjean
Louis .............................. Edmond Gréville
Pola .............................. Pola Illery
Fred .............................. Gaston Modot
Bill .............................. Bill Bocket
Drunken old man in café .............. Paul Olivier

The advent of sound in the late 1920's clearly constituted a major development in the cinema, but not all filmmakers welcomed the talking picture with enthusiasm. Among those who were apprehensive concerning the effects that sound might have on the art of the motion picture was poet, novelist, scenarist, former actor, and director René Clair. By 1930, Clair had directed eight silent films, among them the highly regarded experimental short *Entr'acte* (1924) and *Un Chapeau de paille d'Italie* (1927; *An Italian Straw Hat*). In 1928, Clair had begun work on a scenario for a sound film for a French-German company but dropped the work in 1929, believing that the coming of sound would mean the end of cinema as he had known and loved it. For Clair, cinema was poetry: The art of film was an art of images, a *visual* means of stimulating the viewer's imagination and of evoking a kind of dreamworld into which the spectator could escape. Clair feared that the intrusion of dialogue would result in the production of films that were nothing more than pedestrian reality, filmed theater (and such films were in fact made) in which the spoken word would nullify the importance of movement, expression, rhythm, and visual invention. Having seen Harry Beaumont's *The Broadway Melody* (1929) in London, Clair became aware of the artistic possibilities of the sound film. He returned to Germany to finish *Prix de beauté*, which starred the American beauty Louise Brooks, and which was eventually released in 1930; unfortunately, the producers had his scenario rewritten, except for the final scene, and called in another director to shoot the film.

*Under the Roofs of Paris* was not only Clair's debut in sound film, but it was also the first sound film of any real importance to be produced in France (the release of André Hugon's *Les Trois Masques*, 1929, the first "all-talking" film made in France, preceded the release of *Under the Roofs of Paris* by a year). *Under the Roofs of Paris* stands as Clair's initial answer to the problems which, from his perspective, he saw posed by the coming of sound; some of the techniques that Clair used in the film in order to respond to the challenge were more successful than others.

The plot of *Under the Roofs of Paris* deals with the pursuit of Pola (Pola Illery) by Albert (Albert Préjean), a songwriter who earns a meager living selling copies of his compositions in the streets of Paris. The effects of the Great Depression on life in France are made clear in the film, and the life which is seen is that of working-class folk whose possessions are few and whose pleasures are simple. Pola also catches the eyes of Albert's friend Louis (Edmond Gréville) and Fred (Gaston Modot), the leader of a ring of cheap crooks. Crime offers a better living than honest labor when times are hard, and Fred is obviously more prosperous than either Albert or Louis. Fred succeeds in at first gaining the upper hand in the quest for Pola's affections, but Albert follows Pola to her apartment late one night, and, when Pola finds that her key is missing (Fred had stolen it from her purse), Albert is able to persuade her to spend the night with him. Eventually, Pola agrees to marry Albert, much to the latter's obvious delight. Bill (Bill Bocket), however, a neighborhood pickpocket and burglar, had, at the suggestion of Fred, left a valise in Albert's apartment, a valise which, unknown to the trusting Albert, contains stolen silverware. The police raid Albert's apartment, find the valise, and carry him off to jail. Meanwhile, Pola turns to Louis for solace, and they soon fall in love. Bill later confesses the innocence of Albert, but upon his release, Albert sees that things have changed. In a magnanimous gesture of true friendship, Albert defers to the love which exists between Louis and Pola and returns, not unhappily, to hawking his songs on streetcorners.

While *Under the Roofs of Paris* is indeed a sound film, it is not dialogue that Clair exploits as one of the new dimensions available to him. In fact, the dialogue is not at all memorable. Clair permitted his cast to improvise their lines, such as they are, and he quite obviously avoids using speech except occasionally for the sake of exposition; even in these cases, the spoken word is of no crucial value. On the other hand, in several scenes, the viewer *sees* people speaking but must imagine, as Clair intends the audience to do, what the characters are saying, since their words are not audible. A most notable example of Clair's defiance of the vogue of the new cinema, of his somewhat playful refusal to give in to the exigencies of the spoken word, is the scene late in the film when Pola rushes to tell Louis that Fred has challenged Albert to a fight. Their animated conversation takes place behind the glass doors of a café, and if the viewer understands the distress of Pola and Louis, it is because of the efficacy of facial expression and gesture. Instead of having his characters dazzle the audience with their witty repartee, Clair makes effective use of a stock tradition of silent comedy, the sight gag. The scene, played in gesture only, in which the two policemen search Albert's apartment only to have the heavy valise fall on one of them from the top of an armoire, is pure silent slapstick. When Albert and Fred are preparing to settle their claims on Pola, Fred pulls a knife. Albert does not have a knife on him, so several of Fred's thug friends offer Albert an assortment of knives of various shapes and sizes. Albert, however, is not really too keen on settling things with knives anyway, and he uses a series of Chaplinesque gestures to indicate that none of the weapons meets his exacting specifications.

Clair draws on the conventions of the silent film for another of his most effective devices in *Under the Roofs of Paris*—crosscutting. Clair often shows parallel development by cutting from one scene to another, depicting action that is taking place at the same time but in different places. A famous sequence illustrates well this editing technique. After Pola has agreed, somewhat reluctantly, to marry Albert, he makes preparations for the day when Pola will come to his apartment to stay. First, Pola is in her apartment, packing; she places her worn bedroom slippers in her suitcase. The next shot is a new pair of fancy slippers which Albert carefully lays beside his bed. He has also bought flowers and food for the nuptial celebration, but these signs of Albert's apparent future happiness will have a sad fate. When the police, appropriately dressed in black, search Albert's apartment, they trample the slippers, flowers, and food with their heavy boots. From this point on, Clair uses crosscutting to indicate the passage of time and the loss of Albert's dream by juxtaposing shots of the flowers, bread, and cheese with shots of Pola and Louis having dinner (the beginning of their romance) and of Pola and Louis in her apartment. Time passes, and Albert's hopes are dashed; the flowers wilt and the bread becomes stale; eventually, in the last shot of the sequence, mice scramble over the remains of what was to have been a humble wedding feast.

If Clair employs editing techniques which he inherited from presound cinema, it is nevertheless to his credit that he also demonstrates superb use of camera movement, something that many thought would be lost to the technology of the microphone and clumsy sound apparatus. *Under the Roofs of Paris* begins (after a prologue of sorts) with a long pan, as the camera descends from the rooftops of the working-class neighborhood, down into the narrow streets, to Albert as chorus-master, leading a group of people in singing the film's title song. The music becomes louder as the camera moves closer to the group of singers. Later, Clair moves his camera on a vertical pan up the wall of the apartment house, enabling the viewer to look into each apartment and eavesdrop as everyone sings or hums or plays snatches of "Under the Roofs of Paris" (even the nasty Fred whistles the tune). Finally and fittingly, the film ends with a reverse pan away from Albert, who is back on the streets, singing again, and the point of view moves away from the singers and up once again to the rooftops. In several amusing sequences, Clair's camera follows his characters by focusing on their legs and feet, not only to register their movements but also to express their attitudes. When Albert follows Pola from the café to her apartment, Clair follows their feet through the streets. Moments later, after Pola has agreed to share his apartment for the night, Pola's coquettishness is shown to good advantage as she and Albert climb the stairs to his room. She stops, evidently having second thoughts, retreats, Albert moves down to block her withdrawal, they hesitate, then she finally decides to go on up; this little episode is related entirely without dialogue.

It is, in fact, music and Clair's manipulation of sound other than dialogue which account for the place of *Under the Roofs of Paris* as a landmark in the development of the sound film. Music is of paramount importance to the spirit of the film: popular music, Albert's street songs, the music of the café-dance hall scenes, the skill of the blind accordionist who accompanies Albert as he leads his audience in song. Background music assists the development of the narrative insofar as it supports the visual action (for example, suitably dramatic music is provided when the police arrive to break up the fight between Albert and Fred), and it presents a unifying element between scenes, most effectively when there is parallel development. Allusion has already been made to the crosscutting from Albert preparing his apartment for Pola's arrival to Pola in her room packing for her departure. In addition, Clair cuts from Louis and Pola enjoying an evening together in a café to Albert in his cell to the police taking Bill to the station, and the same tune accompanies all three of these scenes, advancing the narrative and reinforcing the visual message that the action in the three scenes is more or less simultaneous.

When Albert and Louis escape from the police after the fight with Fred, they take refuge in a nearby café, posing as the proprietors. Thus, the stage is set for a wonderful scene, one of the highlights of the film. An unsung hero of the cast, Paul Olivier, contributes an excellent performance as an old man who has obviously been drinking in the place for some time. He is a reluctant and bewildered witness to a series of events which tax his befogged understanding, and he plays a principal role in a sterling example of

Clair's skill in exploiting the comic potential of music and mime. The fight between Albert and Louis over Pola is punctuated by the music of Gioacchino Rossini's "William Tell Overture" emanating from a record cued by Albert before the fight starts. The record gets stuck during the fight, and the old man holds his head in agony, eventually becoming so distraught that he swears off wine and switches to water. Albert's abiding friendship for Louis is underscored, after the fight, by his playing a recording of "Under the Roofs of Paris," affecting a smooth transition to the denouement of the film. Happiness is not irretrievably lost, even though Albert did not win Pola.

One should note some other instances of Clair's clever use of nonverbal sound. When Pola and Albert spend the night in Albert's apartment, Pola climbs into Albert's bed alone, Albert turns out the light, and the screen goes to black. At this point, *Under the Roofs of Paris* becomes a sound film in a literal sense, as what is going on can be determined only from what is heard—namely, arguing and noises. When the lights come on again, one can easily conclude, from the expressions of Pola and Albert, that Albert's advances in the darkness have been repulsed. The following morning, the alarm clock in the room goes off. The viewer sees Albert reaching out to grab what he thinks is the clock. Instead, he touches Pola's shoe; nevertheless, the ringing stops—Pola has at that instant stopped the alarm. It is not difficult to see that Clair had no intention at all of producing, with *Under the Roofs of Paris*, a "talkie," in the sense of solving the problem of integrating dialogue into film. What interested him was the marriage of sound and the art of images, of rhythm, of movement, of imaginative editing. Static scenes of long conversations were better left to the theater. If the director's will to avoid dialogue seems at times to be too self-conscious and a bit perverse, it must nevertheless be said that *Under the Roofs of Paris* constitutes an extremely important contribution to a crucial period of transition in the history of the cinema.

The mood which the film creates may remind the viewer of American musical comedy. The tone of *Under the Roofs of Paris* is light, and despite the bittersweet ending, viewers are left with a positive feeling: to paraphrase Albert's song, "What's done is done, the past is past, we must go on." The vision of what has been called "the little world of René Clair," as seen in *Under the Roofs of Paris*, affirms the values of loyalty, friendship, and optimism. The acting of Albert Préjean, who appeared in several of Clair's films—*Paris qui dort* (1923; *The Crazy Ray*) and *An Italian Straw Hat*, among others—and Gaston Modot—familiar to connoisseurs of French film as Schumacher in Jean Renoir's *La Règle du jeu* (1939; *The Rules of the Game*) and as The Man in Luis Buñuel's *L'Âge d'or* (1930)—is particularly distinguished. Pola Illery's work more clearly betrays the transition from silent film in that her expressions and gestures are at times overdrawn.

After *Under the Roofs of Paris*, Clair went on to make many fine films in France—most significantly, *Le Million* (1931), and *À nous la liberté* (1931)—in Britain, in the United States during World War II, and in France again after the war. His last film, *Les Fêtes galantes* (1965), was never released in the United States. René Clair remains one of the major creative figures of world cinema, leaving a legacy of technical innovations, critical writings, and a love of fantasy, humor, and romance, tempered with occasional insights into the serious side of the human condition.

*Gordon Walters*

# AN UNFINISHED PIECE FOR PLAYER PIANO

*Origin:* U.S.S.R.
*Released:* 1977
*Released in U.S.:* 1982
*Production:* Mosfilm Studio
*Direction:* Nikita Mikhalkov
*Screenplay:* Alexander Adabashyan and Nikita Mikhalkov; based on the play *Platonov*, by Anton Chekhov
*Cinematography:* Pavel Lebeshev
*Editing:* no listing
*Art direction:* Alexander Adabashyan and Alexander Samulekin
*Sound:* Valentin Bobrovsky
*Music:* Eduard Artemyev
*MPAA rating:* no listing
*Running time:* 100 minutes

*Principal characters:*

| | |
|---|---|
| Platonov | Alexander Kalyagin |
| Sophia | Elena Solovei |
| Sasha | Eugenia Glushenko |
| Anna Petrovna | Antonia Shuranova |
| Sergei | Yuri Bogatyrev |
| Dr. Triletsky | Nikita Mikhalkov |
| Shcherbuk | Oleg Tabakov |
| Glagolyev | Pavel Kadochnikov |
| Yakov | Sergei Nikonenko |
| Gerasim Petrin | Anatoly Romashin |

Along with Andrei Tarkovsky and Andrei Mikhalkov-Konchalovsky, director Nikita Mikhalkov is one of the most important filmmakers of the 1970's to emerge from the Soviet Union. Mikhalkov followed in the footsteps of his famous older brother, Mikhalkov-Konchalovsky, whose *A Nest of Gentry* (1969) and *Uncle Vanya* (1971) earned for him critical acclaim. Like many modern directors, Mikhalkov attended film school. From 1966 to 1971, he studied with Mikhail Romm at the Moscow Film School. He made his film debut with 1974's *At Home Among Strangers*. This marked the first time he worked with cameraman Pavel Lebeshev, who would go on to become an important part of Mikhalkov's films. With Mikhalkov's second film, *Raba lyubvi* (1976; *A Slave of Love*), he moved into the ranks of world-class directors. Mikhalkov further established himself with *An Unfinished Piece for Player Piano* in 1977, *Pyat Vecherove* (1978; *Five Evenings*), and *Neskolko dnei iz zhizn I. I. Oblomova* (1980; *Oblomov*).

Mikhalkov draws heavily upon Russia's rich literary works for his subject matter, and he prefers to work with period stories. All of Mikhalkov's films are swathed in nostalgia, but at the same time, Mikhalkov injects a modern sensibility into his subject matter. Though the films are dated historically, they often address contemporary concerns.

The source for *An Unfinished Piece for Player Piano* is Anton Chekhov's first published play, *Platonov* (1923). The play contains typical Chekhovian motifs: decadent aristocracy, a decaying house, a sense of impending doom. Mikhalkov perfectly captures the essence of all that is Chekhov through his lyric cinematography and his expert direction of actors. His adaptation of Chekhov is a definitive vision. Just as Chekhov was able to capture the tragicomic in his play, so too does Mikhalkov depict the varying nuances of bittersweetness in this superbly crafted ensemble piece.

The opening shots for the film place it within a historical framework and signal to the audience that this is a prerevolutionary film. A freeze-frame of the countryside comes alive before one's eyes as it is transformed from a sepia-toned photograph to a colorful, moving frame. It is a lazy summer day, and a group of aristocrats pass the time over the samovar, playing cards. The estate belongs to Anna Petrovna (Antonia Shuranova), the young widow of a famous Russian general. Her once resplendent country mansion is now overgrown with weeds. Servants who were loyal when her husband was alive are now defiant and lazy. Anna spends the day making idle conversation with Dr. Triletsky (Nikita Mikhalkov); Sergei (Yuri Bogatyrev), her foolish dolt of a stepson; Glagolyev (Pavel Kadochnikov), an aging admirer; and Gerasim Petrin (Anatoly Romashin), a wealthy patron. Anna Petrovna has invited neighbors to attend a summer fete, for which she has planned all sorts of surprises, including Gypsies.

Dr. Triletsky watches the first guests arrive through a set of binoculars. It is Misha Platonov (Alexander Kalyagin), a portly schoolteacher, and his plump, adoring wife, Sasha (Eugenia Glushenko). Both are the picture of middle-class respectability. When Platonov and Sasha greet Sergei, he gushes about his new bride, Sophia (Elena Solovei), who is off rowing with Glagolyev. The Platonovs' congratulations are interrupted by peals of laughter from Anna Petrovna. Her mirth is bewildering to the three. After an awkward moment, Dr. Triletsky breaks the mood by saluting Anna with gunshots from the balcony of the mansion. This is a device that Mikhalkov uses over and over again. As the tension mounts and the situation becomes increasingly uncomfortable, a final confrontation is avoided by a series of comical interruptions.

As the guests gather inside Anna Petrovna's drawing room, Platonov spies Sophia rowing with Glagolyev. A stunned look is on his face. When Sophia enters the house and is introduced to Platonov, she does not recognize him as the man she used to love. In the seven years that have passed, both have changed. Sophia stares in disbelief at Platonov. She asks him if he is still an individual, if he still strives for things. Platonov's bitter, savage response is to mock her condescending questions with cruel answers. He belittles his wife, and himself. The room becomes still as Platonov launches his tirade. The only other sounds heard are the sounds of summer: flies buzzing, wind blowing, and pure silence. The use of ambient sound to punctuate dramatic moments is another clever device Mikhalkov repeatedly uses.

Later that afternoon, the guests are joined by two buxom sisters who bring along their French-speaking young male cousin. As they enter the house, Shcherbuk (Oleg Tabakov), a wealthy, landowning neighbor, joins them. He is very fond of women and drink. Sophia and Platonov steal away as the new guests enter the room. They convene in a dark closet, lit only by the matches Platonov occasionally strikes as he lights his cigarettes. Artificial lighting, such as matches and fireworks, is used whenever Platonov and Sophia are alone. This aesthetic device is perfect for the two former lovers, who do not really want to see each other as they really are. Platonov and Sophia sadly confront each other with the people they have become. Sophia has married an utter fool; Platonov abandoned his studies and settled for a simple, unintellectual woman. They both agree that theirs is a trite story; girl once loved boy, boy used to love girl. Beneath their casual words, it is apparent that they still care deeply for each other.

The guests once again go outside and wander around Anna Petrovna's grounds. Petrovna joins Platonov on a hammock and showers him with words of love. The dignified Petrovna has been having an affair with Platonov, but now he urges her to forget about him. Anna Petrovna knows that he is thinking of Sophia. If Sophia snubbed Platonov to settle for simpler things, she is shown to have her share of hot air.

Sophia and Sergei try to impress the guests by announcing their plans to help the peasants. She will feed all the peasant babies for one morning, while Sergei will donate some used clothing. Platonov laughs hysterically at Sophia's plans, much to her chagrin. Although Anna Petrovna's Gypsies never materialize, another surprise awaits the guests. As the aristocrats sit on the balcony sipping tea, a peasant magnificently plays the piano for their enjoyment. After a few chords, he walks away, but the piano is playing all by itself. After a few moments, the guests become bored with their toy. This is one of the many diversions set up in the film that the gentry discards with rapidity. Cards, charades, costumes, liaisons, player pianos, all of these are games in which the characters frantically engage because they have no other idea of how to spend their time. This is Mikhalkov's way of gently mocking their atrophy. The nobility had become vestigial organs in Russian society at this time, with no plans, and no energy to change. In their world, everything is unfinished business.

The guests all spend the latter part of the afternoon, which has become rainy, inside the house. They pass the time by flirting, getting drunk, and playing dare. The titillating mood of the afternoon is interrupted by the entrance of a peasant, who has walked through the rain to find Dr. Triletsky. He beseeches Triletsky to help his wife, who is seriously ill. Triletsky ignores his pleas.

The whole scene is solemnly watched by the young Parisian boy. Together, the boy and the peasant function as Mikhalkov's criticism of the class distinctions that formed the foundation of Russian society. Mikhalkov gives the young boy and the peasant a sanctioned spirituality that he denies his other characters. Although the boy is a very minor character, several shots of the boy are included at important moments in the film. In one instance, the boy is alone in front of a pond. Lonely music can be faintly heard. The scene is reminiscent of François Truffaut's *L'Enfant sauvage* (1970; *The Wild Child*) in terms of its style. Mikhalkov includes a shot of the angelic-looking boy as he sleeps in the final shot of the film. This is where he embellishes Chekhov's story. He chooses to end the film with hope, instead of resignation.

The theme of class distinction comes up at the dinner table later that evening, where a perfectly splendid meal is interrupted by politics. Shcherbuk, the portly landowner, is bemoaning the fact that the blue bloods are dying out, while working-class scum is overpopulating the earth. His discourse is cut off by Gerasim Petrin, who has not yet said a word in the film. He has made his fortune through labor, and he chides all the idle aristocrats at the table for their inefficiency. After Shcherbuk leaves the room in tears, one by one all the characters confess their sense of frustration and disillusionment with this paltry life.

Platonov calms the group by telling them a love story. As he recounts how he and a woman once shared a strong, passionate love, the guests are enraptured. He concluded his sad tale by explaining how the resplendent lovers grew up and became only ordinary people. Sophia cannot contain her reaction to this story, and she leaves the table. Later that evening, Sophia and Platonov will rekindle their lost romance. Sophia's bumbling husband, Sergei, sees the reunited lovers as they plan to run away together. Sergei runs to Anna Petrovna, a mother figure for the stepson only a few years younger than she. Yet when Anna Petrovna tells Sergei of her love for Platonov, Sergei tears away from her with disgust. He makes plans to leave his deceased father's wretched estate. He packs his bags and sits in the carriage near the stables. He yells for some assistance in getting horses, but his cries are ignored by the apathetic servants. Though the aristocratic class is mobile, they have become paralyzed by their inertia.

Meanwhile, it is early dawn. Platonov is all alone as the sun rises. In the distance, he sees a train moving. He is struck by his own inability to move on and to change. Suddenly, his life seems a worthless endeavor. When he encounters Sophia, he rejects her love. He proceeds to wake up the entire household with his anguished cries. He screams over and over, "I am lost. I am thirty-five. All is lost."

Although the audience has seen Dr. Triletsky's anguish about being ineffective as a doctor and listened to Anna Petrovna's musings about the importance of financial solvency over love, Platonov's frantic, yet amusing attempt to kill himself by diving into two feet of water is a culmination of all the remorse that is mentioned over and over again. Thus, this pathetic suicide attempt is doomed to failure. Sasha jumps in the river after him, and her loving embraces and tender words soothe the wounded Platonov's pride. Anna Petrovna and her guests have wandered down to the river in search of Platonov. The pajama-clad guests sleepily embrace Platonov as they trudge up the hill together. They all gaily comment about how things never change, how they are always the same. Sophia has joined Sergei, and the two are asleep in the carriage without horses. Their attempt to flee becomes an early morning nap.

The ignorance of the aristocracy who think that things will never change is important in all of Chekhov's works in general, and in *An Unfinished Piece for Player Piano* in particular. As a playwright, Chekhov was always able to capture two very opposed emotions, scorn and compassion, at the same time. This is Mikhalkov's special gift as well. All the characters are exalted and then debased. Their foibles, their illicit affairs, all of these are humorous. Yet the characters' frantic attempts to break out of their stupor, and their sincere search for meaning, are very poignant.

Mikhalkov's direction of his gifted cast is superb. This film really is an actor's dream, full of fleshed-out characters that really breathe life into the Russian aristocracy they portray. Critics soundly praised the film as a superb adaptation and as a poignant, amusing work teeming with many talented actors. The year of *An Unfinished Piece for Player Piano*'s American release, audiences would find another loose version of the story in Woody Allen's *A Midsummer Night's Sex Comedy* (1982).

Alexander Kalyagin, who also appeared in Mikhalkov's *A Slave of Love*, is marvelous as the nobly ignoble Platonov, a man who strives for the finer things in life in spirit, but who enjoys the coarser pleasures in reality. Mikhalkov's direction of Kalyagin makes the one-hundred-year-old play contemporary. Platonov could easily pass for a Federico Fellini character. Elena Solovei, who also starred in *A Slave of Love* and *Oblomov* portrays a winsome, lovely Sophia. She bears a startling resemblance to Diane Keaton in her acting style. Antonia Shuranova plays a classically theatrical role as Anna Petrovna, the knowing woman who has a vulnerable side beneath her carefree manner. Eugenia Glushenko and Yuri Bogatyrev are perfectly cast as Sasha and Sergei. They portray simpletons but with a fragility that is extremely touching.

Mikhalkov acted prior to attending film school, and it is his ongoing interest in performers and in the mechanics of acting that makes him very adept at conveying all that is Chekhov.

The characters' frequent outbursts aside, there is a stasis to *An Unfinished Piece for Player Piano* that is part and parcel of Chekhov. People do not change, things remain the same, but Mikhalkov paints a portrait of the thwarted aristocracy that is totally engrossing. Mikhalkov's vision of this world is perfectly orchestrated. The use of lighting and music gives the film a lyric quality. Pavel Lebeshev's cinematography is impressionistic—the shots of the river or of the fireworks that light the sky all have a solitary, mournful beauty. A tension is built up between the use of interior and exterior spaces. All the characters long to escape from one another, but once they are in the world of nature, they are trapped by their isolation from the world. This sense of anomie is conveyed on a stylistic as well as a thematic level.

Eduard Artemyev's haunting music is not used to underscore charged moments, but rather contemplative ones. *An Unfinished Piece for Player Piano* is not only a film to be watched, but also a film to be listened to. The world outside the estate is very subtly referred to through the lilting music and images. The whole texture of *An Unfinished Piece for Player Piano* is dreamily perturbing. What begins as a summer frolic becomes a quest for the ephemeral. Mikhalkov's touch is as light as Chekhov's. The whole film has a naturalness to it. He is never heavy-handed with the actors or the story, which he cowrote. Instead, he prefers to probe gently the internal changes, the emotional states of flux in this doomed world of aristocracy. His characters blithely think that things will never change; Mikhalkov knows that they have.

*Laura Gwinn*

# THE UPRISING (DER AUFSTAND)

*Origin:* West Germany and Costa Rica
*Released:* 1980
*Released in U.S.:* 1981
*Production:* Joachim von Vietinghoff
*Direction:* Peter Lilienthal
*Screenplay:* Peter Lilienthal and Antonio Skármeta
*Cinematography:* Michael Ballhaus
*Editing:* Siegrun Jäger
*Art direction:* no listing
*Sound:* Mario Jacob and Luis Fuentes
*Music:* Claus Bantzer
*MPAA rating:* no listing
*Running time:* 96 minutes

*Principal characters:*

Son .............................. Agustín Pereira
Father ........................... Carlos Catanía
Mother .......... María Lourdes Centano de Zelaya
Major ............................ Oscar Castillo
Uncle ............................ Guido Sáenz
Sister ........................... Vicky Montero
Miriam ........................... Saída Mendieta Rúiz
Darwis ........................... Orlando Zelaya Pérez
Ígnacio .......................... Flavio Fernández
Roger ............................ Roger Barrios
Children ......................... the Lorio children

A dramatic feature recounting the last weeks of the Nicaraguan revolution, *The Uprising* offers a close-up look at the subject from the viewpoint of the participants, and it accurately captures the mechanics of how it happened—how wretchedly poor, hideously terrorized ordinary citizens conducted a street-by-street and house-by-house war to win their country back from the dictator Anastasio Somoza and his National Guard. The film has the advantages and the disadvantages that come with the filmmakers' decision to let the people tell their own story and to serve as translators for the victors' tales of heroism.

Peter Lilienthal is one of the "New German Filmmakers," a cofounder of the cooperative filmmaking and distribution company Filmverlag der Autoren. Lilienthal has a special relationship with Latin America. He spent his adolescence in Uruguay in exile from the Nazi terror, and he later returned to live in Allende's Chile. There he met Antonio Skármeta, a Chilean novelist in exile who, like Lilienthal, lives in Berlin. The two have collaborated on several projects with explicitly political themes.

Lilienthal looks for the political through the personal, telling stories of political crisis and change through the decisions of one person or family. For example, *La Victoria*, on which Skármeta collaborated, was about a Chilean middle-class girl pulled both ways by the conflicts of Allende's Chile. *Calm over the Countryside* (also done with Skármeta) concerned a progressive son and a reactionary father in an imaginary Central American revolution. *David* told the story of a rabbi's son who survived Nazi Germany.

Lilienthal's other films have a style strikingly different from this street-war story—a style marked by dreamy montage, ambiguity about the line between reality and fantasy, and rejection of simple chronology. In contrast, *The Uprising* is made with a ruthless simplicity and an acceptance of the victors' perspective that is perhaps too trusting. Lilienthal went to the Nicaraguan university town of Léon four months after victory and made the film with residents, not actors.

The story is a stripped-down melodrama. The son is in the National Guard, his father is a Sandinista. Eventually the son rejects the Guard's promise of training in the United States and sides with the Sandinistas in time to join in the retaking of Léon. As the soldiers flee with hostages, he faces the sight of his real father being used as a protective shield by his superior officer in the Guard.

The dramatic center of the film, however, is not in the father-son crisis; rather, it is in the taking of the stockade at the center of Léon, an impregnable concrete block. The reenactment—done with gusto by the residents—is a remarkable demonstration of urban warfare. Because the National Guard controlled the streets, the people broke holes in walls between houses. They rigged a fire hose through the houses until they could spray the place with gasoline and torch it.

It takes a unified group of people to achieve such teamwork, and the film strives to depict the conditions that created solidarity of that order. What is shown of the Guard's practices—including a massacre in a church and the casual gunning down of passersby, children, and suspects' neighbors—brings home the swift erosion of any neutral ground in a war pervading all aspects of daily life. This realization, however, raises other questions that the film does not answer.

In a shattered local economy, how did people get through a day? How was bread delivered? How did fuel trucks travel through mined streets? Were medical supplies available? Was potable water hard to find? These are questions that recent documentaries from El Salvador, including *El Salvador: The Decision to Win* and *Carta de Morazán*, attempt to address, but this fictionalized version of life under siege, which could have used its scripting license to probe the domestic strains of personal life, instead features characters that are all either fighting men or women engaged in male heroics. The makeshift survival tactics that were vital to revolutionary victory are simply ignored. (This is not merely Lilienthal and Skármeta's problem; in such documentaries from Nicaragua as *Patria libre o morir* and *Women in Arms*, Nicaraguans interviewed prefer to emphasize military skills over the wit required to get daily bread.)

Certainly the revolutionary heroics were verifiable. Nevertheless, a significant question of motivation is never satisfactorily answered: How did the Guard get recruits? How did they convince boys "from the neighborhood" to terrorize their own people?

Lilienthal and Skármeta's answer is simple: with a combination of promises (recruits will receive an education) and threats (the entire family of any deserter will be shot). The son in the story is the vehicle to demonstrate those techniques, but the boy is a special case—a trained technician, not someone like the sons of the tragic mothers in black who descend on a Guard training camp to demand their sons back. The appeal of military authority for ordinary soldiers who not only joined up but who also stayed to kill with ferocity, month after month, is never probed, except with contempt for the Guard officer's languid sadism.

There are other ways in which Lilienthal and Skármeta fail to exploit the possibilities that fiction offers over documentary. No scenes tell the viewer about the daily life within the National Guard. Has this young man any friends in the Guard? What is life in the barracks like? Other aspects of the fiction confuse more than they clarify. The family has a spacious home, for example, but makes claims to the same devastating poverty that afflicts neighbors with much more cramped quarters.

It is understandable that the Nicaraguans who participated in the film should want to stress street action over scrounging and Sandinista heroics over the Guard's barracks chatter. The restaging could possibly have been therapeutic for some. Lilienthal found, for example, that a young girl suffering terrible bombing nightmares was cured of her fear by the "replay," by discovering that war could be turned into a game, and thus controlled. A more psychologically convincing film, however, would have gone beyond and behind the participants' own enthusiasm.

In explaining the how and why of street fighting in this revolution, *The Uprising* explores the psychology of a polarized society seeking a radical solution. The weaknesses of the present Nicaraguan regime can be detected in the very weaknesses inherent in this film. The single political issue is the conflict between the people and Somoza, the resolution of which cannot take anyone very far in establishing a new kind of government.

*Pat Aufderheide*

# UTAMARO AND HIS FIVE WOMEN (UTAMARO O MEGURU GONIN NO ONNA)

*Origin:* Japan
*Released:* 1946
*Released in U.S.:* 1972
*Production:* Shochiku
*Direction:* Kenji Mizoguchi
*Screenplay:* Yoshikata Yoda; based on an idea by Kanji Kunieda
*Cinematography:* Shigeto Miki
*Editing:* no listing
*Art direction:* Isamu Motoki
*Music:* Hisato Osawa and Tamezo Mochizuki
*MPAA rating:* no listing
*Running time:* 106 minutes

*Principal characters:*
Utamaro ........................ Minosuke Bando
Okita ............................ Kinuyo Tanaka
Seinosuke ........................ Kotaro Bando
Takasode ......................... Toshiko Iizuka
Oran ........................... Hiroko Kawasaki
Kano ........................... Mitsuaki Minami
Yukie ............................... Eiko Ohara
Shozaburo ..................... Shotaro Nakamura
Takemaro ...................... Minpei Tomomoto

In the latter half of the eighteenth century in Tokyo, one of the most legendary of Japanese artists arose from the middle classes. His name was Utamaro, an *ukiyo-e* printmaker whose dynamic drawings of women upset traditional aesthetics. The women he drew came from all classes and were of all types. Kenji Mizoguchi's film *Utamaro and His Five Women* invokes a host of issues associated with this figure, his times, and his art. The film, by the director's own admission, is one of his most personal works, for unquestionably Mizoguchi saw himself as a modern-day Utamaro and cinema as a twentieth century substitute for woodblock prints. The threats of competition and censorship under which Mizoguchi had to labor were frighteningly explicit in Japan after the war, with new film companies fighting for the market and with a diligent American bureaucracy perusing every script before passing it on to production.

In fact, *Utamaro and His Five Women* was initially rejected by the censorship board, which had outlawed period films, fearing any resurrection of feudal or nationalist feelings. Mizoguchi successfully argued that the hero of his film was no military leader and might be considered to be a prophet of democracy and even of women's rights. His problems with this project, however, were by no means over. Required to commence shooting as soon as possible, Mizoguchi and his trusted writer, Yoshikata Yoda, found themselves grappling with the most complicated script they had ever undertaken. Essentially, Utamaro (Minosuke Bando) is a passive character in the eye of a storm of women whose frantic lives touch his artistic sensibility. He lives near them in order to draw them. In consequence, Mizoguchi must center his attention on the tales of Utamaro's women, and he must tell these tales passionately enough to be able to see their effects registered on the face (and, by extension, in the art) of Utamaro. Juggling three major stories, two minor ones, and their impact on a single hero is one of the film's greatest accomplishments. Although both Mizoguchi and Yoda believed that the plot was not perfectly executed, it is both elegant and audacious in its complications.

The film opens with a parade of courtesans traipsing through the streets of Edo. One couple, Yukie (Eiko Ohara), the daughter of the great artist Kano (Mitsuaki Minami), and her fiancé, Seinosuke (Kotaro Bando), is window-shopping for artworks. Seinosuke is impressed by the woodblock prints of Utamaro, until he reads an epigraph on one that advertises its realism at the expense of Kano and all traditional artists. As Kano's disciple, Seinosuke demands satisfaction and tracks down the store owner, who is passing the time in teahouses and brothels of the geisha quarters. When Oshin, a fat courtesan, reveals that Utamaro is probably with Okita (Kinuyo Tanaka), one of his models, the nervous store owner sends her to warn the unsuspecting artist. At his modest studio, Utamaro and his friend Takemaro (Minpei Tomomoto) wait for Okita, who is strolling with her lover Shozaburo (Shotaro Nakamura). She enters just ahead of Oshin. Against all advice, Utamaro decides to leave Okita and go to the geisha quarters, because, he says, he wants to witness the tatooing of Takasode (Toshiko Iizuka), a poor courtesan.

The outraged Seinosuke wants to fight Utamaro to the death, but he agrees to a "drawing duel" instead. He swiftly sketches a figure that all admire. Utamaro, after expressing his utmost admiration, improves the sketch with a few strokes. While the astonished Seinosuke gazes speechlessly at the drawing, Utamaro leads his friends to another, nearby house, where the tatooing is in progress. The tatooer has found himself incapable of touching Takasode, for never has he worked on such a matchless skin. Utamaro, too, is transfixed by this lovely courtesan's body and, despite his reputation as a serious artist, insists on drawing the cartoon for the tatoo on Takasode's back. The result is stunning. Utamaro is gleeful to see his drawing alive on a moving body, and the spectators exclaim that no other artist mingles so with the people.

Meanwhile, Seinosuke tells Yukie that he has decided to break with Kano's refined tradition and follow Utamaro. Yukie knows that this will destroy their marriage plans and pleads with him to reconsider, but her father enters and expels the youth. Seinosuke proceeds immediately to Utamaro's studio, which he is surprised to find so functional and impoverished. Nevertheless, he asks to be taken in and is not refused. When Utamaro returns to the geisha quarters, he is pleased to find his associate Takemaro courting the lonely Oshin. He is less pleased to learn that Okita's Shozaburo has eloped with the tatooed Takasode. No one will inform the volatile Okita, and she only learns of it from a newspaper hawker broadcasting the affair. She buys up all the papers and announces her determination not to relinquish her lover.

Later that night, Utamaro discovers Yukie outside his studio in search of Seinosuke. Quickly he sends Takemaro to recall Seinosuke from the geisha quarters while he entertains this distraught lady. Takemaro returns alone, reporting that Seinosuke refuses to see Yukie. All then go to convince him, but Utamaro soon realizes that Okita has seduced the inebriated Seinosuke and will not release him. Yukie is inconsolable but will not return to her father's house.

Now Utamaro begins to argue with Okita, his favorite model, who counters by claiming that he is jealous. His drawing suffers until even his friends and vendors grumble about his lack of inspiration. They devise a plan to shake him from his lethargy. Early in the morning they conduct him to the estate of a wealthy, decadent daimyo to witness a bizarre ritual. Carefully hidden, they observe this provincial governor reviewing a harem of a score of girls, who disrobe and wade nearly naked into the sea to fish with their bare hands. Utamaro is so excited by this sight that he leaves his cover. One girl particularly attracts him, and he is persuaded to retreat only by the promise that somehow he will be allowed to meet her. The meeting is arranged, and the demure Oran (Hiroko Kawasaki), daughter of a poor samurai who sold her to the daimyo, consents to model her exquisite body for Utamaro.

Okita finally learns by rumor the whereabouts of Shozaburo and Takasode and leaves immediately to seek them out. Seinosuke feels abandoned until Utamaro arranges for him to run into Yukie, who he assumed had returned to her father. The couple makes up, but only briefly, for a dramatic event disrupts the whole community. Utamaro is arrested for outraging the local magistrate with some of his drawings. Five days later he returns handcuffed, sentenced to fifty days of idleness. Further misfortune now befalls him: Seinosuke has finished his drawing of Oran and gone off with her, leaving Yukie again in tears.

Okita at last reaches the distant resort district to find Takasode alone. They argue over Shozaburo, who is off quietly fishing. Takasode tries to escape with Shozaburo, but Okita has hired men to kidnap him. Brought before Okita, Shozaburo remembers their love and returns with her to Tokyo.

At Utamaro's studio, Yukie is concerned about Seinosuke's absence. She is reassured that he is merely on a trip to see artworks. The mood is happy, for Oshin has finally obtained enough money to buy her freedom, and she and Takemaro can now be married. When a letter from Seinosuke arrives asking Utamaro for money to get him over his illness, Yukie decides to give him her money and sets out with Takemaro to do so personally. In a distant town across the mountains, they learn the truth: Seinosuke and Oran are together and plan never to return. Takemaro scolds Oran and escorts the again disconsolate Yukie home. There, Utamaro's vain entreaties that Yukie return to her father are interrupted by Okita, who saunters in bragging about her hold on Shozaburo. Suddenly Yukie is gone. Utamaro sends Okita after her, and together with Takemaro, who has just come in, she narrowly prevents a suicide.

When Takemaro inadvertently reveals to Okita that Takasode has been seen nearby, she abandons Yukie and races home. Finding Shozaburo gone, she picks up a large knife. In an empty alleyway, Takasode and Shozaburo, walking arm in arm, are confronted by the desperate Okita. When Shozaburo cannot decide to which woman he belongs, Okita stabs him, then turns on Takasode. Yukie and Oshin rush in to tell Utamaro the horrible news. Then Okita herself arrives, distracted. Calmly, she justifies herself, claiming that, like Utamaro, she has refused the mediocre path and has "gone to the end" in her love as he has in art. With Oshin sobbing and Yukie claiming to have seen the truth about women for the first time, Okita announces that she must end her life. "Be kind to the woodblock print of Okita," she tells Utamaro, as she walks out to her death. Bursting with feeling, the shackled Utamaro cries out, "I want to draw; I want to draw so much."

The fifty-day sentence finally comes to an end. Takemaro breaks out the sake to celebrate with Utamaro's friends, but Utamaro refuses. "Sake can wait," he exclaims, his eyes glistening. "Bring my drawing materials. I must render Okita's spirit, a courtesan's tatooed body, Oran fishing—I'll draw them all." Over the ending credits, prints of women rain down, one after the other. For Mizoguchi, who had just experienced the public horror of the war and the private trauma of seeing his wife committed permanently to a mental institution, Utamaro represented the triumph of art over life and love. Takasode's elopement worries Utamaro because she carries his cartoon on her back; the film's greatest calamity, Okita's confession of the double murder and her wandering off to suicide, is met by Utamaro's stunned remark, "I wish I could draw." When his manacles are removed, he refuses to take time to celebrate, calling immediately for his tools.

This was an artist Mizoguchi could understand. Moreover, Utamaro's was in art in which he had more than a passing interest, for *ukiyo-e* prints were in many respects the equal of film. First, they were a middle-class obsession and their subjects chronicled, nearly narcissistically, the diversions and lives of the people who bought them: mainly courtesans, teahouse women, and theatrical entertainers. Moreover, *ukiyo-e* was a collaborative art and an industry in which a ruling master tried to instill his vision in a host of coworkers (engravers, colorists, pressers). Most of all, it was popular, and its greatest practitioners felt caught between the hallowed aesthetic traditions of painting, represented in the film by the great Kano school of art, and the drive toward stylishness, immediacy, and even fad.

In the midst of conflicting aesthetics, of industrial pressures, and of the volatile lives of those with whom they lived, Mizoguchi and the Utamaro he represents in his film carry on a private search for artistic validity. More than a search, it is the fulfillment of a nearly biological destiny. Utamaro is addicted to drawing and to perfecting his drawing, Mizoguchi to filmmaking. Such is not necessarily the healthiest addiction, as neither man was beyond a certain sadism and masochism in his relationships with others. Utamaro could paint only when he was passionately in love; Mizoguchi could film only when he had driven his actors and assistants mad. Both were commoners who entertained the loftiest notions of art and of their position in art.

Stylistically, *Utamaro and His Five Women* is vintage Mizoguchi. Exemplary episodes can be picked out in every reel. The opening shot tracks against the ritual movement of the women. Other camera movements operate independently of the actors altogether, as when the film slides from the tearoom of the brothel across to an interior room, where Takasode, naked, awaits her tatoo. Other scenes are rendered in single tableau, particularly Yukie's pathetic search for her lover. Despite these and many other transcendent scenes, Mizoguchi believed that the film lacked visual thrust and coherence. He simply did not have the time to set up the compositions he had hoped would echo many of Utamaro's actual drawings. In the immediate postwar era, he, and all directors, had to employ a quick and serviceable style. Fortunately, Mizoguchi's is always an interesting and evocative style; he himself, however, would admit that only at the end of the decade (perhaps because Miyagawa had joined him as cameraman) did he once again become satisfied with his work. If *Utamaro and His Five Women* cannot lay claim to being in the first rank of Mizoguchi's output, it, more than any other film, attests the validity of the effort to achieve the sublime in art.

*Dudley Andrew*

# VALERIE AND THE WEEK OF WONDERS (VALERIE A TÝDEN DIVŮ)

*Origin:* Czechoslovakia
*Released:* 1970
*Released in U.S.:* 1974
*Production:* Jiří Becka for Barrandov Film Studio
*Direction:* Jaromil Jireš
*Assistant direction:* Eliska Stibrova and Ota Koval
*Screenplay:* Ester Krumbachová and Jaromil Jireš; based on the story by Vítězslav Nezval
*Cinematography:* Jan Čuřík
*Editing:* Josef Valusiak
*Production design:* Josef Calta
*Art direction:* Ester Krumbachová; set decoration, Jan Oliva
*Makeup:* Ladislav Bacílek
*Costume design:* Eva Lackingerova
*Sound:* Emil Polednik
*Music direction:* František Belfin
*Music:* Lubos Fiser
*MPAA rating:* no listing
*Running time:* 85 minutes

*Principal characters:*

Valerie ....................... Jaroslava Schallerova
Grandmother/Elza ................ Helena Anyzová
Eagle ............................. Petr Kopriva
Weasel/the Constable/Richard/Bishop .... Jiří Prymek
Priest ............................... Jan Klusak

*Valerie and the Week of Wonders* is one of the high-quality films made during the period of artistic freedom that existed in Czechoslovakia in the 1960's. Directed by Jaromil Jireš, who also cowrote the screenplay, it is a masterpiece of Czech filmmaking art.

Jaromil Jireš was born in 1935 and began his film career in 1961 with the release of his thesis film, *Sál ztracených kroků* (*Hall of the Lost Footsteps*). His first feature film was *Křik* (1964; *The Cry*). For the next several years, Jireš made no feature films. He did, however, contribute to making a collective film, *Perlicky na dne* (1965; *Pearls at the Bottom*). In addition to Jireš, the collaborators included Věra Chytilova, Jiří Menzel, Jan Němec, Ivan Passer, Evald Schorm, and Juraj Herz, all of them among the best of the new generation of Czech filmmakers. Jireš contributed a short piece about a Gypsy girl and a young laborer, called "Romance." During this period Jireš also made a short documentary film, *Obcan Karel Havlíček* (1966; *Citizen Karel Havlíček*), for the Documentary Film Studio in Prague. The film concerns the life of a famous nineteenth century Czech journalist, politician, and patriot.

In 1968, Jireš returned to filmmaking with *Žert* (*The Joke*), based on the 1967 novel by the Czech writer Milan Kundera. *Žert*, a story of political injustice and revenge, stands out as one of the most powerful critiques of Stalinism produced in Czechoslovakia. The invasion of Czechoslovakia in August 1968 by troops of the Warsaw Pact nations, interrupted work on the film. When Jireš completed and released the film in 1969, it met with immediate success.

The process of "normalization" which followed the 1968 invasion ended the brief taste of freedom that Czech filmmakers had experienced. Authorities permitted only a few of this new generation to continue their work. By some twist of fate, Jireš was one of that number. In 1969, he made what must be considered his best film, *Valerie and the Week of Wonders*, which is based on a novel by the Czech surrealist poet Vítězslav Nezval. This complex, poetically structured film, filled with a young girl's fantasies, was in total contrast to anything that Jireš had done previously.

*Valerie and the Week of Wonders* won the Grand Prix at the Bergamo Film Festival in 1970. In Czechoslovakia, however, the film had a very negative reception. Official film critics strongly rejected the work and asked how an ostensibly committed Marxist-Leninist such as Jireš could produce such a film. Jireš himself was subjected to vicious attacks in the press. Despite these official attitudes, Jireš soon made another film, *A pozdravujte vlašťovičky* (1971; *And Give My Love to the Swallows*), which was based on the diaries of a seventeen-year-old girl, Marie Kuderikova, who was executed by the Nazis during World War II.

The viewer who expects *Valerie and the Week of Wonders* to be a logical action film will be both disappointed and confused. It bears no resemblance to a traditional Hollywood product; there is no real plot. The film is the story of a thirteen-year-old girl, Valerie (Jaroslava Schallerova), who lives through a week filled with dreams, nightmares, fantasies, strange occurrences, human hate, and human love. Essentially *Valerie and the Week of Wonders* is an exercise in translating into film the hopes, dreams, and fears of a young girl who is on the verge of sexual self-awareness. The film cannot easily be summarized except descriptively as a series of vignettes or dreams.

Jireš creates this dreamlike atmosphere by moving, seemingly illogically, through several totally unrelated scenes. The music, composed by Lubos Fiser, enhances and complements the surrealistic quality of the narrative. At times, especially in the opening scene, the music is as important as the visual component in establishing the mood of the film.

Equally important is the work of Ester Krumbachová, the art director as well as one of the screenwriters. Krumbachová's use of colors in the film, white for innocence and black for evil, appears rather simple and conventional, but the manner in which she makes use of these to express a person's changing character, as, for example, the grandmother, is remarkable for the nuances it evokes. Her touch is evident throughout the film. A director in her own right as well as a screenwriter, she remains one of the best film art designers in Czechoslovakia; her collaboration is frequently requested by the best Czech directors. Krumbachová, unfortunately, was one of the artists affected by the post-1968 "normalization" and has not been able to work as often as her talents deserve.

As the film begins, Valerie is living in a large old house, alone with her grandmother (Helena Anyzová). There are no parents. Among her most prized possessions is a pair of bell-shaped earrings. Valerie's grandmother, however, urges her to get rid of these earrings because they were a gift to Valerie's mother from the Constable (Jiří Prymek).

Living alone with her grandmother in a distinctly rural setting, Valerie is strongly affected in her awakening adolescence by the earthy peasant attitudes, not only sexually, but also by the local religious views which are thoroughly mixed with deep-seated superstitions. It is the mingling of these three sets of attitudes that gives rise to the week of wonders.

One day two different groups of people arrive in town, a troupe of actors in strange costumes and a number of missionaries clothed in religious garb. As they parade through the town, Valerie is at her window. She observes one of the actors dressed in a long, black cloak, white-faced with vampirelike teeth painted on. This strange figure captures Valerie's imagination, and she transforms him mentally into the Eagle (Petr Kopriva), who gives her some pearls that he has discovered.

In this half-horror story, no one, with the exception of Valerie herself, is as he or she appears to be. All of the principals are several characters in the imagination or fantasies of Valerie. The Constable appears variously as a vampire, the Weasel, Richard, and a Bishop. He apparently is known in different guise by Valerie's grandmother, who later discovers that he is someone long believed to be dead.

At this juncture, Valerie receives a letter from the Eagle, in which he claims that his parents were killed by his uncle, the Constable. The Eagle writes that he fears for Valerie and asks her to come to the local church to hear a sermon concerning virgins, asking her to meet him there. Although Valerie attends church, the Eagle does not appear. The sermon is delivered by the Bishop—that is, the Constable. Returning home, Valerie meets the Constable, who wraps her in his black cape and escorts her into his underground kingdom. With this, the week of wonders begins.

Here Valerie sees her grandmother with her former lover, the Priest (Jan Klusak). Valerie attempts to convince herself that this is only a dream, but from this point, the viewer is never certain what is a dream or fantasy and what is reality. The Constable talks with Valerie's grandmother, who desperately wants to be young again and who is willing to put Valerie in jeopardy to do so. At dinner, the Priest tells Valerie that her father was the Bishop, who also had a son, the Eagle. Later, when the Priest tries to seduce Valerie, she takes a pearl from her earring, places it in her mouth, and is saved. These pearls, given to her by the Eagle, will later save her from other perils.

The next morning, news arrives that the town is suffering from the outbreak of a mysterious plague that is killing all the chickens; further, the Weasel is dying because he cannot drink the blood from the sick chickens. Valerie, in the underground kingdom, discovers a coffin in which her grandmother is lying—as a vampire. A young woman now appears in the house, claiming to be Valerie's distant cousin Elza; in fact, she is Valerie's grandmother, now much younger. She kidnaps Valerie, taking her to a tower, and wants to take away Valerie's earrings. She is disappointed, however, because the earrings are empty: The Eagle has already given the pearls to Valerie. At this time, the Eagle himself appears and tells Valerie that the Weasel is his father, who is also her father.

Valerie decides to save her father from death, stealing a chicken in the marketplace and taking it to the tower. As she feeds him the chicken's blood, he begins to metamorphosize from the Constable to the Weasel. During this transformation, he briefly has the visage of a handsome, young, red-haired man. Shortly afterward, Valerie receives a farewell letter from the Eagle, in which he states that the Weasel is neither her father nor his.

At this point, Valerie decides to stay with her girlfriend Hedwiga, who has been bitten by the Weasel. Hedwiga complains that she is in the vampire's power. The following scene, which may be viewed as an example of childhood innocence or as overtly lesbian in content, with Valerie and Hedwiga together in bed kissing and caressing each other and sleeping in each other's arms, was severely attacked by proregime critics in Czechoslovakia as being immoral and against Socialist principles.

The following day, a pearl again saves Valerie from being burned as a witch by the Priest. Shortly afterward, she again saves the Weasel from being killed. Weasel the man now metamorphosizes into weasel, the animal.

The next morning, Valerie talks with her old grandmother at breakfast. From the conversation it becomes evident that the grandmother has never gone away, that she has just returned from church, and that she has never heard about the actors or missionaries that Valerie has seen in town. Again the question of what is fantasy and what is reality is raised.

At this point, a young man tries to shoot the weasel, who immediately transforms into the Constable. Valerie's grandmother, who appears to be dying, now confesses to her that her mother had a lover—a young gamekeeper—and that they had two children. The grandmother became jealous when Richard told her that the children were his. She then drove Valerie's mother out of the house, keeping the little girl with her while Richard disappeared with the boy.

A coach with a young man and a young woman now drives up. Valerie recognizes the young man's face as that into which the Constable had transformed when he was dying. Presumably this is Valerie's father and the woman is her mother.

As the film concludes, Valerie returns the earrings to her mother and the week of wonders comes to an end. A celebration now takes place in a meadow by a lake, a beautifully rendered scene ending with a song which is a refrain heard several times before—"Good night my brunette/Good night and sweet dreams/When you awake, my love/Do not disclose your secret." As the music concludes, Valerie is sleeping in her white bed in the middle of the meadow and the trees.

In *Valerie and the Week of Wonders*, Jaromil Jireš dared to make a film without a single trace of Socialist Realism, choosing instead to rely on symbolism and an evocative imagery. This powerful, highly original film is a strong reminder of the New Wave in Czechoslovakia which produced so many notable films during the 1960's.

*Dagmar Berry*

# VAMPYR

*Origin:* France and Germany
*Released:* 1932
*Released in U.S.:* 1943
*Production:* Carl Theodor Dreyer and Nicolas de Gunzburg for Carl Theodor Dreyer Filmproduktion
*Direction:* Carl Theodor Dreyer
*Screenplay:* Carl Theodor Dreyer and Christen Jul; based on the story "Carmilla," by Sheridan Le Fanu
*Cinematography:* Rudolph Maté and Louis Née
*Editing:* no listing
*Art direction:* Hermann Warm, Hans Bittmann, and Cesare Silvagni
*Music:* Wolfgang Zeller
*Running time:* 83 minutes
*Running time in U.S.:* 70 minutes
*Also known as: Castle of Doom*, *Not Against the Flesh*, *The Strange Adventure of David Gray*, and *Vampire*

*Principal characters:*

David Gray .......................... Julian West (Baron Nicolas de Gunzburg)
Marguerite Chopin ............... Henriette Gérard
Doctor ............................ Jan Hieronimko
Bernard ......................... Maurice Schutz
Léone ........................... Sybille Schmitz
Gisèle ............................ Rena Mandel
Joseph ............................ Albert Bras
Jeanne ............................ N. Babanini
Nurse .............................. Jane Mora

The two major literary sources for vampire films have been Bram Stoker's *Dracula* (1897) and Sheridan Le Fanu's short story "Carmilla." Tod Browning made the first sound vampire film, *Dracula* (1931), by adapting to the screen Hamilton Deane's stage adaptation of Stoker's novel. Browning's film was successful because of Bela Lugosi's captivating performance, Karl Freund's evocative photography for the first and last parts of the film, the novelty of the vampire story, which had been relatively unexplored during the silent film era (although F. W. Murnau's *Nosferatu*, 1922, remains one of the classics of the genre), and the thrilling combination of eroticism and horror. Of significance also was the greater amount of fear that sound film could bring to audiences than could silent film because of its greater proximity to the natural world and because real silence, silence created in the context of normal sound, could be orchestrated and manipulated to intensify suspense and a dread of the unknown.

Carl Theodor Dreyer, the Danish film director, who had already earned a high perch in film history with his powerful *La Passion de Jeanne d'Arc* (1928; *The Passion of Joan of Arc*), was stimulated to make a similar type of film and so chose Le Fanu's story as the basis for his work because Browning had already appropriated Stoker's vampire world. Dreyer also derived the idea for his hero's dream about his burial from "The Room in the Dragon Volant," which had appeared along with "Carmilla" in a collection of Le Fanu's stories, *In a Glass Darkly* (1872). Perhaps Dreyer chose to make such a film as a relief from the dramatic intensity of his film about Joan of Arc. One should remember that horror films were not yet an established genre and that Browning's *Dracula* was considered a serious feature film. Undoubtedly, the kind of film that Browning made appealed to Dreyer because it offered an opportunity to exploit the poetic and expressive capabilities of the medium. It also allowed him to deal with his perennial subject of good and evil, though projected into the outside world as a morality play and not internalized as a psychological conflict within his characters. Whatever the causes, Dreyer created a strange film in the context of his own career and certainly an anomaly in film history. *Vampyr* was poorly received at its opening in Berlin on May 6, 1932, and the film was not released in the United States until 1943, when it was distributed in a shortened version with a new and unfortunate sound track as *Castle of Doom* and *Vampire*.

Dreyer's sojourn into the vampire world is far less dramatic and far less focused on its human characters than Browning's—it sustains throughout a dreamlike atmosphere, a poetic intrusion into the nightmare world of fear and anxiety. Like the dreamworld, his film is inhabited by shadowy creatures, by bizarre shapes and symbols rather than by creatures of flesh and blood. This is both its strength and weakness—the film is moody and visually haunting, but, at the same time, it is lifeless and even a little dull. The power of the horror genre, when at its best, is to impose the nightmare world upon the world of the living; Dreyer's world is one sapped of life.

Dreyer selected for this film a largely amateur cast—the only exceptions were Sybille Schmitz, who played the role of Léone, and Maurice Schutz, who played the father, Bernard—which further distances the characters for the viewer. Baron Nicolas de Gunzburg, who contributed to the financing of the film, played the role of David Gray under the pseudonym of Julian West: His singularly stiff deportment leaves the film lifeless at its very center. The distancing of the characters is increased by keeping them away from the camera for large portions of the film; with the exception of the prolonged close-up of Sybille Schmitz as she brilliantly enacts Léone's vampiric transformation, the most striking moments show characters moving though the landscape of nightmare in middle and long shots. At the same time, characters are never brought into immediacy by speech or verbal communication. *Vampyr* was Dreyer's first sound film, but the work is largely conceived in visual terms, with dialogue brief and barely audible—the performers were directed to mouth the lines, and the dialogue was later dubbed in for English, German, and French versions of the film. What sustains the film on an aural level is a moody and evocative musical score by Wolfgang Zeller.

On a visual level, the film is often impressive, frequently intriguing, and sometimes infuriatingly elliptic. *Vampyr* was made in France, where Dreyer had his cinematographer for *The Passion of Joan of Arc*, Rudolph Maté, shoot the film along with Louis Née. Maté had worked under Karl Freund, the cinematographer for Browning's *Dracula*, in Berlin, where both had also photographed Dreyer's *Mikaël* (1924; *Chained*). One of the art directors for Dreyer's film was Hermann Warm, who had also been a designer for Robert Weine's *Das Kabinett des Dr. Caligari* (1919; *The Cabinet of Dr. Caligari*) in Berlin, as well as the designer for a number of other notable German films. Such connections explain why these early vampire films by Browning and Dreyer are visually rooted in the German Expressionistic tradition. To these, one might add F. W. Murnau's *Nosferatu—Fine Symphonie des Gravens* (1922; *Nosferatu the Vampire*), which also was made in Berlin and influenced by Expressionism. When Dreyer was making *Vampyr*, however, Murnau's film had long been unavailable because of its copyright infringement of Stoker's novel.

Browning's film, because of financial exigencies, is stagey and cinematically impoverished for most of its middle part, while Dreyer's film maintains its dreamlike and eerie quality from beginning to end. What also distinguishes Dreyer's film from that of Browning, and relates it to Murnau's film, is the location shooting which takes Expressionism out of the artificial studio sets and imposes it on the real world before the camera. Dreyer's Gothicism is a result of light and shadow, of dim and foggy vistas, of a camera that uncertainly moves and creeps along the buildings and landscapes. Much of the film was shot at dawn and dusk. Dreyer was impressed by the foggy image achieved when light inadvertently shone in the camera and so used this effect intermittently throughout the film. This technique is indicative of a generally elliptic and confusing quality in the film, both in its visual images and in its plot. Dreyer used Le Fanu's story in the most casual way and substituted little else for what he left out—instead of the camera and editing following the plot, what plot there is seems to develop fitfully out of the changing visual images, which themselves seem to function and connect with one another largely for effect.

The film begins with titles that tell of David Gray's strong interest in the supernatural and prepare the viewer for a strange event that once happened to him. On a shadowy and mysterious night, Gray takes a room at an inn in the village of Courtempierre, where his sleep is interrupted by the intrusion into his room of an elderly man. The stranger cries in anguish, "She must not die," and leaves behind a package to be opened after his death. Gray soon departs also, wandering through the night to find the man and offer help. He makes his way to an old factory, where, amid other strange sights, he sees the disembodied shadow of a one-legged gamekeeper move about and finally rejoin the actual body of its owner; then, a white-haired and bespectacled figure welcomes an elderly woman. These last two figures are later revealed to be the doctor (Jan Hieronimko) and Marguerite Chopin (Henriette Gérard), the vampire whom he serves. Gray finally makes his way to the castle of his nocturnal intruder, where he watches through the window as the old man is shot, apparently by the gamekeeper, whose shadow is seen firing a rifle. The coachman is sent to fetch the police, while Gray remains to help Léone, the dead man's mysteriously ill daughter, and her sister, Gisèle (Rena Mandel).

Gray opens the package that their father had left him and finds a book on vampires. His reading is interrupted by the discovery that Léone is missing from her bed. In a striking long-shot, the viewer sees her sprawled across a bench outside the house, Marguerite Chopin bent over her throat. Chopin is forced to flee, and the young woman is returned to the house, where she undergoes a remarkable transformation, her face becoming a mask of lust and evil as she gradually bares her teeth and turns leering at her sister. The carriage returns with the dead coachman, followed soon after by the doctor, who asks Gray to help the stricken Léone with a blood transfusion. While Gray is incapacitated, the doctor gives Léone a bottle of poison, but, before she can drink from it, Gray rushes in and saves her. The doctor quickly departs, forcing Gisèle to go with him, and Gray follows. Once outside, Gray collapses from weakness and begins to dream a strange and powerful dream in which he sees himself dead in a coffin and watches through a small window in the lid of the coffin as he is carried to his grave.

While all this has been occurring, a male servant in the household, Joseph (Albert Bras), has been reading the book about vampires and has discovered the truth about Marguerite Chopin. Gray awakes and immediately joins the servant in opening the lid to Chopin's coffin and driving a stake through her heart. As soon as the old woman is transformed into a skeleton, Léone rises in her bed and says that she is free. The doctor and gamekeeper are suddenly threatened by the ghost of the murdered father, whose gigantic face appears behind the window amid a raging storm. The gamekeeper is killed, falling down a flight of steps, and the doctor runs off in terror. While Gray finds Gisèle and leads her to freedom, the doctor makes his way to a mill, where he is trapped by the servant and suffocated beneath a cascade of flour. Gray and Gisèle enter a small boat and make their way across the river through a thick fog. They debark and enter the sunlight through a bower of trees.

*Vampyr* sustains an eerie and strange mood, a feeling of uneasiness and muted fear. Dreyer creates a fluid visual poem of striking and evocative images, some of which have permanently etched themselves in cinematic memory. The classic shot of the reaper, with the scythe balanced over his shoulder, ringing the bell for the ferry at the beginning of the film; the emblem above the inn of the impaled angel seen against the cloudy sky; Léone draped across the bench with her throat exposed to the vampire—these and other images create for the viewer a sinister and macabre atmosphere that at the same time is haunting and beautiful. The editing of the film is sometimes truncated and quizzical, but the camera moves through the landscape in individual scenes with a fluid mobility that guides the viewer's attention, conveys subjective perspectives of characters, searches out information, and creates a singularly fluid rhythm through the landscape of nightmare. The landscape itself, scarcely belonging to the natural world, is an indistinct place of shadow and fog, of unnatural bursts of illumination, of distorted figures and symbols—it is a world of fantasy and dream.

Vampirism has been the most popular motif in the horror genre because the vampire figure is such a repository of human fears and desires. The vampire is the *nosferatu*, the undead who allows audiences unconsciously to confront their fears of death and the dead. This figure who lives through the centuries, untouched by time, spreads foul contagion from person to person, embodying the unseen forces of disease and illness that suddenly strike people down. Sleeping by day, the vampire is a dream figure, a nightmare shape who haunts the dark and threatens the imagination during sleep. A seductive figure, in male or female shape, who entices others to give up their wills, to expose their flesh to his or her bite, to offer their blood, the vampire is a sexual figure who gives men and women license to sin—as victims of the vampire and as his vicarious doubles, they play out their masochistic and sadistic drives. Steeped in superstition, a creature who defies the laws of nature, the vampire is a potent symbol of the irrational and unknown.

Most of these themes appear together in vampire films, though undoubtedly the sexual aspects of the vampire figure have been most exploited. Le Fanu's "Carmilla" has been especially ripe for such treatment with its implicit lesbianism, and Hammer Studios in England has made a trio of films based on the story, *The Vampire Lovers* (1970), *Lust for a Vampire* (1971), and *Twins of Evil* (1971), which borders on the pornographic. By making Carmilla into Marguerite Chopin, Dreyer moved far away from Le Fanu's story. The brief scene between the two sisters in his film gives only a momentary touch of the erotic to his world. Chopin is old, very old. She does not even make death attractive. The old dowager, supported by her cane, moves about with great difficulty. She makes death and seduction seem ugly and repulsive. Dreyer's camera and superficial story stay away from her as much as possible—the doctor and his one-legged gamekeeper are hardly sufficient substitutes. Ultimately, there is no real center of evil in Dreyer's film. With Gray, the viewer moves from place to place, never certain about what he is seeing; the camera looks for answers, searches out explanations, but finds little. Dreyer has created his mood poem about an indistinct and threatening world, the very emptiness of which is cause for profound anxiety.

*Ira Konigsberg*

# VARIETY LIGHTS (LUCI DEL VARIETÀ)

*Origin:* Italy
*Released:* 1950
*Released in U.S.:* 1965
*Production:* Federico Fellini and Alberto Lattuada for Capitolium Films
*Direction:* Federico Fellini and Alberto Lattuada
*Screenplay:* Federico Fellini, Ennio Flaiano, Alberto Lattuada, and Tullio Pinelli; based on a story by Fellini
*Cinematography:* Otello Martelli
*Editing:* Mario Bonotti
*Art direction:* Aldo Buzzi
*Music:* Felice Lattuada
*Running time:* 93 minutes

*Principal characters:*
Checco Dal Monte .............. Peppino De Filippo
Liliana Antonelli .................. Carla Del Poggio
Melina Amour..................... Giulietta Masina
Adelmo Conti .......................... Folco Lulli
Johnny ............................ John Kitzmiller
Edison Will............................ Giulio Calli

If it had any other director's name on it, *Variety Lights* would probably be seen as a well above-average example of late Italian neorealist cinema, thanks to its apparently committed study of an aspect of postwar Italian life—in this case, the hand-to-mouth existence of a troupe of engaging but not especially talented vaudeville performers. As the first film to be directed by a thirty-year-old former gag writer and assistant to a number of other neorealist directors, Federico Fellini, it has acquired a different sort of interest. Beneath its realist surface, it is possible to detect a number of themes and visual motifs that will characterize the director's later work.

*Variety Lights*, like most neorealist films, interweaves two plots, the one public, the other personal, examining the social conditions that shape its characters' lives, and at the same time paying close attention to the personal destiny of one of two characters. The public side of *Variety Lights* is Italy's dying provincial variety theater circuit, whose mixture of grossness and sentimentality had always fascinated Fellini, but of which, contrary to a number of beliefs, he had had no direct experience. The troupe in the film consists of a director, Adelmo (Folco Lulli), who gives dramatic recitations; a singer-comedian, Checco Dal Monte (Peppino De Filippo), who somehow believes that he is destined for greater things, though he is already in his mid-forties and has yet to achieve them; Melina Amour (Giulietta Masina), a dancer and impressionist who is Checco's companion, and is busy building up a savings account so that they can settle down and buy a little delicatessen; a plump and aging soubrette who sings tacky songs about the South Pacific; a turbaned and supposedly Indian illusionist whose constant companion is a goose; and a chorus of four female dancers who are neither particularly attractive nor particularly skillful.

This company is first seen at its final performance in a rundown provincial theater, where the audience is unappreciative and where the local hotel manager is in the process of sequestering the week's receipts as a way of settling unpaid food and lodging bills. Despite their remonstrances, the troupe members leave without their pay. To one member of the audience, Liliana Antonelli (Carla Del Poggio), a redhead who once won a seventy-hour dance marathon and a local beach beauty contest, the "variety lights" seem genuinely magical, if only because they will take her away from provincial life. Despite rebuffs, she attaches herself to the company and travels with them to their next engagement.

Prospects do not seem much brighter at the next town, since the theater manager has neglected to send transport to the station and the company has to walk into town—until, that is, Liliana spends her savings on hiring a horse cab for them. At the theater, the manager finds that the company is smaller than he had been led to believe, and Liliana is hastily drafted into the chorus. She turns out to be the star of the show, especially when her dress splits to reveal her underwear, and the remainder of the company is driven offstage by cries of "We want the redhead!" To Melina's intense but suppressed jealousy, Checco begins to pay court to Liliana, and, when they return to Rome at the end of the tour, he attempts to impress her by taking her to the theatrical cafés. Convinced that he can set up a show with Liliana as the star, Checco takes her to a smart nightclub where he hopes to meet a big impresario. The evening, however, is a disaster: Checco's white tie and tails are mocked by the resident comedian, and Liliana goes off with another impresario whose interest in her is less than professional.

Despite the warnings from Adelmo and Melina, Checco hangs on to his fascination with Liliana and to his belief that he can set up his own touring company. His landlord has thrown him out on the street with his possessions, and a glimpse of Liliana's gold-digger personality beneath her sweet, provincial exterior rather tarnishes his dream. Wandering the streets of Rome by night, Checco comes across a black American trumpet player, Johnny (John Kitzmiller), a gypsy singer, a sharpshooter, and a number of other street artists around whom he is convinced he can build his company. When he takes them all to Liliana's pension in the middle of the night, she is highly skeptical. Nevertheless, Checco persuades the reluctant Melina, against her evidently better judgment, to hand over their savings, and he sets up a new company. When he invites an impresario to see a rehearsal, Liliana fails to show up; when she finally does, she reveals that she has accepted a place in a major touring company being set up by the man she met in the nightclub. To preserve the last vestiges of his dignity, Checco waives the penalty clause in her contract. With his dreams—public and private—in ruins, Checco meets Liliana one last time, as she boards an express for Milan. The express pulls out before Checco can tell her of his "success," and the disconsolate Checco boards a stopping train for the South of Italy on which members of his old company are assembled. As the train departs, a pretty young ingenue appears to be impressed by Checco's patter.

Like many neorealist films, the structure of *Variety Lights* is essentially circular, with the briefly optimistic upswing of the middle of the film cancelled out by a return to the starting point as Checco appears to be about to launch on a new, disastrous liaison. In common with many later Fellini characters, Checco does not change in the course of the film. What does happen, though, is that the viewer grows to like him in spite of, and perhaps even because of, his faults; in many respects, he is a seedy, failed version of Guido, the supposedly autobiographical central figure of *8½* (1963).

There are, however, major problems in trying to see *Variety Lights* as a "Fellini film," not the least of which is the fact that he is credited as only one of four screenwriters (though with sole credit for the original story), and as codirector with Alberto Lattuada, a filmmaker who, with a number of commercial and critical successes to his name, was undoubtedly Fellini's senior. Lattuada had come into the Italian film industry slightly earlier than Fellini and, with Luigi Comencini and Mario Ferrari, had founded the Italian film archives in 1940. As a neorealist, his reputation rested on two solid critical and commercial successes, *Senza pietà* (1948; *Without Pity*) and *Il mulino del Po* (1949; *The Mill on the Po*). He also collaborated along with Fellini, Dino Risi, Michelangelo Antonioni, and Cesare Zavattini on the compilation film, *Amore in città* (1953; *Love in the City*), in which his sketch, "Gli italiani si voltano" is both the weakest and the most heavily marked by the neorealist aesthetic, consists almost entirely of candid shots of pretty girls coming out into the spring warmth without the thick clothing of the winter months. Indeed, a large amount of Lattuada's later work, while undoubtedly of a much higher standard than the *Love in the City* sketch, has had a strong erotic strain to it, in, for example, *La mandragola* (1965; *The Love Root*) with Rosanna Schiaffino; *La lupa* (1953; *The She-Wolf*) with Kerima and May Britt; and his later *Così come sei* (1978), the film that "discovered" Nastassja Kinski.

Fellini had worked with Lattuada on the screenplay of three of his earlier films, *Il delitto di Giovanni Episcopo* (1947; *The Crime of Giovanni Episcopo*), *Without Pity*, and *The Mill on the Po*, and it had been at Lattuada's suggestion and with Lattuada's support that Fellini received a codirecting credit on *Variety Lights*. Not surprisingly, Lattuada has been somewhat resentful of the tendency of film historians to see the film as Fellini's, (one source even credits him as Fellini's assistant director!). The senior director was, he claims, responsible for most of the direction and the choice of shots; indeed, one of the most apparently Felliniesque characters in the film, the black trumpet player Johnny, whom Checco meets on the street during his nocturnal ramble, was played by John Kitzmiller, an actor who had already appeared in Lattuada's *Without Pity*. "It is not right," says Lattuada, "that Fellini, having had this extraordinary success and having had his merits as a director recognised, should try to rob me of the paternity of *Variety Lights*. . . . I don't deny his input, but we have equal shares in the film's creation."

*Variety Lights* did not open in the United States until May of 1965 when, in the aftermath of the success of *La dolce vita* (1960) and *8½*, it played in a double bill with Jean Rouch's *Chronique d'un été* (1961; *Chronicle of a Summer*) at the New Yorker cinema in New York City. To his great credit, A. H. Weiler of *The New York Times*, who found the film to be "wholesome corn" but "highly palatable fare," not only recognized its double authorship, but also found that the film "in its story line, hews more to the type of films subsequently made by Mr. Lattuada."

Nevertheless, *Variety Lights* will probably find its place in cinema history as "Fellini's first film," and it is worth looking at some of the elements in it which link it to the director's later, solely authored films. The most obvious among these is the theatrical setting—something which Lattuada is fully prepared to concede as being mainly Fellini's contribution—which figures in almost all of the newcomer's later films, reaching the proportion of a leitmotif in *Fellini Satyricon* (1969) and *Amarcord* (1973). Another theme that strongly marks later Fellini films is the contrast between provinces and capital, with Checco's relative sophistication and renown in small-town Italy taken from him when he finds himself in the capital, most notably in the part-comic, part-painful scene in which, dressed in white tie and tails but with his beret still on his head, he is mocked as an outmoded "penguin" in the smart, highly priced nightclub where he tries to impress Liliana. In Checco, one can also see the prototype for a number of later Fellini heroes—Fausto in *I vitelloni* (1953), Augusto in *Il bidone* (1955)—who are interesting for their weaknesses, failures, and half-realized shortcomings, and who are all summed up in the Guido of *8½*.

The world in which Checco operates is one that is familiar as much from the great neorealist films as from Fellini's later work—an environment that is partly mocked and half lovingly observed for its seedy charm. The reality of the provincial variety show that opens the film is in marked contrast to the glittering neon of the credits and to the jaunty words of the title song: "Lights of variety . . . how beautifully they shine . . . this is happiness!"

Nevertheless, it is enough to seduce the wide-eyed Liliana. As the viewer watches, however, any remaining layers of glamour are stripped away from the "lights of variety": a leaking roof drips on the dancers and the audience boos a tacky Carmen Miranda number. Liliana's "big break" at the end of the film promises little improvement: A fat singer is wound up into place by bored stagehands, and Liliana appears, posing in bouffant knickers and metallic breast cups. It is as before—more lavish, perhaps, but as tacky.

The most obviously Felliniesque element in the film, however, is the parade of grotesque characters who hover at the film's margins: the applause leader and elderly drummer in the opening show; the old magician followed everywhere by his goose; the fat cabdriver at the station who refuses to give the troupe credit, the obstreperous man in the audience who blows raspberries at Melina's act, but is moved to tears when she dons a Guiseppe Garibaldi head; and the duo of very small, fat impresario and very tall, thin one which turns up at Checco's rehearsal.

In the final analysis, though, it is by the character of Checco that the film stands or falls. Here again, the mixture of derision and sympathy is one that will be familiar to any devotee of later Fellini films. Checco is clearly despicable, trying to seduce Liliana as soon as she tells him of her desire to be a star, and beginning the same hopeless process at the end. He mistreats Melina, as other Fellini characters will mistreat the women played by Giulietta Masina, and takes her money through the use of a kind of emotional blackmail (in a scene which, in its staging, is reminiscent of Guido's confrontation with his wife at the screening in *8½*). Checco is pathetic in his belief in his own powers of seduction and talent. Yet two things bring him within the range of the viewer's sympathy. First, he is, like Fausto in *Il bidone*, so palpably not what he thinks he is, and second, he seems, perhaps uniquely for a male Fellini character, to be endowed with some of the grace that will surround Gelsomina in *La strada* (1954): When, for example, he collapses during the rehearsal, it is the children who gather around him, as they will later gather around Gelsomina.

If, in the end, *Variety Lights* does not quite measure up to one's expectations of a neorealist picture because of a number of almost fantastic elements and a strongly determined moral structure, that probably has more to do with the kind of retrospective idea one has of the movement. Neorealism was, above all, a reaction to the horror of World War II, and it was designed to find the deeper realism that lay beneath the more obvious surface. "Neo-realism," Fellini has said in an often-quoted definition, "is a way of seeing reality without prejudice, without conventions coming between it and myself—facing it without preconceptions, looking at it in an honest way—whatever reality is, not just social reality but all that there is within a man." This definition exactly fits *Variety Lights*.

*Nick Roddick*

# VERONIKA VOSS (DIE SEHNSUCHT DER VERONIKA VOSS)

*Origin:* West Germany
*Released:* 1982
*Released in U.S.:* 1982
*Production:* Thomas Schuhly and Rainer Werner Fassbinder for Laura Film and Tango Film, in cooperation with Rialto Film, Trio Film, and Maran Film
*Direction:* Rainer Werner Fassbinder
*Screenplay:* Peter Märthesheimer and Pea Fröhlich
*Cinematography:* Xaver Schwarzenberger
*Editing:* Juliane Lorenz
*Art direction:* Rolf Zehetbauer
*Costume design:* Barbara Baum
*Music:* Peer Raben
*MPAA rating:* R
*Running time:* 105 minutes

*Principal characters:*

| | |
|---|---|
| Veronika Voss | Rosel Zech |
| Robert Krohn | Hilmar Thate |
| Dr. Katz | Annemarie Düringer |
| Henriette | Cornelia Froböss |
| Josefa | Doris Schade |
| Dr. Edel | Eric Schumann |
| American soldier | Gunther Kaufmann |
| Max Rehbein | Armin Mueller-Stahl |

*Veronika Voss* was released four months before director Rainer Werner Fassbinder's premature death at the age of thirty-six and was hailed as his swan song (a metaphor found also in the film); it was the last film he was to bring through postproduction. In a climactic sequence, the fading film star Veronika Voss delivers *her* song, a memorable rendition of "Memories Are Made of This." This sentimental song, popular in the 1950's, evokes the goals of that era. These goals, it becomes evident, are not part of the protagonist's life. On the contrary, Veronika Voss's "longing," *Sehnsucht* in the original German title, has nothing to do with the romanticized bliss described in the lyrics of the song but is a wordplay meant to equate her longing or nostalgia with her drug addiction.

The best-known of the German filmmakers to achieve international recognition in the 1970's, Fassbinder made many minor films about his own generation before embarking on a series of films about Germany's social and economic development immediately following World War II. By commercial standards, these films are considered to be more valuable and accessible than his earlier works, incorporating larger budgets, color cinematography, and professional screenwriters who collaborated on scripts based on Fassbinder's own skeletal ideas. The commercial value of *Veronika Voss* was helped by the Golden Bear it received at the 1982 Berlin International Film Festival.

Although Fassbinder stopped writing his own scripts for his films, he maintained control of their visual style, which varied radically, from the black-and-white formality of *Fontane Effi Briest* (1974; *Effi Briest*) to the garish and chaotic *Die dritte Generation* (1979; *The Third Generation*). While lack of consistency made Fassbinder's development difficult to predict, one thematic element remained consistent throughout all of his films: his interest in outsiders and how they were discriminated against—socially, for sexist reasons, or for reasons of sexual preference. The protagonists in his films are either women or homosexuals—groups which, incidentally, have been critical of Fassbinder's portrayal of them.

For *Veronika Voss*, Fassbinder developed a historical fiction based on the life of Sybille Schmitz, an actress who began her career at the production company of Ufa under the direction of such legendary figures as Max Reinhardt and Carl Theodor Dreyer. Unlike many performers and filmmakers who fled Germany after the Nazi takeover in 1933, Schmitz remained and continued her career. She committed suicide in 1955, a time when West Germany had recovered under the *Wirtschaftswunder*, the economic miracle that provided the background for Fassbinder's *Die Ehe der Maria Braun* (1978; *The Marriage of Maria Braun*) and *Lola* (1981), which, together with *Veronika Voss*, form a postwar trilogy. (If, however, *Lili Marleen*, 1980, is to be included in such a group, it must be expanded to a quartet.)

Noted for his experiments with narrative form and antidramatic melodrama, Fassbinder exposes the causes of events rather than building toward them. After quickly revealing the central problem in *Veronika Voss*, he concentrates on a stylish black-and-white production. The result is a film that transcends its melodramatic story of drug addiction and the paradox of former Nazis exploiting one of their own film heroines.

The film opens in a motion-picture theater, where a silent film is being watched by its star, Veronika Voss (Rosel Zech). (Director Fassbinder can be seen sitting at the rear of the cinema.) Robert Krohn (Hilmar Thate), a sports reporter, is sitting behind Veronika. When he later sees her on a streetcar, he recognizes her as a fellow film buff whom he had observed mouthing in synchronization the words of the film they were viewing. Only later does he realize that she is Veronika Voss, the actress in the film. When Robert tries to approach her, she runs away from him, apparently frightened. Intrigued and mystified, Robert notes the door behind which she has sought refuge: a doctor's apartment.

Robert tells Henriette (Cornelia Froböss), his companion of many years, about the woman in the cinema. They decide to investigate her present circumstances and thus discover the reasons for her mysterious behavior. Gradually, they uncover a tale of drug addiction and exploitation, and their involvement eventually results in the murder of Henriette. Veronika, it becomes apparent, is a fragile woman who appears to have lost all of her friends and, further, has developed a fear of friendship or help. The one person to whom she seems to be devoted is Dr. Katz (Annemarie Düringer). This devotion is motivated by Veronika's need for drugs: Feigning therapeutic concern, Dr. Katz administers regular injections of morphine. In exchange for the treatment, Veronika has transferred her personal property to Dr. Katz; now her entire estate belongs to the doctor.

Dr. Katz also is treating several similar cases with illicit drugs that she receives from a bureaucrat in the Ministry of Health. In a subplot, an aging couple, former concentration-camp victims, owe money for drugs to Dr. Katz. In their search for evidence against the doctor, Robert and Henriette are led to them and become messengers for the couple's final payment to Dr. Katz. Their ultimate payment is, like that of Veronika, life itself, but the love and shared suffering imaged in their suicide pact serve to highlight all the more starkly Veronika's miserable isolation.

Dr. Katz is but one of many who benefits from Veronika's misfortune. Veronika's husband, Max (Armin Mueller-Stahl), enjoys the prestige of being a witness to her misfortune and inevitable demise as a star. He meets with Robert over a beer in order to explain a simple psychological law at work with actors: When the roles run out, they drink. All of the former star's seemingly benevolent friends and protectors are portrayed as vultures, intent on using Veronika and plundering the wealth she had accumulated in better days. They obviously enjoy basking in the glow of her stardom, although Veronika has been robbed not only of her belongings but also of her ability to practice her profession. When she is given a small film role, she fumbles her lines and must resort to glycerine tears to show emotion. In everyday life, she is equally incapable of a genuine emotional response. After seducing Robert one evening, she experiences a breakdown, but rather than being an emotional reaction, it is actually the beginning of withdrawal symptoms.

Veronika's *Sehnsucht* or longing for popularity is an extension of her addiction. The perhaps tenuous equation, longing = addiction, is meant to reflect the great power that the unreal world of film has to spellbind an adulating public. If a sports reporter such as Robert were not also addicted to glamour, he would not be attempting to cover a story which, according to his editor, would be better left to the society editors. By situating an actress with an addiction between the public and its object of desire, the cinema,

Fassbinder creates a mirror image for the proposed metaphor of film as the opiate of the people, and, however much filmmakers are thought to sublimate social desires through art, his characters seem to prefer real drugs to satisfy their needs. There is disconcerting irony in watching Fassbinder's dark wit at work in such a film, since his death was attributed to drugs. Furthermore, Fassbinder was the most prolific and promising of the contemporary German filmmakers, and this film about Veronika as the specter of the once great German cinema invokes the loss not only of a brilliant contemporary filmmaker but also of the great tradition of German Expressionism, which Fassbinder appreciated and tried to resuscitate. In interviews, he frequently expressed such intentions.

The seemingly inconsistent characterization of Veronika as victim-turned-persecutor is a standard technique in Fassbinder's plot development. When Veronika borrows three hundred marks from Robert for an impulsive purchase, only to return the expensive broach later for a cash refund, she exhibits her adeptness in applying the methods of her persecutors. When asking for the loan, she charmingly confesses to Robert that she likes to seduce helpless men.

Her own helplessness is evident when the opportunity for an acting comeback arises, exposing her to Dr. Katz's contempt. While Veronika waits for the limousine that she imagines will pick her up, as it had in her glorious past, Dr. Katz stands behind her, mocking her deluded pretensions. Thus, the bon voyage party given later by Dr. Katz in Veronika's villa on the pretext of Veronika's departure for Hollywood is a cynical showcase for Veronika's vanity, illusions, and childlike reveling in the spotlight. It is her own weakness that permits her exploitation.

The doctor and her friends subsequently depart for a two-week vacation in Italy, leaving Veronika locked in a narrow chamber with a supply of pills. While the travelers visit Saint Peter's Square in Rome, where the pope is dispensing his blessings *ad urbem et orbem*, Veronika listens on the radio to the ringing of the Easter bells and realizes that she must commit suicide with the pills scattered across the dresser in front of the mirror. Through a barred window she can barely see the outside world. In an earlier version of the film's conclusion, Veronika tries to get someone's attention outside, beyond those bars: Her appeal for help, scrawled on a scrap of paper, blows down the street and remains ignored. In the final version, the film concludes as Robert reports to his editor that the story has eluded him.

*Veronika Voss* illustrates how a politically motivated, socially provocative film can accommodate an artistically elegant *mise en scène*. The film is an indictment of the survivors of the Third Reich, who, hiding behind their respectable positions and professions, continue their atrocities in postwar Germany. This message is encapsulated in Dr. Katz's response to a visit from Henriette, who visits the doctor in hopes of entrapping her, to obtain evidence of her drug dealing. Dr. Katz responds to the request for drugs by saying, "Actually, instead of morphine, I should prescribe someone to love you." The meaning of this kindly statement is soon revealed: In the subsequent scene, the doctor watches Henriette leave and has her killed. The all-powerful maintain their power by violently removing those who get in the way—or by manipulating them through such illegal means as the exchange of drugs for possessions.

Screenwriters Pea Fröhlich and Peter Märthesheimer have developed a script that deliberately maligns the focus of Fassbinder's accusation, the medical profession. Fassbinder leaves no doubt that the guarantors of public health have contributed generously to the country's postwar malaise.

The added presence of the American armed forces, a characteristic element in Fassbinder's later films, contributes to the portrait of manipulation in postwar German society. The background sounds of the American Forces Network on the radio render an image of a frivolous military presence. An American soldier (Gunther Kaufmann), who lives in Dr. Katz's house, seems to contribute to the illicit drug trafficking by boxing ampules, thereby tying the American presence more closely to the social corruption.

Fassbinder uses the characterization of Robert and Henriette, and their relationship, to serve as a sharp contrast to Veronika and her relationships with self-serving, faithless friends. Robert and Henriette enjoy an intimacy and affection that Fassbinder underscores in close-ups, which allow the camera to add dimension and credibility to their behavior. Henriette's lack of jealousy and her tolerance of Robert's interest in Veronika illustrate the more human qualities of such people, opposed to the greed and lack of concern of those who prey on Veronika.

Along with his own troupe of relatively unknown actors, who later became stars through the vehicles he created for them, Fassbinder was fond of using German stars from the 1950's. Before learning of her death, Fassbinder had wanted to cast Sybille Schmitz in one of his early films; this film about her is a tribute. By choosing her as the victim of the impact of capitalism and reconstruction on postwar Germany, Fassbinder was able to equate the *Wirtschaftswunder* with the death of the German cinema.

Using an actress as the pivotal figure allowed Fassbinder to glide back and forth between the dreams and realities of filmmaking. By making a film about Sybille Schmitz, Fassbinder has turned Veronika's dream of a comeback into a reality. He did not go so far, however, as to employ another era's grande dame to play the title role. (Billy Wilder cast Gloria Swanson as the fading star of *Sunset Boulevard*, 1950, with which the film is often compared.) That gesture, combined with the stylized cinematography, would have rendered the film a mausoleum of the 1950's. (In fact, precisely because they were not widely known, most of the actors brought no contemporary associations to the film.)

The most effective device used by Fassbinder to strengthen the film's message, as well as the characterizations, is lighting. While other characters dwell in semidarkness or blinding light, Veronika's primary scenes are illuminated with shifting lights or flickering candles, serving as both a metaphor for her own reputation and an illustration of her distorted perspective. As her character disintegrates, the lighting fades. In her final scene, locked in her chamber, the light threatens to bleach her out of existence as she comes closer to her inevitable suicide.

Fassbinder's skillful use of lighting in this work was the culmination of many experiments with light and shadow in both color and black-and-white. Yet more important than the experimental nature of this work is its ability to call upon the stylistic developments of the German film tradition, specifically those of director Josef von Sternberg, whose handling of lighting in cinema transcends simple plot development by creating special relationships between object, characters, and action. Fassbinder further employs lighting as a narrative element—even to the point of having Veronika tell Robert that cinema is only light and shadow. Indeed, that claim is at the heart of the film, which begins in the darkness of a theater and culminates in its star fading to white light.

*Karen Jaehne*

# VICES AND PLEASURES (VIZI PRIVATI, PUBBLICHE VIRTU)

*Origin:* Italy and Yugoslavia
*Released:* 1976
*Released in U.S.:* no listing
*Production:* Filmes/Jadran Film
*Direction:* Miklós Jancsó
*Screenplay:* Giovannà Gagliardo
*Cinematography:* Tomislav Pinter
*Editing:* Roberto Perpignani
*Art direction:* Zěliko Senečić
*Music:* Francesco de Masi
*MPAA rating:* no listing
*Running time:* 104 minutes
*Also known as: Private Vices, Public Virtue*

*Principal characters:*

| | |
|---|---|
| Prince | Lajos Balázsovits |
| Sofia | Pamela Villoresi |
| Duke | Franco Branciaroli |
| Mary | Ann Savoy |
| Therese | Laura Betti |
| Colonel | Ivica Pajer |
| First priest | Umberto Silva |
| Second priest | Zvonimir Črnko |

Miklós Jancsó's *Vices and Pleasures* dates from that period in the director's career, during the early 1970's, when he alternated his filmmaking between Italy and his native Hungary. The script by Giovannà Gagliardo, his usual collaborator on his Italian films, is loosely based on the notorious Mayerling scandal, itself the subject of several films in Hollywood and elsewhere; but it is given a characteristic visual and thematic treatment that marks it as the work of one of the most original cinematic stylists in the world today. The film deliberately employs some of the conventions of soft-core pornography in order to further its political statement; one consequence of this (which may or may not have been intended) was that it proved to be by far the greatest popular success to date for a director whose appeal is normally to a small and specialized audience, both in Hungary and elsewhere. It has not yet been given a public release in Hungary, though the reasons for this are more likely to derive from its sexual explicitness than from its political content, which is not significantly different from that of the films which Jancsó has made in his native country.

The films made by Jancsó before *Vices and Pleasures* had been marked by a systematic, almost obsessive intent to reduce the total number of shots in a single film to the absolute minimum—a search which reached its logical conclusion in the eleven shots sufficient to tell the story of *Elektreia* (1974) and which led many critics to accuse Jancsó of "formalism" and of being preoccupied with style for its own sake at the expense of theme and characterization. *Vices and Pleasures* returns to something much closer to the normal number of shots found in a feature film (around 350 in this case), though it contains several bravura sequence-shots, several minutes in length, in which the endlessly tracking camera circles and weaves its way through groups of characters who are themselves moving in complicated, almost ritualistic patterns, in the manner of his earlier films.

The themes and many individual elements of the film are familiar from Jancsó's previous work, for he is the kind of director who is constantly remaking the same film (though always with significant variations and fascinating shifts of perspective) rather than branching out into new subject matter and settings. The major themes are the nature and exercise of power; the relationship between victims and oppressors; deceit, lying, and humiliation as techniques of political control; and the possibility or otherwise of revolt and the birth of a new society. The method is deliberately nonrealistic, drawing freely on dancing, song, music, elaborately choreographed movements, and even gymnastics and acrobatics, as much as on the traditional narrative techniques of the cinema. The main innovation is in the use of images and actions that are more usually associated with pornographic films and that go far beyond the relatively circumscribed use of both male and female nudity in Jancsó's earlier films.

The film opens with the deliberately shocking image of the nude Prince (Lajos Balázsovits) romping in the paradisiacal gardens of one of the country estates belonging to his father, the Emperor, while a uniformed band plays military music in the background. The setting is left vague, but is presumably somewhere in the Austro-Hungarian Empire, and the time is presumably the beginning of this century. The Prince is openly contemptuous of his father and delights in scandalizing him with his behavior; he also neglects and insults his wife, choosing as his sexual partners those women most likely to be disapproved of by society—his former nanny (who is still a young woman) and his own half-sister. He expresses his hatred for his father by spitting on his portrait and encouraging his friends to defy and disobey the Emperor as well. As they talk, dance, and sing revolutionary songs, they learn that some of their companions have been arrested for sedition.

An envoy sent by the Emperor arrives, and the Prince is ordered to return to the capital. Instead, he and his friends mock and humiliate the messenger, turning garden hoses on him and having him chased by dogs.

This conflict between representatives of established authority, usually wearing uniforms, and oppressed or revolutionary groups who have only their own wits and ingenuity to protect them is found in Jancsó's previous films; in his earliest work, it is the cunning and unscrupulousness of the authorities that triumphs, but *Fényes szelek* (1968; *The Confrontation*) and *Még kér a nép* (1971; *Red Psalm*) both suggest that the ultimate victory will be with the (usually youthful) opponents of the status quo. Here, the fact that the Prince and his followers lack both weapons and a basis of political power ensures that their opposition must be indirect, working through the subversion of conventional symbols of authority and the ridiculing of established moral and social values: In this context, then, the erotic, even pornographic elements of the film become weapons in the struggle for political freedom.

With the help of a group of circus performers (one of whose clowns sports a mask representing the features of the Emperor) the Prince schemes to corrupt the youthful members of the local aristocracy and thus cause a scandal that will bring discredit on the social system as a whole. He invites them to a party that, with the help of drugs freely added to the champagne, quickly degenerates into an orgy. Here the visual pattern of the film is at its most elaborate, with the camera endlessly weaving its way among groups of young people, dancing or making love, linking the disorganized and random activities in an overall visual harmony and giving them shape and rhythm. The Prince and his friends move through all this, taking photographs that can be used as evidence later. Meanwhile, the Colonel (Ivica Pajer), sent by the Emperor earlier, waits patiently in the background, eating and drinking as he surveys the chaos of naked bodies and the overt flouting of the Emperor's authority.

Finally the Colonel makes his move and, supported by priests as well as his own soldiers, attempts to arrest the Prince. The latter's friends rally to his support, mobbing the troops, teasing and provoking them. They successfully undermine the Colonel's control over his men, using songs, dances, sexuality, and even the chanting of English nursery rhymes to bewilder and confuse them and thus short-circuit the habitual patterns of their response to orders and authority. The Colonel himself is then subjected to a series of ritual humiliations: He is forced to perform "rabbit jumps" along a table, stripped of his uniform, made to wear the clown's "Emperor" mask, and thrust into unseemly conjunction with a hermaphrodite who is a member of the circus troupe.

An idyllic sequence follows in which both the innocence and the vulnerability of the young people are indicated as they dance in slow motion, sing, and play at blowing soap bubbles, while the soldiers regroup and ominously circle around them, controlling and limiting their movements. Once again the Prince and his friends disorient and disconcert the troops, breaking up their organized ranks and making fun of another official who has arrived to try to restore order. The Prince feigns madness and then claims that it is his father who is really the criminal and who has driven him to these excesses in sheer self-defense.

In another ambiguously idyllic—and here more overtly despairing—scene, the Prince finds a brief, personal contentment in making love to the hermaphrodite. The candlelight atmosphere, backed by soft music, is drowsy, quiet, almost hallucinatory—and is quickly ended. More troops arrive, and the Prince and his closest supporters, including his lover Sofia (Pamela Villoresi), are shot. In keeping with Jancsó's typically cold and distanced treatment of death in his films, the shootings are deliberately artificial and unreal, with each of the victims dying from a neat bullet hole in the exact center of the forehead. The military band plays to signal the triumph of the established order, and the political significance of the deaths is covered up in the claim that the Prince committed suicide because his position as heir to the throne prevented him from marrying the lower-class girl that he loved. His body is photographed beside the body of one of the women from the circus as "evidence" of this, and the film ends with a slow-motion shot of the funeral cortege.

*Vices and Pleasures* mediates in a fascinating way between the bleakness of Jancsó's films of the mid-1960's, such as *Szegénylegények* (1965; *The Round-Up*) and *Csend és kiáltás* (1968; *Silence and Cry*), with their apparent despair at the possibility of any meaningful change in the established system of political oppression, and the revolutionary euphoria of *The Confrontation* and *Red Psalm*. The mood and techniques of the film, together with the tactics of the revolutionaries, are similar to the latter works, and yet the final impact is, disturbingly, closer to that of *The Round-Up*: The Prince is living in a fool's paradise, where his gestures of defiance are doomed to failure from the start. The ultimate control, despite brief and easily assimilated setbacks, is always with the established powers and, when they choose to make their move, nothing can stand in their way.

As always with Jancsó's films, the center of interest lies in the director himself and his idiosyncratic (and often controversial) treatment of some of the fundamental political and social concerns of contemporary life. Script and camera work (cinematography is by Tomislav Pinter rather than Jancsó's usual János Kende) are, without doubt, important, but they are part of the ongoing pattern of the film, often crystallized only in the moment of shooting, and always subordinated to Jancsó's own obsessive vision. The actors, though always talented (supremely so, in the case of his Hungarian films) are likewise allowed little scope to impose their own personalities: They are pawns on the chessboard of Jancsó's art, as the characters they represent are pawns of the unseen, yet omnipresent, powers that decide their fate.

*Graham Petrie*

# VIDAS SÊCAS

*Origin:* Brazil
*Released:* 1963
*Released in U.S.:* 1969
*Production:* Luiz Carlos Barreto, Herbert Richers, and Darulo Trellers
*Direction:* Nelson Pereira dos Santos
*Screenplay:* Nelson Pereira dos Santos; based on the novel by Graciliano Ramos
*Cinematography:* Luiz Carlos Barreto and José Rosa
*Editing:* Rafael V. Justo
*Art direction:* João Duarte
*Music:* Leonardo Alencar
*MPAA rating:* no listing
*Running time:* 100 minutes
*Also known as: Barren Lives*

*Principal characters:*
Fabiano . . . . . . . . . . . . . . . . . . . . . . . . . . . . . . . Átila Iório
Sinhá Vitória . . . . . . . . . . . . . . . . . . . . . . . . Maria Ribeiro
Older boy . . . . . . . . . . . . . . . . . . . . . . . . . . . Gilvan Lima
Younger boy . . . . . . . . . . . . . . . . . . . . . . Genivaldo Lima
Landowner . . . . . . . . . . . . . . . . . . . . . . . . . . Jofre Soares
Soldier . . . . . . . . . . . . . . . . . . . . . . . . . . Orlando Macedo

Nelson Pereira dos Santos is often considered to be the "conscience" of the Brazilian *Cinema Novo* movement. His 1955 *Rio 40 graus* (*Rio 40 Degrees*), with its critical yet poignant look at the lives of five young peanut vendors in Rio de Janeiro, served as a veritable cinematic lesson to a new generation of Brazilian filmmakers who sought to develop a strong national cinema based less on subservience to Hollywood traditions than to a committed vision of Brazilian socioeconomic reality. *Rio 40 Degrees* served as a model not only in terms of its focus but also, and perhaps more important, in terms of its collaborative production strategy: low budgets, location shooting, and the use of nonprofessional actors. In thematics and production, dos Santos successfully and forcefully followed the example of postwar Italian neorealism. Besides directing key films, including *Rio, zona norte* (1957; *Rio Northern Zone*), *O boca de ouro* (1962; *Gold Mouth*), and *Mandaracaru vermelho* (1961; *Red Cactus*), dos Santos contributed to the development of *Cinema Novo* in other ways, including production (for example, he produced Roberto Santos' *O grande momento*, 1958, *The Grand Moment*) and collaboration on many films (he edited, for example, Glauber Rocha's film *Barravento*, 1961, *The Turning Wind*).

*Vidas sêcas* is universally considered dos Santos' masterpiece. Based on the novel by Graciliano Ramos, the film not only responds to the sociopolitical context in which it was made but also represents an important, and ultimately universal, affirmation of faith in the ability of humanity to overcome adversity no matter how difficult. In contextual terms, *Vidas sêcas* was the director's contribution to a debate raging before 1964 (the date of the military *coup d'état* that overthrew João Goulart) concerning the pressing problem of agrarian reform. In terms of its broader meaning, it is a filmic statement that ranks with films such as John Ford's *The Grapes of Wrath* (1940) and Vittorio De Sica's *Ladri di biciclette* (1948; *The Bicycle Thief*) in its expression of a transcendent human spirit.

Set in the impoverished Brazilian Northeast during a two-year period between 1940 and 1942 (roughly the time of Ramos' novel), *Vidas sêcas* portrays the life of a peasant family forced to flee its land because of a drought. The family is composed of Fabiano (Átila Iório), Sinhá Vitória (Maria Ribeiro), two small sons (Gilvan Lima and Genivaldo Lima), the dog Baleia, and, initially, a parrot. The film opens with them walking across the scorched, desertlike land, searching for a resting place. Their desperation is evidenced by Vitória's killing of the parrot for sustenance—an act which she rationalizes by observing that the poor bird was worthless since it could not even talk. After walking for days, they come upon an apparently abandoned small ranch; with the arrival of winter showers, they decide to stay, optimistic that their plight will improve. The ranch's owner (Jofre Soares) soon returns and orders them to leave but changes his mind when Fabiano offers his services as a cowherd.

The bulk of the film deals with their life on the ranch, Fabiano's work with the herd, Vitória's caring for the house and the children, and the boys' admiration for and imitation of their father. The dog Baleia is also a central character, given an almost human personality; her death near the end of the film is one of its most poignant moments. The tranquillity of the family's life on the farm is broken only in the sequences in which they go into the nearby town. In the first case, Fabiano goes to receive his payment from the landowner, only to be cheated. The fact that the landowner is eating throughout their conversation introduces the theme of ritual anthropophagy into the film. After he leaves the owner, Fabiano is impeded from selling some pork by the local tax collector, backed up by the "yellow soldier" (the name given him in the Ramos novel; played by Orlando Macedo).

Later, the whole family goes into town on feast day. Vitória, the children, and Baleia go to Mass, although the boys and the dog find the church an uninviting, repressive place; Fabiano does some business and is intimidated by the soldier into playing a game of cards. Unable to function effectively in the urban setting, Fabiano is once again cheated and robbed during the game. When he resists, the soldier and his men beat him and throw him in a dark, sweltering jail cell, where he spends the night while festivities continue outside and Vitória and his family wait in a lonely and uncertain vigil. *Vidas sêcas* ends much as it begins. With the onset of another drought, the family is forced to leave the ranch, now without Baleia, whom Fabiano was forced to kill because she was sick and dying. The film closes with the family walking across the hot, dry desert in search of a better life.

Dos Santos creates an intense empathy with his seemingly brutish characters through the successful transmutation of Graciliano Ramos' subjective third-person narrative into film. The novel uses an indirect free style—that is, a mode of discourse that begins in the third person and then modulates into a more or less direct, but still third-person, presentation of a character's thoughts and feelings. In the film, interior monologue and the indirect free style disappear in favor of sparse direct dialogue. Fabiano and Vitória's internal wrestle with language itself, for example, is dropped; instead, the viewer is given the fact of their inarticulateness, which does not mean that they do not communicate, but rather that they have difficulty expressing themselves verbally. The parrot is killed near the beginning of the film because it could not talk. In reality, the parrot had much in common with the film's human characters.

The film plays on diverse cinematic registers to transmit the characters' and the dog's perspectives on their situations. Most obviously, it utilizes subjective point-of-view shots that alternate the person seeing with what the person presumably sees. Such shots are associated with each of the four human protagonists and with the dog. One sequence alternates shots of Baleia looking and panting with shots of cavies (South American rodents) scurrying through the brush. This "humanization" of the dog corresponds to the "animalization" that the humans suffer throughout the film.

*Vidas sêcas* also creates subjective vision by camera movement: Handheld traveling-shots evoke the experience of traversing the *sertão* (desert backlands); a vertiginous camera movement suggests the younger boy's dizziness and fall. Other procedures involve exposure (overexposed shots of the sun blind and dizzy the character and the spectator), focus (Baleia's vision goes out of focus after Fabiano shoots her), and camera angle (the boy inclines his head to look at the house, the camera inclines as well). One particularly striking sequence effectively using both camera angle and subjective camera records the older boy's struggle to understand the concept of "Hell" after hearing a local healer use the word. The brush around him, filmed from his perspective, visually represents Hell as defined by his mother. It is also noteworthy that the camera films the dog and children at their level, without patronizing them, so to speak, by using high angles. Luiz Carlos Barreto's cinematography, the result of a search for a "Brazilian" light adequate to portraying the violence and misery of the Northeast, is dry, harsh, and washed-out.

The film's sound track is ingenious throughout, providing an example of what Noël Burch has called the "structural" use of sound. Rather than relieving the austerity of the images with a lush musical score, dos Santos' sound track offers only occasional diegetic music (that is, music that arises in the course of the narrative, such as the violin lessons for the landowner's daughter and the music of the *bumba-meu-boi* ceremony), along with extremely harsh sounds (the squawking of the parrot, the grating creak of the oxcart); there is no nondiegetic musical score at all. The director obviously did not want to render poverty palatable by allowing spectators to lose themselves in the music and forget the provocative rawness of the facts depicted.

The nondiegetic sound of the creaking wheels of an oxcart accompanies the film's credits. The sound is later visually explained, as Fabiano is seen arriving in town on the oxcart as the sound is heard. At this point, the sound forms part of an aural pun by means of which the creaking of the cart modulates into the sound (diegetic) of the scraping violin of the landowner's daughter, thus equating elite culture and oppression. The sound of the oxcart becomes, through the course of the film, a kind of auditory synecdoche that encapsulates the Northeast, both by its denotation (the oxcart represents the technical backwardness of the region) and by its connotation (the very unpleasantness of the sound constitutes a certain structure of aggression). The wheel of the oxcart also operates metaphorically, in that its circularity recalls the cyclical droughts and never-ending misery of the region.

The ox (*boi*) pervades the entire film. The sound of the oxcart opens and closes the filmic text; midway in the film, the date 1941 is superimposed on a clay ox molded by one of the boys. When Fabiano must decide whether to join an armed gang, the sound, in the background, of a cowbell tempers his decision. He decides not to kill the "yellow soldier" partly because he hears one of the last surviving oxen in the brush. Fabiano makes the family's sandals from cowhide, and the family depends on the herd for food. In short, the family's very survival depends on the ox.

The *bumba-meu-boi* celebration is a traditional folk-dance pageant in which the people symbolically divide an ox and offer it to local dignitaries. Although the celebration is a remnant of mythic rites of vegetation representing a moral value deriving from religious traditions and economic activity, in more modern society the festival has lost much of its primitive poiesis and mythological significance, but the ox's social value remains. The *bumba-meu-boi* celebration expresses a social and economic collectivity; it is a totem that reflects the socioeconomic structure and the deepest values of those who participate in it. In *Vidas sêcas*, dos Santos uses the ox and popular culture in a critical sense, rather than a merely representational one.

The ultimately repressive nature of the *bumba-meu-boi* pageant is revealed through the superimposition of image and sound, as the sequence contrasts the celebration with shots of Fabiano suffering behind bars. When the dancers finally say, "Let's cut up the ox," the camera focuses not on them, but on Fabiano. When the ox is divided and symbolically served to the ruling classes, so, too, is Fabiano, who represents the collectivity, served up and devoured in a ceremony of ritual anthropophagy.

The *bumba-meu-boi* can be seen in this context as the ceremonial representation, the *mise en scène*, of a situation of oppression, for the dancers offer not only what is in some sense the product of their labor (the ox) to the oppressors, but also, symbolically, offer themselves. Popular culture, the director seems to be saying, is politically ambiguous: Whereas it does offer an alternative to elite culture, it can also alienate by simply representing, rather than challenging, the people's oppression.

In the novel's jail episode, Fabiano thinks to himself that, if it were not for his wife and children, he would join a band of *cangaceiros* (rural bandits) and kill the men who command the "yellow soldier." Although in the novel Fabiano never has the opportunity to carry out his revenge, the film offers him such an option. In jail with Fabiano is an enigmatic second prisoner who soothes the cowherd's wounds and comforts him during the long night. In sharp contrast to Fabiano, who grimaces in pain and curses his jailers, the second prisoner, although wounded himself, shows no sign of pain or fear. He speaks not a word. When not helping Fabiano, he gazes calmly out of the jail window, confident that he will not be in jail long. At daybreak, the band to which he belongs rides into town and frees him, thereby also causing Fabiano's release. They later meet again on the road outside town, and the young man offers Fabiano his horse and invites him to join the band. The cowherd refuses, feeling a greater responsibility for his family.

The spectator does not really know who the members of the band are. They share none of the visual characteristics of *cangaceiros* (codified, for example, in Lima Barreto's *O cangaceiro*, 1953). The narrative simply never explains who they are, what they do, where they come from, or for whom they work. It is clear only that they represent a threat and an alternative to the ruling classes. Through this abstraction, the director introduces an option merely latent in the novel: armed struggle. The availability of this option is reinforced visually in a shot of Fabiano on horseback, framed against the sky with a rifle in his hands. Although the cowherd rejects the option, the image remains vivid in the film's discourse.

The ultimate dignity of Fabiano and his family is reinforced near the end of the film when he encounters the "yellow soldier" lost in the brush near the ranch. Although the desire for revenge is great, Fabiano, hearing the last surviving ox nearby, forgets his past humiliation and allows the soldier to go, preferring to care for his family. Their dignity, adaptability, and capacity for endurance is further strengthened in the film's final sequence, in which both Fabiano and Vitória, on the road again and determined to improve their lives, resolve that they can no longer go on living in the same manner.

In purely cinematic terms, Nelson Pereira dos Santos' film, with its soberly critical realism and its implicit optimism, represents early *Cinema Novo* at its best. Rarely has a subject—in this case hunger, drought, and the exploitation of a peasant family—been so finely rendered by a style. Rarely have a thematic and an aesthetic been quite so fully adequate to each other.

*Randal Johnson*

# UNE VIE

*Origin:* France and Italy
*Released:* 1958
*Released in U.S.:* 1962
*Production:* Agnès Delahaie and Annie Dorfmann for Agnès Delahaie Production and Nepi Film
*Direction:* Alexandre Astruc
*Screenplay:* Alexandre Astruc and Roland Laudenbach; based on the story by Guy de Maupassant
*Cinematography:* Claude Renoir
*Editing:* Claudine Bouché
*Art direction:* Paul Bertrand
*Music:* Roman Vlad
*Running time:* 105 minutes
*Running time in U.S.:* 86 minutes
*Also known as: The End of Desire* and *One Life*

*Principal characters:*

| | |
|---|---|
| Jeanne Dandieu | Maria Schell |
| Julien de la Mare | Christian Marquand |
| Rosalie | Pascale Petit |
| Fourcheville | Ivan Desny |
| Ghilberte Fourcheville | Antonella Lualdi |

To appreciate Alexandre Astruc's adaptation of Guy de Maupassant's novel *Une Vie* (1883; *A Woman's Life*), it is helpful to know something of Maupassant's work, although the film does not require familiarity with the novel. Best known as a short-story writer, Maupassant was in his own time regarded as a "saucy" storyteller, subversive of Victorian morality. Literary critics have described his stories as psychological studies, or linked them, for their anti-idealist tendency, with the naturalist school led by Émile Zola. More recently, critics have seen these elements as aspects of a larger, less easily defined inspiration more akin to the English mainstream, with its compromises between social and psychological elements and a lyric feeling for scenery and settings. Maupassant's dry ironies, his sense of social assumptions seeping into people's souls, can be seen as a French opposite to George Eliot's ideas of moral responsibility, central to the English "Great Tradition." For its sense of sad figures in a landscape, *Une Vie* has been compared to the works of Thomas Hardy. Its slow, depressing story secured for it a niche as a classic untainted by any suspicion of mere frivolity.

Astruc's film begins with a boating accident which throws Jeanne Dandieu (Maria Schell) into the arms of Julien de la Mare (Christian Marquand). She has enjoyed a secluded upbringing on her parents' Normandy estate and is innocently confident of a happy life as her natural lot. Neither she nor her ailing mother heeds hints that Julien's honorable intentions are not entirely unconnected with his crushing load of debts.

Their wedding is happy enough. As the newlyweds slip away from the ball in the mansion and romp in a cornfield, they seem to have found a balance between her domesticity and his wildness. Their marriage settles into its routine. Jeanne has her maid Rosalie (Pascale Petit) for company and is patiently confident that her devotion will gradually soften Julien's brooding silences and shorten his long, solitary hunting trips through the forest.

Rosalie becomes pregnant, and one icy day, in the pigpen, she is abruptly delivered of a child. Julien becomes increasingly sullen. Venturing to his bedroom one lonely night, Jeanne finds Rosalie with him. Suppressing her anger, she understands that solitude imprisons each of them. Julien banishes Rosalie but without attaching himself to Jeanne. She entices him into her bed so that she can find consolation in the joys of motherhood, and has his son. The seasons pass.

New neighbors appear: an old acquaintance of Julien, Fourcheville (Ivan Desny), and his wife, Ghilberte (Antonella Lualdi), a woman as athletic as Julien and as dashing as he must have been before debts and marriage depressed him. When Ghilberte's husband catches her making love with Julien in a mobile cabin on a clifftop scenic spot, he pushes the cabin over the edge of the cliff. Jeanne's melancholy voice-over concludes the film with the final phrase from the novel: "Life is neither as good nor as bad as people think."

There the film ends, omitting the last quarter of the book, in which Jeanne's son Paul grows up to become a reckless gambler, almost as if rebelling against maternal overprotectiveness, and gambles away the family estate. Rosalie returns and comes to dominate, but also to sustain, Jeanne with her peasant caginess. Eventually Jeanne is reconciled with Paul, and, together with Rosalie, will mother her grandson.

The film also omits the spiteful priest, conspicuous in the book, and ignores Maupassant's implicit indictment of a traditional French combination of Catholic misanthropy and (in Jeanne's parents) freethinking idealism in the tradition of Rousseau. These omissions, however, hardly amount to a betrayal of Maupassant's novel, whose essence and structure lie not in its plot or its ideological criticisms but in its sense of years and seasons passing. These essential aspects are fully accommodated by Astruc's rambling linear narrative. In any case, Maupassant's treatment of motherhood is thin and theoretical.

As a commercial proposition, the subject belongs to the "tradition of quality" (adaptations of literary classics) deplored by François Truffaut. Furthermore, the basic theme of female patience and possessiveness has considerable potential for a "woman's film," whose "weepie" aspects need not necessarily be merely sentimental. From this point of view, the subject is a provincial, luxurious counterpart of another grueling saga with Maria Schell, who had starred in René Clément's highly successful *Gervaise* (1956).

If Astruc ignores the ideology, he emphasises and develops the personal theme in a more timeless way. His first version of the film began with Jeanne and Julien already married. He feels trapped by her and asks only to be left alone; but her selfless love is stifling, possessive, deadly. He reacts by tormenting her. This version of the film banished hope practically from the beginning—and suspense along with it. The trap has closed from the moment of their marriage. The producers objected to the combination of brutality and no dramatic progression. Astruc was asked to reedit the film, rendering it softer and therefore slower.

In some respects, this montage would seem to have reverted to Maupassant's evocation of an uneventfully oppressive existence, albeit with ominous overtones, emphasizing passive drift over contestation. Julien seems to have developed something of a death wish. He is withdrawn and enigmatic, and although the absence of hope and suspense is more diffuse and indefinite, it seems all the more pervasive, but lacking dramatic clarity. Perhaps, at first glance, this was the reason that the film, Astruc's third, rather baffled the public, the critical body generally, and most of his admirers. A brief digression into the history of film criticism will explain why they expected something closer to the spirit and style of later French directors such as Jean-Luc Godard and François Truffaut.

In a 1948 essay, Astruc had proclaimed *le caméra-stylo*. He demanded films whose formal and stylistic finesses would express an auteur's thought, without necessarily going through the supposed necessities of story, realism, or spectacle. This linkage of film with thought, as distinct from physical reality, effectively prevailed over French film historian André Bazin's theory that film was dependent upon the material basis of photography. At this time, Astruc, not Bazin, was regarded (rightly) as the driving force of French film's theoretical evolution away from realism.

Since then, among auteurists, the term *caméra-stylo* is sometimes reduced to "calligraphic" camera movements or specifically cinematic "interventions" such as jump cuts. Sometimes it is actually opposed to what is called the "pro-filmic"—that is, the choice or construction of an action for photographing, or movement, change, and rhythms occurring in front of the camera. Hence, those who understood *caméra-stylo* as formal innovation and lunging camera work thought *Une Vie* bafflingly like an old-fashioned mainstream spectacle, for its camera is often motionless, or its long tracking movements retain a discreetly constant distance from the action, as characteristic of the old follow shot.

Actually, Astruc's idea of *caméra-stylo* included all aspects of audiovisual style: postures, gestures, movements, staging, topography, and so on. The movement of an actor's head or body could be as richly calligraphic as the camera's. He challenged the prevalent distinction between the auteur (the artist with a vision) and the *metteur en scène* (the director as a craftsman who merely stages a story for motion pictures). He believed that the vision embraced every aspect of the visual. In *Une Vie*, he was particularly fascinated by those moments in the middle of scenes, where one comes to sense that something within these people is about to happen which will set their impulses, and lives, off on an unexpected course. Often the camera does nothing, so as to allow the viewer to savor the almost imperceptible change within the actors and their behavior toward one another.

Astruc's opening scene makes his method perfectly clear. Two women run laughing across sloping fields. The wind agitates their dresses—one sunflower yellow, the other a delicately introverted pink—as it strokes the long grasses, stippled with small gold flowers. As they run fluttering downhill, converging and diverging, they contrast with a new background: a long, gray beach, leading to a luminous, listless sea. The new background constitutes a visual event, a new statement about nature's, and life's, beautiful indifference, into which this youthful energy will fall and shrink.

The same visual idiom determined the wedding trajectory from a lavish ball to a cornfield, and Astruc declared a special concern with harmonizing the changes in color tonality between interiors and exteriors. Another scene is constructed around the changing hues, and their moods, as an oil lamp moves closer to or further from the faces and fabrics which it illuminates. David Thomson, in *Movie Man*, analyzes the *mise en scène* of Jeanne and Julien's first meeting on the quay. He finds its meaning in its changing configuration of internal pictorial relationships. There is a slight lack of harmony between Julien's movements and the camera's. The slowness of the tracking movement which develops suggests Julien's as yet only sluggish curiosity. At one moment his movements are brusque, casual; at another he stands stolidly in Jeanne's way.

Cameraman Claude Renoir contributed the principle of contrast between the dramatic mood and the atmosphere of the setting, or the feeling of the color scheme. Reviewers made many comparisons with paintings: inevitably, Dutch landscapes and French Impressionists, Jan Vermeer and Auguste Renoir, even Pierre Bonnard and Henri Matisse. The pictorial intensity is underlined by long silences and the terse, sparse dialogue and commentary. Spoken by Jeanne in the first person and in the past tense, it contrasts with the detached long-shots and the immediacy that comes from movement. More questionable is the background music's resort to the distinctly anachronistic sounds of a saxophone.

Although the film's subject was not initiated by Astruc, his comments indicate how carefully considered was his treatment. Without denying the accepted view of Maupassant as a realist, he was fascinated by Maupassant the poet, the "madman"—in effect, a visionary, albeit expressing himself, like Van Gogh, through the detour of realism. Astruc sought to bring out the novel's anticipation of the anguished bitterness running through Ernest Hemingway and John Steinbeck. For him, Maupassant's work resembled William Faulkner's novel *The Wild Palms* (1939) in that it is not so much the portrait of a woman changing through the seasons of her life as the passage of the seasons and life as reflected through a woman's fate.

If by spreading the events across many years, Astruc eliminated the possibilities for a "well-constructed" bourgeois drama, he opened the story's rhythms to what he called "the total and cyclical dimension of life." His landscapes bear the colors of the seasons (cornfields, snow) and thus of time. Godard thought that the film seemed to have been "meditated on the whole scale of Normandy," much as F. W. Murnau's *Tabu* (1931) seemed to contain within itself all the space of the Pacific and Sergei Eisenstein's *Que viva Mexico!* (1932) the real space of Mexico.

For Astruc, the film resembled all of his work to date in being a moral drama rather than a psychological one. Each of the two characters has made a mistake that he or she cannot redress. Julien has married through lassitude and to amortize his debts. Jeanne has married a man who is out of her class as an animal: too strong, handsome, and masculine for her. Her attempts to conquer him by patience are vitiated by a cloying masochism. These disparities between the characters are somewhat masked by Maria Schell's innate style and by her refusal to play an *undignified* victim. Yet any close relationship was beyond psychological adjustment, for reasons connected with Astruc's second theme. The misunderstandings between Julien and Jeanne are beyond rationality and arise from the irreducible incompatibility of their disparate natures. For Jeanne, marital happiness is a necessary intellectual construct, the project that gives her life its meaning. Julien's death ends her project, therefore her chance of happiness, and the film. Julien is earthy, instinctive, as natural and immediate as an animal. Astruc relished the further paradox, that Maria Schell's acting style, as the victim, was active and therefore masculine in principle, whereas Christian Marquand's was more inward and feminine.

In its concern with a woman's condition, *Une Vie* pairs with Astruc's following film, *La Proie pour l'ombre* (1960; *Shadow of Adultery*). Where that delves into a modern woman's confused principle of independence, *Une Vie* bids farewell to a nineteenth century woman's principle of dependence.

Between a feminist optic, criticisms of women, and criticism of Woman, there are fine lines and paradoxical tensions. It would be perfectly possible for Astruc's films to combine a feminist agenda with the misogyny of which he was often accused by gallant males—wrongly, he protested. The feminists of a few years later would have had little patience with his emphasis on biological nature—explicitly in his interviews, implicit in the natural environment presented here. In contrast to French talk of misogyny, some English critics assumed that the film expected an uncritical sympathy with Jeanne, so that Julien was simply an unfeeling male. Actually, Astruc's Julien has far more soul, and experiences far greater suffering, than does Maupassant's, albeit its forms, or presentation, render him drably nihilistic. His affair with Ghilberte registers more like the no-future pastimes of two splendid but heartless animals than a new springtime of his feelings. Hence, other critics spoke of misanthropy rather than misogyny. They found Jeanne and Julien equally inflexible and absolute—too much so to allow the changes and nuances which make drama interesting.

Astruc insisted that he detested "the cinema of denunciation." Rather, he felt an absolute need to imbue even simple or monstrous subjects with beauty, through which he could intimate a kind of reconciliation with the world. This love of making beauty, as a power in itself, would link the film's "philosophical distance" with another kind of distance: the "aesthetic distance" particularly celebrated by Aestheticism and the French Symbolists, with their long trail of influence through the years. Astruc's own defense of *mise en scène* drew on such ideas, notably the intoxication of artists with "pure" sensation (the color yellow, conspicuous as a motif in *Une Vie*). French critic Jean-André Fieschi insightfully compared Astruc's style to that of the Symbolist poet Stéphane Mallarmé. Both strike the spectator as highly wrought and rigorous, yet so enigmatic that their meanings seem fragile. They generate, not a continuous expression of the subject's urges, moods, and emotions but, on the contrary, "the sensation that our understanding and the thing understood can coincide for an infinitesimal moment only. . . . Our wonderment comes from the miraculous blossoming of this coincidence."

From this perspective, the identifying characteristic of Astruc's style would be its unusual separation of beauty (his aesthetic interests) and severity (his moral side). The latter brings him close to French New Wave directors Eric Rohmer and Claude Chabrol.

While many admirers of Astruc's theories found *Une Vie* bafflingly like conventional cinema, reviewers generally found it overly remote from its characters and undramatic. Jean de Baroncelli called it "frozen, strained, distinguished, intelligent, elegant, but never for one second affecting." The film's detractors can argue that through some spiritual-aesthetic coldness, Astruc allowed landscape distance to overpower or stiffen the characters. Its supporters could declare that, on the contrary, it is Astruc who is exceptionally sensitive to what is sometime called "the acting picture" and the lyric dialectic of drama and scenery. One could posit a certain academicism, not in Astruc's theories of life or film but simply in his pictorial style here.

Equally reversible are arguments about the film's moral and dramatic tensions. It can fairly be said that Maria Schell's strong playing eclipses both Jeanne's negative side and Julien's positive side, so that the story hangs, one-sidedly, in midair, and the "woman's view" smothers everything except the landscape. Others can claim that a "hesitation waltz" exists between drama, philosophy, and lyric.

The larger public took the negative view, as this high-budgeted film fared poorly at the box office, reinforcing the critical consensus. Nevertheless, the film was championed by such as Godard, and a significant minority of critics have insisted that its time will come.

*Raymond Durgnat*

# LE VIOL

*Origin:* France and Sweden
*Released:* 1967
*Released in U.S.:* 1968
*Production:* Göran Lindgren and Mag Bodard for Parc Film, Argos Films, and Sandrews
*Direction:* Jacques Doniol-Valcroze
*Screenplay:* Jacques Doniol-Valcroze
*Cinematography:* Rune Ericson
*Editing:* Sophie Bhaud
*Art direction:* Jan Boleslaw
*Music:* Michel Portal
*MPAA rating:* no listing
*Running time:* 90 minutes
*Also known as: The Rape*

*Principal characters:*

Marianne Pescourt . . . . . . . . . . . . . . . . Bibi Andersson
Walter . . . . . . . . . . . . . . . . . . . . . . . . . . . . Bruno Crémer
Henri Pescourt . . . . . . . . . . . . . . . Frédéric de Pasquale
Jacqueline . . . . . . . . . . . . . . . . . . . . . . . Katerina Larsson

*Le Viol*, which can be directly translated as "the rape," is an intellectual guessing game disguised as a thriller, a one-set chamber piece with superb performances for adults who enjoy a bit of tease.

The film opens with a spot of light directed on what appears to be a Vassarelly print of concentric circles and squares. The focus changes with a harsh, background jazz score, and the husband, Henri Pescourt (Frédéric de Pasquale), is seen in the bedroom pulling on a pair of boots next to his sleeping wife, Marianne (Bibi Andersson). It is seven o'clock in the morning, and he whispers to her that he will be home around seven o'clock in the evening and leaves their apartment with his hunting gear.

In the hallway outside the apartment, a mysterious-looking man dressed in trenchcoat and dark glasses (Bruno Crémer) appears on the staircase with a package in his hand. A close-up of Marianne asleep is followed by the appearance of the maid, Jacqueline (Katerina Larsson), who arrives with Marianne's breakfast at nine o'clock in the morning and informs the sleep-logged wife that she will return to prepare for the party at six o'clock that evening.

Outside the apartment, the maid is seen leaving by the elevator. Footsteps are heard, and soon the mystery man is loitering once more outside the door.

Marianne finally wakes to subliminal images of sexual violence, warms her breakfast coffee, and prepares her bath. Meanwhile, the mystery man is inspecting his lethal-looking gun in the exterior hallway. Marianne phones her friend Alberte and arranges an afternoon meeting while the waiting man descends the building's steps to avoid several noisy children on their way out.

As Marianne begins playing a haunting guitar piece on the record player and steps into her bath, the doorbell rings. She hurriedly pulls on a white, three-quarter-length robe and admits the unknown man who feigns delivering a package for her husband. As she goes for a pen to sign a receipt, Marianne has another subconscious, violently erotic flash. In a moment it becomes reality as the mystery man quickly ties and gags her, then deposits her on the couch, white on white. With dispatch he closes the white curtains, rearranges Marianne's dishabille, snaps the silencer on his gun, inspects the rest of the apartment, and sits.

Soothingly stating that she has nothing to fear if she remains calm, the man answers the phone and reports to an accomplice. This done, he removes his trenchcoat and studies a large photo of a smiling Marianne submerged up to her neck in water, which decorates one area of the living room wall. Giving a lecture on his gun, he puts it away to light a cigarette, informing Marianne that someone will call each half hour to check. The man then removes his dark glasses, leather gloves, and Marianne's ankle trusses. After she promises to remain calm, he removes her gag. Sullenly thanking him, Marianne requests that he remove her wrist bindings as well. The man discusses her husband and his own job, claiming that he is only a soldier, stupid and disciplined. The phone rings for another progress report, then Marianne's captor discusses "morality" before prowling around the ultramodern room, examining objects and wall photos. Finally, he asks for a drink, they go to the kitchen in search of ice, then return to the living room, where he plays a little sadomasochistic game of offering her a whiskey and the release of her hands if she will do anything he asks. She refuses, then he asks if she would comply to save her husband. Finally her wrists are released and the two share drinks and cigarettes while the camera plays with objects: the print on the wall, Marianne's face. He asks her name and requests lunch. She balks. He slaps her face, violently, and soon Marianne is preparing his lunch, then watching him eat it, her wrists bound again. She makes coffee, there is another phone check.

After lunch, he inspects her library, expressing an interest in her first editions. He visits the bathroom, leaving her tied on the bed in front of the television. He towers over her on the bed, frees her hands again, and the phone rings. It is an unscheduled call, Marianne's friend Alberte. She begs off from their appointment with the excuse of a migraine.

It is three-thirty, and they are back on the couch, where he asks her to read aloud to him several passages that he has chosen from her books. The readings concern games between people, interpretations of reality. Marianne suddenly observes that he did not eat like a gangster. At four o'clock, he takes out his gun to check on noises he hears in the kitchen. Alone, Marianne tries to use the phone. He shoots the glass vase adjacent to the phone to smithereens, then hustles Marianne into the bedroom and locks her in. After slowly inspecting the photo of Marianne, semisubmerged, he returns to the bedroom, where he states that he will not take advantage of her. She tells him that she wants him to do so. The photo of Marianne comes alive, her image completely submerging itself.

The man is seen in a bathrobe answering the living-room phone. Back in the bedroom, Marianne has his gun leveled at him. After commenting that it is hard to dress a corpse, Marianne hands back the gun. Soon her captive is dressed again, and her husband then calls, suggesting nothing was ever amiss.

Marianne and her captor embrace by the door, and he leaves. Marianne systematically goes about picking up the pieces of glass from the broken case and puttying the bullet hole in the wall, obliterating all traces of the encounter. In the bedroom she sees the rumpled bed and recalls the violent/gentle lovemaking that took place.

The maid arrives, and Marianne asks her to tidy up the bedroom. The butler arrives. The maid refuses to go to the basement wine cellar, claiming that she might get raped. Henri arrives home to find Marianne dressing for their party. The guests arrive, and Marianne appears like a dream in a lovely white gown. One of the guests comments that she has never looked so beautiful. There are drinks and small talk until the final guest arrives. It is Walter, an old family friend, and Marianne's captor of the afternoon. He refuses a whiskey, claiming he never drinks it. Marianne asks if he went hunting with the other men, and Walter replies that he had work to do. Dinner is served.

The European version of *Le Viol* apparently had a sequence at the end, deleted from the version seen in the United States. That night, after the dinner party, Marianne sleeps restlessly beside Henri. Finally, she tells him that a package arrived for him. He drowsily indicates that it can wait until morning. The doorbell rings and Marianne goes to answer it, finding Walter standing in the open doorway.

What is truth? What is reality? What is morality? Jacques Doniol-Valcroze is obviously having fun with these concepts in *Le Viol.* Did the events of the day actually happen, or were they only the figments of imagination of a wealthy, bored Parisienne housewife? If they did happen, are they to be construed as rape or as carefully orchestrated adultery? There is the evidence of the broken case, the puttied bullethole, the rumpled bed, and yet one is not sure.

*Le Viol* is a subtly ordered, meticulous record of an event which may or may not have happened. Its luxurious, French-apartment setting is icily modern, almost frigid in design. It is a most interesting environment in which to set Bibi Andersson's restless, middle-aged, upper-class woman. Her sleepy, sexy, disheveled look throughout the film casts the only bit of body warmth present in the otherwise sterile and perfect surroundings. The decor, coupled with Michel Portal's perfectly attuned atonal jazz score, is a fitting setting for the tensely unfolding day's events.

A Swedish-French coproduction, shot in Sweden, *Le Viol* shows off the talents of Bibi Andersson, better known for her many fine performances in the films of Ingmar Bergman (she considers *Le Viol* to be one of her best), and shows off the rough masculinity of Bruno Crémer, an actor occasionally seen in films but more familiar in France for his many stage performances.

Jacques Doniol-Valcroze, the director, was the cofounder, with André Bazin, as well as editor-in-chief of the highly influential film magazine *Cahiers du cinéma.* Prior to that, he was a film critic and actor in the films of Jean Cocteau, Jacques Rivette, and Alain Robbe-Grillet. His previously directed films include *L'eau a la bouche* (1960; *A Game for Six Lovers*), a weekend romp between four young lovers and their two servants, reminiscent of both Jean Renoir's *La Règle du jeu* (1939; *The Rules of the Game*), and Bergman's *Sommarnattens leende* (1955; *Smiles of a Summer Night*) and the romantic comedy *Le Cœur battant* (1962; *The French Game*). While considered, with Jean-Luc Godard and François Truffaut, to be among the "Cahiers" group of filmmakers, Doniol-Valcroze is the least-known of the group, and his more recent work, including *Le Viol,* has a more psychological and philosophical cast and might better be compared to the films of another old Cahiers confederate, Eric Rohmer.

*Kathleen Karr*

# LES VIOLONS DU BAL

*Origin:* France
*Released:* 1973
*Released in U.S.:* 1975
*Production:* Michel Drach for Violons Associates
*Direction:* Michel Drach
*Screenplay:* Michel Drach
*Cinematography:* Yann le Masson and William Lubtchansky
*Editing:* Geneviève Winding
*Art direction:* no listing
*Music:* Jean Manuel de Scarano and Jacques Monty
*MPAA rating:* no listing
*Running time:* 110 minutes
*Also known as: Violins at the Ball*

*Principal characters:*
Michel's wife/Michel's mother ....... Marie-Jose Nat
Michel ..................... Jean-Louis Trintignant
Michel as a boy/Michel's son .......... David Drach
Michel Drach ........................... Himself
Grandmother .................. Gabrielle Doulcet
Jean ............................... Christian Rist
Nathalie ......................... Nathalie Roussel
Monsieur Robert .................. Paul Le Person

The title *Les Violons du bal*, under which this film was released in the United States, translates literally as "violins at the ball" and idiomatically—by writer-director Michel Drach—as "others call the tune."

As part of the subgenre of French films of the 1970's that explored the ramifications and the extent of French collaboration during the Nazi occupation of France during World War II—a cluster that includes Louis Malle's *Lacombe, Lucien* (1974), Michel Mitrani's *Les Guichets du Louvre* (1974; *Black Thursday*), and the Marcel Ophüls documentary, *Le Chagrin et la pitié* (1971; *The Sorrow and the Pity*)—*Les Violons du bal* is a strongly autobiographical reminiscence. Although somewhat less abrasive than its generic brethren, it nevertheless performs their characteristic function of chipping away at the myth of grand, across-the-board Gaullist resistance by demonstrating instances of betrayal of French Jews by other French citizens.

The Germans remain an unseen enemy throughout *Les Violons du bal*; there are virtually no real on-screen German characters. Although less overtly threatening, perhaps, it is the French countrymen of the protagonist and his family who are—implicitly, at least—the real enemies in the film.

One sequence even shows Parisian Jews being herded into buses while French aristocrats socialize with the Germans behind closed doors.

Drach's idiosyncratic, personal narrative strikes an uneasy balance between Pirandellian playfulness and autobiographical intimacy. As an intriguing intellectual treatment of dangerously volatile material, it tips more often toward the aesthetically whimsical side, avoiding—perhaps to its detriment—the affective possibilities of its scenario.

Several of Drach's audacious structural devices, craftily chosen and fully realized, serve—paradoxically—both as aesthetic distancing mechanisms and as bridges between past and present: the interspersing of two stories, one, Drach's reminiscence of his family's attempt to flee German-occupied France, the other a dramatization of his attempts to get film producers to finance his film about same; the shooting of the childhood sequences in color, prettified for and by the camera, while the film-financing footage is shot in grainy black-and-white *cinéma vérité* style; and the reverberant casting, which employs actors (including members of Drach's real-life family) in multiple roles as well as multiple actors in the Drach role. All contribute to the film's resonant, multilayered texture.

A painter before entering film as an assistant to his cousin, director Jean-Pierre Melville, Michel Drach directed shorts and television programs—in addition to serving as assistant to Jean Cocteau—prior to stepping into feature directing. His first full-length film, *On n'enterre pas le dimanche* (1959), won the annual Prix Delluc.

*Les Violons du bal*, Drach's sixth feature film, was the official French entry at the 1974 Cannes International Film Festival, at which Marie-Jose Nat—Drach's wife, who plays both herself and Drach's mother in the film—was honored as Best Actress. Subsequently, the film became the first Drach work to be released in the United States.

When the film opens, with what at first seems to be a simple framing device, Drach appears as himself—a bearded and leather-jacketed, forty-four-year-old, obsessive film director—making plans for the production of a film about his childhood. He scouts locations—sparking his memory by visiting the sites of experiences of his youth—and discusses with his wife (Marie-Jose Nat) and his young son (David Drach), who are also playing themselves, the possibility of them playing his mother and himself as a boy in the film.

Drach screen-tests his wife and son and casts them in the film. As he continues his search for actors, props, and locations, the black-and-white image occasionally blossoms into color, creating a gallery of virtual flash-forwards, demonstrating the director's subjective vision and components of his upcoming film-within-a-film.

His entreaties to producers—the first French, the next Italian—for financing are met with the standard objections: The film is not commercial, the audience is not interested in the past, the project needs a star in the lead role.

The last objection is met immediately and head-on, with an adroit editing touch. Drach, playing himself, bows his head in momentary frustration. When he lifts his head again, the face is that of bankable actor Jean-Louis Trintignant. Subsequently the exchange of role from Drach to Trintignant is driven home with a visual metaphor. Drach hands Trintignant the key to his apartment as they move on parallel escalators going in opposite directions—while multiple mirrors reflect the image of the two men converging into one. After walking backward on a forward-moving band to accommodate the handoff of the key, Drach disembarks, leaving Trintignant to go it alone. The project now has its star and can commence.

Regardless of Drach's motives for oscillating between the two stories, the effect invites skepticism. The film contains within its complex structure what amounts to an appeal for the viewer's sympathy for the filmmaker, who reveals to the viewer that he had to go through unspeakable frustrations and tribulations simply to bring the project to fruition.

What helps the viewer to overcome his reservations about the film is the fact that the interweaving of the two stories—punctuated by frequent jump-cut parallels—does make thematic sense, enabling the film to make several well-observed filmic statements about the selective retention and retrospective embellishment of memory, as well as about the mysterious relationship between reality and its dramatic reconstruction for the screen.

Furthermore, although both stories are fairly well realized, it is the relationship between the film's two thrusts—rather than the individual narratives themselves—which is the distinctive accomplishment of *Les Violons du bal*. Hearing Drach's articulated remembrances and then seeing them in the intercut sequences of his re-created youth reveals intriguing insights into the ways that the past is cosmeticized for the sake of present *mise en scène*.

The sustained film-within-a-film sequences are shot in pastel-dominated color, befitting the idealized, ingenuous vision of nine-year-old Michel during his family's 1939 uprooting. As if to establish immediately that his film is a decidedly subjective vision—a reflection of reality rather than a carefully researched, historically representative depiction—Drach presents, in the film-within-a-film's very first sequence, a shot of the family that he soon discloses to be their reflection in a mirror.

The comforts and concerns of bourgeois family life are about to be turned upside down. Michel, who lives with his mother and grandmother, is subjected to vocal and physical humiliations at school and at play, but he does not yet understand what a Jew is, or that he is one, or that his Jewishness is the reason for his victimization.

His brother Jean (Christian Rist, who is also seen playing a student demonstrator smuggled to Lyons by Trintignant in the black-and-white present) has an affair with a woman refugee, then disappears to join his father in Spain, in the underground. His pregnant sister Nathalie (Nathalie Roussel), rejected by the mother of her wealthy, Gentile fiancé because she is Jewish, becomes a fashion model in occupied Paris, where she is seen fraternizing with Nazi officers while awaiting an opportunity to escape.

Michel's mother changes the family name and finds a new apartment in an effort to remain inconspicuous. When the environment becomes intolerably hostile to Jews, she sends Michel to the provinces for a few months to live with the family of a farmer, Monsieur Robert (Paul Le Person). Michel's mother and his grandmother (Gabrielle Doulcet, who appears earlier as an old woman who emerges from the Paris metro and is stopped by film director Drach) join him after arranging an escape into Switzerland.

The seemingly hospitable farmer, however, characterized as one of the few French locals willing to shelter the fleeing Jews during the Occupation, lies repeatedly to the fugitives whom he is harboring and takes their money, leaving the three of them penniless as they head for the Swiss border, losing and jettisoning their remaining possessions along the way.

During the climactic escape sequence—a moderately suspenseful but derivatively mounted passage completed with snarling dogs pulling pursuing Nazis armed with machine guns—the three generations of escapees make their way through barbed-wire fences, dense woods, and the mistiest fields ever to appear in anything other than a travel brochure.

This last sequence is probably the most bothersome to the film's detractors, who see the lush lyric, prototypically tasteful depiction of the family's melodramatically miraculous escape as ludicrous. They see the scenic beauty, the mother's finely tailored clothes and immaculate coiffure, and the stately camera setups as incurable romanticism rather than as the appropriately rendered perceptions of a young boy.

The effect of the pastel prettiness and picture-postcard poses on the successful escape is to blunt its suspenseful edge. In this manner Drach's sublimated escape from a problem-plagued, black-and-white present to a color-drenched, dramatic, but nearly idyllic past almost undermines the denouement of his sentimental melodrama.

Drach's cast, including himself, are a uniformly responsive and effective ensemble. Marie-Jose Nat is both terrifically photogenic and appealing in her roles, although her depiction of the mother—lovely, graceful, unflappable, brave, resourceful; in short, perfect—might be seen as overly idealized, even given Drach's intent. Jean-Louis Trintignant lends his ever reliable presence, but little else, to a singularly shallow and undemanding role. David Drach handles in impressively assured fashion his key role as the young Michel.

Lest anyone forget that his film has been an unmistakably personal recollection, Michel Drach makes the point—visually—one final time. He clacks a film clapboard in front of his face, embedding in the viewer's memory the image of the director as not only the auteur of *Les Violons du bal* but also its content.

*Bill Wine*

# THE VIRGIN SPRING (JUNGFRUKÄLLAN)

*Origin:* Sweden
*Released:* 1960
*Released in U.S.:* 1960
*Production:* Alan Ekelund for Svensk Filmindustri (AA)
*Direction:* Ingmar Bergman
*Screenplay:* Ulla Isaksson; based on a fourteenth century ballad, "Töres dötter i Wänge"
*Cinematography:* Sven Nykvist
*Editing:* Oscar Rosander
*Art direction:* P. A. Lundgren
*Music:* Erik Nordgren
*Running time:* 88 minutes

*Principal characters:*

| | |
|---|---|
| Herr Töre | Max von Sydow |
| Mareta | Birgitta Valberg |
| Ingeri | Gunnel Lindblom |
| Karin | Birgitta Pettersson |
| Thin shepherd | Avel Düberg |
| Mute shepherd | Tor Isedal |
| Boy shepherd | Ove Porath |

Although Swedish director Ingmar Bergman has since tried to dismiss his 1960 film *The Virgin Spring* as a bad imitation of the work of Japanese director Akira Kurosawa, the film remains a powerful and moving experience for virtually anyone who sees it. Bergman usually writes the scripts for his own films, but *The Virgin Spring* is one of the exceptions. A few years before that film he had collaborated on the script of *Nära livet* (1958; *Brink of Life*) with Ulla Isaksson and had been pleased with her work. He therefore was glad to have her write the script for *The Virgin Spring*, a retelling of a medieval folk song about the rape and murder of an innocent girl and her father's vengeance.

Isaksson has written that she wished to retain the original story of the song as well as "its simultaneously cruel and beautiful visual nature," but that it was necessary to add a large amount of characterization and psychological motivation to make a full-length film out of the song, which consists of only thirty-three short stanzas. Throughout the writing, her aim was to ensure that the song be "both preserved and communicated." She says that the main theme that she added to the song for the filmscript is the tension between Christianity and paganism in Sweden in the Middle Ages.

It is with this theme that the film begins. Ingeri (Gunnel Lindblom)—a dark, unkempt, and pregnant young woman—interrupts her early morning chores in a farmhouse to invoke the name of the pagan god Odin. Soon the viewer meets the main occupants of the house: Herr Töre (Max von Sydow) and his wife, Mareta (Birgitta Valberg), whose daughter Karin (Birgitta Pettersson) does not appear for breakfast. Mareta reports that she is ill, but Töre insists that she not be allowed to stay in bed. It is obvious that this is an argument that has occurred frequently and that Töre thinks that his wife spoils their daughter. It is also obvious that Ingeri greatly resents Karin and the favored treatment that she receives. Ingeri's exact position in the house is not made clear. Although she is referred to once or twice as Karin's stepsister, she is treated as a servant, and she does not hide her resentment of Karin from anyone.

This is an especially important morning for Karin because it is the day she is to ride to the church with the Maria candles, and Töre insists that since she was well enough to go to a dance the night before she must go to the church with the candles. When he goes to her room, however, the viewer sees that he spoils his daughter almost as much as his wife does, but he does not let her stay at home. Even though she is late, she leaves for the church with the candles, wearing one of her best dresses. Ingeri is sent along to accompany her.

Thus is set up one part of the drama of *The Virgin Spring*: a Christian family with an innocent but spoiled daughter, who is envied and hated by a pregnant but unwed "stepsister," who is a follower of a pagan god. Once Karin and Ingeri set out on their journey, however, the film enters its second act. At the edge of the forest, Ingeri stops and lets Karin go on alone. Karin soon meets three shepherds who say they are brothers. One (Avel Düberg) is thin and does the talking for the three; another (Tor Isedal) is mute; and the last (Ove Porath) is a boy of about fourteen years.

The shepherds convince the innocent Karin to stop and share her food with them. The audience immediately recognizes the danger in the situation and watches in fear as Karin dismounts from her horse. Also watching is Ingeri, who has followed Karin but not made her presence known. It takes Karin some time to realize her peril, and Bergman carefully constructs the scene so that the intensity of feeling develops but is not excessively drawn out. Karin's fear does not begin until she notices that one of the sheep bears the markings of her neighbor. At that point the brutality of the two older shepherds begins as they cut off Karin's means of escape and then rape her. The depiction of the rape was quite explicit by the standards of 1960, and that scene was edited for American prints of the film at the time. Considering what has reached the screen in succeeding decades, however, it is clear that the rape scene, which can now be seen in its entirety, is neither gratuitous nor prurient. After the rape, the two older shepherds kill Karin, stamp on the candles that she was carrying, and take her fine, embroidered dress. The boy, however, is sickened by the events.

The third act of the film begins with the sort of coincidence that is perhaps only acceptable in a folktale or fable. As the three shepherds travel on, they seek and are given shelter in Töre's house, although they do not know he is Karin's father. They eat with the family and the farm workers, but no one suspects what they have done until late in the evening when they offer to sell Karin's dress to Mareta, telling her that it belonged to their sister. Mareta immediately recognizes what this means, but she betrays no emotion. After she leaves the shepherds, she lifts the heavy bar and locks the room they are in from the outside. Then she goes to Töre and tells him.

As in the scene in which the viewer saw Karin stop to share her food with the shepherds, it is now clear what will happen next, but Bergman draws out the sequence that leads to Töre's vengeance upon the murderers. There are two important elements in the prelude to vengeance. First, the viewer sees Ingeri again watching as Töre descends the stairs. This time, however, she does not remain hidden but instead goes to Töre and confesses her "sin," as she herself calls it: She wished for evil for Karin and she watched but did nothing. Töre has nothing to say to her, however, except to enlist her help in the ritualistic purification he begins as preparation for what he has to do.

As the viewer continues to expect violence, Töre goes to the bathhouse and cleanses himself with water and branches he has stripped from a tree. He then dons a heavy leather apron that he probably uses when he slaughters animals. With Mareta he goes to the room where the shepherds are, and—in a scene that is too long though not overly violent—kills each one. He apparently does not intend to kill the boy, but when he throws him against the wall, the boy dies immediately. This entire scene is rather dark and completely wordless until Töre finally asks God to forgive him for what he has done.

The last act takes Töre and Mareta to Karin's body. Töre says that he cannot understand God, but he asks His forgiveness again. Then he swears to build a church on the spot and, as they lift the body, a spring begins to flow out of the ground: This was a key element of the song and is the source of the film's title. Almost the last shot of the film shows the faces of the grieving parents as they hold their dead child. All three faces are fully lighted by the sun.

*The Virgin Spring* is a spare, carefully controlled film; background music is kept to a minimum, and there are few signs of self-indulgence or unnecessary effects. In this way it resembles the ballad upon which it is based. The use of light and dark is particularly appropriate and often has the simplicity of the ballad also. The contrast between the dark hair and skin of Ingeri and the fair skin and blonde hair of Karin is notable throughout, but other effects are somewhat more subtle, such as the shadow of a tree branch covering Karin's face at the moment she dies. The acting is good but not exceptional because the style of the film resembles that of a fable, and the actors and actresses are not called upon to give deep performances. The exquisite cinematography of Sven Nykvist is exceptional and began a series of highly accomplished films in the 1960's that Nykvist photographed for Bergman.

Even though Bergman is no longer satisfied with *The Virgin Spring*, and no one would say that it is his best film, it received critical acclaim upon its release, including the Academy Award for Best Foreign-Language Film, and it remains an important and affecting work. Even a minor film by a master such as Bergman is of superior cinematic significance.

*Timothy W. Johnson*

# VIRIDIANA

*Origin:* Spain and Mexico
*Released:* 1961
*Released in U.S.:* 1962
*Production:* Gustavo Alatriste for Uninci S. A. and Uninci Films 59
*Direction:* Luis Buñuel
*Screenplay:* Luis Buñuel and Julio Alejandro
*Cinematography:* José F. Aguayo
*Editing:* Pedro del Rey
*Art direction:* Francisco Canet
*Music:* George Frederick Handel's *Messiah* and Wolfgang Amadeus Mozart's *Requiem*
*Running time:* 90 minutes

*Principal characters:*

Viridiana .............................. Silvia Pinal
Don Jaime .......................... Fernando Rey
Jorge ............................ Francisco Rabal
Ramona ...................... Margarita Lozano
Lucia ............................... Victoria Zinny
Rita .................................. Teresa Rabal

In 1961, a cartoon appeared in a Mexican newspaper to mark the return of Luis Buñuel to filmmaking in his native Spain. The first frame showed an expressionless Buñuel coming ashore to a welcome mat smilingly proffered by Generalissimo Francisco Franco himself, while on the horizon a small figure shouts loudly about hypocrisy and betrayal. In the second frame, Buñuel, now smiling mysteriously, hands Franco a gift-wrapped package marked "Viridiana" and leaves; the small figure is still shouting abuse. In the final frame, Buñuel has gone, the package has exploded, the generalissimo is left in that charred and torn state beloved of cartoonists, and the small figure on the horizon has his hand over his mouth in an "Oops!" gesture.

The cartoon is an exact depiction of what actually happened when Buñuel, after an exile of a quarter of a century in the United States and Mexico, was persuaded to return and make a film. The Spanish government, though evidently nervous, was glad to welcome back Spain's best-known filmmaker at a time when the regime was trying to establish a better international image (to benefit, among other things, from the extraordinary growth in international tourism that was taking place at the time). The invitation to Buñuel to return was first made by filmmaker Carlos Saura, whose first feature, *Los golfos* (1959), had represented Spain at the Cannes

Film Festival, which Buñuel also attended. What finally decided Buñuel, however, was the enthusiasm of the young Mexican producer Gustavo Alatriste, who was anxious to do a coproduction with a Spanish company (in this case, Uninci Films 59 of Madrid).

Buñuel was cooperative with the Spanish authorities, agreeing to every change demanded in the script of *Viridiana* (which he wrote in conjunction with Julio Alejandro, a young Mexican writer who had also collaborated with him on an earlier film, *Nazarín*, in 1958). Buñuel even altered the end when it appeared to offend the censors' sensibilities. The censors were shown a rough cut but postproduction on the film was not completed in Paris until a few days before the 1961 Cannes Film Festival. The Spanish authorities were confident about the finished film, however, and did not ask to see it before allowing it to represent Spain at Cannes. On May 17, 1961, the festival's closing night, the film was screened, causing the jury to revise all previous prize decisions and award it the Gold Palm (jointly awarded to Henri Colpi's *Une Aussi Longue Absence*). Spain's representative José Muñoz-Fontan collected the prize on behalf of his government.

By the time Sr. Muñoz-Fontan had returned to Madrid, the predominantly religious censorship authorities had had an opportunity to see the film and were outraged. All references to the Cannes prize were banned in the Spanish press, the film was suppressed, and Sr. Muñoz-Fontan was fired. Outrage at the film was not confined to Spain: It was attacked by Catholic (and non-Catholic) critics throughout the world for being willfully sacrilegious, copies were seized in Italy, and a number of hostile critics suggested that Buñuel needed psychiatric help. Buñuel's own comment on the situation is characteristic: "I didn't set out to be blasphemous, but then Pope John XXIII is a better judge of such things than I am. . . . When you're sixty-one, you're not interested in behaving childishly, and as I have no pre-conceived position I refuse to get caught up in the scandal surrounding my film."

It is as well, looking at the plot of *Viridiana*, to remember that this is a Spanish film that came out at the very beginning of the period of Spanish "modernization." Otherwise, it is difficult to appreciate the intensity of the shock and outrage that greeted it. Viridiana (Silvia Pinal), a young novice, is approached by her mother superior shortly before she is to take her final vows, which will then cut her off completely from the world. The girl's uncle, Don Jaime (Fernando Rey), who has paid for her religious education, is asking that she visit him at his country estate. The mother superior presses Viridiana to go: It is her last chance to see the old man before taking her vows, and he is in poor health. Viridiana, who can barely remember Don Jaime, is reluctant to leave the convent but demurely obeys the mother superior. Arriving at Don Jaime's estate, she shows more obedience than affection. Her knowledge of the world is sketchy, and she brings all of her convent habits with her, sleeping on the floor of her bedroom and taking only a coarse nightdress and a crown of thorns in her suitcase. The scene of her undressing for bed, however, hints at what is to come: The camera dwells lovingly on her thighs as she takes off her stockings, and Silvia Pinal's performance is such that piety and sensuality are both present in the moment. Don Jaime is a lonely old man, both kindly and tyrannical; he plays religious music on the harmonium and treats his dead wife's wedding clothes with a mixture of reverence and fetishism.

Overcome by Viridiana's beauty, Don Jaime asks her to marry him. Shocked, Viridiana refuses. She does, however, accede to his request that she do him one small favor on her last night in the house: dine with him in his dead wife's wedding dress. During dinner, however, he arranges for the servant Ramona (Margarita Lozano), who may well have been his mistress, to drug Viridiana's coffee, but he is unable to possess her while she is asleep, as he had intended, contenting himself instead with worshiping her in the wedding dress, much as he had worshiped the uninhabited dress in the privacy of the loft.

The next morning, Don Jaime tells Viridiana that he did make love to her while she slept. Horrified, she flees the house. As she is about to board the bus for the convent, two *guardia civil* (policemen) stop her and tell her that Don Jaime has committed suicide by hanging himself with a skipping rope he had given to Rita (Teresa Rabal), Ramona's daughter (and perhaps Don Jaime's). Viridiana feels somewhat responsible for Don Jaime's death (as indeed she is) and returns to the estate, resolved to devote herself to a life of charity there rather than a life of prayer in the convent. She scours the surrounding towns and villages for beggars and paupers and sets up a charitable community on the estate, much to the disapproval of Don Jaime's estranged son Jorge (Francisco Rabal), who has returned to set the estate in order and make it economically profitable once more. Viridiana's plans backfire because the beggars are not prepared to fit in with her charitable equations (charity requires gratitude; gifts of food call for work and submissive behavior). Secretly, they mock her; as one of them, Enedina, remarks, "She has a heart of gold but she's a bit simple!" When Viridiana and Jorge are absent, the beggars move into the house and hold an orgy in the dining room, smashing plates and glassware and desecrating Don Jaime's treasured possessions (including the wedding dress). When Viridiana returns in the midst of the orgy, she is seized by Hobbly, one of the beggars. With Jorge knocked unconscious and tied up, Hobbly rapes Viridiana. When Jorge comes to, he manages to persuade a leper to free him and kill Hobbly. The police arrive and order is restored. At the end of the film, Viridiana, whose experience of the ways of the world is now complete, abandons any idea of returning to the convent and settles into a *ménage à trois* with Jorge and Ramona, who has become Jorge's mistress. The film ends with them playing a hand of cards, though Buñuel had wanted to end with Viridiana replacing Ramona in Jorge's bed. The religious music that has dominated the film's sound track (the orgy and rape are accompanied by George Frederick Handel's *Messiah*, with the verse "And He shall reign for ever and ever" playing over the latter) is replaced by a scratchy modern pop song, "Twist your cares away."

It is a characteristically abrupt Buñuelian ending for a film that preaches no definite moral. As he did so often with his films, Buñuel developed the original idea for *Viridiana* from a single image: that of a young woman drugged by an old man. As the idea developed, the young woman became a novitiate nun, her obsession became charity, the charity involved taking in a community of beggars and the beggars betrayed her by ravishing her fine linen and tableware. The plot had by then acquired the three key ingredients of any Buñuel film: sex, religion, and death. The world portrayed in the film is, as befits Buñuel, a contradictory one. Don Jaime clearly has evil intentions toward Viridiana but is not in himself an evil man—a fact that Buñuel establishes with masterly simplicity: Standing beside a water tank with his niece, Don Jaime casually rescues a bee from drowning. Viridiana's purity, on the other hand, has the selfish blindness of all true obsessions, religious or otherwise, and her refusal to behave like a human being toward Don Jaime on their first meeting makes her a most unattractive character. The beggars, for all of their violence, are not unlikable, and there is a fair degree of sympathy in their refusal to fit in with Viridiana's rules ("If you want to stay," she admonishes them bossily, "you'll have to be more humble"). Jorge, finally, is no saviour or message carrier, merely a rather selfish young man who casually throws out his girlfriend Lucia (Victoria Zinny) and equally casually seduces Ramona. Buñuel thus avoids the temptation to show Viridiana rescued from self-denial by the wondrous discovery of sex; her first encounter with it is violent, her second (on which the film ends), perfunctory and loveless.

There is a short scene just after Jorge's arrival at the estate that encapsulates the moral position of the film. Jorge sees a peasant's cart rumbling by, a dog tied to its axle by a short length of rope. Out of compassion, Jorge frees the dog, which the peasant claims was tied there to prevent the animal from being run over. The dog does not seem particularly grateful for being freed, and the scene ends with another cart passing in the other direction, unnoticed by Jorge, with another dog tied to it. There is no point in Jorge's saving the dog—it will change nothing—yet it was a good thing for him to do: One should never miss the opportunity to help, even if helping changes nothing. It is this lesson that Viridiana learns: To engage with the world, not with some abstract notion of how the world should be. It is better to do something imperfectly than to fester in perfect inaction. This engagement causes her a mixture of pain and pleasure, frustration and satisfaction, but that is better—more real—than self-incarceration. The world will never be perfect, but it *is* the world, and it is all one has.

As a film, *Viridiana* is more carefully structured than many earlier Buñuel films, with a prologue (at the convent), a first section (with Don Jaime), an interlude (during which Viridiana is visited at the estate by the mother superior—a character, it should be noted, that is much more "worldly" than she), a second section (Jorge and the beggars), and an epilogue (the card game). Religious imagery recurs throughout, but generally in an ironic context. Jorge peels an apple with a small switchblade that opens out of a Crucifix (a detail much criticized at the time, but which, Buñuel points out, is something readily available in any Spanish town). Most memorable of all, the beggars' orgy freezes for a moment into an exact reenactment of Leonardo da Vinci's *The Last Supper*—a moment that is undoubtedly blasphemous but that perfectly fits the ambiguous imagery of the film as a whole.

*Viridiana* is, as the work of a director then more than sixty years old, both a remarkably youthful film and one that shows him to be prepared to change and develop a method of filmmaking which, in its directness and adaptability, could never really have been described as a style. Buñuel, indeed, was not a filmmaker who was concerned with placing his signature on the look of a film: He was concerned with presenting an accurate picture of the world. Though *Viridiana* shows few of the Surrealistic moments that characterize both his early and his late films, it is entirely in keeping with the very Spanish brand of Surrealism that dominated Buñuel's entire life: to show, by the uninflected presentation of a number of situations, the truth which lies beneath the reassuring surface of reality. *Viridiana* is a film about the uselessness of living life by a set of predetermined rules and the dangers of not doing so.

*Nick Roddick*

# I VITELLONI

*Origin:* Italy and France
*Released:* 1953
*Released in U.S.:* 1956
*Production:* Lorenzo Pegoraro for Peg Films and Cité Films
*Direction:* Federico Fellini
*Screenplay:* Federico Fellini, Ennio Flaiano, and Tullio Pinelli
*Cinematography:* Otello Martelli, Luciano Trasatti, and Carlo Carlini
*Editing:* Rolando Benedetti
*Art direction:* Mario Chiari
*Music:* Nino Rota
*Running time:* 104 minutes
*Also known as: The Young and the Passionate*

*Principal characters:*

Moraldo .......................... Franco Interlenghi
Alberto .......................... Alberto Sordi
Fausto .......................... Franco Fabrizi
Leopoldo .......................... Leopoldo Trieste
Riccardo .......................... Riccardo Fellini
Sandra .......................... Eleonora Ruffo
Fausto's father .......................... Jean Brochard
Sandra's father .......................... Enrico Viarisio
Olga .......................... Claude Farère
Michele .......................... Carlo Romano
Giulia .......................... Lida Baarova
Woman .......................... Arlette Sauvage
Singer .......................... Maja Nipora

Now recognized as one of the best directors in the history of cinema, Federico Fellini was merely a neophyte filmmaker when he cowrote and directed *I vitelloni*. He had been one of two directors on one film, *Variety Lights* (1950), and had directed another, *Lo sceicco bianco* (1952; *The White Sheik*), by himself, but neither film was well received by either the critics or the public. *I vitelloni*, however, was an immediate success and gained an international reputation for the young director. The film, which tells the story of five aimless young men, is based in part upon the life of Fellini himself and other men he knew in his native town of Rimini, Italy. Fellini infused this simple story with such style and artistry that it is regarded by many as one of his two or three best films.

The film has been shown in the United States under the Italian title as well as under the Hollywood-style title of *The Young and the Passionate*.

Since *vitelloni*, derived from the word for veal, or young cow, is an idiomatic term in parts of Italy for men who are past their teenage years but still retain their adolescent behavior, a more accurate translation of the title would be "The Big Loafers" or "The Overgrown Teenagers," as critic Edward Murray has suggested. The five protagonists of the film are about thirty years old but still live with their parents and do not hold jobs. The film is the story of their accepting or avoiding responsibilities.

The viewer first sees the *vitelloni* in an opening shot of them walking through a town square late at night, and is then introduced to them individually by a narrator during a "Miss Siren" contest at a café. Fausto (Franco Fabrizi) is described by the narrator as the "leader and spiritual guide" of the group, but one soon suspects that this description must be at least partly ironic because Fausto is making advances to a young woman, who accuses him of breaking promises to a woman named Sandra (Eleonora Ruffo). The other *vitelloni* are Riccardo (Riccardo Fellini, the director's brother), who sings and acts as master of ceremonies at the event, Alberto (Alberto Sordi), Leopoldo (Leopoldo Trieste), and Moraldo (Franco Interlenghi), the character who is most closely identified with Fellini himself. As the film progresses, the viewer learns more about each of the characters except Riccardo, who remains only vaguely defined.

Fausto's character emerges quickly. Riccardo announces that Sandra, who is Moraldo's sister, has won the beauty contest. When she faints soon afterward and a doctor is called to examine her, Fausto deduces the cause and goes home to pack his suitcase, telling his father (Jean Brochard) that he is leaving town to take a job. Before Fausto can leave, however, Moraldo arrives to tell him that Sandra is pregnant. His father then insists that Fausto stay and marry Sandra.

The wedding takes place, and Fausto and Sandra leave for Rome. A montage then shows the other four *vitelloni* that night after they separate. Leopoldo, who thinks of himself as a poet and playwright, begins writing at his desk, but he soon stops and begins talking to the maid in the house next door. The fact that none of the young men has a job is emphasized when Moraldo, who is sitting alone in an empty square, sees a young boy on his way to work at the railway station. He is surprised to find that this boy goes to work every morning at three and that he does not complain about it.

The next day Alberto borrows money from his sister, Olga (Claude Farère), who works at an office during the day and does extra typing at home at night. He takes the money and goes off with the others to the racetrack. Some time later, Alberto accidentally discovers that Olga is seeing a man who is married but separated from his wife. Alberto takes a superior tone with her and tells her that she must stop seeing the man.

When Fausto and Sandra return from Rome, Sandra's father (Enrico Viarisio) gets Fausto a job in a small shop owned by his friends Michele

(Carlo Romano) and his wife, Giulia (Lida Baarova). The shop sells religious articles, a singularly inappropriate position for the reluctant Fausto, as the viewer sees in the next scene. He goes to see a film with Sandra but leaves in the middle of the showing to follow a woman (Arlette Sauvage) who was sitting next to him and had asked him to light her cigarette. When he returns to the theater, the film is over, and Sandra is waiting outside in tears.

The narrator then announces that time has passed and reveals the film's flippant attitude toward its protagonists by saying, "In the next few months the most important things that happened were that Riccardo grew a moustache, and Alberto grew sideburns. . . . While Fausto shaved his moustache off."

In the subsequent sequence, it is Carnival time, and the *vitelloni* go to the ball, all dressed in costumes except for Fausto, who wears a tuxedo. Riccardo and Leopoldo indulge in clumsy flirtations, and when Fausto is greeted by a slightly inebriated Giulia, he looks at her low-cut gown and asks her to dance, causing her to retreat in embarrassment. The ball ends with a scene emblematic of the lives of the young men—Alberto dressed as a woman, drunkenly dancing with a huge papier-mâché head. When Alberto reaches home, he finds that Olga is leaving with her lover and their mother is crying. In order to console her, he promises to get a job, but he is obviously upset when she endorses the idea.

The next day, Fausto arrives late for work. When the opportunity presents itself, he tries to kiss Giulia. She is upset by his advances and gets away from him. That evening, Michele tells him that he and his wife love each other and that he no longer wants Fausto working there. Fausto tells his friends that he was fired because he refused the advances of his employer's wife, and he convinces Moraldo to help him steal a large angel from the shop. They try unsuccessfully to sell the angel to a nun and a monk and finally leave it with Gidizio, the town fool.

The father of Sandra and Moraldo finds out what has happened and becomes enraged with both Moraldo and Fausto, but finally they are forgiven. When Sandra and Fausto's baby is born, the narrator informs the viewer, the family is less concerned with Fausto.

Leopoldo's inevitable moment of dashed hopes is presented with similar equanimity. He takes the other *vitelloni* to the theater with him to see the actor Sergio Natali, who has taken Leopoldo's play to read and evaluate. After the performance, Leopoldo finds that the old actor has read very little of his play and is interested in him only as a sexual partner. Meanwhile, Fausto has gone to a hotel room with a singer (Maja Nipora) from the theatrical troupe. When he goes home to Sandra, she is still awake and sees him wiping lipstick off of his face. She begins crying, and the next morning before Fausto awakens, she leaves with the baby. When Fausto finds that she is gone, he spends a frantic day looking for her. Finally, he finds her at his father's house. His father whips him with a belt for what he has done, and then Sandra and Fausto go home together with the baby. Sandra expresses some sympathy for Fausto, but she tells him very definitely that the next time she will beat him herself.

In the final sequence, Moraldo arrives at the railroad station early in the morning and boards the train. He is leaving, he tells another boy, although he does not know exactly where he is going or what he is going to do.

Fellini has said about this film that it is "the story of adolescents who cannot see anything more in life than satisfying their animal desires—sleeping, eating, fornicating. I was trying to say there is something more, there is always more. Life must have a meaning beyond the animal."

This attitude is reflected in the film, especially in the narration, but also in two or three speeches of Fausto's father and Michele. *I vitelloni* is not, however, a condemnation of its protagonists, and it does not portray them unsympathetically. The use of subjective camera angles in many scenes, for example, involves the viewer with the characters, preventing an entirely censorious attitude toward them.

Each of the *vitelloni*, except Riccardo, has a moment or two of self-awareness when he realizes some small truth about his character and his situation. Only Moraldo, however, seems changed by this revelation. The others, it seems, will continue to live the same lives as before.

The strengths of *I vitelloni* are not only in the interesting characters and the underlying theme in the screenplay created by Fellini with Ennio Flaiano and Tullio Pinelli, but also in the performances, which are emphasized by Fellini's characteristic attention to faces and the use of reaction shots.

Federico Fellini has continued to make films that are highly regarded by both critics and the public, *Otto e mezzo* (1963; *8½*) and *Giulietta degli spiriti* (1965; *Juliet of the Spirits*) among them, but many feel that he has never surpassed the quality of *I vitelloni*.

*Timothy W. Johnson*

# VIVA LA MUERTE

*Origin:* Tunisia and France
*Released:* 1971
*Released in U.S.:* 1971
*Production:* Jean Velter for Isabelle Films and Hassene Daldoul for SATPEC
*Direction:* Fernando Arrabal
*Screenplay:* Fernando Arrabal and Claudine Lagrive; based on the novel *Baal Babilonia*, by Arrabal
*Cinematography:* Jean-Marc Ripert
*Editing:* Laurence Leininger
*Art direction:* no listing
*Music:* Jean-Yves Bosseur
*MPAA rating:* no listing
*Running time:* 90 minutes
*Also known as: Long Live Death* and *Hurrah for Death*

*Principal characters:*

Fando ............................ Mahdi Chaouch
Mother ............................ Nuria Espert
Aunt Clara ............................ Anouk Ferjac
Father ............................ Ivan Henriques
Teresa ............................ Jazia Klibi

Fernando's Arrabal's *Viva la muerte* first appeared in the manner of a cult film. Like a very different film, *The Rocky Horror Picture Show* (1975), it played only midnight showings at the St. Marks Theatre in New York. Because it retains its special audience and its so-called underground reputation, *Viva la muerte* also retains its original title and is almost never translated, somewhat like a similarly "special" film, *Taxi zum Klo* (1981). Whereas *Taxi zum Klo* provokes its audience with its presentation of real and contemporary situations, *Viva la muerte* instead presents grotesque, surrealistic, and alienating images that refer to a time and place few remember and even fewer have experienced. It is important, then, to know that the Spanish Civil War (1936–1939) provides the necessary context within which the film's often almost unbearable imagery becomes something more than a privileged reference to the director's personal psychology.

The Spanish Civil War was a most brutal war by any standard: Members of the same families became bitter enemies, neighbors routinely slaughtered one another, and more than 500,000 people were killed, many by execution. Within this context, the bizarre occurrences, the dreams, visions, and memories, the apparent visual fetishes, all become not only believable but also paradigmatic. Beneath the cruel surface of his film, Arrabal exposes not simply the unusual or the abnormal, but rather the universal response to tyranny, and he does this not only within the state but also within the private world of the family. The very harshness of the film's images, however, has evoked a variety of critical response. Whereas some critics consider *Viva la muerte* disgusting, ugly, or simply a failure, others find the film to be monumental, beautiful, or artistically significant. Certainly, in part, this mixed response derives from the mixed nature of the film itself. Arrabal, for example, is known as a playwright and not a filmmaker (*Viva la muerte* is his first film). Furthermore, this film about Spain, made by a Spanish exile, actually appears in French and was shot in North Africa. This apparent confusion aside, *Viva la muerte* has a basically simple story to tell.

A young boy, Fando (Mahdi Chaouch), living with his grandparents, mother (Nuria Espert), and aunt (Anouk Ferjac), tries to discover the fate of his father (Ivan Henriques), betrayed to the police (by the mother). The father, it appears, represented everything that Francisco Franco, the winner in the Civil War, hated: At various times the father is referred to as an anarchist, a Jew, a Communist or "Red," and an atheist. Fando cannot understand how this paradigmatic enemy of the state was also the gentle father he remembers. Consequently, the film cuts back and forth between scenes of the boy's daily life at home, playing with friends or at school, and the various memories or visions which seem to intrude themselves into his mind. These imaginary sequences have a double nature: They reflect Fando's fearful and confused response to a world too complex to be understood by a sensitive child. Thus, his mother can appear as both a pure Madonna and a sadistic slut. Fando's visions also reflect the violent split within Spanish society during the war. There could be no middle ground: One must be either Nationalist (a supporter of Franco and the Fascist Right), or Republican (a supporter of the elected government or the Communist Left). Fando, a child of about twelve in the film (though Arrabal was actually only four when the war started), becomes a middle ground on which the opposing sides may battle.

The film reveals the child's inchoate desires as an entire society's almost subliminal response to the war which has divided it. He is clearly attracted by his mother, by her erotic beauty, and, at the same time, repelled by her continual justification of her treachery toward her husband. Still too young to comprehend completely the meaning of his desires, Fando finds himself yearning simultaneously for his beautiful mother and for his missing father. Like so many Spaniards of the period, he can make no simple choice—choosing sides is like the parting of the nail from the flesh, as the unknown poet of the medieval epic the *Poem of the Cid* (thirteenth century) put it.

This brutal image has cast its shadow over the entire history of the Spanish people. From the medieval poet of the *Poem of the Cid* to the modern poetry of Federico García Lorca, from the Inquisition to the Civil War, the

Spanish people seem to have a peculiar affinity for violence. The theater of Arrabal is very much a descendant of Antonin Artaud's Theater of Cruelty. Artaud believed that theater must be violent enough to crush the spectator, to hypnotize him, and to shake his complacency. Arrabal's film, which concentrates on the cruelest possible images and events, continues this violent tradition.

The violence and cruelty, however, are necessary in order to place Fando's concerns within their proper context. The struggle between his parents reflects the larger struggle which is tearing apart the Spanish nation during the Civil War. The war, in fact, points to an even larger historical canvas, the centuries of repression which almost always characterized Spanish life. Not only must Fando come to terms with the complex events surrounding his father's imprisonment, but he must also confront the tormented and distorted sexuality he finds in his own home. Even the credit sequence suggests a confusion of private and public concerns, of subjective and objective points of view, or of the roles of child and adult.

While the credits appear briefly, almost humbly, written across the screen, they appear over a series of grotesque drawings by Arrabal's friend Roland Topor. The drawings are outrageous images of caricaturelike figures involved in various sexual activities or suffering the most obscene tortures. Although the pictures suggest the work of a tormented soul, they are accompanied by the innocent voice of a child singing a Danish nursery song. The contrast between the innocent young voice (whose words cannot be understood and thereby suggest the audience's distance from the events they are about to see) and the gruesome drawings establishes Fando's perspective and locates him psychologically within his universe. While he struggles to understand his own experience, he must also participate in the larger historical events he cannot possibly comprehend.

The film begins by pointing to the double nature of Fando's experience. In the distance, a truck filled with soldiers careens down the side of a mountain. The camera zooms in on Fando as he listens with surprise to the soldiers' shouts that all traitors will be executed and therefore, "viva la muerte." This shout, actually the battle cry and motto of the Moors who formed Franco's Spanish Legion (those guilty of the worst atrocities), sends Fando running home. The camera movement, which takes the viewer closer to Fando, also prepares the viewer for his response, the first of many interpolated visions. This first vision is a reddish colored image of his father's head being crushed by grotesquely brutal executioners. This cruel image is replaced by Fando's mother, now back in the present, who talks to him of death and heaven, while he lovingly caresses her feet. A second vision shows the mother showering, now all in blue, first to the sounds of a flute and then to increasingly abandoned but joyful music. Matching the building tempo of the music, the shower is transformed into a wildly erotic dream in which the water seems to become more viscous, like milk or semen.

Subsequent sequences introduce new contrasts and increase the complex network of associations. When Fando punishes himself, with the help of a smiling Aunt Clara, for his lustful desires, he suddenly dreams that he is tumbling out of a basket. This image of escape and rebirth contrasts significantly with the images of sexual repression and medieval self-discipline. The fact that Fando projects his pubescent desires onto members of his family strains even further those traditional relationships which his parents' politics have disrupted. Added to this is the discovery that Fando is suffering from tuberculosis. The disease saps his strength and makes it difficult to react to each new event in his life. Instead, he substitutes his sometimes obviously feverish visions or fantasies.

When Fando discovers some of his father's old letters, he remembers the arrest. While the father sits calmly with his pipe (Dr. Plumb), the police swarm through the gate of their house brutally assaulting him. The mother, dressed in black, leans against a white wall. In the background is the Danish nursery music from the opening credits. The music suggests Fando's uncomprehending innocence before this terrifying scene. The moment becomes even more frightening, however, as the memory gives way to a vision of his father's possible fate. He imagines his father buried up to his neck in the sand while horsemen ride over his head. As in the first vision it is most often the head, the mind or the spirit of dissent, that is destroyed.

Each sequence is carefully structured, fluctuating between reality, memory, or fantasy, but developing along a clearly defined line. Reading another of his father's letters provokes a new, even more terrifying vision. The father is carried away by executioners while the mother looks on excitedly. In the background is the music of a *saeta* (Passion of Jesus). Suddenly, the mother is transformed into a maniacal witch, glorying in her vengeance as her whipped husband falls between her legs. This frenzied scene is replaced by the present as the mother explains to Fando that his father was a "Red" and an atheist. Fando, however, is unable to accept his mother's explanation, and this leads to his most important memory of his father: a trip to the beach. This memory, in turn, evokes an equally gentle image of the mother, now as a Madonna, giving her blessing to him and to his friend Teresa (Jazia Klibi). Unfortunately, this image cannot endure. These peaceful and gentle images are shattered as the Madonna-mother assumes a grotesquely malign appearance. Now she appears with a knife between her lips, winking, as if conspiring with her son, the police, or even the audience. Fando's response to this vision is to return to his memory-vision of the beach, where he and his father kiss with their tongues in a striking image of communion.

As the tuberculosis becomes more debilitating, Fando's fantasies become more bizarre, intruding themselves into almost every memory and eventually obliterating almost all the present action. The increased distortion of traditional chronology, however, reflects not only the course of Fando's disease but also his more intense confusion as he struggles against the various influences which assault him. He remembers cruel traditions (the grandfather's "bleeding"), the massacre of rebellious workers (who refuse to wear muzzles while working in the field), and the executions (including that of the great poet and playwright García Lorca). These memories also provoke wild fantasies of revenge. Thus Fando envisions a priest being emasculated and then forced to eat his own genitals, or he imagines himself drowning an entire city in his urine. Present reality also becomes more explicitly cruel. When the grandfather dies, Aunt Clara insists that Fando whip her until she bleeds, after which she squeezes his testicles until he screams. Finally, watching Aunt Clara masturbate, Fando bites the head off a small lizard. This gruesome response to sexual passion (like Aunt Clara's sadomasochism), underlines the intense passions lying just beneath the surface of Spanish society. Arrabal's vision of Spain insists on these violent juxtapositions. There can be no simple reconciliation either of opposing political forces or of sexual desire and its expression.

The final series of fantasies are the most grotesque. At one point, Fando imagines his mother defecating on his father, and he imagines himself eating some filth from Aunt Clara's shoe, as she covers him with spaghetti while he holds out his arms like a crucified Christ. These brutal and punishing images culminate in a final bloody fantasy. The mother castrates and slaughters a bull and then wraps Fando, now an adult, in its flayed carcass. Hanging passively like a side of beef, while a brass band plays loud and raucous music, Fando seems finally lost, defeated by his mother's overpowering influence. In another dramatic cut, back to the present, however, Fando is in the hospital, about to be operated on for the tuberculosis which has continued to drain his strength. He awakens from his surgery and is gently wrapped in a blanket by Teresa. She places him on a cart and, with her ever-present pet turkey trailing behind, leads him up to the mountains (where the film began), to find his father, who is supposedly alive and fighting with the Resistance. Just as Teresa's gentle wrapping contrasts with the previous scene in which his mother sewed him into the bloody carcass of a bull, the melody of an exhilarating Gloria contrasts with the brutal and repetitive notes of the brass band. The pet turkey seems to stand for the incongruous innocence of these children; it is the burden that every Spanish child must drag along through life. The film concludes here on this final ambiguous note. Unlike all the other visions this last scene seems real. The suggestion is that although viewers are not told whether Fando's father lives, he will nevertheless free himself both from the disease, which has drained him, and from the constraints of his repressive Spanish heritage.

Because the final scene, though a fantasy, seems so real, one can take this for Arrabal's indication that Fando, like himself, has broken free. The liberating spirit of the father, alive or dead, finally triumphs over the enervating world of the mother (with which one associates Spanish tradition and even Fando's disease). It is Fando's imagination that permits him to break free, an imagination which, though brutal and alienating, releases the creative forces which have been repressed for so many years. The film, then, ends on a hopeful note, just as the book that inspired it, *Baal Babilonia*, ends with the word "yes."

*Martin Kabat*

# VLAD THE IMPALER
## The True Life of Dracula
## (VLAD TEPEŞ)

*Origin:* Romania
*Released:* 1979
*Released in U.S.:* 1980
*Production:* Romaniafilm
*Direction:* Doru Năstase
*Screenplay:* Mircea Mohor
*Cinematography:* Aurel Kostrakiewicz
*Editing:* Adina Georgescu Obrocea
*Art direction:* Guţa Ştirbu
*Costume design:* Ileana Oroveanu
*Music:* Tiberiu Olah
*MPAA rating:* no listing
*Running time:* 147 minutes
*Running time in U.S.:* 107 minutes

*Principal characters:*
Vlad Tepeş ........................ Stefan Sileanu
Mînzila ........................ Ernest Maftei
Stoica ........................ Emanoil Petruţ
Mohammed ........................ Alexandru Repan
Albu ........................ Teofil Vîlcu
Yunus Beg (Katavolinos) ....... Constantin Codrescu
Mahmud Pacha ........................ Ion Marinescu
Count Szilagyi ........................ György Kovacs
Chief of the merchants ....... Constantin Bărbulescu

Almost a century after the publishing of Bram Stoker's novel—which has become an inexhaustible source for makers of films about bloodsucking monsters—it was time for the truth to be told about Dracula, also through the most popular art of cinema.

"Dracula" is the name given by foreigners to Romanian prince Vlad Tepeş (Vlad the Impaler), who ruled in Wallachia (a province in the south of today's Romania) between 1456 and 1462. During his brief reign, he proved to be an untiring fighter for the independence of his country from the greatly expanding Ottoman Empire, and inside the country, he provided justice and was a fierce enemy of lies, theft, and murder, of laziness and hypocrisy. Vlad tried and, in a way, succeeded in establishing in Wallachia an absolutist regime, as was done by Louis XIV in France two centuries later. Vlad decided to defeat the resistance of the powerful boyars, who were arbitrarily making their own laws on their lands, and force them to support the state economically. Vlad also decided to do away with crime so that each of his subjects should live in safety, and he severely punished any opposition to his decrees. It was not exactly the punishment (impalement) that shocked the people of those times; in the middle of the fifteenth century, savagery and cruelty of the most refined kind were present everywhere in Europe. What impressed Vlad's contemporaries was the impartiality of the sentence, applied equally to enemies inside and outside the country, to common people and to great boyars. The consequences of applying this humiliating punishment (by contrast, the ax and the block would have been considered a glorious death) were seen after a very short while: All the social classes observed the laws; honesty and order were introduced, the roads became safe, and trade flourished. Skillfully handling his small army, Vlad the Impaler succeeded in giving a bitter lesson to Sultan Mohammed II, who entered Wallachia with a huge army. After ruling for six years, in a difficult moment, Vlad took refuge in Transylvania with his ally King Matthias Corvinus. The latter, misled by rivals who schemed against Vlad, threw him into prison, where he was to spend twelve years. He would only rule in Wallachia for another two months, after which he was killed by one of his rivals to the throne.

The documents preserved from that period, as well as the legends kept in the oral tradition of the Romanian people, invariably point to a feeling of admiration for this stern prince. As regards the name "Dracula" (which is supposed to mean "the devil's son"), it is a distorted variation of the nickname of Vlad's father, who was a knight of the Hungarian Order of the Dragon. The graphics of the respective decoration reminded people of a devil (in Romanian, *drac*)—which in those times was sufficient evidence for a person to be suspected of doing business with the Evil One.

There is no doubt that Vlad the Impaler's deeds were commented on throughout Eastern Europe with due exaggerations in the countries where he was regarded with enmity. It was, in fact, in the folklore of this geographical area in which vampires originated. From the frightening bedtime fairy tales to stories meant to frighten adults, Vlad the Impaler was consistently characterized as the culmination of this ancestral folk background. Thus, a concrete identity for the fictitious bloodthirsty character was established. The life of the Wallachian prince and the way in which his character was distorted until he entered into this undesired legend can be found in the film *Vlad the Impaler: The True Life of Dracula*. In the film, Vlad (Stefan Sileanu) quickly attains the throne by taking advantage of a moment of confusion. The Saxon merchants of Transylvania recover their goods stolen by thieves, and they receive a proposal regarding the free traffic of goods. The open conflict between Vlad and the great boyars takes place in the state council. The beggars and the parasites are invited to a princely feast, and when the party is in full swing, the doors are closed and the house is set on fire. A group of boyars rebel, but they are defeated and impaled. Romanian goods are confiscated in the city of Braşov and thus "the economic war" between Vlad (by now identified as "the Impaler") and the German merchants begins. The latter grant hospitality to the great boyars led by Albu (Teofil Vîlcu), who are running away, as well as to Wallachia's crown prince. They subsequently start a campaign of slander against Vlad. The alliance with Matthias Corvinus, the new king of Hungary, solves "the economic war" in Vlad's favor. Yet, the latter does not agree to be the king's vassal. An attempt to assassinate Vlad is stopped by provost marshal Stoica (Emanoil Petruţ). Three years later, three Turkish messengers are shipped back to the sultan with their turbans nailed on their heads. Sultan Mohammed II (Alexandru Repan) sends a sly ambassador, Yunus Beg (Constantin Codrescu), who is either to convince Vlad to make an alliance with the Turks against Hungary or to lure him into a trap and take him prisoner. Yunus Beg and his soldiers, however, end up being impaled. In a rage, Mohammed gathers his armies and comes to Wallachia himself in order to give the throne to Radu, Vlad's brother and his hostage. In the meantime, the crown prince, Dan, crosses the mountains in Wallachia, but he is defeated and executed, while the plotting boyars are impaled. On their way, the Turks only find deserted villages and poisoned wells. In the night, Vlad, having penetrated the Turkish camp, succeeds in creating such a panic there that the Turks end by killing one another. Mohammed withdraws with what is left of his army. Yet, Vlad is caught by surprise as a result of a dirty trick played on him by his brother Radu, and in order to prevent the massacre of innocent people, he gives up the throne. In the meantime, with letters fabricated by the merchants of Braşov, Vlad's enemies have persuaded Matthias Corvinus that Vlad has betrayed him. When Vlad appears, accompanied only by Stoica, the soldiers take him prisoner. While trying to settle things, his faithful servant is killed before Vlad's eyes. An epilogue describing his twelve years in prison and his tragic death concludes the film.

In his second film (the first centered on an actual episode from World War II), director Doru Năstase could easily have been tempted by the spectacular elements in the facts known about Vlad the Impaler. On the contrary, the tone of the film is one of sobriety. The events are narrated by a chronicler concerned with objectively rendering facts, without allowing room for speculation. Screenwriter Mircea Mohor did not allow himself to ramble beyond historical data (for example, nothing is known about any wife or mistress of Vlad; therefore, there is no feminine presence in the film, no element to soften for a moment the harshness of the main character). The role of a man born two centuries too early, who untiringly fights to apply his ideas about the state, about society, and morals, is particularly difficult. That is why both critics and audiences warmly greeted the sober performance required by the director, and the result obtained by an actor unknown until then—Stefan Sileanu—who succeeded in appearing both volcanic and ice-cold. The same sobriety is present at a visual level—there is nothing ostentatious in the settings and costumes—these are the interiors and the clothes which could be found in everyday Wallachia in the fifteenth century. The tragic element—the impaling stake—that accounts for the nickname of the Wallachian prince is a discreet presence, not an obsession. It is exploited fully only once, in a scene which is memorable from a visual point of view, when Sultan Mohammed is welcomed by a forest of stakes bearing what is left of his men, making up a mocking arch of triumph.

Some Romanian critics have disapproved of this sobriety, characterizing the film as "illustrativist" and even "uncinematic." Yet, the conception of the film is simple, not simplistic, while the editing alone, with intelligent cut-ins on sound, photography, and ideas, contradicts such allegations. The same is true of the climax—the sequence showing the panic in the Turkish camp and the incredible slaughter following—handled with the tact of a director skilled in battle scenes and in routs with hundreds of extras. This strong tempo is followed by a slower moment, and again a strong tempo, in which the celebration of victory introduces the joy of Vlad and of those close to him. After having helped the prince to take off the Turkish disguise which had allowed him to squeeze into the enemies' camp, the hated garments are trampled upon. From the rhythm of that very treading, a *hora*, a type of national dance, takes shape, a superb solution of manifesting the joy of fulfilling one's duty toward one's country. Cinematic and convincing also is the end of the film, when, after the murder of his counselor, Stoica (Emanoil Petruţ), who dies looking at his master, whom he was unable to protect, the camera stops on Vlad's face, which reflects his understanding that this is actually his own end.

None of Vlad the Impaler's countrymen expected this film to put an end to the fabulations about the prince: Dracula is too profitable a character to be abandoned. Yet the Romanians have thought it necessary to achieve a dissociation between the monstrous count and one of their most admired leaders. For that reason, the film *Vlad the Impaler* must be mainly regarded as a polemic gesture.

*Aura Puran*

# VOLPONE

*Origin:* France
*Released:* 1947
*Released in U.S.:* 1947
*Production:* Île de France Productions
*Direction:* Maurice Tourneur
*Screenplay:* Jules Romains and Stefan Zweig; based on the play by Ben Jonson
*Cinematography:* no listing
*Editing:* no listing
*Art direction:* A. Barsacq
*Music:* Marcel Delannoy
*Running time:* 98 minutes

*Principal characters:*

| | |
|---|---|
| Volpone | Harry Baur |
| Mosca | Louis Jouvet |
| Corvino | Fernand Ledoux |
| Canina | Marion Dorian |
| Voltore | Jean Temerson |
| Leone | Alexandre Rignault |
| Corbaccio | Charles Dullin |
| Columba | Jacqueline DeLubac |

Maurice Tourneur is, quite rightly, considered one of the American cinema's greatest visual stylists, a director who composed each shot, each scene in his films as painstakingly as any painter. Such Tourneur productions as *The Wishing Ring* (1914), *The Pride of the Clan* (1917), *The Poor Little Rich Girl* (1917), *The Blue Bird* (1918), *Prunella* (1918), and *Treasure Island* (1920) have become classics of American silent film. In classifying Tourneur as one of the most important of early American film directors, however, there is an inclination to forget or to dismiss the films which he directed after leaving the United States and returning to his native France.

Born in Paris, France, on February 2, 1876, Maurice Tourneur began his professional career as a magazine illustrator and as a designer of posters and other materials. He worked in the theater from 1900 until 1912, when director Émile Chautard (who, like Tourneur, was to come to the United States) invited Tourneur to act in some of his film productions. From Chautard, Tourneur learned the elements of film production, became a director with the Eclair Company in France, and, in 1914, came to the United States as a director. His first American film was *Mother* (1914), shot at Fort Lee, New Jersey.

From 1914 until the 1920's, Tourneur directed some of the most polished of American feature films; in the September, 1918, issue of *Motion Picture Magazine*, he noted that he had "brought stylization to the screen." Tourneur was to continue to direct major American features through 1926, but somehow those later films, such as *Lorna Doone* (1922) and *The Christian* (1923), lacked much of the unique quality of Tourneur's earlier features. In 1926, the director was working for Metro-Goldwyn-Mayer on *The Mysterious Island*, featuring Lionel Barrymore, and was told by the studio that a producer would be supervising his work. Tourneur refused to be supervised, Metro-Goldwyn-Mayer insisted, and the result was Tourneur's sudden departure for his native France.

Tourneur's first non-American feature in thirteen years was *L'Équipage* (1928), filmed in France in 1927 but not released in the United States until 1929, under the title of *The Last Flight*. *L'Équipage* was followed by a German silent, *Das Schiff der verlorenen Menschen* (1929; *The Ship of Lost Men*), featuring Marlene Dietrich and Fritz Kortner, a superb production deserving of far more recognition that it has received. Tourneur's first sound feature was *Accusée, levez-vous* (1930), starring Gaby Morlay and Charles Vanel. It was followed by, among others, *Partir!* (1931), *Les Deux orphelines* (1933, featuring Yvette Guilbert in a film based on the same story line as D. W. Griffith's *Orphans of the Storm*, 1921), *Koenigsmark* (1935; *Crimson Dynasty*, shot in both English and French and starring Pierre Fresnay), and *Samson* (1936).

Immediately prior to the Nazi takeover of France, Tourneur directed one of his best foreign-language features and the only one of his French films readily available in the United States. That was *Volpone*, based on English dramatist Ben Jonson's greatest comedy, first performed in 1606, and filmed by Tourneur in late 1939 and early 1940. *Volpone* has been filmed several times and was revived as the Broadway hit play *Sly Fox* (with George C. Scott in the leading role), but there can be little question that Tourneur's version is the definitive one.

Tourneur's *Volpone* is faithful to Ben Jonson, but through it runs a special hint of Gallic wit. It is bawdy, at times degenerating to slapstick, but it moves along at an exhilarating pace, well acted on sets of a lavish scale.

Volpone (Harry Baur), a rich Venetian merchant, decides to "punish" his friends, at whose hands he has suffered when it appeared one of his ships has been sunk. Assisting Volpone in his machinations is his rascally servant Mosca (Louis Jouvet). Volpone pretends to be dying in order to watch the actions and reactions of his "friends," as they jockey for positions as his heirs. Each has been told privately that he will be the sole beneficiary of Volpone's will, and each is overly anxious to please his benefactor. The silk merchant, Corvino (Fernand Ledoux), is happy to send his attractive young wife, Columba (Jacqueline DeLubac), to "nurse" the ailing Volpone, while Corbaccio (Charles Dullin) disinherits his own son and names Volpone beneficiary of his estate. Volpone's scheme appears to be unfolding without a hitch, but in a final, riotous carnival sequence, it is Volpone himself who finds himself stripped of his wealth and kicked out of his own home by the conniving Mosca.

Aside from Tourneur's direction, *Volpone* is a joy to watch thanks to the superb playing of Harry Baur and Louis Jouvet as Volpone and Mosca. Harry Baur (1880-1943) was a classic actor in French theater and film, with his better-known performances in the latter being in *Rothschild* (1934), *Les Misérables* (1934), *Le Golem* (1936), *Un Grand Amour de Beethoven* (1936; *The Life and Loves of Beethoven*), and *Un Carnet de bal* (1937). Both Baur and his Jewish wife were arrested during the Nazi occupation of France, and Baur died, under mysterious circumstances, in 1943. Louis Jouvet remained away from France during the Nazi occupation. Born in Brittany in 1887, Jouvet was a passionate disciple of the theater, who made occasional, but major, contributions to such films as *La Kermesse héroïque* (1935), *Les Bas-fonds* (1936; *The Lower Depths*), *Un Carnet de bal*, *La Marseillaise* (1938), and *Hôtel du Nord* (1938). Of the cinema, Jouvet once remarked, "It is an American industry, but a French art." He died in Paris in 1951.

Because of the war, *Volpone* was not released in the United States until 1947. Despite heavy editing for censorship, it delighted the critics. In *The New York Times* Bosley Crowther called the production, "a rollickingly naughty motion picture. . . . It has a gusto that is to be admired." The West Coast news magazine *Fortnight* commented, "*Volpone* is bawdy, breathless, alternately sly and bold, and thoroughly captivating." *Cue* called the production "one of the brightest and most entertaining film comedies of the year." The National League of Decency condemned the film, because "despite pretense of moral purposes, this film portrays vice attractively and ridicules virtue. It contains blasphemous references to religious practices and indecent and suggestive scenes."

Maurice Tourneur continued to work during the Nazi occupation of France, directing five features, the last of which was *Cécile est morte* (1943). After World War II, he directed two films, *Après l'amour* (1948) and *L'Impasse des deux anges* (1948). Tourneur died in Paris in 1961.

*Anthony Slide*

# THE WAGES OF FEAR (LE SALAIRE DE LA PEUR)

*Origin:* France and Italy
*Released:* 1953
*Released in U.S.:* 1955
*Production:* Louis Wipf for Commerciale Cinématographique/Filmsonor, Véra Films, and Fono Roma
*Direction:* Henri-Georges Clouzot
*Screenplay:* Henri-Georges Clouzot and Jérôme Géronimi; based on the novel by Georges Arnaud
*Cinematography:* Armand Thirard
*Editing:* Henri Rust, Madeleine Gug, and E. Muse
*Art direction:* René Renoux
*Music:* Georges Auric
*Running time:* 156 minutes

*Principal characters:*

Mario .............................. Yves Montand
Jo .................................. Charles Vanel
Bimba ............................ Peter van Eyck
Luigi ................................. Folco Lulli
Linda .............................. Véra Clouzot

Except for the early 1900's, France has traditionally found the American film market to be nearly impenetrable. In the mid-1950's, however, the box-office barrier to Gallic films collapsed as "art houses" sprang up in most major urban centers to showcase exceptional works from abroad. One of the first hits to triumph in these specialized American theaters was Henri-Georges Clouzot's taut thriller *The Wages of Fear*.

It is easy to see why *The Wages of Fear* (remade in 1977 by William Friedkin as the expensive box-office flop *The Sorcerer*) proved to be so accessible to American audiences. Its vigorous narrative, multilingual dialogue (including much awkward English), and American derivations (its plot somewhat resembles Raoul Walsh's *They Drive by Night*, 1940) contrasted sharply to the stylish, leisurely manner for which the French cinema was known. At the same time, there was enough foreignness to the film to satisfy exotic fancies: Layers of Latin American ambience, pop existentialism, and anti-imperialist raillery coat its tense action.

The story is simplicity itself. An oil well, owned by an American petroleum company (the S.O.C.), has caught fire. Only a massive explosion can cover and thereby extinguish the flames, but the nitroglycerin needed for the job is stored in the sleepy, squalid South American town of Los Piedras, located three hundred bumpy, hilly miles away. To truck the volatile explosives to the disaster site would be too dangerous for the company's employees, so the company's managers decide to enlist four drivers from Los Piedras' ecumenical, vagrant population. The reward: two thousand dollars apiece.

The opportunity is welcomed by the dozens of men stranded without jobs or hope in Los Piedras. The four drivers chosen, divided into two teams, are a motley crew: There is Luigi (Folco Lulli), an ebullient Italian mason whose plaster-dust cough will be cured only in more felicitous climes; Bimba (Peter van Eyck), a Germanic type with nerves of steel; Jo (Charles Vanel), a middle-aged, amoral cutthroat; and Mario (Yves Montand), the film's romantic, virile protagonist whose hope it is to see again the Paris Métro.

Clouzot, who gathered many of his ideas during a trip to Brazil, engages for nearly an hour in a detailed dissection of character and milieu. Considering how depressing Los Piedras is and how base are its inhabitants, this long exposition is at times intellectually torturous, but it certainly gives firm support to the visual and narrative pyrotechnics to come.

It is for its second half, however, that *The Wages of Fear* is best known. The premise itself is enough to generate tension: Two trucks, loaded with explosives, must avoid every rock and pothole on the torturous mountain road leading to the oil field. To make matters worse, the trip begins at night, in the dark. At first, the Mario-Jo team takes the lead (the two trucks must keep apart, lest one mistake destroy both crews), but Jo proves to be a complicating factor: The tough gangster turns out to be a coward. Thus, the Luigi-Bimba team passes them and thereby must face each obstacle first.

There are three such hurdles. The first is a wooden overhang which the trucks must use to negotiate a difficult turn. Bimba's wheels spin on the rotten wood, passing perilously close to the edge, but he and Luigi manage with only moderate difficulty. Mario, however, must contend not only with the useless Jo but also with a heavier truck. The complications pile up in classic Aristotelian form: The boards creak; Mario drives too close to (and even overhangs) the edge; his wheels slide sideways in the mud; a hook on the truck's side catches a platform-supporting rope. Just as Mario pulls away, the entire half-bridge collapses, tumbling noisily into the ravine.

All four men pool their resources and nerves to confront the second obstacle: a massive boulder blocking their path. Bimba's solution is tremblingly simple: use the nitroglycerin to blow it out of their path. With string, hammer, and Thermos bottle, Bimba jerry-builds an ingenious detonating device. The fuse is lit—but nothing is ever simple in a Clouzot thriller. The men suddenly think: What if exploded rocks hit the vehicles? The trucks are quickly backed down the hill, but Luigi decides to extinguish the fuse. He is too late. The explosion is massive; stones rain down on the trucks and their cargo. The dreadful downpour stops, but one rock tumbles solitarily toward a can of nitroglycerin left by the roadside. It stops inches from the can. Luigi is safe, and the nerve-rattling voyage continues.

The film's third crisis begins with a brilliantly underplayed moment. Luigi and Bimba have pulled far ahead of Mario and Jo. Suddenly, the latter two see a mushroom cloud thunder up in the distance. Luigi and Bimba are dead.

Jo and Mario arrive to find no trace of their comrades, only denuded, bent trees and a hole filling with petroleum from a pipe severed like a huge, mangled artery. The remaining two drivers must traverse the unfathomed ditch. Jo wades into the muck and guides his companion as he drives through. Jo falls, however, and Mario refuses to stop; Jo's left leg is crushed. So obsessed is Mario with continuing that he leaves a moaning, unattended Jo by the roadside. Mario then rigs a stake-and-rope device to pull his now-stuck truck from the rising goo. Only after breaking free does he take aboard an anguished, hallucinating Jo. The road becomes smoother, Mario arrives at the well, and Jo dies on his shoulder, mumbling something about a fence with nothing on the other side.

There is no respite, however, in Clouzot's cynical vision. As Mario, in relief and elation, returns home, he drives carelessly and soars off a cliff. The film ends with Mario dead, the Métro ticket in his hand.

Clouzot favors a cynical, misanthropic tone for his superbly crafted suspense films, making him an Alfred Hitchcock without humor. Nowhere is his vision more bleak than in *The Wages of Fear*. He mocks culture by placing those who cling to it (with Métro tickets and natal languages) in an uncaring, savage environment. He fashions a male-dominated world (complete with the woman-as-object, Linda, played by his wife, Véra Clouzot), but then emasculates its most macho citizen, Jo. He seems to praise the more honest camaraderie of the other drivers, yet he allows it to degenerate into selfishness and foolish chance-taking. He transforms what could have been the fascinating, if dingy, Los Piedras into an existential hellhole, where fate toys with its prisoners as sadistically as does a small boy whom the viewer sees piking roaches in the film's opening image. Most distressingly, he builds increasingly sympathetic characters, then promptly kills them off.

Everyone seems to be exploited in this film—the natives, Mario's girlfriend, the drivers, the land. Nevertheless, *The Wages of Fear* succeeds, first because it possesses a roller-coaster-like narrative, even though it is painted an ominous black. Second, the film conjures the dark, disquieting nightmares of personal vulnerability in the face of uncivilized corruption.

Finally, and above all, *The Wages of Fear* is a cinematic tour de force, with numerous images that both haunt and compel: the overexposed, hot whiteness of Los Piedras; the diagonal lines of shadows in the restaurant's porch area, which both imprison the characters and foretell their doom; the small stone rolling threateningly toward the very large danger of a nitroglycerin can; Bimba shaving, moments before his death; the tracks of Bimba and Luigi's blasted vehicle ending abruptly, as if the truck had flown away; Jo (who, at his first appearance, is dressed immaculately in white) emerging, tar-covered, from the petroleum pool; a backlit Mario arriving at the oil field, staggering and collapsing before a roaring conflagration.

These potent images are matched by the film's vigorous editing. For example, continuing dialogue links a series of disparate moments into a clever montage, compressing what could have been an overlong, introductory interchange between Mario and Jo. More often than not, however, the editing of *The Wages of Fear* concerns itself less with contracting time than with expanding it to create tension: the series of close-ups as Jo anticipates an explosion from falling rocks; the multiple perspectives on the collapsing platform; the crosscutting between Mario's return trip and a "Blue Danube" waltz in the café.

It was reported that sundry logistical problems harassed Clouzot during this shoot near Nîmes and that he, in turn, placed demands upon his actors that verged on the sadistic (Charles Vanel, for example, was supposedly required to flounce about for hours in the petroleum pool). Nevertheless, *The Wages of Fear*—the unprecedented winner, in 1953, of both the Gold Palm for Best Film at the Cannes International Film Festival and the Berlin Festival's award for most popular film—is an overwhelming, if acrid, masterpiece of cinematic manipulation.

*Marc Mancini*

# THE WALLS OF MALAPAGA (AU-DELÀ DES GRILLES)

*Origin:* France and Italy
*Released:* 1949
*Released in U.S.:* 1950
*Production:* Alfredo Guarini (AA)
*Direction:* René Clément
*Screenplay:* Jean Aurenche and Pierre Bost; based on an original screen story by Cesare Zavattini, Suso Cecchi D'Amico, and Alfredo Guarini
*Cinematography:* Louis Page
*Editing:* Mario Serandrei
*Art direction:* Piero Filippone
*Music:* Roman Vlad
*Running time:* 95 minutes
*Also known as: Beyond the Gates* and *Le Mura di Malapaga*

*Principal characters:*

| | |
|---|---|
| Pierre | Jean Gabin |
| Marta | Isa Miranda |
| Cecchina | Vera Talchi |
| Joseph | Andrea Checchi |
| Maria | Ave Ninchi |
| Bosco | Robert Dalban |
| Police commissioner | Carlo Tamberlani |
| Pickpocket | Checco Risoni |

*The Walls of Malapaga* contains ingredients familiar from Jean Gabin's films of the 1930's, notably *Quai des brumes* (1938), *Le Jour se lève* (1939), and *Pépé le Moko* (1937). A world-weary loner, hounded by fate, knowing that he must succumb, finds a brief respite with a woman (who offers him temporary affection), and is then captured or surrenders. The René Clément film, however, is less complex than its predecessors, the characters' personalities less well defined; even the plot is somewhat schematic.

Pierre (Jean Gabin), on the run because he killed his girlfriend, arrives in Genoa in the hold of a freighter. Suffering with a toothache, he finds a young girl, Cecchina (Vera Talchi), who speaks French and helps him locate a dentist. He is about to surrender to the police, when he sees Cecchina's mother bringing food to the jail, and he follows her to the café, where she waits on tables. The woman, Marta (Isa Miranda), is also a fugitive: She is running from her estranged husband, who pursues her, trying to take custody of Cecchina. Marta makes friends with Pierre, letting him sleep in her attic, and they begin a short-lived romance. Pierre's identity card is found on a thief who picked his pocket when he arrived; the police have been tracking him while he had begun to think he was safe.

Gabin's character in *The Walls of Malapaga* is old and graying; his cynicism hardened into a mask that is not easily removed. Director Clément appears to have taken the Gabin personality of the 1930's, "the tragic hero of the contemporary cinema," as André Bazin called him, as a given, an icon, and, knowing that audiences would recognize this figure immediately, did not believe that he had to embellish the *persona*. This is the Gabin of the grizzled countenance, the slouch hat, the clothes crumpled from traveling, with his hands in his pockets and a cigarette drooping from his mouth. Gabin comes with a set of easily recognized characteristics, on which Clément capitalized without exploring their significance beyond the most superficial observations.

In many of his previous films, Gabin's characters had been impelled by a fatal obsession: to rescue Françoise (Jacqueline Laurent) from M. Valentin (Jules Berry) in *Le Jour se lève*, Nelly (Michèle Morgan) from Zabel (Michel Simon) in *Quai des brumes*, to escape the Casbah with his paramour in *Pépé le Moko*. In the Depression-dominated 1930's, Gabin came to embody an impulse to escape from spiritual and economic entrapment. He fails, but he makes the effort; his is a soul that is not easily conquered. No such romantic quest motivates Pierre's actions in *The Walls of Malapaga*. He is simply a fugitive at the end of his rope, a man who has killed his sweetheart, because she said he was too old for her—she wanted a younger man. Pierre, the rejected, middle-aged lover is a new type; the part heralded a change in the sort of roles Gabin would play from then on, roles that would combine elements of his former *persona* and this revamped incarnation. Still amorous, still pursued by destiny, the parts he played in *Leur dernière nuit* (1953) and *Touchez pas au Grisbi* (1954) are among the best examples of his work in this interim phase of his career.

The earlier Gabin roles were ironic, self-mocking. He was allowed moments of humor; he could even kick up his heels from time to time. *The Walls of Malapaga* offers no such release. With the exception of a brief sequence in which Pierre takes Marta for an outing, the film is unremittingly somber and doom laden. This is partially the result of the locale; set in postwar Genoa, the film presents Marta and Cecchina as so impoverished that they live in a bombed building. Around them, in the vast wrecks of the buildings that still stand, huddle the destitute survivors of the war. (When the city was a merchants' republic, hundreds of years ago, the "mala pagas," the bad payers, were thrown into this corner of Genoa—a sort of debtors' exile—so it is fitting that Pierre, who owes a debt to society, should find himself caught in this slum.)

From the beginning, the scenario is careful to establish Pierre as an outsider. He is shown in the hold of the cargo ship. He is dirty, ragged, in pain, and hidden until he can reach the comparative safety of a foreign port. Thereafter, he is separated from human society by his status as an alien and his inability to converse in Italian. It is only because Cecchina speaks French that they strike up an acquaintance. Pierre has decided to surrender when he sees Marta delivering a meal to one of the prisoners. He knows that he will be caught sooner or later; without money or friends, he would rather capitulate in the first place than live as a fugitive.

Pierre does enjoy a reprieve from flight when he eats at the dingy trattoria where Marta works. She spots his lira as phony but passes the money on to the owner. So delighted is Pierre with her kindness that he buys flowers for the diners with the change, then sits talking and drinking with the *patron* until it is time for Marta to go home.

Isa Miranda's Marta is typical of many of the women who play against Gabin: rueful, experienced, yet still hopeful—like Arletty in *Le Jour se lève*. She is a less tough version of Suzy Prim in *Les Bas-fonds* (1936; *The Lower Depths*) and a shabby reflection of Mireille Balin in *Pépé le Moko*. These women even look alike, with their dark hair (Prim's hair was dyed blonde) and their expressions by turns wistful, hard, knowing, and eager. Miranda won the Best Actress Award at the Cannes Film Festival for her role in *The Walls of Malapaga*.

The most memorable personality of *The Walls of Malapaga* is the daughter, Cecchina, played with luminous intensity by Vera Talchi. Fascinated by Pierre and anxious to serve as his interpreter, she scampers in front of him, showing him the way to the dentist, watching him from a building across the street, her eyes betraying the crush she has on the stranger. Later, when Pierre is a part of her household, albeit a transient one, Cecchina does not comprehend her own disturbed emotions; she is torn between the appealing Frenchman and her devotion to her mother. Watching the police leading Pierre away, Marta pats her daughter's hand, comforting her for the loss they will both feel keenly. Grave and confused, the pigtailed thirteen-year-old aptly symbolizes youthful longings and frustration.

Clément's direction is meticulous and economical. The Genoa he depicts is not simply a busy seaport: Its Malapaga section represents wrecked lives and hopes—lives that may improve, like convalescing invalids, hopes that may someday come to a happy fruition but that are presently in limbo. That limbo is symbolized by the city walls themselves, bleak and scarred, with labyrinthine streets and their ancient tenements. Clément's camera escapes these confines once—on the day that Pierre takes Marta on the town. The viewer sees the harbor, then a smart store where Pierre buys Marta a dress, a crowded bus where they flirt across the other passengers. For a while they lie by the water in the moonlight, the open air suggesting freedom, then conclude the day with dinner at an attractive restaurant. Too soon, however, they are back behind the walls of Malapaga, with the police closing in.

Clément made his film in the Genoese streets, so the look of the film is completely authentic. This interest in cinematic naturalism, which started in Italy with Roberto Rossellini's *Roma, città aperta* (1945; *Rome, Open City*) was paralleled in the United States by films such as Henry Hathaway's *Call Northside 777* (1948) and Elia Kazan's *Boomerang!* (1947) and *Panic in the Streets* (1950), which used locales in Chicago, Stamford, Connecticut, and New Orleans to impart a semidocumentary flavor to their narratives. They were part of an informal international movement designed to get the camera—and the story—out of the studio and into realistic locales, to open up the cinema so that it reflected the real-life concerns of the changing world.

*The Walls of Malapaga* won the Academy Award for Best Foreign-Language Film in 1951.

*Judith M. Kass*

# WAR AND PEACE
# (VIONA I MIR)

*Origin:* U.S.S.R.
*Released:* 1966-1967
*Released in U.S.:* 1968
*Production:* Mosfilm Studio (AA)
*Direction:* Sergei Bondarchuk
*Screenplay:* Sergei Bondarchuk and Vasily Solovyov; based on the novel by Leo Tolstoy
*Cinematography:* Anatoly Petritsky
*Editing:* Tatiana Likhacheva
*Art direction:* Mikhail Bogdanov and Gennedy Myasnikov; set decoration, G. Koshelyov and V. Uvarov
*Music:* Vyacheslav Ovchinnikov
*MPAA rating:* no listing
*Running time:* 480 minutes
*Running time in U.S.:* 373 minutes

*Principal characters:*
Pierre Bezuhov . . . . . . . . . . . . . . . . . Sergei Bondarchuk
Natasha Rostova . . . . . . . . . . . . . . . Lyudmila Savelyeva
Prince Andrey Bolkonsky . . . . . . Vyacheslav Tikhonov
Anatole Kuragin. . . . . . . . . . . . . . . . . . . Vasiliy Lanovoy
Hélène Kuragina. . . . . . . . . . . . . . . . . . . Irina Skobtseva
General Kutuzov . . . . . . . . . . . . . . . . . . . Boris Zakhava
Napoleon . . . . . . . . . . . . . . . . . . . . Vladislav Strzhelchik
Count Rostov . . . . . . . . . . . . . . . . . . . . . Viktor Stanitsin
Countess Rostova . . . . . . . . . . . . Kira Ivanova-Golovko
Nikolay Rostov . . . . . . . . . . . . . . . . . . . . . Oleg Tabakov
Dolokhov . . . . . . . . . . . . . . . . . . . . . . . . Oleg Yefremov
Liza . . . . . . . . . . . . . . . . . . . . . . Anastasiya Vertinskaya

To film *War and Peace* would be, at best, a Herculean task, but to film it as magnificently as did Sergei Bondarchuk marks an accomplishment that few filmmakers have achieved. Shot in the Soviet Union with the complete cooperation of that nation's government, Bondarchuk's beautifully wrought adaptation of Leo Tolstoy's 1886 epic novel depicts, against the backdrop of the Napoleonic invasion of Russia, the ultimately ineffectual struggle of individual heroes in the face of the larger and more telling historical forces.

It is estimated that the four-part film, which required one hundred indoor and 103 outdoor sets, cost in excess of one hundred million dollars and required five years to complete. A specially edited version was dubbed into

English and released in two parts. This unforgettable two-night cinematic experience, the only version to be shown in theaters in the United States, was extremely popular and highly profitable, as well as critically acclaimed, winning an Academy Award for Best Foreign-Language Film.

Leo Tolstoy's *War and Peace* has been considered by many critics the high point in the development of the modern realistic novel. Scrupulously faithful to the novel, the film, too, was an inspired undertaking, considered by some to be the most constant star in the Soviet Union's galaxy of cinematic achievement. Tolstoy's vast array of characters comes to life on Bondarchuk's filmic canvas: The awkward yet lovable Pierre (Sergei Bondarchuk) and the prettily naïve Natasha (Lyudmila Savelyeva) develop and mature in tandem with the larger sweep of events in their country, a country fated to twist in the grip of Napoleon Bonaparte's will to power.

As the nineteenth century began, Europe was surrendering itself to that power. By 1805, it was obvious that only two nations, Russia and England, would stand their ground against Napoleon's campaign for empire, a campaign that was to last eight years before its resolution.

As the film begins, the viewer is introduced to two of the film's central characters, Prince Andrey Bolkonsky (Vyacheslav Tikhonov) and Pierre Bezuhov. Andrey is a nobleman, unhappily married to Liza (Anastasiya Vertinskaya). He looks forward with anticipation to war with France, hoping to escape, through war, from his domestic dissatisfaction. His friend Pierre is the ugly, illegitimate, unrecognized son of a count.

On his deathbed, Pierre's father summons his son, whom he has previously ignored, and blesses him, telling him that he is leaving all of his enormous wealth to him. Overnight, Pierre finds himself a young man of great fortune and importance. His oafish ways are suddenly overlooked, and he finds himself, for the first time, desirable in the eyes of women. Hélène Kuragina (Irina Skobtseva), a dazzling court beauty, takes an interest in him. Pierre easily wins her, and they are married, but she turns out to be unfaithful. Her lover Dolokhov (Oleg Yefremov) goads Pierre into a duel. By chance, it is Dolokhov who is severely wounded. Pierre, stunned, demands a legal separation from Hélène.

At the border, Andrey, in his first conflict with the enemy at Austerlitz, is wounded and captured by the French but is released soon afterward because of his rank and because Napoleon (Vladislav Strzhelchik) hopes to negotiate with Russia. Andrey returns home to find his young wife dying in childbirth. Not long after Liza's death, Andrey attends a splendid ball at the Rostov estate in Otradnoye, and there he meets the radiant young Natasha Rostova. They immediately fall in love, but when Andrey asks for her hand in marriage, her father, Count Rostov (Viktor Stanitsin), asks them to postpone their wedding for a year, during which time Andrey is to travel abroad while Natasha, who is judged to be too young for marriage, will journey to Moscow with her father.

In Moscow, Natasha meets the dashing young Anatole Kuragin (Vasiliy Lanovoy), brother of the heartless Hélène. Like his beautiful but false sister, Anatole is a handsome cad, pursuing Natasha so impulsively and romantically that she succumbs and promises to elope with him that night. Although Natasha is not aware of the fact, Anatole is already married. Pierre learns of this situation and harshly enlightens her as to the true character of her would-be seducer, then locks her in her room. Shocked and shamed, Natasha believes that, because of her betrayal, she can no longer marry Andrey, and she breaks off their engagement. Filled with grief, she becomes ill and will see no one but Pierre, who remains devoted to and protective of the girl.

Meanwhile, the temporary armistice fails, and Napoleon leads his victorious army boldly across the border and onto Russian soil. Pierre visits the front lines at the Battle of Borodino and is so aghast at the ill-planned strategy and cruelty of the war that he vows to slay Napoleon. General Kutuzov (Boris Zakhava), commander-in-chief of the Russian armies, is forced to retreat, but plans a scorched-earth policy to prevent the French from living on the land they conquer as they advance on Moscow.

The Russian people devastate their lands as they flee the unimpeded advance of the French army. Kutuzov orders everyone to evacuate Moscow, and as Napoleon advances, flames and smoke fill the air in the wake of the destruction perpetrated by the departing Russians. Pierre refuses to leave and wanders through the desolate ruins, hoping to find and assassinate Napoleon.

Andrey is severely wounded at the Battle of Borodino and is brought to a tent where his wounds can be dressed. On the stretcher next to him is a soldier whose leg is being amputated. Andrey recognizes the man: It is Anatole Kuragin. Andrey's hatred for the man who ruined his happiness turns to pity. He is brought to Moscow—ironically, to the lodge of the very house where Natasha is staying. Later, as the Rostovs join the exodus from Moscow, the dying Andrey, whose presence is still unknown to Natasha, travels with their party. Eventually, Andrey and Natasha meet, and he forgives her as he dies in her arms.

Napoleon tries to negotiate a treaty with General Kutuzov, but he is unsuccessful. When supplies and reinforcements on which he had counted fail to arrive, Napoleon is forced to order the now completely demoralized French to retreat. The cruel Russian winter descends upon the French troops as they desert Moscow, disabling them even more. Pierre, who has been captured by the French, is taken along with them as they retreat. Many of the starving soldiers are grateful to die, so disordered and ghastly have their lives become. General Kutuzov attacks the remnants of the once glorious French army at Berezina, and Pierre is freed.

It appears that Pierre is also free of his estranged wife, who is now dead—a victim of venereal disease. He returns to Moscow and there meets Natasha, who is living with friends. The affection that these two have had for each other has been strengthened and tempered, through eight years of pain, into love.

Sergei Bondarchuk was extremely competent in his three-part role of director, cowriter, and lead actor of the film. As director, he proved himself able and effective in exposing the subtle shades of Tolstoy's many characters while managing the larger-than-life scope and spirit of the tale. As writer, he, along with Vasily Solovyov, did an enviable job of successfully adapting Tolstoy's great epic novel to the cinema. As actor, Bondarchuk was exceptional as Pierre (although he seems, initially, too old in the role of Pierre as a youth). In contrast, Lyudmila Savelyeva as Natasha is at her best as the very young girl, but she fails to develop and mature as Natasha grows older. Vyacheslav Tikhonov's performance as Prince Andrey is sensitively wrought, and Vasiliy Lanovoy as Anatole, the daredevil cad, is suitably handsome and roguish.

The costumes are authentic and exquisitely designed. Many are copies of museum pieces—the resources of the Hermitage museum were fully utilized during production. Furniture and accessories were reproduced in detail, and many authentic period pieces were borrowed when their reproduction proved infeasible.

The three great battle sequences of Austerlitz, Borodino, and the destruction of Moscow, extending through most of part 2, are awesome, both in their realistic depiction of nineteenth century tactics and in their incredible choreography, involving many thousands of soldiers and horses—the almost unbelievable carnage of the Battle of Borodino lasts nearly an hour. The mood of absolute devastation in such sequences, as well as the killing, burning, and horror of the retreat from the winter-besieged Moscow, finds a neat balance in the exquisite civility and grace of the initial lyric ballroom sequence in which Natasha and Andrey first meet. The contrast between these two sets of sequences reinforces the basic contrast between the personal and familial events and those occurring on the larger historical plane. Although Natasha and Andrey's first meeting lasts twelve minutes—a full reel—it is, in a sense, dwarfed by the almost interminable battle scenes, just as the heroic efforts of individuals, in Tolstoy's view, are ineffective when seen against the movements of masses and the forces of history.

The subject matter, the scope, the realism, and especially the setting make it eminently fitting that *War and Peace* was filmed on Soviet soil by Russian artists. A heroic endeavor on a heroic theme, it will stand as one of the most ambitious productions in the history of Soviet cinema.

*Larry Lee Holland*

# WAYS IN THE NIGHT (WEGE IN DER NACHT)

*Origin:* Poland and West Germany
*Released:* 1979
*Released in U.S.:* 1983
*Production:* Hartwig Schmidt for Westdeutscher Rundfunk
*Direction:* Krzysztof Zanussi
*Screenplay:* Krzysztof Zanussi
*Cinematography:* Witold Sobociński
*Editing:* Liesgret Schmitt-Klink
*Art direction:* Tadeusz Wybult and Wolfgang Schunke
*Makeup:* Halina Sienska and Christiane Sonnenberg
*Costume design:* Anna Biedrzycka and Delia Friedrich
*Sound:* Richard Kettelhake
*Music:* Wojciech Kilar
*MPAA rating:* no listing
*Running time:* 98 minutes

*Principal characters:*

Friedrich ........................ Mathieu Carrière
Baroness Elzbieta.............. Maja Komorowska
Hans Albert ......................... Horst Frank
Mattei Amidei............... Zbigniew Zapasiewicz
Friedrich's mother.................... Imgard Forst
Charlotte.......................... Diane Korner
First officer......................... Peter Kuiper
Second officer ............. Andrzej von Schoenaich
Third officer ...................... Peter Drescher
Schultz ........................... Claus Enskat
Farm manager................. Edward Dziewonski

Toward the end of Krzysztof Zanussi's *Ways in the Night*, a Jew is literally uncovered or forced to strip so that Nazi officers can "determine" his race. The now discovered Jew, Amidei (Zbigniew Zapasiewicz), a convert to Catholicism and a man who knows more about German literature than almost any German, is quickly led out and shot. This event is presented without any special sentiment and apparently with only mild outrage. In fact, the stripping of Amidei and his execution are seen most poignantly through the eyes of a German officer, Friedrich (Mathieu Carrière), who is the film's protagonist. The camera generally remains in long-shot—which, while it does not adequately reflect Friedrich's sympathy for Amidei, nevertheless retains the cool, almost dispassionate tone of the film. Further, it suggests a major theme of the film, the distance people keep from situations which threaten to violate a carefully cultivated self-image.

No matter how far Zanussi seems to remove the audience from this action, however, he still raises the specter of the Holocaust and places it at a critical moment in the film. This creates an implicit dialogue between the characters in the film and the audience, upon which Zanussi plays. Whereas the audience understands the historical significance of every event, the characters are locked within the smaller spatial and temporal circle of their own private lives. Each action in the film, in fact, as well as its *mise en scène* or background, suggests a larger context of which the characters are poignantly oblivious. Thus, the impact of the Holocaust, though alluded to only briefly, radiates outward from a single moment in the film and becomes a critical part of the context through which the film's major struggles are acted, analyzed, and resolved.

*Ways in the Night*, like many of Zanussi's other films, including *Struktura kryształu* (1969; *Structure of Crystals*), *Żyćie rodzinne* (1971; *Family Life*), *Za ściana* (1971; *Behind the Wall*), and *Iluminacja* (1973; *Illumination*), defines the various dimensions in a struggle between antagonists. In this particular film, the struggle is a romantic one, a frustrating and unfulfilled romance between Friedrich, one of a small number of officers in the Wehrmacht stationed at the Polish town of Malogoszcz in 1943, and a Polish baroness, Elzbieta (Maja Komorowska). Just as in *Structure of Crystals*, however, there is an intellectual argument which complicates the romantic plot. The intellectual argument, in fact, has a double nature. On the one hand, there is Friedrich's constant debate with his cousin Hans (Horst Frank), a fellow officer and former teacher at the university, who wants Friedrich to put aside his genteel scruples and seize the glorious moment offered by the war. Elzbieta, on the other hand, insists that the war makes any private passion inconceivable, especially between enemies. Friedrich's romanticized desire for Elzbieta is tossed between Hans' perverse claim that all things, especially aesthetic judgments, are relative and Elzbieta's absolute insistence that one can never compromise principles. Thus, Friedrich finds himself caught in a strangely triangular version of the ancient debate between intellect and emotion.

Zanussi, himself a former scientist, structures his film around this traditional paradigmatic conflict almost as if he were conducting an experiment. Friedrich, caught in the web of World War II, is unsuited for the role that history assigns him. He is naturally an aesthete, a highly cultured man who can recognize a wrong note in a Frédéric Chopin sonata or quote Provençal poetry. As a German officer, however, he is forced to participate in the brutalities of war and to associate with people for whom he has contempt. The romance is an alternative he naturally embraces. Thus, he tries to convince Elzbieta both that their similar backgrounds should permit them to transcend the factitious existence forced upon them by the war and that the war is after all only another historical ripple, a temporary obstacle, which will eventually lead to a better world.

An added complication is that Friedrich has a fiancée in Germany, whom he marries toward the end of the film. Like the murder of the Jew Amidei, however, the brief scenes of Friedrich's wedding are stiff and seem dominated by a fatalistic acceptance of anticipated misfortune. If Friedrich does make a brief angry response at the arrest of Amidei, he seems almost to take no notice of his new wife, Charlotte (Diane Korner), when she sadly leans her head upon his shoulder. That he remains obsessed by the baroness, even at his wedding, is suggested by the very next shot, which shows Friedrich returning to Malogoszcz to see Elzbieta one more time. It is later learned that Charlotte's pessimism was justified: Like so many millions, Friedrich will die on the Russian front.

Before returning home for his wedding, Friedrich had participated in a battle with partisans which led to the death of Hans and the capture of a man who turns out to be Elzbieta's husband. After Hans's death, Friedrich angrily kills a partisan and finds himself for the first time forced to deal with war "up close." This shocks his aesthetic sensibilities: He is no longer a tourist in a museum admiring a work of art from a proper distance. When he next sees the baroness, she begs him for help in freeing her husband (though she says that he is her brother). Realizing that she manipulated him and betrayed information to the partisans, he brutally demands payment in advance and assaults her. His madness, however, lasts only for a moment, and he quickly stops himself. Soon afterward, he leaves for home and his wedding to Charlotte.

Friedrich's return to Malogoszcz, on the way to the Russian front, is filled with new and resonant imagery, the significance of which is only realized at the very end of the film. Beginning with the murder of Amidei, the "clean" war has ended. The rhythm of the war has become more intense; the slow evenings during which the officers played cards while Friedrich courted Elzbieta are clearly over. The battles with the partisans and Hans's death, which in turn leads to Friedrich's assault of Elzbieta, all suggest a tightening spiral of violence and despair. By the time Friedrich returns to Malogoszcz, the war has taken its full toll. The baroness' husband has died (from injuries received during torture), and her estate is in ruins. Friedrich visits her in a church and gives her a family ring and a sealed letter. As he walks out of the church, the camera follows him briefly, and then he walks out of the picture. The camera, however, remains where it is and then continues to pan the graveyard. By separating the camera from its natural object, Friedrich, Zanussi has symbolically already buried him. Events, like history, now pass him by.

Every event in the film gains in significance not only because of the way it fits into a larger, historical context, but also because of the way Zanussi manipulates the *mise en scène* to suggest new layers of meaning. In almost every sequence, in fact, despite Friedrich's naïveté, the *mise en scène* provides an oblique commentary on the action. A long conversation about aesthetics, for example, takes place in a bathroom. It is a peculiarly inappropriate location for a discussion of beauty. Nevertheless the irony here is subtle because Zanussi takes his characters seriously and treats them sympathetically. Even Hans, once a lecturer in philosophy and certainly a cultured man, who now espouses the idea of the *Ubermensch*, the Nazi as Superman, and who refers to the Poles as "subhumans," is never reduced to a stereotype. In some respects, Hans reflects the problem that many, like the French philosopher Jean-Paul Sartre, associated with the German thinker Martin Heidegger: Heidegger's very genius was corrupted by his willingness to accept the Nazi cause. The acceptance of Nazism, in fact, suggests a flaw so profound that it calls a man's entire nature into question: This is Elzbieta's position. As Friedrich's loyal cousin, however, Hans remains a sympathetic character, even if Zanussi's choice of a bathroom for their discussion must suggest a subliminal judgment.

This double perspective, the Nazi viewed externally and historically and, at the same time, viewed internally and emotionally by sympathetic friends, lies at the heart of Zanussi's film. When two partisans are hanged, Hans, with a sardonic smile, takes a candid photograph of Friedrich standing in front of the gallows. Though Friedrich is angry, and clearly disassociates himself from the hanging, he is nevertheless "there" in a physical and even metaphysical sense. Similarly, when Friedrich chases an escaping partisan into a stable, he emerges from the barn covered with manure. The camera does not pause; rather, it quickly records the abashed look on Friedrich's face and then continues the action. Thus, despite his innocence and his good intentions, each event further fixes Friedrich within the context of the war and of the uniform he wears.

Zanussi's careful control of every detail in a scene is beautifully realized when Friedrich, who despite Hans's warnings has continued to court Elzbieta, emerges from some woods on her estate holding a book of poetry. She rides by on a white horse which, along with the lush growth of the park, gives the entire scene the appearance of something from a nineteenth century romantic novel. The setting, however, only reflects Friedrich's desire. As the camera closes in on the dialogue between Friedrich and Elzbieta, isolating their personal situation from the larger context of the park, the double perspective reappears. Friedrich, as always, tries to woo the baroness by exhibiting a common culture which should, in his opinion, join them. Elzbieta, on the other hand, refers to his culture as German schizophrenia; despite the extraordinary cultural heritage of Germany, their soldiers are no more than bandits. Their culture cannot hide the plain fact that their violence makes them barbarians.

The conflict here, between Elzbieta and Friedrich, perfectly expresses Zanussi's own point of view. In their opposing arguments, they reflect the tension between an individual and society as a whole. Friedrich wants to separate himself from the "collective guilt" of the Germans, but Elzbieta refuses to permit it. As Zanussi has said in interviews, the individual must either accept the consequences of his society's actions or oppose them completely, even by rebellion. Thus, the two terms of the equation, represented in the baroness' many arguments with Friedrich, admit no possible ground for compromise. The scene in the park, which for Friedrich appears almost as a romantic reverie, ends suddenly as Elzbieta slashes at him with her riding crop and rides off while he stands there helplessly, a perplexed and forlorn look on his face. This look on Friedrich's face is immediately contrasted with the sly, knowing look on the face of Hans, who has apparently watched the entire scene. Until the moment the camera cuts to Hans, in fact, the entire scene appears to be taking place in some secluded spot. Now, it turns out, they are only a few feet from Elzbieta's château, in which the officers are quartered, and their private meeting has actually taken place in public. It is a small surprise but one typical of the way Zanussi manipulates the narrative to reveal subtle nuances or little details which nevertheless control the viewer's reaction to each event.

The story of Friedrich's stay in Malogoszcz, in fact, is placed within brackets which frame the main action and alter the viewer's initial responses. The first shot in the film is a disorienting high-angle view of a rainy street. From there the camera moves inside an apartment which turns out to belong to Friedrich's mother (Imgard Forst), who is being visited by Friedrich's fiancée Charlotte. They have received a letter from Friedrich, who writes from Malogoszcz. The mother, who is bitter at the declining quality of life in Germany, has begun to despair. She doubts the outcome of the war and refuses to repair her broken piano. This will have special significance as the film unfolds, for the piano, especially the music of Chopin, is the link through which Friedrich approaches Elzbieta. As a final testament to her growing despair, the mother refuses to keep Friedrich's letter and, though it shocks Charlotte, she burns it.

At the end of the film, after the main action has been concluded, Zanussi suddenly jumps to the present. Friedrich's daughter is being interviewed by a historian who has found the ring and letter which Friedrich had given Elzbieta. The daughter, however, shows little interest in the ring and does not even choose to open the letter, instead destroying it. Not only does she not want to retain relics, but she also actively rejects the past. Like so many Germans she chooses to bury a past which only brings painful memories. She is like those Alain Resnais warns against in *Nuit et brouillard* (1955; *Night and Fog*): those who close their eyes to the past and thereby permit it to recur. What is striking here, however, is the ease with which the daughter chooses not to uncover her father's past, especially this love story in which his deepest nature has been revealed and refined. The audience, it turns out, is more profoundly moved by her father's story than she is. As she points out, justifying her lack of interest, she never really knew her father, and there is no reason to start now. On the surface, this appears as discretion, an unwillingness to open a private letter from her father to another woman, but as the final credits come up Zanussi's camera slowly tracks away from her, suggesting both her disassociation from what was meaningful in the past, and a rejection of her point of view.

Although one cannot help but be ambivalent toward Friedrich, if only because, like the baroness, one cannot overlook the uniform he wears, nevertheless his story is a full one and it is clear that he made more of an attempt to understand the war than his daughter ever will. Friedrich and Elzbieta, fixed as they were in a brutal and annihilating moment, nevertheless are more alive than the daughter who turns her back on the past. Zanussi's film, although generally a remarkably sympathetic view of German officers from a Polish filmmaker, is actually addressed to the daughter and to her generation. The film, in fact, like the ring and the letter, offers that generation a more tender and intimate vision of the past. Whether any of them will respond meaningfully remains uncertain.

*Martin Kabat*

# WE ALL LOVED EACH OTHER SO MUCH (C'ERAVAMO TANTO AMATI)

*Origin:* Italy
*Released:* 1975
*Released in U.S.:* 1977
*Production:* Pio Angeletti and Adriano De Micheli for Dean Cinematografica and Delta
*Direction:* Ettore Scola
*Screenplay:* Age-Scarpelli and Ettore Scola
*Cinematography:* Claudio Cirillo
*Editing:* Raimondo Crociani
*Art direction:* Luciano Ricceri
*Music:* Armando Trovajoli
*MPAA rating:* no listing
*Running time:* 136 minutes
*Running time in U.S.:* 124 minutes

*Principal characters:*
Antonio .......................... Nino Manfredi
Gianni.......................... Vittorio Gassman
Luciana ......................... Stefania Sandrelli
Nicola......................... Stefano Satta Flores
Elide ............................ Giovanna Ralli
Catenacci............................ Aldo Fabrizi
Vittorio De Sica ......................... Himself
Federico Fellini.......................... Himself
Marcello Mastroianni..................... Himself

*We All Loved Each Other So Much*, while not in the same class with the greatest works of the man to whom it is dedicated, Vittorio De Sica, is nevertheless a warm, loving, amusing, perceptive tribute to friendship; its director, Ettore Scola, also pays his respects to the language of the cinema and to other gifted Italian filmmakers, from Michelangelo Antonioni to Luchino Visconti.

The story, unraveled in flashback, focuses on three comrades who meet while fighting as leftist partisans during World War II, the thirty years of their friendship, and the deterioration of the society around them. Antonio (Nino Manfredi) is a simple, good-natured, politically motivated yet naïve hospital attendant; Gianni (Vittorio Gassman) is a clever, opportunistic lawyer who marries into a family of dishonest builders; and the bespectacled Nicola (Stefano Satta Flores) is a radical, intellectual film buff who idolizes the work of De Sica, specifically *Ladri di biciclette* (1948; *The Bicycle*

*Thief*). Their lives constantly cross and recross over the years, as they meet at various intervals to argue and reminisce. Also, they are bound by their friendship with, and love for, the beautiful Luciana (Stefania Sandrelli).

Luciana first meets Antonio while she, a struggling actress, is a patient at the hospital in which he works. He promptly falls in love and recites medical terminology to impress her, but their relationship is volatile, and she soon leaves him. A diehard romantic, he never forgets her. Throughout his life, Antonio remains a humble orderly emptying bedpans, as well as a hapless revolutionary constantly finding himself in pointless brawls. Yet, in the end, he is content with his life. Years later, he and Luciana are reunited. She is a film-house usherette, and together they watch a scene from the 1964 version of *Of Human Bondage* in which Laurence Harvey and Kim Novak reveal to each other their innermost thoughts. The words on the screen are a projection of the silent feelings of Antonio and Luciana.

Early in their relationship, Antonio had lost Luciana to Gianni, but the lawyer soon dropped the actress to marry Elide (Giovanna Ralli), the daughter of a client, Catenacci (Aldo Fabrizi), a wealthy, ostentatious, conniving construction magnate. Elide is at first a gawky, simpleminded country girl. Later, as a result of her husband's neglect, she develops into a chic but alienated bourgeoise who perceives herself as a film heroine; after seeing Monica Vitti in Antonioni's *L'eclisse* (1962; *The Eclipse*), she begins hanging up empty picture frames and communicating only by tape recorder. Gianni outlives his wife and all of her relations and finally comes to control the family business. He is rich, but he is also lonely.

The third friend, Nicola, is at first a high school history teacher. His life becomes inexorably altered when he sees *The Bicycle Thief*. He is soon fired from his job for staunchly defending the Italian neorealists; he abandons his wife and child in rural Italy and goes to Rome, where he has an affair with Luciana and achieves fame for a short while on a quiz show similar to *The $64,000 Question*. Here, Nicola is asked about his favorite film, and he correctly names *The Bicycle Thief*'s child star: Enzo Staiola. Then, he is shown a photograph of the boy crying and is told to explain the still. The film buff correctly answers that De Sica had cigarette butts placed in Staiola's pants and accused him of being a bum. In this manner, the director ingeniously got the desired reaction from the boy, a nonprofessional actor. Nicola is overruled by both emcee and judges, though the "right" answer is that the boy's father has been beaten up for stealing a bicycle. Nicola sues the show five times but keeps losing. He is the classic failed intellectual, a man whose insights no one else finds particularly interesting. All that is left for him is disillusionment.

Luciana serves as a link among Nicola, Gianni, and Antonio. Throughout her life, she unsuccessfully pursues her career as an actress, but her closest taste of fame comes in a bit role in the Federico Fellini classic *La dolce vita*

(1960). In a wonderful sequence, Scola re-creates the filming of *La dolce vita*'s famous Trevi Fountain scene—complete with the presences of Fellini and Marcello Mastroianni.

*We All Loved Each Other So Much* is not without its implausibilities. Nicola is perhaps too obviously cheated on the quiz show; later, De Sica himself is shown affirming what the judges overruled, yet the poor film buff is never officially vindicated. Nevertheless, the film succeeds on several levels. First, it is a humanistic essay on friendship. Scola's three comrades represent three separate classes: Antonio is a politically active proletarian; Gianni is a bourgeois opportunist; and Nicola is a radical intellectual. While the film is not overtly political, these characters begin, as do many Italians, as Communists. Gianni, however, renounces his ideals out of lust for money, and Nicola becomes content to relate more to the motion-picture screen than to the realities around him. Antonio remains closest to his ideals, but he is in no way able to cause change in his society. It is the devious, pretentious Catenacci who obtains and keeps the power. The most revealing line in the screenplay is "We tried to change the world, but the world changed us." What remains unchanged is their friendship. They may often disagree vociferously, yet this does not destroy whatever bond exists between them. The years pass, and they age, but their love is not spoiled.

Scola also points out that wealth and status do not guarantee happiness. Gianni shuns Luciana to marry into a monied family and is outwardly successful, but he never learns to communicate with his wife. In his middle age, he is sad. Antonio, however, remains content with his lot, even though he may have spent his life as an insignificant hospital attendant. Quite simply, he likes his job.

Most interesting of all, the film is about cinema—specifically, the vibrancy of the neorealists and the Golden Age of Italian filmmaking, with special attention paid to Michelangelo Antonioni, Roberto Rossellini, Luchino Visconti, Federico Fellini, and, in particular, Vittorio De Sica. The latter created such profoundly moving, perceptive human dramas and fantasies as *Shoeshine* (1946), *The Bicycle Thief*, *Miracola a Milano* (1951; *Miracle in Milan*), and *Umberto D* (1952). Scola, like De Sica, is a humanist, and *We All Loved Each Other So Much* arises out of this sensibility. The film is also a film buff's delight: Films and directors are mentioned by name; snippets from films are shown; two directors and Italy's most famous male actor make cameo appearances. One amusing bit in the film happens during the shooting of *La dolce vita*—a police official who issues the filmmakers permits shakes hands with Fellini and remarks, "I've always admired your films, Mr. Rossellini."

Ettore Scola first became involved in the motion-picture industry in 1953. He wrote screenplays for a decade and directed his first feature, *Se permettete parliamo di donne* (1964; *Let's Talk About Women*), in 1964.

Other credits include *Brutti, sporchi e cattivi* (1976; *Down and Dirty*) and *Una giornata particolare* (1977; *A Special Day*). His work here is comically stylized, with an emphasis on slow motion, stop action, jump cuts, and asides. The film opens with such a montage. Antonio, Nicola, and Luciana arrive in a beat-up Fiat at Gianni's estate. They check the address and look over a wall as their host walks onto a terrace. Then, suddenly, this entire sequence is repeated. Gianni's appearance on the terrace is followed by a reaction shot of his visitors. He then comes out of his mansion a third time, walks to his swimming pool, removes his robe, climbs onto a diving board, and jumps into the air. Scola freezes him in midair as Nicola tells the viewer that this is the finale of a story that started thirty years before. At various points, the director copies the styles of the aforementioned filmmakers: For example, after this opening, he cuts to a shot of Italian partisans set to attack a German convoy; the cinematography is low-contrast and black-and-white—previously, it was color—and the feeling is highly evocative of Rossellini. Later, Nicola seduces Luciana while demonstrating to her Sergei Eisenstein's genius: A montage of an orange crate rolling down Rome's Spanish steps is reminiscent of the famous baby-carriage sequence on the Odessa Steps in *Potemkin* (1925).

Art director Luciano Ricceri captures a distinct sense of time passing, of Italy from the 1940's through the 1970's; his re-creation of the *La dolce vita* Trevi Fountain scene is magical. Vittorio Gassman and Nino Manfredi, two consummate actors, offer splendid performances: They effectively convey how the passage of time alters the individual.

*We All Loved Each Other So Much* was first screened at the 1975 Cannes Film Festival. The film had a New York opening in May, 1977, and received generally favorable reviews.

*Rob Edelman*

# WEEKEND
# (LE WEEK-END)

*Origin:* France
*Released:* 1967
*Released in U.S.:* 1968
*Production:* Comacio/Copernic/Lira Films/Ascot Cineraïd
*Direction:* Jean-Luc Godard
*Screenplay:* Jean-Luc Godard
*Cinematography:* Raoul Coutard
*Editing:* Agnès Guillemot
*Art direction:* no listing
*Music:* Antoine Duhamel and Wolfgang Amadeus Mozart
*Song:* Guy Beart, "Allô, allô tu m'entends?"
*MPAA rating:* no listing
*Running time:* 105 minutes

*Principal characters:*

| | |
|---|---|
| Corinne | Mireille Darc |
| Roland | Jean Yanne |
| Saint-Just | Jean-Pierre Léaud |
| Pianist | Paul Gégauff |
| Joseph Balsamo | Daniel Pommereulle |
| Gros Poucet | Yves Afonso |
| Emily Brontë | Blandine Jeanson |
| Cook | Ernest Menzer |
| F.L.S.O. leader | Jean-Pierre Kalfon |
| F.L.S.O. members | Juliet Berto/Anne Wiazemsky/Yves Beneyton |

Jean-Luc Godard's fifteenth feature film, *Weekend*, is a virtuoso treatment of the modern world's apocalypse, measured in the highway litter of burned cars and pillaged bodies caused not by nuclear missiles or armored sweeps across continents, but by petty selfishness and casual indifference. Scripted by Godard, the film is also incredibly humorous, not only because the characters are caricatures but also because they frequently step out of character to comment on the action in the film, an irony that is amplified by the director's frequent use of intertitles that contain puns on the film's dialogue. Made in the late 1960's, when discussion of the imminence of revolution was fashionable, *Weekend* also depicts the emerging postapocalypse society as a mixture of Sigmund Freud and old motion-picture titles, and Friedrich Engels and native American culture. On the purely formal level, Godard employs long tracking shots, 360-degree panning sequences, flash-forwards, flashbacks, and performers in various roles to make *Weekend* his most flamboyant, and perhaps his most successful, film.

"A film found on the trash heap," announces one of the first intertitles in the film, and the couple introduced in the first sequence, Roland (Jean Yanne) and Corinne (Mireille Darc), are indeed morally repulsive. They learn of the impending death of her father and plan to visit to ensure their part of the inheritance, a legacy that they have effected by steady, but small, doses of poison. As if this gradual patricide were not enough, it appears that each of them is conspiring with a lover against the other. Corinne's lover is also her analyst, who listens to her account of an orgy that may or may not have occurred, while Roland warns his lover not to call him at home. Unloving and unlovable, they care only about their present and future possessions, a trait seen as a universal curse, since within the film's first fifteen minutes, a fistfight erupts between two motorists over a sideswipe. Roland and Corinne watch the fight from their apartment balcony with the detached interest of spectators at a prizefight. The private automobile and the questions of status, taste, and money which surround it are an important theme in the film and a literal vehicle for its plot. A dented fender becomes the cause of a shouting match between Roland and Corinne and their neighbor. The traded insults, in turn, lead to a wrestling match that degenerates into a comical shoot-out as the irate husband appears on the scene with a shotgun and a barking spaniel. Seen from a distance of years, Godard's foresight is remarkable in that he focuses throughout on the middle-class obsession with brand names and designer labels. The fight in the parking lot starts when the neighbor's young son, dressed in a "wild Indian" headdress, insults Roland's car as an old, cheap model. Corinne cites the neighbors' fancy dress as being no excuse to act arrogantly toward her. The tussle has all the earmarks of a Laurel-and-Hardy routine, but with the irony imposed by Godard's social sarcasm, and it is only the start of the decline toward anarchy.

Once on the highway, the camera tracks for one extended sequence to show the line of cars and motorists halted by a severe tie-up. As Roland and Corinne pass by the waiting motorists, the audience is shown the enraged reaction of the others and the universal assortment of people and animals. There is no real dialogue, only the jeers of the angry; the unusual sight of some people playing chess, cards, or ball; a man adjusting the sails of his boat; and cages of wild animals. There are also traces of disaster: abandoned and overturned cars on the grass embankment under the trees, like a faint memory of the defeat in 1940. The cause of the tie-up appears as the sound track's music reaches a crescendo: a fatal accident involving several cars, some of which are burning. There are bodies sprawled alongside the road, but the speeding motorists, like Corinne and Roland, take advantage only of the right-of-way granted them by a traffic policeman.

In one of the film's few close-ups of the major characters, Roland and Corinne discuss the chances of the mother changing the will, but any sympathy for Corinne or Roland is minimized by a folk tune played on a concertina and the fact that the visuals are often shot through the windshield. Lost in a small village on their way to her parents' home in Oinville, in itself an abstraction for a French town, they witness an incident that Godard introduces as an example of the "class struggle." A red tractor, driven by a farmer loudly whistling "L'Internationale," somehow helps cause the crack-up of a young man's sportscar. A fashionably dressed young girl (Juliet Berto) accuses the farmer of killing her handsome, rich young lover simply because of his attributes. Told that he was driving too fast, the girl starts to insult and kick at the man's tractor, whereupon he starts to insult her. The camera pulls away from this action to show individuals watching the fight in static close-up. A further, perhaps unnecessary, irony is supplied by the union of the girl and tractor driver when Roland and Corinne ignore her plea for a lift.

The road to Oinville is increasingly littered with abandoned and destroyed cars, punctuated by corpses bedecked with theatrically red blood. There are also the occasional hitchhikers. Roland stops to examine the legs of a female hitchhiker, and her male companion emerges from his hiding place brandishing a revolver and demanding a lift. Firing his gun almost at random, like a lion tamer in a circus, the man announces himself as Joseph Balsamo (Daniel Pommereulle), the son of Alexandre Dumas and God. His name itself is a reference to the eighteenth century mesmerist Count Cagliostro, and Balsamo also announces that he is the "minister of the interior," in clear reference to Luis Buñel's early silent films. Dressed in a red herdsman's smock and gesturing wildly with his revolver, Balsamo states that he is destined to proclaim the end of the "grammatical era" and the start of flamboyance in all the arts, "especially in the cinema." Tired of his chatter, Corinne and Roland demand proof of his powers, and Balsamo complies—a rabbit appears miraculously under the car's dashboard. Offering them whatever they desire, Balsamo demands a trip to London, so Corinne and Roland reel off a series of wishes—a head of naturally blond hair, a fancy limousine, a fleet of jet planes, a weekend with James Bond. Their desires annoy Balsamo, who belittles the couple as petty and selfish bourgeois unworthy of his attention. When Roland and Corinne chase him out of their car in a fury, Balsamo responds by making a herd of sheep appear in their midst. This sequence is the most benevolent one in the entire film, and the traces of true mystery and divine powers surrounding Balsamo may be indicative of a direction that Godard decided not to take. *Weekend* soon returns to its recurrent image—the car crash.

The screen blacks out and one hears the sound of screeching tires and the slam of metal on metal. Amid the wreckage and burning bodies, Corinne emits a spine-tingling scream and then cries loudly, not for a crushed leg or a bloodied Roland, but for her Hermes pocketbook. Rarely has such a strong sequence been undercut by such a caricatured line of dialogue. To underline the degeneration of his major characters as representatives of the French bourgeoisie, they are contrasted with Saint-Just (Jean-Pierre Léaud), who declaims about the relationship between liberty and violence. Clad in the tricolored plumes and jacket of a late eighteenth century gentleman and Jacobin, Saint-Just is also a victim of Godard's sly irony, since he proclaims his speech while referring to a modern paperback. Corinne and Roland's degeneration is not merely intellectual; they ignore the dead who litter the roadway except to steal the odd jacket or designer pants. Most of the people who cross their path are equally reprehensible. Motorists quiz them on their politics before refusing to give them a lift, and a tramp rapes Corinne while Roland concentrates on his cigarette.

The only disinterested person who gives them a lift is a roving pianist (Paul Gégauff), who delivers a lecture and concert in the middle of a farmyard. He plays a Mozart sonata and discusses the quality of the music and the fate of Wolfgang Amadeus Mozart in terms that are accurate and trenchant. Godard's camera performs two 360-degree pans while the farmhands listen or go about their chores. Art is not always so well received in Godard's vision of destruction; Corinne and Roland do not hesitate to incinerate Emily Brontë (Blandine Jeanson) when she insists on asking them riddles rather than indicating the way to Oinville. This apparently casual barbarism is laced with an absurd humor, since Roland complains of his role in a film in which one meets "sick people," and a troupe of "Italian actors from a coproduction" announce themselves to all passersby—this in a film that happens to be a Franco-Italian coproduction.

Following the musical interlude, Corinne and Roland are picked up by an open van collecting rubbish in the French countryside. Since the workers are an Algerian and an African, Godard turns the sequence into an illustrated lecture on the Third World. While a voice-over discusses revolutionary movements in the former colonies, the camera focuses first on the face of the Algerian, and then the African. A disconsolate Roland and Corinne, who have to do the actual work of trash collection, sit atop the trash heap, which includes a blue cloth decorated with fleurs-de-lis. The sequence is very static and includes a virtual précis of Friedrich Engels' 1884 treatise, *Origin of the Family, Private Property and the State*, an indication of Godard's later, short-lived Marxism. During this lecture, there is a curious flash-forward to a group of hippies seated by a river.

Despite their travails, Roland and Corinne do arrive at Oinville, only to learn that the mother intends to keep the estate for herself. Unable to change her mind, Roland kills her in an offscreen murder, the visual accompaniment of which is a close-up of a butchered rabbit drenched with watery red dye. During their discussion of the millions that they will inherit, Roland and Corinne for the first time in the film say that they love each other. To destroy the evidence of their crime, they place the body in an implausible wreckage of cars, a tree, and a glider which they set afire. Roland and Corinne, however, soon run into their logical successors, the members of the Liberation Front of the Oise-Seine (F.L.S.O.).

Armed with automatic weapons and sporting "hippie" clothes and long hair, this liberation front owes its doctrines not to Mao Tse-tung or Karl Marx but to Sigmund Freud and Attila the Hun. They machine-gun some of their victims and take the rest as captives, subjecting them to peculiar rites that have intimations of Corinne's earlier confession to her analyst-lover. The F.L.S.O. cook (Ernest Menzer) is also a shaman who sports a gigantic carving knife and a bloodstained smock. Although there are hints of a bucolic pantheism in a Whitmanesque ode to the ocean accompanied by the drumbeats of the group's leader (Jean-Pierre Kalfon), the reality of this new tribal life is depressing. The members of Front accept the situation of primitive warfare in a devastated landscape that they have helped to create. Women captives are exchanged as barter, and armed clashes are common; even worse, the Front literally lives off its slaughtered captives. Accepted as the leader's mate, Corinne calmly appreciates the meal composed of dead English tourists and parts of her husband.

*Weekend* may well be Godard's most successful experiment, since it excited real debate among both critics and filmgoers. Whether seen as an "appallingly funny indictment" or simply an extended session of "bourgeois baiting," *Weekend* is certainly a film in which themes and formal structure are almost perfectly matched.

*Lenny Rubenstein*

# WELCOME, MR. MARSHALL (BIENVENIDO, MR. MARSHALL)

*Origin:* Spain
*Released:* 1952
*Released in U.S.:* 1953
*Production:* Vincente Sempere
*Direction:* Luis G. Berlanga
*Screenplay:* Juan Antonio Bardem, Luis G. Berlanga, and Miguel Mihura
*Cinematography:* Manuel Berenguer
*Editing:* Pepita Orduña
*Narration:* Fernando Rey
*Art direction:* Francisco Canet Cubel
*Music:* Jesús García Leoz
*Songs:* Ochaita, Valerio, and Solono
*Running time:* 86 minutes

*Principal characters:*

| | |
|---|---|
| Mayor | José Isbert |
| Village priest | Luis Pérez de León |
| Don Luis | Alberto Romea |
| Manolo | Manuel Morán |
| "Songbird of Southern Spain" (Carmen Vargas) | Lolita Seville |
| Schoolteacher | Elvira Quintillá |
| Doctor inventor | Félix Fernández |
| Delegate general | José Franco |
| Town crier | Joaquín Roa |
| Secretary | Fernándo Aguirre |

*Welcome, Mr. Marshall*, filmmaker Luis García Berlanga's second solo effort as a director, was made when he was thirty-one and just beginning a long and controversial career in the Spanish cinema. Prior to this film, he had codirected *Esa pareja feliz* (1951; *That Happy Pair*) with Juan Antonio Bardem. *Welcome, Mr. Marshall* was greeted with highly favorable notice at the Cannes International Film Festival, but it has not received the critical recognition that it deserves. While the film is admittedly flawed, it is important as an early example of modern cinematic satire; it preceded more successful efforts in the genre, such as Jack Arnold's *The Mouse That Roared* (1959) and Norman Jewison's *The Russians Are Coming the Russians Are Coming* (1966), by several years.

*Welcome, Mr. Marshall* not only established Berlanga as a director but also raised the stock of Spanish cinema on the international scene. Berlanga's other notable efforts are several. In 1956, there was *Calabuch* (*The Rocket from Calabuch*). His *Placido* in 1961 assured his status in the United States when it was nominated for an Academy Award for Best Foreign-Language Film. These films, like all of his works, were coscripted by Berlanga, usually with Bardem, an important director in his own right, with whom he shared credit for both story concept and screenplay on *Welcome, Mr. Marshall*. With *El verdugo* (1963; *Not on Your Life*), Berlanga ventured beyond satire to the outer edges of *film noir*, and he completely shocked audiences with his erotic film *Life Size Love Doll* in 1977.

In many ways, *Welcome, Mr. Marshall* is the satiric antithesis of *The Mouse That Roared* and *The Russians Are Coming the Russians Are Coming*. The expected "invaders" of a small village in the Spanish heartland are a welcomed group of American diplomats on tour to study Spain's needs on behalf of the famous post-World War II European Recovery Act, headed by then United States Secretary of State George C. Marshall. The curious delight in this theme comes from the recognition that Spain in reality was altogether excluded from participation in the Marshall Plan, given its neutral status during the war and the tremendous diplomatic pressures directed against the nation by the Soviet Union after the war because of Spain's Fascist leanings under the rule of Francisco Franco. Berlanga masterfully plays on the underlying irony by including a brief clip of a propagandistic newsreel extolling the virtues of the Marshall Plan in providing Italy with astronomical quantities of war-recovery goods. In counterpoint to the primary theme, Berlanga keeps the audience's intellect alert by playfully injecting innumerable little vignettes that comment on the universality of human nature.

The film opens on a spring day in a town in the region of Castile. The viewer later learns that the town is called Via del Campo, although the mayor (José Isbert) calls it Via del Rio, thereby reflecting his aspirations for the town. In fact, it is a town that is unknown and will remain so, whatever its name. It could be anyplace, anywhere; Berlanga places great emphasis on this point.

The film opens with a freeze-frame segment that stops the action in the town square while an anonymous voice-over narrator introduces the characters and establishes the story line. The narrative is interrupted in this fashion several times thereafter to fill in thematic elements; the film ends with the narrator making a final observation: "[The town] is just an ordinary little pueblo."

In some ways, the town fits the stereotype of the quaint Spanish village: It is one of those out-of-the-way places in which it seems as though time has stopped. Indeed, this is literally the case, as Berlanga pointedly reminds the viewer that the clock in the town-hall tower has not worked in years. The mayor goes to great lengths to erase this image in his preparation to greet the Americans. He appoints a citizen (who proves to be delightfully inept at his task) to operate the hands of the big clock manually and sound its bells with a hammer as appropriate.

On one level, *Welcome, Mr. Marshall* is a film about international perceptions, how the people of one nation perceive those of another nation—particularly through films. In Berlanga's opening sequence, the viewer is informed that the mayor, a fan of American Westerns, is awaiting the arrival (at the local movie theater) of the weekly film—which is, needless to say, a Western. Berlanga makes use of this motif in several ways. First, he uses it to introduce the newsreel mentioned above, a sort of twisted Shakespearean play-within-a-play (in this case, film-within-a-film) that takes on farcical dimensions; second, it establishes a basis for an absurd Western dream-scene in which the mayor participates; and third, it comments on the stereotypes and false perceptions fostered by the popular cinema.

Within *Welcome, Mr. Marshall*, Berlanga employs several devices to distinguish his film from the conventional films which it implicitly criticizes. The editing, for example, is often deliberately abrupt; Berlanga supplies few transitional devices to link sequences. In addition, this practice frequently enhances the film's comedic effect. Indeed, perhaps Berlanga's greatest accomplishment in *Welcome, Mr. Marshall* lies in his fusion of so many diverse comedic elements into a cohesive montage, one that makes a succinct and universal statement about the words and actions of men. That the audience can see caricatures of themselves and laugh is to his credit. His exaggeration of reality utilizes nearly all the elements of comedy, yet it is not overdone, and the director stops short of the vulgar. One sees touches of the absurd, of burlesque, of farce, and even moderate doses of slapstick—all of which work to unify Berlanga's conceptualization rather than detract from it as might be expected. It is a style reminiscent in many ways of that of Berlanga's countryman, Miguel de Cervantes, and his masterpiece, *Don Quixote de la Mancha* (1605, 1615), though the heroic element is missing. A more experienced director might have been leery of putting so much variety in the celluloid salad. Yet, with all of this, the viewer is never led to doubt the film's more serious side.

Characterization plays an important role in Berlanga's method. The mayor, a beret-clad and not obnoxiously lecherous old gentleman, owns half the town. He is unashamed of his eccentricities. He bears a striking resemblence to Pablo Picasso. The "Songbird of Southern Spain" (Lolita Seville) is simply that and has no other dialogue. Only briefly does the viewer come to know her as Carmen Vargas. The "songbird," who escapes neither the fancy nor the fantasies of the mayor, is on tour and, in her brief stopover, is delegated the role of entertaining the Americans when they arrive. Manolo (Manuel Morán), the agent extraordinaire, is Carmen Vargas' promoter, who surprisingly becomes a bit of a philosopher-mediator between the town's pro-American and anti-American factions. Don Luis (Alberto

Romea), the town nobleman, and the village priest (Luis Pérez de León) form the opposition to the "Welcome, Mr. Marshall" fiesta being planned. The delegate general (José Franco) is the high-level Spanish bureaucrat who forces the action with threat, innuendo, and false promises. Other characters include the schoolteacher (Elvira Quintillá), the doctor inventor (Félix Fernández), and the town crier (Joaquín Roa). Much of the cast forms what becomes, in true democratic fashion, a politically inexperienced town council, not unlike the familiar American form of town governance. The mayor's power lies not so much in swaying the vote of the council, but rather, in his financial and eccentric base; that is, he does as he pleases, council support or not—almost like a benevolent dictator.

The action of Berlanga's film focuses primarily on the festivities being planned by the pueblo. It is here that Berlanga plays on the theme of cross-cultural perceptions. It is decided that the Americans will expect to see a "traditional" Spanish village, with the townspeople attired in appropriate clothing à la Hollywood, dancing in the streets, and strolling musicians. Costumes are rented and Moorish architectural façades are built and appropriately placed to dress up the original structures. In the village cantina, the wall is adorned with a large bull's head. On the opposite side of the wall stands the remainder of the bull on a platform, intact and seeming only a little discontent out of its pasture. Thus, the town becomes a motion-picture set to conform to the expectations of its visitors. In effect the preparations become a reeducation for the townspeople, who are taught that this is the way Americans expect Spaniards to be.

The village teacher is a stock character who reads a long, impressive list of American accomplishments, resources, and production capabilities before a meeting of the town. The priest has his own list concerning the Americans that articulates specific numbers of people in various Protestant denominations and concludes with a large number of doubtful believers. In the midst of all this, the agent forewarns the town power structure that "Americans won't have enough time [to appreciate the fiesta in their honor] because they never have enough time."

On the day before the Americans' arrival, the town goes into full dress rehearsal. The day culminates with the people standing in line in the town square to register their names on the gift list with the mayor, for he has told them that for their support and cooperation, each will receive a gift of his choice, purchased with the American money expected to pour in. "You are permitted only one thing from the Americans," the mayor tells the more greedy waiting in line. (The townspeople have also been told that they will be expected to help pay for the fiesta.) The list finally becomes a collective one of desirable rather than utilitarian goods. Only one person, the town nobleman, does not submit his name to the list.

With the anticipation of the big day upon the principals, the night is a restless one in which Berlanga takes the viewer into the dream fantasies of the mayor, the nobleman, and the priest. The clergyman's dream leads him initially into an ominous courtroom where the proceedings are obviously aimed at him. His jury is composed of several dark-robed inquisitor types with conical hats; "KKK" is stenciled on the backs of their robes. The dark side of the dream fades to an airdrop with American planes whose crewmen push out tractors that resemble sleighs filled with toys. These "gifts" fall to the ground hanging from parachutes.

Meanwhile, in his dream, the nobleman, who repeats throughout the film that his complaints are against the "original" Americans (that is, the Indians) who killed his ancestors, winds up being prepared for cooking in a large pot as American natives take him captive. Finally, there is the mayor's dream, in which he finds himself in a Wild West saloon as town sheriff and gunslinger while the "Songbird" sings "Oh! Susanna" in sultry Spanish.

The day of the fiesta and the arrival of the Americans finally comes. The costumed villagers line the main road and fill the windows, throwing streamers and confetti—a sort of ticker-tape parade in miniature. At last, the Americans are spotted; their caravan of shiny new Chryslers passes under the town's large "Bienvenidos" sign. Amid the cheering and fanfare, the American caravan never slows down, continuing through and out of town with the last Chrysler displaying a "Goodbye" sign on the rear.

Berlanga leaves the viewer with the townspeople, again standing in line before the mayor, each bearing his respective token payment of livestock or vegetables or a household item to help subsidize the expenses of the "Welcome, Mr. Marshall" fiesta. Even the proud town nobleman, without bitterness, gives up his sword, a family heirloom, to assist the town's debt.

Because of the timing of the film's release, Berlanga found the fictional irony of his work extending into reality. Negotiations concerning the establishment of American military bases in Spain were then under way, and Berlanga's work did not serve the purposes of either country. The deal between the two nations was finally consummated in 1953, with Spain receiving a rather generous bonus (nearly $100,000,000) for its cooperation.

*Welcome, Mr. Marshall* set the modern standard for cinematic satire and ensured Berlanga's place among the masters of the genre. Its topical satire is still timely, as relations between the United States and the European community remain uneasy, but its deftly ironic treatment of universal human foibles will prove yet more enduring.

*Cecil Costilow*

# WESTFRONT 1918

*Origin:* Germany
*Released:* 1930
*Released in U.S.:* 1931
*Production:* Nero Films
*Direction:* G. W. Pabst
*Assistant direction:* Marc Sorkin
*Screenplay:* Ladislaus Vajda and Peter Martin Lampel; based on the novel *Vier von der Infanterie*, by Ernst Johannsen
*Cinematography:* Fritz Arno Wagner and Charles Metain
*Editing:* no listing
*Art direction:* Erno Metzner
*Sound:* Guido Bagier
*Music:* no listing
*Running time:* 90 minutes
*Also known as: Comrades of 1918* and *Shame of a Nation*

*Principal characters:*
Karl .............................. Gustav Diessl
Karl's wife........................ Hanna Hoessrich
Karl's mother ........................ Else Heller
Bavarian ......................... Fritz Kampers
Student .................... Hans Joachim Moebis
Lieutenant ....................... Claus Clausen
Man from Hamburg ............... Gustav Püttjer
Yvette .......................... Jackie Monnier
Butcher's son ...................... Carl Balhaus

The history of the Weimar Republic is a history of extremes. Within little more than a decade, virtually no sector of the German population was spared the effects of radical shifts in political, economic, and social structures. The years immediately following the war were marked by a sharp reaction to nationalism and a general turn to the Left. Soon, however, rampant inflation and the consequent destruction of the social order resulted in ever-growing political polarization. By the early 1930's, the process had come full circle with the renewed triumph of nationalism, particularly in its National Socialist interpretation. Within this context, the war was one of the most important ideological issues. Whether used as a lesson for the inevitable results of nationalism and militarism or as evidence of leftist treachery (the "stab in the back" theory), it was often in the forefront of the political disputes in the Weimar Republic.

G. W. Pabst's *Westfront 1918* fits awkwardly in this strained environment.

It was attacked by the Right for its unglamorized and even treasonously defeatist portrayal of the Great War, and by the Left for its trivialization of the social and economic disorders that resulted in nationalism. Its historical significance, however, is precisely a function of this seemingly compromised point of view and its disengagement from the pervasive revisionist attitudes toward the war. *Westfront 1918*'s effectiveness was confirmed by the speed with which it was banned after the National Socialist rise to power in 1933. Yet the film's orientation is hardly radical; it reflects established middle-class values—friendship, love, and moral obligation—offering a revealing insight into the naïveté still extant so late in the Republic.

*Westfront 1918* falls within the tradition of the war film along with films such as King Vidor's *The Big Parade* (1925) and Lewis Milestone's *All Quiet on the Western Front* (1930). This genre provided the parameters by which it was judged and all too often dismissed, but in retrospect, it is a context that demonstrates the integrity of Pabst's vision and directorial style. *Westfront 1918* refrains from the romantic drama that characterizes most war films of this period and instead portrays the war as a disruptive, gritty, and tedious ordeal. Unlike the more successful *All Quiet on the Western Front*, *Westfront 1918* avoids sensationalist pathos and emotionalism, providing instead a sober *exposé* of the consequences of war. While Pabst's relentless vision is tempered by an underlying theme of transcendental values, his cinematic style, previously marked by a growing objective tendency, here approaches its most realistic level. Erno Metzner's authentically detailed sets are enhanced by Fritz Arno Wagner's long takes and tracking camera, and although this style is an important shift from Pabst's usual reliance on carefully composed images of nearly symbolic import, it is consistent with the film's narrative structure and extended by his subtle handling of the actors.

Based on Ernst Johannsen's pacifist novel *Vier von der Infanterie*, *Westfront 1918* examines the experiences of war through the lives of four soldiers: a naïve, idealistic university student (Hans Joachim Moebis); Karl (Gustav Diessl), a recently married engineer; a jovial Bavarian farmer (Fritz Kampers); and the Lieutenant (Claus Clausen), a fittingly nationalistic member of the military aristocracy. Their varied backgrounds, personalities, and perceptions provide a diverse yet complementary view of the war's disruptive effect on the individual, the family, and society. The bulk of the film focuses on the day-to-day drudgery and tensions of life at the front, but insights into the broader implications of war emerge particularly through the student and Karl.

The film opens with the student's first love affair—a relationship with a French barmaid, Yvette (Jackie Monnier)—and their subsequent separation as the battle begins and he goes to the front with his unit. The obvious contradiction of a German soldier's love for a Frenchwoman expresses the dissonance between individual perceptions and needs, between national declarations and the requisite duties of citizens. Moreover, the battle lines and physical separation of the two lovers vividly portray the disruption of everyday life. These factors build an active tension that is relieved only when the student volunteers for a mission behind French lines in order to be reunited with Yvette.

These opening scenes suggest the beginning of a narrative that emphasizes characters and their emotional interactions, but this is not Pabst's overall strategy. Rather, he dwells on the collective and often mundane events that bind a group of ordinary men together. The tangential and contrasting episodes of the student's and Karl's personal lives punctuate the film's predominant focus on this collective experience and the pervasive imagery of trenches and barren, battle-scarred landscapes.

Against a backdrop of food lines and columns of eager recruits, Karl makes a surprise visit home only to discover his wife (Hanna Hoessrich) in bed with the butcher's son (Carl Balhaus). Karl's mother (Else Heller) intercedes, extending the wife's excuse of loneliness caused by Karl's long absence to the more pervasive disruption caused by the war, thus addressing the central theme of the film. Whereas the student is driven by his longing for Yvette, Karl's consequent bitterness propels him back to the front with renewed zeal.

Pabst continually draws a contrast between human actions and external events. The lyricism of the initial love scene between the student and his French lover is shattered by an air raid and the subsequent start of battle, a device that is repeated in a quiet interlude at the front. As the troops sit listening to the Bavarian sing, the French suddenly launch an artillery barrage, and in the course of the attack, the Germans are virtually destroyed. The savagery of this process is individualized in the fate of the student, who, returning to his unit after an emotional farewell with Yvette, is killed not by an anonymous shell but in brutal hand-to-hand combat.

During the battle, Karl undergoes a profound emotional change as he is forced to listen to the screams of a wounded French soldier, until he himself is wounded. Meanwhile, the shell-shocked lieutenant stumbles through the corpses and rubble in a daze. Pabst uses these solitary moments as transitions to scenes of mass horror, in which images of destruction fill the screen and the war's insanity is depicted through overwhelming numbers of dead and dying. The camera tracks relentlessly through the expanses of the battlefield, revealing endless craters, shattered timbers, discarded weapons, barbed wire, and piles of corpses. These scenes are remarkable for the intensity of their near-documentary realism and are among the most powerful and persuasive in the film.

Pabst's careful orchestration of unending horrors with character counterpoint emerges in a dialectical fulfillment when Karl and the lieutenant are brought to a field hospital in a bombed-out church. The screaming of countless wounded men accompanies the lieutenant's confused wanderings; here, as in the battlefield scene, the devastating impact of war's atrocity is evoked as much through the multiplicity of the depicted events as through the continuous method of its cinematic presentation. Karl, meanwhile, lies dying next to a wounded French soldier, and he hallucinates a scene of reconciliation with his wife. Shortly after his death, the theme of reconciliation is extended as the Frenchman takes the dead man's hand and declares their comradeship. The film's closing title—"Ende?"—repeats this ironic note.

Despite the pathos of these closing scenes, Pabst tends to emphasize the broader implications of war, particularly the massive scale of destruction, rather than dwell on the sentimentality of individual tragedy. This orientation is consistent throughout the film, as demonstrated by one of the most dramatic scenes, the student's death in hand-to-hand combat. Although the scene certainly derives some of its impact from the narrative context of the student's previous character development—personal traits of naïveté and idealism, his relationship with Yvette, his hopes and aspirations—the violence of his final struggle and death is deemphasized as the camera moves away from the fight to reveal the victims of countless identical conflicts in the battlefield. The student is simply one of many, and Pabst accentuates the many. In contrast to this dispassionate approach, *All Quiet on the Western Front*, from the same year, relies heavily on personal drama and emotionalism in its depiction of war. In 1930, when the two films were released, Milestone's melodramatic intensity found greater critical success than did Pabst's emotional distance. Today, however, Milestone's style seems dated, whereas Pabst's unflinching portrayal of the day-to-day rigors of war remains powerfully honest.

In addition to minimizing the role of narrative conventions, Pabst relies heavily on long takes and the moving camera to evoke not only a sense of place but a sense of realism as well. André Bazin's analysis of the implications of these techniques provides a relevant context for understanding the cinematic structure of *Westfront 1918*. Bazin argues that the moving camera produces an ever-shifting series of spatial relationships and encourages viewers to enter visually and explore the image in a manner that parallels the perception of the outside world. Compared to the limited information available in static short takes, Bazin argues, the moving long take results in enhanced perceptual realism. It is this technique on which Pabst relies to intensify and sustain scenes of near-documentary realism.

*Westfront 1918* stands as one of the high points of the realist narrative cinema in Germany. Both in theme and in production design, the film marks an important point in Pabst's own development of a realist film style, components of which were already evident as early as 1925 in *Die freudlose Gasse* (*The Street of Sorrow*). *Westfront 1918*, together with his production of *Kameradschaft* (1931) the following year, established Pabst as one of the leading influences on subsequent realist developments, particularly the British school of realism exemplified by Basil Wright and John Grierson.

Pabst's directorial style in *Westfront 1918* is singularly appropriate to the urgency of his pacifist message. Although the film was criticized for not displaying a more polemical or emotionally evocative indictment of war, its impact arose through its unsensationalized presentation of an event that was mystified and caricaturized by both extremes of Germany's political spectrum. Pabst's highly developed realist style provided an unwavering gaze at the horrors of war and its destruction of the human community, creating a film remarkable for the universality of its vision.

*William Uricchio*

# WHEN THE GREEKS (TON KERO TON HELLINON)

*Origin:* Greece
*Released:* 1981
*Released in U.S.:* 1983
*Production:* A. Papefstratiou for Cinetic/Greek Film Center
*Direction:* Lakis Papastathis
*Screenplay:* Lakis Papastathis
*Cinematography:* Theodoros Margas
*Editing:* Vangelis Youssas
*Art direction:* Nikos Politis
*Costume design:* Nikos Politis
*Sound:* Lycorgous Vayakis, Thanassis, and Arvanitis
*Music:* Georges Papadakis
*MPAA rating:* no listing
*Running time:* 100 minutes

*Cast:*
Alexis Damianos, Kostas Arzoglou, George Sampanis, and Stavros Mermighis

Perhaps the nationalism of a once great people who have undergone a series of suppressions is more acutely felt than that of a still mighty nation. Certainly their sense of national pride, of national identity, becomes schizophrenically bound up in their past glories and in their more feeble attempts to attain the benefits of modernity, as they perceive them.

It is precisely that duality that characterizes the nationalist impulse in twentieth century Greek culture and that lies at the heart of Lakis Papastathis' *When the Greeks*. The film, Papastathis' feature debut (he had previously made three shorts), examines the bandits of the *fin de siècle*. Andreas Bellis describes this era (in the 1982 edition of the *International Film Guide*) as a "deliberately darkened period in Greek history." According to Bellis, these bandits were the remnants of a self-styled army, which had joined with the liberation armies of the 1821 revolt against the Turks. When Greece was then liberated, part of this "army" was absorbed by the official state army under King Otto of Bavaria. Nevertheless, many of their comrades kept apart and maintained the bandits' traditions for some one hundred years afterward. It was thought of as a national liberation movement, in exile in its own land and enjoying extremely strong popular support—the stuff of legend.

It is the transitional period leading to the eventual downfall of the bandits that is Papastathis' concern. *When the Greeks* presents an arc of events which traces that downfall, as personified in the trajectory of his hero, a bandit chieftain called the Captain, while also presenting the clash of two parallel views of Greek nationhood. For Papastathis, this was clearly a conflict of class as well, pitting the landless bandits and their supporters among the peasantry against the landed gentry and the growing bourgeoisie. The upper classes would ultimately prevail, and their vision of Greek nationhood would dominate subsequent Greek culture.

Papastathis introduces this class-oriented, materialist reading of history in his precredit sequence, a selection of clips from a silent film version of the legendary vengeance and near beatification of the bandit woman Maria Pentayotissa. The silent film clips, with their hypnotically insistent flickering, are counterpointed with a narration which is balladlike in tone, simultaneously invoking Maria's legend and explicitly rejecting the earlier film's mystification of it. At key moments of violence, Papastathis freezes the silent film and adds a cartoonish tinting of large, fiery blocks of red and orange. The resulting stylized flames of revolt suggest that the film to follow will be agitprop. It actually is not, and the effect, though oddly beautiful, is misleading and simplistic, because, instead of delivering an overtly revolutionary tract, Papastathis leads the viewer into a world of hieratic, often cryptic gesture.

The film narrative begins at the home of a wealthy landowner, a young liberal. A salon is in progress in which tribute is paid repeatedly to the greatness that once was Greece. Paradoxically, the young landowner's wife plays modern European music at the piano, and his guests are all dressed in evening clothes, the perfectly assimilated Victorian ideal of proper attire and conduct. Indeed, only the children wear the skirted *foustanella*, the traditional garb of the mountain peasants and bandits. When the Captain and his men enter the house to seize the young master, only his son, no more than ten or twelve years old, stands up to them.

The irony is unmistakable. While to the bourgeois guests the *foustanella* is a costume fit for children, it is only the earnest courage of the child which reflects the Greece of the epic heroes, evoked moments before in the boy's recitation. At the same time, the contrast between the children's *foustanellas*—clean, white, prettily embroidered—and the soiled, sweat-stained clothing of the bandits underlines the difference between a culture which is lived and one which is merely invoked piously.

It is immediately clear that there is a chasm of difference between the bandits and the bourgeoisie. The Captain and his men, dirty, ragged, bearded, emerge from the darkness, as if they were part of the night itself. (Indeed, Papastathis will identify them throughout the film with natural phenomena, even with the earth.) Throughout the remainder of the film, they will be seen in sunlight. By contrast, the houseguests are immaculately attired and seen only in glaring, artificial light. They are posed awkwardly, grouped according to the conventions of nineteenth century portraiture. Moreover, their outrage at the kidnaping, which seems theatrically artificial, centers entirely on concerns of property—the size of the ransom, the invasion of the home.

From this point, the film moves into bright sunlight, the world of the bandits, the world of the Mediterranean culture of which they are a natural part. The young landowner is taken to a cave, where he is witness to the first of a series of ritual gestures which run through the film like a leitmotif. A young peasant comes to see the Captain and, by way of pledging his allegiance to the bandits, prostrates himself, rubbing his clean shirt and *foustanella* with the reddish-brown earth of the cave. It is a gesture which acknowledges the superior authority of the Captain and the band and, at the same time, invokes a mystical oneness with the earth of Greece.

As the young landowner's voice-over narration, which begins after the actual kidnaping, states, it is imperative for the bandits to stay on the move. Thus begins a series of sequences of the bandits walking through the hill country, their captive riding, his hands tied before him, on a mule. At each stop the bandits engage in conversations about the nature of the Greek people, their culture, their earth. Significantly, the first of these takes place on a promontory overlooking the Mediterranean, in the blaze of noon. The Captain's voluble second-in-command invokes the glorious history of the Greeks, who, according to the story told, existed before Adam. Another recounts the legend that when Lord Thomas Elgin sent the Turks (a hated enemy with whom Greece is yet again at war during the film's time frame) for the remaining "marbles" (the Elgin marbles), they, poetically enough, cried for their sisters who had been taken away. The link between the bandits and the ancient Greek warriors is made explicit in a line of dialogue which clearly states that they were as brave as Achilles and the other warriors. By contrast, the bourgeois explains that he came from a family of merchants, thereby restating the class dichotomy which is central to the film.

Again the bandits take to the rugged footpaths of the mountains, this time coming to a mountaintop overlooking the vast wooded expanses of the Greek countryside. Here, in a small whitewashed church, the Captain participates in a solemn wedding ceremony while his men wait outside. The resulting sequence, perhaps the finest in the film, is a beautiful but eerie ritual of renewal, of new beginnings, an encapsulation of the film's central concerns.

The Captain moves into the church, his rough appearance amplified by the rifle slung over his shoulder. He carries himself with a reticence which underlines his status as an outsider, but which, nevertheless, suggests the great dignity of the man. The young bourgeois is seen framed briefly in the doorway, an even more alienated figure, awkward and disheveled. The ceremony is performed with a painfully slow intensity, punctuated by an occasional cut to the bandits waiting patiently outside. A lone violinist stands inside the rough country church, framed by the sunlit doorway suggesting the ritualistic power of tradition. A slow, almost mournful but authentic ceremonial dance of the wedding party moves outside and around the courtyard, while the violinist trills and the merchant sings solfeggio, detached, perhaps a bit amused by the simplicity of what he has witnessed. The Captain speaks gravely of saving their history, adding that he is thinking of the children, and Papastathis cuts, beautifully, to the newlyweds' skirts as they walk away from the camera with the priest and the fiddler. He then cuts once more, to a lovely long-shot of the foursome, the priest and the couple in an oxcart, the fiddler walking behind, as they move out into the green of the hills, the afternoon light just starting to fade.

If the wedding sequence is the emotional and aesthetic high point of the film, it is also the last moment in the film in which the bandits are seen as being in harmony both with nature and one another. From this point on, things begin to fall apart, starting almost immediately with the next scene, a skirmish with government troops. Papastathis stages the encounter on a flat plain which offers a few scattered rocks for ground cover and a nearby wood all around. The young bandit, who had come to the Captain in the cave to swear his allegiance, strides forward to taunt the government forces. A dark-uniformed soldier stands, and they exchange insults across the opening. Suddenly, a shot rings out and the young bandit falls, scrabbling on the ground in a moment reminiscent of his gesture of self-abasement in the cave. The two ragged groups of combatants surge forward and back in a brief flurry of gunfire then, as suddenly as it began, the battle is over, the government troops in retreat (more, one suspects in confusion than fear or defeat).

During this skirmish, the merchant, in terror, hurls himself to the ground and grovels in fear, a moment which, like the young bandit's death, reminds one of the cave scene. It is an appropriate echo, for it is only after the battle that the merchant discards his battered derby and takes on the responsibility of carrying the bandits' water gourd, a symbolic acceptance of the group of which he has previously been an unwilling part.

The next sequence, the funeral of the young bandit, is another beautifully staged ritual, as stylized as the wedding. As a group of women bathe the corpse, the Captain sits at the foot of a hill and sings slowly, solemnly. The dead youth's face is painted white, and he is dressed in fresh clothing before the bandits bear him away in a moving long-shot in which their presence is the only sign of life in a dark, almost black image.

The funeral takes on an added significance now as the bandits, seen at the lip of a promontory, partake of what will be a last supper, in the biblical as well as literal sense. It is the last time they will be seen together, and it is at this gathering that the Captain's second-in-command will decide to betray him, a decision which is signaled with a kiss. A deserter from the army has brought them a newspaper with information about an offer of amnesty to those who turn in other bandits and agree to fight against the Turks. Papastathis cuts to a series of close-up reaction shots, ending with the Captain, impassive, and his lieutenant, thoughtful. In the distance, one hears the faint sound of cowbells, a reminder of the security of family life that these men have abandoned. The lieutenant kisses the Captain and walks away, offcamera. The Captain decides to go home one last time, and he, too, leaves the seeming warmth of the group's circle; as one of the bandits explains, "He doesn't want his enemies to laugh or his friends to cry."

The circle has been broken in the most literal sense. The Captain has read, correctly, the meaning of the kiss, and he must, perforce, ambush and kill the lieutenant and the other bandit who joins this renegade. Papastathis stages this ambush on a rock face, reminiscent of those familiar from the Westerns of American director Anthony Mann, a sheer drop threatening all the men while, simultaneously, providing the Captain with the high ground necessary to carry out his lethal endeavor.

Back at the campsite, the merchant is told that he will be returned to his family. Again there is a ritual of cleansing as he is bathed, shaved, and dressed in new clothing, again the westernized dress of the bourgeoisie, by the bandits. Each of them in turn embraces him, an eloquent and bittersweet moment that reminds the viewer how much he has become a part of the group.

As the merchant is led through an earth-brown valley by the Captain and another bandit, the distant music of a military band, music which is recognizable, grows louder. It is John Phillip Sousa's "Washington Post March," an ironic comment on the increasing influence of American power in post-World War II Greece. The army band approaches, led by another captain, this one in dark blue military garb, a scarlet cape tossed jauntily over one shoulder. He climbs atop a boulder and begins to read a declaration of nationalist intent which invokes, once more, the prowess of the ancient Greek warriors. The other bandit hurls his rifle down, shrieking curses and hurling clouds of dirt at the departing band, scrabbling in the dirt (another repetition of that image of Greek earth as mother/cruel mistress). The Captain follows the band, however, as in a trance, and Papastathis holds the spot as long as he can, keeping both captains in the frame, the wind snapping at the military man's cape in a violent parody of the gentler breezes of the wedding scene.

Finally, Papastathis brings his film full circle, returning once more to the gray-brown of the black-and-white footage of the precredit sequence, to a plain, a plain dotted with the tents of a military encampment. The merchant walks beside the Captain, the army captain at his other arm. The bandit chief looks dazed, weary for the first time in the film; he stumbles and the two avatars of the "new" Greece pick him up. On the sound track, the merchant says that the Captain joined the army but sang no more, and that he never heard his voice again. Papastathis holds the shot until they are offscreen and all that remains are a few soldiers, ironically dressed in *foustanellas*. The modernization of Greece is triumphant, and its picture of a bourgeois nationalism, with only lip service to the roots of the Greek nation, is the one that remains.

*George Robinson*

# WHERE CHIMNEYS ARE SEEN (ENTOTSU NO MIERU BASHO)

*Origin:* Japan
*Released:* 1953
*Released in U.S.:* no listing
*Production:* Yoshishige Uchiyama for Studio 8 Productions and Shin Toho
*Direction:* Heinosuke Gosho
*Assistant direction:* Akira Miwa
*Screenplay:* Hideo Oguni; based on the novel *Mujaki na hitobito*, by Rinzo Shiina
*Cinematography:* Mitsuo Miura
*Editing:* Nobu Nagata
*Art direction:* Tomoo Shimogawara
*Sound:* Yuji Dogen
*Music:* Yasushi Akutagawa
*Running time:* 108 minutes
*Also known as: Chimney Scene*, *Four Chimneys*, and *Three Chimneys*

*Principal characters:*
Ryukichi Ogata....................... Ken Uehara
Hiroko Ogata....................... Kinuyo Tanaka
Kenzo Kubo .................... Hiroshi Akutagawa
Senko Azuma ................... Hideko Takamine
Yukiko Ikeda......................... Chieko Seki
Chuji Tsukahara.................... Haruo Tanaka
Katsuko Ishibashi.................... Ranko Hanai
Ranko Nada ........................ Eiko Miyoshi
Isamu ......................... Zekou Nakamura
Daisuke ......................... Shigeru Ogura

Along with Yasujiro Ozu, Mikio Naruse, Hiroshi Shimizu, and Yasujiro Shimazu, his mentor at Shochiku's Kamata Studio in the early 1920's, veteran director Heinosuke Gosho (1902-1981) was one of the leading exponents of the *shomin-geki*, the drama of the everyday life of the lower and middle classes. His career spanned forty-three years, beginning in 1925 with *Nanto no haru* (*Spring in Southern Islands*), his directorial debut, and ending in 1968 with *Meiji haru aki* (*A Girl of the Meiji Period*). During that time he made nearly one hundred films and worked in a wide range of genres. His first films to attract critical attention—*Sabishiki rambo-mono* (1927; *The Lonely Roughneck*), *Karakuri musume* (1927; *Tricky Girl*), and most of all, *Mura no hanayome* (1928; *The Village Bride*), which is regarded as his earliest masterpiece—demonstrated his sympathy for the oppressed and downtrodden, as well as his commitment to bringing realism to the Japanese cinema of the day.

Gosho's long and successful career, however, was by no means untroubled. Illness (tuberculosis), projects unsuited to him, conflicts with the studios, and resistance to the wartime policy of militaristic Japan all took their toll. Nevertheless, his art flourished, especially in the 1930's and 1950's. His most notable films of the 1930's include Japan's first successful "talkie," the comedy *Madamu to nyobo* (1931; *The Neighbor's Wife and Mine*); *Izu no odoriko* (1933; *Dancing Girls of Izu*), a lyrical adaptation of Yasunari Kawabata's classic tale of doomed adolescent love; and *Jinsei no onimotsu* (1935; *Burden of Life*), a family drama about the antipathy that a salaryman nearing retirement age feels toward his last dependent, his nine-year-old son. In the 1950's, Gosho created three of his most accomplished works: *Osaka no yado* (1954; *An Inn at Osaka*), about the failure of a young insurance company employee and those around him to find meaningful lives for themselves in materialistic postwar Japan; *Takekurabe* (1955; *Growing Up*), a bittersweet love story set in the red-light district of Tokyo in the 1890's; and *Where Chimneys Are Seen*, his most celebrated work, and one of the finest representatives of the *shomin-geki* mode.

Winner of the *Kinema Jumpo* "Best One" Award in 1953, followed by the International Peace Prize at the Berlin International Film Festival, *Where Chimneys Are Seen* is a perfect example of Gosho's cinema. Like all of his films, it is characterized by a great number of separate shots (primarily medium shots and close-ups), a frequently mobile camera, careful attention to atmosphere and setting, excellent direction of actors, and a special mixture of humor and pathos, sentiment and irony, and realism and lyricism that has come to be known simply as "Goshoism." This mixture is the most distinctive feature of Gosho's style and is responsible for making the audience want to laugh and cry at the same time. It derives not only from Gosho's compassion for human beings and his desire to show their lives as they really are, but also from his ability to touch the emotions of his audience deeply. If *Where Chimneys Are Seen* is, as many believe, Gosho's greatest work, it is in good measure because he sought to do justice to the strength, humor, and determination of the common people to carry on after the war.

Based on Rinzo Shiina's novel *Mujaki na hitobito* (1952), *Where Chimneys Are Seen* focuses on the interconnected lives of two couples in a lower-middle-class neighborhood in Senju, a poor industrial section of Tokyo. The plot is simple. A childless, middle-aged couple struggling to get ahead—Ryukichi Ogata (Ken Uehara), a clothing dealer, and his wife, Hiroko (Kinuyo Tanaka)—is left unexpectedly with a baby. Its parents are Hiroko's former husband, Chuji Tsukahara (Haruo Tanaka), whom she has long thought to be dead, and his mistress, Katsuko (Ranko Hanai). Not knowing Tsukahara's whereabouts, the Ogatas are forced to take care of the baby. Its incessant crying, however, soon puts a great strain on them and on their upstairs renters, Kenzo Kubo (Hiroshi Akutagawa), a young tax collector, and his girlfriend, Senko Azuma (Hideko Takamine), a bargains announcer on the radio. Exhausted and depressed by the strain, Hiroko tries to commit suicide, but Kenzo saves her life and offers to find Tsukahara. After a frustrating and difficult search, he discovers him living in abject poverty. By this time, the Ogatas have grown accustomed to the baby and even have come to accept it. Thus, when it falls acutely ill, they lovingly nurse it back to health with the support of Kenzo and Senko and some of the neighbors. Furthermore, when Katsuko, who has left Tsukahara, arrives to reclaim the child, they refuse to give it to her, though the implication is that they will do so later. In short, by the end of the film, the baby proves to be a positive force in the lives of the Ogatas and their two renters. Now Senko, far from being indifferent to Kenzo as she once was, has grown to love him for the kind and gracious person that he is. They will probably marry. The Ogatas have also learned a lesson in love and look to the future with optimism. Perhaps they will even have a child of their own.

*Where Chimneys Are Seen* begins splendidly. Following an aerial view of smog-filled Tokyo is a series of staccato shots of smokestacks—the chimneys of the title. First, four chimneys are seen, then three, then two, then one. In the next shot, the camera pans from the industrial section of Tokyo where these chimneys dominate the landscape to the poor neighborhood of tenement houses adjacent to it, the home of the protagonists. In this manner Gosho not only sets the scene but also introduces the central metaphor of the film: the chimneys themselves. Appearing throughout the film, sometimes they are barely visible in the background; at other times, they are in prominent view. In either case, the chimneys are a familiar sight to the neighborhood, especially to the protagonists, who discover that, depending on where one is, their number seems to vary from one to four (an illusion which Gosho's rapid-fire editing in the opening shots wittily duplicates). It is this illusion, in fact, that leads Ryukichi to remark at the close of the film that life itself is very much like the chimneys. That is to say, life is whatever one chooses to make of it. This observation, along with the implication that there are no absolutes in life, that everything is relative, emerges as one of the principal themes of the film.

Important as this theme may be, Gosho's first and most abiding concern in *Where Chimneys Are Seen* is his depiction of the everyday lives and innermost feelings of his characters. This he does not only with warmth and sympathy but also with humor that is sometimes sweet, sometimes ironic. Take, for example, his delineation of the Ogatas, the two most significant characters in the film. Before the arrival of the baby, when they are almost idyllically happy, in spite of their modest means, the humor is decidedly sweet. Thus, Gosho shows their attempts on two separate occasions (once during

Ryukichi's lunch hour) to do what any loving couple desires to do—make love—but the outside world interrupts. In an even more amusing incident, Ryukichi asks Hiroko to help him by reading aloud numbers from one of his accounts. Yet her litanylike recitation irritates him almost immediately, so he ends up finishing the job himself. No harm is done, however, because the Ogatas are perfectly comfortable with each other—quirks and all.

After the arrival of the baby, Gosho's affection for the Ogatas in no way diminishes, but now his humor becomes gently ironic so as to enable the audience not only to identify with them but also to view them with a certain amount of objectivity; hence the scene in which they discover the baby.

Having returned home, the Ogatas are stunned to find an abandoned baby on their living-room floor. At first the baby is smiling and happy, but soon it begins howling. While Ryukichi covers his ears, Hiroko desperately tries to prepare something for it to eat. To make matters worse, the noise alerts one of the neighbors, who drops by and—misunderstanding the situation—congratulates the couple on becoming parents. As the scene ends, Ryukichi tries to eat his meal, but one look at the still crying baby is all that is needed to drive him out of the room. Hiroko is left to tend the child.

Throughout the scene, Gosho's humor derives from two main sources. First, the basic situation—two adults at the mercy of an uncooperative baby—is inherently comic. So, too, is the dramatic action, which contrasts the Ogatas' helpless scurrying around with the baby's static position on the floor, a position that visually reinforces the fact that this infant is truly an immovable object, one with which the Ogatas will have to reckon.

Inherently comic though the situation and dramatic action may be, it is primarily Gosho's editing and *mise en scène* that sharpen the humor and are responsible for the audience's involvement in and detachment from all three characters. In terms of editing, the scene, which consists mostly of medium and long-shots, is punctuated regularly by close-ups and extreme close-ups. Of these shots, none perhaps is more ironic and resonant than the group of extreme close-ups of the baby. In the first such shot, which takes place at the beginning of the scene, the baby smiles the broadest of smiles, thereby winning over the audience immediately—even if the Ogatas are left cold. Yet once the baby starts to cry—and continues crying, as it does in scene after scene without letup—the extreme close-ups become oppressive. The audience wants some distance, if only in the form of a medium shot. In this way, Gosho puts his audience in roughly the same position as the Ogatas, but with one all-important difference: While now identifying with them (and even finding their predicament still comic), the audience never completely loses sympathy for the baby, no matter how long and how loudly it cries.

Similarly, Gosho's *mise en scène* tends to balance audience sympathy equally between the Ogatas and the baby. Consider, for example, his use of deep focus in the establishing shot of the scene. In the mid-foreground of the frame, the baby lies on the floor, alone and helpless, while in the background the Ogatas stand frozen in place, staring at it uncomprehendingly. By including all three characters in the frame, thereby establishing their spatial relationship to one another, Gosho manages to suggest that they are all victims of the situation. If at times during the course of the scene the childish behavior of the Ogatas (such as Ryukichi's covering his ears and going off by himself to eat in peace) seems to risk the loss of audience sympathy, it is only temporary, for Gosho makes it clear that the situation would test the mettle of anyone. Indeed, the audience—understanding the Ogatas perfectly, yet still feeling sympathy for the baby—can only laugh or cry, and hope that somehow all will turn out well. In short, the audience has had its first sample of "Goshoism" in *Where Chimneys Are Seen*.

Invariably, Goshoism expresses belief in the compassion and goodness of the common people. Nowhere is this better illustrated than in the penultimate scene. When the Ogatas refuse to hand over the baby to Katsuko, she runs, distraught, from the house, losing one of her sandals. Yukiko (Chieko Seki), Senko's thoroughly Westernized friend, follows her. In a scene that is quintessentially Gosho in its mixture of pathos and humor, Yukiko, dressed in a fur coat, fancy hat, and high heels, offers the hobbling, kimono-clad Katsuko one of her shoes. At first not knowing whether to laugh or cry, Katsuko takes the shoe, acknowledging Yukiko's effort to comfort her. Yet when she sees Yukiko walking lame, she returns the shoe and thanks her: She, too, is capable of generosity. By the end of the scene, much to the audience's delight, the two women are barefoot and walking side by side. Not only does this resolution demonstrate Yukiko's and Katsuko's goodwill and, by extension, imply that the baby will be returned to its mother, but also it reveals the generosity of spirit that Gosho considers typical of ordinary people.

Like all of Gosho's work in the *shomin-geki*, *Where Chimneys Are Seen* ultimately celebrates everyday life as the most authentically human existence—that is, a life not distorted by false values. To be sure, this existence—as the lives of the Ogatas and their renters indicate—is often filled with hardship, but if happiness is to be attained, it can be attained only by accepting whatever life has to offer and by extending compassion to others. Indeed, Gosho perceives happiness to be something as simple as taking pleasure in learning how to balance a pencil on its end (as Kenzo and Senko do), or in accepting responsibility for an abandoned baby.

Two basic shots, which recur with variations throughout the film, not only express Gosho's attitude toward life but also crystallize his art. The first is a carefully composed shot of the Ogatas' neighborhood, two rows of tenement houses behind which a steep hill rises, spanning the frame. Each time Gosho returns to this shot, a man is pulling his cart over the hill. Though this shot ostensibly serves the narrative by fixing the time of day, its real purpose is to concentrate the audience's attention on the image itself and on the truism that it eloquently visualizes: Life goes on. Clearly meditative in style, this shot represents Gosho at his most Ozu-like; at the same time it is typically Japanese in its evocation of pathos.

The second shot is no less meditative in effect, but its style is unique to Gosho. Here, in the film's most audacious bit of humor, Gosho superimposes the sound of a rooster crowing over the image of three chimneys. Quite obviously, this shot announces a new day, yet its incongruity of sight and sound (and its witty juxtaposition of the urban and the rural) once again prompts the audience to reflect on Gosho's meaning, this time an ironic one. Like all the other chimney shots, this shot conveys the beauty and mystery of life, but in addition it implies that one must be able to appreciate these qualities even in the least likely places. Indeed, life truly is whatever one chooses to make it. In conclusion, these two basic shots, besides reaffirming Gosho's celebration of life, demonstrate his reliance on humor and pathos in order to bring warmth and vitality not only to *Where Chimneys Are Seen* but also to all of his studies of the common people.

*Arthur Nolletti, Jr.*

# THE WHITE HELL OF PITZ PALÜ (DIE WEISSE HÖLLE VOM PITZ PALÜ)

*Origin:* Germany
*Released:* 1929
*Released in U.S.:* 1930
*Production:* Aaga Films/Sokal
*Direction:* G. W. Pabst and Dr. Arnold Fanck
*Assistant direction:* Marc Sorkin
*Screenplay:* Dr. Arnold Fanck and Ladislaus Vajda
*Cinematography:* Sepp Allgeier, Hans Schneeberger, and Richard Angst
*Editing:* no listing
*Art direction:* Erno Metzner
*Music:* silent (original version), Giuseppe Becce (1935 version)
*Running time:* 90 minutes

*Principal characters:*

Maria .......................... Leni Riefenstahl
Hans............................ Ernst Peterson
Dr. Johannes Krafft ................ Gustav Diessl
Maria Krafft........................ Mizzi Gotzel
Christian Klucker .................... Otto Spring
Aviator............................. Ernst Udet
Man in the bar..................... Kurt Gerron

The act of donning lederhosen, grabbing a pickax, binding a coarse rope around your midriff, and climbing straight up the side of an inaccessible peak has occasionally provided the stuff of film fantasy for American filmgoers—from Charles Chaplin in *The Gold Rush* (1925), Stan Laurel and Oliver Hardy in *Swiss Miss* (1938), Ronald Colman in *Lost Horizon* (1937), Clint Eastwood and Richard Burton in *The Eiger Sanction* (1975), Julie Andrews in *The Sound of Music* (1965), to Dwayne Hickman and Frankie Avalon in *Ski Party* (1965). In Germany, however, this passion for mountain climbing and the lure of distant snow-white mountaintops has elicited an entire genre of so-called mountain films, which were popular with German audiences of the 1920's and early 1930's and were revived in a slightly different form as fantasy entertainment in the postwar Germany of the 1950's.

Dr. Arnold Fanck was a geologist, filmmaker, and mountaineer who, in 1920, reacted against the claustrophobia of the German Expressionist cinema: With Homunculus, the Golem, Caligari, and Cesare stalking through Walter Reimann's studio-bound sets, Fanck sought an escape through the snow. In an effort to remove the camera from the studio, Fanck began producing and directing films that were shot beyond the confines of artificial settings, aiming his camera at the frozen natural reality of the mountain ranges of Germany and Austria. The result was a variety of melodramas with Expressionist touches and fresh outdoor settings, a genre that proved highly successful. Among the mountain films directed by Fanck in the 1920's and early 1930's were *Das Wunder des Schneeschuhs* (1920; *Marvels of Ski*), *Im Kampf mit dem Berge* (1921; *Struggling with the Mountain*), *Fuchsjagd im Engadine* (1922; *Fox Hunt in Engadine*), *Der Berg des Schicksals* (1924; *Peak of Fate*), *Der heilige Berg* (1926; *The Holy Mountain*), *Der grosse Sprung* (1927; *The Big Jump*), *Stürme über dem Montblanc* (1930; *Avalanche*), *Der weisse Rausch* (1931; *The White Frenzy*), and *S.O.S. Eisberg* (1933; *S.O.S. Iceberg*). The most quasi-mystical of the genre was a film directed, not by Fanck, but by his actress discovery, Leni Riefenstahl—*Das blaue Licht* (1932; *The Blue Light*).

With the degradation and rape of Germany by the Treaty of Versailles, the fragile and impotent decade of the Weimar Republic in the 1920's, and the shattering hopelessness of the worldwide Depression, the mountain films represented a psychic hope to an embittered population. In these Alpine tales of crippled passions and heroic ideals, the mountain became an amoral nemesis to be overcome. To scale and conquer an overpowering mountain peak became a metaphor for the struggle for life and meaning in a bankrupt German society and culture. Into this void of despair, in which films such as *Geheimnisse einer Seele* (1925; *Secrets of the Soul*), *Sylvester* (1924; *New Year's Eve*), and *Die letzte Mann* (1924; *The Last Laugh*) retreated inward into a psychology of the self, the mountain films offered a sweet balm for the collective German psyche and a hope for a new order and a better world. To conquer and vanquish the ever-present looming mountain, personal conflicts must be set aside and replaced with idealistic heroic virtues: courage, stamina, self-sacrifice, and unbridled enthusiasm.

In this triumph of the will, the mountain will be defeated and the innate superiority of the mountaineer (as opposed to the staid villagers below him) will shine through the freezing snow. This emphasis on superhuman triumphs and heroic accomplishments and the accent on well-scrubbed youthful mountaineers reflected the cultural attitudes that made possible Adolf Hitler's landslide election of 1930.

A kind of cultural schizophrenia is apparent in the narrative construction of the mountain films, in which natural mountain scenes jar with closet Expressionism. As Fanck, who was aware of this defect in his earlier films, was planning *The White Hell of Pitz Palü*, he sought another director to handle the dramatic sequences, while he concentrated on the mountain climbing sequences. The ploy worked: The film proved to be an enormous success, an international hit. It helped that the director whom Fanck chose was one of the paramount directors of the German silent film, G. W. Pabst.

Pabst was highly regarded as a practitioner of the "New Realism," a reaction against the Expressionist tendency in German film, a retreat from intense, studio-bound subjectivity. Pabst had already directed such films as *Die freudlose Gasse* (1925; *The Joyless Street*), *Die Liebe der Jeanne Ney* (1927; *The Love of Jeanne Ney*), and *Die Büchse der Pandora* (1928; *Pandora's Box*). In *The White Hell of Pitz Palü*, Pabst toned down the melodramatic excesses and created interesting camera angles and editing contrasts. Yet the mountain Pitz Palü forever loomed in the camera eye, dominating every scene. Pabst, eyepiece in hand, fell into the cinematic crevice, overpowered by the forces of Expressionism in natural settings. For Fanck, *The White Hell of Pitz Palü* was the triumph of his career. For Pabst, it was hackwork.

The story begins on the mountain and does not come down. Maria (Leni Riefenstahl) and Hans (Ernst Peterson) are spending their honeymoon in a cabin on the Pitz Palü, where Hans relates to Maria the tragic tale of Dr. Johannes Krafft (Gustav Diessl), a doom-laden wreck of a man who spent his own honeymoon in the same cabin with his bride (also named Maria). During an avalanche, Krafft lost Maria to the mountain. Since that time, Krafft has devoted his life to searching for his lost bride, stalking the Pitz Palü. Hans tells Maria that Krafft is known in the mountains as "the Ghost of Pitz Palü." At this point, Krafft suddenly appears in the doorway. He shares the cabin with them, and all three sleep in the same bed. Maria is attracted to Krafft and his obsession with Pitz Palü and ignores Hans. In the morning, Krafft leaves a note telling of his intention to scale Pitz Palü. First Hans, and then Maria, rush to join him on his ascent. Undeterred by a warning by Krafft's old mountain guide, Christian (Otto Spring), that an avalanche is expected on the mountain, the three mountain climbers go off.

After they rest from an arduous climb on a cliff, Hans insists that he should take the lead on the next leg of their ascent up the mountain face. As they begin their climb, an avalanche occurs. Hans loses his grip and falls off the mountain. Krafft rescues him, breaking his leg in the process. A blizzard develops, and the three are stranded on a mountain ledge—Hans in the first stages of freezing to death and Krafft applying a splint to his broken leg. Some students spot them and attempt a rescue, but the blizzard sweeps them off the mountainside to their deaths on the mountain's north wall. In the village below, Christian organizes two rescue parties to look for the students and the Krafft party. The students are discovered frozen to death. Meanwhile, the Krafft party awaits rescuers on the ledge. The famous German war ace Ernst Udet (played by himself), alerted to their plight, takes off in his biplane and scans the mountain passes in search of them. Udet spots Maria, Hans, and Krafft and signals the villagers as to their location. Krafft sees Udet fly away and gives up hope; wrapping Hans in his jacket, he leaves the young couple. The villagers arrive and rescue Hans and Maria, and Christian discovers a note from Krafft in Maria's coat.

The note reads, "Dear old Christian, don't try to find me. Save the others. I have gone to her." In the last shot of the film, Krafft is seen frozen in the ice caves of Pitz Palü.

Like the translucent sheen of ice that clouds Krafft's body at the end of the film, a cocoon of fatalism swathes the entire film (much in the same way as Fate engulfs the Expressionist film canon that the mountain films were outwardly reacting against). The brutal, ice-covered precipice of Pitz Palü becomes the embodiment of predestination in the film, casting its shadow over Krafft, Maria, Hans, and the villagers.

Just as Krafft is drawn to the mountain in a futile search for his dead bride, so Maria and Hans are drawn to the mountain's awesome mystery. The villagers, too, live their dangerous and precarious lives under the mountain's spell. The unearthly pull of Pitz Palü is imaged by the framing of the mountain through the rustic windowpanes of the cabin window. In tremendous long-shots of imposing magnitude, Pitz Palü dwarfs human figures and affairs, rendering human beings as tiny, insignificant forms on the mountainscape. Minute lines of skiers appear as dots on the white, snow-covered slopes, villagers in the search party are minuscule black forms arising from the icy, mountain mist, students are thrown into the abyss by an avalanche like papier-mâché puppets.

Indeed, the mountain itself is invested with qualities of will and feeling: A title introducing Maria and Hans in their honeymoon cabin refers to Pitz Palü as having "seen grim tragedy . . . and great happiness," while in another title, the mountain is endowed with a respiratory system: "Palü roars defiance . . . her icy breath becomes an armor of freezing vapor." Pitz Palü is also given to motherly rage: "As if angered by prayers soaring upward, Palü thunders with fury . . . resolved to keep her prey." (Quite a reversal from another well-known film taking place in snowy expanses—*Nanook of the North*, 1922.) In that film, although nature is amoral and a trial to man, the human characteristics still belong to the Eskimo family and not the natural elements. In addition, *Nanook of the North* is a celebration of man's survival against nature and not an exploration of man's insignificance and submission to primal forces beyond his reason.)

If Pitz Palü is given human characteristics, the human characters are, in turn, depicted as automatons, doomed to act out their obsessions without stopping to reason. Significantly, Johannes Krafft is a doctor who has abandoned his profession to stalk Pitz Palü in search of his lost bride. As Hans explains to Maria, "He's been searching for her until he's half mad . . . Palü draws him like a magnet. People call him the Ghost of Pitz Palü." Yet Hans and Maria are no less possessed than Krafft; the mountain is devouring their souls. Although they are newlyweds, Maria finds more excitement lying on her back and gazing at a melting icicle than frolicking with Hans outside their honeymoon cabin. Once they scale the mountain, Hans virtually becomes a living corpse. Wrapped in tattered clothing and casting his eyes heavenward as he freezes to death, Hans, in his glazed expression and stiff posture, resembles no one so much as Paul Wegener in *Der Golem* (1920; *The Golem*) or Conrad Viedt in *Das Kabinett des Dr. Caligari* (1919; *The Cabinet of Dr. Caligari*). The reason that the characters seem consumed with Pitz Palü and are drawn to its mysteries is left unexplained. Just as the mountain is there, so, too, are they lured to it. Pitz Palü has become a substitute for human emotions.

It is appropriate, then, that any human feelings which the characters do possess should be displayed through the nature surrounding them and not by their blank, cypherlike expressions. In the sequence in which Maria, Hans, and Krafft are lying in their cabin bed, nature takes over—the misty dawn breaking through the mountain clouds reflects emotions of attraction and jealousy that are not present on the faces of the actors. The gray mist of clouds is seen parting through the rising sun, and then there is a cut to Krafft lying awake in the cabin bed. There is a cut back to the parting clouds and then back to the cabin bed. Maria, still asleep, turns toward Krafft. The camera cuts back to the clouds moving through the mountains. Back in the cabin bed, Maria rests her head on Krafft's arm. Krafft does not remove his hand. There is a cut back to the moving clouds. In the cabin, Hans awakes. He glances over and sees Maria sleeping with Krafft's arm around her. Once more, there is a cut—but to storm clouds blocking out the sunlight. The playing of the cabin scene is very restrained, allowing the forces of nature to give the best performance of the film, playing out the emotions of the protagonists.

This catatonic technique allows Fanck and Pabst to demonstrate an attraction between Maria and Krafft by framing and cutting, but with no real emotion passing between them. Maria and Krafft are constantly shown together in the same frame, Hans either offscreen or not in the scene. (There are cutaways to Hans, alone, chopping wood or Hans silently freezing on the cliff.) Krafft and Maria are revealed as kindred spirits in that they are always seen performing tasks together—the two chopping wood for the stove in the cabin, Maria touching Krafft's arm as he relates his tragic tale to her, Maria assisting Krafft in applying a splint to his injured leg, Maria coming to Krafft's rescue as she ties up a delirious Hans. Maria holds the same name as Krafft's bride, and they are both seen gazing as though hypnotized at melting icicles. Yet ultimately it is the force of the mountain that binds them together.

In this mystical battle of submission versus reason, the villagers who collectively band together to rescue the mountaineers are portrayed as well-intentioned but inferior to the members of the Krafft party, who submit their will to the power of Pitz Palü. The villagers are seen as ineffective against the forces of nature, their search parties dwarfed in extreme long-shot against the face of the mountain expanse. They are also belittled in a title card that refers to them as "heroic pygmies."

In fact, for all of their efforts, it is not the villagers who rescue the Krafft party. Rather, it is an individual with a link to the glory of the German heroic past, a figure from the shining exploits of World War I, Ernst Udet, the famous German aviator and war ace. While the villagers are seen as puny ants in comparison with Pitz Palü, Udet is shown in low angle close-ups as he calmly flies through the mountain passes in search of the abandoned mountain climbers. With Udet soaring, Germany's heritage on his wing, the storm magically subsides and the sun emerges, allowing Udet to spot the Krafft party. When Udet salutes the villagers and the stranded trio before he disappears into the clouds like an airborne Lone Ranger, the guide, Christian, looks up into the clouds longingly. Now the linkage is complete: With Udet and Pitz Palü, the forces of emotionalism have become bound with the nationalist heroism of Germany's past. German audiences of 1929 clearly identified with this simpleminded heroism: The glory of Germany was fresh and ready to be tapped, erasing the last ten years of despair and heartlessness with the heroic rituals of the Hitler cult.

After *The White Hell of Pitz Palü*, the nationalistic strain became even more intimately linked with the mountain film. In his next film, *Avalanche*, Fanck dwelt lovingly on mountain-peak cloud formations and displays that anticipate the opening shots of Reifenstahl's *Triumph des Willens* (1935; *Triumph of the Will*). In *Berge in Flammen* (1931; *The Doomed Battalion*), a mountain climber capitulates to his destiny by defeating an enemy force and becoming an idealized war hero. In *Der Rebell* (1933; *The Rebel*), an outcast triumphs to become leader in a rebellion of German mountain climbers against a thinly veiled depiction of the French as a ruthless enemy subjugating the German nation.

It took three years for Dr. Johannes Krafft's ice tomb to thaw, but the heat of passion that burned down the Reichstag finally melted the ice. As the ice cleared from the white hell of Pitz Palü, it was not Dr. Johannes Krafft who emerged from the crypt. Instead, it was Adolf Hitler.

*Paul Brenner*

# THE WHITE SHEIK (LO SCEICCO BIANCO)

*Origin:* Italy
*Released:* 1952
*Released in U.S.:* 1956
*Production:* Luigi Rovere for APDC-OFI
*Direction:* Federico Fellini
*Assistant direction:* Stefano Ubezio
*Screenplay:* Federico Fellini, Tullio Pinelli, and Ennio Flaiano; based on a story by Michelangelo Antonioni, Fellini, and Pinelli
*Cinematography:* Arturo Gallea
*Editing:* Rolando Benedetti
*Art direction:* Raffaelo Tolfo
*Makeup:* Franco Titi
*Sound:* Armando Grilli and Walfredo Traversari
*Music:* Nino Rota
*Running time:* 86 minutes

*Principal characters:*

| | |
|---|---|
| Wanda Giardino Cavalli | Brunella Bovo |
| Ivan Cavalli | Leopoldo Trieste |
| Fernando Rivoli | Alberto Sordi |
| Marilena Velardi | Fanny Marchio |
| Ivan's uncle | Ettore Margadonna |
| Fernando's wife | Gina Mascetti |
| Cabiria | Giulietta Masina |

*The White Sheik* is perhaps the least celebrated of Federico Fellini's early films. Coming after his collaboration with Alberto Lattuada on *Luci del varietà* (1950; *Variety Lights*), *The White Sheik* is the first film he directed alone, and it shows, despite its slight reputation, the artist in complete control of his medium. Combining the lives of ordinary people with an examination of the underside of show business, as in *Variety Lights*, *La strada* (1954), and several other films, *The White Sheik* explores its characters' illusions, the contrast between their dreams and the reality in which they find themselves, with subtlety, irony, and affection. Fellini is trying to define his distinctive approach to cinema, attempting to shift the focus of postwar Italian films away from the neorealism that presents characters as formed primarily by society. Fellini makes his protagonists more individualistic.

Ivan Cavalli (Leopoldo Trieste) and his bride Wanda Giardino Cavalli (Brunella Bovo) arrive in Rome from the provinces for their honeymoon and check into a seedy hotel. Ivan has prepared a meticulous itinerary for their visit, beginning with meeting the family of his uncle (Ettore Margadonna), whom Ivan constantly identifies as an influential man at the Vatican, followed by an audience with the Pope, along with two hundred other couples, and a tour of all the city's major sights. While Ivan takes a nap, Wanda sneaks away to meet the man of her dreams, the White Sheik, hero of a series of *fotoromanzi*, comic books with photographs instead of drawings. Wanda, signing herself Impassioned Doll, has corresponded with the actor-model, portraying the White Sheik, and he has invited her to look him up.

Wanda takes a drawing she has made of her idol to the offices of Blue Romance, publisher of such gaudy tales as "The Starry Abyss," "Souls in Torment," "Hearts in the Tempest," and "In the Whirlpool of Love." The editor, Marilena Velardi (Fanny Marchio), is enchanted by the devotion of this wide-eyed innocent. Wanda accompanies the actors, all dressed in exotic Middle Eastern costumes, to a shooting location on the beach at Fregene. There she introduces herself to Fernando Rivoli (Alberto Sordi), presenting him with her drawing. Fernando is flattered by her infatuation and neglects his work to spend time impressing her. He gets Wanda into a slave-girl costume and into the scenes the company is shooting.

The film cuts back and forth between Fernando's efforts to seduce his young admirer and Ivan's attempts to placate his puzzled relatives. Ivan, while searching frantically for Wanda, explains that she is not feeling well, trying to keep his relatives from discovering that she is missing.

Wanda's idyll with Fernando ends when his harridan of a wife (Gina Mascetti) arrives. Left behind at the beach, Wanda catches a ride to Rome with a sleazy man whose advances she rejects. Meanwhile, Ivan wanders off with a sympathetic streetwalker. Wanda, distraught at the mess she has made of her life, tries to end it by jumping off a bridge, only to land in a few inches of the River Tiber. Taken to a mental hospital, she is reunited with Ivan in time to be rushed to another audience with the Pope. Ivan's relatives are pleased finally to meet his bride.

The contrast between illusion and reality is a common theme not only for Fellini but also for Michelangelo Antonioni, who collaborated with Fellini and Tullio Pinelli on the story on which the screenplay of *The White Sheik* was based. Wanda filters all of her experiences through the romantic illusions fostered by popular culture, and Ivan is equally entrapped by his perception of conventional respectability.

The discrepancy between Ivan's and Wanda's view of the world is made clear when they are first seen at the train station upon their arrival in Rome and are separated by a train window. The romantic illusions that they should share are underscored by their riding to their honeymoon hotel in a horse-drawn carriage, but the horse's name is Whitey, a foreshadowing of Wanda's true love. Wanda's fascination with the exotic becomes obvious when they reach the hotel and she stares at two Indian women instead of heeding

Ivan's request to speak to his relatives on the telephone. Wanda drifts off to their room, and the closing of the elevator doors again points to the barriers between the couple.

The conflicting forces working on Wanda are displayed when she walks to the Blue Romance office and passes movie posters, symbols of her dream world, while church bells, representative of her obligations to her husband's world of respectability, are heard in the background. Marilena tells Wanda that dreams are one's true life, but Fellini shows otherwise.

Wanda's first sight of her hero is appropriately romantic. Fernando is suspended high in the air, singing in a swing that is hanging between two very tall, phallic pines. (He has left his sword beside one tree.) Towering above Wanda, he represents the distance between this small-town girl and the fulfillment of her dreams. A character or object suspended between earth and sky is a typical Fellini touch, as with the helicopter carrying the statue of Christ in *La dolce vita* (1960). Fernando, flabby, wearing too much makeup, is a comic caricature of a swashbuckler; this pathetic imitation of Rudolph Valentino emphasizes the falsity of Wanda's dreams. He can only be seen as heroic from far away. Fernando says that their meeting makes him feel the reality of life, but this foolish clown has no conception of reality, avoiding his responsibility to his work in order to show off for Wanda.

When Fernando transforms Wanda into Fatma, faithful slave girl, she has reached the apex of happiness. It does not matter if her hero is frightened of the White Sheik's white stallion. Fernando puts her into a boat, and she says that she is not herself anymore. He has also fallen for the illusion and speaks to her as would the White Sheik. He has even invented a sort of mythology about himself, claiming, when Wanda learns that he is married, that his wife seduced him with a magic potion to keep him from his true love. Yet even on a romantic boat on a romantic sea, reality cannot be seduced, and a sail boom hits Fernando in the head when he tries to kiss Wanda. The boom of truth hits Wanda as she learns that Fernando was a barber before becoming the White Sheik, as he blames Wanda for his failure to work, and as his wife shows up and he calls Wanda a slut and slaps her. Wanda's illusions about the White Sheik are punctured further when she discovers that Fernando's wife did not use a magic potion to entrap him. (Fellini's characters frequently suffer through similar crises on beaches or, as does Ivan when he meets the prostitute, in piazzas late at night.)

Wanda's disillusionment with the White Sheik is shown when she passes the empty swing where she met Fernando, but it is not the loss of her romantic illusions that causes her to attempt suicide: She is simply afraid to face Ivan. Her gazing at statues of angels on the bridge before jumping off proves that her illusions are intact. She intends to die tragically because of a broken heart, like a romantic heroine. Before jumping, she dictates a farewell message to the hotel porter in the clichéd language of Blue Romance.

He stops her to ask how to spell "abyss": Her illusions are more silly than destructive.

Playing a role as much as Wanda does, the very respectable Ivan is living in a different kind of dreamworld where everything supposedly falls into a perfect order. Fellini makes clear at the beginning of the film that Ivan is not as much in control of his destiny as he thinks when his hat, symbol of his dignity, is knocked off at the train station. His warning to a porter to handle his suitcase carefully because the contents are breakable reinforces the flimsiness of his illusions. Ivan is obsessed by appearance, criticizing Wanda for going to their hotel room without him because it looks bad for a lady to be alone with a porter. Their behavior to his influential uncle must be perfect, Ivan explains, since he intends to be town secretary of Altavilla Marittima in two months. Indeed, he has his whole life planned out, just as he has a schedule for all of their activities in Rome. This schedule ends with the couple's having a good night's rest; no time for romance is included.

Chaos quickly enters Ivan's well-ordered world when Wanda sneaks off for her rendezvous. She has left a bathtub overflowing; a black priest speaks to Ivan in an incomprehensible tongue; Ivan goes looking for Wanda and gets in the path of a military band (representative of his belief in order); he is pushed by the crowd following the band, and his dignified hat is trampled. Later, for the sake of his relatives, whom Fellini always shoots as a group as if they are about to pounce on Ivan, he must pretend to be having a telephone conversation with Wanda. Ivan goes to the police for help but will not give his name, for fear it will get into the newspapers. The ink he accidentally smears on his face represents the potential blot on his reputation and his loss of control over his life. Leaving the police station, he becomes entangled with a marching squad of police. He cannot, therefore, fit in with the order of the military or of the law. These two ordered groups contrast with the disarray of the actors when Wanda first meets them. (Such processions of people, both organized and disorganized, appear throughout Fellini's films.) It becomes clear that Ivan's respectability is all pretension; his going with the prostitute indicates his hypocrisy, his general weakness. He has completely lost control of his life and faints when he hears that Wanda is in a mental hospital.

Given their misperceptions of reality, it is appropriate that the couple is reunited in an asylum. Ivan's relatives have had doubts about his sanity, as have a policeman and a taxi driver. At the hospital, Ivan does not want to hear any explanations. Concerned foremost with what he calls the honor of the family, he wants only to get to the Pope as quickly as possible. The Church has no religious significance here; organized religion is important merely for fitting into its ordered place in the superficial lives of people such as Ivan.

Some critics have said that the couple is freed of illusions at the end of the film, but Ivan is as much a slave to his schedule and to appearances as he was at the beginning, arriving at Piazza San Pietro on time and greeting his relatives as if nothing has happened. For her part, Wanda tells Ivan that he is now her White Sheik. She cannot love him simply as Ivan; she must hold on to her romantic dreams. The final shot of a statue of an angel hovering over the procession climbing the steps of Saint Peter's Basilica emphasizes this point. Such fools need the protection of angels.

The style of *The White Sheik*, like that of all Fellini's early efforts, is very simple, but deceptively so. His use of objects such as Ivan's hat and Fernando's swing to make thematic points visually indicates the director's assured control. Likewise, his cutting between Wanda's and Ivan's scenes displays his skill at ironic juxtaposition, as when he shifts from Fernando's attempts to seduce Wanda to Ivan and his relatives at a performance of Wolfgang Amadeus Mozart's *Don Giovanni* (1787). Though Fellini satirizes the foolish illusions of his protagonists and offers no hope that they will ever be free of them, his satire is gentle and good-natured, with none of the misanthropy of his later films.

In *The White Sheik*, Fellini explored themes which he was to develop more fully in later films; he was already well on his way to attaining a masterful visual style. It is not surprising that perhaps his best film, *I vitelloni* (1953), was his next project. Another of his masterpieces, *Le notti di Cabiria* (1957; *The Nights of Cabiria*), is an expansion of the story of a minor character in *The White Shiek*, Cabiria (Giulietta Masina), the prostitute friend of the woman who goes off with Ivan. The most important achievement of this film is Fellini's ability to capture the rhythm of ordinary lives in a way not seen before in Italian cinema.

*Michael Adams*

# THE WHITE-HAIRED GIRL
# (PAI MAO NU)

*Origin:* People's Republic of China
*Released:* 1970
*Released in U.S.:* no listing
*Production:* no listing
*Direction:* Sang Hu
*Screenplay:* Shanghai Dance School, "White-Haired Girl" Unit; based on the stage opera by the Lu Hsun Art Academy
*Cinematography:* Shen Xilin
*Editing:* no listing
*Art direction:* no listing
*Music:* no listing
*MPAA rating:* no listing
*Running time:* no listing

*Principal characters:*
Yang Bailao.......................... Dong Xilin
Xi'er.............................. Mao Huifang
Landlord Huang.................... Wang Guojun
Wang Dachun...................... Ling Jiaming

From the mid-1960's into the early 1970's, the Cultural Revolution in China created a unique political condition in which the cultural future of China, in particular film productions, came under the jurisdiction of a former actress, Lan Ping, who became Chiang Ching after she was married to Mao Tse-tung. It is impossible to separate the making of *The White-Haired Girl* (1970) from the influence exerted by this influential woman. If there ever was a real studio boss in China, it was she, and this was her pet project. As the wife of Chairman Mao, she attained a political height that rivaled that of the former Empress Dowager. Under her watchful eyes, the Chinese film industry experienced a blazing authority that resulted in productions coming to a halt with studios "purified" by their closing. Chiang Ching had her own set of ideas of what politically correct films should be, and she was responsible for both undermining the immense progress made in Chinese cinema and creating a unique and exclusively Chinese film form: the revolutionary ballet film. *The White-Haired Girl*, along with the equally well-known *The Red Detachment of Women* (1960) and *East Is Red* (1964), bore the stamp of her particular vision.

The legend of *The White-Haired Girl* originated in Northwest Hopei, China, during the period of the anti-Japanese resistance. When the area was liberated by the eighth route army, the legend was embroidered to include the participation of the Red soldiers. The original story tells of a young peasant girl whose hair turned white as a result of her ordeals at the hands of tyrannical oppressors. The first theatrical version was written as a stage opera by the Lu Hsun Art Academy of Yenan in 1944. This version told of the girl's rape, her subsequent pregnancy and delivery in the mountains, and the suicide of her father. In 1950, the first film version was produced in a naturalistic manner. This film treatment includes the rape and the pregnancy, but in it the child dies at birth. Chiang Ching's film ballet rejected what she felt was a portrayal of the peasants as feeble and inferior people. In the final rendition, she removed the rape and the child, and instead of committing suicide, the father is beaten to death by henchmen. While these changes emphasized a more positive theme of active resistance and reconstruction in new China, it can be added that for purely practical purposes, since the story was choreographed into a ballet, it would have been difficult to allow for a pregnant ballerina. Working with the Shanghai Dance Institute, Chiang Ching managed to bring together many of the puzzling contradictions within revolutionary China. While Party members of good standing were suddenly sent to the farms for reeducation in political and cultural purity, Chiang Ching insisted that it was revolutionary to put a peasant's toes into a pair of ballet slippers.

The ballet film follows a simple plot. During the war of resistance against the Japanese, the peasant Yang Bailao (Dong Xilin) and his daughter Xi'er (Mao Huifang) are preparing for the Chinese New Year. Their landlord, Huang (Wang Guojun), a most despicable man, comes to demand payment of debts incurred by peasant Yang. When Yang is unable to pay, he is beaten to death by the landlord's henchmen, and Xi'er is claimed by the despot as a "prize." Wang Dachun (Ling Jiaming), Xi'er's neighbor and childhood sweetheart, is filled with hatred and leaves the poor village to join with the eighth route army. Mistreated by the landlord, Xi'er escapes into the mountains. Xi'er suffers from hunger and constant hardship until her hair and garments turn white (the symbol of purity and righteousness). The eighth route army comes to the village and arouses the peasants to expose traitors of the revolution. Huang the landlord is arrested for his many heinous crimes and sentenced to death. The lovers are reunited, but Xi'er has become a revolutionary. She takes up the rifle and joins the eighth route army for the class struggle.

As cinema, *The White-Haired Girl* has many failings. It offers old-fashioned choreography that sometimes borders on tediousness, with a special emphasis on the gesture of a clenched fist. Actors are forced to play one-dimensional characters with melodramatic expressions, and close-ups of heavily made-up faces in revolutionary zeal are often cartoonish, unrealistic, and unbelievable. *The White-Haired Girl* also has a weak score and suffers from a lack of cinematic creativity. It is simply a filmed stage piece with a static and unimaginative camera that routinely cuts off the dancer's head or feet in mid-shots. The editing shows a similar amateurishness: Cuts from shot to shot are often abrupt and awkward. As the critic R. G. Davis observed, "The simplicity of the ballet and the clumsiness of the camera combine to produce neither a ballet story nor a filmic story, but rather a programmatic series of images." It is as if the ideological power of film, coupled with the ideological powers of the Gang of Four, created such a panic that filmmakers limited themselves strictly to "safe" projects.

Certainly, many have witnessed the decline of once-revered filmmakers after the Communist rise to power. While some were simply accused and "retired" from their activities, others paid dearly during the Cultural Revolution. Even the greatest actors, such as Shi Hui and Chao Tan, were imprisoned, the former forced to take a fatal swim against his will. It is not surprising that even the staunchest preferred to work in the safety of ballet-record films or simple newsreel-type documentaries. Those who resisted could find themselves in prison cells. The history of China's film industry has been fraught with social strain and strife amid a national state of continual war. From its earliest existence, there has been no business like Chinese show business. To survive, a filmmaker had to bribe government officials for script approval, pay under the table to bankers to extend production credits, go underground to escape invading armies, Koumintang armies, Red armies, and beat off thugs and gangsters lest one's studio be burned to the ground. It is practically a miracle that this film industry survived, let alone that it created an artistic tradition that rivals those of the great national cinemas. It must be noted that in the midst of havoc, the Chinese almost always manage to create a beautiful tune, a new line of poetry, or a new approach to express their social criticisms and common wisdom. In like manner, the Cultural Revolution fathered the school of "Theatrical Realism" by seeking to enhance the Communist ideology that films are not a form of entertainment but are, rather, politically didactic, useful in enhancing the revolutionary consciousness of the masses. As a puzzling contradiction, a film such as *The White-Haired Girl*, while it pales in comparison to other Chinese classics, remains the film that is most identified as a Chinese film with an exclusively Chinese film language.

As a rule, Chinese filmmakers have sought to produce a distinctive national film language since the first Chinese fictional film, *The Suffering Couple*, was made in 1913. By the 1930's and the 1940's, Chinese filmmaking reached a golden period. China had an industry that produced notable pictures that featured great stars: In the 1930's, there were *The Highway* (1934), *Song of the Fishermen* (1934), *Street Angel* (1937), and *New Women* (1934), the latter starring the legendary Ruan Ling-Yu. The 1940's culminated in such classics as *Horse over the Cliff* (1947) and *Crows and Sparrows* (1949).

While the period of filmmaking before the Revolution was a dynamic one, a valid criticism remains: The films were unduly influenced by Western culture. Some of the themes found in those Chinese films, while transformed into Chinese patterns, nevertheless had their roots in Western literature, and at times these films blatantly replicated their Western counterparts. The task before Chiang Ching, during the Cultural Revolution, was to purify Chinese art, not only purging it of the influence of the West, but also, more to the point, ridding it of the petty bourgeoise forms that emanated from these influences. China, according to the Gang of Four, was in danger of having its revolution betrayed by its art forms. Mao Tse-tung, in his talks on art and literature in Yenan, emphasized the importance of heroic resistance; a film such as *The White-Haired Girl* is meant to be proletarian in story, in form, even in distribution, so that the popular model to which the masses in China have been subjected for generations is reshaped into a revolutionary battle cry. It must be added that while the conceptual debate of art's role in politics and vice versa continues, China during the Cultural Revolution was experiencing more than a crisis in its art forms. The Cultural Revolution was in fact a euphemism for the bitter struggle between the left wing and the pragmatists, who are less concerned with ideological purity than with the modernization of China.

*The White-Haired Girl* is a revolutionary ballet filmed from a stage production. The phenomenon of putting before an audience of farmers and peasants (who hardly ever pirouetted on their way to work) a group of slippered "heroes" and "heroines" was certainly an experiment that stretched the boundaries of the proletarian revolution in those days. R. G. Davis suggested that since "bound feet were outlawed in China when the Revolution came, in 1949, and since bound feet had been fetishized sexually, the slippered feet of the ballerinas at work may thus have an important cultural echo and attraction." Whatever the motive, there is no question that dance, on the international level, has been affected by this peasant ballet, in particular as it reflects movements in everyday work and home habits. This is an enduring achievement of *The White-Haired Girl*.

*Daniel Kwan*

# THE WHOLE SKY (SARA AKAASH)

*Origin:* India
*Released:* 1969
*Released in U.S.:* 1982
*Production:* Cineye Films
*Direction:* Basu Chatterji
*Screenplay:* Basu Chatterji; based on the novel by Rajendra Yadav
*Cinematography:* K. K. Mahajan
*Editing:* G. G. Mayekar
*Art direction:* no listing
*Music:* Salil Chowdhury
*MPAA rating:* no listing
*Running time:* 100 minutes

*Principal characters:*

Samar ............................ Rakesh Pandey
Prabha ........................... Madhu Chanda
Samar's father ....................... A. K. Hangal
Samar's mother ...................... Dina Pathak
Samar's elder brother.................. Mani Kaul
Bhabhi ............................ Tarla Mehta
Munni ........................... Nandita Thakur
Samar's college friend ................. Jalal Agha

During the 1970's, Basu Chatterji, the prolific director of *The Whole Sky*, created his own kind of "middle cinema," halfway between the escapist extravaganzas of India's commercial cinema and the socially conscious, aesthetically innovative movement known as the New Cinema. The genre he carved out for himself in more than twenty films in the decade of the 1970's is that of the light, romantic comedy, naturalistic in style, and directed toward an educated, urban, middle-class audience whose problems he treats with a light, affectionate touch. Yet Chatterji's first film, *The Whole Sky*, was quite different in style and became a milestone in the development of the Indian New Cinema. The film is a sharply observed portrait of a young college student who refuses to accept the wife his parents have pressured him into marrying. In many ways, it constitutes a strong indictment of oppressive, traditional patterns of marriage and power relationships within the joint family.

*The Whole Sky* was shot on a small budget, entirely on location, in black and white, without the stars or obligatory song-and-dance numbers of the Indian formula film. In the manner of its production as well as in its style and handling of subject matter, Chatterji's film was a striking contrast to the prevalent modes of commercial cinema. Like many subsequent New Cinema films, Chatterji's directorial debut was made possible by a loan from the government-funded Film Finance Corporation, under an innovative policy for encouraging the production of serious, experimental, low-budget films. *The Whole Sky* was released in 1969, a watershed year for India's New Cinema. The film's critical and popular success not only launched Chatterji's career but also—along with Mrinal Sen's *Bhuvan Shome* (1969; *Mr. Shome*)—initiated the Hindi wave of the New Cinema. For the New Cinema, filming in Hindi meant potential access to audiences much larger than the limited audiences of regional cinema. (Among India's sixteen official languages, Hindi is the most widely understood and has long been the dominant language of the commercial film.)

Chatterji made *The Whole Sky* with a crew of young graduates from India's national film school. His own film education, like that of many of the younger New Cinema directors, came through film societies and books. Living in Bombay, India's film capital, Chatterji worked for almost twenty years as a cartoonist for *Blitz*, a weekly leftist tabloid; he was especially inspired by the comedies of Czech directors Miloš Forman and Jiří Menzel and the work of Satyajit Ray, at that time India's only filmmaker of international stature. Such films were not commercially released in Bombay but were widely circulated on the film-society circuit. Just as most of Ray's finest films have been based on contemporary Bengali-language fiction, so New Cinema directors working in Hindi drew on modern Hindi fiction, a practice long abandoned in commercial cinema. The *nai kahani* (new story) movement in Hindi literature played an especially invigorating role for directors such as Basu Chatterji, Mani Kaul, and the late Awtar Krisha Kaul. Chatterji based *The Whole Sky* on a novel by *nai kahani* writer Rajendra Yadav, which was published in 1960.

As the film opens, a traditional Hindu wedding ceremony is in progress, interrupted by a series of flashbacks which rapidly reveal how Samar (Rakesh Pandey), the bridegroom, has been pressured into an arranged marriage. Only midway through his college studies, Samar is an idealistic young man who sees himself as a budding leader, following the path of his guru (portrayed by Chatterji himself in a brief Hitchcockian cameo appearance) and inspiring other young men to struggle in the tradition of India's patriotic leaders. His marriage, however, rudely shatters his daydreams. Through the fantasies and flashbacks of the opening sequence, Chatterji quickly establishes the main figures in Samar's life, economically sketches in their motivations, and deftly outlines the web of joint-family constraints which ensnares the helpless Samar. His mother (Dina Pathak) believes that it is time to bring another daughter-in-law into the large household to help with the many chores. His father (A. K. Hangal), still struggling to pay off debts incurred by the marriage of Samar's sister Munni (Nandita Thakur), is eager for the dowry money he expects a bride to bring. Over Samar's protests, the father makes emphatically clear that Samar's first duty must be to the family. Samar's older brother's wife Bhabhi (Tarla Mehta) urges Samar to accept the marriage in a teasing, semiseductive style that suits the traditional relationship between a sister-in-law and a younger brother-in-law. She, too, stands to gain from the marriage—a new bride in the house will not only relieve her of much burdensome work but also raise her status to that of senior daughter-in-law. Finally, there is Prabha (Madhu Chanda), the bride herself: She is a high school graduate and will therefore be the first educated woman in the family. She and Samar are total strangers. As the ceremony progresses, it is clear that Samar's thoughts are only of escape from this unwanted marriage.

Instead, he finds himself alone with Prabha on their wedding night. As he contemplates the distance between them, another couple appears—young, romantic lovers, on *their* wedding night, in a scene taken from a well-known popular film. The screen bride bends to touch the groom's feet, in a traditional gesture of wifely submission. Prabha completes the action, in a perfect match-cut—but only in Samar's imagination. In life, she stands, patiently waiting, shyly turned away from Samar. Samar's own shyness prevents him from making a first move. His expectations turn to uncertainty and fear. Finally, unable to bear his mounting agitation, he runs out of the room in anger. He escapes to the roof, where he has the whole starry sky to himself. Not a word has been exchanged between the groom and the lovely young bride.

Chatterji traces the descending spiral of relations between Samar and Prabha as Samar's confused emotions are reinforced by the interplay of domestic politics within the joint family. When Samar is teased and then admonished by his family for not sleeping with his wife, he retreats further into hostility toward Prabha. He refuses to speak to her or to eat the first meal she prepares for him, which Bhabhi, the jealous senior daughter-in-law, ruins by covertly adding extra salt. When Samar's sympathetic sister, Munni, tries to engineer a rapprochement by arranging an outing to see a film, Samar's speed leaves Prabha walking twenty paces behind him, and when a college friend standing in front of the theater asks if Prabha is his new bride, Samar hastily denies it and moves on without entering the theater. Back home, the family heaps more and more household tasks on Prabha. Samar's continued rejection and cruelty toward her apparently sanctions their exploitation of her. The family comes to assume that whatever is wrong with the marriage must be her fault. Meanwhile, Bhabhi, jealous of Prabha's beauty and education, eggs Samar on in his sullen rejection while playing the role of his confidante and adviser. When Prabha is away visiting her parents, Samar daydreams about her, and his feelings begin to soften: He actually looks forward to her return. When she does come back, however, he is unable to break through his false pride. Once again expecting her to make the first move, he is disappointed and retreats further into his stubborn anger.

The tension reaches a peak when Prabha unwittingly uses a lump of sacred clay for cleaning some pots. Samar slaps her before the entire family and speaks to her for the first time, abusing her and calling her an atheist. Finally, an insult from her mother-in-law, who accuses her of immorality because she spends much of her time looking out a window, leads Prabha to escape at night to the roof, where she sobs uncontrollably. They have long been sleeping in separate rooms, but Samar, on this night, cannot sleep. He goes up to the roof and discovers Prabha, weeping. He reaches out and comforts her. They talk together for the first time and spend the night holding each other under the whole sky.

Chatterji's film at one level is a depiction of Samar's inner turmoil, but at another it is an examination of the rigid structures, and the possibilities for cruelty, within the traditional joint family. Samar thinks of himself as a modern and progressive young man, yet he is not free to reject his parents' wishes. Like the male protagonists of many other New Cinema films, Samar wants to rebel but cannot. The potential cruelty of the authoritarian traditional family is underscored in the subplot of Samar's unhappily married sister, Munni. She is Prabha's only friend in the family, partly because of her own unhappy experience in marriage. Munni has had to return home after her husband took up with another woman. When the husband, after being abandoned by his mistress, comes to claim Munni, her father insists on sending her back despite her desperate protests, which are supported by other family members. With traditional authority behind him, Munni's father sends her off in misery.

The oppressive potential of the traditional joint family is shown most strongly in the treatment accorded Prabha. In the North Indian pattern of marriage, a daughter leaves the protection of her own family to enter a family of strangers, generally far from the home where she has grown up. As a new bride, she enters at the lowest niche of the family power structure, totally under the authority of her in-laws. She may become part of a system of sequential oppression in which older female members of the family take out their repressed anger on the newest woman to enter the household.

The enmity between sisters-in-law in the joint family is a cultural cliché often true in life, but one that has been exaggerated into a stereotype in commercial films. In his handling of the character of Bhabhi, Chatterji suggests the pattern of the former victim turning into an oppressor, but in both the writing and direction of the role, he succumbs to the cinematic stereotype of the wicked sister-in-law, weakening the effect of the character.

In other respects, however, Chatterji makes telling use of references to the romantic clichés of commercial cinema. He shows humorously and incisively the enormous role that films play in the lives of young people. Samar's images of romance and sexuality are all derived from films. On his wedding night, a film image of the perfect wedding night comes between the reality of him and Prabha. During Prabha's absence, when he begins to long for her, he visualizes their coming together in standard film clichés of young lovers chasing each other and playing on a swing. When he goes with friends to the cinema, the viewer sees a typical scene of young lovers singing to each other. At the film's climax, when he is trying to decide, at last, whether to approach the weeping Prabha, Samar recalls the same scene in a flashback; this time, however, it helps to impel him to action. Through his use of these recurring film images, Chatterji not only comments on the role of films in the inner life of the young but also underscores the gulf between Samar's adolescent emotions and the adult role into which he has suddenly been forced. The romantic film images which are his "teachers" are as childish as Samar's own emotions. Nothing in his experience has prepared him to deal with the feelings and responsibilities he now confronts.

Chatterji represents Samar's conflicting emotions partly through expressionistic techniques within the film's basically naturalisitc framework. The film is composed of many short episodes, acutely observed and often linked through abrupt and surprising transitions. Its style was influenced both by 1960's European experimentation and by the earlier tradition of German Expressionism, but at the time it was made, in the context of Indian cinema, *The Whole Sky* was stylistically fresh and innovative. Chatterji uses freeze-frames, slow motion, aural or visual flashbacks, and quotes from and allusions to other films in order to convey Samar's romantic fantasies and fears, and as counterpoint to the emotional poverty of Samar's and Prabha's actual encounters. In one of the film's most dramatic sequences, depicting Samar's tensions on his wedding night, Chatterji rapidly cuts together fragmented images of faces and symbolic objects (shot with distorting lighting, wide-angle lenses, and reversed to negative film) into an expressionistic crescendo reflecting Samar's mounting agitation. Later in the film, the influence of German Expressionism operates less effectively. In an attempt to convey the complexity of Samar's tortured emotions beneath his rigid exterior, Chatterji shows Samar in reality and in imagination contemplating a rushing train. The train represents Samar's secret fear that his abusive behavior may lead Prabha to commit suicide, perhaps by throwing herself under a train. The recurrent use of the train motif, accompanied by Samar's guilt-ridden thoughts in voice-over, is heavy-handed and one of the film's least successful strategies.

Through the use of location shooting, rare in Indian cinema at the time, Chatterji situated his drama in the small city of Agra, with its narrow lanes and its ironically evoked associations with that monument to romantic love, the Taj Mahal. The claustrophobic atmosphere of the joint family's small, middle-class house is effectively established through his filming of the cramped quarters, especially the narrow stairwell on which Samar and Prabha repeatedly squeeze past each other as though they were strangers. The house is depicted as a place without freedom or privacy, a prison from which the confused Samar escapes—to the countryside, to the cinema, and up to the roof.

The film's final rooftop scene, when Samar for the first time speaks to Prabha and comforts her, serves to resolve the emotional tension between them, but this tender resolution obscures the film's hard look at the inequities of an oppressive system of familial authority. The viewer has not been prepared for Samar's sudden and quite melodramatic turnabout, which offers a happy ending that conforms to the conventions of Indian commercial cinema. Throughout the film, Samar has been driven by childish emotions. The viewer has seen no evidence of his inner growth. The sight of Prabha's tears provides him the opportunity for the first time to act the part of the grown-up, to comfort and cradle and caress her, and behave at last like a "man." Yet Prabha's tears, her patience and fortitude, are in the mold of the long-suffering heroine of folklore and popular cinema. She has won him as a husband but through endurance and tears, not through a process of growth and mutual discovery. Indeed, the conclusion seems to reinforce the traditional stereotype of the patient and submissive Indian woman. When Samar mumbles that no one is to blame for what has happened, though perhaps it was his fault, and Prabha, despite all that she has endured, accepts these few words as sufficient recompense, the evasive ending undercuts the well-observed and incisive critique that has preceded it. The viewer is left with a powerful but flawed film which, in its resolution, seems to evade the responsibilities previously assumed with distinction and with courage.

*Mira Reym Binford*

# WHO'S THAT SINGING OVER THERE? (KO TO TAMO PEVA)

*Origin:* Yugoslavia
*Released:* 1980
*Released in U.S.:* 1984
*Production:* Centar Film
*Direction:* Slobodan Šijan
*Screenplay:* Dušan Kovačević
*Cinematography:* Božidar Nikolić
*Editing:* Lana Vukobratović
*Art direction:* Veljko Despotović
*Music:* Vojislav Kostić
*MPAA rating:* no listing
*Running time:* 83 minutes

*Principal characters:*
Krstić .............................. Pavle Vuisić
Miško ........................ Aleksandar Berček
Singer ........................... Dragan Nikolić
Mr. Moustache .................. Danilo Stojković
Bride ............................... Neda Arnerić
Bridegroom ....................... Slavko Štimac
Aleksa Simić....................... Milivoje Tomić
Hunter ............................. Taško Načić
Bald man..................... Borislav Stjepanović
Young Gypsy ....................... Nenad Kostić
Older Gypsy ..................... Miodrag Kostić

In 1981, *Who's That Singing over There?*, Slobodan Šijan's first feature film, won the Prix Georges Sadoul as the Best Foreign Film Shown in France, was screened during "Un Certain Regard" at the Cannes International Film Festival, and played to high praise at festivals in Rotterdam, Mannheim, Cairo, Chicago, Vevey in Switzerland (where it won a Special Jury Prize for Comedy), and Montreal (where it won the Prix Spécial of the Jury). Šijan's film presents a robust and diverse cross section of Serbian country folk on a dilapidated bus bound for Belgrade on April 5, 1941, a few days before the Germans invaded Yugoslavia during World War II. The title refers to the film as a whole, which is presented as a "song" sung, and thus narrated by, two young Gypsy musicians, who are part of this picaresque misadventure. The title becomes both ironic and significant by the end of the film, when the viewer learns that the only survivors of the journey are the Gypsies, that nomadic minority group in Yugoslav culture which has traditionally lived outside the social mainstream.

Slobodan Šijan, born in Belgrade in 1946, was graduated from the Film Division of the Faculty of Dramatic Arts in Belgrade in 1975, having studied under the acclaimed director Živojin Pavlović. With a degree in painting as well, from the Academy of Pictorial Arts, Šijan's job was to help manage the film programs for the Belgrade Students' Cultural Center. Unlike many other Yugoslav directors, who began with documentary films, Šijan is representative of a new generation of directors since the late 1970's who got their start through television films. He has five telefilms to his credit, and even *Who's That Singing over There?* began as a television project, later expanding into a feature film.

It is clear from this film and from his two subsequent features that Šijan has a special flair for a picaresque and vibrant form of comedy in the tradition of Aristophanes, François Rabelais, and Giovanni Boccaccio in literature, and Luis Buñuel and John Ford in film. Unlike Roman comedy, which emphasizes romance, the Aristophanic approach concerns a middle-aged or older character who creates his own world and proceeds to live in it despite its opposition to an existing order. This individualistic and anarchistic brand of comedy certainly holds true for Šijan's second feature, *Maratonci trče počasni krug* (1982; *The Marathon Runners Run Their Lap of Honor*), which, like *Who's That Singing over There?*, was scripted by the popular Yugoslav playwright Dušan Kovačević. In this film, based on Kovačević's hit play, five generations of men (the women have all died off) in a family which runs a mortuary business create their own chaotic and patriarchal community, organized according to their own rules. A film full of devilish black humor (the family is not above helping its customers toward death in order to improve business), Šijan's second feature, like Aristophanes' plays, is topical. By opening with documentary footage of the assassination of King Alexander in Marseilles in 1934, Šijan not only relates history, and his story, through the theme of death, but also sets up his film to be taken metaphorically as a reflection on Yugoslav society in the troubled period between the world wars.

His 1983 film *Kako sam sistematski uništen od idiota* (*How I Was Systematically Destroyed by Idiots*) is also in the Aristophanic satiric and nonromantic tradition of comedy. Based on a novel about a real-life character, it concerns a middle-aged Yugoslav male dissident who in 1968 grieves the loss of Cuban revolutionary Che Guevara and his austere form of Marxism. Believing that Yugoslav socialism has become decadent, Šijan's protagonist wanders the countryside and Belgrade trying to preach and live the gospel according to Che. Unlike Aristophanes, who usually has his characters triumph over their surroundings, Šijan presents endings in which his protagonists become victims of their times. "Che," for example, dies having seen none of his ideals realized. In this sense, Šijan's work is squarely within a tradition of Yugoslav cinema which since the 1960's has often used black humor and comedy for satiric purposes without offering a "happy ending." The emphasis on an almost entirely male society is also typical of both Yugoslav society, which has traditionally been strongly patriarchal, and Yugoslav cinema, which has seldom involved itself with the portrayal of women other than as sexual objects or as traditional, subservient home creatures. Finally, like Buñuel, Šijan shows a degree of affection for his obsessed males, whom he also feels free to satirize almost to the point of caricature. As in the spirit of Aristophanic comedy, the result of Šijan's films is one of acceptance, rather than rejection, of human folly.

*Who's That Singing over There?* is presented from start to finish as a spontaneous folk song composed by two wandering Gypsies. As the film opens, one tall Gypsy (Miodrag Kostić) playing an accordion and a short lad (Nenad Kostić) whose face is obscured by his hat look straight at the camera and thus at the audience. They sing about dawn rising and a bus that will go to Belgrade. The choral line repeated throughout the film is "I sing to sing my pain away." In this direct manner, Šijan establishes a link with the audience as in a theatrical performance: What is about to unfold is a song, a play, a folktale, and a film.

In a barren rural landscape shot in dull pastels throughout the film by cinematographer Božidar Nikolić, many of the passengers are introduced, one by one, as they await the bus. (The words, "Somewhere in Serbia, April 5, 1941" have previously appeared on the screen.) There is a would-be singer-playboy (Dragan Nikolić), complete with greasy dark hair and a pencil moustache, headed for an "audition" in Belgrade. A pudgy middle-aged man in a suit, who becomes tagged Mr. Moustache (Danilo Stojković) jots odd Serbian words in a notebook, comments on the superiority of German products, and, as the film proceeds, shows definite pro-Fascist leanings. A bumbling hunter (Taško Načić), who appears unable to hunt anything other than personal misfortune, arrives next. A bald man (Borislav Stjepanović) is the pathetic remains of a man with a tubercular cough who senses his own insignificance.

With the young Gypsy's Jew's harp serving as punctuation, the bus—a faded, red wreck of a machine with a stovepipe smokestack, pulls into view. The lettering on the side of the bus identifies it as "Krstić and Son," and it is immediately clear that the bearlike, boozy-faced Krstić (Pavle Vuisić) and his crew-cut, idiotically grinning son, Miško (Aleksandar Berček, who received a Best Supporting Male Actor award for this performance at the 1980 Pula Festival), operate their own society within their bus.

Krstić is a patriarchal benevolent tyrant who rules with a democratic spirit. When questioned concerning why he allows Gypsies on his bus, he replies that anyone who buys a ticket can ride (including pigs, kept in the back). Before long, Krstić has picked up the other riders. Aleksa Simić

(Milivoje Tomić) is an old peasant and a World War I hero; a priest also appears, as does a young married couple who are catching a ride to Belgrade for their honeymoon. At this point, the cast is gathered for the kind of picaresque journey that is both realistic and metaphoric in the spirit of Buñuel's *Subida al cielo* (1951; *Mexican Bus Ride*) and John Ford's *Stagecoach* (1939). Each character is a type, halfway between a stereotype and an archetype, yet because of the subtle warmth of Kovačević's script, the well-rounded performances of the actors, and Šijan's balanced directing, the film never gives way to easy farce.

*Who's That Singing over There?* is one of those rare examples of ensemble acting at its best. No one person, including Krstić, dominates the film. Šijan and Kovačević orchestrate their tale so that each figure stands out with his or her own character and so that each is accorded equal attention as the journey progresses. It must be remarked that most of the film actors in Yugoslav cinema can be considered to belong to a single ensemble; most of the actors have worked with one another in many films over the years. Šijan builds on this unusual fact to encourage a hearty interaction among the cast in scenes that often call for group response.

Like Yugoslavia itself on the eve of war, the bus, with its representative motley crew of passengers, rambles toward a dark destiny. Six major events occur on the trip. First, Miško, the son, drives the bus blindfolded on a bet from one of the passengers to the dismay of all but Krstić, who collects the money (miraculously there is no accident). An old peasant plows up that section of the road which passes through his land and tries to collect a toll (he finally is paid, but again Krstić makes a profit). Third, while a flat tire is being repaired, the passengers experience death, revenge, and love, as they join the funeral procession of a murdered schoolteacher whose relatives swear bloody revenge and as, one by one, the entire male group gathers on a hill to watch the young married couple below in the act of consummating their marriage. Fourth, after Mr. Moustache falls into a river and disappears (he later returns wet but unharmed), Krstić calls for a feast by the river, a festive moment in which all differences are momentarily forgotten as the group eats, drinks, and dances together. Fifth, the Yugoslav army arrives, borrows the bus, and drafts Miško, leaving the group to spend a night by the river, an opportunity which the singer uses to move in on a young bride (Neda Arnerić) who is having second thoughts about spending her life as a peasant's wife. Finally, once the bus has been returned and the group sets off again, the passengers immediately suspect, and then begin to beat up, the Gypsies when the old peasant discovers his wallet is missing (racial prejudice is thus revealed, since the wallet was accidently left with the hunter, who is cast off the bus).

Šijan shoots his tale with a balance between close-up shots inside the bus, giving the viewer a feeling for the immediacy of each character's concerns, and long-shots, in which the bus is seen in relation to the bleak landscape. The lonely tranquillity of the landscape, like Monument Valley in John Ford's *Stagecoach*, helps to put the comic chaos of the society within the bus into perspective. Šijan's use of the Gypsies to narrate the feelings of the moment also serves both to divide the film into "acts" and to frame what is happening in a form—music—that will outlive the characters passing through the landscape. Furthermore, the simple camera work and subdued colors (the film was for the most part shot at dawn or dusk) help to create the feeling of Yugoslav folk paintings. Šijan thus succeeds in creating an unusual balance between robust ensemble comedy that at times approaches *commedia dell'arte* and a much more melancholy sense of inevitability. This tension helps set the film apart from other worthy road films which attempt to suggest something of a nation's identity at a certain moment in its history (such as *Bye Bye Brazil*, 1980, or *La Nuit de Varennes*, 1982, *That Night at Varennes*).

The conclusion is swift and effective. While the passengers are occupied with beating the Gypsies, one hears the sound of bombers overhead. The camera lingers on the face of Mr. Moustache, the pro-German member of the group, and then quickly cuts to the faces of the others one last time. There is a sudden blackout. As the smoke and dark clear into sepia lighting, the bombed-out wreckage of the bus in the rubble of Belgrade can be seen. While it appears impossible that anyone could have survived, the two Gypsies, more tattered than ever, climb over the top of the bus and approach the camera in the same way in which they began the trip (and thus the film and song). This time they have no hats, so that they appear as individuals. As sirens whine in the background, they sing once more. The last lines tell of the earth shaking and everything collapsing, culminating in the choral line, "I sing to sing my pain away."

Šijan's ending cuts short the ironic human comedy of the bus ride and Krstić's small society on wheels. With the singing Gypsies, Šijan not only adds to a strong interest in these survivors and outsiders as captured in both Yugoslav literature and film (Aleksandar Petrović's 1967 film *Skupljači perja*, *I Even Met Happy Gypsies*, is the best-known example); he also closes his film with a degree of triumph for individuals, though surrounded by the evidence of destruction, and of song and film to capture that triumph.

*Andrew Horton*

# THE WILD CHILD
# (L'ENFANT SAUVAGE)

*Origin:* France
*Released:* 1970
*Released in U.S.:* 1970
*Production:* Marcel Berbert for Les Films du Carosse and Les Productions Artistes Associés
*Direction:* François Truffaut
*Screenplay:* François Truffaut and Jean Gruault; based on "Mémoire et rapport sur Victor de l'Aveyron," by Jean Itard
*Cinematography:* Nestor Almendros
*Editing:* Agnès Guillemot
*Art direction:* Jean Mandaroux
*Music:* Antonio Vivaldi
*MPAA rating:* G
*Running time:* 85 minutes

*Principal characters:*
Victor de l'Aveyron ............. Jean-Pierre Cargol
Dr. Jean Itard .................... François Truffaut
Mme Guérin ....................... Françoise Seigner
Professor Philippe Pinel ............... Jean Dasté
Orderly ............................. Pierre Fabre
Rémy ................................ Paul Villé
M. Lémeri ......................... Claude Miller
Mme Lémeri ........................ Annie Miller

As an opening title to the film makes clear, *The Wild Child* is based on historical fact: It deals with the discovery of a "wild child," about twelve years of age, in a forest in the Aveyron area of France in the summer of 1798, and with the attempts made during the next few years to educate and socialize him. Almost every word in the film, both in the dialogue and in the offscreen commentary, is taken from the journal of Dr. Jean Itard, now regarded as an important pioneer of many techniques of modern education and child psychology, who was principally responsible for the boy's education and upbringing. During his short lifetime (he died at around the age of thirty), the boy became the subject of often acrimonious debate between those who held that it would have been kinder to leave him in the "natural" state in which he had existed prior to his capture, and those who maintained that no human being can enjoy any kind of meaningful existence outside some social framework. While showing himself sensitive to both positions, François Truffaut (who chose to play the role of Itard partly as a means of reassurance for the shy gypsy boy he had selected as Victor) respects throughout Itard's own viewpoint that the effort of socialization had to be made, whatever the difficulties, even if he allows himself a certain sly irony at some of the doctor's foibles and preconceptions.

The film opens with an iris shot—a technique rarely used since the silent period, but one which Truffaut revives as a regular method of cinematic punctuation throughout the film. Like the use of black and white, which almost every major American and Western European film director had discarded by 1970, it gives the film a deliberately archaic and formalized quality, distancing the viewer from an overready emotional identification with the characters and imposing a perspective of objective detachment within which one can judge the philosophic and moral issues that the film raises.

A peasant woman gathering mushrooms in the woods is frightened by the almost animallike apparition of a naked, unkempt boy (Jean-Pierre Cargol). A search party, headed by dogs, is organized by the local villagers; after a lengthy chase the boy is run to earth and smoked out of a hole in which he has taken shelter. A newspaper report of his capture comes to the attention of Dr. Jean Itard in Paris; meanwhile, the boy is kept chained up in a hut by his captors, who view him as little better than a wild beast. The local children make fun of him, but he responds favorably to the kindness shown him by an old peasant, Rémy (Paul Villé).

The boy is taken to Paris, where he is placed in an institute for deaf-and-dumb children. Itard and his colleague Professor Philippe Pinel (Jean Dasté) start to carry out tests on his physical and mental abilities, attempting in particular to discover if he is capable of speech. Shocked at the continuing mistreatment of the boy, both by the other children and the wardens, who pocket a lucrative income by putting him on display to Paris socialites as a freak, Itard offers to make himself wholly responsible for his education and expresses his confidence that the boy is intelligent and capable of learning.

Up to this point, the film has contrasted the boy's successful adaptation to his conditions of existence in the forest with the largely insensitive and unsympathetic treatment he receives from almost every stratum of French society. Although Itard rescues him from this, he does so in a spirit of scientific detachment rather than of affection or emotional warmth: The boy is an object of study for him, albeit one to be treated with kindness, respect, and dignity. The slightly amateurish stiffness of Truffaut's acting becomes an unexpectedly positive element of the film in this respect: Itard seems genuinely unaware that the boy might need love and physical affection from him as well as being taught to read and write, and he leaves these aspects of the boy's care to his motherly housekeeper, Mme Guérin (Françoise Seigner).

Itard's initial experiments are (perhaps perversely from a modern point of view) designed to break down those qualities that enabled the boy (whom he christens Victor) to survive years of isolation and hardship in the forest:

his imperviousness to heat and cold, his apparent insensitivity to pain, his lack of "normal" human emotions. Victor's love of nature is channeled into the socially acceptable form of walks in the countryside; he is taught to wear shoes and clothes, and to eat with a spoon and drink from a mug.

Having established what, from his point of view, are the necessary foundations for civilized social behavior, Itard begins to show himself remarkably open to following the direction of Victor's own interests and talents, rather than imposing on him a rigid and preconceived course of study. He attempts to stimulate the boy's curiosity and to invent games that will provide an opportunity for education as well as amusement. Nothing, however, seems capable of provoking him into speech, even though he has an acute sense of hearing and can respond to musical rhythms. Despite his patience and his willingness, on the whole, to let Victor develop at his own pace, Itard cannot always control his frustration at being unable to break down what is, for him, the crucial barrier that separates human beings from animals. This results in occasional confrontations in which he tries to push Victor further than the boy is able, or willing, to go, and from which both have to be rescued by the intervention of Mme Guérin.

Itard then decides to tackle the problem in a different manner, by making use of Victor's taste for order and tidiness and the fact that he possesses a good visual memory, and by rewarding him for his cooperation with a glass of water, as this seems to provide the boy with an intense physical satisfaction. Victor is instructed to collect and place in the correct position certain household objects, a task which he performs very capably as long as he has a picture of the object to guide him. When asked to respond to either the spoken or the written word for the object, without the assistance of a picture, the boy is unable to understand what is required of him, and Itard has to admit failure in this respect.

Next, Itard has a wooden alphabet constructed for Victor, in the hope of teaching him, through play, to recognize and distinguish between the letters. Victor proves adept at arranging the letters in the correct order, but once again he relies wholly on his visual memory in doing so and cannot take the crucial step of understanding the letters as signs for something beyond themselves. Itard's discouragement at the partial and fluctuating degree of success that he has achieved leads him once more to make excessive demands on his pupil, though he eventually heeds Mme Guérin's advice that the boy needs more time for relaxation and pleasure.

Itard's system of rewards and punishments (praise and a glass of water for cooperative behavior; rebukes and, as an extreme measure, imprisonment in a dark closet for lack of cooperation or defiance) seems to have had some effect in "socializing" Victor: One moment of rather mixed triumph for his teacher occurs when the boy, reacting to one of these punishments, weeps for the first time. Other "firsts" include his first articulated sound, *lait* (milk), and his invention of a holder for a piece of chalk. Itard, however, becomes obsessed with discovering whether his pupil possesses what he calls "a natural feeling of justice," and he resolves to test this by punishing him unfairly and studying the boy's reaction. Instead of praising him, therefore, when he next performs a task correctly, he rebukes him and tries to force him into the dark closet; Victor resists and, in the ensuing struggle, bites Itard on the arm. The delighted Itard concludes that the boy does indeed possess an instinctive moral sense, and congratulates himself on having helped to foster and direct this.

Shortly after this Itard falls ill and is unable to take Victor out for his daily walks. Frustrated by his confinement, the boy takes an early opportunity to run away, but his months of socialization have destroyed his capacity to survive in the wild: He is unable to climb trees and take shelter in them with his earlier skill, nor can he subsist on the diet that had satisfied him previously. His attempts to steal a chicken almost lead to his capture, and he is soon cold, miserable, and hungry.

Meanwhile, the disconsolate Itard is writing to the Ministry responsible for Victor's welfare to report his disappearance, though he insists that the boy was making excellent progress and was rapidly becoming a useful member of society. As he writes, the exhausted Victor appears at the window and allows Itard to pursue and catch him. Mme Guérin welcomes the boy with great affection, and he responds to her caresses. Itard, more restrained, yet moved by his pupil's return, also briefly caresses him, telling him that he has "come home" and that he is a "man" now, not a "savage." He is a young man of "great expectations" and, as Mme Guérin leads the boy upstairs, Itard reminds him that they will continue with his lessons soon. The last shot of the film is an iris closing in on Victor's impassive face.

On its original appearance, *The Wild Child* proved somewhat disconcerting to many of Truffaut's admirers, who disliked its apparent emotional detachment, and even coldness, and compared it unfavorably in this respect to the warmth, vitality, and sympathetic understanding of such earlier films as *Les Quatre Cents Coups* (1959; *The 400 Blows*) or *Jules et Jim* (1961; *Jules and Jim*). Some critics also believed that it was strange for the director whose feature-film career had begun with a passionate and powerful defense of a child mistreated by an uncaring society to be apparently condoning the forced socialization of another child in this film, seeming to accept uncritically that this was in the child's own best interests.

The verbal structure of the film—Itard's voice-over commentary and the dialogue—certainly presents Itard's arguments for his treatment of Victor in a generally positive light, though there is also a considerable element of self-questioning and self-doubt involved. Against this, however, the images and music of the film remind one continually of what Victor loses in his assimilation to the social framework. Itard, who is constantly shown indoors, his back turned to the natural world, writing at a desk with the aid of artificial light, can respect but never fully share his pupil's total immersion in the world of trees, grass, water, rain, open air, and moonlight: The contrast is perhaps most vigorously expressed in those scenes that show Victor romping on all fours across the meadows while Itard, sedately dressed in frock coat and top hat, strides purposefully ahead, following the path to his chosen destination.

The music, too, based on contrasting themes from Antonio Vivaldi, sets an exuberant outburst from the mandolin, accompanying moments of successful achievement of a social task, against a wistful, poignant, recorder theme heard when Victor is reminded of the natural world that he has been forced to leave behind him. The total effect, then, is not one of unconditional endorsement of "society" and "conditioning" over "nature" and "freedom," but a much more subtle balance that constantly sets the very real gains that Victor makes in a society whose values are by no means accepted without criticism, against a reminder that this society has lost touch with a vital area of experience with which Victor retains strong, though gradually fading, contact. Unlike Werner Herzog, whose *Jeder für sich und Gott gegen alle* (1974; *The Mystery of Kaspar Hauser*) deals with a very similar, and historically almost contemporaneous, theme, Truffaut is not primarily concerned with exposing the artifice and corruption of civilization by presenting it through the uncomprehending eyes of a "child of nature."

The "classicism" of both Truffaut's theme and his style in this film (which marked the beginning of a regular collaboration with the cameraman Nestor Almendros) can be seen in retrospect to mark a turning point in his own career and in the fortunes of the French New Wave, in whose success he had played such a prominent role. His subsequent films, until his untimely death in 1984, were generally much more restrained and conventional than the freewheeling and sometimes deliberately outrageous works with which he first gained international recognition: By 1970 too, the initial ferment of the New Wave had died away, and the next decade was, for all except a few perennial mavericks such as Jean-Luc Godard and Jacques Rivette, to see in the French New Wave, a period of consolidation and even an accommodation to the commercial norms once so vigorously rejected and denounced.

*Graham Petrie*

# WILD STRAWBERRIES (SMULTRONSTÄLLET)

*Origin:* Sweden
*Released:* 1957
*Released in U.S.:* 1959
*Production:* Allan Ekelund for Svensk Filmindustri
*Direction:* Ingmar Bergman
*Screenplay:* Ingmar Bergman
*Cinematography:* Gunnar Fischer
*Editing:* Oscar Rosander
*Art direction:* Gittan Gustafsson
*Music:* Erik Nordgren
*Running time:* 90 minutes

*Principal characters:*

Professor Isak Borg................Victor Sjöström
Sara, the hitchhiker/
Sara, Isak's cousin.................Bibi Andersson
Marianne...........................Ingrid Thulin
Evald.........................Gunnar Björnstrand
Agda.............................Jullan Kindahl
Anders...........................Folke Sundquist
Viktor.........................Björn Bjelvenstam
Isak's mother.....................Naima Wifstrand
Sigfrid............................Per Sjöstrand
Isak's wife.......................Gertrud Fridh

In the mid-1950's, Swedish director Ingmar Bergman began to be noticed by the international film community. After *Sommarnattens leende* (1955; *Smiles of a Summer Night*), and *Det sjunde inseglet* (1956; *The Seventh Seal*), won special prizes at the Cannes film festival, he was regarded by most film critics as one of the major talents in world cinema, and his next film, *Wild Strawberries*, was eagerly awaited. The reception given it was enthusiastic. It won four international film prizes and a nomination (in the screenplay division) for an Academy Award. The screenplays of these three films and their successor, *Ansiktet* (1958; *The Magician*), were published in English translation in a single volume in 1960, further enhancing Bergman's international reputation.

The subject of *Wild Strawberries* is an old man's realization of his own character, and the themes of the film include age, youth, and compassion. These are developed through the story of the old man's one-day journey in his car, combined with dreams, memories, and flashbacks. By the end of the journey (and the film), the viewer has learned the man's story and his character and has seen that he has come to know himself better than ever before. The device of the journey permits Bergman to have the man encounter several different types of people who embody several different attitudes toward life and toward other people.

The protagonist of *Wild Strawberries* is a seventy-eight-year-old professor and physician, Isak Borg (Victor Sjöström). On the morning of the day he is to be honored in a ceremony in the city of Lund, he awakens from a strange and disturbing dream in which he sees a large clock without hands. When he tries to check the time by looking at his own watch, he finds that it, too, has lost its hands. In the most terrifying part of the dream—indeed, so terrifying that it wakens Isak—a horse-drawn hearse spills its casket on the street. When Isak walks over to look, the corpse is himself, and it reaches out a hand and pulls him down toward the casket.

When Isak awakens, he tells his housekeeper, Miss Agda (Jullan Kindahl), that he is going to drive to the ceremony rather than take the airplane as planned. Agda is herself seventy-four years old and has worked for Isak for forty of those years. In her not-at-all-pleased response to Isak's announcement of his change in plans, Agda reveals much of her own character and the nature of her relationship with Isak. Though she is a relatively minor character in the film, the part of Agda is excellently delineated and acted, as are those of most such secondary characters in the films of Ingmar Bergman.

On his journey to the site of the ceremony, Isak meets several people; among the most important are two members of his family. His son's wife, Marianne (Ingrid Thulin), accompanies him, and he stops along the way to visit his ninety-six-year-old mother (Naima Wifstrand). Marianne has been staying with Isak for about a month since she left her husband, Isak's son Evald (Gunnar Björnstrand). During the journey, Marianne tells Isak that she left Evald because she is pregnant and Evald does not want them to have a child. She had hoped that Isak might help them, but Isak had then only told her that he did not want to be pulled into their troubles. Marianne tells Isak that he lacks compassion and consideration, and when she sees him with his mother later in the journey, she says that she sees that all three generations—the mother, Isak, and Evald—are lonely, cold, and almost dead.

The greatest contrast to Isak in the people they meet on the trip is Sara (Bibi Andersson), a spirited young female hitchhiker whom they take with them most of the way. Sara is accompanied by two young men who are both in love with her. The two, Viktor (Björn Bjelvenstam) and Anders (Folke Sundquist), are much like each other except that Anders believes in God and plans to become a minister while Viktor considers himself a rationalist and plans to become a doctor. The youthful high spirits of the three contrast greatly with the coldness and age of Isak, a contrast he notices and which begins to change his evaluation of himself.

Further emphasizing that contrast and further heightening Isak's self-awareness are flashbacks in which the viewer sees that Isak was once in love with a young woman named Sara (also played by Bibi Andersson). When he first sees her in a flashback, she is picking wild strawberries. The viewer learns that although Sara is secretly engaged to Isak and considers him kind and sensitive, she is also attracted to the "fresh and exciting" Sigfrid (Per Sjöstrand), Isak's brother. As the film progresses, the viewer finds that Sara married Sigfrid and that Isak's later marriage was quite unhappy, his wife (Gertrud Fridh) accusing him of coldness, indifference, and selfishness.

Some of the above revelations come in a dream that Isak has as he naps in the car while Marianne drives. Also embodied in that dream is another terrifying event. Isak finds that he is being given an examination by some sort of medical board. Asked to diagnose the illness of a woman, he says that she is dead. She immediately rises and laughs at him.

Isak and his companions finally do reach Lund, and Isak is honored in the ceremonies that are seen by Miss Agda, Marianne and Evald, and the three young hitchhikers. Isak learns from Evald that he has asked Marianne to stay with him: He cannot live without her. Isak also tries to change his cold personality somewhat, but his efforts are not really understood. When, for example, he apologizes to Miss Agda for his crossness to her that morning, she thinks that he is ill. Only Marianne seems to understand fully how he now feels. Finally he retires to bed and dreams of the long-ago days and the wild strawberry patch. At the end of the film, the viewer sees the old Isak looking at his parents when they were young. A beatific smiles comes to his face.

Any discussion of *Wild Strawberries* must acknowledge that second only to Bergman in significance of his contribution to the film is Victor Sjöström in the role of Isak. Sjöström had begun his career at the age of sixteen and had been both an actor and a director in Sweden. During the 1920's, he directed several films in Hollywood under the name of Seastrom. When he appeared in *Wild Strawberries*, he was nearly eighty years old. His performance in the film is deep and affecting; indeed, some critics thought that his performance made the old man seem more human and sensitive than the script required. Most, however, agreed that the role was a fitting end to his career. He died less than three years after the film was released.

To Ingmar Bergman, as both director and screenwriter, belongs most of the credit for the other virtues of the film. The images photographed by Gunnar Fischer are continually striking; Bergman has, in fact, always produced visually striking films, no matter who was his cinematographer. The acting in all of the parts, large and small, is universally excellent. It is, incidentally, a bit of a shock to most viewers who know Bergman's *The Sev-*

*enth Seal* to see Max von Sydow, who played the metaphysical medieval knight in that earlier film, playing a quite small role as a gas station attendant in *Wild Strawberries*.

When *Wild Strawberries* was first released, some viewers and critics professed to be puzzled by the film; Bosley Crowther in *The New York Times* wrote that it was "so thoroughly mystifying that we wonder whether Mr. Bergman himself knew what he was trying to say." Most, however, found that Bergman mixed the various episodes, dreams, and flashbacks artfully to make a masterful work of art—a judgment confirmed by the fact that the film is still widely shown and appreciated.

*Timothy W. Johnson*

# DER WILLI-BUSCH-REPORT

*Origin:* West Germany
*Released:* 1979
*Released in U.S.:* 1981
*Production:* Visual Filmproduktion Elke Haltaufderheide
*Direction:* Niklaus Schilling
*Screenplay:* Niklaus Schilling
*Cinematography:* Wolfgang Dickmann
*Editing:* Niklaus Schilling
*Art direction:* Christa Molitor
*Music:* Patchwork, BSW-Combo, and Fanfarenzug Wanfried
*MPAA rating:* no listing
*Running time:* 120 minutes

*Principal characters:*
Willi Busch . . . . . . . . . . . . . . . . . . . . . . . . Thilo Prückner
Adelheid Busch . . . . . . . . . . . . . . . . . . Dorothea Moritz
Teacher . . . . . . . . . . . . . . . . . . . . . . . . . . . Kornelia Boje

*Der Willi-Busch-Report* was Niklaus Schilling's fourth film. Schilling, born in 1944 in Basle, Switzerland, became a resident of Munich in 1965. He began his career as a television reporter and cameraman. In 1971, he made his first film, *Nachtschatten* (1971; *Nightshade*), followed by *Die Vertreibung aus dem Paradies* (1976; *Expulsion from Paradise*) and *Rheingold* (1977). Although the subjects of all four films differ greatly, there is one thing that they share. They are pure cinema, luring audiences into subtle traps and offering them one surprise after another. Schilling's films are always a strange mixture of reality and fantasy, of bizarre dreams and cool facts. Their common background is modern Germany, which on the surface seems to be a wonderland. Yet behind the façade, the old wounds of the Third Reich and World War II have not yet healed.

*Der Willi-Busch-Report* is set against the reality of the borderline that splits Germany politically into two parts, East and West. The film's protagonist, who lives practically on the border between the two Germanys, is a young man named Willi Busch (Thilo Prückner). Willi, whose name recalls one of Germany's greatest satiric poets of the nineteenth century, tries hard to keep his business going. This business is a small newspaper that Willi and his sister Adelheid (Dorothea Moritz) have inherited from their father. Before 1945, this paper, *The Werra Post*, had had a large circulation; at that time, it was sold in East Germany as well. During the postwar decades, however, the circulation has dropped to a few thousand copies a day. Willi's one aim in life is to save his newspaper from ruin. Being *The Werra Post*'s one and only reporter, he sets out to find stories that will win readers back from the country's largest yellow-press paper, *Tag* (day). If things do not happen in this quiet place at the world's end, one has to make them happen. Thus, Willi first destroys telephones in the town's few telephone boxes in order to write about the "new vandalism" of the time. He then invents a strong headline for his dying paper: Small Girl (Five) Prophesies: Germany Will Be United Again. This not only helps to sell the paper but also brings busloads of people hungry for such sensationalism to the small town in West Germany's easternmost province.

Yet people soon tire of the little girl's prophetic words, and Willi has to find fresh fodder for his readers. When a friend of his dies while making love to the local prostitute, Willi disposes of the body near the frontier and spreads the rumor that the dead man was a secret agent for "the other side." This makes things start happening, but Willi is soon overwhelmed by the events which he has set in motion. In the end, with a rifle in his hand, he tries to storm the frontier.

Although the German frontier is a subject that few German films have tackled, it becomes quite palpable in the hands of Niklaus Schilling. On first glance the film belongs to the tradition of political spy thrillers such as *The Spy Who Came in from the Cold* (1965) or *Torn Curtain* (1966). The story that Schilling tells in his film seems to fit into this mold: There are wild pursuits by car and helicopter; there are dead men and strange signals in the night. Yet actually Schilling's film belongs mainly to a different category of film, which has a long tradition in German cinema, the so-called *Heimatfilm* (local drama—but this translation is not exact). The *Heimatfilm* is a genre of many shades. Most *Heimatfilme* were set against the beautiful background of the Bavarian Alps and forests and very often told the touching story of a poor but honest girl who fell in love with a nice forest ranger or a duke who roamed the mountains and woodlands in disguise. The great days of the *Heimatfilm* were in the late 1940's and the 1950's. Then, when the new German cinema was born, its directors neglected this genre as much too trivial and silly. Yet the *Heimatfilm* never died. During the last two decades, a new kind of *Heimatfilm* has developed. Its heroes changed and were no longer innocent young girls who yearned for dukes in disguises, but young men and women living in a remote corner of Germany, in the "provinces." The new *Heimatfilm* usually describes the dreams and illusions of these people, who long to escape the narrowness of their provincial surroundings but often fail to realize their hopes. In the old *Heimatfilm* there was always a happy ending, where the young man and the brave young woman faced a rosy future together. Not so in the modern variety of this genre. There are other solutions to one's problems than wedding bells: To have faced a challenge and survived it is as much a good ending to a story as riding to church in a coach with four white horses.

In the modern sense of the word, then, Niklaus Schilling's film is a *Heimatfilm*. Set in that remote part of West Germany, the Werra Valley—named after the little river Werra, which comes from the Eastern part and crosses the border without problems (very different from what people have to face who want to travel from one part of the country to another)—*Der Willi-Busch-Report* describes the life and death of people in the province. Here time seems to have stood still. Nothing moves; days roll by without outward excitement. Everything seems to be caught in an everyday routine. Even the frontier, with its ugly face of barbed wire and watchtowers, has superficially become as distant and "normal" as the setting and the rising of the sun.

Schilling's main character, Willi Busch, refuses to get lost in the daily monotony. His strange adventures and efforts to save his small newspaper are truly an attempt to escape the gray routine of provincial life and the depressing boredom of life in a small town. In order to escape from the prison of his responsibilities—earning money and continuing with the newspaper—and from the monotony of an uneventful life, Willi Busch invents wild stories which slowly become reality. The things that happen turn out to be much more frightening than all the visions Willi Busch had ever had. His dreams are transformed into nightmares, and in the end Willi Busch does not know what is real or what is one of his bizarre visions.

As with most German films, there is also a political side to *Der Willi-Busch-Report*, which is reflected by the border between Germany and Germany. Here, history and daily politics mingle. The frontier that parts Germany in two halves is a result of history, the most visible leftover of the Third Reich and its consequences. The border remains a constant bone of contention. Its grim face is part of Germany's present history. Although it has been a reality for decades, people have not grown accustomed to it. *Der Willi-Busch-Report* demonstrates how absurd, how cruel, and how terrifying this artificial gap between people who share their past still is. One of the great assets of Schilling's film lies in the way that it shows this part of German life without painting matters in black and white. The border creates unusual situations such as the possibility that spies swarm across the country and even threaten provincial citizens, who seem to have nothing to hide. The border is, furthermore, such a monster in its inhuman ugliness that people will believe anything in order to nourish their hope that one day it will disappear. Thus, the tragicomic scenes with the small girl who talks of the reunion of the country have a genuine power: The people who came to see the girl are moved by a glimmer of hope that her prophecies may come true.

In 1981, Niklaus Schilling was awarded the Max Ophüls Prize of the city of Saarbrücken for the Best Film of 1980. The Max Ophüls Prize had only been recently created, and *Der Willi-Busch-Report* was the first film to receive this award. The jury praised the film's great originality and the director's successful attempt to create pure cinema, a mixture of comedy and drama, of real life and imagination, of excitement and thought. The film's main actor, Thilo Prückner, was awarded the prize for Best Acting. His acting is a highlight in this film on modern Germany, which is a portrait of a country that still suffers from its self-inflicted wounds.

*Margarete von Schwarzkopf*

# WINTER LIGHT (NATTVARDSGÄSTERNA)

*Origin:* Sweden
*Released:* 1962
*Released in U.S.:* 1963
*Production:* Allan Ekelund for Svensk Filmindustri
*Direction:* Ingmar Bergman
*Screenplay:* Ingmar Bergman
*Cinematography:* Sven Nykvist
*Editing:* Ulla Ryghe
*Art direction:* P. A. Lundgren
*Music:* no listing
*Running time:* 80 minutes

*Principal characters:*
Märta Lundberg .................... Ingrid Thulin
Tomas Ericsson................ Gunnar Björnstrand
Jonas Persson..................... Max von Sydow
Karin Persson .................. Gunnel Lindblom
Algot Frövik ........................ Allan Edwall
Fredrik Blom ...................... Olof Thunberg

Swedish director Ingmar Bergman's 1962 film *Winter Light* is one of his chamber films. In an analogy to chamber music, the term denotes an intimate film with a rather small cast in which the action is limited to a very few settings and a short time period. In fact, the time period covered in *Winter Light* is not much longer than the film itself: The film uses eighty minutes to portray about three hours on a November Sunday. The restrictions of time, place, and number of characters in a chamber film can produce a concentration of effect or an almost claustrophobic feeling. For this film, the concentrated effect is aptly described by its American title, *Winter Light*, even though a literal translation of the Swedish title is "The Communicants." The film has much the same bleak tone that winter sunlight often offers, and Bergman has remarked that the light is the protagonist of the film.

The film opens with Tomas Ericsson (Gunnar Björnstrand), the pastor of a small church, beginning a midday Sunday service. Bergman then goes outside for a series of shots of the church and its surroundings before returning inside for the rest of the service. In the congregation are only nine people, but the viewer sees the whole service before learning much about any of them, although some slight indication of what is to come is given by several shots that show that Fredrik Blom (Olof Thunberg), the organist, is not at all interested in the service and wants only for it to be over as soon as possible. He reads a magazine during the service and occasionally checks his watch.

After the service is over, one begins to learn that Tomas is in a state of crisis. Although not all the facts are set before the viewer immediately, one gradually finds that his wife died four years ago and that he has had a long affair with an assistant schoolteacher, Märta Lundberg (Ingrid Thulin), a rather plain woman who wants to help Tomas even though he does not want help from her. This aspect of their relationship is first indicated soon after the service, when Märta offers Tomas a hot drink and he insists that he does not need it. He also tells Märta that what is troubling him is God's silence.

Adding to Tomas' mental distress is the fact that he is suffering from a severe cold or influenza, and adding to it even more is a visit after the service from Jonas (Max von Sydow) and Karin Persson (Gunnel Lindblom). Jonas barely speaks, but Karin explains to Tomas that her husband is extremely troubled. He has heard that the Chinese are taught to hate and that they will soon have the atomic bomb. This worry has destroyed Jonas' will to live. Tomas is able to offer Jonas only a few platitudinous statements, but he knows these statements are inadequate, so he persuades Jonas to come back for more talk after he takes Karin home.

At this point, all looks rather dismal, but there is worse to come, and it comes in three very direct, powerful scenes. In the first, Tomas reads a long letter that Märta has sent him. Because they find it hard to talk to each other, Märta writes, she will try a letter to tell him what she thinks is important. For the reading of the letter, Bergman uses a very daring device. After Tomas opens and starts to read the letter, one sees, in a medium close-up, Märta speaking the entire letter as she looks directly at the camera. This shot lasts nearly five minutes, which is twenty or thirty times the length of an average shot in feature films. This technique gives the words an uncomfortable intensity that approximates the way that they affect Tomas. The shot is interrupted at one point to show a flashback of what Märta is describing. In the letter, Märta describes an experience that made her realize the lovelessness of Tomas, but she also says that she believes her great task in life is to show her love for him, although she does not know how to do it.

In the second major scene, Jonas returns to talk to Tomas. Instead of offering a Christian answer to the man's dread, Tomas confesses his own lack of faith, saying that he is a poor wretch himself. He concludes by telling Jonas that they have given each other gifts. "You've given me your fear, and I've given you a god I've killed." None of this seems to console Jonas, however, and he leaves without having said much.

The third of the major scenes occurs after the word has been received that Jonas has killed himself, and Tomas and Märta have been to the site where the body was found. They stop by the schoolhouse in which Märta lives. While she goes upstairs, Tomas waits in the classroom on the first floor. Märta returns to Tomas, and what follows is a scene described accurately by critic Robin Wood as "human beings totally exposed to each other, raw nerved and vulnerable, among the most painful and ugly [scenes] in all cinema." Märta tries to persuade Tomas to marry her, but Tomas responds with a list of things about her that he despises, ending by saying that he is tired of everything that has to do with her. Then he says that he should leave before he says something worse. Märta's response is one that the audience can share; she simply wonders how anything could be worse.

After this scene, however, Tomas surprises Märta by asking her to accompany him. He must stop to tell Jonas' wife of her husband's death and then go to another small town for a three o'clock service. When he arrives at the church, he finds that only Blom, the organist, and Algot Frövik (Allan Edwall), the hunchbacked sexton, are there. Blom suggests that there is no need for a service without a congregation, and Algot explains to Tomas his ideas about the suffering of Christ. He echoes Tomas' earlier statement, when he says that it was the silence of God and the lack of understanding of man, not the physical pain, that caused Christ's real suffering. The film ends in a most surprising way. The service begins, and Tomas speaks: "Holy, holy, holy, Lord God Almighty. The whole earth is filled with His glory." Then there is a very quick fade out, and the film is over.

Critic John Simon, in his book *Ingmar Bergman Directs*, which is devoted to *Winter Light* and three other Bergman films, says that there are three possible interpretations of this ending in which the pastor who has confessed his loss of faith continues his preaching. The Christian interpretation concludes that Tomas has regained his faith. Another interpretation is that Tomas has become so cynical that he continues to mouth words that mean nothing to him. The interpretation which Simon favors is the existential one, which holds that Tomas continues his ministry despite his lack of religious belief because he has become aware of human aloneness and suffering and seeks to mitigate this condition through the only means of communication or sharing that he knows. The difficulty with this interpretation, however, is the lack of evidence that Tomas has truly become more aware of the realities of the human condition.

Bergman has said that in *Winter Light* he wished to provide a kind of correction for what he regarded as the too simplistic and too optimistic ending of his previous film, *Såsom i en spegel* (1961; *Through a Glass Darkly*), but he has also indicated that he does not think that the ending is completely pessimistic. One can notice that, to a certain extent, the position of Tomas parallels that of Bergman himself. Through many films Bergman has examined the silence of God and despite his doubts he continues in his art of filmmaking.

Two incidents helped Bergman shape the film that became *Winter Light*.

He was working on a plot that concerned the silence of God and that took place in a church, but it was quite different from the plot of *Winter Light*. Bergman went to a number of churches with his father, who was a clergyman, and at one, a minister announced that he was going to conduct an abbreviated service because he was ill. Bergman's father insisted that a full service be held. Bergman also met a minister who told him how devastated he had been when one of his parishioners committed suicide the day after he had talked to the minister. Bergman used these incidents to help shape the script that he was writing.

The four main roles of Tomas, Märta, Jonas, and Karin are played by actors who had appeared in several of Bergman's films and had become a sort of Bergman stock company. All except Gunnar Björnstrand, who plays Tomas, play roles considerably different from most of their previous ones, but all are excellent in making credible the characters that Bergman had created.

The critical reaction to *Winter Light* was quite varied. Some thought it one of Bergman's best films, while others said that its only real virtue is that it is short. When Bergman showed it to his wife, she said: "Yes, Ingmar, it's a masterpiece; but it's a dreary masterpiece."

*Timothy W. Johnson*

# WITHOUT ANESTHESIA (BEZ ZNIECZULENIA)

*Origin:* Poland
*Released:* 1978
*Released in U.S.:* 1979
*Production:* Film Polski, Society for Film-Making, Unit "X"
*Direction:* Andrzej Wajda
*Screenplay:* Andrzej Wajda and Agnieszka Holland
*Cinematography:* Edward Kłosiński
*Editing:* Halina Prugar
*Art direction:* Allan Starski
*Music:* Piotr Derfel and Wojciech Młynarski
*MPAA rating:* no listing
*Running time:* 131 minutes

*Principal characters:*

Jerzy Michalowski............Zbigniew Zapasiewicz
Ewa Michalowska.................Ewa Dałkowska
Jacek Rosciszewski..............Andrzej Seweryn
Agata ............................Krystyna Janda
Wanda .........................Emilia Krakowska
Bronski .........................Roman Wilhelmi
Editor-in-Chief ..................Kazimierz Kaczor
Maid ............................Stefania Iwinska
Ewa's lawyer...........................Jerzy Stuhr
Olenka.......................Aleksandra Jasieka
Ewa's mother ..........................Iga Mayr
Ewa's sister......................Halina Golanko
Jerzy's lawyer ...............Magda Teresa Wojcik

Andrzej Wajda's *Without Anesthesia* is about a very personal problem, divorce, and the impact in modern Poland of political pressures on such a dilemma. A subtheme in the film, coscripted by Wajda and Agnieszka Holland, is the presentation of truth, since the divorce becomes a judicial matter, and the major character is a well-known journalist. The opening credits are seen in typewritten characters against a background of scenes of guerrilla war in Africa. The emphasis on the public perception of world events and television is continued, when the film begins, by the televised image of the reporter, Jerzy Michalowski (Zbigniew Zapasiewicz), being interviewed as the guest in the first program of a new television series. That program is being scrutinized by four very different pairs of eyes: two network programmers, who question the value of the program and specifically the choice of guest; Jerzy's wife, Ewa (Ewa Dałkowska), who is preparing to meet him at the airport; and her young lover, Jacek Rosciszewski (Andrzej Seweryn), who busily scribbles in his notebook as the program unfolds. Within the film's first half-hour, the basic interrelationship between the personal and the political in Poland has been outlined and given dramatic flesh.

Jacek is Jerzy's rival in a number of ways; they sit on the same editorial committee, which decides on literary awards, and Jacek craves his own chance to pontificate on nationally televised talk shows. At one point in the program, Jerzy Michalowski speaks of the importance of his wife and children in his life. He is about to discover exactly how important they are—his wife plans to leave him. She tells him of her plans shortly after picking him up at the airport on his return from a journalistic assignment abroad. Ewa literally leaves him at the door of their house when she tearfully tells him that she and their younger child have moved out. Their older daughter is away at school, in Moscow. Jerzy wanders through their multiroom apartment, staring at the empty rooms from which clothes and furniture have been taken, occupied now by half-filled cartons. Left with the remnants of his happy home life, Jerzy tries to get Ewa and the child back.

As part of his effort, he visits Ewa's friend Wanda (Emilia Krakowska), a dentist, whose clumsy assistant seems to be eavesdropping on their conversation. Wanda discovers a decayed tooth, and the film's title derives from the fact that Jerzy refuses anesthesia, though he later faints from the pain. Wanda cannot help him regain Ewa, and the young lawyer (Jerzy Stuhr) who represents her is cynically fatalistic. He tries to talk Jerzy into conceding defeat and tells him that anything can be proved against anybody in court. Besides the political implications of this boast, the confusion of lawyers and clients in his crowded office hints at a mechanistic, bureaucratic, and possibly corrupt administration of justice.

Ironically, Jerzy engages in battle with his rival, Jacek, at a meeting of the literary prize committee on which they both sit. Two diametrically opposed books, one highly critical of the status quo in Poland, the other relatively optimistic, have been nominated for the annual award. Despite somewhat murky rhetoric, it becomes clear that Jacek champions the book that takes a more positive (that is, sugarcoated) view of Polish life than does Jerzy. The debate grows heated, each insulting the other, and the older Jerzy is warned by his associates that the decision has already been made and that he should save his energy for more important battles.

Consumed by rivalry, Jacek watches his own performance on a television talk show and nervously asks Ewa to judge his performance. A young intellectual with a modest, two-room apartment, it is obvious that he is much more concerned with besting his rival than he is consumed with love for Ewa, an older woman who tends to mother him. Exactly why she has chosen to leave Jerzy or what attracts her to Jacek remains unclear, except for her vague aspirations to return to research work and his moderate, but clear, egotism. Much more detailed in the film is the impending destruction of Jerzy as an established journalist. Whether independently or in tandem with the divorce, the political forces around Jerzy are raising the stakes of his battle.

Jerzy's classroom at the local university is empty, and it is rumored among the students that he has been forced to resign. Jerzy calms his students with a lie, telling them that the cancellation of his class was a clerical error and nothing more. Popular with his students, emboldened to take dissident views on literary matters, and forthright in his opinions on a journalist's task, Jerzy seems ripe for premature retirement. When he goes to his news office, he discovers that he has to share an office with a new colleague and that he is no longer on the circulations list for American and West German news weeklies. When he tries to get a United Nations assignment that he had initially refused, he is told that it is no longer available. Jerzy begins to drink more regularly, and he looks more despondent, a far cry from the confident guest on the television show seen at the opening of the film.

Ironically, the slow collapse of his professional life has an effect on his dilemma with his wife. One of the students who attends an impromptu party at his apartment stays on for a few days; she is a statuesque, silent blonde, Agata (Krystyna Janda). Overcome with a hangover from a night of heavy drinking and generally passive, Jerzy accepts her presence unthinkingly. She becomes a factor in the distorted view that some people have of him. A loyal maid (Stefania Iwinska) who secretly brings his infant child for a visit sees the lanky Agata wandering through the apartment. Meanwhile, Wanda immediately assumes that Agata is his new lover. All Jerzy wants to know, however, is the whereabouts of his wife and child, so as to effect some kind of reconciliation. In a grotesque way, he does effect a happy meeting with his wife. While waiting to see his child, Jerzy spots his wife and Jacek. In a rage, he attacks the younger man, banging him over the head with the toy that he had bought for his child. A brief scuffle develops, and the aghast Jacek watches Ewa embrace Jerzy. Jerzy invites her to a dinner which he elaborately prepares, and it goes remarkably well, at first. Ewa, however, feels herself falling prey to Jerzy's easy charm and leaves abruptly.

The larger social aspect of Jerzy's disintegrating life is amplified by the sudden appearance of his friend Bronski (Roman Wilhelmi), who has been reassigned to a new job, partially because of his ties to Jerzy. Nervously joking about the tuxedo that he will need in the foreign service, Bronski asks to borrow Jerzy's formal wear and talks about the system of reassignments by which trained and experienced personnel are shifted to totally unsuitable jobs. Another clue to the political aspects of Jerzy's problems is the sudden appearance of his older daughter Olenka (Aleksandra Jasieska). She says that she has been told about the pending divorce at her school in Moscow, but it appears that neither parent has reported the news to the school. The implication is not lost on Jerzy, who nods grimly at the connotations of this revelation.

The climactic scene is the divorce proceedings between Ewa and Jerzy before a tribunal of three judges. Ewa's aggressive lawyer states that the husband's behavior was to blame for the wife's departure with the youngest child. Affairs with other women are cited and, as witnesses, the lawyer calls on the maid, the dental assistant, and Ewa's sister (Halina Golanko). Upset by the divorce and intimidated by the lawyer, the maid cannot remember whether she saw Agata in the apartment after or before Ewa left him. The dental assistant testifies to a flirtation that the audience knows to be false, while Ewa's sister reports a similar tale. Jerzy refuses to let his attorney (Magda Teresa Wojcik) cross-examine any of the witnesses extensively and keeps his eyes steady on those of his wife in the opposite dock. Even as the presiding judge reads the verdict, he strides out of the courtroom. Ewa rushes after him, her face a mask of tears and grief, but he is deaf to her cries. Whether Ewa still loves him, but is motivated by the changing political climate, or whether she is unable to reconcile her own ambitions with his self-satisfied life, or whether she simply needed an extramarital affair remains unclear in the film. What is more definite is that the court proceedings have galvanized Jerzy into a firm rejection of his wife. He returns to his old apartment to live with the young student Agata.

The political mystery surrounding him, however, is not so easily resolved. Although there are strong hints of a purge, not only of Jerzy but also of his friends, the conclusions are left to the audience. In this light, it is instructive that Wajda considers *Without Anesthesia* to be one of the three films, along with *Popiół i diament* (1958; *Ashes and Diamonds*) and *Czlowiek z marmuru* (1977; *Man of Marble*), in which he has most clearly mirrored the concerns and interests of the majority of Polish film audiences. Jerzy Michalowski dies from an exploding stove at the film's close. Here, too, there is ambiguity, since it remains unclear if it is an accident. There have been several references to a faulty cooker, although Jerzy's movements near the stove remain unclear and could indicate suicide, since the explosion occurs when Agata has left the house on an errand.

The doyen of Polish filmmakers, Andrzej Wajda has depicted his nation's history in films that range from the Napoleonic period to the turmoil surrounding the Solidarity trade-union movement. A product of postwar Polish society, he has demonstrated a formidable talent in making films that lie on the borderline between the permissible and the impermissible.

*Lenny Rubenstein*

# WITHOUT PITY (SENZA PIETÀ)

*Origin:* Italy
*Released:* 1949
*Released in U.S.:* 1949
*Production:* Carlo Ponti for Lux Films
*Direction:* Alberto Lattuada
*Screenplay:* Tullio Pinelli, Federico Fellini, and Alberto Lattuada; based on an idea by Ettore Maria Margadonna
*Cinematography:* Aldo Tonti
*Editing:* Mario Bonotti
*Art direction:* Piero Gherardi
*Costume design:* Piero Gherardi
*Music:* Nino Rota
*Running time:* 94 minutes

*Principal characters:*

Angela Borghi .................... Carla Del Poggio
Jerry Jackson...................... John Kitzmiller
Pierluigi............................ Pierre Claudé
Marcella ......................... Giulietta Masina
Giacomo .............................. Folco Lulli
South American captain .............. Lando Muzio
Richard ............................ Daniel Jones
Baron Hoffman....................... Carlo Bianco
Sister Gertrude...................... Enza Giovine
Bandit ............................ Romano Villi
Bandit ........................... Mario Perrone

Alberto Lattuada's *Without Pity* is one of the minor masterpieces of neorealism, as well as one of the director's best films. Though produced in the heyday of neorealism, it differs from films such as Luchino Visconti's *La terra trema* (1948; *The Earth Trembles*) or Vittorio De Sica's *Ladri di biciclette* (1948; *The Bicycle Thief*) in several interesting ways. Like them, it presents a faithful, almost documentary portrait of a particular time and place, in this case postwar Livorno, more specifically, the pine forest of Tombolo, headquarters of the occupying American Army—and of crime, bootlegging, and prostitution as well. *Without Pity*, however, unlike more familiar neorealist films, uses cinematic techniques and a plot that are much indebted to classic Hollywood films, particularly gangster films and *film noir*. In fact, it is precisely its eclectic style which has caused it to be overshadowed by purer examples of neorealism.

While the film's theme of interracial love is unusual for its time, the figure of the naïve, kindhearted, American black soldier recurs in several of the period's films, including Roberto Rossellini's *Paisà* (1946; *Paisan*). In the cultural context of postwar Italy the black is not viewed as an object of racial prejudice, but rather as someone generous and better off, to be exploited somewhat affectionately for American material advantages such as money, food, and clothing. Yet because he is a suffering victim within his own culture, he reveals America's failure to eradicate old-world evil.

As the film begins, Angela Borghi (Carla Del Poggio) is stowing away on a Livorno-bound train, determined to find her brother, when a shoot-out occurs, wounding a black American soldier, Jerry Jackson (John Kitzmiller). Seeking help for him, she is charged with vagrancy and is sent to a women's prison with a truckload of prostitutes. One of them, Marcella (Giulietta Masina), leads the others in an escape and befriends Angela, sharing her scanty sleeping accommodations in the apartment of Giacomo (Folco Lulli) and introducing her to Pierluigi (Pierre Claudé), who runs the bootlegging operations. Jerry drives by and recognizes Angela. Seeing them talking, Pierluigi decides to exploit Jerry's feelings for her in order to enlist him as a bootlegger, arguing that she will get in trouble unless Jerry provides her with money. While delivering stolen goods, Jerry is caught by the military police and imprisoned. Meanwhile, Marcella persuades Angela, who believes that her brother is dead, to support herself by becoming one of Pierluigi's prostitutes. Jerry escapes from the military prison, but his friend Richard (Daniel Jones), accompanying him, is killed. Jerry returns to look for Angela, pursued by the military police. A young prostitute kills herself after Pierluigi refuses to give her money, and Angela, enraged, attacks him. She sees Jerry from the window, but Pierluigi goes out looking for him, and he disappears. On the beach of Livorno, Marcella, who has finally saved up enough money to depart for America with her fiancé, bids Angela a tearful farewell. Afterward, on the beach, Angela encounters Jerry, and they lament their inability to raise enough money to follow Marcella's example. Later, at the club, Angela tells Jerry that she has overheard Pierluigi planning to deliver a large sum of money at dawn. In the morning, she goes off to church to pray. Jerry holds up Pierluigi, takes his money and truck, and joins Angela in the church. Pierluigi returns with his gunmen (Romano Villi and Mario Perrone), however, and in the ensuing scuffle Angela leaps in front of Jerry to save him from a bullet and is killed. Jerry, distraught, places her body in the truck, drives awhile, then plunges the car through a fence and down a hill, killing himself.

The film's basic rhythm is operatic; moments of quiet lyricism alternate with violently edited confrontations. At first, Angela seems the typical neorealist heroine. Staring vacantly at the landscape, dirty and disheveled, she yawns, makes faces at a dog, spits, and empties dirt from her shoes. Yet quickly the mood turns dramatic as a military truck crashes through a fence, and the chase is on. In these action-packed sequences, Lattuada uses a montage which aims at involving the spectator's emotions. The film's finale provides a good example of his method. As Jerry and Angela leave the church, they encounter one of Pierluigi's two gunmen, who have come for the money. As Jerry resists, grabbing the bandit's gun, Lattuada suddenly cuts to a close-up of Angela screaming, then an extremely brief shot of the second gunman pointing his gun, then back to Angela throwing herself in front of Jerry, the gunman firing, and finally Angela slumping dead at Jerry's feet. After Jerry decides to drive off the cliff, the spectator sees a similar sequence: The crash consists of a medium shot of the truck breaking through the fence, then a very brief, extremely low-angle shot from underneath its wheels before it rolls down the hill, filmed from alternating viewpoints. In scenes such as these, Lattuada creates a Hollywood-style suspense and excitement that are not usually found in the slow-paced neorealist films, most of which employ long sequences without cuts, demanding more attention from the spectator.

Lattuada's expressionistic, *film noir* lighting also reflects the Hollywood influence. Ominous shadows, strong diagonal lines, and nighttime settings reinforce the evil atmosphere generated by the character of Pierluigi, who, though himself similar to a certain type of *film noir* gangster, incarnates a purer form of evil. Marcella compares him to a piece of chalk, for he always dresses in white and never displays emotion. In one sequence, Pierluigi is on his way to meet Jerry and Angela at Giacomo's apartment, intent on corrupting Jerry. Pierluigi climbs the staircase, followed by his shadow, before pausing at the landing, his face momentarily eclipsed by the broad, diagonally slanting steps of the next flight. Suddenly another huge, ominous shadow appears from around the corner, followed by its source—Jerry's assailant, who appears ever so briefly before Pierluigi, irritated, tells him to go away. When Jerry arrives at the building and starts up the stairs, he pauses in mid-flight to greet Pierluigi. Jerry's innocence is underscored by his forthright shadow, which, in contrast to the others, is straight behind him, undistorted.

Pierluigi's ominous character is emphasized in another scene as Jerry and Angela are leaving Luna Park. From their point of view, the spectator sees Marcella with Giacomo in his truck, but then, expecting a counter-shot of them from Marcella and Giacomo's point of view, the spectator sees them through the far window of the truck, with Marcella and Giacomo in the foreground. This is somewhat disorienting, but the reason soon becomes apparent: When Giacomo drives off, Pierluigi is revealed, parked behind the empty space, and the strange shot is retrospectively revealed as having been from Pierluigi's point of view. Lattuada, by showing that an apparently objective shot of Jerry and Angela was in reality a subjective one from

Pierluigi's point of view, points up the near omniscience of the latter's presence, the impossibility of escaping his evil designs.

The film's sound track by Nino Rota, famous for his later collaboration with Federico Fellini, utilizes black spirituals such as "Nobody Knows the Trouble I've Seen," "I Got a Robe," and "Swing Low, Sweet Chariot." Twice during the film, "I Got a Robe" is sung: once by Jerry as he leaves Luna Park with Angela, and once by the group of predominantly black prisoners in the military prison. When modulations of these songs appear on the sound track, they link the suffering of prostitutes with that of the American blacks. In fact, even apart from the sound track, the similarity between Jerry, the black American soldier, and Angela, the blonde, Italian prostitute, is striking. In a café, Baron Hoffman (Carlo Bianco) reads their palms, claiming that the lines are almost identical. They regard each other with a protective sympathy, each trying to save the other from harm. Both are involved in fights while in the prisons from which they escape. Both are generous to a fault: Jerry spends wildly on a gang of ragamuffins at Luna Park; Angela gives alms in the church. Ultimately, each is caught in Pierluigi's web.

The film is not, then, a neorealist examination of a love relationship doomed because of racial disparity. It is a pessimistic statement about the triumph of an evil that transcends mere social causes. The similarity between Jerry and Angela reflects the underlying similarity between Italy and the United States, and the film's eclecticism, its marriage between Italian and American styles, is part of its meaning. There is no possibility of a new beginning, be it a radically new cinematic style or a boat to America. In Pierluigi's universe, suicide is the only escape from evil and corruption.

*Joan Esposito*

# WOMAN IN THE DUNES
# (SUNA NO ONNA)

*Origin:* Japan
*Released:* 1964
*Released in U.S.:* 1964
*Production:* Kiichi Ichikawa and Tadashi Ohono for Teshigahara Productions; released by Pathé Contemporary Films
*Direction:* Hiroshi Teshigahara
*Screenplay:* Kōbō Abe; based on his novel
*Cinematography:* Hiroshi Segawa
*Editing:* F. Suisui
*Art direction:* no listing
*Music:* Tohru Takemitsu
*Running time:* 123 minutes

*Principal characters:*
Man .............................. Eiji Okada
Woman .......................... Kyoko Kishida

The allegorical *Woman in the Dunes* poses many questions, foremost among them whether man lives to work or works to live. Absorbing in its implications, the stunningly photographed black-and-white film is both simplistic and complex. Only the second feature to be directed by painter Hiroshi Teshigahara, the work is a parable about the nature of freedom, a story of man versus nature, and a love story between Everyman and Everywoman. In the view of some critics, it is primarily a study in horror.

Scripted by Kōbō Abe, from his best-selling novel of the same title (winner of the 1960 Yomiuri Literature Award), the 1964 film opens to find a man (Eiji Okada) hunting insects on a desolate stretch of beach. When he misses his bus back to the city, he asks local villagers if they know of lodgings where he might spend the night. They lead him to a sand pit, inviting him to climb down a ladder into its depths. The woman (Kyoko Kishida) who lives there, in a flimsy shack, must shovel sand daily in order to survive; otherwise she will be drowned in a sea of sand. She allows the stranger to stay the night, and greets him the following morning with the words, "Please don't blame me. Remember, you came here of your own accord." Wandering outside, the man discovers that the ladder is gone. A prisoner of the sand pit, he has been brought to the woman of the dunes as an intended mate. At first perplexed, and later angered, the man schemes to escape, but as the film progresses, he undergoes an evolution. Ultimately, when he can escape, he chooses not to do so.

Insistent that in narrative and theme the film is simplistic, requiring no analysis, director Teshigahara has said, "The battle against the lifeless sand, which becomes almost alive through its constant shifting, can be interpreted as the never-ending battle of man against his environment." Indeed, the sand permeates every nuance of life in the pit, as well as every frame of the film. Yet if the story line seems to find the man coming to terms with his surroundings, it also underlines other perceptions which have, through the decades, drawn exhaustive critical scrutiny which continues today, since the film regularly enjoys retrospective screenings.

A film of ironies, since the man who was a collector is himself captured—collected—*Woman in the Dunes* has also been examined as a love story, since, in time, the man is drawn to the woman he initially found drab. Feminists have also drawn significance from the fact that the woman accepts her fate while the man, like a bad-tempered child, incessantly struggles. Peace seems to come only when he grows resigned to his new life. That resignation appears to be derived from many things, including the fact that the world he had known lets him down (that is, no one ventures into the dunes looking for him when he does not report back to his office job in the city). He is also given to ponder whether he was any more free in the city than in the dunes.

Though they eventually become allies, the man and the woman discover each other only after days (time is never made clear) alongside each other in the pit. For reasons that are part of the film's inherent mystery, the woman must shovel sand not only for her survival, but also to ensure the very existence of the village. Each day, villagers cluster at the pit, drawing up the sand that the woman has shoveled. The villagers turn the sand into bricks, which are then sold to cities. "Don't you find all this meaningless? Moving sand to live—living to move sand?" the man angrily asks.

At first confused and arrogant and certain that rescue is imminent, he is also puzzled by the unassuming woman, who toils daily without question, despite even personal sorrow, including the death of a lover (whom the man has replaced) several months earlier. Dependent upon the villagers for food and water (and, on occasion, liquor and tobacco), the couple is constantly taunted by those who draw up the buckets of sand. At one point, in punishment for an escape attempt, the man must make love to the woman in view of a village audience that gazes downward into the pit; this act is done in exchange for water.

The days stretch on, one into the other. This passage of time in itself frustrates the man, who is given to cry out, "Time is important to me!" Obsessed with escape, he manages to weave a rope; with the use of a grappling hook, he even climbs to safety. After leaving the pit, however, he inadvertently wanders into quicksand (another of the film's many ironies). Hearing his cries, the villagers come to his aid. After pulling him out, they return him to the pit.

Confounded by the woman, and sometimes cruel to her, the man is also surprised when she grows increasingly attractive to him. Their lovemaking, at first hesitant, grows in passion, as if to suggest a life force within the deathly dunes.

Still, the thought of escape persists, causing the man to build a trap for a crow (to which he plans to attach a message). When the woman becomes ill with abdominal cramps—she is pregnant—the trap becomes unnecessary. After taking the woman away to receive medical attention, the villagers fail to take the rope ladder which leads into the pit. The man, who has been left alone, climbs to freedom. Yet once away from the pit, he has second thoughts. After returning to the sand pit which was once his purgatory, he studies the trap. Water, apparently drawn from the pit's depths, has gathered inside. In the film's closing sequence, the man stares at his own reflection in the water, apparently awaiting the return of the woman and, perhaps, marveling at the new life that has collected in the desolate dunes.

A film in which man discovers fulfillment, and even a sense of belonging, in a primitive world, *Woman in the Dunes* is a tour de force for performers Eiji Okada and Kyoko Kishida. The exceedingly handsome Okada first garnered acclaim as the architect-lover in Alain Resnais' landmark French New Wave film, *Hiroshima mon amour* (1959). He was also critically hailed for his performance in the 1963 American film *The Ugly American*. Kyoko was noted mostly for her work on the stage.

Along with the two performers, *Woman in the Dunes* is dominated by the ever-present sand. The film's cinematography, by Hiroshi Segawa, with its high-contrast lighting and textured look, makes the sand the film's third "performer." Magnified hundreds of times in numerous close-ups, the grains tumble through the roof of the shack and continually sift down the sides of the pit. They are everywhere—on utensils, dishes, clothing, and even bodies, from which they are constantly brushed—sometimes with sensual strokes. When not obsessed with grains of sand, the camera focuses on grains of skin. Compelling in look as well as theme, *Woman in the Dunes* includes boldly photographed (for the time) lovemaking sequences, as well as breathtaking vistas of the seemingly never-ending dunes.

The winner of the Special Jury Prize at the 1964 Cannes International Film Festival, *Woman in the Dunes* was also nominated for an Academy Award as Best Foreign-Language Film. It is a film that seems destined to endure—a film that dares to ask questions which linger long after the end credits.

*Pat H. Broeske*

# THE WOMAN NEXT DOOR (LA FEMME D'À CÔTÉ)

*Origin:* France
*Released:* 1981
*Released in U.S.:* 1981
*Production:* Armand Barbault for Les Films du Carosse and TF1 Films
*Direction:* François Truffaut
*Screenplay:* François Truffaut, Suzanne Schiffman, and Jean Aurel
*Cinematography:* William Lubtchansky
*Editing:* Martine Barraque
*Art direction:* Jean-Pierre Kohut-Svelko
*Music:* Georges Delerue
*MPAA rating:* R
*Running time:* 106 minutes

*Principal characters:*
Bernard Coudray................Gérard Depardieu
Mathilde Bauchard..................Fanny Ardant
Philippe Bauchard..................Henri Garcin
Arlette Coudray..............Michèle Baumgartner
Mme Odile Jouve.................Véronique Silver
Thomas Coudray ...............Olivier Becquaert
Doctor ...................Philippe Morier-Genoud
Roland Pugnet ..................Roger Van Hool

François Truffaut's *The Woman Next Door* is a moody and disturbing tale of obsessive love uneasily yoked with a perceptive portrait of the suburban bourgeoisie. The film saddles quite ordinary people with extraordinary romantic dilemmas (traditionally the subject matter of French farce) which lead to tragic results.

A pall of pessimism is cast over the film from the beginning by the sadly retrospective narrative voice of Mme Odile Jouve (Véronique Silver), the manager of a tennis club in a village just outside Grenoble. Among the club's members are a merchant-marine engineer, Bernard Coudray (Gérard Depardieu), his wife Arlette (Michèle Baumgartner), and the Coudrays' young son, Thomas (Olivier Becquaert). Theirs is a content, middle-class existence, free of major problems or rifts but also devoid of any true joy.

Things suddenly change when a married couple rents the house next door. The neighbors are Philippe Bauchard (Henri Garcin), an air traffic controller, and his younger and hauntingly attractive wife, Mathilde (Fanny Ardant). Startled and strangely intense looks pass between Bernard and Mathilde when the families first exchange introductions, and from then on,

Bernard makes an unsubtle effort to avoid contact with the strange beauty—even failing to show up at a housewarming dinner that Arlette prepares for the Bauchards. Enigmatically, Mathilde finds these snubs enticing; when she makes attempts to contact Bernard by telephone, he rudely cuts her off.

When Bernard and Mathilde meet accidentally at a supermarket, the audience learns that they are not, in fact, new acquaintances who have only recently been introduced to each other. Eight years before, they carried on a passionate love affair, and now, despite their fears (Bernard is particularly fearful), they resume their romance, meeting secretly at a hotel in the city. During an afternoon at the tennis club, Mathilde learns the story behind Mme Jouve's limp: Following a jilting in her youth, the poor woman attempted a suicide plunge. It is Mme Jouve who introduces Mathilde to a homosexual publisher, who hires her to illustrate a children's book.

Involved in a promising career (and with Bernard's wife pregnant with a second child), Mathilde finds the termination of their relationship inevitable, but Bernard responds to these rebuffs with increased attention. Indeed, Bernard becomes so reckless that Mathilde finally suggests to Philippe that they take a North African holiday. At the bon voyage party, Bernard's possessiveness borders on insanity: He publicly beats Mathilde and professes his love for her.

Following this embarrassing incident, Bernard seems resigned to the end of the affair, but Mathilde now suffers from his romantic obsessiveness, as if by contagion: returning from her vacation in time for the publication of her book, she has a nervous breakdown during an autograph-signing party. With his wife hospitalized and seemingly fated to perpetual catatonia, Philippe asks Bernard to drop in on her to help her snap out of it. With the Coudray household now moved into the city, Bernard and his wife look upon these visitations as the therapeutic duty of any ex-neighbor. Indeed, Mathilde seems to recover; she is released and resumes her married life with Philippe in Grenoble.

One night, awakened by strange sounds, Bernard leaves his sleeping wife to find the source of the noise. In the vacant house next-door, he discovers Mathilde. After exchanging a minimum of words, they fall into each other's arms and make love. While they are still locked in their embrace, Mathilde pulls a pistol from her purse and shoots Bernard in the head and then herself.

*The Woman Next Door* could be dismissed as simply a sordid country-club romance were it not for the pervasive sense of impending disaster created by the manner in which the story is told, a narrative mood underscored by Georges Delerue's pensive score and by William Lubtchansky's cinematography. Starting with Mme Jouve's gloomy voice-over introduction during an aerial shot of a police ambulance rushing to the site of the murder-suicide, the story is sprinkled with small situations that teeter on the brink of disaster. Early in the film, for example, young Thomas scampers about the Bauchard house under the supervision of the strange Mathilde, and she has the expression of a child-murderess or someone who would giggle if the boy fell upon the exposed nails of a broken packing crate. Later, Bernard sends Thomas on a mission through the rear hatch of the family car after locking himself out—with the engine running.

Doomed love and romantic obsession are constant themes in Truffaut's films; *Le Peau douce* (1964; *The Soft Skin*) and *L'Histoire de Adèle H.* (1964; *The Story of Adèle H.*) are two good examples. Relationships that ultimately end with a woman responsible for a murder-suicide are an extension of the premise set forth in *Jules et Jim* (1962; *Jules and Jim*). In *The Woman Next Door*, Truffaut again adapts this tragic scenario, and the result is a film which, despite its moments of undeniable power, is ultimately forced and unconvincing. Stage-trained Fanny Ardant had her film debut in the title role. Although her strange allure provides motivation for the hapless Bernard, she does not give a performance that is sufficiently multidimensional to explain why she is driven to murder the man fate has forbidden her to love. The fault is ultimately Truffaut's, however, for he has imposed his aesthetic will on his material instead of giving it a life of its own.

*Tim Kennedy*

# THE WOODEN GUN (ROVEH HULIOT)

*Origin:* Israel
*Released:* 1979
*Released in U.S.:* 1985
*Production:* Eitan Even, Richard Sanders, and John Hardy for Makor Films/Hardy-Sanders Motion Pictures
*Direction:* Ilan Moshenson
*Screenplay:* Ilan Moshenson
*Cinematography:* Gadi Danzig
*Editing:* Zion Abrahamian
*Art direction:* Eytan Levy
*Music:* Yossi Mar-Haim
*MPAA rating:* no listing
*Running time:* 91 minutes

*Principal characters:*
Yoni .............................. Eric Rosen
Mother .............................. Judith Sole
Teacher .............................. Leo Yung
Palestina .............................. Ophelia Strahl
Principal .............................. Louis Rosenberg
Father .............................. Michael Kfir

Since 1972, a group of serious young directors has committed itself to capturing the Israeli reality on film. Among the films produced by this group, known as Kayitz (New Israeli Cinema), Ilan Moshenson's *The Wooden Gun* ranks as one of the finest works.

The story, set in Tel Aviv in 1950, examines two adolescent gangs that play "war games." The film addresses itself to the national myth of being a soldier. It reflects the contradiction between the military priorities necessary to protect the state and the ethical values that promote aliyah (the ingathering of Jews to Israel). As social historian Amos Elon points out in his book *The Israelis*, "Early Zionism was predicated upon faith in peaceful change. The discovery that this was nearly impossible has profoundly affected the Israeli temper. As in other liberation movements, whether social or national, the Zionist mystique of redemption has become powerfully intertwined with a mystique of violence. The resulting dissonance is today a main characteristic of Israel."

This clash is played out in the mind of Yoni (Eric Rosen), a sensitive ten-year-old boy who gradually learns the meaning of responsibility. Director Moshenson concentrates on the Israeli effort to deny the Holocaust and the stigma of Jewish victimization, especially through the children's insensitivity and intolerance. Yoni and his friends treat the new immigrants as pariahs, invaders of their proud land.

Moshenson reveals the power structure that infects the whole society, finding ultimate sanction in the family as well as in the children's gangs, and exposing the cruelty and complexity of domination in both worlds. Only in his depiction of Palestina (Ophelia Strahl), a Felliniesque madwoman, ravaged by the events of World War II, does he lapse into sentimentality and obtrusive symbolism.

Behind the opening credits flash images of war, immigration, and economic conditions. These three subjects constitute the major themes of the film.

The story proper opens as the sounds of a waltz by Johann Strauss emanate from an apartment window. Outside, Yoni and his friends sneak up and ambush a lone child. Although the group had agreed that it was against the rules to gang up on a single child, the boys now decide that "it is war" and cast the rules aside.

At school, lessons seem boring and the children become restless. Only the school play holds their attention. Reenacting the battle between the Jews and the Romans, Yoni and his friends elect to play Romans.

Another activity that absorbs the children is watching the arrival of new immigrants. Disgusted by their aura of victimization, the boys think they should have stayed in Europe. In contrast to their suffering, the students exude a sense of innocent arrogance, declaring that the Jews of the Diaspora should have eradicated the Gentiles.

Yoni knows little about World War II or the Holocaust. Although his mother (Judith Sole) keeps the radio tuned in hopes of hearing the names of lost relatives and travels to Haifa to meet boatloads of new arrivals, she will not discuss matters directly, telling Yoni, "When you grow up."

At school, Yoni and his friends are taught about ancient wars; in fact, Jewish history seems to be a chronicle of ceaseless attacks. The boys are being groomed to be good soldiers and indoctrinated with the goal of winning back East Jerusalem with its sacred Wailing Wall. Even at home, the importance of strength is communicated as Yoni's father (Michael Kfir) hand wrestles with Yoni and talks of his brave war experiences. Only Yoni's mother opposes this emphasis on fighting.

Yoni's nemesis is the gang leader, a fat boy whom Yoni has named "Einschwein," a term of denigration which, his teacher (Leo Yung) explains, was used by the Nazis. The boys in his group have obtained a wooden gun whose chain link bullets have killed a bird. The children debate the use of the gun and decide that it is permissible to use it if they aim only at their enemy's legs.

In addition to picking on one another, the boys sometimes go down to the beach and taunt the crazy Palestina, who lives in an isolated hut and sings songs about the destiny of Palestine.

As the war games become more aggressive, some of the children break into Yoni's apartment. Now Yoni's father takes a stand against the pranks. Still Yoni will not concede. His father then whips him with a belt, ironically demonstrating the use of power at the same time that he opposes it.

With the arrival of the Independence Day celebrations, the students run off to fight their ultimate battle. The rival leader, Kaufman, wounds Einschwein with a switchblade. Yoni, determined to seek revenge for this deed as well as for his own previously broken arm, attacks Kaufman with the wooden gun. When hit, Kaufman falls limp and bleeding. Frightened because of his deed, Yoni runs off, arriving at Palestina's hut. While she washes his bleeding knee, he gazes at her walls filled with old photographs of Jewish victims. The boys, still playing their games, arrive and throw stones. Yoni now experiences what it feels like to be a victim. Simultaneously, he realizes that his actions have been little different from those of a Nazi.

Outside, his friends yell that Kaufman is okay and Yoni is a "hero," but Yoni knows better: Leaving the hut, he begins to climb the hills as the boys call out, "Come back. Come back to us." Nevertheless, Yoni has grown apart from them now. With new understanding, he ascends the hills.

Although the effect of war on the psychological development of the young has appeared in other films, namely *Forbidden Games* (1952) and *The Search* (1948), the theme takes on special significance in an Israeli context. Here the children are not waifs, but rather the desensitized offspring of brutalized adults. The details—Independence Day pageants, radio announcements for lost relatives, school trips to Jerusalem—are specifically Israeli, but the message is universal. By intelligently confronting the values of a past era, Moshenson has provided a compelling lesson for the present.

As might be expected, *The Wooden Gun* was a box-office disaster in Israel and, like other films critical of the body politic, was well received elsewhere, especially at the Berlin International Film Festival. Even though the film experienced a lack of attention at home, it is an impassioned plea to Israelis to reassess contemporary values and to readjust the balance between the emphasis on strength and the necessity for human concern.

*Patricia Erens*

# THE WORLD OF APU (APUR SANSAR)

*Origin:* India
*Released:* 1958
*Released in U.S.:* 1959
*Production:* Satyajit Ray and Amiyanath Mukerjee for Satyajit Ray Productions
*Direction:* Satyajit Ray
*Screenplay:* Satyajit Ray; based on the novel *Aparajito*, by Bibhuti Bannerji
*Cinematography:* Subrata Mitra
*Editing:* Dulal Dutta
*Art direction:* Bansi Chandragupta
*Music:* Ravi Shankar
*Running time:* 103 minutes

*Principal characters:*
Apu.......................... Soumitra Chatterjee
Aparna .......................... Sharmila Tagore
Pulu .......................... Swapan Mukherji
Kajol.......................... Aloke Chakravarty
Aparna's mother.......................... Shefalika
Aparna's father................ Dhiresh Mazumder
Landlord.......................... Dhiren Ghosh
Aparna's brother ............... Abhijit Chatterjee
Apu's neighbor.......................... Belarani
Office associate .............. Shanti Bhattacharjee

*The World of Apu* is the final film of Satyajit Ray's Apu trilogy. Since the appearance of *Pather panchali* (1955), Ray's films have the distinction of being the only Indian films to have attracted significant attention in the United States. Ray's career as a filmmaker was inspired by his enthusiasm for Italian neorealist films and by his contact with the great French director Jean Renoir. Thus, Ray's visual style and often the subject matter of his work clearly indicate the influence of the major European traditions of cinematic realism, and his films are therefore more accessible to the Western viewer than one might expect. Although he was graduated from the University of Calcutta, where he majored in economics, he later studied painting with Rabindranath Tagore, the Hindu poet. A poet's sensibility and the eye of a painter are evident in Ray's keen sense of shot composition and camera placement as well as in his preoccupation with the fundamental questions of the human condition. The scope of the Apu trilogy is vast, encompassing the youth of an Indian boy in *Pather panchali*, his adolescence in *Aparajito*

(1957), and his attainment of maturity and wisdom in *The World of Apu*. All three films deal vividly with terrible poverty, hardship, and the loss of innocence. Perhaps the most important theme of the Apu films is that of learning to cope with the inescapable presence of death. From one perspective, the trilogy may be seen as cyclic in structure, but from another point of view, the conclusion of *The World of Apu* breaks the cycle and presents the protagonist in the optimistic light of a new life.

The structure of *The World of Apu* is itself carefully conceived. The film begins with a prologue, which is presented before the title and credits appear on screen. Part 1 introduces Apu (Soumitra Chatterjee) as a young, ambitious, but impoverished writer, who is able to survive in Calcutta only by giving private lessons and by pawning his books. In part 2, an old friend, Pulu (Swapan Mukherji), visits Apu and invites him to the country, where they will attend the wedding of Aparna (Sharmila Tagore), Pulu's cousin. In an unexpected turn of events, Apu himself becomes the bridegroom, and the wedding of Aparna and Apu and the circumstances which bring it about constitute the third part of the film. The fourth and central section of the film is in fact the story of the happiness of Apu and Aparna, but part 5 begins with the death in childbirth of Apu's beloved bride. Apu changes drastically, and his aimless wanderings and scenes of the difficult childhood of his son, Kajol (Aloke Chakravarty), are depicted also. The final section of the film features Apu's return to the village where Kajol lives with his maternal grandparents (Dhiresh Mazumder and Shefalika). The film ends with Apu returning to Calcutta, having accepted the responsibility of fatherhood and having allowed love to be part of his life once again.

The narrative of *The World of Apu* is quite simple. The beautiful understatement of the film's plot, dialogue, and acting may surprise the American viewer who is accustomed to a very different film tradition, one which relies more on action than upon subtle characterization, psychological analysis, and the relationships between human beings and the world in which they find themselves. Nevertheless, the attentive, patient spectator will be rewarded. The Apu whom one meets at the beginning of the film has recently been cut loose from the relative security of formal education: He cannot afford to complete the work necessary for his bachelor's degree. Lack of a job, money, and security, however, neither dampen his spirits nor cloud his romantic vision of himself as a struggling young writer preparing himself for "greatness." The film's first scenes show an Apu almost reveling in his poverty: bathing in an early morning downpour, bantering cheerfully with his landlord (Dhiren Ghosh) over the question of back rent, chatting with an elderly neighbor (Belarani), pensively playing his flute. Pulu represents the real world—the world of steady, respectable work and responsibility. The two men even differ in appearance: Pulu gives the impression of being more Westernized and urbanized than Apu. He has put on weight, dresses in trousers and an open-necked shirt which contrast with Apu's traditional attire, and his horn-rimmed spectacles give him a serious mien. As different as Apu and Pulu may seem, however, the warmth of their friendship is obvious. Like the teacher who praised Apu's writing and encouraged him to continue with it, Pulu knows that his old friend has unusual talent.

Pulu invites Apu to Aparna's wedding. Apu is charmed by Pulu's description of the beauty of the distant village where the ceremony is to take place, and they soon set out on a journey. Oddly enough, the tables are turned upon their arrival in the rural setting. Apu seems ill at ease amid the relatively primitive customs and surroundings. On the day of the wedding, the groom-to-be falls victim to a strange fit of anxiety and disorientation. According to tradition, should the wedding not take place, Aparna will be cursed. Pulu, now clad in white ceremonial garb, pleads with Apu to be the substitute groom. Apu is at first appalled by such an unreasonable request (he wants nothing to do with barbaric customs of this sort), but after a time, he relents, because, as he later says to Aparna, he thinks that he is doing something noble. Apu and Aparna are thus united as strangers in a bizarre marriage which appears to hold no promise of happiness for either of them—he is hopelessly poor, she is accustomed to comfort.

The love of Apu and Aparna is literally and figuratively the heart of the film. Aparna is seen weeping alone in Apu's wretched Calcutta apartment, but she hears a baby crying and looks down into a refuse-littered courtyard. Her vision of the mother tenderly caring for the child seems to bring her out of her homesickness and culture shock into a realization of what she must do and of what her role is. What develops from this point is, for both her and Apu, nothing less than bliss; what began as an arranged marriage of the most peculiar sort becomes a study in mutual devotion.

All the more tragic, then, is Aparna's death. Apu has taken an office job and has sent Aparna home to her mother to have their child. The messenger who is waiting for Apu outside his apartment one afternoon after work brings the news which nearly ends Apu's life in the true sense of the word. He considers suicide but instead leaves Calcutta and begins a five-year-long rejection of everything that he has known before. One is reminded at this point of what he has said to Pulu earlier in the film: He was happy in his poverty and lack of responsibility and ties. All he needed then was his novel and his dream of success as a writer. Now, he wanders by the sea, into the forests, staring at sunsets—apparently looking for answers in nature. The novel is literally thrown to the winds: Apu's gesture of scattering the pages of the manuscript into a remote valley and his expression state quite clearly that life has absolutely no meaning for him at all. Cruel irony is to be found, however, in the subject of the unfinished novel. As Pulu has observed, it was an autobiography of sorts. The novel was to tell the story of a boy who loses his father (Apu's father died when he was ten; he later also lost his mother and sister) and later comes to the city to study. The hero of the novel has, as Apu describes him, ambition and the seeds of greatness, but he fails in his pursuit of success. Even so, he learns that failure is not the end. He does not try to escape from reality or reject life—instead, he discovers that the real point of life is facing reality, no matter how harsh it may be. As Apu abandons the manuscript upon which he has worked so hard and with such hope, he fails to recognize the relevance of its lesson to his own situation.

While Apu is indulging his own grief, Ray shows by means of parallel editing what has become of the son whom Apu has never seen. Kajol is an undisciplined child, and his grandfather is understandably bitter about what he believes to be Apu's selfish neglect of the boy. Pulu finds Apu in the mountains of central India, where he has taken a job in a mine. Pulu tries to convince his friend that he and his son need each other. Eventually, for reasons which are no more immediately apparent than were the motives which encouraged him to marry Aparna, Apu agrees to return to the village to meet Kajol. He does make a genuine effort to win the boy's affection, but without success. In frustration, Apu takes his leave of the grandfather and walks away from the home. In the background though, Kajol watches, and ultimately the boy learns that this stranger is his father. The film ends with an unforgettable shot of Kajol on the shoulders of a happy Apu as they begin a journey back to Calcutta, back to the film's point of departure. The musical theme which was stated at the beginning of the film is heard again.

Apu, it turns out now, has lived his novel instead of writing it. In spite of the terrible grief which he suffered after Aparna's death, his newfound devotion to Kajol constitutes an affirmation of life's value—a simple moral to the tale, banal perhaps, but most viewers will recognize the validity of the film's message and accept it. Apu has seen all too clearly that life is not reasonable. He has firsthand knowledge of the contingency of existence. His own life has been changed by a series of absurd twists: the mysterious madness of Aparna's intended groom; the marriage which began as a vaguely felt obligation on Apu's part and which became a union of profound devotion; Apu's sudden, vaguely motivated desire to be a father to Kajol; and the boy's equally unexplained change of heart at the end of the film. Love, like life, cannot be explained: It must be embraced when it is offered. Apu has been torn between loyalty to himself and the goals which he has set and obligations to others and what they expect of him—between a consciousness of the past and the forces of tradition as well as the promise of the future. In fact, the subject of his never-completed novel had embodied these tensions. At the end of the film, Apu has, at least for the time being, put aside his longing for literary fame in order to accept enthusiastically a new role as father—a role which he takes upon himself because he wants to and not because of the insistence of others. It is in this sense that the life cycle which Apu has known has been broken, for Kajol will not be, as his father was, an orphan. The film suggests, then, that despite the essential forces which determine one's life, one can, in some fashion, take charge of one's destiny. Apu's acceptance of his responsibility, as was the case with Aparna's acceptance of her lot as wife, comes from within. To this extent, Apu is master of his fate, and of Kajol's as well. Finally, Apu's union with his son belies what he has said to Pulu. Apu knows now that life must not be simply a matter of self-fulfillment and of avoiding commitments: He has learned from Aparna and through Kajol that life is living for others; true fulfillment comes only in love.

Since so much of *The World of Apu* has to do with self-analysis and with the attempt to understand one's relationship to others and to the grand scheme of things, it is not surprising that the close-up and the long take are basic to Ray's photographic repertoire. There are, it is true, important conversations and confrontations in the film, but more often than not, it is what one can read in the expressions of the characters that is most revealing and most touching. Ray's favorite strategy is to move the camera in, usually from a medium shot to a close-up, or to begin with a close-up and pull the camera back while the viewer listens to what is being said. Frequently, during a conversation, the camera focuses on the person being addressed rather than on the speaker, thus emphasizing reaction rather than words. Indeed, there are numerous critical passages in the film in which there is no dialogue at all. In a key sequence of the film, Aparna and Apu have arrived in Calcutta after their marriage. She dutifully follows her husband into their new home, which is much unlike that to which she has been accustomed. Apu leaves her alone for a moment, and Aparna sits down on the bed and looks out the window. She is seen from the side, in close-up, her head turned away from the camera, as she begins to cry softly. The camera pulls back slowly to show her in a medium shot that is held for several seconds. Aparna hears the baby crying in the courtyard below; there is a cut to a high-angle shot of what she sees in the courtyard, followed by a cut to an extreme close-up of Aparna's face at the window. This shot too is held so that one can absorb Aparna's reaction to what she has observed. Actually, this last shot also bears a certain symbolic content. Aparna looks down at the mother and child through a gaping hole in the curtain over the window, the hole and the curtain which were the subject of the first shot of Apu's apartment near the beginning of the film. The curtain then served as a concrete representation of Apu's wretched poverty; at this point, Aparna is literally framed by the hole in the curtain and by the bars on the window, a prisoner of poverty herself. This series of shots exemplifies not only Ray's extraordinary use of the camera but also his gift for composition within the frame, and there are countless such examples in the film of the director's visual sense. The last sequence of the film begins with a shot of Apu in close-up to the left of the frame. To the right of the frame, at some distance, stands Kajol. The issue at this moment in the narrative is the bond which is to develop between Apu and his son. In this shot, they are already united in the balance and harmony of the composition, the head and shoulders of Apu and the tiny figure of Kajol, by a broad, triangular expanse of deep shadow which is cast by the grandparents' house, which is to the right and almost completely out of frame.

Ray's masterful exploitation of the long take (a technique which he may well have learned from his admiration of Vittorio De Sica and Renoir) can be illustrated by an analysis of one of the most powerful sequences in *The World of Apu*. After he receives word of the death of Aparna, Apu falls into a state of lethargy; he lies on his bed for hours at a time. What follows on-screen is a series of unusually long takes which serve as a marvelous example of Ray's skill at editing in the camera. The first shot of the sequence is an extreme close-up of Apu in profile, looking right, in the darkness of his room. A clock is ticking; this sound becomes increasingly loud, then stops abruptly. Apu's eyes turn to the left of the frame, to where the clock must be. This first shot is held for fourteen seconds. The second shot begins as the camera pans slightly to the right to take in Apu's face as it is reflected in a small shaving mirror. The lower right-hand corner of the mirror, to the bottom and right of the frame, catches a bright spot of light. A train whistle is heard. When he hears the whistle, Apu slowly turns his head to the left; his face bears an expression of despair, and his eyes nearly close. This shot lasts twelve seconds. The train whistle serves as a sound bridge into the next shot, which has a duration of eight seconds. There is a fade from the darkness of Apu's room to a low-level shot of railroad tracks, and the viewer sees Apu in close-up to the right of the frame, looking sullenly left and down at the tracks. This shot is relatively brief, lasting only three seconds. The camera pans slowly left to include the expanse of sky above Apu's head, a representation of emptiness, which, interestingly enough, remains on the screen for eleven seconds. A train whistle and the sound of an approaching engine increasing in volume are heard. A train, still at some distance, enters the frame at lower left—a shot held only for one second—and then the camera pans slowly to the right to the close-up of Apu again, looking left. He lowers his head slowly, and the camera moves in. The time consumed by this shot is eight seconds. The sequence comes to an end with the roar of the passing train and the piercing squeal of a pig, which has been struck by the locomotive. Apu is distracted by the animal's scream and quickly turns his head. Ironically, his life has been saved by the death of the pig, for it is now too late for him to throw himself in front of the train. This wonderful sequence obliges the viewer to participate actively in what is taking place on-screen: There is no dialogue, no voice-over narration to explain what is on Apu's mind. That he is about to commit suicide is a point which Ray makes through an extraordinary juxtaposition of shots, pacing, frame composition, the orchestration of sound, and Soumitra Chatterjee's eloquent expressions.

In some ways—especially in its cinematography—*The World of Apu* has a Western look; yet the film gives the viewer a genuine sense of Indian life, customs, and values at the midpoint of the twentieth century. Ray does not make direct statements in the film about political and social problems, something which is perceived as a failing by some critics. Nevertheless, urban poverty and marginal living conditions, the exotic ambience of rural India, and even the lasting influence of British presence play important parts in the film. (Apu uses English phrases to emphasize a point, and the viewer will undoubtedly be amused to hear the strains of "For He's a Jolly Good Fellow" accompany the ceremonial arrival of Aparna's bridegroom.) Ravi Shankar's music, which enhances the narrative in ways which the American viewer may not always appreciate, often adds an effectively eerie quality to a film which has much to do with the mystery of human existence. The viewer has the best of both worlds, for Satyajit Ray's artistry, the film's message, and the talent of actors such as Chatterjee and Tagore easily transcend temporal and cultural boundaries.

*Gordon Walters*

# WOYZECK

*Origin:* West Germany
*Released:* 1979
*Released in U.S.:* 1980
*Production:* Werner Herzog for Werner Herzog Filmproduktion
*Direction:* Werner Herzog
*Screenplay:* Werner Herzog; based on a play fragment by Georg Büchner
*Cinematography:* Jörg Schmidt-Reitwein
*Editing:* Beate Mainke-Jellinghaus
*Art direction:* no listing
*Music:* Antonio Vivaldi and Benedetto Marcello
*MPAA rating:* no listing
*Running time:* 82 minutes

*Principal characters:*

Woyzeck .............................. Klaus Kinski
Woyzeck's mistress..................... Eva Mattes
Captain ..................... Wolfgang Reichmann
Doctor ........................ Willy Semmelrogge
Drum major ..................... Josef Bierbichler
Andres ............................. Paul Burian

As *Woyzeck* opens, Klaus Kinski comes comically into view, dressed in a shabby, old-fashioned soldier's uniform similar to the prisoner-of-war costumes of the American film *Stalag 17* (1953). The actor who was so threatening as the mad conquistador Aguirre and the vampire Nosferatu in Werner Herzog's earlier works is running energetically through the streets of a quaint German village, made sinister by its utter emptiness. An officer suddenly appears and forces the awkward soldier to go through his paces, doing Army calisthenics—useless, rigorous, and still comical. Then the middle-aged private passes the limit of his endurance, and the officer insists that he continue his push-ups, repeatedly kicking the exhausted soldier in the head. The theater of *commedia dell'arte*, with its stock character of the zealous soldier, turns into the alienating political theater of Bertolt Brecht, with its proletarian archetype of the oppressed soldier whose eagerness stems from fear and forlorn hope. Kinski's plastic face registers suffering, mute and intense, the suffering of the abused donkey under the whip. The theater of Brecht is transformed into the cinema of Werner Herzog, centering—as always—on the individual pushed to the extreme edge of human life.

From the beginning, Herzog's cinema has been the art of an outsider. Disavowing the readily available imagery of television and mass-audience films and the constant conditioning to mediocrity that they impose on their viewers, Herzog has always seemed to be attempting to re-create the cinema afresh. With visionary screen imagery reflecting the visions which afflict his outcast heroes, his protagonists have been those who will not or cannot be conditioned by their civilizations: dwarves, madmen, feral children, even a vampire who cannot quite succeed at being human. Up until his remake of the 1922 masterpiece *Nosferatu*, Herzog even avoided the use of the normal sources for film scripts—literature, drama, and other films—so that each work seemed wholly a product of his own imagination.

By remaking *Nosferatu* and by filming *Woyzeck*, Herzog begins to unravel his own riddle: He has not, as it first appeared, sprung full-blown from the German mystic tradition; he also has roots in a heritage of radically experimental German theater arts—from Georg Büchner and Bertholt Brecht in drama, and from F. W. Murnau and Fritz Lang in film. This fierce and extremist heritage, destroyed by Adolf Hitler (the ultimate media manipulator and conditioner of minds), has been revived in new forms. Herzog represents, if not quite the vanguard, at least one of the most extreme positions.

With *Woyzeck*, Herzog uses one of the earliest works of this tradition, a fragment of a play by Georg Büchner, who died at the age of twenty-three in 1836. Büchner wrote in common German instead of the aristocratic High German of the bourgeois theater of his day; even more scandalously, his protagonist was a man of the lowest class, a character based on a real soldier who had recently been executed for murder, and whose legal defense was a precursor of the "insanity plea." When *Woyzeck* was written, with its Marxist and Freudian prefigurations, Karl Marx was a teenager, and Sigmund Freud's mother was still a baby. A century later, Bertolt Brecht acknowledged Büchner's seminal influence on his own radical theater.

While Herzog is not by any standard an orthodox "Brechtian," being more inclined to mysticism than to Marxism, his *Woyzeck* inherently pays tribute to both Brecht and Büchner by centering on a man pushed over the edge by the specific cruelties of social class, demonstrated schematically in the precredit sequence described above. At the same time, the material reflects Herzog's own style and obsessions. The weird characters so typical of his previous work are present again: There is an obscene little doctor (Willy Semmelrogge); the actor who played the hypnotized drunk in *Herz aus Glas* (1976; *Heart of Glass*) reappears here as a ranting, misanthropic drunk; the protagonist himself is a soldier going mad, like the hero of Herzog's first film, *Lebenszeichen* (1968; *Signs of Life*). Also present are the conditioned "trick" animals (such as the dancing chickens of *Stroszek* (1977), who mock human attainment by their mindless imitations: At a street fair, the viewer meets a dancing monkey dressed as a soldier, and a "counting" horse. Only a cat, which the doctor flings from a window and which Woyzeck catches, retains its own nature. Thus, Woyzeck refuses to be the soldier-monkey and allies himself with the only domestic animal that sets its own limits on how far it will allow itself to be "trained."

As in most of Herzog's work, at the center is the hallucinating hero, whose very hallucinations free his mind from the truisms and common sense assumptions that, to Herzog, evidently cause blindness to the true nature of things. Clearly seeing the bare bones of the world, the hero can respond only by destroying that portion of his world that he can touch. Woyzeck's army pay is a mere subsistence, even for a bachelor, and thus the soldier supports his mistress (Eva Mattes) and infant son by serving as a guinea pig for the horrid doctor, who attempts to justify his contempt for humankind (and in particular, the "lower classes") by ugly experiments bent on proving that a working man is worth no more than a donkey.

The doctor has kept Woyzeck on a diet of peas for three months and gives the soldier a bonus for every new evidence of aberrance that he manifests. Woyzeck, half-starved and denied even the basic human pleasure of a varied diet, is indeed growing aberrant, but his madness has the clarity of a fasting saint's. The system has begun to reveal itself to him. When his captain (Wolfgang Reichmann) chides him for keeping a mistress, Woyzeck responds: "A penniless man doesn't have any use for morals." Beset by visions of a deadly white fire over the town and of a totally empty world, Woyzeck's lunacy—his breakout from the prisons of class and condition—proves him to be something more than a dancing monkey or a counting horse. Upon discovering his mistress' unfaithfulness, he loses the last worldly joy remaining to him and becomes a tragically free man.

In contrast, his mistress is a "normal" poor woman, forced into a form of whoredom by the social framework: A penniless woman does not have any use for morals. She betrays Woyzeck with a handsome, wealthy drum major in splendid uniform, who gives her gold earrings for her favors. Yet, because she is no more a trained monkey than is Woyzeck, she mourns her betrayal of a good man for a dazzling one and tells her children a story which reflects Woyzeck's own apocalyptic visions: A poor little girl is left all alone in a dead and empty world in her story. When Woyzeck stabs his mistress by the river's edge, in a slow-motion tableau wherein her body is invisible below the frame line, and Woyzeck's upper body fills the screen, the knife in Woyzeck's hand always comes back into the frame shining clean, as though his mistress had already been, somehow, emptied of blood.

*Woyzeck* unfolds with an austere economy of time and image: The tale is told briefly, in short, sharp episodes, filmed in a limited spectrum of cool, neutral colors (as in Herzog's *Nosferatu, the Vampyre*, 1979, and in contrast to most of his earlier color films). The imagery, too, is restrained, with only a few of the director's typically extraordinary settings: Woyzeck in a field of tall, green, as yet unblossomed flower buds; Woyzeck wading further and further into the river to retrieve his knife, raving aloud; his mistress' body carried in slow motion to a coffin by the river. Not an extravagant film, it is tightly elegant in its bleakness, the landscape of Kinski's face, an extremist face in which a change of expression, seen in close-shot, performs the same narrative function a a gun battle in a Western, taking the place of scenery.

Regardless of Kinski's superb performance, the film is deliberately unemotional, a cool, pastel-toned refutation of the German Expressionist tradition of dark lighting, heavy shadows, and overt appeals to feeling. The slow-motion tableaux of both the murder and the discovery of the body are climactic moments that are somehow less expressive than the events leading to them—they have the remote grandeur of an alien religious ceremony. Once again (as he did in *Nosferatu, the Vampyre*), Herzog uses stately Baroque music at the moment of violence to disown the passion of the visual image, to alienate the audience from sharing the feelings of the characters at those very moments when the characters are most overtly manifesting their feelings. This alienating device may appear Brechtian, but Brecht employed alienation to allow the audience to engage in political analysis, rather than being manipulated into emotion. The effect is quite different in Herzog; it hints that serious cinema is an awe-inspiring religious rite designed, for modern man, to replace the ceremonies of institutionalized religions. Alternatively, along with the pallid color scheme, Herzog's use of distancing devices may well indicate an experiment on the director's part, an attempt to avoid using his medium to condition the audience with ready-made emotions, or with the normal sort of pretty film images that are the visual equivalent of popular show tunes. *Woyzeck* is neither an indulgent work nor an ingratiating one. It does not demand the audience's sympathy, but, rather, its unflagging attention.

*Naomi Wise*

# WR—MYSTERIES OF THE ORGANISM (WR—MISTERIJE ORGANIZMA)

*Origin:* Yugoslavia
*Released:* 1971
*Released in U.S.:* 1971
*Production:* Svetozar Udovicki for Neoplanta Film
*Direction:* Dušan Makavejev
*Screenplay:* Dušan Makavejev
*Cinematography:* Pega Popović and Aleksandar Petković
*Editing:* Ivanka Vukasović
*Art direction:* Dragoljub Ivkov
*Music:* no listing
*MPAA rating:* X
*Running time:* 80 minutes

*Principal characters:*

| | |
|---|---|
| Milena | Milena Dravić |
| Jagoda | Jagoda Kaloper |
| Vladimir Ilyich | Ivica Vidović |
| Radmilović | Zoran Radmilović |
| Stalin | Michael Gelovani |
| Tuli Kupferberg | Himself |
| Jackie Curtis | Himself |
| Betty Dodson | Herself |
| Nancy Godfrey | Herself |
| Jim Buckley | Himself |

*WR—Mysteries of the Organism* mixes equal parts of politics, comedy, and human sexuality to create an unusual, perhaps unique, cinematic artifact. It is a film of collage, juxtaposition—collisions of ideas that remind one of pioneering Russian director Sergei Eisenstein's notion of montage as a combustion engine driving the film onward. In the early 1970's, *WR—Mysteries of the Organism* was an international *cause célèbre* that brought notoriety to its Yugoslav director, Dušan Makavejev.

*WR—Mysteries of the Organism* was the fourth feature film of Makavejev. (He had made short films from 1953 until his feature debut in 1966.) That he has made comparatively few films—with gaps of inactivity lasting as many as seven years—is largely attributable to his films' eccentricity, but it is also caused by his recurrent controversial presentation of explicit sexual activity. *WR—Mysteries of the Organism*, for example, includes documentary footage of sexual intercourse (apparently shot as part of scientific research and not by Makavejev). Makavejev's ebullient attitude toward sexuality has often led to censorship, both explicit and implicit, which retarded his career. In the decade following the release of *WR—Mysteries of the Organism* in 1971, Makavejev made only two films: the scandal-provoking and scatological *Sweet Movie* (1974) and *Montenegro* (1981). Although *WR—Mysteries of the Organism* is probably the best-known and most frequently revived of Makavejev's features, *Montenegro* was broadly released in the United States and even appeared on cable television, although some sexual scenes were censored.

Of the many elements comprising *WR—Mysteries of the Organism*, the least unconventional is the amusing narrative of a young Yugoslav woman, Milena (Milena Dravić; a well-known actress in Yugoslavia, Dravić also appears in Makavejev's first feature, *Čovek nije tijka*, or *Man Is Not a Bird*, released in 1965). Milena is a forthright, freethinking feminist with strong feelings about sexual liberation. The apartment she shares with Jagoda (Jagoda Kaloper) has been decorated with, among other things, a photograph of radical psychoanalyst Wilhelm Reich. "W. R.," Milena explains, stands both for Wilhelm Reich and for "world revolution." Following Reich, Milena believes that social revolution can be liberating only if it is accompanied by personal, sexual revolution.

Putting the theory of sexual revolution into practice, Milena decides to liberate sexually a haughty ice skater from the Soviet Union. Named after Lenin, Vladimir Ilyich (Ivica Vidović) is presented as the model Communist Party member: tall, stiff, blond, filled with Party-line platitudes to suit every situation. With acid satire, Makavejev attacks the remnants of Stalinization in Soviet Russia by characterizing this Party representative as a repressed—and repressive—prig. Indeed, Vladimir suggests nothing more than the model Nazi of German propaganda films of the 1930's.

Nevertheless, Milena and Jagoda mount a campaign to seduce Vladimir. A naked Jagoda serves him milk and cookies while Milena launches into a libertine polemic. Vladimir is unaffected. Milena and he then stroll through a barren landscape and board a deserted boat. When Milena kisses him, he knocks her to the deck—a repressive response to a tender gesture. Only after this violent outburst does Vladimir succumb to his desire for Milena; they have sexual relations (off-screen), but at the moment of orgasm he decapitates her with his ice skate.

The film's narrative segment abruptly shifts its tone at this juncture, the lighthearted sexual adventure turning much darker with Vladimir's brutal act. Nevertheless, Makavejev's basically joyous view of the world would not permit a gloomy denouement. The viewer sees Milena's head sitting on a tray in the morgue as the lab technicians discuss the crime. Once they exit, the viewer is startled to witness Milena's head suddenly come to life as she renews her polemic on sexual freedom. Even in death, she remains committed to combatting repression, especially that form of repression which cloaks itself in revolutionary rhetoric. The film concludes with Vladimir singing a mournful ballad to a white horse. The viewer is returned to Milena in the morgue; she smiles broadly and infectiously, and the film dissolves to a photograph of her mentor, Wilhelm Reich. For most audiences, this moment is a strangely uplifting one. Even though the protagonist has been savagely murdered, the conclusion of the film is somehow optimistic.

To describe simply the plot is misleading, however, for many elements interrupt the narrative, commenting on the action or suggesting associations for the viewer. The most significant extranarrative material in the film is documentary footage dealing with Reich. Makavejev traveled to Maine to interview Reich's widow and several others, including citizens from the town near Reich's Orgone Institute. Through these interviews, the viewer comes to understand how Reich's radical ideas about sexuality made the former colleague of Sigmund Freud a subject for persecution in the United States of Dwight D. Eisenhower's presidency. Townspeople in the 1950's called Reich a Communist (which he was not; he eventually voted for Eisenhower). The Food and Drug Administration confiscated and burned his books, declaring his Orgone Box (a wooden and metal device for collecting psychic energy) a hazard to public health. Jailed for these offenses, Reich died in prison in 1957. Makavejev's material on Reich also includes interviews with contemporary Reichian psychologists and footage of men and women engaged in Reichian therapy, screaming and contorting their bodies to release psychic tension.

Milena's story becomes a Reichian moral fable when intercut with this documentary footage. The film suggests that Reich's key insight—the necessary linkage of sexual and social revolution—has been neglected by the Soviets, as represented by Vladimir. The October Revolution, which held such promise for personal liberation in the 1920's, has turned sour and spawned yet another repressive social regime. Makavejev's mockery of the Soviet Union continues a tradition of Yugoslav conflict with nearby Russia: Since Marshal Tito's resistance to Joseph Stalin in the late 1940's, Yugoslavia has remained one Eastern European Communist nation that resists easy inclusion in the Soviet Bloc.

Makavejev's iconoclasm, however, does not stop with one major world power. Interwoven with the Reich documentary and the Yugoslav narrative is a third component: footage of New York City's "underground" or "counterculture," circa 1971. These scenes, incorporating real-life members of the counterculture "playing" themselves, indicate that Makavejev is no more trustful of the American status quo than he is of the Russian one.

*WR—Mysteries of the Organism* begins on the streets of New York, with Tuli Kupferberg, an underground poet and songwriter, dressing in ragged army fatigues and helmet and arming himself with a lifelike toy rifle. Kupferberg was one of the 1960's and 1970's inheritors of the "beatnik" legacy: distrustful of established mores, anathema to the middle class. Where the beats were "cool," however, Kupferberg was "hot"—exuberant, almost beatific. He, like so many of the subsequent "hippie" generation, had a certain rampant exuberance that, in *WR—Mysteries of the Organism*, seems closely allied with Reich. Kupferberg's revolution was a personal one, pursued without the aid of conventional revolutionary groups such as the Communist Party. His role in Makavejev's film is to patrol Manhattan, confronting businessmen and businesswomen while the Fugs (an underground folk-rock group to which Kupferberg belonged) sing the ironic "Kill for Peace" on the film's sound track. "Guerrilla" theater such as Kupferberg's was closely allied with the antiwar movement of the Vietnam era. It frequently accompanied demonstrations and was one expression of the nonviolent attitude of the hippies.

Each of the New York scenes features someone on the fringe of conventional society. Frequently they are outsiders because they share with Reich a liberated attitude toward sexuality. For example, painter Betty Dodson discusses her explicit representations of men and women involved in sexual acts; Nancy Godfrey makes a plaster cast of a man's penis; and members of the staff of the underground newspaper *Screw* go about their editorial duties without any clothes on. The latter argue that unfavorable reaction to their paper derives from people's fear of total freedom. One of the best-known personages of New York scenes is transvestite Jackie Curtis. Curtis had come to prominence in films by Andy Warhol and Paul Morrissey. He appears in several scenes in *WR—Mysteries of the Organism*: walking through Times Square with a male companion, riding in the back of a car, narrating the story of the first time he had sex with another man, and so on.

These instances of "abnormal" sexuality expand Makavejev's exegesis on contemporary sexuality. Some writers have criticized Makavejev's use of this side of sexuality, arguing that he is presenting little more than variations of casual, mechanical sex, devoid of genuine affection. Indeed, contemporary Reichians in the United States reacted quite unfavorably to *WR—Mysteries of the Organism* when it was originally released. They believed that Makavejev had misrepresented Reich by emphasizing his later, more eccentric work and his controversial views on sexual freedom. Furthermore, one psychologist believed that, in cutting from the Reich documentary to the sequences of sexual aberrations shown in the New York footage, the film misleadingly implies that the two are directly associated. Makavejev did a great disservice to Reich, that psychologist argued, by dissociating sex from love, emphasizing the former to the detriment of the latter.

Other critics disagreed, contending that Makavejev's films are celebrations of positive emotions and that the unusual sexual activity discussed and sometimes shown is merely a device for better understanding all sexuality. *WR—Mysteries of the Organism* is a film trying to break down old psychosexual boundaries in the hope of achieving a healthier attitude toward sexuality.

One distinctive feature of *WR—Mysteries of the Organism* is its use of archival footage—a technique that surfaced early in Makavejev's work. *Nevinost be zaštite* (1968; *Innocence Unprotected*), for example, illustrates Makavejev's affection for oddities culled from cinema archives. *Innocence Unprotected* takes the first Serbian sound film (from 1942) and completely reworks it, adding documentary footage of the actors today and handpainting many of the scenes from the original black-and-white film. Makavejev's interest in such "found" footage reveals itself in *WR—Mysteries of the Organism* when he incorporates scenes from a propagandistic Soviet fiction film. These scenes (tinted blue by Makavejev) feature an actor (Michael Gelovani) in the role of Stalin, who is presented with maudlin sentimentality as Lenin's only true successor. Makavejev reedits and recontextualizes this film so that it suggests that Stalin led a regime that was repressive both socially and sexually.

The most distinctive feature of Makavejev's style is his sometimes puzzling use of both sound editing and image editing. Like Eisenstein, he cuts, not simply to construct a conventional narrative, as in the classic Hollywood style, but rather to suggest new and sometimes startling associations of normally disparate elements. When, on the boat, Vladimir strikes Milena, for example, the camera shows her fall to the deck. She looks up toward Vladimir. In conventional cinema, the next shot would be from her point of view, looking toward him. Instead, Makavejev cuts to the fictional Stalin. This modification of traditional cutting links Vladimir with Stalin and characterizes both as violent and repressive. Not all—or even most—of Makavejev's editing communicates symbolic meaning so bluntly. Indeed, many viewers are confused by the rapid montage of images that he assembles. Meaning is often both allusive and elusive; Makavejev's montages are always cohesive, but not always coherent.

A secondary function of Makavejev's editing is to produce a narrative "distanciation" that has caused some writers to compare Makavejev to French director Jean-Luc Godard. Like Godard, and following Bertolt Brecht, Makavejev breaks up the narrative of *WR—Mysteries of the Organism* with an amalgamation of the material described above (that is, documentary and archival footage). These interruptions break viewer identification with the characters, placing them at one remove (hence, "distancing" them). In theory, the film audience sees Milena and Vladimir not as flesh-and-blood people but as emblems of their sex, social class, nationality, and so on.

Brecht and Godard use this distance to promote a specifically Marxist reevaluation of social structures. Makavejev's motives are neither so obvious nor so pure. One can make manifold associations from Makavejev's films:

No one interpretation seems entirely correct, and, indeed, parts of his films are quite perplexing. Makavejev collects the detritus of human experience, the characters living on society's fault-lines, and assembles them into a peculiarly fascinating collage. *WR—Mysteries of the Organism* is one such collage: peculiar, sometimes perverse, but compelling, intriguing, arresting.

*Jeremy G. Butler*

# XALA

*Origin:* Senegal
*Released:* 1974
*Released in U.S.:* 1975
*Production:* Films Domirev/Société Nationale Cinématographique
*Direction:* Ousmane Sembène
*Screenplay:* Ousmane Sembène; based on his novel
*Cinematography:* Georges Caristan
*Editing:* Florence Eymon
*Art direction:* no listing
*Music:* Samba Diabara Samb
*MPAA rating:* no listing
*Running time:* 123 minutes
*Also known as: The Curse* and *Impotence*

*Principal characters:*

El Hadji Abou Kader Beye ............ Tierno Leye
Awa Adji ............................ Seun Samb
Rama ................................ Miriam Niang
Oumi N'Doye ......................... Younousse Seye
N'Gone .............................. Dieynaba Dieng
Modu ................................ Ilimane Sagnan
Blind beggar ........................ Douta Seck
President ........................... Makhourédia Gueye

*Xala* is one of Ousmane Sembène's most successful films—in both critical and financial terms. A complex satire about the ruling black bourgeoisie in Senegal, the film not only showed at festivals throughout the world but also won commercial screenings (often being the first African film to do so) in many countries in the West. Sembène, who has been called "the father of African cinema," was the first black-African filmmaker to create a stir internationally, while his films have been made in a country where a film industry as such, at the time, did not exist. It is a tribute to both his talent and his determination that even under those difficult conditions his films have won acclaim. Sembène started as a fisherman, then taught himself to read and write in French, the official language of Senegal, and began writing novels. In 1960, he decided to go to Moscow to study film under the renowned directors Mark Donskoy and Sergei Gerasimov. On his return to Senegal, his first short films were in French, but he gradually moved to using Wolof, the native language of Senegal, in films such as *Mandabi* (1968) and *Emitaï* (1971). For *Xala*, Sembène returned to French because of the film's subject matter, although within the film he raises political points about the coexistence of the two languages in Senegal.

The film opens on an independence day, the day that Africans take power in an unnamed country. The French leave the chamber of commerce to make way for their African counterparts, who on entering the chamber remove their African robes and don European suits and ties. The French, even though no longer formally in power, soon return to present each member of the board with a briefcase stuffed with bank notes. The stage is carefully set for Sembène's satire, with indications already firmly present that the African businessmen are all too ready to step into French shoes.

The story itself revolves around El Hadji Abou Kadar Beye (Tierno Leye), a prominent businessman and a member of the board of the chamber of commerce. El Hadji, as a sign of his wealth and power, is about to take a third wife, the young and desirable N'Gone (Dieynaba Dieng). It is a move that causes considerable stirrings in his domestic arrangements: Awa Adji (Seun Samb), his first wife, is as resigned to polygamy as a good follower of Islam should be, but Oumi N'Doye (Younousse Seye), his second, more Europeanized wife, is jealous of the proceedings. Yet El Hadji presses on with a lavish, pompous wedding which consolidates his status. His moment of grandeur is cut short, however, when on his wedding night he discovers that he cannot consummate the marriage. El Hadji is suffering from temporary impotence: He has the "xala."

El Hadji consults various Marabouts to find a cure, but, despite several suggested remedies, fetishes, and potions, nothing seems to have an effect. Meanwhile, his sexual impotence is affecting his work. Various deals go wrong, he gets further and further in debt, and finally he is thrown off the board of the chamber of commerce. Oumi packs up and leaves him, and, when El Hadji's personal life and business life are disintegrating, a blind beggar (Douta Seck) steps forward, claiming that since he is the source of the xala, he can cure it. He explains that El Hadji ruined him many years ago, so he placed a curse on him. The cure is for El Hadji to strip and be spat on by the band of beggars who have assembled at his house. This purification rite duly takes place in a bizarre and sickening climax to the film.

Sembène's film is really a parable on contemporary Senegalese society, where independence can be seen as merely a process of replacing one lot of rulers, the French whites, with another set, the Senegalese blacks. Sembène depicts Senegal as a country where two cultures clash—the traditional African and the modern European—but where neither way of life provides the real answers to the social and economic problems that dominate Africa. He reserves his bitterest satire for the black businessmen who revel in all the consumerist value of the West; men who speak French, wear suits, drive around in limousines, making fetishes of their possessions. El Hadji, for example, feeds his Mercedes with bottled water. Sembène, a committed Marxist, very consciously structures his films to highlight his political theories. He argues that since independence, French colonialism has been replaced by a new "cultural imperialism," which encourages false, consumer-oriented aspirations and continues to exacerbate the class and caste divisions of Africa. In this sense, the black rulers are no better than the French ones—poverty and oppression continue unchanged. Thus, in *Xala*, it is fitting that it is a band of beggars, the dispossessed of the country, who are able to cure El Hadji's disease while revenging themselves on the rich through the nature of the cure.

While on the surface, *Xala* is a satire about the black bourgeoisie inheriting the mantle of the colonists, it is also in a deeper sense a parable about the development of Africa. Each of the women in the film, for example, represents a different stage in Africa's history. Awa Adji, the first wife, is the embodiment of traditional Africa. She wears the traditional colorful robes of African women and speaks Wolof in her own home; she is submissive to her husband as duty dictates, but she is nevertheless proud and dignified in her role. Sembène may be showing her oppression, but she herself is sublimely unaware of it. Her relationship with El Hadji is a supportive one—she has stood by him through his second marriage and will stand by him through his third. She is still with him even at his final humiliation at the hands of the beggars. Yet she is conscious of her own status and what is due to her as the first wife. When El Hadji drives with her to Oumi's house to take them both to the wedding, she refuses to enter the house of the second wife, recognizing that to do so would diminish her, and she stands firm in the face of considerable persuasion from her husband and Oumi. Yet later, at the wedding, she is supportive of Oumi, helping her to face up to her jealousy, again maintaining the duties of the first chosen toward the co-wives. Like African traditions themselves, Awa Adji has many qualities that Sembène would like to see preserved, while he would like to abolish the oppression that accompanies them. Oumi N'Doye, on the other hand, with her wigs, makeup, and dark glasses, is the epitome of Europeanized Africa. She lives in a modern house, reads Western fashion magazines, and delights in gossip about film stars. Her relationship with El Hadji is based on sex and money, and she continually nags him for more of both, becoming almost a caricature of the prevailing image of a Western wife. When El Hadji is facing financial ruin, she unhesitatingly packs a truck with her valuable possessions and returns to her family. Like all those dominated by cultural imperialism, she is interested only in wealth, with sex being the commodity that she effectively sells to El Hadji.

N'Gone, El Hadji's third wife, has little substance. She is rarely seen other than as an object—a doll to be dressed by her aunt or undressed by El Hadji. Just as her wedding present from her groom, a car, is never unwrapped, N'Gone is the essence of unattainable desire—a wife whom El Hadji will never be able to possess. She represents the faceless future of Africa as it is desired by the middle classes, neither African nor European, but an insubstantial amalgam. She is insubstantial, precisely because she is unattainable.

In complete contrast to N'Gone (and of the same age) is Rama (Miriam Niang), Awa Adji's daughter. Vibrant and alive, she represents the potential of Africa. She is independent, driving around on her moped, and not afraid of her father, standing up to him, arguing for Wolof and against polygamy. Yet, at the same time, she is protective toward her mother, sensitive to her wants and needs. Significantly, Rama speaks in Wolof, championing the true independence of her country from the French. She is even able to influence her father. When he faces the board to argue against his removal, for the first time in the film, he wants to address his colleagues in Wolof. The board refuses, however; only French is spoken at the chamber of commerce. There is an important scene where Rama confronts her father in his office, a scene which exemplifies not only Sembène's politics but also his cinematic ability to juxtapose images tellingly. Rama has been concerned about Awa Adji and asks her father to visit her. As she stands up to leave, the camera catches sight of a map on the wall behind her. The map is drawn in the exact same colors as Rama's traditional boubou outfit—blue, purple, green, and yellow—yet the map is a boundaryless one; it is a Pan-African map and speaks volumes for Sembène's identification of Rama with the hope for the future.

It is indicative of Sembène's ability that while these women in the film evidently represent important facets of the allegorical side of the film, they are never reduced to mere ciphers but have a strong, impressive presence. Equally masterful is Sembène's handling of the beggars. While they are present throughout the film—being abused, rounded up, or ill-treated by the police—they are always taken for granted as part of the background of contemporary Africa. It is only toward the end of the film that Sembène gradually allows the audience to become aware of their pivotal role. For Sembène, the future lies with the dispossessed and their ability to revolt. In the film, this band of men provide some of the most vivid images. Led by a blind man, they consist of men with missing limbs, men deformed by leprosy, and men whose only means of motion is to crawl. It is a potent contrast to the wealthy middle classes, with their plethora of wives, houses, and cars. Yet Sembène clearly indicates that there are others besides the beggars in this revolt. A messenger from the countryside on his way to the city to buy supplies is carted off with the beggars and subsequently joins them; likewise, a seller of the Wolof-language newspaper is forced to join the gang. With these devices, Sembène creates a dramatic and political link with the urban and the rural poor and also with the media. Significantly, both of these men are present at the climactic showdown with El Hadji.

El Hadji's cure is disgusting, and Sembène spares no feelings in showing the beggars spitting on the naked man, leaving great white gobs all over his body. This denouement leaves the audience in no doubt that it is a political, not a psychological, disease that has infected El Hadji. His xala represents not only his own inability to consummate his third marriage but also the inability of the Senegalese middle classes to solve the country's political and social problems. For Sembène, independence and black rule are not enough: What is needed is a total restructuring of the economy to eradicate oppression and class and caste divisions. *Xala* is a powerful statement of that message.

*Sally Hibbin*

# XICA
# (XICA DA SILVA)

*Origin:* Brazil
*Released:* 1976
*Released in U.S.:* 1977
*Production:* José Oliosi and Aírton Correa for Distrifilmes and Terra Filmes in association with Embrafilme; released by Embrafilme
*Direction:* Carlos Diegues
*Screenplay:* Carlos Diegues and João Felício dos Santos
*Cinematography:* José Medeiros
*Editing:* Mair Tavares
*Art direction:* Luis Carlos Ripper
*Music:* Roberto Menescal and Jorge Ben
*MPAA rating:* no listing
*Running time:* 117 minutes

*Principal characters:*

Xica da Silva .......................... Zezé Motta
João Fernandes .................... Walmor Chagas
Intendant ............................ Altair Lima
Hortênsia .......................... Elke Maravilha
Sergeant .......................... Rodolfo Arena
José ........................... Stepan Nercessian
Count of Valadares.................... José Wilker
Teodoro.......................... Marcus Vinícius
Priest..................... João Felício dos Santos

Carlos Diegues, one of the leaders of the Brazilian *Cinema Novo* movement, refers to his sixth feature, *Xica*, as a multicolored butterfly resting on the solemn white wall of a colonial church. The image is appropriate, for the film is a dynamic, colorful, noisy, playful celebration of a little-known historical figure who was brought forth in a context of political repression, under a military regime that gave perhaps less cause for joy and commemoration. The film is an ode to the creative spontaneity of the Brazilian people, a spirit which, the director suggests, transcends any specific political situation. It reflects an optimism and faith in the vitality of the Brazilian people as the moving force of the country's history.

The film's popular reception in Brazil was enormous, being seen by more than eight million spectators in its first two and a half months of exhibition; this figure is extraordinary in a country with only slightly more than 2,500 film houses. It was equally well received by popular critics. The film is not, however, without its detractors, who base their critique on political problems that they see as inherent in it. Such diverse reactions derive, ultimately, from the ambivalence of *Xica*'s conception: a comedy about slavery, a defense of the irrational set in a political context, a historical reconstruction in which fantasy and myth are more important than historical accuracy.

*Xica* is a fictional re-creation of events that occurred in the state of Minas Gerais in eighteenth century colonial Brazil. Like Diegues' first feature, *Ganga Zumba* (1963), which depicts a slave revolt in seventeenth century Brazil, it deals with Brazilian history and, more specifically, with slavery and the possibility of freedom. History and freedom, in fact, are two of the major threads running through virtually all of Diegues' production. *Os herdeiros* (1969; *The Heirs*) is a mural of Brazilian political history from 1930 to 1964, and *Joana Francesa* (1973; *Joana the Frenchwoman*) deals indirectly with the aftermath of the Revolution of 1930. Freedom is a theme in many films: freedom from slavery—*Ganga Zumba* and *Xica*; freedom from economic marginalization—*A grande cidade* (1965; *The Big City*); from foreign domination and neocolonialism—*Joana Francesa* (1974) and *Bye Bye Brazil* (1980); freedom to love, regardless of age—*Chuvas de Verão* (1977; *Summer Showers*). Diegues' concern with freedom is also evident in his defense of cinematic pluralism, which has led him to experiment with different styles and modes of discourse, ranging from the slow, deliberate realism of *Ganga Zumba* to the carnivalesque exuberance of *Xica*, from the "non-Cartesian," nonlinear *Os herdeiros* to the musical comedy *Quando o carnaval chegar* (1972; *When Carnival Comes*), from the political didacticism of early short films to the "Hollywoodian" *Bye Bye Brazil*.

In the eighteenth century, the Portuguese crown inaugurated a contractual system for the extraction of diamonds and other precious stones from the rich mineral areas of Brazil's interior, guaranteeing, through the concession of contracts, a monopoly for a person of the king's choosing. The most famous of the successive holders of contracts for diamond extraction was João Fernandes de Oliveira (Walmor Chagas), who first obtained his contract in 1739. João Fernandes implanted modern, efficient methods of extraction, discovered new beds of precious stones, and accumulated a wealth approaching that of the Crown itself. His wealth and power were soon seen as threatening to the Crown, and he was forced to return to Lisbon in 1773.

While in Brazil, João Fernandes took as his lover the slave woman Francisca (Xica) da Silva, freed her, and watched her become one of the most powerful courtesans of colonial Brazil. For several years, until João Fernandes' downfall, Xica da Silva dominated the politics, economics, and fashion of the region. Her rise to power and frequent extravagant behavior scandalized the aristocracy of the diamond-mining region as well as the Portuguese court. In fact, little is known about Xica da Silva, since after her fall the people of Arraial de Tijuco (now the town of Diamantina) undertook a virtual exorcism, burning most of the documents concerning her. The myths surrounding Xica and her love of freedom are the bases of Carlos Diegues' film. The earlier *Ganga Zumba* is a story of the slaves' love of freedom; *Xica da Silva*, observes Diegues, is about the possibility of freedom through love.

The story's major contradictions are worked out in an essentially political space. In an early, rather bucolic scene shot in soft focus, João Fernandes, traveling to Tijuco to assume his position as Contractor, stops along the road and plays a flute with several itinerant musicians. The European music is strangely out of place in the rugged interior of Brazil; the incongruous refinement and solemnity of European culture contrasts sharply with the "primitive," yet authentic, vitality of the local culture and ambience. Unaware that they are speaking to the new Contractor, the musicians openly discuss the economic and political situation of the region. When they realize that he is João Fernandes, one of them looks directly at the camera and excuses himself, saying that in reality artists should have nothing to do with politics. Rather than eliminating politics from the film, the musician's statement brings them to the fore and creates a specifically political context for its analysis. The assertion also sets up João Fernandes and the colonial institutions he represents as conservative, essentially repressive elements that would almost certainly agree with the musician's disclaimer. The director has suggested that *Xica* is perhaps even more political than some of his earlier, more explicitly political, films, since it is a reflection on the nature of power and how one enters the different arenas of power. The film is political, albeit not in the traditional sense of political cinema. In it, existing political, economic, and moral hierarchies are upended in ribald fashion by the exuberant and quick-witted Xica. The film's politics are of festive, carnivalesque commemoration.

The film deals with Xica's rise to power, her vindictiveness and extravagance while in power, and her subsequent fall from power. She is an object of the desire of the most important men in the village, including the Intendant (the holder of civilian power; played by Altair Lima), the Sergeant (the holder of military power; Rodolfo Arena), and, finally, the Contractor himself (the holder of economic power). She first attracts João Fernandes' attention through the premeditated exposure of her body as the Contractor meets with the Intendant and the Sergeant. Soon afterward, buying Xica from the Sergeant, João Fernandes' other slaves comment wryly that he has become her slave sexually. Social hierarchies are thus comically overturned through Xica's frontal, festive attack on the ruling class's solemnity.

As Xica ascends, rumors of her strange behavior abound, both in the mining district and in Lisbon. After complaining of never having seen the sea, João Fernandes builds her a private sailing ship, which can be used only by blacks. In another social inversion, no whites are allowed except as musicians and servants. While she pretends to enjoy herself on the ship, the film audience learns that the Sergeant's son José (Stepan Nercessian), who had earlier left for Vila Rica to participate in a revolt against colonial rule, has been accused of subversion and is now hiding in a local monastery for black monks. One also learns that a dam built by João Fernandes to aid in the extraction of diamonds has burst and killed many workers. The Contractor had been warned of such danger but obviously preferred profit to safety and failed to heed the warnings. The Intendant's wife, Hortênsia (Elke Maravilha), a pallid, whiny, petty woman, begins to conspire against Xica out of jealousy and overt racism.

Shortly thereafter, a pompous revenue agent, with the equally pompous name José Luis de Menezes Abrantes Castelo Branco de Noronha, the Count of Valadares (José Wilker), arrives from Lisbon to inspect João Fernandes' dealings and to investigate reports of Xica's behavior. He and Xica immediately dislike and distrust each other. He makes racist jokes about her color saying that things should be cleared up (in Portuguese, the word for "clear," *claro*, also means "light colored"). Xica reacts in high carnivalesque fashion by wearing white-face makeup to dinner and suggesting that the count not eat the chicken with "brown sauce." The count, dressed in European finery and an absurd white wig, is totally out of place in tropical Brazil and constantly refers to the primitive and strange customs he witnesses.

To save João Fernandes and her own position, Xica attempts to convince the bandit Teodoro (Marcus Vinícius) to organize an army to fight the count. She then prepares an exotic African banquet to seduce him and thus convince him to leave. Her efforts fail, and the count publicly reads the decree that João Fernandes has been recalled to Lisbon. It is at this point that the true limits of Xica's power are revealed. After João Fernandes rides off, the townspeople turn on her, and some of the boys begin to stone her.

Xica flees to the monastery where the rebel José is hiding. She believes that her life is over and that she is once again a nobody. José tries to convince her that she herself is life and that together they will show that they can overcome all obstacles. The film ends with a replay of shots of Xica going happily to the church, carrying in her hand the papers granting her freedom. She thus reverts to her previous carnivalesque attitude toward the world.

The importance of Xica's trajectory from slave to powerful free woman to social outcast rests in the contrast she represents to the rigidity of the representation of the ruling class. She disrupts their corrupt political machinations and their social rituals. She parodies and ridicules their staid yet hypocritical behavior. In contrast to their formality, she is a dynamic, creative, personable, and quick-witted woman who exudes a tremendous vitality and energy. She creates an alternative "second life" for those who are repressed by the ruling classes. She enters the "official" stratum of power only to subvert it through what might be called her "gay relativity." She ridicules the hypocrisy of the Church and even suggests at one point that it be painted black. She takes public, and often hilarious, revenge on those who had humiliated her earlier.

Brazilian anthropologist Roberto da Matta suggests that relationships of power must be seen in relative terms. The ruling classes attempt to find ways to control the masses and yet have them content enough to avoid revolts. Several levels of power—military, civilian, spiritual, economic—are evident in *Xica*. Matta points out that it is precisely when the holder of economic power (João Fernandes) is asserting himself that Xica enters into action to change her situation in life. Through the premeditated exposure of her body, disrupting an official meeting of the holders of power, she manages to align herself with the most powerful man in the village—most powerful since he is closest to the seat of power, the Portuguese court. She is a slave who is aware of the value of her body (the only thing she possesses), and she uses her "erotic power" effectively. Matta also points out that it is precisely João Fernandes who feels most strongly the contradiction between individual rights and authoritarianism, since it is he who must reconcile his personal enrichment with that of the Crown. In his freedom of economic movement and in his opposition to the desires of the Crown, João Fernandes creates an unofficial link with the bandit Teodoro. The conflict comes to a peak when he has to decide whether to align with Teodoro in the formation of an army to fight the count. He decides to reject such a possibility.

Xica herself does not enter the spheres of power through political knowledge and action, as does the rebel José, but rather through the use of her body. If José has an intellectual, political knowledge of Brazil, Xica has a practical knowledge. She is repressed in individual political terms, but at the same time, she is remarkably free in terms of her own carnivalesque sensuality and sexuality. Xica gives pleasure, joy, and strength to those around her. That is her most powerful weapon. The politically powerful men she deals with exercise the power of the strong, Xica the power of the weak. Her power is carnivalesque since it results in the leveling of social forces and hierarchies.

*Xica* often evokes political struggle through cultural differentiation. The director develops this struggle through an opposition between the stodginess of alien European culture and the vitality of Brazilian popular culture. Through the valorization of dance, music, and cuisine, the film inverts the existing social and economic hierarchies. Banquet images are typical of the carnivalesque, and in the tropical banquet, Xica offends the count, she ridicules his greed and hypocrisy. As Xica ascends, she becomes increasingly alienated from her own culture, even to the point of ordering other slaves to desist with the "noise" of their highly rhythmic, percussion-based music.

Only after her fall from the graces of official culture is she restored to the fullness of her previous self.

Although some critics have said that Carlos Diegues' portrayal of Xica as a sexual creature has racist overtones, there is also, to the director's credit, a critique of racism throughout. Racism pervades the power structure, especially the Church and the representatives of the Portuguese Crown. The Intendant's wife is perhaps the most petty incarnation of racism in the film. Lily-white, she feels threatened by Xica's vitality and ascent. While many critics have been troubled by Diegues' comic treatment of slavery, the careful observer will note that as João Fernandes rides into town, he passes a slave in chains. When he rides out of town at the end of the film, the slave is still chained in the same position. That is the reality of slavery in Brazil. Xica's link with the ruling classes has changed nothing. *One* slave, Xica herself, has been liberated. The film's ending, though offering no concrete solutions, opens the possibility of other forms of social and political transformation.

*Randal Johnson*

# YESTERDAY GIRL
# (ABSCHIED VON GESTERN)

*Origin:* West Germany
*Released:* 1966
*Released in U.S.:* 1967
*Production:* Kairos-Film/Alexander Kluge with Independent-Film
*Direction:* Alexander Kluge
*Screenplay:* Alexander Kluge; based on "Anita G.," by Kluge
*Cinematography:* Edgar Reitz and Thomas Mauch
*Editing:* Beate Mainka-Jellinghaus
*Art direction:* Bernhard Hoeltz
*Music:* no listing
*Running time:* 88 minutes

*Principal characters:*

| | |
|---|---|
| Anita G. | Alexandra Kluge |
| Pichota | Günther Mack |
| Mrs. Pichota | Eva Maria Meineke |
| Judge | Hans Korte |
| Young man | Peter Staimmer |
| Social worker | Edith Kuntze-Peloggio |

*Yesterday Girl*, Alexander Kluge's first feature, was the film that firmly established the existence of a New German Cinema. It was voted Best Film at the prestigious Venice International Film Festival in 1966, which made it the first German film to be awarded an official prize there since the war. Also at Venice, an informal critics' poll enthusiastically named the director's sister, Alexandra Kluge, Best Actress for her performance in the lead role. Earlier the same year at the Cannes International Film Festival, critics had paid special attention to three German entries: Volker Schlöndorff's *Der junge Törless* (1966; *Young Törless*), Jean-Marie Straub's *Nicht versohnt* (1965; *Not Reconciled*), and Ulrich Schamoni's *Es* (1965; *It*). The impressive success of *Yesterday Girl* at Venice consolidated the impression that a new movement was replacing the moribund postwar German cinema. These films were made by a young generation of directors and showed an unexpected vitality in style and subject matter. Like the French New Wave seven years earlier, which achieved public recognition when François Truffaut's *Les Quatre Cents Coups* (1959; *The 400 Blows*) and Alain Resnais' *Hiroshima mon amour* (1959) both won prizes at Cannes in 1959, the New German Cinema was taken seriously at home only after it had made an international name for itself with critics at film festivals in Venice, Cannes, and New York City.

There are many points of comparison between the French New Wave and the New German Cinema. Just as the young François Truffaut denounced the French "Cinema of Quality" (quality was used as a term of disparagement for the heavily mannered cinema of the Occupation and the postwar decade), so, too, the Oberhausen Manifesto of 1962, which Kluge helped draft and which twenty-five young directors signed, called for a complete break with the past, an end to *Papaskino*. Similarly to the *politique des auteurs*, the Manifesto called for an *Autorenkino*, where the director, not the writer or producer, would have complete creative control, analogous to a novelist. In both countries, new sources of funding were demanded and gradually obtained from the government to revitalize the film industry and make it possible for inexperienced directors to get a start; the need for film schools was stressed (Kluge later became director of one); and protection was sought from the domination of imported films. Both movements were concerned with redefining their national cinemas through films that would address problems of contemporary life and that would win over the public to experience films in new ways. The sense of urgency to put an end to sterile conventions and to experiment with traditional cinematic representation went hand in hand with the need to speak to pressing problems of national and personal identification. In the German films, easily the most insistent theme remained the search for identity. This is invariably bound up in one way or another with the problem of the two Germanies, meaning both the divided, postwar Germany and the contemporary history of Germany, which was characterized by a repression of the war years because of the impossibility of reconciling the past with the present.

The search for identity, and its futility in West German society, is at the heart of *Yesterday Girl*. The protagonist is a twenty-two-year-old woman who has moved from East Germany to the West and who insists on the importance of the past in her life. The film shows her repeated failures to come to terms with the norms and expectations that allow one to be a member of society in West Germany. The most poignant visual image, aside from the earnest face of Anita G. (Alexandra Kluge), is the suitcase that holds all of her belongings. As she is evicted from place after place during the film, the suitcase represents both her homelessness and her desire for normal status.

*Yesterday Girl* chronicles the story of Anita G. in a highly elliptic manner. There is no plot in the standard sense, because there is so little exposition and there are so many fragments interpolated without explanation. Yet by means of repetition, occasional explanatory titles, and voice-over narration, a number of important aspects of Anita's story stand out. It would be more accurate to say that her story is observed rather than understood, since the viewer is never able to comprehend her motivation. Reviewers of this film never fail to mention Kluge's debt to Jean-Luc Godard, particularly to *Vivre sa vie* (1962; *My Life to Live*). Although stylistically there are direct quotations from that film as well as from *À bout de souffle* (1960; *Breathless*), Anita is a much more enigmatic or abstract character than are Godard's heroines. She is not romanticized, and she is unfathomable in psychological terms.

The film has a circular design. Its first real sequence is a courtroom hearing that results in Anita's being sent to a detention center; it ends with Anita checking herself into a similar institution in order to be rehabilitated. In four or five years, she has been told, she should be ready to go out into society again. The viewer learns from the judge (Hans Korte) at the beginning of the film, as he reads from Anita's statement, some important facts about her past: She is twenty-two; she was born in 1937; she grew up in East Germany and moved to the West in 1957 to better her condition in life; she is Jewish, and her grandparents suffered because of it in 1938; her parents still live in Leipzig but had their factories possessed by the State when the Communist regime took power. The judge insists to Anita that the past has no bearing on the present and that she should forget it, whereas her statement indicated that she thought her family history was responsible for her present situation. She has lost her job and is in court because she stole a cardigan sweater, the theft of which she did not even try to conceal. When the judge asks about her motivation and whether she feels guilty, she replies that she took it because she was cold, that she simply felt like doing it. She says almost nothing during the hearing, and her face reveals very little, except perhaps a desire to please or obey. The judge looks perplexed. The audience doubtless feels perplexed about the lack of explanation or concern on Anita's part, and also about the trivial nature of the crime.

Next, Anita is seen in a series of static shots at different angles in the detention home. A female warden speaks directly into the camera, in extreme close-up, and explains the probation rules. Anita gets a job selling language-learning records. Her boss explains that she will be selling something educational, which fits in with her basic desire to learn. The discussion with her boss is intercut with *cinéma vérité* style shots of Anita selling the records in the street, a tracking shot over family photographs (hers?), and Anita in a store trying on coats. Because his wife is suspicious about Anita, one learns by voice-over narration that her boss has decided to settle the problem by bringing a minor complaint against Anita.

A title follows: She wants to improve herself. Anita seems to be working as a cleaning lady; she is fired from that job too. It is unclear whether Anita has again taken something petty, or whether she is unjustly accused. She is thrown out along with her suitcase for not paying the back rent. Next, the song "Red Roses for a Blue Lady" is heard in a café where, à la Godard, Anita awkwardly and comically meets a young man (Peter Staimmer), and they return to his room. They make love under a blanket in the middle of the bed, a quotation from *Breathless* but without the humor. Another title announces that she wants to begin a new life. She goes to the university and sits in on different lectures, where she invariably falls asleep. She has an appointment with a professor about her desire to enter the university, but he talks over her head and tells her that she does not have the educational background to apply. She returns to him, asking for practical advice for herself, in the guise of asking on behalf of a friend. Once again, he can speak only in abstract terms. This is the theme of the 1960's *par excellence*: Education must be relevant. Here, as in the courtroom and in the detention hall, Anita learns nothing that she can use in her everyday life.

She meets a man who wants to teach her, Pichota (Günther Mack), and they have an affair. In another scene of educational futility, he instructs her in reading train schedules; then he tries logic, which she does not follow because she does not agree. Anita lies about where she lives; she has checked into another hotel. She discovers that she is pregnant. After a conversation with Pichota, shot at a distance and inaudible, she takes her suitcase again and walks back and forth, in the city, on a highway and bridge, entering hotels and exiting instantly through a very effective use of jump cuts to indicate immediate, serial eviction. Finally, it is night and car lights follow her, still carrying her suitcase. The lights stop at a door marked Police. She enters, and from there another cut takes her to an institution that looks like a jail. She puts on a uniform, gives up her belongings, and gives an interviewer almost exactly the same information that the judge had read from her statement at the beginning of the film. In other words, the past has indeed affected the present. The last shot has Anita looking directly into the camera, expressionless.

Until the final sections of the film—the exhausting search for a place, mostly in long-shot, and inside the prison—Anita still seems optimistic. In fact, her optimism may make her seem like an irrational character, someone who is not responding normally to her environment. The acting of Alexandra Kluge is a crucial factor in sustaining interest in the character of Anita, for it is impossible to assess the expressions on her face, and one is always looking to her face for answers which are not forthcoming. At the end, she does not look tragic either; she manages to have no expression without losing visual interest. This greatly aids the abstract dimension of the film.

*Yesterday Girl* could be described as the film equivalent of a *Bildungsroman* that has been frustrated. The quest for knowledge and the tradition of the educational novel are central to the theme of the wanderer as it appears here—except that the protagonist is a woman, which is not typical, and the protagonist does not learn. She is constantly searching for education, but she never finds knowledge that she can use, as represented by the circular structure of the film. Not only does the protagonist not learn, but the audience does not learn either. There is no stabilizing, external viewpoint that organizes all the fragments and assesses their value. The absence of a reliable source of knowledge is doubtless another of the film's central themes, and it is realized with great virtuosity in the style that Kluge adopted. The film is constantly varying its style, working toward realism in many dialogue scenes and away from realism at other moments. The opening hearing is shot in a fairly realistic manner, with the sound echoing appropriately for a large, barren room, until the judge begins to talk about the specifics of the theft. Suddenly the sound of his voice and the image of his face are very unrealistically out of sync. Pixillation is used at one point to indicate the passing of time and to lend a kind of mechanical quality to the street. Animation is used to create an effect that is both comic and abstract. Overall, the style is quite dazzling and unpredictable; this is in keeping with a story built of fragments and an unpredictable protagonist. Often the film seems to be a first-person narrative, but it is antipsychological at the same time. Not much has been learned about Anita G. by the end of the film, and it is impossible to persuade oneself of the contrary because of her unreadable look that is the last image, before an enigmatic quotation from Fyodor Dostoevski that would seem to indicate that guilt is unassignable to individuals.

*Janet Bergstrom*

# YIDDLE WITH HIS FIDDLE (YIDL MITN FIDL)

*Origin:* Poland
*Released:* 1936
*Released in U.S.:* 1936
*Production:* Joseph Green for Greenfilm
*Direction:* Joseph Green and Jan Nowina-Przybylski
*Screenplay:* Joseph Green
*Cinematography:* Seweryn Steinwurzel
*Editing:* no listing
*Art direction:* Jacob Kalich
*Music:* Abraham Ellstein and Itzik Manger
*Running time:* 92 minutes

*Principal characters:*
Yiddle .............................. Molly Picon
Arye .............................. Simche Fostel
Issac .............................. Max Bozyk
Froim .............................. Leon Liebgold
Teibele .............................. Dora Fakiel
Gold .............................. Samuel Landau
Widow .............................. C. Lewin

*Yiddle with His Fiddle* is a good example of the Yiddish films produced in Poland before the beginning of World War II. Codirected by an American-Jewish immigrant, Joseph Green, the film reveals a higher technical and artistic standard than the majority of the Yiddish films produced in the United States at the time. In part, this can be attributed to the greater technical advantages available to Green in Europe and in part to Green's careful supervision. Particularly praiseworthy are his choice of actors, their sensitive performances, the location shooting, and the use of moving camera, which contrasts greatly with the theatrical performances and static, studio-bound cinematography which were often the order of the day in Yiddish-language films made in United States.

The story concerns a young girl's efforts to help support her aging father. In order to achieve this, she disguises herself as a boy and travels with a group of itinerant musicians. She falls in love with one of the other musicians, and many comic scenes revolve around mistaken identity. The film also reflects the difficulties of being female in a man's world.

The film opens on market day in Kazimierz, Poland. After a long pan of the countryside, the camera tracks down the center of the main aisle providing close-ups of the faces of Jewish men and women. Among the group is

Yiddle (Molly Picon), who plays her fiddle in hopes of earning a few coins. Trying to cheer up Arye (Simche Fostel), her aging father, she brings him a herring. They have been evicted, but she tells him that the sky will now be their roof.

Her plans are to wander the countryside, but her father is concerned about her safety as a young woman. Relieving his anxiety, she dons male clothes. The two hitch a ride with a hay cart and, perched high on the hay, Picon sings, "Yiddle, fiddle, schmiddle/Yiddle with his Fiddle." Henceforth, she will be Yiddle.

The two arrive in a small town, where musicians already command the streets. Yiddle and her father move to a poor courtyard. Arguments ensue, but finally Yiddle wins everyone's heart with a melodious Yiddish tune. At night, the two rest in an abandoned shack with a pair of musicians. One, Froim (Leon Liebgold), sings a love song, and Yiddle dreams of being in a lovely meadow with this handsome young man.

A series of dissolves chronicle their movement from town to town. Slowly they gain notoriety. Yiddle tries to maintain her disguise. Boasting that she can drink with the best of them, she succeeds only in getting sick. Ignored by Froim, who thinks that she is a weak-livered man, she becomes alternately whiny and flirtatious.

The four find a job at a small-town wedding. Yiddle hears gossip about the beautiful, young bride and the old, rich bridegroom, who is in his third marriage. Yiddle wanders into the house bustling with preparations and discovers the crying fiancée, Teibele (Dora Fakiel). Meanwhile, the traditional wedding merrymaker has arrived. In a traditional ceremony, he improvises a song to the bride, warning her of the realities of married life. (The merrymaker could be brutally honest in his renderings.) A series of rituals follows, completing the wedding ceremony. The guests break into a dance, and the commotion reaches a frantic pace. Suddenly, everyone realizes that the bride Teibele has disappeared with the musicians.

The group is headed for Warsaw, where Teibele hopes to find her true love, Yossel, but Yiddle is jealous lest Froim win her for his own. In Warsaw, Teibele is discovered as a potential new star, but, frightened of appearing onstage, she flees with Yossel. Yiddle puts on a dress and appears in her place. To no one's surprise, she is a huge success as a comedienne and a songstress.

A montage of headlines chronicles Yiddle's rising career. Her name appears in Hebrew lights. Froim, who now knows her true identity, shuns her for fear that he will hamper her career. Despite her fame and fortune, Yiddle cannot forget Froim. Then, on a cruise to the United States, Yiddle hears her song. When she discovers Froim among the ship's musicians, the lovers are finally reunited.

*Yiddle with His Fiddle* reveals many of the elements common to Yiddish cinema—a world peopled almost entirely by Jews who are played by Jewish actors and actresses, the use of Hebrew melodies familiar to most audience members, the comic interludes, the sentimentality, the strong-minded women, and the expected happy ending.

Also of great interest is the depiction of Jewish ceremonies, seldom portrayed in Hollywood films. The wedding scene is a particularly memorable episode. In her autobiography, Molly Picon recalls the actual circumstances of its filming in a poor rural village named Kazimierz: "The wedding scene in *Yiddle with His Fiddle* took more than thirty consecutive hours to film. The food had to be truly kosher, because we hired the Orthodox Jewish men, women, and children of Kazimierz to be the guests. As we filmed, they ate, and for the successive shots of the table, the food had to be replenished, over and over again. Our poverty-stricken guests couldn't figure out what was happening." Commenting on this film years later, Norman Jewison, director of *Fiddler on the Roof* (1971), noted, "*Yiddle* was fifty years ahead of its time."

Picon's spritelike figure and freshness added immensely to the popularity of the film. Already a well-known entertainer, Picon, unlike many Yiddish performers, was able to make the transition to film. Indeed, *Yiddle with His Fiddle* was so successful that Picon went on to make another Yiddish-language film with Joseph Green: *Mamele* (1938). In addition, Picon's filmography includes two silent films: *Das Judenmadel* (1921; *The Jewish Maiden*) and *Mazel Tov* (1923), both made in Austria with Yiddish intertitles. She also has appeared in *Come Blow Your Horn* (1963), *Fiddler on the Roof* (1971), and *For Pete's Sake* (1974).

In addition to the charm and entertainment of this work, *Yiddle with His Fiddle* also offers a glimpse of the Jewish life in Eastern Europe which vanished, never to return, after the Holocaust—the sense of family solidarity, the respect for elders, and the security of a shared tradition.

Joseph Green continued to produce Yiddish films in Poland until the outbreak of World War II; all are of high quality.

*Patricia Erens*

# YOJIMBO

*Origin:* Japan
*Released:* 1961
*Released in U.S.:* 1961
*Production:* Tomoyuki Tanaka and Ryuzo Kikushima for Kurosawa Films; released by Toho
*Direction:* Akira Kurosawa
*Screenplay:* Ryuzo Kikushima, Hideo Oguni, and Akira Kurosawa
*Cinematography:* Kazuo Miyagawa
*Editing:* Akira Kurosawa (uncredited)
*Art direction:* Yoshiro Muraki
*Music:* Masaru Sato
*Running time:* 110 minutes
*Also known as: The Body Guard*

*Principal characters:*

Sanjuro Kuwabatake ............... Toshiro Mifune
Gonji ............................. Eijiro Tono
Tazaemon ...................... Kamatari Fujiwara
Tokuemon ....................... Takashi Shimura
Seibei ......................... Seizaburo Kawazu
Orin ............................ Isuzu Yamada
Yoichiro ...................... Hiroshi Tachikawa
Ushitora ......................... Kyu Sazanka
Unosuke ....................... Tatsuya Nakadai
Inokichi ......................... Daisuke Kato
Kohei .......................... Yoshio Tsuchiya
Nui ............................. Yoko Tsukasa
Homma .......................... Susumu Fujita

*Yojimbo* is Akira Kurosawa's most popular film. It can be enjoyed by an audience unacquainted with Japanese cinema in general or with Kurosawa's oeuvre in particular, but it can be most fully appreciated only when those contexts are supplied.

In the Japanese cinema, there is a sharp distinction between the *jidai-geki*, the period-film, and the *gendai-geki*, the film of contemporary life. Usually set in the Tokugawa period (1603-1867), the enormously popular *jidai-geki* genre has its counterpart in drama and in the novel, and has recently been successfully adapted to television. A subgenre of the *jidai-geki* is the *chambara*, or sword-fighting film (known in the West as the samurai film, though, in fact, not all the swordsmen-heroes of such films are samurai). Thus, when Kurosawa made *Yojimbo*, he was working in a tradition that encompassed literally thousands of works in a wide variety of art forms. In *Yojimbo*, he plays against many of the assumptions and conventions of that tradition while retaining its *mise en scène*, and his innovations have greatly influenced subsequent *chambara* films, though not always in ways that he would approve.

The plot of *Yojimbo* is quite simple. Sanjuro (Toshiro Mifune), a wandering nineteenth century samurai, comes to a small town that is terrorized by the conflict between two warring gangs. One gang is employed by Tokuemon (Takashi Shimura), the local sake merchant, who controls prostitution in the town, the other by Tazaemon (Kamatari Fujiwara), the silk merchant, who controls gambling. Previously, they have worked together, respecting each other's territories, but now both desire exclusive control of the town. Sanjuro, based in the shop of Gonji (Eijiro Tono), a humble sake seller, offers his services as a bodyguard to Seibei (Seizaburo Kawazu), the silk merchant's henchman or gang chieftain. His real intention, however, is to play one side against the other. While not employed by either side—he demands a large sum of money for his services—he perches on a fire tower and watches the fighting below, pronouncing the spectacle "interesting."

The sake merchant's side is bolstered by the arrival of the henchman's younger brother Unosuke (Tatsuya Nakadai). Handsome, vain (he sports an English-style muffler), and psychopathic, Unosuke is armed with a pistol—the only one in town, a fearsome novelty. Sanjuro ostensibly changes his allegiance to this side, becoming the bodyguard of Ushitora (Kyu Sazanka), the sake merchant's henchman. When the conflict between the two sides appears to be flagging, Sanjuro heats it up by killing a half dozen of the sake merchant's men, blaming the carnage on the other side.

Sanjuro's cynical maneuvering is entirely successful; he is undone only by an act of kindness. Kohei (Yoshio Tsuchiya), a poor farmer, has gambled away his wife, Nui (Yoko Tsukasa). When Sanjuro kills the sake merchant's men, he also frees Nui, telling her to leave town with Kohei and their small child. When Kohei foolishly sends Sanjuro a note of thanks, Unosuke discovers it. Sanjuro, supremely in control to this point, is given a terrible beating and is imprisoned. He escapes, however, and, nursed back to health by Gonji, returns in time for the climactic battle. The sake seller and the village coffin maker look at the dead bodies lying everywhere; Sanjuro observes with satisfaction: "Now it will be quiet in this town." The film ends as it began, with the masterless samurai on the road again.

Even in this bare plot summary, Kurosawa's subversive approach to *jidaigeki* conventions is apparent. The central conflict between the silk merchant and the sake merchant and their respective contingents is one in which both sides are equally at fault. The many antagonists on both sides are presented without any redeeming qualities whatsoever. The hero, instead of challenging the forces of evil head-on, in typical heroic fashion, is principally engaged in provoking the two sides to kill each other off. Indeed, many critics, including Donald Richie, the foremost Western authority on Kurosawa, have argued that Sanjuro is not even morally superior to the craven antagonists whom he observes and occasionally dispatches with a bit of swordplay. In Richie's words, "Mifune is just as monstrous as any of the monsters. . . . For reasons entirely nonmoral . . . he decides to help the bad destroy each other."

This view is a serious misreading of the film. If it is clear that Kurosawa intended a contrast between Sanjuro and the stereotype of the samurai hero, it is equally clear that Sanjuro is not the amoral character described by Richie and others. Such an interpretation of *Yojimbo* not only violates the humanistic intent that persistently informs Kurosawa's work (with the possible exception of *Kagemusha: The Shadow Warrior*, 1980) but also runs very much against the grain of the film.

First, it is important to note that not all the townspeople are evil. Gonji is an entirely sympathetic "little man," capable of heroic self-sacrifice. The coffin maker, a weak and selfish man, is nevertheless capable of doing good. The family whom Sanjuro reunites can stand for many similar victims of the conflict between the rival gangs. Even among the contesting gang members, there are degrees of evil. Thus, Kurosawa is not presenting in *Yojimbo* an amoral world in which no one is good, in which there are only the strong and the weak.

Mifune's character, moreover, while not that of the traditional samurai hero, is clearly intended to be sympathetic. In the opening moments of the film, he is seen only from the back. Kurosawa thus opens with a cliché of the action-film genre, which he quickly deflates by showing the hero's hand reaching up to scratch his head. This gesture is but one of several mannerisms which Mifune maintains throughout the film—he also chews on a toothpick—to deflate the heroic stereotype. At the same time, Sanjuro is no mere caricature. His swaying walk (sometimes interrupted by a comic shake of the shoulders, as if to straighten himself) and his swordsman's carriage are impressive. He is a supremely self-confident figure, resembling in some ways the bearded doctor of *Red Beard* (1965), whose forbidding exterior conceals a compassionate heart.

When Sanjuro enters the town for the first time—it appears deserted, the boarded-up "main street" recalling the Westerns on which Kurosawa drew for inspiration—he sees a dog trotting along in a businesslike manner, carrying a severed human hand in its mouth. This wonderfully grotesque image establishes the tone of the film. It is both horrible and comical—the contrast between the jauntiness of the dog (a mood reinforced by the music) and the nature of its burden is particularly funny. It is also a stylized image that prepares the audience for Kurosawa's highly stylized, even theatrical treatment of the conflict that follows.

Here again, Kurosawa subverts the *jidai-geki* conventions. The sword-fighting scenes in the traditional *jidai-geki* film are stylized, even elegantly choreographed, rather than graphically bloody and violent. Kurosawa retains that dancelike quality, even exaggerating it in certain scenes for comic effect, as when one gang advances toward the other with shouts and sword thrusts, then hastily retreats in comic terror at the slightest sign of resistance. Sanjuro watches these antics from his perch on the fire tower, looking down on the narrow street like a spectator watching a ballet. At the same time, however, Kurosawa's sword-fighting scenes are more realistic, more bloody—at once more exhilarating and more sickening than the traditional *chambara* scenes.

Indeed, *Yojimbo* is, in a sense, a film about the nature of violence and, by extension, the nature of war. Kurosawa's attitude toward his subject is conveyed in that opening image of the dog carrying the severed hand. *Yojimbo* is one of his most amusing films, yet the humor of the film, aside from the intrinsic pleasure it provides, is intended to serve another purpose as well. Like the stylized elements—the choreographed sequences for example, the watchman who runs out at intervals and clacks his blocks together, as if to introduce the next act of a play—the humor has a distancing effect. It allows Kurosawa to show real violence, to show how sickening it can be, without forcing the audience—as a director such as Sam Peckinpah does—to become sadistic voyeurs. It also saves the film from didacticism.

Kurosawa has often said that he hates violence, that it is perhaps this very hatred of violence that allows him to depict it so convincingly. His treatment of violence throughout his films, however, is more complex than this statement might suggest. Unlike many artists who have a genuine horror of suffering and cruelty, Kurosawa can also depict violence as exhilarating, a triumph. Always a great admirer of competence, he gives the swordsman his due. When, early in the film, Sanjuro takes on a ragtag bunch of thugs, including a giant who carries an enormous wooden mallet (another image which mixes horror and comedy), Kurosawa encourages the audience to celebrate Sanjuro's victory. With brutal swiftness, he cuts off an arm here, disembowels a foe there, and then assesses the damage in a casual, workmanlike manner: "Two coffins. . . . No, maybe three."

Yet Kurosawa leaves the audience with a more haunting image: the image of the psychopathic Unosuke, smiling as he shoots a helpless enemy with his pistol. Even Sanjuro's victory over Unosuke in their Western-style showdown, in which he whips out a knife and throws it unerringly into the gun arm of his overconfident opponent, cannot efface this image. The conflict in the town is an allegory of war, in which advanced technology—the pistol, the atomic bomb—renders the mastery and heroism of the swordsman useless. The carnage in *Yojimbo* anticipates the much greater carnage at the end of *Kagemusha*, when wave after wave of the Takeda cavalry is slaughtered with rifles imported from Europe, until the field is covered with dying horses and men.

Kurosawa made *Yojimbo* immediately after *Warui yatsu hodo yoku nemuru* (1960; *The Bad Sleep Well*). One of Kurosawa's most pessimistic films, *The Bad Sleep Well* deals with the pervasive corruption in postwar Japan. The hero of the film (again played by Toshiro Mifune) is faced with a moral dilemma: In order to combat effectively the utterly unprincipled businessmen whose shiny offices and veneer of civic virtue conceal their ruthless practices, he must become like them, a driven man ready to employ any means necessary to achieve his end. He cannot do this—he is too good, too human—and, as a result, he is tortured and murdered, and the case he has built against high-placed wrongdoers dies with him.

In *Yojimbo*, Kurosawa once again suggests, more indirectly, the evil that can be traced to immaculate corporate offices. The conflict in *Yojimbo* is a power struggle between two prototypes of the corporation man; they remain faceless for virtually the entire film while their proxies terrorize the town and kill off one another. Their greed is ultimately self-destructive: The barrels of sake are opened to run into the mud; the warehouse of fine silks burns to the ground. The sake seller and the coffin maker, representatives of the common man, are left alive and Sanjuro leaves town. The black humor of his final judgment ("Now it will be quiet in this town") is a kind of antidote to the bleak, highly dramatic climax of *The Bad Sleep Well*.

*Yojimbo* is an excellent production in every way. As in many of Kurosawa's films, the music is brilliant, and the cinematography, in particular, has been highly praised: The film was photographed by Kazuo Miyagawa, who also worked with Kurosawa on *Rashomon* (1950). Kurosawa's own innovative techniques, such as the use of telephoto lenses to film the sword-fighting scenes, making the actors appear closer together and the action more intense, also add to the distinctive look of the film. The popularity of *Yojimbo* prompted a sequel, *Sanjuro* (1962). Ironically, it was *Yojimbo* that inspired Italian director Sergio Leone's "spaghetti Western" *Per un pungo di dollari* (1964; *A Fistful of Dollars*), the film that catapulted Clint Eastwood to fame. In this roundabout fashion, Kurosawa may be said to have more than repaid his debt to the American Western.

*John Wilson*

# YOL

*Origin:* Turkey
*Released:* 1982
*Released in U.S.:* 1982
*Production:* K. L. Puldi and E. Hubschmid for Güney Film/Cactus Film, in association with Maran Film
*Direction:* Şerif Gören
*Screenplay:* Yilmaz Güney
*Cinematography:* Erdoğan Engin
*Editing:* Yilmaz Güney and Elisabeth Waelchli
*Art direction:* no listing
*Music:* Sebastian Argol and Kendal
*MPAA rating:* PG
*Running time:* 114 minutes
*Also known as: The Road* and *The Way*

*Principal characters:*

| | |
|---|---|
| Seyit Ali | Tarik Akan |
| Mehmet Salih | Halil Ergün |
| Ömer | Necmettin Cobanoğlu |
| Ziné | Şerif Sezer |
| Emine | Meral Orhonsoy |
| Mevlüt | Hikmet Çelik |
| Meral | Sevda Aktolga |
| Yusuf | Tuncay Akça |
| Gulbahar | Semra Uçar |

*Yol* may have won the Gold Palm at Cannes in 1982, but it lacks the chic sophistication associated with that prize; it also lacks the exotic naïveté of much Third World cinema. *Yol* is a story film, Hollywood-on-the-Bosporus filmmaking, and if a film so rich in melodrama is infused with social and political comment, this is typical of filmmaking in Turkey.

*Yol*'s notoriety at Cannes derived as much from the conditions of its making as from the content of the film. All filmmakers have trouble finishing their films, but when Yilmaz Güney arrived at Cannes, emotion ran almost as high as it does among Turkish film fans (posters of him are sold on the street alongside those of Turkish independence hero Mustafa Kemal Atatürk). Güney—longtime star of Turkish film and himself a veteran director as well as a novelist and playwright—has spent much of his adult life in prison for his role in Turkish politics, both as an artist and as a supporter of dissidents. (One charge against him was abetting terrorists.) He wrote *Yol* and directed production by remote control, through the services of a dedicated friend, Şerif Gören. After escaping form light-detention prison, he edited the film in Europe. Given only temporary immunity by the French to show the film at Cannes, he promptly disappeared and went into hiding after the festival, with the Turkish government in pursuit.

The enthusiasm at Cannes, however, was not entirely dependent on offset dramatics; the film builds its own power, from the opening sequence of a group of light-detention prisoners getting their papers for a week-long leave. These are not political prisoners, but rather thieves, murderers, brawlers—common criminals. When they leave prison, they go home to another kind of hell—domestic life in a country torn apart by social change.

Four men's family crises are intercut with crudely effective editing. In one, Mehmet Salih (Halil Ergün) tries to regain his wife, Emine (Meral Orhonsoy), and their children from the in-laws who hate him. They suspect, correctly, that he abandoned his wife's brother to die in a burglary attempt; only vengeance will satisfy family honor. In another, Seyit Ali (Tarik Akan) must avenge his family's honor after his wife, Ziné (Şerif Sezer), becomes a prostitute. In a third, Mevlüt (Hikmet Çelik), a young man bursting with self-important modernity, chooses an ultratraditional wedding, sternly ordering about his already abjectly submissive fiancée, Meral (Sevda Aktolga), on the same day that he visits a brothel. Finally, in the fourth tale, Ömer (Necmettin Cobanoğlu) returns to his village in Kurdistan—an area in chronic revolt against central Turkish authorities—during a skirmish that catapults him reluctantly into the role as the head of the household and abolishes his dreams of a marriage for love.

Each of these miniplots is rife with sex and death. In part, this thundering approach to entertainment draws on popular film tradition in Turkey. Güney starred in a long series of blood-and-thunder epics, playing doomed heroes. Experience tells; the crises unfold expertly. The centerpiece scene is one often featured in advertising, in which the avenging husband forces his unfaithful wife to trek across a canyon in a blizzard; the trek starts out as an attempt to kill her, but it is a death easier intended than accomplished. Other action sequences—such as the brothel scene, with its raw humor, or the terrifying scene of an angry crowd in a train—bring tensions to a head just as effectively.

*Yol*'s melodrama, however, is as much life as it is art. These stories have the crudeness of truth; every week Turkish newspapers carry feature stories of the kind of domestic conflict that animates *Yol*. The cost of social upheaval is registered deep within the family and the causes are not difficult to find. More than half of the Turks live in cities, and most of them moved there from peasant villages. Urbanization in Turkey comes complete with urban blight. It is no wonder that the men are confused when they go home—they are caught between traditional obligations and the imperatives of new conditions. Güney's analysis of this cultural crisis—one involving a fundamental challenge to traditional sex roles, among other things—is not systemic; he focuses on the men, and he finds them caught in cruel binds yet behaving bestially to their women. The women in the film are flatter characters, more passive than the men; in Güney's script, they are the victims of the victims. The approach makes for a more mechanical development of plot and character than if Güney had chosen to focus on one family's crisis and investigate it from all sides of the sex-role tangle, but for a film whose perspective is that of the men in the family, it is surprisingly unflattering to men.

Güney is well-known in Turkey for his outspoken criticism of the military government—a short introduction to the film draws a parallel between state prison and the prison of tradition. The introduction ends pontifically, "They are *all* prisoners of the state." Certainly, the role of the state in fostering oppression in Turkey is undeniable. The military has everything to do with daily life in Turkey. With mass migration, unemployment, and desperate poverty, social unrest can only be controlled by force if the power relationships are going to stay the same.

Nevertheless, the film's political implications are less interesting than its multifaceted depiction of the collapse of traditional domestic life. That collapse is at the core of the film's drama, and it is why *Yol* travels well—sex, death, and family conflict are universal themes.

*Yol* may be truly international cinema, a film that can be "read" by Western audiences without translation because its style is so familiar. Güney learned it from Hollywood: "I started making films under the influence of American cinema," he has said. "I learned the techniques of cinema from American movies." Yet this comment does not mean that the film is not authentically Turkish. Güney comes honestly by the style, and it has even become part of Turkish national culture. His populist film vocabulary is a deliberate choice—a product of decades of interplay with his home audience. Further, it is not his only effort in this direction; this film is much less experimental in style than earlier work of his that has garnered international attention.

The film's accessibility, though, also means that foreigners can miss the subtler ways that traditional values are enforced and conflict expressed—those marking ways in which Turks are not "just people like you and me," but people with a different culture. As a result, some of the traditional sanctions seem peculiarly arbitrary and cruel, only a "prison" and not the shards and remnants of a formerly coherent way of life. Further, the film's violence can be read as a denigrating characterization of Turkish people rather than the result of intolerable conflicts.

Around the familiar themes, though, is a wealth of material that brings home the shock of the new in Turkey and gives the film a cultural specificity. The breadth and geographic diversity of the country is astounding (this is a kind of travelogue as well), even when it is filmed with a greeting-card gloss. Mud shacks, mountain huts, and neon-lit city streets with congested traffic and Parisian-style store windows are all part of the same country. In homes, the wealth of visible tradition—in gaudy folk decorations, in home-made dresses, in gestures of deference—clashes with such emblems of modernity as trim business suits and electrical appliances. There are, too, guns and uniforms, everywhere: The shock of the new comes with a military escort.

The film packs a greater political punch in Turkey than internationally, and it testifies to the importance of popular art on social issues. In Turkey, it can mean five years in prison simply to acknowledge, as *Yol* does, that Kurds and the Kurdish language exist. Further, in Turkey it is incitement to unrest merely to assert—especially with all the authority of film fame—the humanity of ordinary people.

*Yol*, with its sentimental lapses and wooden moments, its peasants, and its unfamiliar landscapes, is unlikely to become an art-house crowd-pleaser, but it is a rare exploration of the effects on private life of earthshaking social change, and it tells four tales well.

*Pat Aufderheide*

# THE YOUNG GIRLS OF ROCHEFORT (LES DEMOISELLES DE ROCHEFORT)

*Origin:* France
*Released:* 1967
*Released in U.S.:* 1968
*Production:* Gilbert de Goldschmidt for Parc Film and Madeleine Films
*Direction:* Jacques Demy
*Screenplay:* Jacques Demy
*Cinematography:* Ghislain Cloquet
*Editing:* Jean Hamon
*Art direction:* Bernard Evein
*Costume design:* Jacqueline Moreau and Marie-Claude Fouquet
*Choreography:* Norman Maen
*Music:* Michel Legrand; lyrics by Jacques Demy
*MPAA rating:* G
*Running time:* 126 minutes

*Principal characters:*
Delphine Garnier............... Catherine Deneuve
Étienne........................... George Chakiris
Andy Miller .......................... Gene Kelly
Maxence.......................... Jacques Perrin
Solange Garnier................. Françoise Dorléac
Bill ................................... Grover Dale
Yvonne......................... Danielle Darrieux
Simon Dame ....................... Michel Piccoli

*The Young Girls of Rochefort* was a follow-up to director Jacques Demy's earlier all-singing film *Les Parapluies de Cherbourg* (1964; *The Umbrellas of Cherbourg*). It takes that film one step further by also being totally danced. In this lovely and unusual film, there is not one word of spoken dialogue and not one step that is not choreographed. One of the few original motion-picture musicals to be produced in the 1960's, *The Young Girls of Rochefort* shares elements of the musical, love, and fairy-tale genres. With dancer-director Gene Kelly as a principal performer, the film is clearly a tribute to American musicals of the 1940's and 1950's, as well as a fond and nostalgic remembrance of Kelly's own work.

*The Young Girls of Rochefort* is also notable for its always mobile, expressive camera work and for its pastel-colored set and costume designs, which transformed the real-life island resort of Rochefort-sur-Mer into a storybook fantasyland.

*The Young Girls of Rochefort* was the fourth feature directed by Demy.

Beginning as an assistant to commercial cartoonist Paul Grimault and to theatrical director Georges Rouquier in the 1950's, Demy became known to international film audiences with the debut of *Lola* (1961). This was followed by the episode "Lust" in the multipart film *Les Sept Péchés capitaux* (1962; *The Seven Capital Sins*), *La Baie des anges* (1963; *Bay of the Angels*), *The Umbrellas of Cherbourg*, and *The Young Girls of Rochefort.* Demy quickly established and maintained a reputation for a lighthearted and romantic style, as well as for surprisingly simple narratives touched with whimsy and fantasy.

Demy's films are also characteristically marked by sweetness and poignancy as his characters yearn for, find, and lose love and ultimately journey to recover that lost happiness. It is the ceaseless search for that delicate entity, "true love," together with the almost certain knowledge that love will win out in the end, that forms the thematic core of his films. To Demy, predictably happy endings are not merely convenient ways of tying up loose plots; rather, they represent the potent interaction of fate, destiny, and the inevitability of love. Many critics have noted a pattern of circularity in his films. *Lola* begins with Michel driving his fancy car into Nantes and ends with him driving out with Lola as his new passenger. *Bay of the Angels* begins with the protagonists entering a casino and ends as they exit. *The Umbrellas of Cherbourg* begins in the morning at one ESSO gas station and ends, at night, at another ESSO station. Time might pass, but stories begin and end in familiar locations, and in between the characters are transformed.

*The Young Girls of Rochefort* begins as two young boat salesmen, Étienne (George Chakiris) and Bill (Grover Dale), lead a veritable assault on the island resort of Rochefort-sur-Mer. Their army of workmen and entertainers and their flotilla of shiny new boats arrive on a Friday night; they will depart early Monday morning at the conclusion of a trade show and festival.

Everything appears to be normal—except that Étienne and Bill seem to be most unusual salesmen. They come to a sleepy little town, spread their glittery show magic around, and leave only after three couples have been united in love. One glance at the little village reveals a fairy-tale land that is decidedly different from the real world that lies—out of sight—at the other end of the ferryboat ride. Demy's cinematic Rochefort is a triumph of art direction and costume design. Art designer Bernard Evein had designed all of Demy's films. For this film, a real island town was transformed by painting every structure to be used in the set according to a detailed color scheme. A wide range of colors was chosen: yellows, reds, greens, blues—the entire rainbow. Colors were chosen only in their soft, pastel shades. Structures were complimented with matching street furniture, offset with contrasting awnings and accented with care. Costume designers Jacqueline

Moreau and Marie-Claude Fouquet created hundreds of costumes to match Evein's pastel color schemes.

The ambience of fantasy and romance is accentuated by Demy's use of singing and dancing. As in his previous popular opera, *The Umbrellas of Cherbourg*, in which automobile mechanics sang about the drudgeries of the day and lovers sang out their plans for the future, the people in Rochefort express every thought in song. Demy's lyrics are often mundane and trivial, but so is "ordinary" speech. The songs are either conversational or introspective—"thinking out loud." The dancing is even more amazing. Norman Maen's frenetic choreography and Ghislain Cloquet's soaring camerawork weave ordinary movement and dramatic gesture into a kinetic tapestry. The singing, the dancing, the colors, and the geographic separation from the remainder of the world guarantee a perfect home for Demy's fated lovers.

The expressive style of the film is established from the beginning. Étienne and Bill arrive at the town square and supervise as their workers set up the show. The camera angles are high as the men move about rhythmically, carrying metal poles and creating the scaffolding for the show. The camera glides in leisurely, arching movements, moving in to capture a detail, and sliding out for more perspective. Music swells, and groups of women clad in purple, pink, and blue dance down the street. Men, women, children, tradesmen—all the people of the town move, sway, and travel in all directions. The vibrant mixture of camera positions and angles records the excitement of the town, introduces the geography, and captures both the exuberant and deeper romantic themes. Camera positions and vistas were of paramount importance when Demy selected Rochefort as the site for his film: He knew that there were not structures in the town which were tall enough to block or obscure his camera movements.

When the upbeat music in the construction sequence changes to low and somewhat solemn piano music, the camera moves up the exterior of a building and into a classroom. The teachers, twin sisters named Delphine and Solange Garnier, are played by real-life sisters Catherine Deneuve and Françoise Dorléac. They are teaching a class, but soon the children leave and Delphine is left to meditate on her search for a good man while Solange sings about how boring her life has become. Their mother, Yvonne (Danielle Darrieux), runs a small café nearby. She still yearns for her former love, Simon Dame (Michel Piccoli). She does not know that M. Dame runs the piano and music store only a short distance away.

While Solange and Delphine fantasize about their future lovers, those fortunate young men are moving inexorably toward them. Maxence (Jacques Perrin) is a young sailor on leave who has painted a portrait of his ideal woman: It is the exact image of Delphine. Andy Miller (Gene Kelly) is a concert pianist who almost immediately finds the manuscript of a concerto written by Solange. These three couples—Simon and Yvonne, Delphine and Maxence, and Solange and Andy—will be propelled by destiny (and Jacques Demy's story construction) until each is permanently entwined by Monday morning.

Although Gene Kelly, George Chakiris, and Grover Dale had all had notable successes in American musical film, none of them was able to sing in French. In fact, the overall casting for *The Young Girls of Rochefort* was curious. Only Danielle Darrieux (in the relatively small role as Yvonne) could sing well enough in French to use her own voice. For a film in which every note was sung, thirteen roles, including all but one principal, had to be dubbed. In addition, neither Catherine Deneuve nor Françoise Dorléac had had training as dancers. The design of their numerous dance routines could merely minimize that problem.

Surprisingly, though, these problems cause little damage to the film. *The Young Girls of Rochefort* is an ensemble piece. There are no central characters and no principal plotline. Instead, the stories of each couple intersect, overlap, and reflect on the others.

What does matter with this film is its physical production. As the story progresses, the fluid photography, expressive editing, and always amazing sets take on an emotional quality of their own—a vibrancy and excitement that is purely cinematic.

Outside the café, after introducing the Garnier sisters and then introducing Maxence, who sings to his portrait and despairs at ever knowing his true love's name, Demy again turns his camera to the hustle and bustle of the street. The sequence is a clear illustration of Demy's desire for movement, excitement, and vitality: A group of soldiers moves to the left, a woman dressed in yellow seems to be following, and acrobats come in from the right. A woman in red walks from the right. Everyone is moving, dancing, twirling, and seemingly gliding through the air. Soldiers leap around corners, arms and legs akimbo, in clear references to dances in American films such as *An American in Paris* (1951) and *On the Town* (1949).

In another sequence, Solange learns that a famous pianist is in town to visit Simon Dame. Andy has not arrived yet, so she walks down the street and nearly bumps into him. Played by Gene Kelly, who embodies much of Demy's love for American musicals simply by his presence, Andy bends to pick up her papers while time slows down and people in the background walk in slow motion. By all the conventions of film musicals, these two people are already in love. Solange runs off, leaving her precious concerto like a latter-day silver slipper in Andy's hand. Dazzled and euphoric, Andy dances near an old lady in a shop, twirls on one foot, dances a duel with some kids down the block, and interacts with some soldiers. The camera work is high and mobile, backing up to give him space for exuberant kicks and coming in close for quieter moments.

Almost two decades had passed since the musicals of Metro-Goldwyn-

Mayer and Gene Kelly were at their height, and the dancer's movements are somewhat diminished. Nevertheless, the dances are identifiably Kelly's. He always loved working with children, and his work on the sidewalks of Rochefort, teaching them to dance, is reminiscent of his work with children in *Anchors Aweigh* (1945) and *An American in Paris*. More than anything, Kelly liked the concept of "character dancing"—the notion, now thoroughly accepted, that dance steps and gestures can be used to express the innermost feelings and emotions of a character. This dance of newfound love, like similar dances in the rain, on roller skates, and along the moonlit banks of the Seine, is beautifully evoked in Demy's delicate tribute. Kelly's romantic *pas de deux* with Solange amid the gleaming white pianos in Simon Dame's store is also (not coincidentally) reminiscent of the dances of love in his earlier films.

In *The Young Girls of Rochefort*, the plot is almost insignificant. When Étienne and Bill discover that their entertainers have quit, they hire Delphine and Solange to take their place. The subsequent musical number is the surprise hit of the weekend fair, and the boys invite them to join the traveling show. Still waiting for their perfect love, the girls hesitate; then fate intervenes. Their mother finds Simon, Solange finds Andy, and with a little help from her friends, Delphine drives off to find her artistic sailor, Maxence.

As daylight begins to break on a new week and a new world, the festival trucks complete their circular route, heading off the island and back to the real world. Three couples have been touched by love and fate and are moving toward a happy (if undefined) future.

In Jacques Demy's lovely rose-tinted world, everything ends happily ever after. Yet there are questions in his happy ending. How would his characters fare in a world whose color scheme also admits black, flaming red, screeching orange, and the darker emotions such colors evoke? Demy would probably dismiss such concerns. After all, with the muses, cupid, and lady luck all on his side, his never-never land is under control.

*Ted Siminoski*

# YOUNG TÖRLESS (DER JUNGE TÖRLESS)

*Origin:* West Germany and France
*Released:* 1966
*Released in U.S.:* 1967
*Production:* Franz Seitz for Seitz Filmproduktion and Nouvelles Éditions de Films
*Direction:* Volker Schlöndorff
*Screenplay:* Volker Schlöndorff; based on the novel by Robert Musil
*Cinematography:* Franz Rath
*Editing:* Claus von Boro
*Art direction:* Maleen Pacha
*Music:* Hans Werner Henze
*Running time:* 90 minutes

*Principal characters:*

Törless .......................... Matthieu Carrière
Basini .......................... Marian Seidowsky
Beineberg .......................... Bernd Tischer
Reiting .......................... Alfred Dietz
Božena .......................... Barbara Steele
Mathematics teacher .................. Jean Launay
Mrs. Törless ............... Hanne Axmann-Rezzori
Mr. Törless ...................... Herbert Asmodi

Volker Schlöndorff is a director whose career spans, or rather parallels, the period of West German filmmaking known as the New German Cinema. The American premiere of Schlöndorff's first feature film, *Young Törless*, in 1967 at the New York Film Festival—together with Alexander Kluge's *Abschied von Gestern* (1966; *Yesterday Girl*)—signaled the first American recognition of the new cinema. Later, Schlöndorff's *Die Blechtrommel* (1979; *The Tin Drum*) would be the first of two German films—the other being *Die Ehe der Maria Braun* (1978; *The Marriage of Maria Braun*), by Rainer Werner Fassbinder—to achieve a financial breakthrough in American box-office receipts by passing the one-million-dollar mark. *The Tin Drum* was also the only German film to win an Academy Award—for Best Foreign-Language Film of 1979—a measure of how far the New German Cinema had come. At a budget of six million deutsche marks (about three million dollars), the film showed as well how far Schlöndorff had come from his humble origins.

The New German Cinema was conceived on February 26, 1962, with the signing of the so-called Oberhausen Manifesto by twenty-six young filmmakers. This manifesto was a kind of blueprint, an outline of the direction in which these filmmakers hoped to develop. In signing the manifesto, the younger generation of filmmakers broke with the film establishment, recognizing that postwar West German film production was on the brink of its demise. Nationalized under the Nazis, film production had been broken up and German distribution companies became monopolized by the Americans. To compete against the tide of Hollywood films pouring into West Germany, German filmmakers stuck to tried-and-true formulas: *Heimat* films, adventure films based on the novels of Karl May, and *Sissi* films with Romy Schneider glorifying the imperial past. German films of this period were referred to as a cinematic wasteland, a cinema of barbarians. With the advent of television, film theaters closed down at an alarming rate, audiences declined, and fewer and fewer films were produced. This was the state of affairs which the young filmmakers had inherited and which they intended to alter.

Determined to remain outside the German film establishment, these younger filmmakers set for themselves new standards of artistic quality and established new methods of financing, production, and distribution. Producing as well as directing their own films, the young filmmakers were restricted to very low budgets (under one million deutsche marks) and often assembled their own casts and crew from among their friends or amateur actors and technicians, maintaining the same company from film to film and in time creating their own star system and stars: Hanna Schygulla, Eva Mattes, Bruno Ganz. Because of problems connected with funding, many younger filmmakers had received their training in the making of short films.

Volker Schlöndorff was something of an exception. Though not one of the signers of the Oberhausen Manifesto, he was among the first to reap its benefits. His training differed, however, from that of most of his fellow directors. Born in Wiesbaden in 1939, Schlöndorff attended high school and the university in France and studied film for a year at the Institut des Hautes Études Cinématographiques. Beginning his career with television reports from Algeria and Vietnam, Schlöndorff spent the period from 1960 to 1965 as assistant to such noted French directors as Jean-Pierre Melville, Louis Malle—on *Zazie dans le Métro* (1960)—and Alain Resnais—on *L'Année dernière à Marienbad* (1961; *Last Year at Marienbad*). Through this training, Schlöndorff achieved a high degree of technical precision, which other directors of the first generation of New German Cinema perhaps lacked, and his films occasionally reflect a French influence, though more apparently from the Renoir films that he saw while a student than from the directors with whom he had worked.

Problems in obtaining government funding for films led Schlöndorff in two directions. One solution was the international production (many young German filmmakers were looking to foreign investors for funding). The failure of Schlöndorff's third film, *Michael Kohlhaas—der Rebell* (1969; *Michael Kohlhaas*)—which was funded with American money, with English and French actors (David Warner and Anna Karina), an English scriptwriter, and filmed in Czechoslovakia—convinced Schlöndorff that he should avoid international coproductions in the future. *The Tin Drum*, however, was also an international coproduction, as is *Un Amour de Swann* (1984; *Swann in Love*). In these later coproductions, Schlöndorff maintained greater artistic control, filming *The Tin Drum* in German, despite protests that it should be filmed in English.

Another, happier solution to the funding problem was to film literary classics (although Schlöndorff's admitted love of literature may have encouraged him in this direction). Adaptations from literature were far more likely to receive funding than were original (unknown, untried) scenarios. Many of the new German filmmakers, most notably Fassbinder, Werner Herzog, and Wim Wenders, filmed works of literature. It was Volker Schlöndorff, however, who came to be most recognized for his remarkably faithful adaptations of works by authors ranging from Heinrich von Kleist to Heinrich Böll.

Schlöndorff's fidelity to his sources, his technical creativity and brilliance, and his attempt (virtually unique among his fellow West German directors) to bridge the gap between art and commercial success all came together in two of his greatest successes (and two of the greatest commercial successes of the New German Cinema): *Die verlorene Ehre der Katharina Blum* (1975; *The Lost Honor of Katharina Blum*)—codirected by Schlöndorff's wife, Margarethe von Trotta, a noted director in her own right—and *The Tin Drum*.

These qualities are already present in Schlöndorff's first film, *Young Törless*. Based on the 1906 novel *Die Verwirrungen des Zöglings Törless*, by Robert Musil, *Young Törless* is a psychological study of adolescence and cruelty in a military school in pre-World War I Austria. Viewed by many as a visionary foreshadowing of the coming Nazi period, the novel probably reflects more the influence of the growing interest in the theories of Sigmund Freud in early twentieth century Austria. The film, which has been accused of stressing the political over the psychological, is possibly the victim of those who want to read into the story of victimizer and victim the chronicle of Adolf Hitler and the Nazis, or who at least hope to find the seeds for a mentality that generated a militarism responsible for two terrible wars. Schlöndorff, however, admits to having been attracted to the novel because of his own years at boarding school and because of his fascination with the relationships and power plays among the characters.

The film opens at a small, deserted train station. Törless (Matthieu Carrière), joined by several of his classmates, is seeing off his parents, following their short visit to his military school. The scene, in mood and pictorial quality, perfectly captures the nuances of Musil's descriptive prose. It was shot, as was the entire film, in beautifully stark black-and-white, as much an artistic choice as a result of limited funds: *Young Törless* was shot on a budget of 720,000 deutsche marks. In the warmth of the parents, in the mother's tearful goodbye, in Törless' cool and haughty aloofness, the viewer senses, from the first moments, the emotional tensions that are to follow.

Leaving the train station, Törless and his friend Beineberg (Bernd Tischer) head first to a café for some youthful philosophizing, then to the prostitute Božena (Barbara Steele) for a more adult type of entertainment. Schlöndorff, using a few brief dialogues, a few significant glances, manages to convey all the sexual awakenings and ambiguities, all the philosophical uncertainties of adolescence that novelist Robert Musil unfolds through inumerable pages of interior monologues.

These early scenes are important (though not much happens in them) in giving some clues to Törless' character, because it is he, confused about things felt but not articulated, about the seen and the unseen, the real and the imaginary, who provides the emotional core, the catalyst almost, for the events of the film. These events accumulate slowly and deliberately, Schlöndorff maintaining a methodical control, an emotional coldness, keeping the drama taut, not allowing it to sink to melodrama.

One of the boys at school—Basini (Marian Seidowsky), the soft and sweet Mama's boy, an inveterate spendthrift and chronic borrower—is suspected by Beineberg and his friend Reiting (Alfred Dietz) of stealing. Being the top bullies of the school, they determine to have some fun at Basini's expense. They offer him their protection, promising not to turn him in to the school authorities. In return, Basini must promise to serve them in whatever capacity they should choose and must submit himself to every sort of humiliation and abuse in order to achieve redemption and become an honest human being again.

The game soon degenerates into unspeakable cruelty, Basini being subjected to emotional torments, physical pain, and sexual perversions, all inflicted in a secret attic room at night. The teachers and the other boys seem unaware of what is happening, and indeed, they remain on the periphery of the film, contributing to its claustrophobic and obsessive atmosphere. Though Basini is trapped in this horrible situation, Beineberg and Reiting seem equally unable (as well as unwilling) to bring an end to things.

It is Törless, however, who seems the least able to extricate himself. More spectator than participant, Törless remains involved through curiosity, which prevents his intercession on Basini's behalf. Törless tries to understand what constitutes the dividing line between ordinary people and those—like Basini and Božena—cast out of normal society as a result of their own actions. What brought Basini to steal? How did it feel? How could he actually commit the act? Again, why does he submit to his tormentors? Plagued by these questions, unable to act, Törless is as much victim as oppressor.

While Beineberg and Reiting are away on vacation, Törless questions Basini as to why he committed his crime and why he submits to the bullies. Shocked at the truth in Basini's reply that anyone is capable of anything, Törless suddenly loses interest in the game, and his ever-present but suppressed disgust at the empty cruelty rises to the surface. Dissociating himself from Beineberg and Reiting, Törless refuses to participate any longer. After a particularly grueling session in the gym, to which the other boys have finally been admitted, Törless runs away from the school. Caught and brought back, Törless attempts to explain his part in the torture, his confusions about all the things that are felt but not seen. The teachers attribute everything to overexcitement, and Törless is sent home.

As in many a school story—Lindsay Anderson's *If . . .* (1968), Leontine Sagan's *Mädchen in Uniform* (1931; *Girls in Uniform*)—Törless is caught in an oppressively authoritarian environment. What sets *Young Törless* apart, however, is the fact that the autocratic restrictions are imposed more by the boys themselves than by the school authorities. They feel themselves bound by an exaggerated sense of honor and morals. The decadence in *Young Törless* is not alleviated by the outrageous humor of *If . . .*; repressiveness is not lightened by any of the sweetness found in *Mädchen in Uniform*. The emotional iciness of the characters in *Young Törless*, the experimental nature of the cruelty and, above all, Törless' moral paralysis make the film somehow more ominous than most school stories. In the light of Germany's subsequent history, it is not surprising that many viewers found in *Young Törless* a parable of the militarism and cruelty of the Third Reich.

In filming *Young Törless*, Schlöndorff chose a narrative approach, simplifying the narrative of the book and translating it to the medium of film. In the process, Schlöndorff attempted a streamlining of reality as well, striving for a balance between realism and contrivance—as, for example, in his use of literary dialogue in a realistic setting. The result is a clarity of expression and, at the same time, a dialectic between word and reality—a dialectic of form which matches the dialectic of theme.

In his use of lighting and austere black-and-white images, Schlöndorff pays homage to the early Expressionist films, and in particular to Fritz Lang's *M* (1931). The effect, however, is of a carefully constructed realism, an effect supplemented by Schlöndorff's casting of young unknowns in the leading roles. The acting was universally praised, in particular that of Matthieu Carrière as Törless, whose lean, graceful, austere beauty mirrored the character's sensitivity and haughtiness.

Though a technical perfectionist, Schlöndorff strove for spontaneity in filming *Young Törless*, finding the creative aspect in the moment of looking through the camera. *Young Törless* is filmed with a cool detachment, yet Schlöndorff establishes emotional sympathy for the characters; this emotional appeal set him apart from many of the filmmakers of the first period of the New German Cinema, who concentrated on the cerebral and ascetic.

*Young Törless* was well received, though not a great financial success, and played at several international film festivals, winning the FIPRESCI Prize at the Cannes International Film Festival in addition to several other prizes.

Volker Schlöndorff, easily one of the most talented filmmakers of his generation, has not garnered the enthusiastic response (despite his Academy Award for *The Tin Drum*) granted to his fellow directors Fassbinder, Herzog, or Wenders. He has been widely perceived as a highly skilled but unexciting filmmaker. This perception is perhaps unjust. Certainly, he does not display the unbridled creativity of Fassbinder. When Schlöndorff films a literary work, he remains faithful to his source, while in Fassbinder's case the film may bear little resemblance to the original. Deceived perhaps by the technical polish and apparent realism of Schlöndorff's final product, some critics may fail to observe the technical innovation beneath the surface. Schlöndorff's creativity lies in his ability to translate the essence of a novel from the medium of the printed word to that of film, without necessarily unfolding the book chapter by chapter on the screen. *Young Törless* is the first example of Schlöndorff's success; *The Tin Drum* is the most dramatic.

*Grace Anne Morsberger*

# Z

*Origin:* Algeria and France
*Released:* 1969
*Released in U.S.:* 1969
*Production:* Jacques Perrin for Reggane Films and Office National pour le Commerce et l'Industrie Cinématographique (AA)
*Direction:* Constantin Costa-Gavras
*Screenplay:* Jorge Semprun and Constantin Costa-Gavras; based on the novel by Vassili Vassilikos
*Cinematography:* Raoul Coutard
*Editing:* Françoise Bonnot
*Art direction:* Jacques d'Ovidio
*Music:* Mikis Theodorakis
*MPAA rating:* PG
*Running time:* 125 minutes

*Principal characters:*

Z .................................. Yves Montand
Hélène .............................. Irene Papas
Magistrate .................. Jean-Louis Trintignant
Journalist .......................... Jacques Perrin
Public prosecutor .................. François Périer
Manuel ........................... Charles Denner
Yago ............................ Renato Salvatori
Vago ............................ Marcel Bozzufi
Matt ............................ Bernard Fresson
General ............................. Pierre Dux
Nick ............................ Georges Géret
Nick's sister ........................ Magali Noël
Colonel .......................... Julien Guiomar

The Greek word *ze* means "he lives" and was the word shouted by protesters when they learned of the death of left-wing deputy Grigorios Lambrakis in May, 1963. His death initially appeared accidental but was later found to be the result of deliberate action, and the subsequent investigation finally implicated the army, the police, and even the government. In 1969, Constantin Costa-Gavras, a young Greek filmmaker living in exile in France, made a film, *Z*, which, although set in an unidentifiable Mediterranean country, clearly told the true story of the assassination of Lambrakis.

*Z* was one of the first modern political films to utilize the thriller format to get its message across to a wider audience. The style of Costa-Gavras' film is reminiscent of that of the American gangster films of the 1950's, a style which strikes many resonances with cinemagoers throughout the world and which contributed to the film's achieving commercial distribution. Some critics, at the time that the film was released, argued that this popular format softened the political points that the film made, but others applauded *Z* for its hardhitting condemnation of dictatorships, for its demonstration of the appalling and undemocratic nature of the Greek regime, and for its clear portrayal of the machinations of latter-day Fascists, who, the film suggests, use law-and-order propaganda as a cover for brutal suppression of dissent. *Z*'s use of a rapidly paced investigation to reveal the truth of an incident established a new trend in cinema, evident in films such as Francesco Rosi's *Cadaveri eccelenti* (1976; *Illustrious Corpses*) and, in the United States, *All the President's Men* (1976) and *The China Syndrome* (1979).

Costa-Gavras himself has made extensive use of the thriller format. While studying at the Sorbonne in Paris, Costa-Gavras became interested in film and abandoned his literature course to enroll at the Institut des Hautes Études Cinématographiques. He worked as an assistant to Marcel Ophüls (on *Peau de banane*, 1964; *Banana Skin*), to René Clair (on *Tout l'or du monde*, 1961), and to René Clément (on *La Baie des anges*, 1963; *Bay of Angels*). Costa-Gavras' first film, *Compartiment tueurs* (1965; *The Sleeping Car Murders*), was a fast-moving detective story starring Yves Montand and Simone Signoret—a solidly commercial film whose style laid the basis for the more sophisticated *Z*. His second film, *Un Homme de trop* (1967; *Shock Troops*), about the French Maquis during the Occupation, disappeared after a brief showing in New York. Since *Z*, the political thriller has become Costa-Gavras' trademark: *L'Aveu* (1970; *The Confession*) examines the political purges in Czechoslovakia; *État de siège* (1973; *State of Siege*) looks at the involvement of the United States Central Intelligence Agency in Central America; and *Missing* (1982) investigates American interventions in the coup in Chile.

To understand the impact of *Z*—which opens with a title that states that any resemblance to real people and events is purely intentional—it is necessary to look at the implications of the Lambrakis murder. Lambrakis, a professor of medicine at the University of Athens, was an outspoken pacifist and a leading figure in the growing Greek peace movement. He was leaving a rally in Salonika when he was knocked down by a three-wheeled delivery truck and taken to a hospital, where he later died. The autopsy disclosed that Lambrakis was not killed as a result of the accident but by a blow to the back of his head with a blunt instrument. The resulting investigation revealed a network of complicity in the murder, involving high-level officials in the police and army as well as the tacit cooperation of members of the government. The scandal pushed the leader of the opposition, George Papandreou, into the position of premier, but in 1967 a *coup d'état* overthrew the legally elected authorities and established a military rule, many of whose leading figures were implicated in the Lambrakis affair. For example, the first prime minister after the coup, Constantine Kollias, was in fact the chief prosecutor sent from Athens to try to persuade the investigating magistrate to limit his inquiries. Lambrakis became a symbol of freedom and democracy for the Greeks opposed to the coup.

It is ironic, given the subsequent commercial success of *Z*, that Costa-Gavras had tremendous difficulty raising the money for the film. Most of the major American production companies, including United Artists, with whom Costa-Gavras had a contract, turned the film down for being too political, and the European companies, including those in France, Italy, and Yugoslavia, followed suit, despite the fact that the well-known members of the cast had stated their commitment to working at low salaries. Finally, the money was raised with the help of Jacques Perrin (who plays the journalist in the film). He donated the initial funding from his own savings, the cast agreed to participate on the basis of waiving their salaries until the film was sold, and independent producer Hercules Muccilli added an extra $200,000. *Z* was eventually shot with the help of the Algerian government, with Algerian locations being made to look like Thessalonika, where the action is set. The interiors were finished in Paris, and the film was completed for approximately $750,000. Nevertheless, the international press ignored it while it was being made, rejecting invitations to visit the Algerian locations.The only periodical that covered it was *Elle*, the French women's magazine, which was not interested in the film as much as it was in Costa-Gavras' new bride, Michelle Ray, a former writer for the publication.

Both the large companies and the critics were taken by surprise when the film was first shown at the Cannes International Film Festival. It received the Special Jury Prize and later won an Academy Award and the New York Film Critics Award for Best Director and Best Film. At Cannes, *Z* was sold for $400,000 plus a percentage for distribution rights in the United States, and it grossed more than $1,000,000 in the first few months in Italy alone, totally justifying the faith, commitment, and personal sacrifices of the cast.

*Z*, based on the novel by Vassili Vassilikos, takes up the story of Lambrakis, giving the left-wing deputy the name "Z." When Z is knocked down and dies after a peace rally, an inquiry into his death is started by an investigating magistrate (Jean-Louis Trintignant) and a journalist (Jacques Perrin) looking for a scoop. Yago (Renato Salvatori), the driver of the truck, is discovered to belong to a secret organization which covertly works against the movement led by Z and which has, at times, been used by the police and the government to suppress left-wing activity. Despite threats and pressure from the public prosecutor (François Périer), the magistrate continues probing and finally accuses the general (Pierre Dux) and the colonel of the gendarmes (Julien Guiomar) of aiding and abetting the assassination. The authorities, faced with a public scandal, are forced to take action, and the affair is brought to trial, although several witnesses meet with fatal accidents before they can testify. The trial is a mockery, and eventually the regime takes complete power. The accused are released and reinstated, while those working to reveal the truth are imprisoned or discredited.

The film closes on both a chilling and a hopeful note. As the final titles roll, identifying the various fates of the protagonists and the list of banned works in the country (which includes the music of Mikis Theodorakis, who arranged the score for the film), in the background people are shouting *athanatos* ("not dead," or "immortal"), and the final title translates "Z" as "he lives." Costa-Gavras' lasting message is that although the man himself was killed, the ideal for which he fought lives on.

The cast was well chosen; indeed, the film's believability stems in part from the matching of the actors with the characters they represent. Yves Montand, as Z, is readily identifiable as a liberal and a humanitarian. (In fact, Montand was so type-cast in this persona that when Costa-Gavras used him as an American "adviser" in *State of Siege*, he was criticized for making the CIA too human and plausible.) Irene Papas, the only Greek in the cast, had played so many distraught widows that her part as Z's wife seemed natural. Renato Salvatori, who plays Yago, has a screen history as a bully and a thug, and Jean-Louis Trintignant would have a difficult time being anything other than the principled, upright character that is the essence of the investigating magistrate. It was a clever stroke to call on the cinematic past of the principal actors to give the film an immediate flesh-and-blood credibility which allows the action and unraveling of the plot to dominate the screen.

The film is scrupulously accurate in detail. It was the persistence of the investigating magistrate, who could legally have abandoned his questioning at any point, that brought the facts behind the Lambrakis killing to light. During the aftermath of the murder, it became publicly apparent that the police used secret Fascist groups to control the Communists and their sympathizers. Key witnesses did disappear or fail to make the trial, although the causes of their unavailability were never investigated. Even Yago's homosexual activities (which have been a source of criticism of the film by people who believe that Costa-Gavras is making the connection between homosexuality and Fascism too strong) are based on fact. One of the most powerful facets of the film, for audiences outside Greece, is that it is not until the final rolling credits of banned works that viewers are clearly able to identify the country depicted. Before that, Z's assassination holds parallels with the killing of Ben Barka in France or John Kennedy in the United States, an ambiguity which allows the film simultaneously to condemn authoritarianism wherever it appears and to pinpoint the extreme antidemocratic nature of the Greek regime itself. In this sense, *Z* had a dual impact abroad.

*Z* has also received criticism for the things it left out. In a painstaking collection of documents, *The Lambrakis Affair*, compiled by Ioannis Voultepsis, there is clear evidence for the belief held by many Greeks at the time that both the Greek palace and the United States had an interest in seeing the peace movement destroyed. Furthermore, those critics will argue, the role of the government in suppressing the facts of the case at the trial is not brought out sufficiently in the film or given enough emphasis.

Costa-Gavras' response was to explain that he wanted to use only those facts of the case that had been publicly proved, believing that even that level of truth was sufficient to expose the corruption and political motivation behind the murder. Furthermore, *Z* is a film that was deliberately aimed at non-Greek—particularly American—audiences. In several interviews given at the time of the film's release, Costa-Gavras argued that the military government could not be overthrown purely by activity in Greece itself, that the support and intervention of countries such as the United States were necessary to topple it. In this context, *Z* was clearly an effective plea for foreign recognition and condemnation of the situation in Greece.

*Sally Hibbin*

# ZATOICHI'S CANE SWORD (ZATOICHI TEKKA TABI)

*Origin:* Japan
*Released:* 1967
*Released in U.S.:* 1968
*Production:* Daiei
*Direction:* Kimiyoshi Yasuda
*Screenplay:* Ryozo Kasahara; based on an original story by Kan Shimozawa
*Cinematography:* Senkichiro Takeda
*Editing:* Toshio Taniguchi
*Art direction:* Yoshinobu Noshioka
*Music:* Ichiro Saito
*MPAA rating:* no listing
*Running time:* 93 minutes

*Principal characters:*

Zatoichi . . . . . . . . . . . . Shintaro Katsu
Oshizu . . . . . . . . . . . . Shiho Fujimura
Zenzo . . . . . . . . . . . . Eijiro Tono
Iwagoro . . . . . . . . . . . . Tatsuo Endo
Horse driver . . . . . . . . . . . . Makoto Fujita
Oharu . . . . . . . . . . . . Kiyoko Suizenji
Oryu . . . . . . . . . . . . Masumi Harukawa

In 1962, a handsome, young Japanese matinee idol shaved his head, closed his eyes, found some scruffy clothes, picked up a sword, and became the star of Japan's most popular action series ever. Zatoichi, the Blind Swordsman, is a sightless samurai with a radarlike sense of hearing. Shintaro Katsu, who starred in all twenty-five Zatoichi episodes made for theatrical release through 1973, continued this role on a popular television series.

Based on legends of a lone outlaw of the 1830's, the crew-cut Zatoichi is undoubtedly Shintaro Katsu's best-known role. Sometimes a gambler, sometimes a masseur, at times wanted by the law, Zatoichi is an easily identifiable lower-class hero. Always trying to mend wrongs, he frequently lands in trouble for his generosity. His incredible aural talents, his uncanny ability to sniff out danger and formulate strategy, and his special agility with his cane sword are his only protection as he wanders around the Japanese countryside. He is cool and knows his way around men, but he is rather shy with women. Although he is peace loving, he continually finds himself stalked by straying samurai. Comical sword and dice tricks enhance his actions.

Zatoichi's amazing hearing ability is emphasized throughout the series. On occasion, the camera will zoom into or cut to his ear, throbbing or thrusting as need be, alerting him to the needs of any situation. Not only is he able to locate potentially ambushing samurai in an immediate vicinity, but his "radar" can also scan over longer distances. More than once he has asked a shooting range assistant to tap on a faraway target so that he can judge its location, then bag a bull's-eye with a bow-and-arrow shot that would prove difficult for most skilled marksmen. Since he enjoys gambling, his aural skills give him a special advantage: He can determine dice values by following their roll—and catch cheaters with loaded or hidden dice tricks.

The deadly swordsman's reputation attracts scheming samurai who realize they can establish their own names by defeating him; he also draws goon squads sent by corrupt gang bosses whom he has provoked. Finally, he must remain alert for hooligans who do not know his identity and consider him an easy mark. At times, he is surrounded by challengers whose numbers seem overwhelming, yet he always wins—except for a Chinese version of *Zatoichi yabure! tojin-ken* (1971; *Zatoichi Meets His Equal*), in which he fights a legendary Chinese kung fu hero of his own stature. (This film has two different endings, so that both Chinese and Japanese fans would be able to see their respective hero victorious.)

Even in the earliest episodes, Zatoichi reveals very little about his past. Occasionally a woman reminds him of his mother or sister. An unusual flashback in *Zatoichi umio wataro* (1966; *Zatoichi's Pilgrimage*) depicts him as a five-year-old child playing by a lake, with normal eyesight. In *Zatoichi ro-yaburi* (1967; *Zatoichi's Rescue*), however, he states that he cannot remember being able to see. His mysterious past enhances his legend.

Sometimes Zatoichi earns money as a masseur, a common occupation for blind men in the Edo period. At other times, he gambles or sells his sword skills. Yet he does not necessarily contract to the bidder who offers him the most *ryo*, and will confront a boss (territorial *yakuza* leader) whom he feels has used him immorally. Usually he has very little money; when he possesses more, he frequently gives it away to the needy or victimized.

Zatoichi is a *ronin*, a masterless or unemployed samurai, and prefers to rove rather than accept permanent employment. He is easygoing and good-natured. When aroused, however, he becomes a ruthless swordsman tenaciously fighting injustice. Once in a while, he displays a sardonic streak, as when he severs a pickpocket's arm. Nevertheless, he feels remorse for the trail of blood which follows him, as in *Zatoichi's Pilgrimage*, when he begins a journey to visit eighty-eight Buddhist temples to cleanse his soul of the eighty-eight men he has killed for the sake of justice. He vows to put aside his blade here and in several other episodes. Fortunately, or unfortunately, he is unable to carry out this resolution very long.

Most Zatoichi episodes follow typical samurai genre patterns. To some Japanese, Zatoichi recalls the Tange Sazen series, which was especially popular in the late 1920's and early 1930's. Tange Sazen was the name of a legendary one-armed, one-eyed samurai whose exploits are still retold on film screens. Akira Kurosawa's *Yojimbo* (1961) and *Tsubaki Sanjuro* (1962; *Sanjuro*), made before the first Zatoichi episode, started a genre of light action films featuring scruffy but resourceful heroes. Star Shintaro Katsu had also played a blind masseur unscrupulously grabbing for power in *Shiranui kengyo* (1960; *Shiranui, the Court Masseur*), a forerunner to the Zatoichi series. Many Zatoichi enthusiasts rank *Zatoichi's Cane Sword* among the very best of the series. A synopsis of this film illustrates the electricity of the series.

An unsettled atmosphere is immediately created in the prologue to *Zatoichi's Cane Sword* when Zatoichi (Shintaro Katsu), alone on the road, hears a man rushing by, then finds another dying from a sword wound. Tensed up, he hears a noise and automatically responds with his sword—then realizes he has bisected a bird in flight, a grisly action he immediately regrets. After doing what he can for the victim, Zatoichi continues his journey, and the credits for *Zatoichi's Cane Sword* flash on the screen.

Some time has passed. A passing cart bumps an absentminded Zatoichi into a ditch. A group of actors and performers are inside, and they offer Zatoichi a ride. All are best friends by the time they arrive at the Ebisu Shrine Compound in Tonda, their destination. The horse-faced horse driver (Makoto Fujita) challenges the blind man to a dice game while the others set up their equipment. Suddenly a group of toughs representing Boss Iwagoro (Tatsuo Endo) approaches, demanding a hefty advance and a percentage of the business. Boss Shotaro, a fair and honest *yakuza* leader who had controlled the territory, never charged the poor little troupe, but he died a month earlier, Boss Iwagoro's fiendish men explain, and several laws have changed. Since the group has traveled so far, it pays the necessary tribute.

After this incident, a sympathetic Zatoichi bumps into the troupe's leader and steals his virtually depleted money bag. He instinctively locates a big gambling party and plays three rounds. Even though all the other gamblers appear to be losing, the blind gambler wins a tidy sum. Zatoichi then retires to a little noodle and sake shop, apparently not realizing that he is being followed. There he meets Zenzo (Eijiro Tono), an old man, and boasts how he won eight *ryo*—his ears informing him how the dice were loaded. Suddenly he is attacked by the two men who have been lurking behind since he left the gambling joint. In defending himself, he slits the table counter. When he leaves, he gives the proprietor one *ryo* to attend to the damages and the bodies.

Since Zatoichi has no place to sleep, Zenzo invites him to stay at his modest house. Zenzo's place, like himself, smells of charcoal and iron. Zenzo explains that was once an apprentice swordsmith, but that he is only a country blacksmith now. He examines Zatoichi's cane sword, and recognizes it to be the work of his teacher, Kotatsu of Shimotsuke, a master swordmaker. Learning of the quality of his blade, Zatoichi realizes that it has not been his skill alone which has protected him. Unfortunately, as he listens to the sound of the sword, Zenzo finds a crack three inches from its guard, which will cause the weapon to break with its next usage; a sword of such quality cannot be fixed. Zatoichi regretfully presents the sword to Zenzo as his teacher's keepsake; in turn, Zenzo gives the blind man his door bar to use as a cane.

Zatoichi decides to reform, so he asks Zenzo to help him get a job. Zenzo takes him to an inn, where Zatoichi can work as a masseur. Oshizu (Shiho Fujimura), the "young mistress" of the inn, is Boss Shotaro's daughter, Zatoichi learns; a month ago the good boss was ambushed and killed after visiting a shrine. As befits a boss's daughter, Oshizu is a strong-minded woman. She introduces Zatoichi to the master of the inn, who is the father of the man to whom she is betrothed.

An inspector, a guest at the inn, needs the services of a masseur, so Zatoichi is called. The inspector, a boastful but corrupt man with very stiff shoulders, talks about Zenzo with his guests while Zatoichi works. He explains that Zenzo is currently making his masterpiece, a sword of great quality which the inspector covets. When he was young, Zenzo created five very good swords which were rumored to be even better than his master's work, but he thought it wrong to receive more praise than his teacher, so he took to sake and gambling and was eventually expelled from his class. Boss Shotaro saved him from complete ruination, and Oshizu, who is really Zenzo's daughter, was adopted by Shotaro. The sword which the inspector covets was intended for Shotaro, to repay Zenzo's debt of gratitude, and when Shotaro was killed, Zenzo wanted Seikichi, the boss's son, to have it. Seikichi, however, does not wish to succeed his father. Zatoichi, hearing all of this as he massages the inspector, suspects that he witnessed Shotaro's assassination (at the beginning of the film) by Iwagoro's men, who intended to widen the corrupt boss's territorial control.

Later, Zatoichi goes for a walk and meets his friends from the little theater troupe. He generously returns their money bag, now full of his gambling earnings, simply explaining that it had fallen at his feet. As he and the horse driver prepare to toss dice, several of Boss Iwagoro's mugs attack, and he must use Zenzo's rod to protect himself. Meanwhile, Iwagoro tries to convince Zenzo to sell him the new sword, and wounds the old man when he refuses.

Zatoichi now realizes how corrupt and ruthless Iwagoro really is. He returns to the inn, now "rented" and transformed into a gambling den. Irritated, Zatoichi exposes the crooked games. When Iwagoro is called to quell the commotion Zatoichi has created, he immediately recognizes the masseur. Not knowing the blind swordsman's motivations, he invites Zatoichi to join his gang as his personal bodyguard and virtually forces him to join him for a drink. Upstairs, Zatoichi pretends that he is so drunk he cannot see straight, and he insults the Boss with his ironic overacting.

Shortly thereafter, Oshizu enlists Zatoichi's help as she is being forced to serve the evil inspector. The hired assassin who killed Shotaro, murders Seikichi. When Zatoichi approaches Zenzo's house so that he can consult with the old smith, he again hears the assassin running away. Inside, he finds Zenzo dead and the new sword missing. He locates his old sword, but recalls the old man's warning about its vulnerability. After sneaking through the gate, he must hide as several of the new boss's men pass by.

Both Oshizu and the new sword have been turned over to the inspector by the time Zatoichi tracks him down. Despite his concern for his sword, he attacks, and the inspector defends himself with the prized new weapon. During the struggle a sword breaks—but it is not Zatoichi's. As the inspector falls, Zatoichi realizes that the clever old smith put his new, resilient blade into Zatoichi's handle to decoy his enemy. Snow cascades to the ground. Oshizu gives Zatoichi an umbrella for protection as he sets out.

Zatoichi vows to kill Iwagoro and travels to an area full of barrels. He hides in one but is seen by Iwagoro's men. They seal the top of Zatoichi's barrel, then flip and swirl it. Suddenly a sword blade pierces the barrel, and after several quick slashes, the men fall. Zatoichi is forced to pierce several mats and decimate more men before he comes face-to-face with his chief enemy. Swearing that he has seen many bad men, but none so vile as Iwagoro, Zatoichi lacerates his final opponent.

On his way out of town, he meets the troupe's horse driver once again, and the man wants to finish their constantly interrupted dice game. After a quick toss, Zatoichi throws the dice into his opponent's hands, and wanders off as the film ends.

Though the episodes of the Zatoichi series have been of variable quality, production credits, especially the cinematography, are always of the first class. Zatoichi pictures have been directed by men such as Kenji Misumi, Kihachi Okamoto, Kimiyoshi Yasuda, Satsuo Yamamoto, and Kazuo Mori, directors who have mostly made episodes with a solid reputation within the *chambara* (sword-fighting) genre. Kazuo Miyagawa, Japan's leading cinematographer, shot several episodes. Among the many leading actors who have provided Zatoichi with counterpoint are Tatsuya Nakadai and Masayuki Mori in *Zatoichi's Fire Festival*; Hisaya Morishige, Tokyo's stage Tevye in *Zatoichi goyo tabi* (1972; *Zatoichi at Large*); Toshiro Mifune and Ayako Wakao in the overinflated *Zatoichi to Yojimbo* (1970; *Zatoichi Meets Yojimbo*); Rentaro Mikune in *Zatoichi's Rescue*; Eijiro Tono in *Zatoichi's Cane Sword*; Tomisaburo Wakayama in *Zatoichi senyo kubi* (1965; *Zatoichi and a Chest of Gold*); and Oshima star Kei Sato in *Zatoichi no uta ga kikoeru* (1966; *Zatoichi's Vengeance*).

Shintaro Katsu has played Zatoichi in every film and television episode. Even though he directed only a few episodes, he is the real guiding force for the series. Born in 1931 in Tokyo, Katsu is descended from a long line of samisen players, and remains skilled enough to perform in public concerts. His father plays in Kabuki, but his brother Tomisaburo Wakayama, like himself, is a film star, best known for pushing his galvanized baby cart across the screen for the Kozure okami (Sword of Vengeance) series.

Katsu entered the Daiei studios in 1954 along with Raizo Ichikawa. Although he played major roles, he did not acquire any following until 1961, when he played opposite the late Jiro Tamiya in the *Akumyō* (Tough Guys) series (1961-1963). *Akumyō* capitalizes on the squabbles between the two, with Katsu as the reckless old-fashioned *yakuza* (outlaw), Asakichi, playing off his roguish ultra-Westernized costar. As Zatoichi the next year, Katsu was elevated to superstardom.

Although he starred in two or three Zatoichi episodes a year, Katsu continued to act in other films. *Akumyō* also spawned a popular series, as did *Heitai yakuza* (1965; *Hoodlum Soldier*). In the latter he is a rock-tough Tokyo *yakuza* drafted into, but rebelling against, the Japanese army in World War II. Continually thrashed by authorities until he finally fights back, here he virtually parodies his Zatoichi roles. Katsu is also known for his parts in Hideo Gosha's *Hitokiri* (1969; *Tenchu*), his best role; Kon Ichikawa's *Zeni no odori* (1964; *Money Talks*); Hiroshi Teshigahara's *Moetsukita chizu* (1968; *The Man Without a Map*), from Kōbō Abe's novel; and the 1972 Goyo kiba (Sword of Justice) series, the raciest samurai pornography episodes ever.

In 1967, Katsu founded Katsu Productions, his own production company. For a decade, he continued as one of Japan's most powerful—and most temperamental—performers. Unfortunately, his career then took a downward turn. A drug charge, later dropped, hurt his popularity. He was originally slated to star in Akira Kurosawa's *Kagemusha* (1980; *Kagemusha: The Shadow Warrior*), a role which would have brought him international attention. His fiery temper, however, and artistic disagreements with Kurosawa led to his being dismissed one month after shooting began. In early 1983, his own studio declared bankruptcy. Katsu has yet to affirm his popularity before more recent Japanese audiences. Yet he will always be remembered as Zatoichi.

*Bill Thompson*

# DER ZAUBERBERG

*Origin:* West Germany, France, and Italy
*Released:* 1982
*Released in U.S.:* no listing
*Production:* Franz Seitz for Frank Seitz Film/Iduna-Film/Gaumont/Opera-Film, with Zweites Deutsches Fernsehen
*Direction:* Hans W. Geissendörfer
*Screenplay:* Hans W. Geissendörfer
*Cinematography:* Michael Ballhaus
*Editing:* Peter Przygodda and Helga Borsche
*Art direction:* Heidi Lüdi and Toni Lüdi
*Makeup:* Gerlinde Kunz and Paul Schmidt
*Costume design:* Claudia Bobsin
*Music:* Jürgen Knieper
*MPAA rating:* no listing
*Running time:* 153 minutes (film version), 360 minutes (television version)
*Also known as: The Magic Mountain*

*Principal characters:*
Hans Castorp .................. Christoph Eichhorn
Clavdia Chauchat .............. Marie-France Pisier
Mynheer Peeperkorn .................. Rod Steiger
Ludovico Settembrini ................ Flavio Bucci
Naphta ........................ Charles Aznavour
Joachim Ziemssen .............. Alexander Radszun
Frau Stöhr ...................... Margot Hielscher
Marusja .......................... Gudrun Gabriel
Elly ............................ Ann Zacharias
Dr. Krokowski ........................ Kurt Raab
Herr Wehsal ........................ Rolf Zacher
Popow .............................. Tilo Prückner
Hofrat Behrens ............... Hans Christian Blech
Fräulein Engelhart .................. Irm Hermann

Since the publication of Thomas Mann's novel *Der Zauberberg* (*The Magic Mountain*) in 1924, there have been numerous attempts to produce a film adaptation of his most famous work. As early as 1923 Gerhard Lamprecht directed a silent version of *Buddenbrooks* (1900), *Die Buddenbrooks*, and since then *Königliche Hoheit* (1909; *Royal Highness*), *Tonio Kröger* (1903), *Lotte in Weimar* (1939; *The Beloved Returns*), *Der Tod in Venedig* (1912; *Death in Venice*), *Doktor Faustus* (1948), and some half dozen other works by Thomas Mann have been filmed in Germany alone.

Although Thomas Mann himself was skeptical about the possibility of adequately adapting a novel to the screen and critical of some of the early undertakings, including *Buddenbrooks*, he was not above selling the film rights to major companies in Europe and the United States and even tried his hand at screenwriting, without success. He gave his support to a project to film *The Magic Mountain* in 1928, but it was never produced. About a dozen other directors, including Luchino Visconti and Joseph Losey, expressed interest in adapting the novel, but either their screenplays were rejected by the Mann executors—Erika Mann was involved in almost all of the later film adaptations of her father's works—or they capitulated to the almost insurmountable difficulties of adequately representing the mammoth two-volume epic in a single film.

In 1979, the German producer Horst Wendlandt first approached director Hans W. Geissendörfer with a proposal to film *The Magic Mountain*. Geissendörfer had made a name for himself through solid, unspectacular literary adaptations, such as *Die gläserne Zelle* (1977; *The Glass Cell*), based on Patricia Highsmith's novel; *Die Wildente* (1976; *The Wild Duck*), based on Henrik Ibsen's play; or the eight-part television series *Theodor Chindler* (1979), after the novel by Bernhard von Brentano. As a student he had already worked with the Thomas Mann text, and the first drafts of his screenplay found the approval of the producer and the executors. In the spring of 1980, Wendlandt withdrew from the project—the press had a field day with the many squabbles that accompanied the production of this film—and was replaced by the Munich producer Franz Seitz (who two years later wrote, directed, and produced Mann's adaptation *Doktor Faustus*, 1982).

Seitz organized a twenty-million-deutsche-mark (more than eight-million-dollar) German-French-Italian coproduction with international stars, a project of a magnitude that, with the exception of Wolfgang Petersen's *Das Boot* (1981; *The Boat*), had never been seen in West Germany. It was conceived of as a two-and-a-half-hour feature film, completed in 1981 and released in Germany in 1982, as well as a six-hour television series.

The strength—and the weakness—of the feature film is that it attempts to remain true to the letter and atmosphere of the novel, to distill the essence of a thousand pages into two and a half hours of celluloid. It is an honorable, albeit impossible task. The longer television version can allow itself a certain amount of time to reflect on the contents; the feature film must radically cut out all of the seemingly superfluous frills and embellishments and concentrate on the cinematic plot, a compromise that can never fully satisfy the cineast or the literary purist.

Like Thomas Mann's "initiation story," as he called it, the film relates the tale of Hans Castorp (Christoph Eichhorn), the twenty-four-year-old son of a Hamburg patrician family who, after completion of his engineering studies in 1907, visits his ailing cousin Joachim Ziemssen (Alexander Radszun) at a tubercular sanatorium in Davos, Switzerland. He comes to this "magic mountain" for three weeks; he remains there for seven years.

The film concentrates on three main aspects of the novel: Hans Castorp's total infatuation with Mme Clavdia Chauchat (Marie-France Pisier), a beautiful Russian with Kirghizian eyes; his social intercourse with the other patients, his cousin Ziemssen, and the head physician Hofrat Behrens (Hans Christian Blech); and his intellectual development under the tutelage of the Italian humanist Ludovico Settembrini (Flavio Bucci) and the Jew-turned-Jesuit Communist Naphta (Charles Aznavour).

The love story takes precedence over Thomas Mann's other principal themes: the swan song of the dying haute bourgeoisie of the German Empire, an analysis of the prewar political situation, and a satiric diagnosis of the decadence and destruction of values among the sanatorium patients, a microcosm reflecting the society of pre-World War I Europe.

The film begins not entirely convincingly with Hans Castorp as a fourteen-year-old boy. In a scene charged with latent adolescent homosexuality, Hans Castorp lovingly eyes a fellow pupil (Pribislav Hippe, the "Kirghizian" in the novel) and asks to borrow a pencil. The camera dwells on the silver-sheathed red crayon that the boy loans to Hans, demonstrating the mechanism in such a way that there can be no question about the sexual symbolism.

What is confusing about the scene is that the viewer soon sees Hans Castorp at age twenty-four, with his handsome cousin Joachim Ziemssen, and might suspect a homosexual relationship. This is, however, not at all the case. The "Kirghizian" helps to explain Hans Castorp's immediate fascination with Clavdia Chauchat, who has the same kind of Asiatic facial features.

The film depicts the development of the relationship between Hans Castorp and Clavdia in much the same way as the novel. At first he is shocked and annoyed at her late arrival and demonstrative slamming of the dining-room door (a habit he assumes when she is gone), but he is soon attracted to the charm and radiance she exudes at the "good" Russian table and finally overwhelmed by the fragility of her pale, morbid beauty.

In a concession to the demands of popular cinema, the film shows their one and only night together (it can only be inferred in the novel) after a wild celebration of carnival. Much of the scene leading up to the consummation of their love is lost in translation. Carnival is the season of merrymaking before Lent, and on the last day of carnival it is customary for the celebrants to address one another in the familiar "du" form that is normally reserved for close friends, relatives, and lovers. In the prurient atmosphere of the sanatorium, Hans Castorp has become totally obsessed with Clavdia without ever having been formally introduced to her. Their first encounter echoes that of Hans with his schoolfellow Hippe. On the edge of mental derangement, he stalks through the party rooms shouting for a pencil. He asks Clavdia to lend him one and she answers with the same words that Hippe had used: If he is sure to return it to her. In the ensuing conversation, he declares his love for her and swears never to address her in any way but the intimate "du" form.

The following day, Clavdia Chauchat departs for Daghestan, having promised to return to the sanatorium. This promise becomes Hans Castorp's *raison d'être*, and it holds him in Davos for many years to come, always hoping that she will someday come back. When she finally does, she is in the company of a rich and eccentric colonial Dutch coffee planter, Mynheer Peeperkorn (Rod Steiger). It is only after the strange suicide of Peeperkorn that Hans Castorp returns to the formal "Sie" form in his last words to Mme Chauchat, as if the spell of the Magic Mountain has been broken.

Geissendörfer cast in the role of Hans Castorp—against the original intentions of the producers—a completely unknown young German stage actor named Christoph Eichhorn, who has since starred in a number of pictures. Although he was not universally accepted by the critics, his youthful, awkward, gangling physique and his slightly old-fashioned Northern German features make him an ideal Hans Castorp. He credibly interprets the transformation of the character from a simple, bashful, very average young man into the "Quester Hero" who under the tutorship of Settembrini and in the hermetic atmosphere of death and eros is capable of eloquent expression of thought and emotion.

As the object of his adoration, the Clavdia of French actress Marie-France Pisier is always sovereign, a sensuous woman with an undisclosed past, only a few years older than he is but generations wiser, the unabashed nude model of Hofrat Behrens, a woman who must account to no one for her intemperate behavior.

Hans Castorp is distressed when she returns with Mynheer Peeperkorn. For this part the best-known star in the film, Rod Steiger, was cast. It is a masterful performance, although nearer to Hollywood than the remainder of the film. One has the impression that the role was expanded and Steiger given a free hand to project to the audience.

The characters of Settembrini and Naphta suffer perhaps the most in transfer to the film medium. Thomas Mann uses them as a vehicle for a philosophical debate about the moral and intellectual aims and values of prewar Europe. The analysis must necessarily remain skeletal in the film adaptation. There is no time to carry the thoughts to their logical conclusion, although Geissendörfer has done his best at least to pose the questions. He tries to suggest the madness of the approaching war and the dissolution of reason in a dining room scene of dispute and bickering that rises to the pitch of bedlam.

Italian actor Flavio Bucci is a fine performer, but his Settembrini lacks the magnitude of the character whom Thomas Mann has described as his mouthpiece, although he does capture the humorous-sympathetic side of the part, the mustachioed "organ grinder." French singer Charles Aznavour is very powerful as Naphta, the radical Jesuit who eventually challenges his intellectual adversary to a duel and shoots himself when Settembrini fires into the air.

Despite its numerous and often unavoidable weaknesses as a film, *The Magic Mountain* deserves recognition for the respect and earnestness with which the filmmakers approach the novel. The production values are excellent, with impeccable camera work by Michael Ballhaus, a powerful original music score by Jürgen Knieper, some thirty-five hundred different items of authentic costumes by Claudia Bobsin, and very impressive settings and decorations by Heidi and Toni Lüdi, including the magnificently refurbished Grand Hotel in the Waadtländer Alps, which serves as the Davos sanatorium. If the film perhaps lacks the cinematic sovereignty of Visconti's *Morte a Venezia* (1971; *Death in Venice*), it is nevertheless a valid attempt to capture the quintessence of one of the foremost novels in world literature.

*Stephen Locke*

# ZAZIE
# (ZAZIE DANS LE MÉTRO)

*Origin:* France
*Released:* 1960
*Released in U.S.:* 1961
*Production:* Nouvelles Éditions de Films
*Direction:* Louis Malle
*Screenplay:* Jean-Paul Rappeneau and Louis Malle; based on the novel by Raymond Queneau
*Cinematography:* Henri Raichi
*Editing:* Kenout Peltier
*Art direction:* Bernard Evein
*Music:* Fiorenzo Carpi
*Running time:* 86 minutes
*Also known as: Zazie in the Underground*

*Principal characters:*

Zazie ........................ Catherine Demongeot
Uncle Gabriel ...................... Philippe Noiret
Zazie's mother ..................... Odette Picquet
Man ............................ Vittorio Caprioli
Woman ............................. Yvonne Clech

*Zazie* is the sort of comedy film that is described by critic Gerald Mast as a "riffing" film. "Riff" is a term that he has borrowed from jazz music, and the type of film is one that consists merely of a series of gags somehow related to one topic or situation. Any cohesiveness this sort of comedy has will come from the central topic, from the performer or performers who appear in several of the gags, and from the visual, kinetic rhythm that the film may establish.

The situation within which the events in *Zazie* are arranged is the visit an eleven-year-old French girl, Zazie (Catherine Demongeot), experiences with her Uncle Gabriel (Philippe Noiret) in Paris for thirty-six hours. The film's title, which means "Zazie in the subway," is ironic because, although she desperately wants to ride on it, Zazie finds immediately that the subway is closed because of a strike.

The eighty-six minutes of the film are filled with absurd events, which seldom have much connection with the events that precede and follow them, and with many camera and editing tricks. Some of the filmic devices used are jump-cutting, in which a person seems to move instantaneously from one place to another; fast motion, sometimes with the sound remaining normal and sometimes with the sound also accelerated; an explosion represented by a comic-book-style animated drawing; incongruous elements, such as a sea captain buffeted by waves on top of the Eiffel Tower; and instantaneous substitutions—Zazie, for example, jumps into a garbage can, but, when the lid is lifted, a cat jumps out.

Even when no cinematic trickery is used, the film always seems to surprise the audience. From the first scene on, the viewer continually expects one thing but suddenly receives another. In that first scene, for example, Gabriel is on the railroad platform, and his sister (Odette Picquet) comes rushing toward him, but instead of embracing him with her outstretched arms she rushes on past him to embrace her lover, whom the viewer had not seen.

To attempt to describe this almost plotless film in any detail is fruitless, for part of its design and effect is that few events are more important than the others and, as mentioned before, few events lead to subsequent events. Zazie frequently asks various characters if they are homosexual; one character (Vittorio Caprioli) turns up at various times in different guises, including one sequence as a policeman; a woman (Yvonne Clech), who happens to be stopped in traffic near Zazie, begins talking to her and then becomes a major character in the film; and the film ends with the virtual destruction of the inside of a café with much food slinging, breaking of dishes, and breaking of wine bottles on heads. When she returns to her mother at the end of the film and is asked what she has done, Zazie replies, "I have mellowed." (One element of the humor or surprise in the film is that Zazie frequently shocks the adults with her foul language, but this aspect is missing from the subtitles of the English-language version.)

*Zazie* is based on the best-selling novel by Raymond Queneau. In the novel, the plot was merely the basis for much experimentation with words in which Queneau made fun of French literary language. According to director Louis Malle, he tried in the film to make fun of cinema "language" in much the same way. He said that he wanted to avoid the routine and, in fact, react violently against it. Unlike a standard film that usually lets the viewer know what to expect, this film never accords the viewer that luxury. Malle was also reacting against his own work. He had made two previous films, the second of which was *Les Amants* (1958; *The Lovers*), a romantic and often lyric film that Malle came to consider too naïve, even though it was quite successful. Indeed, he went so far as to say about *The Lovers*, "I tried to kill it with *Zazie*." Because of this, *Zazie* can be seen as an important step in the director's development. None of his subsequent films is anything like it, but the fact that he had tried what might be considered two extremes of filmmaking in his second and third films led him to discover his own voice and to make such highly regarded films as *Le Souffle au cœur* (1971; *Murmur of the Heart*), *Lacombe, Lucien* (1974), and the English-language successes *Pretty Baby* (1978) and *Atlantic City* (1981).

Critical response to *Zazie* was divided when the film was first released, and it remains divided. *Newsweek*, for example, called *Zazie* "inventive, lively, stylish, and fun," and *Variety* praised it as "intellectual slapstick." In French theaters the film was both booed and cheered. On the other hand, Bosley Crowther, then the chief film critic for *The New York Times*, condemned the film as, among other things, a "nasty and irresponsible practical joke," "an evasion of thought," and "tomfoolery with a camera." Crowther concluded by saying that foreign directors should beware of such "aimless and esoteric doodling."

In the years since it was first released, the film has become a classic of its style of comedy for some film critics and historians, who examine it in great detail for such characteristics as its references to other films and its possible use of the language of dreams. Others now dismiss it as "frivolous and baffling" (Ephraim Katz) or point out that Malle did not have the "exact sense of timing" necessary for such "mad comedy" (Roy Armes).

*Julia Johnson*

# ZERO FOR CONDUCT
# (ZÉRO DE CONDUITE)

*Origin:* France
*Released:* 1933
*Released in U.S.:* 1947
*Production:* Jacques-Louis Nounez for Argui-Films
*Direction:* Jean Vigo
*Assistant direction:* Albert Rièra, Henri Storck, and Pierre Merle
*Screenplay:* Jean Vigo
*Cinematography:* Boris Kaufman
*Editing:* Jean Vigo
*Art direction:* Henri Storck; set decoration, Jean Vigo
*Music:* Maurice Jaubert
*Running time:* 44 minutes
*Also known as: Jeunes Diables au collage*

*Principal characters:*

Huguet .............................. Jean Dasté
Pète-Sec .......................... Robert Le Flon
Bed-de-Gaz .......................... Du Verron
Principal ............................. Delphin
Professor ........................... Léon Larive
Mère Haricot ......................... Mme Émile
Prefect .................. Louis de Gonzague-Frick
Fireman ......................... Raphaël Diligent
Caussat ........................... Louis Lefèvre
Colin ........................... Gilbert Pruchon
Bruel ........................... Coco Goldstein
Tabard ...................... Gérard de Bédarieux
Bishop ........................... Henri Storck

*Zero for Conduct* is a surrealist dream, a film which takes place as much inside the heads of the schoolboys depicted in it as it does in what might, by stretching the imagination, be called the real world. The film shows the petty tyrannies in the daily life of a mediocre, provincial boys' school where the students are in open revolt against their teachers. With one exception—the young teacher, Huguet (Jean Dasté), who moves freely between both camps—the instructors are systematically mocked and degraded.

*Zero for Conduct* opens with a few of the boys returning from vacation by train. They, and the audience with them, immediately enter into a fantasy of games and playthings: Illicit cigars are smoked in the no-smoking section; toy balloons erupt from the boys' pockets; goose quills are stuck all over one boy, who performs a grotesque pantomime, and another toots a miniature horn through his nose.

Arriving at their station, the children are lined up with the rest of the boys on the quay and welcomed by the prefect (Louis de Gonzague-Frick), a dried-up authoritarian who cannot even manage to crack a smile; in fact, he does not utter one word throughout the film. The new teacher, Huguet, appears, dropping his suitcases and greeting the prefect effusively.

Thereupon, the stage is set for the students' rebellion: a revolt centered on a nonsensical conspiracy involving hidden marbles, the daily diet of beans, and a boy whose mother dresses him like a girl. In reality, they are rebelling against the despotism of the school administration, which they regard with undisguised hatred. The instructors are seen as distorted interpretations of their personalities, more opinions than personages. The prefect sneaks around peering into windows and going through the boys' effects. The principal (Delphin), who becomes a terrifying wizard in a scene with Tabard (Gérard de Bédarieux), is viewed as a dwarf with a high, squeaky voice; the cook is fat and cranky. Only Huguet, who plays ball with the boys and imitates Charlie Chaplin, is immune from their scorn. He is myopically oblivious to their mischief as he strolls through the playground, ignoring the smoking in the latrine, the plotters literally under his feet.

Huguet exists in a rarefied atmosphere of his own; he endears himself to his students by showing them how to walk on their hands, and when the prefect surprises him in the act, he demonstrates another talent. While still upside down, Huguet draws a cartoon figure, and, in a further depiction of director Jean Vigo's "magic," the sketch comes to life and frolics around the paper. When Huguet takes his charges for a walk, they steal off on their own adventures. This scene is famous because François Truffaut quoted from it verbatim in *Les Quatre Cents Coups* (1959; *The 400 Blows*). Lindsay Anderson cited *Zero for Conduct* in *IF . . .* (1968), and it is worth noting that thirty-six years later, Jean Dasté played still another teacher, Professor Pinel, the mentor of Dr. Itard (Truffaut himself), in *L'Enfant sauvage* (1970; *The Wild Child*).

Huguet does not notice the boys' absence, and, whistling and smoking, wanders on by himself. They rejoin him a few blocks farther on, and all gleefully follow a pretty young woman, who encourages Huguet with a laugh. The sequence is typical of Huguet; he roams around in a daze, far less alert than his students, who must always be on the lookout for prying adults. In the last scene, with anarchy triumphant and the students running amok in the schoolyard during a formal ceremony, Huguet chooses sides and cheers the boys on. He seems scarcely more than a boy himself (certainly no more mature, and in many ways even more endearing).

There are a number of justly famous sequences in *Zero for Conduct*: the aforementioned promenade through town; the insurrection at the film's end, with its joyful celebration of lawlessness and its rebellious nose-thumbing, table-turning rout of authority and convention; and perhaps most famous of all (because it is in itself a quote from Abel Gance's *Napoleon*, 1927), the scene preceding the final rebellion, in which the boys run riot in their dormitory.

Heretofore their sleeping quarters have been merely the locale for high jinks, juvenile expressions of high spirits. Now, however, they go completely wild, throwing bedclothes into the air, carrying Chinese lanterns, reading their manifesto, and leaping across the beds. As a military march plays on the sound track, Vigo slows the action to half speed so that the insurrection appears as a ballet for boys, with bare limbs in flowing nightshirts. Retarding the action in this manner renders it less threatening, more playful. Tabard hoists the boys' flag, a skull and crossbones, on the roof, and the boys squint against the feathers falling from the disintegrating pillows, as Vigo celebrates the uprising with the children.

Vigo's heightened theatrical surrealism is accented by Maurice Jaubert's manipulation of the music for this sequence. The boys' walking song, heard previously, is given a dreamlike rendition on the sound track. As Jaubert says, he then "transcribed it backwards, the last bar before the first and within each bar, the last note before the first. The bit of music in this form was then recorded and recalled little of the original music. The music thus obtained was then used with the film and one found again the shape of the basic melody but the 'transmission' was entirely reversed and derived all its mystery from this simple mechanical operation." The result of Jaubert's "unreal sonorousness" is a haunting chant, part hymn, part anthem—a fitting accompaniment to Vigo's hallucination of youthful abandon.

*Zero for Conduct* shows creativity, youth, and energy in opposition to repression and convention. It was banned in France at the time of its release in 1933 because of what was considered its malicious attack on the French educational system. Cursorily and scornfully reviewed in a few newspapers, *Zero for Conduct* was reviled for its conspicuous interest in the scatological: There are several shots of the pupils in the lavatories; one boy is hauled off the toilet, his pants around his knees, his bare bottom exposed to the shocked gaze of the bourgeoisie. An obscene French word becomes the rallying cry of the boys' revolution. A further outrage occurs in the last scene, when the French flag is thrown to the ground.

*Zero for Conduct* was only shown at film societies and private screenings until it was rediscovered and made available for distribution in 1945. When he saw it in 1947, James Agee stated in *The Nation* that "*Zéro de Conduit* seems to me all but unblemished inspiration, moving freely and surely in its own unprecedented world from start to finish, one of the few great movie poems. . . . Vigo gets deeper inside his characters than most people have tried to on film, and is not worried about transitions between objective, subjective, fantastic and subconscious reality, and mixes as many styles and camera tricks, as abruptly, as he sees fit—always, so far as I can see, using it with force, charm and originality." Agee's response captures the spirit of a film that has come to be regarded as one of the classics of world cinema.

*Judith M. Kass*